THE 2nd DEVONS WAR DIARY

THE 2nd DEVONS WAR DIARY

The 2nd Battalion,
Devonshire Regiment
and its lost men,
1914-1919

Martin Body

PiP
POLLINGER IN PRINT

Pollinger Limited
9 Staple Inn
Holborn
LONDON
WC1V 7QH

www.pollingerltd.com

First published by Pollinger in Print 2012
ebook edition published by Pollinger in Print 2012

Copyright © Martin Body 2012
All rights reserved
The moral right of the author has been asserted

ISBN 978-1-905665-84-6 print edition, paperback
ISBN 978-1-905665-85-3 ebook, ePub edition
ISBN 978-1-905665-86-0 ebook, Kindle edition
ISBN 978-1-905665-87-7 ebook, PDF edition

A CIP catalogue record is available from the British Library

No part of this book may be reproduced, stored in
a retrieval system, or transmitted in any form, or
by any means, electronic, mechanical or otherwise,
without prior written permission from Pollinger Limited

More information available from:
www.pollingerltd.com/bookshop/martin_body.htm

Acknowledgments

I owe a great debt of gratitude to Suzanne Pocock, whose willing help with all aspects of the creation of this book was beyond measure; to my wife, Gillian, for bearing with me and enduring trips to the battlefields of the Western Front; and to Avril Williams, of the 'Ocean Villas Cafe', Auchonvillers, France, for her encouragement. I also thank Phillip Ellis, of the Devon branch of the Western Front Association, for information regarding men from the Newton Abbot area who died during the Great War.
To Lesley Pollinger and Katy Loffman, of Pollinger Ltd., London, I would also like to acknowledge my profound thanks. Their help and encouragement finally made it happen.

Martin Body

This book is dedicated to:

Janice Ann Body, 1954-2009

Pte. 11187 Charles Hulbert Yates, 1893-1916

The soldiers of the 2nd Devons who perished in the Great War

The survivors who bore the physical and mental scars for the rest of their lives

CONTENTS

1 - THE WAR DIARY

2 - A CHRONOLOGICAL LIST OF THE 2nd DEVONS WHO DIED

3 - AN ALPHABETICAL LIST OF THE 2nd DEVONS WHO DIED

4 - GLOSSARY

5 – BIBLIOGRAPHY

The 2nd Devons War Diary

AUTHOR'S NOTE

11187, Private Charles Hulbert Yates, a plumber's mate from 126 Clarendon Street, Paddington, Middlesex, was a member of the Ranelagh Rovers football team, all of whom volunteered for the Army at Marylebone on 6th September 1914. 55 men enlisted in the Devonshire Regiment in London that day, most at Marylebone, some at Fulham, on the only day that the Devons are believed to have recruited in West London. A handful volunteered for Kitchener's 'New Army' and left to start training the next day, while the remainder were sent home to await instructions.

Before war was declared, the British government realised that Regular battalions of its relatively small Army, would find it impossible to replace the expected rate of casualties with a supply of trained 'Long Service' Regular Army recruits, and made a contingency plan to use men who had enlisted under 'Short Service Attestations' to be posted to Regular Battalions, after training. The plan was activated on declaration of war.

So it was that Charlie Yates and his pals were called to commence training at Exeter Barracks with the 3rd Battalion, Devonshire Regiment, on 7th November 1914, the day after the 2nd Devons left to join the British Expeditionary Force in France. At the time Exeter Barracks was overwhelmed with new recruits and Charlie Yates and the lads who had volunteered with him were sent to a satellite camp at Honiton, where they apparently split their time between training and guarding a railway tunnel against 'fifth columnists'.

On 24th March 1915 they were posted to the British Expeditionary Force (B.E.F.) in France, to the 2nd Battalion of the Devonshire Regiment (one of the Regiment's two Regular battalions, the other being the 1st) as part of a draft of men sent to replace men lost in the battle of Neuve Chapelle.

Charles Hulbert Yates, the author's great uncle, served with the battalion until he was killed in action on 1st July 1916 at Ovillers, just one of many 2nd Devons who lost their lives in the Great War. This book tells their story.

Part 1 closely follows the 2nd Devons War Diary, National Archives document WO/95/1712, showing where the Battalion was and what it was doing on every day of the war. There are periods where the entries are sparse because the Battalion was in heavy action and writing up the War Diary was obviously a low priority. This is particularly evident in late March 1918, during the German Spring Offensive, and in late May 1918, when the 2nd Devons made their heroic stand at the Bois des Buttes. To explain the story of those desperate days I have added descriptions of what happened.

Part 2 is a chronological list of all of the men and officers of the Battalion who died in the war, giving as many details of their lives that I have been able to find: employment, family, where they lived, their grave references, whether they were killed in action, died of wounds or just died, etc.

Part 3 is an alphabetical list of the men who died.

From the three parts it is possible to research how the Battalion was employed on any day in the war and to see who died on that day. Alternatively, if details of a particular man or officer are sought, using the alphabetical list (Part 3) it is possible to find the man's date of death, then find his details on the relevant date in the chronological list (Part 2), and finally go to the date in the War Diary (Part 1) to see what the Battalion was doing at the time.

Martin Body

The basic information regarding the 2nd Devons' who died serving with the Battalion is taken from the 'Soldiers Died In The Great War' CD-ROM database (SDGW), which incorporates the eighty-one volumes of the British Army's fatalities, published in 1921 by His Majesty's Stationery Office on behalf of the War Office. This document furnishes names, ranks, serial numbers, whether they were killed in action, died of wounds or died for other reasons, where they were born, enlisted and where they resided, if recorded. It also lists any previous Army units served. This is good information but I wanted to know more about the social backgrounds of the men who died. To obtain this, the most useful sources I found were the Commonwealth War Graves Commission (CWGC) records, the British Army Medal Roll, and the 1891, 1901 and 1911 Census records. Army Service Records would have been useful, but largely appear to be among the records destroyed in the Blitz in 1941.

Martin Body, London, 2012

The 2nd Devons War Diary

11187 Private Charles Hulbert Yates, 2nd Battalion, Devonshire Regiment

12th November 1893 – 1st July 1916

Martin Body

The 2nd Devons War Diary

PART 1

THE 2nd DEVONS WAR DIARY

NOVEMBER 1914

4th November 1914 HURSLEY PARK.
6am. Received orders from HQ 23rd Brigade to be prepared to move for embarkation within 48 hours. At 2.30pm received orders to march off at 2.30am on 5th to embark at Southampton.

5th November 1914 HURSLEY PARK.
2.30am. Battalion paraded and marched off, fully mobilized, in pouring rain. Strength 30 officers, including MO, 983 other ranks, including 6 ASC drivers and Armourer Sergeant. Arrived at Southampton Dock at 7am. Embarked in SS *Bellerephon*, Blue Funnel Line, as also did Brigade HQ. Sailed about 5.20pm, leaving 10 draft horses behind. Sea very calm.

The officers who went to France with the original cadre:
Lt.Col. J.O.Travers, DSO Commanding Officer
Major J.F.Radcliffe, DSO 2nd In Charge
Major J.D.Ingles Adjutant
Lieut. G.Palmer, DCM Quartermaster
Lieut. C.A.Sutton R.A.M.C. Medical Officer
Lieut. H.Eardley Wilmot Machine Gun Officer
Capt. A.J.E.Sunderland 'A' Company
Capt. D.H.Blunt 'A' Company
Lieut. G.N.Belfield 'A' Company
Lieut. F.R.Cobb Sig. Off 'A' Coy
Lieut. R.O.Bristowe 'A' Company
Lieut. F.J.C.Holdsworth Transport Officer 'A' Coy
Capt. G.I.Watts 'B' Company
Capt. M.I.G.Jenkins 'B' Company
Lieut. R.P.Bates 'B' Company
Lieut. G.C.Vaughan 'B' Company
Lieut. R.H.Anderson-Morshead 'B' Company
Lieut. J.R.Cartwright 'B' Company
Major W.M.Goodwyn 'C' Company
Capt. C.J.Spencer 'C' Company
Lieut. R.G.Legge 'C' Company

Martin Body

Lieut. J.A.Park 'C' Company
Lieut. R.B.Featherstone 'C' Company
Capt. C.A.Lafone 'D' Company
Capt. C.H.M.Imbert-Terry 'D' Company
Lieut. O.M.Parker 'D' Company
Lieut. J.A.Andrews 'D' Company
Lieut. A.G.McMullen 'D' Company
Lieut. H.J.Cox 'D' Company

6th November 1914   HAVRE.
9.40am. Began to disembark at 9.40am. Left docks at 1pm for Rest Camp at GRAVILLE, where we pitched camp and stayed night.

7th November 1914   Orders received about 7pm that 23rd Brigade would proceed by train to unknown destination. Battalion to parade at 12pm and march to station.

8th/9th November 1914   Paraded at 12 midnight and marched to station. Commenced to entrain transport at 6am. Train left at 10am. Left 2 men behind sick. Train stopped 1 hour at Rouen where Battalion had coffee. Stopped at Abbeville, Calais, St.Omer and detrained at Strazeele about 10am. Marched to Neuve Berquin at 1pm after dinners and went into billets.
Lt.Featherstone left at Strazeele to act as assistant RSO.

10th November 1914   Remained in billets. Officers of Brigade visited British lines at FLEURBAIX to see trenches in afternoon.

11th November 1914   12am Brigadier (General Pinney) brought us orders to march at 6am with West Yorks Regiment, under Colonel Phillips, to NEUVE EGLISE, about 11 miles. Left billets 5.30am. Arrived NEUVE EGLISE about 10.30am. Billeted in farms.

12th November 1914   Received orders at 9am to take over trenches of West Kent and K.O.Y.L.I. at 5pm. Battalion paraded at 3pm and marched to trenches, which we took over after dark. Had 1 NCO wounded and 1 man broke his ankle. P.A.S.L.I. on our right with Dorsets in support. French on our left with Scots Greys in support.

13th November 1914   In trenches all day. Heavy shelling on both sides. Relieved by West Yorks Regiment between 7pm and 12am . Heavy fighting at Ypres.

14th November 1914   Got back to billets about 2.30am all wet through.

19th November 1914   Two inches of snow on ground. One ma   n killed in trenches.

20th November 1914   In trenches all day. One man killed and two

The 2nd Devons War Diary

wounded.

21st November 1914 Relieved by 2nd Scottish Rifles between 5pm and 7pm. We lost one man killed and 3 wounded during day. Went into billets as Brigade Reserve at LA FLINQUE. Freezing hard.

22nd November 1914 In Billets. German aeroplane captured nearby. Freezing hard.

23rd November 1914 In Billets. Local Reserve.

24th November 1914 Battalion paraded at 4.30 and marched to trenches, taking over from 2nd Scottish Rifles. Had 2 men wounded in taking over.

25th November 1914 In trenches all day. Several men suffering from frost bitten feet, but none wounded.

26th November 1914 One killed and 2 wounded. 2nd Royal Berkshire Regiment attacked German trench on our left and an attempt made to blow up a farm in front of West Yorks on our right. Royal Berks rushed trench and then retired losing 1 officer missing. Farm was partly blown up, no Casualties. 1 company of 2nd Middlesex Regiment came down as support, if wanted, and returned at 2.30am. Artillery fire opened on both sides.

27th November 1914 Lost 3 men killed and 2 wounded. Relieved between 7pm and 9pm by 2nd Scottish Rifles and marched back to ESTAIRES betting into billets about 11pm.

28th November 1914 In billets all day as Corps Reserve.

29th November 1914 Church parade at 10am.

30th November 1914 Paraded at 4.30pm for trenches. 54 men to hospital, nearly all with frost bitten feet. Relieved 2nd Scottish Rifles. One man killed in taking over.

Martin Body

DECEMBER 1914

1st December 1914 Shelling on both sides. (H.M. The King visited Estaires with President Poincare, Prince of Wales, General Office and Staff).

2nd December 1914 Heavier sniping than usual. Two men wounded. (Heard Captain Whipple, 1st Battalion, had died of wounds).

3rd December 1914 Usual sniping. During night obtained shoulder cards off dead German in front of our trenches, of 57th Regiment. Three men wounded during day. Relieved in the evening by 2nd Scottish Rifles and went into billets at LA FLINQUE, Brigade Reserve.

4th December 1914 In billets as Brigade Reserve.

5th December 1914 In billets as Brigade Reserve. Much rain.

6th December 1914 Battalion took over trenches between 5.30 and 7pm from 2nd Scottish Rifles.

7th December 1914 False alarm that Germans were attacking about 6pm. 2nd Middlesex Regiment sent down 2 companies as support, which were sent back at 7pm.

8th December 1914 Quiet day.

9th December 1914 Relieved by 2nd Scottish Rifles between 6 and 8pm and went into billets at PONT RIRCHON as Divisional reserve.

10th December 1914 Whole Battalion had baths and change of underclothing in ESTAIRES.

11th December 1914 Relieved 2nd Scottish Rifles in trenches about 5.30pm. Very wet.

12th December 1914 Brigadier went round our trenches which were very wet and falling in in many places. Our artillery very busy.

13th December 1914 One man wounded. 50 men of 1st Reinforcement arrived and went to transport lines.

14th December 1914 Relieved by Royal Berks about 6pm. The 24th Brigade having gone back to ESTAIRES, the 23rd and 25th took over whole line of 8th Division trenches. Went into Brigade Reserve on LA BASSEE ROAD.

15th December 1914 RED BARN. Billets.

The 2nd Devons War Diary

16th December 1914 Relieved 2nd West Yorks Regiment in C lines about 5.30pm.

17th December 1914 One man killed and one wounded. 53 NCOs and men of 1st Reinforcement joined at Transport Lines.

18th December 1914 CO and Adjutant went to conference at Headquarters 23rd Brigade at 6.45am, subject being proposed attack on German trenches at 4.30pm. Devons leading, 2nd West Yorks Regiment in support and 2nd Scottish Rifles and 2nd Middlesex Regiment in reserve. After short discussion conference dissolved till 12 noon. At latter, Brigadier, CO and Adjutant again met and attack was ordered to hold good as above. CO and Adjutant hastened back to our Headquarters and telephoned to trenches for Company Commanders to whom orders were issued. 'D' and 'C' Companies were to lead supported by 'B' Company. 'A' Company was to come up on right if called upon. Company Commanders only got back to their Companies about 10 or 15 minutes before operations were to commence. CO and Adjutant repaired to trenches with party of West Yorks with bombs at 4pm. 3 of latter wounded on way down. Our artillery opened heavy bombardment of trench to be taken at 4.15. Advance began at 4.30pm. 'D' Company, under Captain Lafone, took German trench. 'C' Company, under Major Goodwyn, started but owing to latter being wounded at once and not having had time to explain scheme to his officers sufficiently the Company lost direction, got too much to the left and were caught up in barbed wire, losing heavily, only Lt. Joy with a few men finally joining 'D' Company. Captain Spencer and Captain Featherstone were killed, Captain Legge missing, believed killed. Major Radcliffe DSO, Major Goodwyn, Lieuts. Park, Andrews and Case wounded, and 121 NCOs and men killed, wounded and missing. We took 27 prisoners in trench and many Germans were killed and wounded.

19th December 1914 Spent early hours removing wounded. 2nd West Yorks relieved us in German trench about 12am or 1am. We returned to our own trenches, and were withdrawn in evening, going into billets at PONT RIRCHON as Divisional Reserve. 2nd West Yorks Regiment were bombed out of the trench we took in the morning and returned to original C lines, losing heavily. Part of 1st Reinforcement joined companies from Transport lines.

20th December 1914 In billets.

21st December 1914 In billets.

22nd December 1914 In billets. Very wet. Lt. Watkins and 40 men of 1st Reinforcement joined HQ.

23rd December 1914 Kept Xmas Day. CO and Adjutant went round. Dinners in various billets. Battalion had innumerable presents of plum puddings etc.

24th December 1914 Relieved 2nd Scottish Rifles in trenches, D lines, between 5 and 7pm. Very wet.

25th December 1914 Informal armistice during daylight. Germans got out of their trenches and came towards our lines. Our men met them and they wished each other a merry Xmas, shook hands, exchanged smokes etc. About 7.30pm sniping began again. We had one man killed and one wounded. Hard frost.

26th December 1914 Report received about 11pm that Germans were going to make attack at 12.15am 27th. Everybody warned and stood to arms.

27th December 1914 At 12am 26th-27th our artillery opened fire and fortunately stopped any attack - if such was contemplated - original report came from deserter. Turned in about 1.30am. Relieved in evening by 2nd Scottish Rifles and went into billets at LA FLINQUE.

28th December 1914 Stood to arms at 6am. 'C' Company moved into new billets. Heavy gale and very wet night of 28th - 29th.

29th December 1914 Quiet day. Stood to arms as usual.

30th December 1914 Quiet day in billets.

31st December 1914 Relieved 2nd Scottish Rifles in trenches in evening.

The 2nd Devons War Diary

JANUARY 1915

1st January 1915 One man killed, two wounded, otherwise quiet day.

2nd January 1915 Relieved by 2nd Scottish Rifles in evening and went into billets as Divisional Reserve at PONT RIRCHON.

3rd January 1915 Very wet. In billets as Divisional Reserve. Draft (of NCOs and men) joined, mostly too old and some very young.

4th January 1915 In billets. Lt. Belfield went to hospital.

5th January 1915 Relieved 2nd Scottish Rifles in trenches in evening.

6th January 1915 One man killed and one wounded. Fire fight, artillery and infantry in trenches and lines.

7th January 1915 Trenches very flooded. (Captains Lafone and Watts, Lieuts. Cobb and Jay, Lt. and Quartermaster Palmer and 2 NCOs, went home on 7 days leave).

8th January 1915 Relieved by 2nd Scottish Rifles and went into Brigade Reserve at and near LA FLINQUE.

9th January 1915 Lt. Anderson-Morshead went to hospital.

10th January 1915 Voluntary service.

11th January 1915 One man wounded in billets on RUE DU BACQUEROT in morning by a premature burst from our own guns. Relieved 2nd Scottish Rifles in trenches in evening. Draft of 75 NCOs and men joined at Transport lines.

12th January 1915 One man killed and one wounded. Got into communication with all Companies by telephone owing to their being separated from one another by floods.

13th January 1915 Very wet. Three killed and two wounded. (5 officers and 2 NCOs returned from leave). Trench is very bad and communication between Companies and parts of Companies impossible.

14th January 1915 Relieved by 2nd Scottish Rifles in evening and went into Divisional Reserve at PONT RIRCHON. Casualties 1 killed (Sgt. Hogg) 1 wounded.

15th January 1915 Draft of 75 NCOs and men joined battalion from Transport lines.

16th January 1915 Grenadiers of each Company practising bomb throwing.

17th January 1915 Generals Davis and Pinney inspected Companies at bomb throwing.
Relieved 2nd Scottish Rifles in trenches between 5pm and 7pm. Lost 1 killed and 2 wounded in taking over. Very cold.

18th January 1915 Very wet and cold with snow and sleet. A Brigade Grenadier Company was started, 1 officer, and 29 NCOs and men from each battalion. We found the CSM but postponed sending any officer. 1 killed 3 wounded.

19th January 1915 Trenches dried slightly. 1 casualty (wounded). Lt. Wright and 30 NCOs and men arrived and joined at Transport lines (Lt. Dunning).

20th January 1915 Relieved by 2nd Scottish Rifles and went into Brigade Reserve at LA FLINQUE. No casualties. (Captains Imbert-Terry and Jenkins, Lt. Bristowe and CSMs Old and King went on leave from 21st to 27th inclusive).

21st January 1915 Draft joined from Transport lines. 2/Lt. Wright attached to 'A' Company.

22nd January 1915 In billets.

23rd January 1915 Relieved 2nd Scottish Rifles in trenches between 5 and 7pm. Had 5 men wounded taking over and Scottish Rifles had 6 wounded. One man badly wounded later (died 24th).

24th January 1915 Enemy Lively. Three killed and six wounded.

25th January 1915 1st Corps on right of our Brigade reported attack imminent. Enemy attacked at LA BASSEE (and lost heavily) at junction of British and French lines. 1 officer and 17 NCOs and men of Brigade Grenadier Company sent to HQ D lines to stay night in case they should be wanted. Casualties: Lt. Anderson-Morshead wounded and 3 rank and file killed and 6 wounded.

26th January 1915 Relieved by 2nd Scottish Rifles. 4 men wounded. G.O.C. Corps visited trench HQ. In evening went into billets as Divisional Reserve at PONT RIRCHON. (Lt. Holdsworth proceeded on 7 days leave).

27th January 1915 CO, Captain Blunt, Captain Cartwright, Sgt. May and 2 NCOs proceeded on 7 days leave. Major Ingles left in command and Lt. Bristowe as Adjutant.

28th January 1915 In billets.

29th January 1915 Frosty day. Relieved 2nd Scottish Rifles in trenches in evening.   Quiet night.   1 man wounded.

30th January 1915   Quiet day except for sniping.   Captain Watkins dangerously wounded.   Sgt. Blake killed.   7 NCOs and men wounded.

31st January 1915   Quiet day except that enemy shelled 'B' Company's supports in morning.   Captain Watkins died at 2.10pm in No6 clearing hospital, Merville.   1 L/Cpl.(Dunsford) of 'B' Company killed in evening.   No other casualties.

Martin Body

FEBRUARY 1915

1st February 1915 Relieved in trenches by 2nd Scottish Rifles Casualties 2 killed 1 wounded.

2nd February 1915 In billets, Brigade Reserve. One man wounded by shell fire.

3rd February 1915 In billets. Shelled but no casualties. CO, Captain Blunt and Lt. Cartwright returned from leave.

4th February 1915 Relieved 2nd Scottish Rifles in trenches. Casualties 3 wounded.

5th February 1915 Enemy shooting considerable amount. 1 killed 6 wounded.

6th February 1915 Very quiet day.

7th February 1915 Relieved by 2nd Scottish Rifles - Casualties 5 killed 4 wounded.

8th February 1915 In billets.

9th February 1915 In Billets. Lt. Parker and Lt. Sutton R.A.M.C. proceeded on leave 10th to 16th.

10th February 1915 Relieved 2nd Scottish Rifles in trenches. Major Ingles, Lieuts. Bates and Vaughan returned from leave.

11th February 1915 Enemy fairly active in shooting line. Casualties 1 killed 4 wounded.

12th February 1915 Considerable firing by day, quiet night. No casualties.

13th February 1915 Relieved by 2nd Scottish Rifles Quiet day. Casualties - 2 killed 5 wounded. (**SDGW contains no record of any 2nd Devons killed in action**)

14th February 1915 In billets, Brigade Reserve. Enemy shelled 'B' Company on RUE DU BACQUEROT.

15th February 1915 'B' Company shelled out of billets on RUE DU BACQUEROT. One billet burnt down with considerable amount of equipment and ammunition. 7 men wounded.

16th February 1915 In billets. One of men wounded yesterday died.
Relieved 2nd Scottish Rifles in line. Draft of 1 officer (2/Lt. Horne, late 3rd battalion at Depot) and 35 NCOs and men joined at transport lines. Very wet.

The 2nd Devons War Diary

17th February 1915 Quiet day. Two men wounded. 2nd Lieuts. Jacob and Lord, promoted from ranks of Artists Rifles, joined at transport lines. Very wet.

18th February 1915 Quiet day. Two men killed and two wounded.

19th February 1915 Relieved by 2nd Scottish Rifles and went into billets as Divisional Reserve.

20th February 1915 Three officers and Draft which joined transport lines on 16th and 17th joined HQ.

21st February 1915 Church parade at 5pm, followed by funeral of Pte. Curtis of 'A' Company who was suffocated in his sleep by fumes from coke fire.

22nd February 1915 Relieved 2nd Scottish Rifles in trenches in evening. Four men wounded. Draft of 90 men joined.

23rd February 1915 Brigadier visited trenches before breakfast and inspected draft after. Casualties.

24th February 1915 Quiet day. Casualties 1 wounded.

25th February 1915 Quiet day. Casualties killed one, wounded one. Relieved by 2nd Scottish Rifles.

26th February 1915 Brigade Reserve. Wagon load of bombs blew up severely wounding 2 (Privates McCarthy and Pike) both of whom died subsequently. They were bicycling behind cart returning from Brigade HQ to Battalion HQ.

27th February 1915 Received orders to march into billets West of MERVILLE for rest tomorrow. Remainder of Brigade to follow later.

28th February 1915 Companies and HQ rendezvous at Transport lines LE DRUMEZ at 9.30am. Battalion marches off at 10am and got into billets about 2 miles West of MERVILLE about 4pm. No arrangements made for billets except an area marked out on map. This area had to be exceeded as the farms and houses had not sufficient room in them for Battalion.

Martin Body

MARCH 1915

1st to 4th March 1915 In billets resting, between MERVILLE and HAVERSQUERKE. Companies route marched etc.

5th March 1915 Conference at Brigade HQ in morning. COs, Adjutants and 1 other officer per battalion.

6th March 1915 As on 1st to 4th.

7th March 1915 Brigade church parade in the rain at 10am at LE SART. 23rd Brigade marched into billets at ESTAIRES in evening. Battalion paraded at 5.45pm and arrived at billets about 12 midnight. Bad march owing to transport of Indian Division being met on road just West of MERVILLE. Battalion got split up and was halted constantly.

8th March 1915 In billets. Preparations made for attack on NEUVE CHAPELLE on 10th.

9th March 1915 In billets. Two conferences at Brigade HQ during day. Battalion paraded at 11.45pm and marched to point from which Brigade marched to point of assembly for attack on 10th. Order of march 'A', 'B', 'C', 'D' and M.G. sections (4 guns).

10th March 1915 Vicinity of NEUVE CHAPELLE.
Left starting point 12 midnight 9th-10th. Reached rendezvous 1.30am. Halted for 1 hour when men had hot tea. At 2.30am started for position of assembly. Brigade marched in following order, 2nd Scottish Rifles, 2nd Middlesex Regiment, 2nd Devon Regiment, 2nd West Yorks Regiment. Arrived at position of assembly behind breast work on South side of RUE TILLELOY. Some difficulty was experienced in finding way across country in spite of ground having been reconnoitred, which pointed to necessity of placing men at intervals to direct troops moving to a given point across country by night. The chief reason way was mistaken was owing to a party of engineers crossing line of march of Brigade, and also to bridges over ditches being too narrow, causing column to become attenuated.
The following was order for attack for 23rd Infantry Brigade - 1st line:
2nd Scottish Rifles on right
2nd Middlesex Regiment on left
In support 2nd Devon Regiment
Brigade Reserve 2nd West Yorks Regiment
7.30am. Wire breaking by field artillery and bombardment of enemy's positions (1st line of trenches) began.
8.00am. 2nd Scottish Rifles began attack from our trenches advancing in most gallant manner in spite of heavy losses.
8.15am. ½ 'A' and ½ 'B' Companies began advance along SIGN POST

The 2nd Devons War Diary

LANE on right in support of 2nd Scottish Rifles ½ 'A' and ½ 'B' advanced along RUTLAND ROW on left to occupy trenches vacated by 2nd Middlesex Regiment. Each party was followed by company bombers. The men of battalion belonging to Brigade Grenadier Company followed in rear of left of Battalion. 2 machine guns followed left half of 'A' and 'B' Companies.
8.45am. Head of ½ 'A' and ½ 'B' Companies on left arrived at head of our communication trench and found that 2nd Middlesex were unable to advance, every man being shot down as he appeared over the parapet. 'B' Company then made 3 attempts to cross to German trenches on right of Middlesex and immediately South of pt.7b, all of which was frustrated, the men being all killed or wounded. Lt. R.P. Bates led the first attempt and was killed, falling on German wire. Lt.Parker, in charge of machine guns, was wounded on way up trench and both machine guns were put out of action before getting into position. Our losses were heavy. A further attempt to advance on the left was stopped for the moment and CO directed C and D Companies to support right of Battalion, which attacked German trench about pt.82. This attack came up on immediate left of right half of 'A' and 'B' Companies, which had followed 2nd Scottish Rifles into trenches 74-17 and our bombers were sent forward to clear enemy out of trench running towards point 76. Enemy were already bombing our men.
9.30am. 2/Lt. Wright led bombing party of 5, cleared enemy out of long stretch of trench and enabled left attack to advance. This was a most gallant performance and 2/Lt. Wright was killed while carrying it out, not however before he had obtained his object. (2/Lt. Wright was shot in the back by a wounded German officer and died on the spot. L/Cpl. Woods, who was backing up his officer, quickly took his revenge). 2/Lt. Windsor was wounded on left and taken back to dressing station where he was killed by a shell.
10.00am. 'A' and 'B' Companies were now joined up and occupied trench 74-76. Lt. R.O.Bristowe was killed just after taking German trench, Captain Watts was wounded and Captain Jenkins dislocated his knee. 2/Lt. Jacob took over command of 'B' Company being only officer left in it.
10.30am. A further advance was now made by 'A' and 'B' Companies and ½ 'C' Company and ½ 'D' Company to 82-21, remaining half of 'C' and 'D' Companies being on north side of SIGN POST LANE, in rear, and a delay ensued while our artillery bombarded trenches 22-78-77.
1.30pm. Orders received to advance to last named points. This was done, many prisoners being made and a machine gun taken. The Battalion then took up position 77-78-22-52-84 with HQ at 18. The ½ of 'C' and 'D' Companies in rear were brought up and Companies reorganised. (2nd Scottish Rifles on our right at pt.19 and 2nd Middlesex on our left at pt.6). We immediately began to consolidate our position.
6pm. Royal Scots (21st Brigade) advanced through our lines (The 21st Brigade had orders to capture line BOIS DE BIEZ - MOULIN DU

PIETRE), but they did not advance far to our front, being apparently unsupported. We were heavily shelled by our guns when east of line 79-78, otherwise we could easily have advanced as Germans were on the run. It was reported that PIETRE and BOIS DE BIEZ were actually occupied by the Worcesters and 2 battalions of Indian troops respectively during the day, but that former had to quit owing to our own shell fire and latter owing to be unsupported. Communication between 1st line of infantry in attack and the supporting artillery certainly wants improving very much. Telephone wires appear to get cut at once.

11th March 1915 Situation in front of 23rd Brigade remained practically unchanged throughout the day till the evening when we extended our left to pt.7. The Grenadiers and Scots Guards passed through our left in the morning. The enemy appeared to be much reinforced regards artillery. Battalion were heavily shelled and had several casualties. 2/Lt. Lord was dangerously wounded in head about 8am by bullet and died in ambulance.

12th March 1915 Battalion was again heavily shelled and 'D' Company had several casualties. Captain C.A.Lafone DSO was killed by a bullet in head about noon. Counter attacks at various points were repulsed.
5pm. Battalion received orders to lead Brigade in attack on line PIETRE - LA RUSSIE at 6.30pm. Battalion was collected as quickly as possible and proceeded via pts 22-7-6-23-92 getting into position, in dark, on enemy's side of our trench, 87-92, with 2nd Scottish Rifles in support. We knew nothing of the ground which we had never been on before. Attack was postponed till 11.30 and then till 1.30. About 1.45am we heard it had been cancelled.

<u>REPORT ON PART TAKEN BY 2nd BATTALION, DEVONSHIRE REGIMENT IN OPERATIONS 10th TO 12th MARCH 1915</u>

9th - 10th 12 midnight
Battalion left LA GORGUE to march to rendezvous, (in CAMERON LANE, pt: M15(d)1.9) of 23rd Brigade: 2nd Scottish Rifles in front followed by 2nd Middlesex, ourselves and 2nd West Yorkshire Regiment.

<u>10th March</u>
1.30am
Reached rendezvous, halted for an hour and had tea.
2.30am
Continued march to point of assembly.
4.30am
In position at point of assembly, 2nd Scottish Rifles and 2nd Middlesex in trenches, ourselves in support behind breast work on RUE TILLELOY square M.28.d.
7.30am
Bombardment of enemy's position began.

The 2nd Devons War Diary

8.00am
2nd Scottish Rifles began advance from our trenches on right of Brigade and 2nd Middlesex on left. Latter failed owing to heavy fire.

8.15am
1/2 A and 1/2 B Companies, under Lt. Cobb, advanced along SIGNPOST LANE in support of Scottish Rifles to occupy trench left by latter. 1/2 'A' and ½ 'B', under Captain Watts, advanced along RUTLAND ROW to occupy trench vacated by 2nd Middlesex. Lt. Parker with 2 Machine Guns followed latter party. All company bombing parties followed their companies, and men of Brigade Grenadier Company followed Battalion.

8.45am
Arrived at head of RUTLAND ROW and found that Middlesex had been prevented leaving trench by fire and had suffered severely. 'B' Company made 3 attempts to advance on right of Middlesex but failed, losing considerably. 18 killed, 21 wounded, Lt. Bates being killed on reaching wire entanglement and Lt. Bristowe also being killed and Captain Watts wounded. The machine guns were rendered useless before coming into action and Lt. Parker was wounded. The C.O. who saw we were held up on left decided to send both 'C' and 'D' Companies to support our right attack, which was on pt. about 82.

9.00am
This attack succeeded, the right half of A and B Companies came up on left of Scottish Rifles. 'A' Company bombers under 2/Lt. Wright bombed the Germans out of trenches, from which left attack had been checked, in a most gallant manner, 2/Lt. Wright being killed during the operation – not however before the left had been enabled to come on.

9.30am
The trench now occupied by us was 17-74-21. Between 9am and 9.30am Captain Jenkins of B Company dislocated his knee, 2/Lt. Jacob being the only officer left with that Company.

10.30am
A further advance was made by 'A' and 'B' Companies and 1/2 C and 1/2 D Companies to 82 – 21, remaining half of C and D being on north side of SIGNPOST LANE in rear and a delay ensued while our artillery bombarded trenches 22-78-77.

1.00pm
We then advanced and reached these points but were prevented going on by our own shell fire only.

1.30pm
Received orders to advance to 22-78-77, the fact of our being there evidently not having got back. Many prisoners were made during advance on last mentioned line and the Germans everywhere appeared to be well on the run.

3.00pm
The rear 1/2 of 'C' and 'D' Companies were now brought up and companies were rearranged along line and HQ were established at point 18. We received orders to consolidate our position which

we proceeded to do, with the 2nd Scottish Rifles on our right, about 19, and the 2nd Middlesex at point 6.

6.00pm
21st Brigade advanced, Royal Scots passing through our line, with orders to capture line BOIS DE BIEZ - MOULIN DU PIETRE. The advance however halted some 200 yards in front of our line. Night of 10th - 11th Enemy's shells passing over us throughout night, but no harm done to us.

11th March
Enemy had evidently brought up considerable amount of artillery and we were heavily shelled. Two shells falling in our HQ killed five signallers and orderlies and wounded six. 'B' Company, to which Captain Terry had been transferred, was heavily shelled in afternoon and had several casualties, otherwise position remained the same till evening, when we extended our left to pt.7.

12th March
Battalion again heavily shelled. 'D' Company had several casualties, 6 killed, 26 wounded. Captain Lafone killed about noon by rifle bullet in head.

4.30pm Received orders to attack the line PIETRE - LA RUSSIE with remainder of Brigade. Battalion was assembled and proceeded via 22.7.6.23.92 getting into position for attack on enemy's side of trench, 87-92, with 2nd Scottish Rifles in support. The front was reconnoitred and an impenetrable fence was discovered about 150 yards in front of us. 'B' Company got close to enemy on left and lost some thirty men wounded and missing. Captain Terry and 2/Lt. Jacob bringing in remainder. We heard the attack was cancelled about 1.45am and took up line of trenches 92-87 with 2nd West Yorks on our right and 2nd Middlesex on our left.

13th March 1915 200 yards S.W. of PIETRE. After attack was cancelled we took up line of trenches 87-92 with 2nd West Yorks on our right and 2nd Middlesex on our left. 'B' Company, which had advanced to within about 50 yards of enemy's position, lost some 30 men wounded and missing. Enemy's field gun shelled us and road by which we advanced at point blank range and we had several casualties. Heavy bursts of fire during night but quiet day. Danger of night attack without having thoroughly reconnoitred ground and without having explained to all ranks exactly what was expected of them was very forcibly brought home to me.

14th March 1915 Trenches all day. Relieved in evening by 1st Lincolns. Went back into billets at and near PONT DU HEM getting in about 11.30pm. Captain Lafone was buried by adjutant and party of Battalion on N.E. side of cross roads near where he fell. Our losses for 5 days, since morning of 10th were 6 officers killed, 3 wounded and 1 accidentally injured and 274

The 2nd Devons War Diary

NCOs and men killed, wounded and missing.

15th March 1915 In billets. Lt. Colonel Travers, DSO, went to hospital in evening with abscess on back, leaving Major J.D.Ingles (adjutant) in command. 2nd Lt. Horne appointed acting adjutant.

16th March 1915 Took over trenches, D lines, from Worcesters and Northamptons in evening (our old lines).

17th March 1915 2 men killed.

18th March 1915 Quiet day.

19th March 1915 Relieved in evening by 2nd Scottish Rifles and went into billets as Brigade Reserve on and near RUE DU BACQUEROT.

20th March 1915 Draft of 4 officers (2/Lts. Bolitho, Bullock, Frossard and Roberts) and 42 other ranks joined.

21st March 1915 Voluntary service in morning. Brigadier inspected draft which joined yesterday. Marched into billets in ESTAIRES in evening and remained in them on 22nd.

22nd March 1915 In billets in ESTAIRES.

23rd March 1915 Left ESTAIRES at 1.50pm and marched into billets at BAC ST MAUR.

24th March 1915 Battalion remained in billets. CO and Company Commanders visited section of trenches to be taken over on 25th.

25th March 1915 Took over trenches south of BOIS GRENIER from 4th Canadian Regiment.

26th March 1915 Trenches. Very quiet day. 2 men wounded. Brigade Major, 2 officers: *R.C.* and *O.S.E.* (handwriting indistinct) No 5 and No 6 section met and discussed defence of new lines.

27th March 1915 Trenches. Enemy threw few shells into BOIS GRENIER. We had 3 men wounded.
28th March 1915 Very fine and frosty, trenches drying well. 2/Lt. Adams went to hospital at 5.00am. Enemy shelled BOIS GRENIER about twelve noon. Our trenches were shelled in afternoon. 2/Lt. Radcliffe and 1 man dangerously wounded. Battalion relieved in evening by 2nd Scottish Rifles and went into billets in Brigade Reserve.

29th March 1915 Billets shelled but no damage done.

Martin Body

30th March 1915 Billets shelled but no damage done.

31st March 1915 Relieved 2nd Scottish Rifles in trenches in evening.

The 2nd Devons War Diary

APRIL 1915

1st April 1915 Cold and bright morning. Aeroplanes in action, both our own and enemy's. One man killed and one wounded.

2nd April 1915 2/Lt. Ferrier-Kerr rejoined from Hospital. Quiet day. One man wounded.

3rd April 1915 Quiet day in our section. Brigadier visited all trenches in morning, the communication trench having been completed, thus making it possible. Very heavy and continuous firing to north-east about 4.00pm onwards.
Battalion was relieved by 2nd Scottish Rifles in evening and went into billets in Brigade Reserve.

4th and 5th April 1915 Brigade Reserve at and near TOULETTE.

6th April 1915 Paraded at 3.05pm and marched into billets in BAC St MAUR in Divisional Reserve. All 23rd Brigade came back as Divisional Reserve. 2/Lt. Case joined Battalion from 1st Lincoln Regiment. He belonged to 3rd Devons.

7th April 1915 Companies at disposal of Company Commanders. 200 men taken for digging in evening 6.00pm to 12.00 midnight under their NCOs and men. Draft of 75 NCOs and men arrived in evening.

8th April 1915 Battalion route marched by Companies.

9th April 1915 Companies at disposal of Company Commanders.

10th April 1915 Battalion route marched by Companies; G.O.C. of Division visited billets in morning.

11th April 1915 Church parade at 9.00am. CO; Adjutant; and 1 officer per Company; visited new trenches.

12th April 1915 Battalion paraded at 2.30pm and was addressed by the Commander in Chief Field Marshal Sir John French, who thanked troops for what they had done at NEUVE CHAPELLE. Battalion paraded again at 6.45pm and marched down to No 3 section taking over from 1st London Regiment: 3 Companies in trenches and 1 in support. Trenches by ANCIEN CHARTREUX.

13th April 1915 New lines good - mostly breastwork. Companies at work thickening top of parapet and putting up parados. Casualties: 1 killed and 1 wounded.

14th April 1915 Certain amount of rain. 2nd in Command of 2nd West Yorks Regiment and 4 officers visited our lines to see the situation as they have to relieve us. Casualties nil. Much work done by Royal Engineers and ourselves.

15th April 1915 Brigade Major visited trenches in morning. Very fine day. One man killed.

16th April 1915 Brigadier visited trench HQ in morning. Busy improving trenches. Enemy aeroplanes over our lines. Quiet day. No casualties.

17th April 1915 Quiet day. Enemy placed a few shells in our neighbourhood in afternoon.

18th April 1915 Brigadier visited our trenches.
Relieved by 2nd West Yorks Regiment in evening and went into Brigade Reserve on the RUE DES QUESNEYS near FLEURBAIX.

19th and 20th April 1915 Companies practising handling of arms, bomb throwing, crossing wire etc.

21st April 1915 As on 19th and 20th. Conference at Brigade Headquarters 2pm to about 3pm. Aeroplanes very busy on both sides.

22nd April 1915 As on 19th and 20th. Had conference with all officers in morning. Aeroplanes very busy on both sides.

23rd April 1915 Work as on 19th and 20th.

24th April 1915 Fine cold day. Battalion paraded at 3.00pm and marched into billets near DOULIEU, about 8 miles in N.W direction. Very comfortable billets taken over from 4th West Riding out in country.

25th April 1915 CO visited all billets (about 24) which extended over some 1½ miles of road. Voluntary church parade in evening at 6.00pm. Report to effect that enemy had driven French back from BIXSCHOETE to north of YPRES and had taken LIZERNE, W of canal - using asphyxiating gases.

26th April 1915 Battalion bathed in batches of 50 at baths between SAILLY and BAC St MAUR. General Davies visited our billets in afternoon. Boxing competition between 'A' and 'B' Companies between 4.00 and 6.30 pm. Sounds of heavy firing in direction of YPRES all day and most of night.

27th April 1915 Battalion route marching by Companies. (Heard Indian Corps had proceeded to YPRES last night) Draft joined - 48 other ranks.

28th April 1915 Battalion did short scheme drawn up by Brigade in morning. Conference of all mounted officers of Brigade at 5.00pm. No definite news from YPRES. Heard 7th Division were to march on YPRES also that 1st Battalion had been engaged and Major Radcliffe, DSO, Lt. Cope and Lt. Prior had been wounded.

The 2nd Devons War Diary

29th April 1915 Companies at disposal of Company Commanders. Brigadier inspected draft in morning.

30th April 1915 Timed route march in morning.

Martin Body

MAY 1915

1st May 1915 In billets near DOULIEU. Enemy bombarded NEUVE CHAPELLE and C and D lines very heavily between 4.00 and 5.00am. Battalion ordered to stand to arms and be ready to move at moment's notice. Transport sent for from south of SAILLY. About 11.00am orders received for normal conditions to be resumed. Sent about 320 NCOs and men to sections 1 and 2 for digging in evening under their platoon officers.

2nd May 1915 Left our country billets near DOULIEU at 10.15am and marched into billets (factory) at ESTAIRES. Conference at Brigade HQ at 5.30pm. Voluntary church parade at 6.00pm. Arrangements made for Brigade to take over C and D lines tomorrow night.

3rd May 1915 CO, A/Adjutant, Company Commanders, and Machine Gun Officer reported at Headquarters 2nd Worcester Regiment on RUE TILLELOY at 7.00am and went round trenches. On return to Brigade HQ at 12.00 noon heard that orders were cancelled and that 23rd Brigade would remain in present billets till further orders. About 9.00pm received orders to take over No 1 section of trenches from 2nd Worcester Regiment tomorrow night. Rained hard during night.

4th May 1915 Conference at Brigade HQ at 11.30am re taking over No 1 section of trenches.
Battalion paraded at 5.30pm and marched to No 1 section of trenches, about 5 miles, in pouring rain. Many working parties working both in rear of and in front of lines. Considerable amount of firing going on all night and some casualties. Pte. Tarr of 'D' Company killed.

5th May 1915 Work going on behind trenches all day and night. A part of 2nd Scottish Rifles was rushed about 10.00pm on, while covering working party in advanced trench. Enemy then retired back to their own trenches. Battalion stood to arms till about 11.30pm. We had one man wounded by shell, trenches being shelled in afternoon. 7 or 8 men of working parties of various regiments wounded in evening.

6th May 1915 Artillery very active on both sides all day. Our Battalion HQ and dugouts of supporting Company shelled in afternoon about 5.00pm but no harm done. The whole of area immediately behind trench is swarming with working parties and officers all day.
Relieved by 2nd Middlesex Regiment in evening and went into billets in RUE DU QUESNE.

7th May 1915 Warned to hold ourselves in readiness to move into assembly trenches in evening for attack following morning. This was however postponed for 24 hours. Quiet day in billets.

The 2nd Devons War Diary

8th May 1915 Uneventful day. Battalion paraded at 8.50pm and marched into K block of assembly trenches just south of RUE DU BOIS. Cold night.

9th May 1915 Neighbourhood of trenches.
4.00am   Cold fine night.
British aeroplane reconnoitred enemy's position. Dawn broke clear and bright, sun rising at about 4.10am.
4.15am   Our guns began ranging shots.
4.30am   Heavy rifle fire broke out on our left flank in direction of ARMENTIERES.
5.00am   Artillery began bombardment of enemy's wire and trenches. The bombardment did not appear to be severe and although the wire was cut in places the enemy were not at all demoralised.
5.40am   The main assault began led by 24th and 25th Brigades. Heavy rifle and machine gun fire.
6.05am   Orders received to advance from assembly trenches. Battalion at once advanced to F block of assembly trenches just south of RUE PETILLON arriving just as 1st London Regiment had evacuated them.
6.15am   Getting into these trenches was awkward as Companies had to move to right in file on RUE PETILLON having been ordered to pass to east of block G (see plan numbered 10 attached). It was here we suffered our first casualties, losing about 10 NCOs and men from shell fire. Order of advance was ½ 'C' and ½ 'D' supported by the other half of 'C' and 'D' in first line. 'A' Company in 2nd line and 'B' Company as Battalion reserve. Machine Gun Section and Battalion bombers followed. 'A' Company carriers (64) under RSM followed in rear of Battalions.
6.45am   The Battalion continued advance following City of London Regiment. The latter were off to right so the Battalion passed them making for east end of D, C, B and A trenches. During this advance we were subjected to a very heavy artillery fire and enfiladed machine gun fire from salient in enemy's trenches on our right, losing heavily. Lt. Baines-Walker 3rd Devons and Lt. Tennant 3rd Dorsets (attached) were both killed and Lt. Vaughan, 2/Lt. Bullock, 2/Lt. Austin and 2/Lt. Corbett wounded. The whole advance was difficult owing to changes of direction and trenches B, C and D not being at right angles to line of advance. The losses during advance to first line trenches were about 200 NCOs and men killed, wounded and missing (latter killed or wounded).
7.30am   Leading Companies arrived in trenches which were full of men of all battalions of 25th Brigade, with scarcely an officer. The whole of 'C' and 'D' Companies were brought up and reorganised and further orders awaited from Brigade.
The CO went to HQ 25th Brigade to find out what they intended to do. General Lowry-Cole had been killed and Brigade Major, Captain Dill wounded, latter however continued to act in coolest manner and CO and he went to HQ 23rd Brigade with Major Carter

Martin Body

Campbell Commanding 2nd Scottish Rifles, the CO Colonel Vandelien having been wounded. Orders were received from Division that a further bombardment of enemy's trenches would take place, at first slow, from 1.00 to 1.30heavy. Most of Battalion Rifle Brigade and some of Lincolns had gained enemy trenches but owing to shell fire and enfilading rifle and machine gun fire they could not be supported.

12.45pm Owing to our troops in and in front of German trenches the bombardment was stopped. The remnants of 25th Brigade were reorganised and withdrawn and the whole battalion brought up into 1st line trenches to replace them. Heavily shelled all the afternoon. The battalion and 2nd Scottish Rifles were told to hold themselves in readiness to assault enemy's trenches after dark but this was cancelled. While awaiting orders at Brigade HQ the CO was buried by a shell which burst on parapet and knocked out for short time, Captain Imbert-Terry being sent for to receive orders.

10th May 1915 12.00 midnight. A heavy fire broke out (on) our troops in part of enemy's trenches, being bombed out and retiring under cover of our fire. Later the Rifle Brigade were counter attacked in force and forced to retire with heavy loss. This retirement we also covered. Thus ended the attack between BOIS GRENIER and LA BASSEE, the 1st Corps and Indian Corps having failed to gain any advantage. Shelling continued on both sides during the day. Morning was spent collecting wounded and remaining dead. (2/Lt. Horne was slightly wounded by shell in afternoon of 9th but continued at duty. Captain Sutton R.A.M.C. (our MO) was wounded by shell during night) of 9th-10th.
We were relieved in afternoon by 1st Worcesters and 1st Middlesex extending left and right respectively. On leaving trenches Battalion was shelled leaving one man wounded. We went into billets at WANGERIE, taking over from 1st Royal Scots Fusiliers, who marched off at 11.15pm. Our total casualties for two days were two officers killed, 6 wounded, 235 NCOs and men killed, wounded and missing.

11th May 1915 In billets refitting. Draft of 99 NCOs and men arrived. 86 NCOs and men sent to R.E. for mining work.

12th May 1915 Brigadier inspected draft. 1st Battalion Sherwood Foresters took over from us in evening and we moved about 1½ miles east into billets. Sent out party to bury 2/Lt. Tennant and NCOs and men by night.

13th May 1915 Rained all day. Divisional Commander, General Davies, visited battalion in morning. We took over No 1 section of trenches in evening from 2nd Middlesex Regiment. One casualty.

The 2nd Devons War Diary

14th May 1915 At 1.00am we bombarded enemy's position heavily for 7 minutes and fired heavily from trenches. Similar bursts took place at intervals all up and down the line. Enemy replied. All quiet by 1.15am. Brigadier visited trench HQ in morning. A repetition of bombardment took place at 2.00pm and 12.00 midnight. Enemy replied to both more or less vigorously, cutting both our telephone lines to trenches during latter. Gunner wire to trenches also cut. One man wounded by shell.

15th May 1915 Artillery bombardment of enemy's position, wire or trenches and both commenced at 5.00am and 9.00am calling forth replies. At 5.00am we cleared our troops away from 1P and right of 1Q. and 1P was again cleared between 10.00am and 12.00 noon, but very few shell were fired. 2/Lt. Horne went to hospital and 2/Lt. Tillet took over duties of acting Adjutant. All spare men in trenches were busy burying dead and collecting arms, equipment, etc.

16th May 1915 2/Lt. E.G.Roberts joined.

17th May 1915 'A' and 'B' Companies relieved by 2nd West Yorks in subsections 1P and 1Q and went into billets on RUE DU BACQUEROT. Captain Jenkins and Lt. Andrews rejoined at transport lines and 2/Lt. Carver joined for 1st time.

18th May 1915 Relieved by 1/6th West Yorks in subsections 1R and 1S and battalion HQ and 'C' and 'D' Companies went into billets on RUE DU BACQUEROT.

19th May 1915 Battalion moved into fresh billets at and near ROUGE DE BOUT.

20th May 1915 Found 3 working parties under RE at night. Captains Cartwright and Terry went home on 7 days leave.

21st May 1915 Ordinary routine drills etc.

22nd May 1915 Draft of 3 officers (Lt. E.G.Bryce; Lt. H.Archer; 2/Lt. R.H.K.Anderson) and 120 NCOs and men arrived. Found 2 working parties in evening under RE.

23rd May 1915 Voluntary church parade in morning. Brigadier inspected draft and latest joined officers at 12.00 noon. Relieved 2nd West Yorks in subsections 1P and 1Q in evening. 'A' and 'B' Companies going into trenches and 'C' and 'D' Companies into billets in support. One man killed going down to trenches.

24th May 1915 Two men wounded. Our artillery bombarded enemy in evening beginning at 8.00pm and continuing at intervals all night.

Martin Body

25th May 1915 Bombardment which commenced yesterday ended about 5.00am. Quiet day after.

26th May 1915 Enemy bombarded us both morning and afternoon with heavy and field artillery setting fire to billet occupied by 1/6th Scottish Rifles, close to Battalion HQ.

27th May 1915 Very quiet day.

28th May 1915 Enemy aeroplanes very active. A draft of 25 men arrived.

29th May 1915 During the day enemy shelled in rear of trenches but did no damage.
Relieved by 2nd West Yorks and went into billets near ROUG DE BOUT.

30th May 1915 Lt. Scott and 2/Lt. Stewart joined the battalion. Voluntary church parade in morning.
Lt. Archer left to take over command of 86 NCOs and men working under the RE.

31st May 1915 Enemy shelled with heavy guns on anti aircraft battery near our billets about 1.00am killing one man and wounding another. Lt. Eales joined. Divisional Commander General Davies visited battalion. Moved into fresh billets on the RUE DU QUESNOY. Garrisoned Post 19 with 1 Platoon.

The 2nd Devons War Diary

JUNE 1915

1st June 1915 Ordinary routine drills etc. One casualty - man accidentally wounded by wooden bullet.

2nd June 1915 Brigadier visited Headquarters. Enemy aeroplanes very active. Battalion furnished working parties of 200 men to work under RE. 2/Lt. Ferrier-Kerr returned from hospital.

3rd June 1915 Divisional General Davies visited HQ. Lt/Col. J.D.Ingles and 2/Lt. C.O.R.Jacob returned from leave.

4th June 1915 Battalion relieved 2nd West Yorks in trenches in evening, left half F section and right section No 1 section.

5th June 1915 Quiet day. Enemy aeroplanes very active. Two men wounded. 2/Lt. T.G.Hillyard joined Battalion.

6th June 1915 Quiet day. No casualties.

7th June 1915 Very foggy morning. Brigadier and C.S.O. Indian Corps inspected our trenches between 6.30am and 9.00am. Major Walter, 10th Lincoln Regiment, 21st Division arrived to be attached to Battalion to see how trench duties etc were carried out etc. Casualties: 2 killed and 1 wounded in morning as fog lifted.

8th June 1915 Very hot very quiet day. Aeroplanes active.

9th June 1915 Quiet day. Enemy transport heard in evening and fired on. One man wounded.

10th June 1915 Quiet day. Relieved in evening by 2nd West Yorks Regiment and went into billets in Divisional Reserve and took over Post 19. Major Walter, 10th Lincoln Regiment, left us.

11th June 1915 Routine work.

12th June 1915 General Davies, G.O.C. Division visited us. Aeroplanes active.

13th June 1915 Battalion paraded and G.O.C. Division presented DCM ribbons to CSM King, Pte. Saltmarsh and Sergeant Leach and congratulated Battalion on work done. Aeroplanes active.

14th June 1915 Church parade in morning. Lt. Cox went on 7 days leave. We made a demonstration opposite sections F and I with artillery fire and moving transport in rear of sections at night etc.

Martin Body

15th June 1915 Furnished working parties of 250 men.

16th June 1915 Relieved 2nd West Yorks Regiment in trenches. Had 150 NCOs and men and 4 officers Divisional MT attached to us to help in trenches. One Sergeant wounded.

17th June 1915 Enemy aeroplanes very active. Enemy shelled road in rear of trench Headquarters in evening.

18th June 1915 Quiet day. 2 men killed, one wounded.

19th June 1915 Trenches shelled with shrapnel but no damage done. Two men wounded.

20th June 1915 Very quiet day. Enemy aeroplanes active in evening. Our artillery opened fire on enemy transport which was heard moving at night. No reply was made.

21st June 1915 Things a little more active on enemy's part. They shelled communication trenches and Post 1A in afternoon and evening and put several trench mortar shells over during night without doing any damage. Lt. Colonel Elwes, 12th Durham Light Infantry, attached to Battalion for instruction in trench duties etc. One man killed.

22nd June 1915 Relieved in subsection F.3 by 2nd Scottish Rifles and remainder of Battalion by 2nd West Yorks. Lt. Cox returned from leave.

23rd June 1915 General Pinney came to say "goodbye" on being promoted from Brigadier to command a Division. Lt. Tillet, 2/Lts. Roberts and Batson proceeded on 7 days leave.

24th June 1915 Officers, NCOs and men of Battalion appeared in recent gazette, having been awarded honours as follows:
Lt.Col. J.O.Travers DSO, mentioned and awarded CMG;
Major (Temporary Lt.Col.) J.D.Ingles mentioned and made Brevet Lt.Col;
Captain C.A.Lafone (killed) mentioned; Captain Eardley-Wilmott mentioned; Lt. F.R.Cobb (now Captain) mentioned and awarded Military Cross; Lts. R.O.Bristowe (killed) and H.J.H.Cox mentioned; Lt. G.C.Wright (killed) mentioned; Sergeant Major Pritchard mentioned and awarded Military Cross; Sergeant Radford, L/Cpl. Roberts, L/Cpl. Middlewich, L/Cpl. Smith and Pte. Wood mentioned; Cpl. Lock awarded DCM.

25th June 1915 Routine work. Heavy thunderstorm and much rain.

26th June 1915 Considerable number of troops on the move. Zeppelin passed over our lines in evening moving east.

27th June 1915 Church parade in morning. 23rd Brigade relieved in trenches by 152nd Brigade and 1 battalion of 154th Brigade. We had to close up in our billets. Lt. Archer and 72 miners joined Battalion from 173rd Company Royal Engineers. Major General Pinney went home on promotion and Brigadier General Clarke took over command of Brigade.

28th June 1915 Lt.Col. J.O.Travers CMG DSO rejoined from sick leave and re-assumed command.

29th June 1915 CO inspected all men in billets in morning. Captain McLeod and 2/Lts. Walker and Bolitho went on 7 days leave.

30th June 1915 Orders received in morning for Battalion to take over trenches ½-2R. 2S. 3P and 3Q tomorrow evening from Northamptons and 5th Black Watch. CO and 2nd in command visited HQ of these battalions and made necessary arrangements.

Martin Body

JULY 1915

1st July 1915 Relieved 2nd Northampton Regiment and 5th Black Watch in trenches and posts No 2E and 3F about 9.00pm. A quiet night.

2nd July 1915 A quiet day. Brigadier General T.E.Clarke visited HQ. 3 men wounded.

3rd July 1915 The Brigadier visited the trenches during the morning. A quiet day. One man wounded.

4th July 1915 A quiet day. One man killed and one wounded. (SDGW does not record a death in the battalion on this day).

5th July 1915 During the day a few shells were dropped behind 'A' Company and during the night a few trench mortar shells. Neither did any damage. 2/Lt. F.E.S.Phillips (3rd battalion) joined for the first time. He remained at HQ for the night and was posted to 'C' Company. He joined his Company in the trenches next day. No casualties.

6th July 1915 Germans shelled in rear of HQ during the morning and afternoon. No casualties.

7th July 1915 Relieved by 2nd West Yorks Regiment. Battalion moved into 2 Brigade Reserve billets on the RUE DU QUESNES and garrisoned posts 21, 22 and 23. There were no casualties.

8th July 1915 Found working party of 400 men.

9th July 1915 Routine work. Found Royal Engineers working party of 400 men.

10th July 1915 Received draft of 35 men. Routine work. Found RE working party of 400 men.

11th July 1915 There was a voluntary church parade in the morning. Found a RE working party of 300 men.

12th July 1915 2/Lt. Neilson joined the Battalion for the first time with a draft of 12 machine gunners. 2/Lt. Neilson was attached to 'A' Company. 2/Lt. Carver proceeded to bombing school for course of instruction in bombing.
Furnished a RE working party of 400 men.

13th July 1915 Relieved 2nd West Yorks in the trenches. It was a very quiet night. There were no casualties.

14th July 1915 Germans shelled a little behind our trenches but did no damage. There were no casualties.

The 2nd Devons War Diary

15th July 1915 Enemy shelled behind our trenches but did no damage. There were no casualties.

16th July 1915 A quiet day. One man wounded.

17th July 1915 Germans were very quiet during the day but after midnight became more active: they sent five trench mortar shells, which however did no damage. One man killed. (**There is no record of a death in the Battalion on this day**).

18th July 1915 Lt. Andrews and Lt. Bryce left for England on leave. A Quiet day.

19th July 1915 Relieved by 2nd West Yorks Regiment and went to billets on RUE DE BRUGES. Enemy took down some of their parapet. A quiet day. Two men wounded and one killed accidentally.

20th July 1915 Found RE working parties. Brigadier visited Headquarters.

21st July 1915 Found RE working parties. Brigadier and Brigade Major dined at Headquarters.

22nd July 1915 Found RE working parties. Divisional General visited Headquarters.

23rd July 1915 Found RE working parties.

24th July 1915 Found RE working parties.

25th July 1915 Moved into No 1 Brigade Reserve. The Battalion garrisoned posts 26 and 27 with one platoon each and 1 machine gun. Posts 4H and 3F were also garrisoned with 1 machine gun and M.G. Detachment each.
'C' Company was in support to the 2nd Middlesex Regiment, 'D' Company in support to the 2nd Scottish Rifles. Both Companies and also 'B' Company being in billets near CROIX BLANCHE. 'A' Company was billeted CROIX MARECHAL. Battalion HQ established at CROIX BLANCHE.
Found RE working parties and had church during the morning.

26th July 1915 Found RE working parties. Brigadier visited Battalion HQ.

27th July 1915 Found RE working parties. Captain Hewlett visited HQ.

28th July 1915 Found RE working parties. Divisional General Davies left to take command of Corps in the DARDANELLES.

29th July 1915 Found RE working parties. Brigadier visited HQ. Lt.Col. Williams, Major Luxmore, Captain Blunt and Captain Llewellyn motored from the 1st Battalion and arrived at Battalion HQ about 5.00pm and stayed about an hour.
Captain J.R.Cartwright left to undergo a course of instruction in staff duties at the HQ 3rd Corps.
Lt. J.A.Andrews took over command of 'C' Company.

30th July 1915 Brigadier visited HQ. Furnished RE working parties.

31st July 1915 The Battalion moved into Divisional Reserve billets near QUATRE CHEMINES.

The 2nd Devons War Diary

AUGUST 1915

1st August 1915 Had church parade in the morning.

2nd August 1915 Furnished R.E. working party of 500 men.

3rd August 1915 Routine. G.O.C. inspected the Battalion.

4th August 1915 Routine. Furnished RE working party. 2 men wounded.

5th August 1915 Routine.

6th August 1915 Received draft of 1 officer and 45 other ranks. Lt. C.G.Carson joined the Battalion for the first time.

7th August 1915 Routine.

8th August 1915 Relieved 1st Sherwood Foresters and 2nd East Lancs in trenches and supporting posts. A quiet night. No casualties.

9th August 1915 A quiet day. One man wounded.

10th August 1915 Divisional General Hudson and Brigadier T.E.Clarke visited the trenches in the morning. Enemy sent about 6 HE shells behind 'C' Company but did no damage, otherwise a quiet day. One man wounded. 5 platoons of the 6th Battalion of the Ox and Bucks Light Infantry were attached to the Battalion for instruction in trench duties (20th Division).

11th August 1915 A quiet day. One man wounded. The 5 platoons were relieved by another 5 platoons of the Ox and Bucks.

12th August 1915 Enemy shelled the trenches for a short time during the evening but did no damage. 5 platoons of Ox and Bucks were relieved by another 6 platoons. One man wounded.

13th August 1915 A quiet day. We successfully sniped the enemy during the day and burst 2 rifle grenades in their trenches. Other platoons of 6th Battalion Ox and Bucks Regiment relieved those in the trenches. One man wounded.

14th August 1915 The enemy were very quiet. We sniped the enemy with success and burst some rifle grenades over their trenches. One man wounded. Ox and Bucks relieved their platoons in the trenches.

15th August 1915 Enemy a little more active than on previous day. One man wounded. Ox and Bucks relieved their platoons in the trenches.

16th August 1915   Enemy very quiet. Ox and Bucks relieved their platoons in the trenches. One man killed and one wounded of the Ox and Bucks.

17th August 1915   No entry in War Diary.

18th August 1915   Furnished RE working party.

19th August 1915   Furnished RE working parties.

20th August 1915   Furnished RE working parties.

21st August 1915   Furnished RE working parties. One man wounded outside post 26 by a spent bullet.

22nd August 1915   Furnished RE working parties. One man wounded.

23rd August 1915   Furnished RE working parties.

24th August 1915   Relieved 2nd Scottish Rifles in trenches and posts.
It was a quiet night except that Germans fired about 6 mortars at trenches. They did no damage and 2 did not explode.
One hit a man on the head and shoulder and fell into the trench but did not go off. On examination these shells appeared to be 77mm shell cases full of TNT. Began work on trenches according to winter scheme.

25th August 1915   A quiet day. Our snipers were successful in bagging several Germans. 2 men wounded.

26th August 1915   Except for a little sniping by the enemy it was a quiet day. Germans were seen working on their parapet - they were soon stopped by our rifle fire. Brigadier visited HQ.

27th August 1915   A quiet day. The enemy were again stopped working by our rifle fire. Good work was done with the aid of Sniperscope.

28th August 1915   Our trench mortars successfully shelled the German trenches, they replied with trench mortars and howitzer shells, but did no damage, only knocking down a traverse and very slightly wounding two men.

29th August 1915   During the night the enemy fired two trench mortar shells which did no damage, otherwise it was a very quiet day. Germans were seen revetting their parapet.

30th August 1915   Several German working parties were seen at work and were dispersed by our fire. The enemy were more active than usual firing several bursts of fire with machine guns and rifles.

The 2nd Devons War Diary

31st August 1915 At 5.30pm the Germans exploded a mine just outside the parapet on the left of 2.R. which was occupied by 'C' Company. As soon as the mine was exploded they bombarded the trenches on either side also the 70 yards line with shrapnel and high explosive; this lasted for about ten minutes. In reply we fired about 30 rifle grenades and the trench mortars fired about 20 shells; the supporting battery also opened fire. The Germans replied with trench mortars and rifle grenades. Our Field Howitzers opened fire on their trenches about 6.30pm firing about 50 rounds. The enemy replied to this with 18 rounds from their howitzers.
4 men were brought to notice i.e:
No. 8439 Pte. H.Hocking, No. 8923 Pte. F.Joint, No. 9347 Pte. E.Webber, No. 14152 Pte. W.Howells.
All the above were men of 'C' Company.
Very little damage was done; 3 men were slightly wounded; one or two dug-outs and the parapet smashed by the mine. The crater was about 40 yards in diameter.
Our bombardment appeared to be very successful, several breaches being made in their parapet.
During the night and next day the Germans were very quiet and were seen working hard on the breaches we had made.
2 platoons less 2 sections of 'A' Company who were in local reserve went up to support 'C' Company if required. The supporting Company of the 2nd Scottish Rifles moved up to Trench HQ. After standing to arms next morning, Companies returned to their original positions.

Martin Body

SEPTEMBER 1915

1st September 1915 Several mine experts visited the trenches during the morning, also representatives from the Division and Brigade. 'C' Company was relieved by 2nd Scottish Rifles about 5.00pm, the remainder of the Battalion was relieved by the 2nd Scottish Rifles about 9.00pm.

2nd September 1915 Furnished RE working parties.

3rd September 1915 Furnished RE working parties. The Brigadier visited Battalion HQ. Received a draft of 30 NCOs and men.

4th September 1915 Furnished RE working parties. 2/Lt. Lloyd and 2/Lt. Wykes joined the Battalion for the first time and were posted to 'D' and 'C' Companies respectively.

5th September 1915 Church parade during the morning. The Battalion was relieved in posts and billets by 7th KOYLI (Kings Own Yorkshire Light Infantry) and 7th Somerset Light Infantry. On being relieved the Battalion moved into billets north of the River Lays (Lys) and was then in Divisional Reserve.

6th September 1915 Lieut.Col. Travers took temporary Command of the Brigade. Lieut.Col. Ingles and the Company Commanders visited the ground in the vicinity of Bois Grenier during the day, as the Battalion was in Divisional Reserve and might have to support the 24th and 25th Brigades should the proposed offensive in this part of the line necessitate the Divisional Reserve being brought up.
The Divisional band played at Battalion HQ during the afternoon.

7th September 1915 The Battalion went for a route march in the morning. Brigadier General Tuson took over command of the Brigade. Lt.Col. Travers returned to the Battalion. Captain Milne and Lt. Haynes of 1st Battalion visited Headquarters.

8th September 1915 Routine.

9th September 1915 Routine. The Brigadier visited Battalion Headquarters.

10th September 1915 Routine.

11th September 1915 Routine.

12th September 1915 Church parade in the morning.

13th September 1915 Routine. Major E.G.Caffin, 9th Yorkshire Regiment, who was attached to the 1st Battalion during the siege of Ladysmith, visited battalion Headquarters.

The 2nd Devons War Diary

14th September 1915   Routine.

15th September 1915   This day was observed as a holiday as far as possible. Battalion Sports were held during the afternoon, in a field near Battalion HQ. The Divisional Band played between 4.00pm and 6.00pm. There were many visitors including the Divisional General.

16th September 1915   A detachment of about 500 men under the command of Lt.Col. Ingles was billeted on the RUE DU QUESNOY till the 18th. This detachment was used for digging; finding working parties about 200 strong each day.

17th September 1915   Routine.

18th September 1915   Routine. The detachment under Lt.Col. Ingles rejoined the Battalion. The Brigadier visited Battalion HQ.

19th September 1915   Church parade during the morning; the Brigadier attended this service.

20th September 1915   Routine.

21st September 1915   Routine. Our guns began a four days bombardment of the German trenches in accordance with the proposed offensive operations.

22nd September 1915   Routine. Bombardment continued.

23rd September 1915   Routine. Bombardment continued. The Divisional Band played at Battalion Headquarters between 4.00pm and 6.00pm. Lt.Col. Travers received a wire from the Brigade ordering him to proceed to the Headquarters 3rd Corps by "car" next morning at 8.30am.

24th September 1915   The whole of the 23rd Infantry Brigade was assembled in the vicinity of the RUE BIACHE and was in Divisional Reserve in preparation for the offensive movement which was to be undertaken next morning by the 8th Division. The 25th Infantry Brigade was to assault the German trenches on a front of about 1200 yards from N.6.d.1.6. to LE BRIDOUX ROAD (BRIDOUX FORT inclusive) at day break next morning. The 24th Infantry Brigade was in support and the 23rd Infantry Brigade as before stated was in Divisional Reserve.

25th September 1915   After a short bombardment the 25th Infantry Brigade assaulted and captured the German trenches between LE BRIDOUX ROAD and N.6.d.1.6. but later had to vacate the captured trenches.
The 23rd Infantry Brigade remained on the RUE BIACHE and did not assume any offensive movement.

26th September 1915 The Brigade still remained in Divisional Reserve. The battalion furnished a working party of 450 men. The following casualties occurred in this working party:

```
8271   Pte.   Price. B.          Killed
8600   Pte.   Baker. B.          Wounded
9300   Pte.   Greenstreet. F.    Wounded
9618   Cpl.   Knowles. C.        Wounded
9297   L/Cpl. Cooper. E.         Wounded
9877   Pte.   Sumner. J.         Wounded
8734   Pte.   Williams. A.       Wounded
6856   L/Cpl. Kingdom. A.        Wounded
11340  Pte.   Litton             Wounded
8329   Pte.   Murray             Wounded
8453   Pte.   Warner             Wounded
```

27th September 1915 The Battalion remained at position of assembly. Lt.Col. Travers rejoined the battalion.

28th September The Battalion moved into billets on the RUE DE QUESNE and also garrisoned CROIX MARECHAL POST with one Company. One Company was also in support to 2nd Battalion Middlesex Regiment and was in billets at CROIX MARECHAL.

29th September 1915 Furnished RE working Party.

30th September 1915 Furnished RE working party.

The 2nd Devons War Diary

OCTOBER 1915

1st October 1915   Relieved 2nd Middlesex Regiment in the trenches and Bottlery Post. A very quiet night.

2nd October 1915   A quiet day. The following casualties occurred:
No. 8739 Pte.R.Warne   Killed
No. 9356 L/Cpl. C.Mitchell   Killed
No. 15514 Pte. C.Reekes   Wounded
No. 9997 Pte. J.Heyburn   Wounded

3rd October 1915   A quiet day.

4th October 1915   Enemy shelled in vicinity of Trench HQ and also front trenches, one gun enfiladed the trenches, a shell going through the parados in 'C' Company's trench.
CSM Ward and Pte.Monday were both wounded by rifle fire.

5th October 1915   Divisional General Hudson visited the trenches. A quiet day.

6th October 1915   Relieved by 2nd Middlesex Regiment and moved into billets on the RUE DE QUESNE, one Company garrisoned CROIX MARECHAL POST and one Company was in support to the 2nd Middlesex Regiment and was in billets at CROIX MARECHAL.

7th October 1915   Furnished RE working party of 220 men.

8th October 1915   Furnished RE working party of 200 men.

9th October 1915   Furnished RE working party of 200 men. 14136 Pte. E.Brown wounded.

10th October 1915   The Battalion was relieved by the 1st Worcester Regiment and moved into fresh billets north of the RIVER LYS.

11th October 1915   Divisional Band played at Battalion HQ.

12th October 1915   Routine.

13th October 1915   Furnished RE working party of 200 men.

14th October 1915   Furnished RE working party of 250 men.

15th October 1915   Brigadier General visited battalion HQ. Furnished RE working parties.

16th October 1915   Routine.

17th October 1915 Relieved 1st Battalion Worcestershire Regiment in the trenches.

18th October 1915 A quiet day. Brigadier General visited Battalion HQ. One man wounded.

19th October 1915 8 platoons of the 8th Battalion KOYLI Regiment relieved 8 platoons of the Battalion. The outgoing platoons were attached to the 8th Battalion KOYLI Regiment thus making two composite battalions.
Major Owen, 2nd in command 8th Battalion KOYLI Regiment was attached to Battalion HQ.
Lt.Col. J.D.Ingles left to take over command of 8th Battalion Devon Regiment.

20th October 1915 A quiet day.

21st October 1915 Enemy opened very heavy rifle fire at one of our biplanes during the afternoon, otherwise enemy were very quiet.

22nd October 1915 The Battalion moved into billets. The platoons of the 8th Battalion KOYLI Regiment in the trenches remaining there, the remainder of the 8th Battalion KOYLI Regiment relieved our platoons in the trenches.
The enemy shelled the right Company with 16 x 4.2 HE shells, knocking down the parapet and wounding one signaller.

23rd October 1915 The Battalion moved into new billets at BAC St MAUR.

24th October 1915 Routine.

25th October 1915 Routine. Captain Holdsworth joined 9th Battalion Devon Regiment.

26th October 1915 Routine. Divisional Band played at 'C' Company's HQ.

27th October 1915 The battalion relieved 2nd Battalion Royal Berkshire Regiment in the trenches.

28th October 1915 The enemy shelled in rear of our trenches with field guns but did no damage. Our guns registered on German lines. 3 men wounded. The ground between the trenches was well reconnoitred. Brigadier General visited the trenches.

29th October 1915 The enemy were quiet. Our guns registered on German trenches during the day. Ground between the trenches was carefully reconnoitred.

The 2nd Devons War Diary

30th October 1915 Our guns registered on German trenches, enemy replied with about 10 or 12 HE and Shrapnel shells from a field gun but did no damage.
Brigadier General visited the trenches. One man killed.

31st October 1915 About Stand-to Germans swept our trenches with Machine Gun fire, a powerful searchlight was played on our trenches at the same time and was used in conjunction with the guns. One Sergeant counted 6 machine guns in what he estimated 600 yards.
The ground was carefully reconnoitred during the night, an enemy listening post was found, when discovered the 3 Germans in the post ran away.
The Corps Commander, General Pulteney visited the trenches with Admiral Sir C.Gust during the afternoon.

Martin Body

NOVEMBER 1915

1st November 1915 The Battalion was relieved in the trenches by 1/7th Middlesex Regiment and moved into billets near FLEURBAIX. One man killed.   (SDGW contains no record of a 2nd Devons fatality on this day).

2nd November 1915 Furnished working party of 50 men.

3rd November 1915 Routine. 2/Lt. Preedy joined the Battalion for the first time.

4th November 1915 The Battalion moved into Divisional Reserve billets near BAC St MAUR.

5th November 1915 Routine. Companies practised the attack on German trenches at BRIDOUX. Furnished RE working parties.

6th November 1915 Routine. Companies practised the attack. Lt.Col. J.O.Travers left to take over temporary command of the 70th Infantry Brigade. Captain C.H.M.Imbert-Terry took over temporary command of the Battalion.

7th November 1915 Routine. Practised the attack. Brigadier General visited the Battalion.

8th November 1915 Routine. Practised the attack, the Brigadier General was present at this parade.

9th November 1915 Routine. Lt.Col. J.O.Travers CMG DSO proceeded on leave to England. Practised the attack at night. General Hudson and the Brigadier-General were both present. Furnished night working party of 25 men.

10th November 1915 Routine. Practised the attack. A party of REs and a digging party of 90 men from 1/5th Black Watch attended this parade. Rugby Football was played during the afternoon against REs at the 8th Division - result 3 points all. Divisional Band played at 'C' Company's billet during the afternoon.

11th November 1915 Relieved the 8th Battalion Yorks and Lancashire Regiment in the trenches N/5.2., N/5.3., and N/5.4.

12th November 1915 A quiet day. Very wet.

13th November 1915 Very wet day. Trenches full of water, front trenches and communication trenches began falling in at many places. Colonel Hayes 2nd Middlesex Regiment, who was temporary in command of the Brigade while Brigadier-General was on leave, visited the trenches. Enemy fired about 6 Shrapnel from a field gun and 6 x 4.2 HE shells at BOUTILLERIE otherwise a quiet day. One man killed.

The 2nd Devons War Diary

14th November 1915 Enemy were more active during the night sweeping the parapet in 'C' Company with Machine Gun fire for about half-an-hour and firing nearly the whole night with rifles.

15th November 1915 The Battalion was relieved in the trenches by 2nd Middlesex Regiment and moved into billets in Brigade Reserve. 'A' Company garrisoned CROIX MARECHAL POST with one Company. 'B' Company was billeted at CROIX MARECHAL and was in close support to 2nd Battalion Middlesex Regiment, the remaining two Companies were billeted near CROIX LECORNEX.
2/Lt. Wilson and 2/Lt. Newton joined the Battalion for the first time.

16th November 1915 Routine. Furnished RE working parties.

17th November 1915 Routine. Furnished RE working parties.

18th November 1915 Routine.

19th November 1915 Relieved 2nd Battalion Middlesex Regiment in the trenches, N/5.2., N/5.3., and N/5.4. Quiet night.

20th November 1915 Artillery were active throughout the day and night - German trenches between N.10.c.2.2. and N.10.c.9.6. being bombarded in order "to destroy mine shafts and to cause as much damage as possible to personnel and material". Machine Guns and Trench Mortars co-operated - Enemy retaliated fairly vigorously - We lost one man wounded by shrapnel.

21st November 1915 Fairly quiet day. Our field guns shelled at intervals but the enemy made very little retaliation. Two men were wounded by splinters of bayonet which was hit by a rifle bullet, another man wounded himself in the hand with a Very Pistol.

22nd November 1915 Quiet day. Moved our line further to left and relieved the 8th Battalion Ox and Bucks Light Infantry Regiment. We now hold a length of trench more suitable for 2 battalions. One man wounded when on sentry.

23rd November 1915 Relieved in the trenches by the 12th Battalion KRRR Regiment (King's Royal Rifle Regiment) and 5th Ox and Bucks Light Infantry Regiment. Relief went off well, though very late. Sergeant Dawe ('A' Company) killed whilst sniping. Battalion moved to billets in BAC St MAUR.

24th November 1915 Marched to VIEUX BERQUIN via SAILLY and ESTAIRES - total distance about 10 miles. Arrived at new billets about 2.30pm.

25th November 1915 Moved again to theatre between HAZEBROUCK and MORBECQUE. Billets very scattered.

26th November 1915 Should have been inspected by the Commander-in-Chief, weather very bad however and inspection indefinitely postponed. Fairly heavy fall of snow. Heavy frost.

27th November 1915 Training commenced.

28th November 1915 Church parade. Weather very frosty.

29th November 1915 Parades in barns owing to bad weather. 2/Lt. Goodman; 2/Lt. Vincent; 2/Lt. Johns and 2/Lt. Hill joined from the 3rd Battalion.

30th November 1915 Brigadier visited Headquarters. Training continued.

The 2nd Devons War Diary

DECEMBER 1915

1st December 1915 Divisional Commander, General Hudson, visited 'C' and 'D' Companies in the morning – Training continued – RE Course for officers commenced.

2nd December 1915 Usual training carried out – A.D.M.S. visited 'A' and 'C' Company's billets.

3rd December 1915 Company training by Platoons.

4th December 1915 Company training by Platoons. Lt. Tillett returned off leave.

5th December 1915 Church parade.

6th December 1915 Company training by Platoons.

7th December 1915 Company training by Platoons. Lt. and Quartermaster Palmer proceeded on leave to England.

8th December 1915 Company training by Companies, this included a route march by Companies. CO, Adjutant and OCs Companies attended a lecture at STEENBECQUE given by Major Hewlett on use of aeroplanes etc.

9th December 1915 Company training by Companies. This included a route march. CO attended a lecture on use of gas.

10th December 1915 Company training by Companies, with route march. CO and OCs Companies attended a lecture on the use of gas.

11th December 1915 Company training by Companies, with route march.

12th December 1915 Church parade.

13th December 1915 Training continued. Battalion drill. Practice in the use of smoke helmets. Battalion route march. CO and Machine Gun Officer attended lecture on Machine Guns.

14th December 1915 Battalion drill and route march. CO and Machine Gun Officer attended lecture on Machine Guns.

15th December 1915 Battalion route march accompanied by 'O' Battery Royal Horse Artillery.

16th December 1915 Road march discipline by half battalions. Field Engineering the C.R.E. attended this parade and gave professional advice. Divisional General Hudson visited Battalion HQ.

17th December 1915 Companies not on outposts practised preliminary attack formations. Mayor of Exeter arrived on a visit to the Battalion.

18th December 1915 The Brigade went for a route march during the morning. Order of march:- 2nd Devon Regiment; 2nd Middlesex Regiment; 2nd West Yorks Regiment; 2nd Scottish Rifles; 1/7th Middlesex Regiment.

19th December 1915 Church parade. Mayor of Exeter left.

20th December 1915 1st day of Divisional Manoeuvres. Order of march of the Brigade:- 2nd West Yorks Regiment; 2nd Middlesex Regiment; 2nd Scottish Rifles; 1/7th Middlesex Regiment; 2nd Devon Regiment. The Brigade moved as far as WARDRECQUES. The Brigade billeted for the night, being covered by the 25th Infantry Brigade.
Battalions occupied billets as follows:-
2nd West Yorks Regiment at ECQUES.
2nd Middlesex Regiment at LE RONS and QUIESTEDE.
2nd Scottish Rifles at BLAMBART-LA SABLAN GRAND-QUIESTEDE.
1/7th Middlesex Regiment at RACQUINGHEM.
2nd Devon Regiment at WARDRECQUES.
Brigade HQ were established at the CHATEAU at CLARQUES.

21st December 1915 2nd day of manoeuvres. The 'enemy' having been driven back to the line RELY-AUCHEL, the 8th Division continued its march via THEROUANNE - COYECQUE - RADINGHEM. The 23rd Infantry Brigade (less 2 battalions), Divisional Mounted Troops (less 2¾ platoons cyclists), 5th Brigade RHA (less 1 battery and Ammunition Column), 57th Battery RFA, 15th Field Company RE and No.1 Section 25th Field Ambulance, formed an advance guard under Brigadier General Tuson.
The 1/7th Middlesex Regiment and 2nd Devon Regiment marched at the head of the main body, the two battalions being under the command of Lt.Col. J.O.Travers, CMG, DSO, Officer Commanding 2nd Battalion Devon Regiment. About 1.00pm when the head of the main body was about 1 mile outside COYECQUE, orders were received that the 23rd Infantry Brigade would attack on a front BOMY inclusive to and exclusive of Road Junction in NW corner of D.6.,1 mile due south of ERNY St JULIEN. The 2nd Middlesex Regiment, 2nd Scottish Rifles, and 1/7th Middlesex Regiment deployed for attack. The 2nd West Yorks Regiment and 2nd Devon Regiment received instructions to remain at COYECQUE where they were to be in reserve. 2nd Devon Regiment billeted for the night at COYECQUE. Brigade HQ were established at BOMY.

22nd December 1915 The Brigade retired and moved into billets in the vicinity of BLARINGHEM. The Battalion was billeted at LE CROQUET.

The 2nd Devons War Diary

23rd December 1915 The Brigade moved to MORBECQUE where Battalion returned to billets.

24th December 1915 Routine.

25th December 1915 Whole holiday. Church parade in the morning. CO visited the men at dinner hour. All the officers dined at Battalion HQ. Christmas greetings sent and received from 1st Battalion.

26th December 1915 Nothing recorded.

27th December 1915 Routine. Company parades.

28th December 1915 Routine. Company parades.

29th December 1915 Routine. Company parades. 2/Lt. H.K.Williams (3rd Battalion) joined for the first time. Appointed signalling officer.

30th December 1915 Routine. Battalion route march combined with tactical exercises in the Field.

31st December 1915 Routine. Company parades.

Martin Body

JANUARY 1916

1st January 1916   At MORBECQUE. Routine. Company parades.

2nd January 1916   Church parade.

3rd January 1916   Routine. Company parades.

4th January 1916   Routine. Company parades.

5th January 1916   Routine. Company parades.

6th January 1916   Routine. Battalion route march.

7th January 1916   Routine. Company parades.

8th January 1916   Battalion route march.

9th January 1916   Church parade.

10th January 1916 Battalion route march.

11th January 1916 The Brigade marched to ESTAIRES. Order of march:
2nd Middlesex Regiment; 1/7th Middlesex Regiment; 2nd Devonshire Regiment; 2nd Scottish Rifles; 2nd West Yorkshire Regiment.
The battalion was billeted in the vicinity of L.17.d.4.5. (sheet 36A. France. 3rd edition. 1/40,000) for the night.

12th January 1916 The Brigade moved to SAILLY, there being half an hour interval between the time each battalion passed the starting point (ie, G.25d.8.7. Map Belgium and France sheet 36. B series 1/40,000. 3rd edition). The Battalion moved into billets near DOULIEU.

13th January 1916 Routine.

14th January 1916 Furnished RE working parties. Routine. Received draft of 30 other ranks.

15th January 1916 Routine.

16th January 1916 Church parade.

17th January 1916 Routine.

18th January 1916 Furnished working parties. The Battalion moved into billets at FLEURBAIX and was in Brigade Reserve. The battalion occupied billets as follows:-
Battalion HQ PERGOLA HOUSE. H.22.d.4.4.
'A' Company H.22.a.4.0. 'B' Company H.28.a.8.3.
'C' Company H.29.c.0.3. 'D' Company H.21.d.6.4.
Reference map sheet 36, Belgium and France.

The 2nd Devons War Diary

19th January 1916 Furnished RE working parties.

20th January 1916 Furnished RE working parties.

21st January 1916 Relieved 2nd Middlesex Regiment in the trenches. N.6/1 to N.6/5 and supporting posts.

22nd January 1916 There is no record of this day's activities in the War Diary.

23rd January 1916 Brigadier visited the trenches in the morning. Artillery was fairly active during the day, about 20 x 77mm HE shells were fired at Battalion Headquarters. (WYE FARM) 8 direct hits were obtained. Three men were wounded. One man was killed looking over parapet.

24th January 1916 Enemy sniped a good deal during the morning but were very quiet during the night. The Division and Brigade Generals visited lines during the morning.

25th January 1916 The enemy shelled a great deal during the day with Field and Heavy guns, little damage was done. 2 men were slightly wounded.

26th January 1916 The Battalion was relieved in the trenches by 2nd Middlesex Regiment and moved into billets at FLEURBAIX.

27th January 1916 Routine. Furnished RE working parties.

28th January 1916 Routine.

29th January 1916 Routine. Furnished RE working parties.

30th January 1916 The Battalion relieved the 2nd Middlesex Regiment in the trenches N.6/1 and N.6/5. One man was wounded in BOTTLERY Communication Trench during the relief. One Company 1st Tyneside Scottish was attached to the battalion for instruction.

31st January 1916 The enemy were active during the day and night especially on the left ('D' Company) firing a large number of shells chiefly 5.9. Hows and 77mm HE shells. The enemy also fired several rifle grenades into this part of the line. One man was killed and another wounded by a sniper. The Company of 1st Tyneside Scottish returned to their unit.

Martin Body

FEBRUARY 1916

1st February 1916 Enemy were again active on the left firing several 5.9 and 77mm shells and rifle grenades into the left Company. 2/Lt. A.W.F.Reed joined battalion for the first time and remained at transport lines.

2nd February 1916 The enemy were less active only firing a few 5.9 and 77mm shells and rifle grenades into the left Company. 2/Lt. H.C.Wilson was wounded in the neck and knee by splinters from a rifle grenade. 2/Lt. A.W.F.Reed was attached to 'D' Company and joined the Company in the trenches.

3rd February 1916 The enemy were very quiet all day. The Divisional and Brigadier Generals visited the trenches during the morning.
The Battalion was relieved in the trenches by 11th Sherwood Foresters and moved into billets on the RUE QUESNOY.

4th February 1916 The Brigadier General visited battalion Headquarters. Furnished working parties.

5th February 1916 Routine. Furnished RE working parties.

6th February 1916 Church parade. Furnished RE working parties.

7th February 1916 Routine. Furnished RE working parties.

8th February 1916 Routine. Furnished RE working parties.

9th February 1916 Routine. Furnished RE working parties.

10th February 1916 Routine. Furnished RE working parties. RSM W.Pritchard left in the evening for HAVRE en route to England.

11th February 1916 Routine. Furnished RE working parties.

12th February 1916 Routine. Furnished RE working parties.

13th February 1916 Furnished RE working parties. Church parade.

14th February 1916 Battalion moved into billets near ESTAIRES. Major A.J.Sunderland rejoined the battalion to take over command, Lt.Col. Travers having received orders to proceed to England for duty.

15th February 1916 The 23rd Infantry Brigade moved to LAVENTIE and relieved the 3rd Guards Brigade. 2nd West Yorks Regiment and 2nd Middlesex Regiment relieved the Guards in the trenches. 2nd Scottish Rifles and 2nd Devonshire Regiment relieved the Guards in billets in LAVENTIE and were in Brigade Reserve.

The 2nd Devons War Diary

16th February 1916 Routine. Major A.J.Sunderland took over command.

17th February 1916 Routine. Furnished RE working parties. Lt.Col. Travers left early in the morning for England.

18th February 1916 Routine.

19th February 1916 The battalion relieved the 2nd Middlesex Regiment in the trenches from ROTTEN ROW inclusive to BOND STREET inclusive and also garrisoned FIREWORKS POST with 1 section and A.1 and FLANK POST with 1 platoon each. Battalion Headquarters were established at RED HOUSE (M.6.d.2.0.) Reference Map Sheet 36. S.W.1. 6th edition.

20th February 1916 A quiet day.

21st February 1916 A quiet day.

21st February 1916 is described above as 'a quiet day', but it was a momentous point in the history of the Great War, for on this day Germany launched its offensive against the French at Verdun. The attack had been expected and extra French Divisions had been rushed in before it commenced, but the Germans pressed their attacks so determinedly that it was feared that Verdun would fall. In desperation the French held on and a war of attrition followed with dreadful casualties suffered by both sides.

France was the senior partner in the alliance, and Joffre insisted to Haig that the BEF would have to launch the Somme offensive alone to take the pressure off the hard-pressed French Army at Verdun. He also insisted that it would have to commence by 1st July 1916 at the latest. Haig would have preferred to attack further north at Ypres and suggested that his force would be more able to succeed if the British offensive could be put back to mid-August. This was dismissed by Joffre who insisted on keeping to the 1st July deadline. Reluctantly, Haig bowed to the wishes of the French Commander-In-Chief.

At a stroke, the strategy of the Somme offensive changed from being an offensive with a real hope of obtaining a major breakthrough which might end the war, to a rescue package for the French Army at Verdun. It should be remembered that in this respect the Battle of the Somme was 100% successful, albeit at a terrible cost in men.

22nd February 1916 The enemy were very quiet. One man wounded.

23rd February 1916 The Battalion was relieved in the trenches by 2nd Middlesex Regiment and moved into Brigade Reserve in LAVENTIE.

24th February 1916 Routine. Major General Pinney visited Battalion Headquarters.

25th February 1916 Routine.

26th February 1916 Routine.

27th February 1916 Church parade during morning.
The Battalion relieved the 2nd Middlesex Regiment in the trenches. 2/Lt. J.C.W.A.Pinney, ADC to General Pinney, was attached to 'C' Company for instruction for 1 month. 2/Lt. R.N.K.Anderson acted as ADC to General Pinney during the absence of his ADC.

28th February 1916 2 men were hit by snipers, 2/Lt. F.B.Lloyd and a private soldier were wounded by a bomb whilst on patrol near German wire.

29th February 1916 Enemy were more active than usual, he fired about 10 x 4.2 Howitzer shells and 20 x 77mm shells at ROTTEN ROW, and 15 x 4.2 Howitzer shells into BOND STREET and PICANTIN AVENUE. The front trench occupied by 'A' Company was also shelled by about 50 x 5.9 shells. Very little damage was done, only one man being wounded by a splinter in the jaw. The shelling was in retaliation to our own artillery fire. One man was wounded while sniping.

The 2nd Devons War Diary

MARCH 1916

1st March 1916 The enemy machine guns were active at night, otherwise a quiet day. 2/Lt. R.A.Wykes appointed Instructor and Commandant 8th Division Trench Mortar School.

2nd March 1916 The Battalion was relieved in the trenches by the 2nd Middlesex Regiment and moved into billets at LAVENTIE. One man accidentally wounded.

3rd March 1916 Routine.

4th March 1916 Routine.

5th March 1916 Church parade.

6th March 1916 The Battalion moved into the trenches and relieved the 2nd Middlesex Regiment. A quiet night.

7th March 1916 Hostile machine guns were active at night. One man wounded.

8th March 1916 Between 1.50pm and 5.00pm enemy fired about 200 x 5.9 shells at old gun emplacements near Battalion Headquarters. One man accidentally wounded.

9th March 1916 A quiet day. Furnished RE working parties. One man wounded on working party.

10th March 1916 Our artillery bombarded the hostile trenches during the morning, the enemy replied by shelling our communication trenches with about 20 x 77mm shells. The enemy traversed our trenches at night with machine gun fire. Captain Jones R.A.M.C. was admitted to hospital sick and was relieved by Captain Blandy R.A.M.C.
The battalion was relieved by the 2nd Middlesex Regiment and moved into billets at LAVENTIE. 2/Lt. S.T.Stephens joined the battalion for the first time and was posted to 'C' Company.

11th March 1916 Routine. Furnished RE working parties. 2/Lt. F.B.Lloyd rejoined from hospital.

12th March 1916 Church parade. Furnished RE working parties. 2/Lt. H.Acomb, 11th Yorkshire Regiment, joined the battalion for the first time and was posted to 'B' Company.

13th March 1916 Routine. Furnished RE working parties. Captain E.G.Roberts admitted to hospital sick. Captain G.L.Jones R.A.M.C. returned from hospital.

14th March 1916 The Battalion relieved the 2nd Middlesex Regiment in the trenches. A quiet night. 2/Lt. C.W.Eales admitted to hospital sick. Each Company had one platoon of 14th Hants Regiment attached to them for instruction. One man wounded.

15th March 1916 At 9.40pm a hostile 4.2 battery fired single shots at the ground just in rear of 'A' and 'B' Companies. No damage was done. Enemy fired several bombs during the night, into the line held by 'D' Company. No damage was done. The Brigade carried out a rocket test at 10.00pm. The enemy took no notice of the rockets.

16th March 1916 Very quiet day. The Brigadier visited the trenches.

17th March 1916 During the morning enemy fired 3 x 77mm shells into the right communication trench. 4 x 77mm shells burst short of the wire in front of 'C' Company during the afternoon. Enemy's machine guns were very active at night.

18th March 1916 The enemy shelled intermittently throughout the day into the vicinity of RUE TILLELOY tram base, Gt. CENTRAL and RED HOUSE (Battalion Headquarters) with 77mm shells. Captain J.A.Andrews was wounded in the leg when in front of his wire. The Brigadier visited Headquarters on his way to the trenches. The battalion was relieved in the trenches by 2nd Middlesex Regiment and moved into billets at LAVENTIE.

19th March 1916 Church parade. 2/Lt. C.O.R.Jacob returned from the base.

20th March 1916 Routine. Furnished RE working parties. 2/Lt. C.W.Eales rejoined from hospital.

21st March 1916 Routine. Furnished RE working parties.

22nd March 1916 Relieved the 2nd Middlesex Regiment in the trenches. Each Company had 2 platoons of the 17th Sherwood Foresters attached to them for instruction. The enemy was unusually quiet, hardly a shot being fired.

23rd March 1916 The enemy was again extremely quiet. 2/Lt. G.Parker joined the battalion for the first time. 2 Brigadiers and various other officers of the 105th Brigade visited the trenches during the day.

24th March 1916 A very quiet day. The platoons of the 17th Sherwood Foresters attached to the Companies returned to their billets. Several officers of the 105th Brigade visited the trenches.

The 2nd Devons War Diary

25th March 1916 A very quiet day. 2/Lt. R.A.Wykes rejoined from the 8th Division Trench Mortar School. One man wounded.

26th March 1916 The battalion was relieved in the trenches by the 15th Battalion Cheshire Regiment and moved into billets at BAC St. MAUR. Three Companies were billeted on the RUE BATAILLE. Enemy were very quiet all day. Captain E.G.Roberts rejoined from hospital. 2/Lt. H.H.Goodman rejoined from 23rd Infantry Brigade Bomb School.

27th March 1916 The Battalion marched to LESTREM STATION where it entrained at 9.5pm and proceeded to LONGUEAU, detraining there at 6.30am on the morning of the 28th.
2/Lt. A.H.Smith, 2/Lt. R.J.Andrews and 2/Lt. G.W.Dibble all joined the battalion for the first time from the cadet school. 2/Lt. A.H.Smith and 2/Lt. R.J.Andrews were posted to 'A' Company and 2/Lt. G.W.Dibble to 'D' Company.

28th March 1916 The Battalion marched to AMIENS after it had detrained at 6.30am and continued through that town to FREMENT where the battalion was billeted with the exception of 'D' Company who were billeted at VAUX.

29th March 1916 'D' Company were brought back and billeted at FREMENT. The whole of the battalion is now billeted at FREMENT.

30th March 1916 Routine.

31st March 1916 Routine.

Martin Body

APRIL 1916

1st April 1916 Routine. There was a conference at Brigade Headquarters of all commanding officers.

2nd April 1916 Church parade at 11.30am for C of E in village.

3rd April 1916 The battalion moved into billets at St GRATIEN (en route for ALBERT).

4th April 1916 The Battalion moved to billets in ALBERT and occupied left Brigade Reserve, relieving the 2nd Battalion Middlesex Regiment. One platoon of 'B' Company was occupying TARA REDOUBT.

5th April 1916 Routine.

6th April 1916 Routine. Furnished RE working parties.

7th April 1916 Routine. Furnished RE working parties.

8th April 1916 Routine. Furnished RE working parties.

9th April 1916 Routine. Furnished RE working parties. Church parade. The Battalion was relieved in billets by the 2nd Lincoln Regiment and moved into new billets at ALBERT. The Battalion after relief went into Divisional Reserve but was under the orders of 70th Infantry Brigade for working parties; half the Battalion working under the 15th Field Company RE and the other half Battalion under the 1st Home Counties RE. Work was carried out on the support and reserve lines daily.

10th April 1916 Working parties. Lt. R.N.K. Anderson was admitted to hospital.

11th April 1916 Furnished RE working parties. The Brigadier visited battalion Headquarters.

12th April 1916 Furnished RE working parties. About 7.30pm the Germans bombarded and raided the trenches held by 1st Royal Irish Rifles. The Battalion stood to arms and was placed under the orders of the G.O.C. 25th Infantry Brigade. Orders were received to stand down at 10.45pm.

13th April 1916 Furnished RE working parties.

14th April 1916 Furnished RE working parties.

15th April 1916 Furnished RE working parties.

16th April 1916 Furnished RE working parties. Captain M.R.M. McLeod proceeded to 4th Army Infantry School to take over the duties of Instructor.

The 2nd Devons War Diary

17th April 1916 Relieved the 11th Battalion Sherwood Foresters Regiment in the trenches during the morning. Enemy fired 6 x 77mm shells into our lines during the day and enfiladed the right company with machine gun fire, otherwise the enemy was very quiet.

18th April 1916 There was a little artillery activity on both sides. A patrol from 'C' Company tried to catch a German patrol which was seen near our lines but was unsuccessful. One of our wiring parties had to cease work owing to hostile machine gun fire. One man wounded. 2/Lt. H.K.Williams reported to 23rd Infantry Brigade for duty with signals.

19th April 1916 During the morning our 4.5 Howitzers shelled the enemy's front line doing some damage. Enemy fired 16 x 77mm shells into our lines doing a little damage. One shell fell into a dug out containing 5 men but all escaped untouched. About 7.00pm the enemy bombarded our trenches with at least 8 guns, little damage was done. We suffered no casualties. Enemy machine guns and snipers were active throughout the night. The following appeared in the London Gazette of the 19th:- Major A.J.E. Sunderland to be Temp. Lt.Col.; 17th March 1916. Received a draft of 40 other ranks.

20th April 1916 Enemy fired 8 x 77mm shells into our trenches during the day, doing no damage. Otherwise a quiet day.

21st April 1916 Enemy fired 18 x 77mm shells at our lines and 11 x 15cm shells. 3 of the latter were blind **(dud)**. One dug out was blown in burying 3 men. They were dug out uninjured. Enemy's machine guns were active at night.

22nd April 1916 Captain Preedy left to undergo a months course at the 4th Army School. The Division on our left carried out a successful raid on the enemy trenches roughly between the hours of 8.00pm and 10.30pm. The enemy retaliated by heavily shelling our trenches, stopping about 11.00pm, damaging the trenches, killing one man, wounding 12 others and wounding Captain E.G.Roberts and Captain T.G.Hillyard. 2 men were killed during the morning by shell fire.

23rd April 1916 The Battalion was relieved in the trenches by the 2nd Battalion Middlesex Regiment and moved into billets in ALBERT.

24th April 1916 Routine. Furnished RE working parties.

25th April 1916 Routine. Furnished RE working parties.

26th April 1916 Routine. Furnished RE working parties.

27th April 1916 Relieved 2nd Battalion Middlesex Regiment in the trenches. A quiet day. Captain Fowler attached to Battalion during the absence on leave of Captain Jones R.A.M.C.

28th April 1916 Enemy was very quiet. He was constantly seen at work on his front and second lines.

29th April 1916 Enemy fired about 12 shells at our trenches during the day, otherwise it was a very quiet day. 2/Lt. L.A.Carey joined the Battalion on first appointment and remained at the Transport Lines.

30th April 1916 About 2.30am the enemy bombarded the trenches of the Division on our right. The enemy also shelled our front line trenches very slightly and formed a barrage lasting about 10 minutes, hostile machine guns were also very active. Our own Artillery replied, some of the shells bursting short, some behind our trenches. The bombardment ceased at 3.25 am. Enemy again bombarded the trenches on our right at 7pm. Our artillery replied. The bombardment ceased about 9.30pm. The enemy machine guns were very active. The enemy again shelled our front trenches and communication trenches doing little damage. One man wounded by our own shell fire. 2/Lt. L.A.Carey joined his Company in the trenches.

The 2nd Devons War Diary

MAY 1916

1st May 1916 The Battalion less 1 Company was relieved in the trenches by the 2nd Middlesex Regiment and moved into billets in ALBERT. 'C' Company was attached to 2nd Middlesex Regiment in the trenches. One man was wounded.

2nd May 1916 Routine. Furnished RE working parties.

3rd May 1916 The battalion was relieved in the billets in ALBERT by the 2nd Royal Berks. Battalion Headquarters, 'B' and 'C' Companies moved into camp in HENENCOURT WOOD. 'A' and 'D' Companies were accommodated in the ALBERT BOUZINCOURT defences for work under C.R.E. (Corps of Royal Engineers) and were under the command of G.O.C. 25th Infantry Brigade. This detachment was under the command of Lt. W.L.Sparkes. One man wounded on RE working party.

4th May 1916 Routine. Furnished RE working parties.

5th May 1916 Routine. 2/Lt. C.W.Eales was accidentally wounded and Sergeant Kearns killed by a bomb accident at 23rd Infantry Brigade Bomb School.

6th May 1916 Routine. Furnished RE night working parties.

7th May 1916 Church parade. 2/Lt. G.W.Dibble proceeded to Bomb School for a course of instruction.

8th May 1916 Routine. 2/Lt. A.E.A.Phillips joined battalion on first appointment from GHQ Cadet School.

9th May 1916 Routine. 2/Lt. A.H.Cornell joined Battalion on first appointment from GHQ Cadet School.

10th May 1916 HQ, 'B' and 'C' Companies joined 'A' and 'D' Companies in the ALBERT BOUZINCOURT DEFENCES during the evening.

11th May 1916 Relieved 2nd Middlesex Regiment in the trenches during the morning. The enemy shelled 'C' Company between 3.50pm and 4.50pm with about 80 trench mortar shells doing a little damage to the trenches and wounding 2 men. One man was saved by his steel helmet.
The enemy snipers and machine guns were more active than usual about 2.00am.
Our own artillery silenced the enemy's trench mortar batteries.

12th May 1916 Enemy were more active than usual. About 34 x 77mm shells, 12 x 15cm shells and 100 light Minenwerfer and rifle grenades were fired into our lines. The enemy opened heavy machine gun and rifle fire upon one of our patrols, one man being killed. Received a draft of 38 other ranks.

Martin Body

13th May 1916 At 1.30pm, 3.30pm, 5.00pm, 9.30pm, 11.30pm, 12.30am and 1.25am enemy fired salvoes of 12 shells (77mm) at our trenches. At 11.00pm and 12.30pm enemy fired about 20 x 77mm shells at our front line. Our artillery retaliated to the enemy's shelling.

14th May 1916 Enemy was not very active during the day. He fired 7 x 77mm shells at Battalion Headquarters; 8 x 77mm shells, 3 trench mortar shells and 3 canisters at our trenches. Beyond killing one man with a canister, little damage was done. The enemy machine guns were fairly active. One man was wounded whilst wiring.

15th May 1916 Relieved in the trenches by 2nd Middlesex Regiment. On completion of relief the Battalion moved into billets in ALBERT.

16th May 1916 Routine. Furnished RE working parties. Received draft of 28 other ranks. 2/Lt. J.A.Rennie and 2/Lt. E.M.Gould joined the Battalion on first appointment.

17th May 1916 Routine. Furnished RE working parties.

18th May 1916 Routine. Furnished RE working parties. Brigadier General Ingles and Colonel Luxmore visited the battalion during the afternoon.

19th May 1916 The Battalion was relieved by 1st Royal Irish Riflesand moved into camp at HENENCOURT.

20th May 1916 Routine.

21st May 1916 Routine.

22nd May 1916 Routine. Captain J.A.Andrews rejoined. The following officers joined the Battalion on first appointment: 2/Lt. H.St.Hill, 2/Lt. E.A.Jago, 2/Lt. H.H.Jago, 2/Lt. J.S.McGowan, 2/Lt. H.W.Jones.

23rd May 1916 Routine. 2/Lt. H.E.Marchant and 2/Lt. C.V.Beddow joined the Battalion on first appointment.

24th May 1916 Routine.

25th May 1916
Routine. During the morning there was a Stokes gun demonstration at which the Corps Commander was present. He presented medal ribbons to 2nd Middlesex Regiment before the demonstration.

The 2nd Devons War Diary

26th May 1916 2nd Devon Regiment and 2nd Middlesex Regiment practised the attack during the morning under the Brigadier. In the afternoon the Battalion carried out a signal test with an aeroplane whilst making the attack. Corps Commander was present and complimented the CO on the way in which everything was carried out and the condition of the Battalion.

27th May 1916 Routine. Moved into billets in MILLENCOURT at night.

28th May 1916 Church parade. Furnished RE working party.

29th May 1916 Routine. Furnished RE working parties.

30th May 1916 Furnished RE working parties. All available officers were taken by bus to FRANVILLERS where the German lines opposite our trenches were marked out on the ground by white flags.

31st May 1916 Routine. Furnished RE working parties. All available officers were taken by bus to FRANVILLERS to study the ground marked out by flags to represent the German lines.

Martin Body

JUNE 1916

1st June 1916 The Battalion moved off at 2.45am and marched to the ground near FRANVILLERS where the German lines were marked out by white flags. Three Divisions practised the attack. The Army and Corps Commanders were present at this exercise. After the attack there was a conference of General Officers and OC Battalions.

2nd June 1916 Routine. Furnished RE working parties. 2/Lt. E.M.Gould proceeded to 23rd Infantry Brigade Bomb School to undergo a course of bombing.

3rd June 1916 Routine. Furnished RE working parties. 2/Lt. C.V.Beddow proceeded to LUCHEX to undergo a short course of sniping under Captain Hesketh Pritchard.

4th June 1916 A draft of 26 other ranks reported from 1st Entrenching Battalion. 2/Lt. H.St.Hill proceeded to 8th Divisional School of Instruction for a Course of Instruction. Church parades were held during the morning.
The battalion relieved the 11th Battalion Sherwood Foresters in the right sub-section trenches during the afternoon. About 5.30pm 6 x 5.9 shells fell near DONNET POST (Battalion Headquarters). No damage was done. There was considerable artillery and trench mortar activity between 5.45pm and 9.45pm in the Brigade on our right. Gas shells could be slightly smelt at Battalion HQ. Between 10.00pm and 12.00 midnight a heavy bombardment could be heard in the vicinity of FRICOURT. The hostile machine guns were more active than usual at night, firing continually.

5th June 1916 Our snipers claimed to have hit one of the enemy. At 3.00pm our trench mortars opened fire on the enemy, who retaliated with field guns and Howitzers. This went on intermittently until 5.10pm when fire from both sides ceased. About 5.30pm our guns again opened fire and the enemy retaliated. At 11.45am and 1.00pm our guns retaliated for hostile shelling. Between 8.00am and 8.15am ten 77mm shells fell at X.7.6. ('D' Company).
At 11.45am six 77mm shells were again fired at 'D' Company trenches. 4 burst in the wire and the remainder behind the front line trenches.
During the afternoon the enemy shelled our trenches with minenwerfer shells, seventy 77mm shells and thirty seven 15cm shells. No serious damage was done but part of the trenches were knocked in.
Between 11.00pm and 12.00 midnight the Divisions on our right and left carried out raids on the enemy's trenches. At 11.00pm the enemy started a heavy bombardment on our front line, support and communication trenches, employing field guns, Howitzers and minenwerfer. At 12.00 midnight the bombardment slackened off a

little but continued until 12.40am.
Considerable damage was done to our trenches.
During the bombardment the following casualties occurred:-
2/Lt. H.E.Marchant   killed
2/Lt. S.D.Carver   wounded
3 other ranks   killed
14 other ranks wounded
It was 2/Lt. Marchant's first tour in the trenches.
2/Lt. Carver was buried by a shell.
'C' Company's Signaller's dugout was blown in. One man escaped but two others were buried and could not be dug out before they had died.
The worst of the casualties occurred in the left Company ('D' Company) as this part of the line is enfiladed. During the bombardment heavy machine gun fire was kept up by the enemy. Two searchlights played in 'No Man's Land' during the bombardment.

6th June 1916 The enemy were fairly quiet. Sixty-four 77mm shells and 12 x 15cm shells were fired. At night the enemy machine guns were active, traversing our front line parapet. During the night, 'C' and 'B' Companies furnished a covering party to a party of about 600 men furnished by the South Wales Borderers and 2nd Middlesex Regiments who, under RE supervision, constructed an advanced trench in front of our line. This work was superintended by Major Betty RE. We suffered no casualties. At the time the enemy were very busy repairing their front line and wire. Captain J.A.Andrews was in charge of our covering party. One man wounded.

7th June 1916 A comparatively quiet day. The enemy registered the new trench with a few 77mm shells. One man was wounded by shell fire.
The following officers were struck off the strength of the Battalion:
Capt. M.R.M.McLeod on being appointed Assistant Instructor at 4th Army School 15/4/16.
2/Lt. E.C.Gardiner on being posted to 4th Field Survey Company 5/6/16.
2/Lt. M.C.Ley, 3rd Battalion, joined on first appointment and was posted to 'D' Company.

8th June 1916 During the morning the enemy fired about fifty 77mm shells at our trenches.
The battalion was relieved in the trenches during the morning by the 2nd Middlesex Regiment and on relief moved into billets in Brigade Reserve at ALBERT.
One man was killed and one wounded. In addition one man was admitted to hospital suffering from gas poisoning. This gas came out of the ground while deepening a new trench dug on the night 6/7th June.

Two signallers attended a short course with RFC in connection with communication with aeroplanes. One man killed and one wounded by shrapnel and another was wounded by an enemy sniper.

9th June 1916   Routine.   Furnished RE working parties.

10th June 1916   Routine.   Furnished RE working parties.

11th June 1916   Routine.   Furnished RE working parties.   Church parades were held during the morning.

12th June 1916   The Battalion was relieved during the evening by 1st Royal Irish Rifles and moved into camp at HENENCOURT WOOD. Furnished RE working parties.

13th June 1916   2/Lt. G.S.D.Carver rejoined from hospital.   'A' Company made up to 240 strong, moved into ALBERT-BOUZINCOURT DEFENCES.   This Company was commanded by Captain Preedy.   A memorial service was held during the evening in memory of the late Lord Kitchener.

14th June 1916   Routine.   Furnished RE working parties.

15th June 1916   Routine.   Furnished RE working parties.

16th June 1916   Moved into the trenches.   Received draft of 48 other ranks.

17th June 1916   Our artillery was fairly active.   Between 9.15am and 10.30am the enemy fired about twenty 15cm shells at our trenches killing one and wounding another man.   About midday the enemy fired several 77mm shells at our trenches.   The enemy machine guns fired throughout the night.   Casualties 1 other rank killed and 4 other ranks wounded.   The Companies were very busy carrying material required for the proposed offensive operations.
2/Lt. R.A.Wykes proceeded to the 23rd Trench Mortar Battery for duty.

18th June 1916   On two occasions our artillery silenced enemy machine gun fire.   The enemy during the day fired about 60 x 77mm shells and several 15cm shells at our trenches.   Enemy machine guns were again active at night.   3 men were wounded. The Companies were again hard at work carrying stores.

19th June 1916   The enemy fired about 40 x 77mm shells and a few 15cm shells at our trenches.   One man was accidentally killed in the trenches.   One man was wounded.   2 men were accidentally wounded at 23rd Infantry Brigade Bomb School.
The Battalion was relieved in the trenches by the 2nd Middlesex Regiment and on relief went into camp at HENENCOURT WOOD.   While

in the trenches a great deal of stores were carried into the trenches.
2/Lt. F.B.Coldwells and a draft of 31 other ranks joined the Battalion in camp. 2/Lt. E.D.Hill proceeded to 23rd Trench Mortar Battery for duty.

20th June 1916 Routine. Furnished RE working parties.
2/Lt. S.M.M.Neilson rejoined the battalion from 23rd Infantry Brigade Trench Mortar Battery.

21st June 1916 Routine. Furnished RE working parties.

22nd June 1916 The Battalion moved into LONG VALLEY V.24.b.2.2. (Map Sheet 57d 1st Edition. France) where it bivouacked.

23rd June 1916 Routine. Furnished RE working parties.

24th June 1916 Routine. Received a draft of 43 other ranks. First day of bombardment preparatory to the attack on German trenches. 'D' Company made up to 240 men from 'A' Company moved into ALBERT DEFENCES. This detachment was under the command of 2/Lt. C.O.R.Jacob.

25th June 1916 Routine. 2nd day of bombardment. Church parades held during the morning.

26th June 1916 3rd day of bombardment.

27th June 1916 Routine. 4th day of bombardment. The Brigadier visited Battalion Headquarters. Temp. Captain R.N.K.Anderson left to take up training duties with reserve battalions at home.

28th June 1916 5th day of bombardment. The Brigadier visited Battalion Headquarters.

29th June 1916 6th day of bombardment. The Commanding Officer addressed the Battalion on the forthcoming operations.
The Battalion moved into the trenches. 'D' Company dug a new assembly trench during the night.
2/Lt. G.W.Dibble and 1 other rank were wounded while digging this trench. One man wounded by shell fire.

30th June 1916 7th day of bombardment. The enemy shelled our trenches intermittently throughout the day with 5.9cm shells, 4.5cm shells and 77mm shells, there were few casualties and the trenches were knocked in, in several places, one shell going through the Battalion Fighting Headquarters which were to be occupied the next day. This damage was repaired by the Regimental Pioneers during the day.
CSM Turner was killed and two men wounded by shell fire.
'C' Company completed the new assembly trench. The Battalion

moved into its position of assembly. 'A' and 'B' Companies moved into the new trench (front line and BORDER STREET). 'C' and 'D' Companies moved into RYECROFT STREET and part of FURNESS STREET. Battalion HQ moved to the Fighting HQ in FURNESS STREET at junction of CONISTON STREET. The 2nd Middlesex Regiment were on the right, 2nd West YorksRegiment in support and 2nd Scottish Rifles in Reserve.

"With God's help I feel hopeful. The men are in splendid spirits. Several have said that they have never before been so instructed and informed of the nature of the operation before them. The wire has never been so well cut, nor the artillery preparation so thorough."
(The Private Papers of Douglas Haig, 1914-1919, page 151).

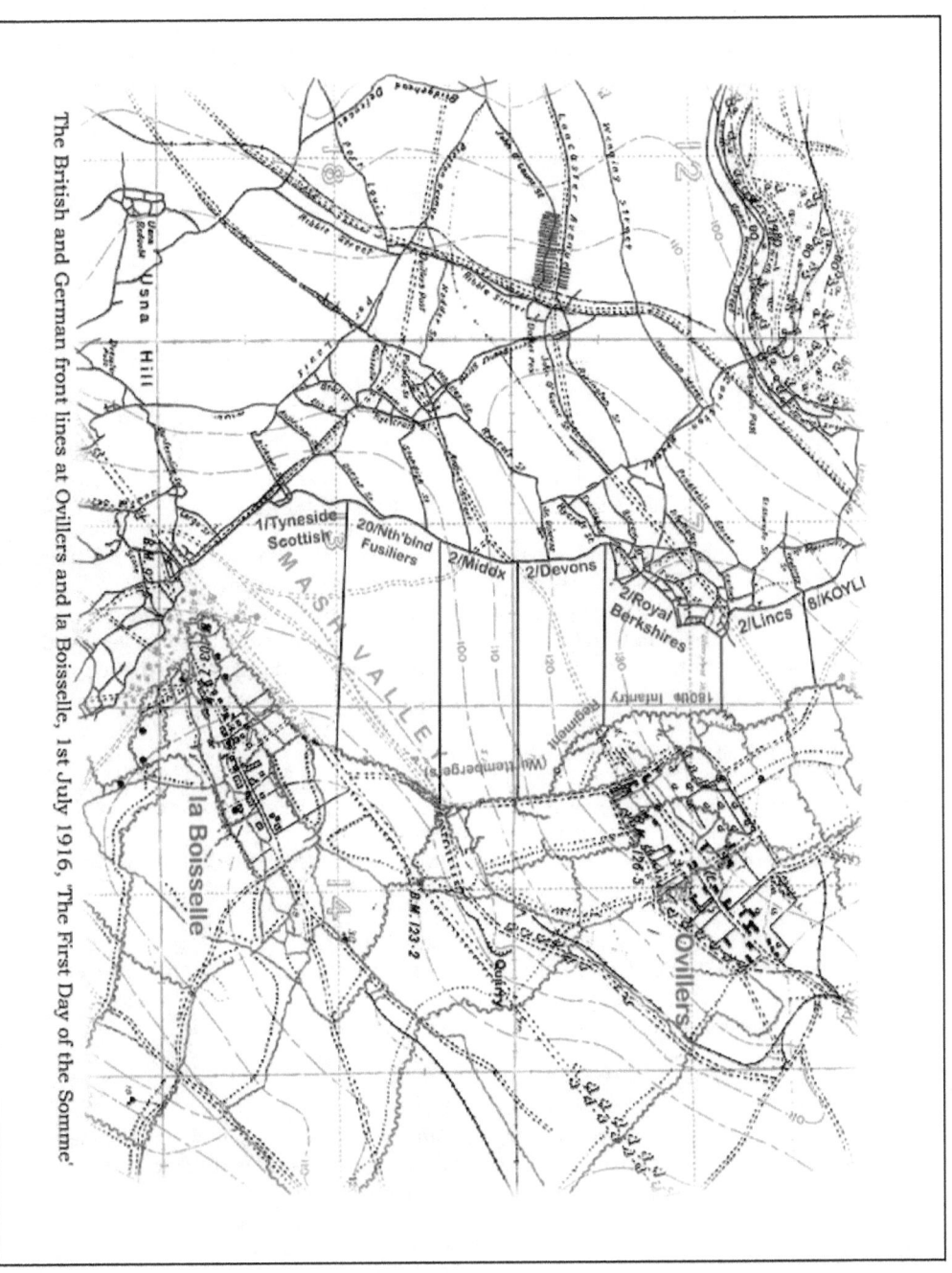

The British and German front lines at Ovillers and la Boisselle, 1st July 1916, 'The First Day of the Somme'

Martin Body

1st JULY 1916 – THE FIRST DAY OF THE BATTLE OF THE SOMME

The First Day of the Battle of the Somme was the most costly day in the entire history of the British Army. The casualties suffered that day, listed below, are taken from the Official History:

Killed/Died of Wounds:
Officers: 993
Other Ranks: 18,247
Wounded:
Officers: 1,337
Other Ranks: 34,156
Missing:
Officers: 96
Other Ranks: 2,056
Prisoners:
Officers: 12
Other Ranks: 573

<u>Total Killed: 19,240   Total Casualties: 57,470</u>

Of the 143 battalions which went into battle that morning, almost exactly 50% of the Other Ranks had become casualties by the end of the day, while the rate among their officers was a staggering 75% being either killed or wounded. The British casualties on that single day amounted to the equivalent of 6 full divisions, or 75 battalions, or 2 casualties for every yard of the 16 mile front stretching from Gommecourt in the north, to Montauban in the south. The 8th Division formed up that morning as follows:

70th Brigade. Left of Divisional Front
8th (Service) Battalion, The York and Lancaster Regiment. Left of Bde. front line.
8th (Service) Battalion, The King's Own Yorkshire Light Infantry. Right of Bde. front line.
9th (Service) Battalion, The York and Lancaster Regiment. In support.
11th (Service) Battalion, The Sherwood Foresters (Notts. & Derbyshire Reg't). In reserve.

25th Brigade.Centre of Divisional Front
2nd Battalion, The Lincolnshire Regiment. Left of Bde. front line.
2nd Battalion, Prince Charlotte of Wales's Royal Berkshire Regiment. Right of Bde. front line.
1st Battalion, The Royal Irish Rifles. In support.
2nd Battalion, The Rifle Brigade (Prince Consort's Own). In reserve.

23rd Brigade.Right of Divisional Front
2nd Battalion, The Devonshire Regiment. Left of Bde. front line.
2nd Battalion, The Middlesex Regiment (Duke of Cambridge's Own). Right of Bde. front line.
2nd Battalion, The Prince of Wales's Own (West Yorkshire) Regiment. In support.
2nd Battalion, The Cameronians (Scottish Rifles). In reserve.

Divisional Artillery
V Brigade, Royal Horse Artillery
XXXIII and XLV Brigades, Royal Field Artillery

The 2nd Devons War Diary

Divisional Units
22nd (Service) Battalion (3rd County Pioneers) The Durham Light Infantry
Nos. 2, 15 and 1/1 (Home Counties) Field Companies, Royal Engineers
24th (1/1st Wessex), 25th (1/2nd Wessex) and 26th (1/3rd Wessex) Field Ambulances, R. A. M. C.
8th Divisional Train (Nos. 42, 84, 85 and 87 Companies, Army Service Corps)

The first objective of the 8th Division on 1st July was the German front line in Ovillers village. The 25th Brigade, occupying the left half of the Divisional frontage, was charged to capture the village itself, before continuing on towards Pozieres, while the 23rd Brigade, led by the 2nd Devons and 2nd Middlesex, would advance along Mash Valley, take the German front lines to the right of the village, then advance to converge with the Albert-Pozieres road, south of Pozieres village. The 2nd Devons and 2nd Middlesex were faced with the unenviable task of having to cross up to half a mile of desolate No-Man's-Land before they even reached the German front line, let alone fighting on through the supporting lines and into the open country leading to Pozieres.

As it turned out, regardless of the week-long bombardment which was supposed to have made the British advance a 'walk-over', it gradually became evident that the attack was a monumental failure. A few isolated groups of men actually reached as far as the second German trench line before being wiped-out, but Mash valley would, from that day, be infamous as one of the major slaughter-houses of the Somme.

1st July 1916

REPORT ON THE PART TAKEN BY 2nd BATTALION DEVONSHIRE REGIMENT
DURING THE ATTACK ON POZIERES ON THE 1st JULY 1916

It was a comparatively quiet night and there was little fire on either side until 6.30am.
At 6.30am our artillery which consisted of guns of all calibres opened an intense bombardment which lasted for one hour. The enemy front and support line came in for most of the shelling. The enemy's reply was not very vigorous, most of his fire being directed on our support and communication trenches.
During the last 7 to 10 minutes of the intense bombardment 'A' and 'B' Companies left the 'NEW TRENCH' and advanced in open order to within about 100 yards of the enemy trenches, closely followed by 'C' and 'D' Companies, who moved down to the new line and advanced from there.
This advance was carried out in four successive waves in the most perfect order: the casualties were not very heavy during this advance. Lt. Temp. Captain E.G.Roberts who was in command of 'A' Company was badly wounded by shell fire while leaving our front line, 2/Lt. L.A.Carey also of 'A' Company was killed at the same time.
Just before the advance began a mist drifted over from the enemy's line towards our own and made observation very difficult. Captain J.A.Andrews was in command of the Front Line and it was due to him, to a great extent, that the advance from

our front line was carried out with such remarkable coolness and precision. At the same time as our Companies advanced towards the hostile trenches, the 2nd Middlesex Regiment on our right and the 2nd Royal Berkshire Regiment on our left, advanced with remarkable coolness and order.

At 7.30am our artillery lifted from the enemy front line trenches on to the trenches in rear. During this pause the hostile artillery fire had gradually increased. As soon as the artillery lifted Captain J.A.Andrews got up and gave the order to advance, hardly had the order been given when he was killed by a hostile bullet which struck him in the head. As soon as the order to advance had been received, the four waves dashed for the German trenches opposite X.8.c.5.2. - X.8.c.8½.3½. - X.8.d.2.4.

Immediately the troops advanced the enemy opened a terrific machine gun fire from the front and from both flanks, which mowed down our troops, this fire did not deter our men from continuing to advance, but only a few reached the German Lines alive. Some of these managed to effect an entry into the German Lines, where they 'put up' a determined fight against enormous odds and were soon killed.

At first and for some little time owing to the mist and dust caused by our shell fire, it was difficult to realise exactly what had happened, although the heavy hostile Machine Gun fire told its own tale. The lines appeared at first sight to be intact, but it was soon made clear that the lines consisted of only dead or wounded, and that no one was there to support the few that had got in, and to carry on with the advance.

The cause of this was eventually discovered: the 2nd West Yorkshire Regiment, who were in support, had been caught by hostile Machine Gun and Shell fire as soon as they advanced from their assembly trenches, and had been cut to pieces.

The Brigade was informed as to what had happened to the Battalion but no information could be given to them as to what had happened to the supporting Battalion, as our runners were unsuccessful in getting in touch with them, neither could any accurate information be given as to what had happened to the 2nd Middlesex Regiment on our right and the 2nd Royal Berkshire Regiment on our left. From observation it was soon ascertained that the Battalions on either flank had also been caught by the hostile Machine Gun fire and had been unable to take the German trenches. This information was communicated to the Brigade. This information was shortly corroborated by our wounded, who began to crawl back to our lines in small numbers. None of the runners sent by Companies reached Headquarters: they were all either killed or wounded.

No accurate information could be ascertained as to the exact number of casualties the Battalion had suffered, although it was clear that there were very few left that had not been hit: the enemy began to snipe our wounded. When it was quite clear that we were not holding the front line, the barrage was brought back on the German front line trenches, and the 2nd Scottish Rifles

were moved forward to the 'New Trench' and were told to hold themselves in readiness to advance.
During this time the hostile shelling had increased and the front line systems of trenches were very badly knocked about. The enemy used a very high proportion of lachrymatory shells which caused a great deal of inconvenience to anyone not wearing gas goggles.
The enemy continued to confine his shelling practically entirely to our front line, support and communication trenches.
About mid-day orders were issued by the Brigade that no further advance would take place till further orders.
Our wounded still continued to crawl in to the 'New Trench' but great difficulty was found evacuating the wounded to the Regimental Aid Post as the trenches were too narrow to allow a stretcher to pass and also the trenches had been so knocked about that in many places one was exposed to hostile Machine Gun and Shell fire.
The Medical Officer went down to the 'New Trench' and bandaged all the wounded while the Stretcher Bearers and parties of Regimental Pioneers from Headquarters carried the wounded back to the Aid Post on their backs and in waterproof sheets. By this means all our wounded which it was possible to get at were removed to First Aid Post where the MO re-dressed their wounds. The supply of orderlies for removing the wounded from the Aid Post was not good. Several messages had to be sent asking for Orderlies to be sent up to remove the wounded.
About 4pm all Adjutants were ordered to report at Brigade Headquarters. The Brigade Major started to dictate orders to the effect that the Scottish Rifles would take over the front line and the remainder of the other Battalions of the Brigade would move into the support trenches. While taking down the orders the 8th Division informed the Brigade that the whole Brigade would be relieved that night, and that orders for the relief would be issued. Adjutants then returned to their Battalions and COs were ordered to re-organise their Battalions.
About 4pm the artillery fire on both sides slackened down considerably.
During the day wounded and unwounded crawled in, in small numbers. The unwounded were organised into parties by Companies.
About 8pm orders were received that the Brigade would be relieved and that in the meantime the 2nd Scottish Rifles would hold the line and the remainder of the Battalions were to move into dugouts in HODDER and HOUGHTON Streets, in the vicinity of Brigade Headquarters and that the Brigade would later move to bivouacs in MILLENCOURT. By this time about 40 men not including headquarters had been collected.
By 10 o'clock all the men had been placed in dugouts.
The CO and adjutant then proceeded to Brigade Headquarters where a conference was held by the G.O.C. 23rd Infantry Brigade, on the operations and the best methods of overcoming the

difficulties which had been met.
The remnants of the Battalion moved off for MILLENCOURT about 11pm. The CO and Adjutant left Brigade Headquarters for Millencourt about 1.30am on the 2nd July and arrived at MILLENCOURT about 3am.

The following Casualties were suffered during the action:-
Captain   J.A.Andrews   Killed(In Command of Front Line)
Captain   A.Preedy   -do-   O.C. 'B' Company
2/Lieut.   L.A.Carey   -do-
2/Lieut.   E.M.Gould   -do-
2/Lieut.   C.V.Beddow   -do-
2/Lieut.   M.C.Ley   -do-
2/Lieut.   E.A.Jago   -do-
43 Other Ranks   -do-
Captain   E.G.Roberts   Wounded O.C. 'A' Company
2/Lieut.   C.O.R.Jacob   -do-   O.C. 'D' Company
2/Lieut.   A.R.Newton   -do-
2/Lieut.   J.A.Rennie   -do-   *(Since died of wounds)*
2/Lieut.   G.Parker   -do-
2/Lieut.   A.H.Cornell   -do-
194 Other Ranks   -do-
2/Lieut.   J.S.McGowan   Missing *(Since reported killed)*
2/Lieut.   G.S.D.Carver   -do-   O.C. 'C' Company *(Since reported killed)*
2/Lieut.   F.B.Coldwells -do-   *(Since reported killed)*
178 Other Ranks   -do-

Two Lewis Guns were lost, the remaining 6 were brought in during daylight under heavy fire, two of these by Privates who were the only men left of their teams.

The following officers took part in the operations:-
Lt. Col.   A.J.E.Sunderland
Captain   A.Tillett
Captain   J.A.Andrews
Captain   A.Preedy
Captain   E.G.Roberts
2/Lieut.   C.O.R.Jacob
2/Lieut.   L.A.Carey
2/Lieut.   G.Parker
2/Lieut.   H.Acomb
2/Lieut.   A.H.Smith
2/Lieut.   A.H.Cornell
2/Lieut.   M.C.Ley
2/Lieut.   J.A.Rennie
2/Lieut.   F.B.Coldwells
2/Lieut.   A.R.Newton
2/Lieut.   C.V.Beddow
2/Lieut.   E.M.Gould
2/Lieut.   F.B.Lloyd
2/Lieut.   H.H.Goodman
2/Lieut.   G.S.D.Carver

The 2nd Devons War Diary

2/Lieut. J.S.McGowan
2/Lieut. G.W.Dibble
2/Lieut. A.E.A.Phillips   Att. to Brigade H.Q.

The undermentioned Officers were detailed to stay behind to replace casualties:-
Major C.H.M.Imbert-Terry D.S.O.
2/Lieut. R.J.Andrews
2/Lieut. S.M.Nielson
2/Lieut. H.St.Hill
2/Lieut. H.H.Jago
2/Lieut. J.H.Vincent
2/Lieut. H.W.Jones

The casualty figures quoted above in the War Diary were, of course, provisional. The actual list of the 2nd Devons who lost their lives on 1st July was to total 10 officers and 163 men killed in action, with a further 6 listed as died of wounds. Over the following two weeks 14 more men died of wounds, most, if not all, from injuries suffered on 1st July.

The German unit facing the 2nd Devons on 1st July was Infantry Regiment 180, who held the southern part of the Somme frontage covered by the 26th Reserve Division. Earlier, this experienced unit had turned Serre into an impregnable fortress and was now entrusted to defend the sector which stretched from Theipval South, as far as the Albert-Bapaume road at Ovillers la Boisselle. This was a well-developed sector and the British bombardment prior to 1st July made no meaningful impression upon the 180th Infantry Regiment's ability to repulse the 8th Division's attack. During the British bombardment they had suffered 95 killed, 187 wounded and 2 missing which, while not being an insignificant number of casualties, did not particularly affect their ability to defend their positions. At 5.45am on the 1st July, the 180th was informed that the British attack was imminent, which gave the soldiers sheltering deep in their dugouts plenty of time to prepare to rush up to their trenches when the British attack commenced.

'The German Army on the Somme 1914-1916' by Jack Sheldon, contains the following extract from the 180th Infantry Regiment's War Diary:
"If the British believe that their fire had shaken and unnerved us, they have deceived themselves......the British attacked Sector Ovillers South in overwhelming strength. The assault unfolded as a series of waves, up to seven of them, which followed in quick succession. Artillery defensive fire came down promptly and the attack in front of the right flank of P5 and in front of P6 and P7 withered away in the combined fire of rifle, machine gun and artillery fire. The enemy suffered extraordinarily bloody casualties."

The area referred to as P5, P6 and P7 is Mash Valley. If one had dared to stand on the 2nd Devon's section of the front line on the morning of 1st July, the German line immediately in front would have been clearly visible curving round to the right, gently sloping up the far side of Mash Valley and running west along the Albert-Bapaume road, atop the La Boisselle spur. From the British positions, the spur does not look like a particularly formidable obstacle, hardly appearing to be of any consequential height at all, and as the 8th Division's assault was to be directed further to the left, directly along Mash Valley towards Ovillers, the minds of the Divisional Commander and his Battalion Commanders were probably focused on their own objectives, never mind the situation on their right, which was the 34th Division's problem. If, however, you stand on the site of the German front line trenches on the La Boisselle spur, you have a grandstand view down onto the battlefield, from where enfilade fire was directed with impunity across the entire width of Mash Valley.

OVILLERS, APRIL 2008

The view along Mash Valley looking towards Ovillers from the site of the British front line. The right flank of the 2nd Devon's 200 yard frontage straddled the lane. The German front line trench, which was their first objective on that fateful day, followed the line of houses from the right and bulged out into No-Man's-Land behind the cemetery. The left flank of the 2nd Devons attack was intended to head diagonally through the area where the cemetery now lies, with their right flank more or less towards the lone white bungalow, half way between the cemetery entrance and the right edge of the picture. With the Germans atop the La Boisselle spur, which is out of picture on the right, with No-Man's-Land averaging a width of around 700 to 800 yards at this point, with no element of surprise, and having been ordered to walk into battle in regimented lines, laden with various stores, extra supplies of grenades, ammunition and so on, as well as their own fighting equipment, the attackers stood no chance whatsoever of succeeding in their task. In the area visible in this photograph, hundreds of men of the 8th Division were killed on 1st July 1916.

MASH VALLEY, APRIL 2008

A view across Mash Valley from the German position at the Ovillers end of the La Boisselle spur. The German trench ran diagonally across the foreground, then followed the road down the hill on the right, before swinging out to the left around Ovillers village, then back around the distant trees on the horizon. To the right centre of the picture is Ovillers Military Cemetery, sitting more or less in the middle of No-Man's-Land. Advancing from left to right, the 23rd Brigade attacked from the British front line trench which ran more or less diagonally across the top of the lighter coloured field behind the telegraph pole, up to the horizon. Any men of the 2nd Devons, 2nd Middlesex and 2nd West Yorks who advanced past the ground now occupied by the Cemetery would have found themselves open to fire from three sides, and any who managed to advance very far into the green field in the right middle distance would have stood very little chance of survival. Remarkably, some 2nd Devons 'managed to effect an entry into the German Lines, where they *'put up a determined fight against enormous odds and were soon killed'*, according to the War Diary.

The 2nd Devons War Diary

2nd July 1916 About midday received orders to move at once to MERICOURT where the Brigade would entrain.
The Battalion marched to MERICOURT and entrained about 8.00pm.

3rd July 1916 Arrived at AILLY about 12.30am and marched to La CHAUSSEE arriving there about 4.00am and moved into Billets. The same evening orders were received from the Brigade to move to SOUES next morning.

4th July 1916 The Battalion fell in about 9.45am and marched to SOUES arriving there about 11.00am
2/Lt. T.R.Johns rejoined the Battalion from 4th Army School of Instruction.

5th July 1916 Were informed by the Brigade that the G.O.C. would inspect the Battalion on the morning of the 6th.
About 8.00pm orders were received to be ready to move at a moments notice.

6th July 1916 About 2.00am received Operation Orders from the Brigade. The Battalion left SOUES at about 10.30am and marched to LONGEAU where the Battalion entrained about 6.45pm for DIEVAL.

7th July 1916 Detrained at DIEVAL about 1.30am and marched to BARLIN where the Battalion moved into Billets about 8.30am.
Lt. H.Archer rejoined the Battalion. Received draft of 92 Other Ranks, this included 20 men of the D.C.L.I.

8th July 1916 Routine.

9th July 1916 Routine.

10th July 1916 Routine. G.O.C. 8th Division inspected the Battalion and congratulated the Battalion on the splendid work it had done and the wonderful bravery shown by all Ranks on the 1st July 1916.
Major C.H.M.Imbert-Terry DSO left to take over Temporary Command of 8th KOYLI

11th July 1916 Routine.

12th July 1916 Routine. 2/Lt. S.G.Blake and 2/Lt. A.M. Rogers, 15th Gloucester Regiment, joined the Battalion.

13th July 1916 Routine. The CO and Company Commanders attended a Staff Tour.

14th July 1916 About 6.45am received orders from the Brigade that the CO, OC Companies and Lewis Gun Officer were to report at Brigade Headquarters at 8.30am to go round trenches, and that the Battalion would move into the trenches that night. At 2.30pm the Battalion was conveyed by Motor Buses to the Brigade Assembly position outside BETHUNE, arriving there about 4.00pm. At 8.30pm the Battalion marched to the trenches and relieved the 14th Hants Regiment in the trenches near CUINCHY.

15th July 1916 About 11.15pm six of the enemy attacked one of our Saps: they threw 3 bombs and were driven off. Later the enemy made another attempt to reach this Sap but was driven off suffering several Casualties.
About 11.30pm about 20 or 30 of the enemy attacked another of our Saps but were driven off by our Rifle Fire suffering several Casualties.
The enemy fired a great number of aerial darts, rifle grenades, shells and trench mortars at our trenches damaging them badly in several places.

16th July 1916 Between 2.00pm and 4.30pm our artillery bombarded the hostile trenches. The effect of our bombardment could not be observed owing to the craters in front of our own line which entirely obscured the view. The enemy replied vigorously with shells of different calibre, Minenwerfer and rifle grenades doing considerable damage to our front, support and communication trenches, knocking in several dugouts. 2 men were killed and 5 others wounded.
During the night our artillery carried out an intermittent bombardment of the hostile trenches.

17th July 1916 From 12.00 noon until 10.00pm the enemy were unusually quiet only firing a few rifle grenades at our trenches, doing very little damage. At 10.45pm the enemy shelled our trenches and attacked 2 of our saps, both these attacks were stopped by our fire and the enemy driven off, the enemy suffering some casualties. At 11.15pm the enemy made another attack on one of our Saps, this was also unsuccessful. At 12.45am a party of the enemy advancing on our line were dispersed by our Lewis Gun fire. Hostile Trench Mortars and aerial torpedoes were very active during the night causing serious damage to our trenches. Casualties 2 men killed 5 wounded.

18th July 1916 At 3.30am the enemy exploded a mine opposite the left Company ('A' Company)
The mine appeared to burst backwards destroying the enemy's parapet and burying several of his garrison. 2/Lt. R.J.Andrews at once pushed forward with one platoon and occupied the far lip of the crater, the enemy offered a vigorous resistance but was driven off with heavy losses. This platoon then retired to the near lip of the crater and immediately consolidated its position. The explosion of the mine caused considerable damage to our forward saps, four of the garrison of one sap were

The 2nd Devons War Diary

entombed.
From 2.30pm to 5.30pm our artillery bombarded the hostile trenches with good effect. The hostile retaliation was feeble and consisted mostly of 77mm shells, light Trench Mortars and Rifle Grenades doing no damage.
The enemy was much quieter, there was practically no artillery fire and the number of hostile rifle grenades fired was considerably less.
Casualties 1 Officer Killed, 5 Other Ranks killed (4 of these were entombed) 15 Other Ranks wounded.

19th July 1916 From 12.00 noon to 3.30pm our artillery carried out a pre-arranged programme. The enemy retaliation was slight. A few 5.9 shells were fired at TOWER RESERVE Line, aerial torpedoes, trench mortars and rifle grenades were also fired in conjunction with 77mm shells, very little material damage being done.
An enemy patrol of 12 men were caught by our bombers and driven back to their own lines.
0 Killed, 1 Other Rank, 13 wounded 1 Officer and 12 Other Ranks.

20th July 1916 A quiet day. There was very little firing by either side. During the night the enemy tried to enter one of our saps but was driven off by our rifle fire.
Casualties. 3 Other Ranks wounded.

21st July 1916 At 3.00am we successfully exploded a mine opposite the left Company ('A' Company). The crater formed was commanded by us from Sap No.5. it was not found necessary to send anyone forward to deny the crater to the enemy who made no attempt to occupy it. On the explosion of the mine the enemy opened a heavy fire on our front line with Minenwerfer, Rifle Grenades and Machine Guns. No damage was done.
During the night we occupied and consolidated the near lip of the crater. During the day the enemy fired a certain number of Trench Mortars, Aerial Darts and Rifle Grenades, but it was noticed that he was much quieter than when we first took over the line. We appeared to have the upper hand.
9 Other Ranks wounded.

22nd July 1916 The Battalion was relieved in the trenches by the 2nd West Yorks Regiment and moved into Supporting Posts and Keeps. Casualties 1 Other Rank wounded.

23rd July 1916 In support.

24th July 1916 In support. Received draft of 26 Other Ranks. 2/Lt. C.Law, 2/Lt. W.H.L.Vesey-Fitzgerald and 2/Lt. A.W.Harrison joined the Battalion.

25th July 1916 In support.

Martin Body

26th July 1916 Relieved the 2nd Scottish Rifles in the trenches. 2/Lt. T.H.Trinaman, 2/Lt. E.C.Jacks, 2/Lt. C.W.C.Hannah,
2/Lt. G.F.Thuillier, and 2/Lt. G.Hosegood joined the Battalion.

27th July 1916 Between 12.00 noon and 1.45pm the enemy fired a large number of 5.9 shells in rear of the right flank of the Battalion.
The enemy were very active firing a large number of Rifle Grenades, Aerial Torpedoes and 77mm Shells at our front, support and communication trenches doing very little material damage. We retaliated with Rifle Grenades, Stokes Mortars and Field Guns. Hostile Machine Guns were very active during the night; our Lewis Guns retaliated.

28th July 1916 Both ourselves and the enemy were very active firing a considerable number of Rifle Grenades, Trench Mortars and Field Guns. 1 Other Rank was wounded.

29th July 1916 About 10.00am the enemy bombarded the Right Company with MINENWERFER and 10.5cm. Shells.
At 3.48pm a party of about 10 to 15 Germans raided one of our Saps, the raiding party with the exception of 1 man, believed to be an officer, were attired in shirt sleeves and wore no boots and were armed with revolvers, clubs and bombs. This party was immediately attacked and were driven out, but managed to drag away one of our sentries who was cut off and had been clubbed. The enemy heavily shelled the vicinity immediately afterwards.
About 4.30pm our 60 pounder Trench Mortars attempted unsuccessfully to cut the wire in front of one of the enemy's saps which it was proposed to raid that night. The enemy replied with 77mm. and 10.5cm. shells. The attempted wire cutting was continued until 8.00pm but was not successful.
At 8.45pm the enemy started bombarding our trenches on the Right Company with Trench Mortars and 77mm shells and after a while with 10.5cm shells. Little notice was taken of this bombardment at first as it was thought to be retaliation for our 60 pounder Trench Mortar Fire.
This bombardment increased in intensity especially on the right, the enemy making use of shells of all calibre and a large number of heavy and light Trench Mortars.
At 9.35pm the Rifle Brigade asked our Machine Guns to open fire on the HOHENZOLLERN Flank. This request was complied with.
About 10.30pm a "S.O.S" message was received from the Battalion on our right (Rifle Brigade) and steps were at once taken to give any assistance that might be required.
About 11.15pm a party of the enemy advanced on our trenches but were dispersed by our Rifle and Lewis Gun fire.
About 11.30pm the hostile bombardment ceased.
Patrols were sent out to try and obtain identification of the enemy but none of the enemy, either dead or alive, were seen.

The 2nd Devons War Diary

30th July 1916 About 2.00am another hostile bombardment started on the left of the Battalion and lasted for about three quarters of an hour.
About 6.15am the enemy rushed one of our saps which was unoccupied, we opened a heavy Lewis Gun fire on the enemy, who retired.
During the afternoon the Battalion was relieved in the trenches by the 1st Northampton Regiment and moved into Divisional Reserve Billets in ANNEQUIN.
2/Lt. C.Law proceeded to the 23rd Infantry Brigade Bomb School for a Course of Bombing.
Casualties for the 29th and 30th. 1 Other Rank taken prisoner, 1 Other Rank Killed, 13 Other Ranks wounded.

31st July 1916 Routine. Furnished RE working parties.
2/Lt. A.E.Rutledge and 2/Lt. C.H.S.Buckley joined the Battalion on 1st appointment.
2/Lt. A.C.G.Roberts promoted Lt. and to date from 22/3/16.

Martin Body

AUGUST 1916

1st August 1916   Routine. Furnished RE Working parties.
2/Lt. R.J.Andrews awarded the Military Cross for conspicuous gallantry at CUINCHY on the 18th July, 1916. The enemy exploded a mine near No. 7 Sap completely filling the sap and part of our front line trench. Lt. Andrews at once lead a party over the top and held the near lip of the crater. He succeeded in driving off the enemy and denying them the crater. He displayed quick grasp of the situation and great dash.
No. 6588 CSM Littlewood E. awarded the DCM for conspicuous gallantry at CUINCHY, 18th July, 1916. When a mine exploded this W.O. was of great assistance to 2/Lt. R.J.Andrews in organizing and leading the party which advanced to the lip of the crater. He showed great coolness and devotion to duty.
No. 5456 RSM King J.B. awarded the Military Cross for continuous devotion to duty and gallant conduct in the presence of the enemy from the commencement of the campaign in France to the 25th June, 1916.
No. 6825 Sgt. E.Bowden, No. 8211 A/Sgt. E.Foster, No. 14206 L/Cpl. E.Budd. No.14367 Pte. T.Pepperell, No. 15502 Pte. W.Sparkes, awarded the Military Medal for conspicuous gallantry and devotion to duty at CUINCHY on the 18th July, 1916. When a mine exploded these NCOs and men showed great courage and coolness in assisting in the capturing and holding of the crater which was denied the enemy.

2nd August 1916   Routine. Furnished RE working parties. 2/Lt. L.Hollingsworth joined the Battalion on first appointment. During the afternoon the G.O.C. 1st Army inspected the 23rd Infantry Brigade near LA BOURSE. On the completion of the inspection he presented medal ribbons to: 2/Lt. R.J.Andrews, No. 5456 RSM King J.B. No. 6588 CSM Littlewood E. No. 8211 A/Sgt. Foster E. No. 14206 L/Cpl. E.Budd, No.14367 Pte. Pepperell T. No. 15502 Pte. Sparkes W.
Before presenting the medal ribbons the G.O.C. addressed the Brigade congratulating the Battalion and the above Officer, WOs, NCOs and men on their gallantry and devotion to duty. The Brigade then marched passed the G.O.C. in Column of Route and G.O.C. granted those presented with medal ribbons the exceptional honour of standing by him as the Battalion marched past.

3rd August 1916   Routine. Furnished RE working parties.
2/Lt. W.W.Drake joined the Battalion of first appointment.

4th August 1916   Routine. Furnished RE working parties.
Received a draft of 158 other ranks.
2/Lt. J.C.Patterson and 2/Lt. W.M.Thomson joined the Battalion for the first time.

5th August 1916   The Battalion moved into Billets in FOUQUIERES.

The 2nd Devons War Diary

6th August 1916   Routine.

7th August 1916   The Battalion relieved the 1st Royal Irish Rifles in the Right Sub-Section. About an hour after the relief the Brigade Major informed the Colonel that the enemy were reported to be working each night in FARMERS HOLE within 50 yards of one of our listening posts and that the Battalion must send out an offensive patrol under an officer to find out exactly what work was being carried out and that the 3" Stokes Mortars would co-operate.
The CO, Adjutant, and OC 'A' and 'D' Companies went down to the line where the work was being carried out. It was found to be in 'D' Company's area and near the junction of 'A' and 'D' Companies.
A raiding party was at once organized from 'D' Company. About 1.10am (8th) a patrol of 1 Officer and 18 other ranks examined this work and it was found to be an old disused trench on which no fresh work had been carried out. The party then crawled up to the enemy's lines and bombed one of his posts and returned without suffering any casualties.
During the day our artillery and 60lb trench mortars fired a few rounds. During the night the enemy was very quiet, but was very busy at work on his front line trenches, our Lewis Gun fire prevented him from mending his wire which he attempted to do.

8th August 1916   The Battalion was relieved in the trenches and moved into Brigade Reserve in Railway Reserve, Central Keep and Village Line, from Junction Keep inclusive to Gordon Alley. Casualties - 1 man wounded.

9th August 1916   In reserve. Furnished Working parties. Enemy dropped a bomb from an aeroplane in the vicinity of Battalion HQ but did no damage.
Casualties - 1 man killed and 2 wounded.

10th August 1916   Furnished Working parties. Casualties - 1 man wounded.

11th August 1916   The Battalion relieved the 2nd Scottish Rifles in the trenches from BOYAU 109 (exclusive) to MUD ALLEY (inclusive) 'A', 'B' & 'D' Companies in the front line and 'C' Company in support in the Reserve Line. Our trench mortars and rifle grenade batteries were very active, doing a considerable amount of damage to his trench and causing his mortars to considerably moderate their activity. Our Lewis and Machine Gunners were also active, both sides sniped a great deal during the night. Patrols which were out inspecting our wire met none of the enemy. Casualties - 1 man killed and 2 accidentally wounded.
Major H.de L.Sprye joined the Battalion for the first time.

12th August 1916 2/Lt. S.M.Neilson, 2/Lt. S.G.Blake (15th Gloucesters) 2/Lt. L.Hollingsworth and 2/Lt. J.C.Patterson left to join the 1st Battalion.
Lt. Archer took over command of 'B' Company.
There was considerable trench mortar activity on both sides, our retaliation to the hostile mortar fire was very heavy.
At 8.05 pm the enemy bombarded the right ('B' Company) and the battalion on our right (2nd West Yorks) with trench mortars and shells of all calibre, this was observed from Battalion HQ and the artillery who were communicated with, at once opened a heavy fire. At 9.00pm the hostile bombardment ceased and a party of the enemy were seen advancing on our right. Lewis Gun fire and a heavy rifle fire was brought to bear on them and they swung off to the right and were not seen again. It was ascertained later that the enemy had raided the Battalion on our right and that 4 of the enemy had been taken prisoners. Our patrols which were out during the night met none of the enemy.
2/Lt. J.C.Patterson was very slightly wounded (at duty) 4 other ranks wounded.
2/Lieut. C.W.Law was admitted to hospital "Sick".

13th August 1916 Field Guns and Trench Mortars were active on both sides. Our rifle grenade batteries were very active and carried out some very good work.
Our bombers and snipers were particularly active and inflicted several casualties on the enemy.
2 parties of the enemy who were observed suffered heavy casualties from our rifle fire and bombs.
The bright moonlight prevented our patrols from going out. The enemy was noticed to be much quieter than usual.
Casualties 1 other rank killed. 8 other ranks wounded.
2/Lt. A.J.Snowden joined the Battalion on 1st appointment.

14th August 1916 Both sides were active with artillery and Trench Mortars the latter especially. The enemy trenches were knocked in in several places and he was prevented from repairing the damage owing to our Lewis Gun and Rifle fire. The enemy succeeded in knocking in one of our Communication Trenches and forced us to stop work on this part of the line for some time. The enemy made several attempts to mend his wire but on every attempt he met with failure and suffered several casualties. Later the enemy tried to put wire out by means of long rods. Our snipers were active and met with considerable success, accounting for several of the enemy.
Casualties: 2/Lt. W.H.L.Vesey-Fitzgerald killed (rifle fire) 2/Lt. H.Acomb 11th Yorks Regiment very slightly wounded (at duty) 1 man killed and 3 other ranks wounded, 2/Lt. H.T.Marshall joined Battalion on 1st appointment.

15th August 1916 Relieved in the trenches by the 2nd Scottish Rifles and moved into Brigade Reserve occupying the same trenches and posts as before. Furnished Working Parties.

The 2nd Devons War Diary

Casualties: 1 man killed, 8 other ranks wounded.
Captain F.W.L.Bissett DCLI reported for attachment to the Battalion.

16th August 1916 2 Officers and 125 Other Ranks proceeded to SAILLY LABOURSE to be attached to 180th Tunnelling Company RE for Spoils Party. Names of Officers, 2/Lt. E.D.Hill and 2/Lt. A.W.Harrison.
Furnished Working Parties. Casualties 1 Other Rank wounded.

17th August 1916 Furnished Working Parties.
2/Lt. A.E.Rutledge and 2/Lt. C.H.S.Buckley granted leave to the United Kingdom from 18th to 24th August.
Casualties. 3 other ranks wounded.

18th August 1916 In reserve. Furnished working party. 2nd Lt. E.C.Jacks attached to 33rd Battery RFA (Royal Field Artillery) until 6 pm 19th inst as liaison officer. Casualties 1 Other Rank wounded.

19th August 1916 2/Lt. G.Thuillier rejoined from 8th Divisional School of Instruction.
Relieved the 2nd Scottish Rifles. In the trenches from BOYAU 109 (exclusive) to MUD ALLEY (inclusive). 'B', 'A' and 'C'. Companies in the front line and 'D' Company in Support in Reserve Trench.
Our artillery was very active on hostile front at G.4.2. and G.4.3.
Retaliation was very weak.
Throughout the night we sent over salvoes of rifle grenades and many Stokes Mortars. Hostile retaliation was very weak, except at G.4.5. where he replied with 8 canisters and several Trench Mortars breaching the parapet in
front line. Our snipers and bombers were very active.
A patrol examined MUD CRATERS at BOYAU 116 and found them unoccupied. Enemy wire was inspected and found to be strong.
We dispersed hostile working party at G.4.b.7.3½.
A connecting trench was dug between Saps No. 4 and 5 at G.4.a.5.5½.

20th August 1916 2/Lt. W.W.Drake, 'C' Company, attached to O Battery as Liaison Officer for 24 hours. Throughout the day our artillery and Stokes Mortars were active upon enemy lines, but in the majority of cases met with no retaliation. We fired numerous rifle grenades and Mills bombs, but the enemy made practically no reply. At 5.00pm our Stokes Mortars in conjunction with those of Battalion on our left bombarded hostile lines. On this occasion enemy replied with Rum Jars, Trench Mortar Shells, Aerial Darts and Rifle Grenades, damaging our front line at G.4.4. and G.4.5. rather badly.
During the night enemy fired a number of Rum Jars, accompanied at the same time with Aerial Darts into NORTHAMPTON TRENCH at

BOYAU 114 and 116.
Patrol examined MUD CRATERS, but none of the enemy were seen.
Listening posts in gallery at G.4.4. report sounds of digging
and same has been reported to Mining Officer.
Casualties - 1 Other rank killed and 2 other ranks wounded.

21st August 1916 Draft of 29 other ranks taken on strength.
Morning very quiet.
At 2.30pm hostile bombardment of our front line with
Minenwerfers and Trench Mortars doing some damage. Our Stokes
and Medium Trench Mortars replied effectively, with artillery
co-operation.
At 4.00pm we bombarded hostile trenches with Stokes and Medium
Trench Mortars and rifle grenades. Enemy retaliated at 6.30pm
with Minenwerfers, doing little damage.
At 7.00pm a hostile Mine was blown in existing Craters at
G.2.a.4½.7. immediately in front of New Trench which joins Saps
Nos 3 and 4.
None of our trenches were blown up and with the exception of
filling up the New Trench and the adjoining Sap No. 3. thereby
burying several men, no material damage was done and the
conformation of front line trenches and Saps were not altered.
The clearing of trenches began immediately after the explosion
and several men, although buried were got out alive. All spare
men of Reserve ('D') Company. With our own pioneers were
immediately put upon the work.
A party of 20 of the West Yorkshire Regiment also worked on the
clearing from 8.30pm until midnight. Soon after midnight the
clearing of the trenches was practically completed and with the
aid of 1 Platoon from Reserve Company to replace casualties, all
trenches and saps were garrisoned as before the explosion.
Saps Nos 1 and 2 and Lewis Gun (Right position) G.4.2. and Saps
3 and 4 and Lewis Gun (Left position) G.4.3. are all in use and
intact.
Immediately after the explosion the enemy bombarded the centre
of Left Companies. (G.4.4. and G.4.5.) with Minenwerfers, Trench
Mortars and Aerial Darts for 15 minutes and considerable damage
was done to our trenches.
It was observed that there was no hostile bombardment of the
area effected by the Mine explosion.
The enemy must have damaged his own trenches when the mine was
blown as there was absolutely no action taken afterwards in this
immediate section G.4.3., and although our men were forced to
walk about in full view of the enemy not a single shot was fired
over. Later the enemy was seen to be throwing earth over his
parapet opposite this point.
2/Lt. H.Acomb killed. 9 other ranks killed. 16 other ranks
wounded.

22nd August 1916 Our trench mortars were very active and our
field artillery shelled intermittently during the day. During

The 2nd Devons War Diary

the night our heavy and light artillery carried out a pre-arranged shoot.
During the afternoon the hostile trench mortars were active for 1 hour doing considerable damage to the centre Company (C Company) trenches. We retaliated vigorously with trench mortars and field guns.
During the night a large number of rifle grenades and bombs were thrown into the hostile trenches.
Our snipers were active all day. It was noticed that the enemy was very quiet at night. Our patrols which were out at night met none of the enemy.
2/Lt. A.B.Kitson, 2/Lt. H.F.Boyse and 2/Lt. R.S.Holmes joined the Battalion for the first time.
Casualties - 4 Other ranks wounded.

23rd August 1916 The enemy were very quiet during the day. We fired the usual number of trench mortars and rifle grenades. During the afternoon the Battalion was relieved in the trenches and moved into Divisional Reserve billets in SAILLY LA BOURSE.
2/Lt. T.L.Lewis and 2/Lt. H.J.Skardon joined the Battalion for the first time.
2/Lt. H.T.Marshall and 28 other ranks proceeded to 23rd Infantry Brigade Bomb School to undergo a course of Bombing.
2/Lt. A.E.A.Phillips proceeded on a Sniping Course.
2/Lt. H.H.Jago and 2/Lt. T.H.Trinman and 5 NCOs proceeded on a course of Physical Training.

24th August 1916 Routine. Furnished RE Working parties.
2/Lt. A.C.Faulkener joined the Battalion for the first time.
2/Lt. G.Thuillier and 8 other ranks proceeded on a course of Raiding.
1st Day of the Divisional Horse Show, the Battalion won the following prizes:-
1st & 3rd Prizes. Light Draught Pairs.
1st Prize. Chargers (Dismounted Units).

25th August 1916 Routine. Furnished RE Working parties.
2nd Day of Divisional Horse Show, the Battalion won the following prizes:-
1st Prize. Heavy Draught. Championship Class.
1st Prize. Best Light Draught Horse.
Casualties. 5 other ranks wounded. 1 other rank killed on Spoils Party.

26th August 1916 Routine. Furnished RE Working parties.
Capt.G.L.Jones, R.A.M.C. proceeded on 7 days Special Leave.
The undermentioned Officers promoted Temporary Captains whilst in charge of a company. Lt. H.Archer 7/7/16, 2/Lt. A.H.Smith 1/8/16, 2/Lt. R.J.Andrews 2/8/16, 2/Lt. J.H.Vincent 2/8/16

27th August 1916 Routine. Furnished Working parties.
2 signallers, No. 2 Squadron RFC for practice in co-operation

with aeroplanes.
During the morning there was a Brigade Divine Service on the completion of which the Corps Commander presented medal ribbons to Officers and men of the Brigade who had not previously been presented with them. Included amongst these No. 8827 Sgt. C.Lock, No.9917 Pte. G.Costello and No. 6759 Pte.P.Parker, who received the Military Medal Ribbon.
1 Other rank proceeded on an Anti-Gas Course.
One man wounded on Spoils Party.

28th August 1916   Routine. Furnished Working parties.
2/Lt. G.Hosegood and 4 other ranks proceeded on Sniping Course.

29th August 1916   Routine. Furnished Working parties.
2/Lt. A.J.Snowden and 2 other ranks proceeded on course of Lewis Gun.
2/Lt. E.C.Jacks, proceeded to 23rd Infantry Brigade Trench Mortar Battery for duty.

30th August 1916   Routine. Furnished Working parties.
7 Other ranks proceeded to 253rd Tunneling Company to be permanently attached, but not struck off strength of Battalion.

31st August 1916   Routine. Furnished Working parties.
7 Other ranks proceeded to 23rd Infantry Brigade Bomb School to undergo a course of Bombing.
2 Other ranks proceeded to 1st Army School of Mortars to undergo a course of Instruction in Trench Mortars.

The 2nd Devons War Diary

SEPTEMBER 1916

1st September 1916 The Battalion relieved the 2nd Royal Berkshire Regiment in the Reserve Trenches, QUARRIES SECTION. 5.30pm
Furnished Working Parties.

2nd September 1916 In Reserve. (BRIGADE). Considerable amount of work done in improving Reserve Trenches and Battalion Headquarters.

3rd September 1916 In Brigade Reserve. QUARRIES SECTION.
2/Lt. C.Law, 'A' Company, having embarked for England (sick) struck off strength from 24.8.16.
1st Corps Commander awarded Military Medals for Acts of Gallantry and Devotion to Duty to :-
No 7193   Pte. W.Raymont   'B' Company
No 16442   Pte. D.J.B.Rees   'B' Company
No 9438   Pte. J.Woolacott   'B' Company
No 11785   Pte. A.G.Dickson   'A' Company
138 other ranks transferred to the Battalion from 1/7th Cyclists Battalion, Devon Regiment.
2 other ranks rejoined from Base.

4th September 1916 In Brigade Reserve. QUARRIES SECTION.
11 other ranks qualified as trained Bombers. 3 other ranks evacuated (sick) and struck off strength.

5th September 1916 Battalion relieved the 2nd Scottish Rifles in the trenches from BOYAU 94 (exclusive) to BOYAU 100a inclusive of HULLUCH ALLEY.
'B' Coy. Right Coy. 'C' Coy. Left Coy. 'D' Coy. Centre Coy. 'A' Coy. Support Coy.
2/Lt. Snowden and 2 other ranks rejoined from Course of Lewis Gun Instruction.
Our Artillery fairly active. Stokes and Heavy Trench Mortars very busy and did good work.
Enemy retaliation on NORTHERN CRATER did no damage.
Two of our patrols were out during the night with the object of capturing a prisoner, but none of the enemy were seen. Several bodies were found out in "No Man's Land" having been there for some months, pocket books and shoulder straps brought in identifying them as ROYAL SCOTS.
Casualties :- 1 Other Rank Killed. 1 Other Rank Wounded.

6th September 1916 In the Trenches.
Lt. Palmer proceeded to BOULOGNE for dental treatment.
2/Lt. H.St.Hill acting Quartermaster.
2/Lt. A.B.Kitson attached to 32nd Battery RFA for 24 hours as Liaison Officer. 2 Other Ranks transferred to Machine Gun Company.

During the night our Artillery was very active shelling hostile front system. Stokes and 60lbs Trench Mortars also very active. Enemy retaliated with several Minenwefers, which did no damage. 3 Officers patrols went out during the night, but none of the enemy were encountered.
Casualties:- 1 other rank wounded.

7th September 1916   In the Trenches.
2/Lt. W.M.Thomson and 1 Other Rank rejoined from 8th Divisional School.
Our Artillery was fairly active during the day and enemy replied with a few Minenwerfers, doing little damage.
Out Stokes and 60lbs Trench Mortars very active, receiving practically no reply. We sent several patrols during the night with a view of capturing a "Bosch", but none of the enemy were encountered.
CASUALTIES:- 1 Other Rank Killed. 2 Other Ranks Wounded.

8th September 1916   In the Trenches.
Our Artillery was fairly active firing in rear of HAIR PIN CRATERS but a large proportion of the shells were blind. They appeared to be 4.5 Howitzers And a good many of them fell in "No Man's Land".
The enemy was also active with Artillery and Minenwerfers and did a considerable amount of damage to our trenches, especially in HIGHLAND TRENCH and ST. ELIE TRENCH.
Our Lewis guns dispersed several hostile working parties during the night. Considerable amount of transport was heard in rear of hostile lines during the night.
CASUALTIES:- 1 Other Rank killed. 1 Other Rank Wounded.

9th September 1916   In the Trenches.
The enemy was fairly active with his Minenwerfer, doing considerable damage again to HIGHLAND TRENCH in his attempt to find our Trench Mortar positions. Our Stokes were very active and caused a great amount of damage to enemy trenches. This he attempted several times during the night to repair, but was prevented from so doing by our Lewis guns.
CASUALTIES. 1 Other Rank Killed. 2 Other Ranks Wounded.

10th September 1916   In the Trenches. 2/Lt. C.H.Buckley 'B' Company proceeded to 8th Divisional School of Instruction.
Hostile Artillery very active. During the morning he bombarded G.11.5. with Minenwerfers and Trench Mortars, completely filling HIGHLAND TRENCH for 30 yards.
Our Artillery retaliated and our Stokes Mortars continued to do good work. Our snipers accounted for 4 of the enemy. We sent several patrols out during the night, but none of the enemy were met. One of these patrols under 2/Lt. G.Hosegood was unfortunately observed by the enemy, this Officer after getting right up to the enemy saps, was killed by machine gun fire.
Casualties:- 1 Officer Killed. 1 Other Rank Wounded.

The 2nd Devons War Diary

11th September 1916 In the Trenches. Our Stokes and 60lbs Trench Mortars have been very active and are causing the enemy considerable annoyance, having damaged his wire and front trench badly.
The enemy retaliated with several Minenwerfers and heavy Trench Mortars, again filling in HIGHLAND TRENCH in two places. He commenced to enfilade our front trenches with 77mm, firing from the direction of ST. ELIE.
During the night he attempted to repair his wire and trenches, but was prevented by our Lewis gun fire.
Hostile sniping appears to have ceased.
Casualties:- Nil.

12th September 1916 In the Trenches. Our Artillery has not been very active, but the Stokes and 60lbs continue to do some good shooting. We have been very aggressive with our rifle grenades and our snipers have done good work penetrating all known hostile loopholes. Enemy sniping seems to have ceased on this front.
The enemy again enfiladed our lines with 77mm From ST. ELIE, but did very little damage.
CASUALTIES:- 5 other Ranks wounded.

13th September 1916 In the Trenches.
2/Lt. A.Winch 'A' Company.
2/Lt. C.B.Rodd 'B' Company.
2/Lt. E.L.Walters 'C' Company.
2/Lt. L.N.L.Tindal 'C' Company joined the Battalion and taken on strength.
Our Artillery has been very inactive, firing only about a dozen 18lb. Shells. Nearly all of which were blind **(dud)**.
Our Stokes and 2" mortars continue to be very active, but hostile retaliation with Minenwerfer has been heavy.
Our snipers seem to have completely subdued hostile sniping.
The enemy retaliated to our Stokes Mortars by again shelling HIGHLAND TRENCH with his Minenwerfer, blocking up 'B' Company's Headquarters and damaging the trench considerably. The enemy was repeatedly prevented from repairing his trenches during the night by our rifle grenades. The night was too light to send out patrols.
Casualties:- 1 other rank killed, 2 other ranks wounded.

14th September 1916 In the Trenches. A draft of 4 other ranks joined the Battalion and taken on strength. Our heavy artillery shelled the Minenwerfer emplacement in the hostile JAEGER TRENCH apparently with good effect as the enemy has not fired from it since.
We continue to be aggressive with our Stokes Mortars and rifle grenades, receiving little retaliation. The enemy fired a good number of 16" trench mortars, which were nearly all blind, several good specimens being obtained.

Two of our patrols were out, but owing to the brilliant moon were forced to come in early.
Casualties:- 1 other rank wounded.

15th September 1916 In the Trenches. Our artillery continues to be inactive. Our Stokes and 60lb trench mortars have been very busy and much good shooting has been done. We also fired many salvos from our rifle grenade batteries, receiving practically no reply.
The enemy fired 6 Minenwerfers from JAEGER TRENCH, but generally he has been very quiet.
A hostile patrol was observed moving in the direction of SAP 98a and was immediately dispersed by our Lewis gun fire. Several small bodies of the enemy have been observed moving in the direction of their front line. A cyclist orderly was also seen and it is thought that a relief has taken place.
Casualties: 1 O.R. killed.

16th September 1916 In the Trenches.
Temp. 2/Lt. J.H.Vincent relinquished the temporary rank of Captain on ceasing to command a company.
Our artillery still very inactive. The Stokes and 60lb trench mortars have been causing the enemy great annoyance and our rifle grenade batteries also have been busy. The enemy still continues to fire Minenwerfer from JAEGER TRENCH, doing a fair amount of damage to HIGHLAND TRENCH. In retaliation for our Stokes the enemy fired a good number of trench mortars into CAMPBELL CUT, a large number of which were blind.
Hostile sniping has ceased. Two of the enemy were accounted for by our snipers.
At 2.30pm the enemy fired a camouflet opposite G.11.1. No damage was caused to our front line, but the entrance of a mining gallery at junction of BOYAU 93 and 94 was shaken in.
Captain A.H.Smith rejoined from hospital and resumed command of 'C' Company.
Casualties:- 2 other ranks killed and 4 O.R. wounded.

17th September 1916 In the Trenches in the morning.
Our artillery still inactive. Our Stokes and 2" mortars bombarded hostile lines intermittently. Our snipers accounted for 2 of the enemy during the morning.
The enemy still continues firing his Minenwerfer from JAEGER TRENCH which always causes considerable damage to HIGHLAND TRENCH and he is beginning to retaliate more with rifle grenades.
At 2.30pm the Battalion was relieved in the trenches by 1st Sherwood Foresters and we moved into billets at FOUQUIERES, being in Divisional Reserve.
The Commanding Officer, Lt.Col. A.J.E.Sunderland, proceeded to Brigade Headquarters, taking over temporary command from vice Brigadier General Fagan while on leave.
Capt. A.Tillett proceeded on leave until the 25th inst.

The 2nd Devons War Diary

Capt. A.H.Smith, 2/Lt. T.R.Johns, 2/Lt. E.L.Walters and 45 other ranks proceeded to 8th Divisional School to practice as a raiding party.
During this last period of 12 days in the trenches a very large amount of good work and many improvements have been made in the trenches by the battalion; especially at Battalion Headquarters where several excellent dugouts were built and the trenches strengthened and improved. It was afterwards appropriately named EXETER CASTLE.
Casualties:- 5 other ranks wounded.

18th September 1916 In Billets at FOUQUIERES. Very wet day. Battalion attended a FLAMENWERFER demonstration in the morning at VERQUIN. Furnished working parties. A draft of 6 other ranks arrived from the Base and taken on strength. 2/Lt. A.W.Harrison and 53 other ranks rejoined the battalion from Spoils Party.

19th September 1916 In Billets at FOUQUIERES.
Furnished working parties.
2/Lt. T.M.Lewis, 'C' Company, transferred to 'D' Company. 2/Lt. C.W.C.Hannah and 1 other rank rejoined from 1st Army School. 7 other ranks rejoined from Bombing School.

20th September 1916 In Billets at FOUQUIERES. Furnished working parties.
2/Lt. A.B.Kitson granted 5 days leave to ROUEN.
Received orders late in the night that the battalion would relieve the 4th Royal Fusiliers in Brigade Reserve at PHILOSOPHE tomorrow morning.

21st September 1916 The Battalion relieved the 4th Royal Fusiliers in the Brigade Reserve of the HULLUCH section at midday.
2/Lt. H.F.Boyce and 1 other rank rejoined from anti-gas course. 6 other ranks rejoined from Spoils Party.

22nd September 1916 In Brigade Reserve, PHILOSOPHE. Furnished working parties.
Lt.Col. A.J.E.Sunderland returned from Brigade and resumed command of the Battalion.

23rd September 1916 In Brigade Reserve. PHILOSOPHE Furnished working parties.

24th September 1916 In Brigade Reserve, PHILOSOPHE. Furnished working parties.

25th September 1916 In Brigade Reserve. Furnished working parties.Lt. A.C.G.Roberts, Transport Officer, proceeded on leave until 3rd October 1916. In the evening the battalion relieved the 2nd Scottish Rifles in the trenches from ESSEX LANE exclusive to BOYAU 77 and WINGS WAY both inclusive. A very quiet night.

26th September 1916 In the Trenches. Throughout the night and early morning the enemy were very quiet until 7.00am when he bombarded our front line and saps from BOYAU 70 to 72a with Minenwerfer and heavy trench mortars, doing a good deal of damage. In spite of retaliation by our artillery the hostile shelling did not cease until 9.15am. Our retaliation did not apparently trouble the enemy and most of our shells were blind. Considerable movement of transport was heard during the night in rear of hostile lines.
Casualties: 1 O.R. wounded.

27th September 1916 In the Trenches. Our artillery generally inactive. Our Stokes and 60lb trench mortars at intervals shelled the hostile front system and caused him considerable annoyance and he retaliated with Minenwerfer and 77mm, doing little damage, however. An officer's patrol went out during the night, but none of the enemy were encountered. A draft of 44 other ranks arrived from the base and taken on strength.
Casualties:- nil.

28th September 1916 In the Trenches. A quiet morning.
In response to Minenwerfer and trench mortar fire, our artillery fired several rounds at 3.45pm. Our Stokes shelled enemy front line and saps with apparent good effect and he retaliated with trench mortars doing no damage. Hostile working parties were dispersed by our Lewis gun fire during the night. In spite of our artillery fire the enemy still continues to use his Minenwerfer emplacement at H.13.c.7.9.
A large amount of work was done to front line during the night to permit of a daylight relief with Scottish Rifles.
Casualties: 2/Lt. C.W.C.Hannah was killed.

29th September 1916 In the Trenches. Morning very quiet.
At 3.00pm the battalion was relieved in the trenches by the 2nd Scottish Rifles and moved into Brigade Reserve billets in PHILOSOPHE. 'C' Company proceeded to GOSNAY for special training. A draft of 45 other ranks joined the Battalion and taken on strength.

30th September 1916 In Brigade Reserve. Routine:- Furnished working parties. Commanding Officer inspected new draft. 2/Lt. A.C.Faulkner and 2 other ranks rejoined from Lewis Gun Course.

The 2nd Devons War Diary

OCTOBER 1916

1st October 1916 Routine. Furnished RE Working Parties. The CO and Adjutant rode to GOSNEY to inspect 'C' Company training for raid.

2nd October 1916 Routine. Furnished Working Parties. The Brigadier, CO and Adjutant motored to GOSNEY at night to inspect 'C' practising a raid.

3rd October 1916 The Battalion relieved the 2nd Scottish Rifles in the trenches during the afternoon.
Our artillery, trench mortars, Lewis and machine guns fired according to programme doing considerable damage to hostile wire and trenches.
The enemy were very quiet and replied very feebly to our bombardments and wire cutting.
One chance 77 mm shell killed 2/Lt. F.B.Lloyd and wounded 2/Lt. E.A.Wykes and A.J.Snowden.
2/Lt. A.E.A.Phillips took over Command of 'D' Company.

4th October 1916 We continued our bombardments and wire cutting. The enemy was again very quiet.
2 other ranks accidentally wounded in a bomb store.

5th October 1916 We attempted a raid on hostile trenches, preceded by a gas attack on the night of the 5/6th. (See report).
Casualties: Capt. A.H.Smith killed. 12 other ranks killed. 3 other ranks Died of Wounds. 21 other ranks wounded during 5/6th.
During the raid the hostile artillery was not very active, most of his fire was directed on the front and support lines.

REPORT ON RAID.

I have questioned the three officers and CSM Radford as to what occurred. The party reached the position of assembly in the front trench without a hitch. There was some difficulty in laying out the tape owing to Stokes Mortars dropping short and also some misunderstanding about cutting our own wire, but the result was not affected thereby as the parties were lined up in front of the gaps at 2.00am 2/Lt. Tindal noted the time.
Some of our 18 pounders were falling short on and in front of the hostile line. The enemy threw bombs and when the men got up to dash in their machine guns opened. One from the base of the sap about H.13.c.5½.½., one firing straight down the tape and one from the left. One of the Officers thought there was a machine gun in the sap about H.13.c.5.¼. and this is confirmed by Captain Tillett who went out afterwards to bring in wounded. The leader of the raid, Captain Smith, was killed at once and most of the leading men were knocked out. The party then became

disorganised and withdrew.
I attribute the failure of the enterprise to the fact that Captain Smith was killed at once and that the enemy were thoroughly alert and prepared.
The gas does not appear to have damaged the enemy or his machine gun.
Captain Tillett and 2/Lt. Tindal went out and brought in 3 wounded men, despite a heavy fire.
This morning at 8.30am Cpl. Dickson and L/Cpl. Wilson went out in broad daylight and carried in two wounded men from close to the hostile wire.
I wish to bring their names to notice.
Casualties were, killed: Captain Smith, other ranks 12. 3 other ranks died of wounds, and 19 other ranks were wounded.

6th October 1916 Our trench mortars fired at intervals during the day, good shooting was observed. The enemy fired a few 77 mm. Shells, but was otherwise very quiet. 4 of our men went out in broad daylight and brought in 2 of our wounded from near the hostile trenches.

7th October 1916 The Battalion was relieved in the trenches during the afternoon and moved into Brigade Support Trenches in German Switch and 10th Avenue. Furnished Working Parties.
2/Lt. H.T.Marshall rejoined from Hospital.

8th October 1916 In Brigade Support.
The CO proceeded on Leave to England.
Major H.F.Hardman, Somerset Light Infantry, joined the Battalion and remained at Transport Lines for the night. Furnished Working Parties.

9th October 1916 Furnished Working Parties.

10th October 1916 In Support. Furnished Working Parties. 2/Lt. H.St.Hill struck off strength, having embarked for England "sick" on the 1st inst. A draft of 6 other ranks joined and posted to 'C' Company.

11th October 1916 In Support. Furnished Working Parties.

12th October 1916 The battalion was relieved in the support trenches by the 14th battalion Argyle and Sutherland Highlanders during the morning, and marched to HOUCHIN CAMP.
2/Lt. A.E.A.Phillips granted leave to UK until 20th instant.

14th October 1916 The Battalion marched to CHOCQUES and entrained for PONT-REMY arriving there during the evening. From PONT-REMY the Battalion marched to HUPPY and moved into Billets at midnight.

The 2nd Devons War Diary

15th October 1916 In Billets at HUPPY. Church Parade. The Battalion was inspected by the OC Major H.F.Hardman.

16th October 1916 In Billets at HUPPY.
Information having been received that the Battalion would probably move this day, the programme of work was cancelled and everyone stood by ready to move in the afternoon. We did not however move until following morning.

17th October 1916 The Battalion formed up at 3am and marched to SOREL, where motor lorries were waiting and conveyed us to VILLE. From VILLE the Battalion marched to MEAULTE and moved into billets.

18th October 1916 In Billets at MEAULTE. Routine. Furnished RE working parties. Very Wet Day.

19th October 1916 In Billets at MEAULTE.
Routine. Furnished RE working parties. Very Wet Day.

20th October 1916 The Battalion formed up and marched into G Camp at MONTAUBAN.

21st October 1916 In Camp at MONTAUBAN. Furnished Working Parties.
Casualties: 3 other ranks wounded.

22nd October 1916 In Camp at MONTAUBAN. Furnished Working Parties.
Casualties: 1 other rank wounded.
Orders were received that the 8th Division and 4th Division on the Right would attack the German trenches in conjunction with an advance by the French Army on the 23rd October, 1916.
The 1st Objective of the 23rd Infantry Brigade was as follows :-
<u>1st Objective</u> N.35.a.5.4½. to N.28.d.6.7.
<u>2nd Objective</u> N.35.a.9½.8. to N.28.d.9½.9.
The attack was to be carried out by the 2nd Middlesex Regiment and 2nd Scottish Rifles, the 2nd West Yorks being in Support and the 2nd Devons in Reserve.
The Battalion moved out of Camp at 12.15am on 23rd inst. and occupied the position of assembly in GAP TRENCH and PUNCH TRENCH.
Lt./Col. Sunderland who had been on leave returned about 12.00 noon on the 22nd and took over Command.
The following Officers accompanied the Battalion into action:

Lt./Col. A.J.E.Sunderland	Commanding Officer
Temp/Capt. Lieut. A.Tillett	Adjutant
Temp/Capt. Lieut. H.Archer	Officer Commanding 'B' Company.
2/Lt. C.H.S.Buckley	Officer Commanding 'C' Company
2/Lt. A.W.Winch	Officer Commanding 'A' Company
Major H.del.Sprye	Officer Commanding 'D' Company

2/Lt. G.F.Thuillier
2/Lt. H.T.Marshall
2/Lt. J.H.Vincent
2/Lt. C.B.Rodd
2/Lt. L.N.L.Tindal
2/Lt. E.L.Walters
2/Lt. W.M.Thomson
2/Lt. A.E.Rutledge
2/Lt. H.J.Skardon
2/Lt. H.H.Goodman
2/Lt. A.C.Faulkner
2/Lt. G.L.Jones R.A.M.C.
2/Lt. E.D.Hill was attached to 25th Brigade HQ as Liaison Officer.
The following Officers remained at Transport Lines to replace Casualties.
Major H.F.Hardman (Somerset Light Infantry)
2/Lt. H.F.Boyce
2/Lt. A.B.Kitson
2/Lt. H.H.Jago
2/Lt. A.W.Harrison
2/Lt. W.W.Drake
Lt. A.C.G.Roberts.   Transport Officer
Lt.& Q/m. G.Palmer

23rd October 1916 The morning of the 23rd broke with a thick fog which did not lift until about noon.
The CO went to Advanced Brigade HQ at 9.00am and returned about 11.00am
In consequence of the fog the attack which should have taken place in the morning was put off until the afternoon.
During the morning we furnished a carrying party which worked under cover of the fog.
The Colonel returned to Advanced Brigade HQ after lunch.
The attack was successfully carried out by the 23rd Infantry Brigade. The enemy did not fire any shells in the vicinity of the Battalion.
The CO returned from Advanced Brigade HQ about 7.00pm
About 11.00pm orders were received that the Battalion was to move at once to NEEDLE TRENCH and that Battalion HQ were to be established at the German Dump, which was Advanced Brigade HQ. Some difficulty was found in getting the Battalion into this trench as the ground was wet and sodden and it was an extremely dark night.
Casualties: 2 other ranks wounded.

24th October 1916 When it was light a considerable number of wounded were discovered near HQ which it had been impossible to move further in owing to the state of the ground and lack of stretcher bearers. The Battalion assisted as far as possible in getting these men away.
The Brigadier returned to Brigade HQ during the morning.

The 2nd Devons War Diary

The CO visited the trenches occupied by the 2nd Middlesex Regiment during the morning and attended a conference later at Brigade HQ.
The Brigadier returned to Battalion HQ in the evening and remained there for the night.
During the night of 24/25th, 'A' Company was employed carrying wounded.
'B' and 'D' Companies carried stores from Brigade HQ to the Battalion HQ in the line during the night.
Casualties: 4 other ranks wounded.

25th October 1916   During the morning orders were received that as a result of the operations on the 23rd and early morning of the 24th October, the Division held ZENITH TRENCH from about N.34.b.9.5. to about N.28.d.5.5. and a line of shell craters running from the Northern end of ZENITH TRENCH (N.28.b.0.1½) to about MISTY TRENCH (N.28.a.6.4.) and that the portion of ZENITH TRENCH lying between N.28.d.5.5. and N.28.b.0.1½ however was still in the hands of the enemy.
This part of ZENITH TRENCH was to be taken by the 25th Brigade and that the 2nd Devon Regiment had been placed at the disposal of the G.O.C. 25th Infantry Brigade to assist in this attack.
The attack was to be carried out as soon as possible after the necessary arrangements had been made, as the weather offered a reasonable prospect of success.
The CO attended a conference at the HQ 25th Infantry Brigade.
At 6.30pm received orders to the effect that the Battalion was under the orders of the 23rd Infantry Brigade and that the Battalion was to be prepared to deliver a counter attack if required to do so, at a moment's notice.
Furnished carrying parties. Major Sprye was admitted to Hospital.

26th October 1916   Orders were received that the Battalion was now under the orders of the 25th Infantry Brigade.
Furnished carrying parties.   CO attended Conference.

27th October 1916   The CO accompanied by the Adjutant, Company Commanders and Company Sergeant Majors visited the trenches the Battalion would occupy prior to the attack. It was found that owing to the bad condition of the trenches and the bad weather, also the fact that there were no Battalion HQ and that sufficient stores had not been taken down, the attack for the moment was not feasible.
Furnished carrying parties.
'C' Company and 2 platoons of 'B' Company relieved the 2nd Royal Berkshire Regiment in LARKHILL and SPIDER TRENCHES during the night. These platoons came under fairly heavy shell fire during the relief.
2/Lt. C.H.S.Buckley was wounded. 3 other ranks killed and 5 other ranks wounded.

2/Lt. E.L.Walters was admitted to Hospital sick.
It was decided that the attack would be carried out at 3.00pm.
on the 29th October, and that the 1st Sherwood Foresters who
were to take part in the attack would not do so, the whole
attack to be carried out by the 2nd Devon Regiment. The attack
was to be carried out as follows:-
'A', 'D' and ½ 'B' Companies were to attack the hostile trenches
from the front; ½ 'B' Company under Capt. H.Archer posted on the
left of the 23rd Infantry Brigade was to attack the enemy from
the rear. 'C' Company was to be held in reserve.
Battalion HQ to be established in the front line.

28th October 1916 Orders were received that the Battalion was
to relieve the 1st Sherwood Foresters in the front line MISTY
TRENCH, arrangements for relief to be made between OC Battalions
concerned.
The relief commenced at 9.00pm. Companies were ordered to
occupy the trenches as follows:-
Right Company: 'B'. Centre Company: 'A'. Left Company: 'D'.
'C' Company in support in RAINBOW TRENCH.
Casualties. 5 other ranks wounded.

29th October 1916 Owing to the Guides supplied by the 1st
Sherwood Foresters not being able to lead the Companies into the
positions they were to occupy it was discovered that 'D'
Company, 'C' Company, 2 platoons of 'B' Company and 2 platoons
of 'A' Company only were in position at 4.50am 29th and that all
these troops were greatly fatigued owing to the fact that they
had been marching in waterlogged trenches since 9.00pm 28th
instant.
The CO informed the 25th Infantry Brigade that he would be
unable to carry out the attack at 3.00pm on the 29th, but that
he would do so at 3.00pm on the 30th.
At 11.00am the missing four platoons were in position but in a
very exhausted condition. The artillery on both sides was very
active. The enemy directed most of his energy in shelling the
Support line only. Few shells burst near our front line. It
rained at intervals during the day and the trenches soon became
very bad. The Brigadier 25th Infantry Brigade sent the Brigade
Major to see the CO at 9.00am to ascertain if the CO still
considered it inadvisable to carry out the attack, informing him
at the time that it would not be possible to carry out the
attack on the next day as the Division was being relieved. The
CO informed the Brigadier that the missing platoons were still
absent and that the remainder of the men were too fatigued and
that under the circumstances it was out of the question to carry
out the attack.
Ration parties bringing up the rations were shelled by the enemy
several animals being injured, one man killed and two others
wounded.
'B' Company's rations were destroyed.
Casualties: 7 killed. 11 Wounded.

30th October 1916 It continued to rain throughout the day and night.
The artillery was again active on both sides, the enemy again shelling the Support line only. One German deserter gave himself up during the night.
Orders were received that the Battalion would be relieved in the trenches by the 10th Sherwood Foresters and that the Battalion would move to C Camp S.23.b.3.3. Relief to be completed by 5.30am
Owing to the Communication trenches being impassable the last Company did not leave the trenches until 7.30am on the 30th.
'A' Company and 2 platoons of 'B' Company came out over the top in broad daylight.
2/Lt. C.B.Rodd and two men were killed and nine men wounded.

31st October 1916 The Battalion arrived at C Camp in a muddy and exhausted condition
Tea was issued to the troops and rifles, equipment, etc. cleaned.
At 2.00pm the Battalion fell in and marched to MANSELL CAMP and again came under the orders of the 23rd Infantry Brigade.
Casualties – 2 men wounded.
Two men who took shelter in a shell hole whilst leaving the trenches stuck in the mud near Brigade Headquarters and it took over an hour to dig them out.

Martin Body

NOVEMBER 1916

1st November 1916   The Battalion moved from Mansell Camp to MEAULTE, where the Battalion was billeted.

2nd November 1916   In billets at MEAULTE. Routine.

3rd November 1916   Moved from MEAULTE to CITADEL CAMP during the morning. During the evening received orders to the effect that the 23rd Infantry Brigade was at the disposal of the 33rd Division to assist in carrying out certain contemplated operations and that the Battalion should be prepared to move in fighting order at short notice. About 10pm received orders that Brigade would probably have to move at 4am the 4th. About 11am received orders to the effect that the Brigade would not move before 9am 4th.

4th November 1916   About 10 a.m. received orders to the effect that the Battalion would move to GUILLEMONT, leaving Camp at 1pm, and that a general attack would be carried out on the 5th by the 6th French Army and our 4th and 5th Armies. The 23rd Brigade would be in reserve in COW and OX line and in the FLERS LINE by ZERO hour, probably 11am on the 5th.
About 11am the Battalion was informed that all previous orders were cancelled and that the Battalion was to "stand by".
About 1pm informed that the situation was normal and that the Battalion need not "stand to".

5th November 1916   CITADEL CAMP. Routine.

6th November 1916   Moved to BRIQUETERIE CAMP.

7th November 1916   Received a Draft of 20 other ranks.
2/Lt. J.D.Harcombe and 2/Lt. H.B.Brooman joined the Battalion from Cadet School, GHQ.
The Battalion moved into the trenches during the night and relieved the 2nd Battalion Royal Welsh Fusiliers.
There was not a great deal of shelling, although the rear Company ('D' Company) had a rather unpleasant journey.
Casualties:- 3 wounded and 1 missing.
The following Officers remained at the Transport Lines.
Major H.F.Hardman
2/Lt. W.M.Thomson.
2/Lt. L.N.L.Tindal.
The trenches were found to be in a fair condition, but very waterlogged.

8th November 1916   In the Trenches. There was considerable artillery activity on both sides. The trenches were greatly improved.
Casualties :- 2 Killed, 1 Wounded and 1 Missing.

The 2nd Devons War Diary

9th November 1916 In the Trenches. Artillery was active throughout the night.
About 2pm the following message was received from the Brigade :- Can you arrange to advance the whole of your two front Companies now in AUTUMN TRENCH on to the crest line in front to-night and dig in. If not the whole line could you arrange for short lines of trenches to be made on same position, prior to joining up later. This is most urgent and G.O.C. considers it imperative. Wire your views at once. AAA A line dug close up to the crest would be sufficient. G.O.C. suggests a covering party with Lewis Guns on the crest line AAA.
The CO wired to the Brigade to the effect that the whole line would be advanced and dug in during the night. The necessary orders were issued to Companies and to assist the 2 Companies in AUTUMN TRENCH in this work, two platoons were allotted to each of these Companies; the whole operation was carried out under the direction of 2/Lt. E.D.Hill.
This operation was most successful carried out during the night in spite of the fact that the troops were spotted and heavily fired on by the enemy as soon as they started work.
By dawn next day the trench was completed, with fire steps, etc. and these communication trenches joined this new trench, later named FALL TRENCH, to AUTUMN TRENCH.
The enemy during the night made a small bombing attack on the new trench, but were easily dispersed.
Casualties: - 2 Killed and 11 Wounded.
The Battalion was congratulated by the Brigadier on the work done.

10th November 1916 Artillery again very active.
The Battalion was relieved in the trenches by the 2nd West Yorks Regiment and on relief moved into Brigade Reserve in the FLERS LINE, less 'C' Company which moved into Camp in TRONES WOOD.
Casualties: - 2 killed, 6 wounded.

11th November 1916 In Brigade Reserve in the FLERS LINE.
H.R.H. The Prince of Wales visited the Battalion and remained for some time.
During the night a field battery on the right of the Battalion was heavily shelled with gas shells and considerable damage done. Only a few shells were fired on the Battalion front and no damage was done beyond cutting the barbed wire.
Furnished Working Parties both by day and night.
Casualties:- 1 man wounded.

12th November 1916 FLERS LINE. Routine - Furnished Working Parties by day and night.

13th November 1916 The Battalion moved to CARNOY Camp during the morning. Received draft of 5 other ranks.
2/Lt. L.Pertwee and 2/Lt. F.R.Brooman joined the Battalion from the Cadet School.

Martin Body

14th November 1916 CARNOY Camp. Routine.

15th November 1916 Moved to CITADEL Camp.

16th November 1916 CITADEL Camp. Routine - Furnished Working Parties.Received Draft of 6 Signallers.

17th November 1916 CITADEL Camp.Routine - Furnished R.E. Working Parties.Casualties:- 3 other ranks Wounded on Working Party.

18th November 1916 CITADEL Camp. Routine. Received Draft of 37 other ranks.

19th November 1916 Entrained at GROVE TOWN about 5pm.

20th November 1916 Detrained at OISEMONT about 4.30am and marched to billets at VERGIES.

21st November 1916 In Billets at VERGIES. Company Training. Received Draft of 32 other ranks.
2/Lt. L.Vinnicombe joined Battalion from Cadet School.

22nd November 1916 Company Training. Received Draft of 6 other ranks.

23rd November 1916 Company Training.

24th November 1916 Company Training.

25th November 1916 Company Training. Received Draft of 8 other ranks.

26th November 1916 Company Training.

27th November 1916 Company Training.

28th November 1916 Company Training.

29th November 1916 Company Training.

30th November 1916 Company Training. At 10.30am the Brigadier inspected the Battalion in marching order.
At 11.15am the Divisional Commander presented MILITARY MEDAL Ribbons to the following:-
No.8258 Sgt. M.Hobbs. For displaying great keenness and intelligence on patrol for which he has frequently volunteered.
No.8826 Sgt. Crispen. For devotion to duty. Has frequently shown great courage in mending telephone wires under heavy fire. This NCO was wounded mending wire.
No.12608 Cpl. A.Holmes. For devotion to duty and showing great daring and resource on Patrol. Always volunteers for any

dangerous work.

No.9937 L/Sgt. R.Roberts. For conspicuous courage and daring on patrol, and readiness to volunteer at all times for work in front of our lines.

No.9428 L/Cpl. W.Kirby. For devotion to duty on the night of 22/23 April 1916 near ALBERT when the telephone wires were being continually cut he showed great promptitude in mending them in spite of heavy shell-fire.

No.6795 Pte. D.Greenslade. For devotion to duty. He has been HQ Orderly throughout the Campaign and has frequently carried messages under heavy shell-fire.

No.8923 Pte. F.Joint. For showing great coolness and devotion to duty on the 31/5/16, when a German Mine was exploded in our lines, he manned the first available bay and carried on.

No.14152 Pte. W.Howells. For showing great coolness and devotion to duty on the 31/5/16, when a German Mine exploded in our lines, he manned the first available bay and carried on.

After the Medal Ribbons had been presented the Battalion marched past the Divisional Commander in Column of route. The men who had been presented with Medal Ribbons were drawn up beside the Divisional Commander as the Battalion marched past.

Martin Body

DECEMBER 1916

1st December 1916 In Billets at VERGIES. Company Training.

2nd December 1916 In Billets. Company Training.

3rd December 1916 In Billets. Church Parade. Received Draft of 46 other ranks.

4th December 1916 In Billets. Company Training.

5th December 1916 In Billets. Company Training.
Lt. J.O'Boyle proceeded to England on Termination of his engagement.
Lt. D.Mackinnon R.A.M.C. took over the duties of Regimental Medical Officer.

6th December 1916 In Billets. Company Training.
2/Lt. J.L.H.Richards joined Battalion for first time.

7th December 1916 In Billets. Company Training.

8th December 1916 In Billets. Company Training.

9th December 1916 In Billets. Company Training.

10th December 1916 In Billets. Church Parade. The CO took over Temporary Command of the Brigade during absence of G.O.C.

11th December 1916 In Billets. Battalion Training.

12th December 1916 In Billets. Battalion Training. Draft of 123 other ranks joined the Battalion.

13th December 1916 In Billets. Battalion Training.

14th December 1916 In Billets. Battalion Training.

15th December 1916 In Billets. Brigade Field Day.

16th December 1916 In Billets. Battalion Training.

17th December 1916 In Billets. Church Parade.
'A' Company proceeded to 8th Divisional School of Instruction. Lt.Col. A.J.E.Sunderland was admitted to Hospital "sick". Major A.Tillett took over Temporary Command of the Battalion.

18th December 1916 In Billets. Battalion Training. 2/Lt. P.Gay and 2/Lt. A.E.Slater joined the Battalion.

19th December 1916 In Billets. Battalion Training.

The 2nd Devons War Diary

20th December 1916 In Billets. Battalion Training. Received Draft of 11 other ranks.

21st December 1916 In Billets. Battalion Training.

22nd December 1916 In Billets. Battalion Training.
2/Lt.Hughes joined the Battalion on first appointment, attached 'C' Company. 2/Lt.P.Gay appointed to command 'D' Company.

23rd December 1916 In Billets. Battalion Training.
1 Officer (2/Lt. Slater) and 52 other ranks proceeded to Musketry Camp, PONT REMY.
2/Lt. C.E.Copplestone joined Battalion on 1st appointment and attached to 'C' Company.
2/Lts. Thomson and Drake went on leave to U.K.
'A' Company returned from Divisional School.
Horse Race in the afternoon, all Officers up.
2/Lt. Roberts - CAMEL, First. Major Tillett - RAJAH, Second.

24th December 1916 In Billets. Church Parades. Xmas Day functions were observed to-day owing to preparations to move back to the line. All Officers dined at HQ.

25th December 1916 Xmas Day. No Parades.

26th December 1916 G.O.C., 8th Division, made his first inspection of the 23rd Brigade at ST. MAULVIS at 10 am.

27th December 1916 Left VERGIES AT 4.30 a.m. and entrained at OISEMONT at 10am and arrived at EDGE HILL (ALBERT) at 3.15 pm. The Battalion then marched to Camp 12 near SAILLY LAURETTE and arrived in a very exhausted condition. 1 Officer and draft of 6 other ranks joined the Battalion. (2/Lt. Bidgway).

28th December 1916 The Battalion fell in at 9.45am and marched to the forward area. Marching was good, due probably to the air being exceedingly cold and the roads hard. Arrived at Camp 16 near MARICOURT at 12.30pm.

29th December 1916 Left the Camp at 12 noon and lorries conveyed the Battalion to MAUREPAS en route to the trenches.
2/Lt.Crane joined the Battalion on first appointment
Debussed at 3.30 pm and marched by Companies as far as COMBLES, thenby platoons to the line.
The following Officers accompanied the Battalion into action:-

Temp. Major A.Tillett	Commanding	
Captain H.Archer	'B' Company	&2nd in Command.
2/Lt. A.Winch	'A' Company	Commanding.
2/Lt. L.Pertwee	'A' Company	
2/Lt. A.C.Bidgway	'A' Company	

2/Lt. H.H.Jago	'B' Company	Commanding.
2/Lt. F.R.Brooman	'B' Company	
2/Lt. T.R.Johns	'C' Company	Commanding.
2/Lt. E.L.Walters	'C' Company	
2/Lt. J.F.L.Hughes	'C' Company	
2/Lt. P.Gay	'D' Company	Commanding.
2/Lt. A.E.Rutledge	'D' Company	
2/Lt. L.Vinnicombe	'D' Company	

29/30th December 1916 Took over the line U.26a.45.85. - U.20.b.2.1. opposite the ST PIERRE VAAST Wood from the 1st Rifle Brigade -
'D' Company in front line, 'B' Company close support and A and C Companies in Reserve.
The trenches are very bad, all full of water. Front line a series of shell holes and held by 10 posts. The night was very quiet and rain fell steadily the whole time.
Casualties:- 4 men wounded during the night by shell fire.

30th December 1916 Raining all the morning. Enemy guns very active on our front and support line. Brigadier General Fagan and the Brigade Major came up to look round the line at 11am. Enemy artillery knocked out a Lewis Gun and crew in the front line.
Casualties:- 1 Killed and 4 wounded.
Slow methodical shelling of our lines continued all the afternoon, during which 1 NCO was wounded. As soon as it was dusk 'A' Company went up and relieved 'D' Company in front line. 'D' Company took over from 'B' in support and 'B' went back to 'A' Company's old area.
At 8pm Captain Archer took 20 men down to the front line to endeavour to improve the trench and assist 'A' Company in pumping water out. 'C' Company supplied a working party carrying pumps up to 'A' Company. On 'D' Company coming into the support trench 2/Lt. L.Vinnicombe went sick, chiefly due to exhaustion. Captain Blencowe (Chaplain) came into the line this evening at about 7pm.
Total Casualties for the day:- 1 Killed and 9 wounded.

31st December 1916 Everything quite normal till about 10am when enemy's guns became active. Company Commanders of West Yorks came to look round. About 3pm, a 5.9 knocked out a Lewis Gun, wounded two and of one man no trace could be found. 'C' Company went up from support and relieved 'A' Company. 'D' went into reserve and 'A' went into support. Evening very quiet. Enemy shelling during the day was above normal and appeared to be concentrated rather on the left of front line, the road (BAPAUME-PERONNE) was heavily shelled during this period - from 7pm to midnight very quiet - artillery unusually quiet.

The 2nd Devons War Diary

JANUARY 1917

1st January 1917 Battalion in the line. The day fairly quiet. At midnight 'B' Company went up from Reserve and relieved 'C' Company in front line.

2nd January 1917 At "stand to" in the morning 2 men were observed approaching No.1 Post. It was thought that they were our own men when about ten yards from the Post it was observed they were Germans. When challenged they failed to put up their hands and ran away. Fire was opened on them and both men fell. One was recovered wounded in about six places. The second man totally disappeared and it is thought he was hit and fell into a shell hole of liquid mud. The man brought in eventually died of wounds. He belonged to the 10th Bavarian Reserve Infantry Regiment (normal). Both men were, it seems, on a ration party and had lost their way and had passed through own line (i.e. the 2nd Lincolns area). Shelling throughout the rest of the day was normal. At 4.30pm the 2nd West Yorks relieved the reserve line - by 7pm the relief was completed. The Battalion went back individually to Camp "Y" MAUREPAS. Two men were reported missing from the march from the line.
2/Lt. A.M.Taylor joined the Battalion on 1st Appointment on the 1st instant and posted to 'A' Company.
2/Lt. L.N.L.Tindal went to 4th Army School and in the afternoon 2/Lt. G.F.Thullier went to Lewis Gun Course at BOUCHON.
2/Lt. A.E.Slater left for England for M.G. Course.
Draft of 28 other ranks joined the Battalion today.

3rd January 1917 Battalion in Camp.
Details furnished a Working Party of 20 men in the morning. In the evening 'D' Company supplied a Working Party for the C.R.E. and another at midnight.
Draft of 5 other ranks joined the Battalion this day.
The following Officers were appointed Temp. Captains from the dates shown :-
2/Lt. A.Winch appointed Temp.Captain 14/10/16
2/Lt. E.D.Hill appointed Temp.Captain 28/10/16
2/Lt. J.H.Vincent appointed Temp.Captain 25/11/16.
Lt. Mackinnon R.A.M.C. reported sick and Captain D.Whyte R.A.M.C. reported for duty.
2/Lt. H.H.Jago took over temporary Command of 'A' Company, vice Captain Winch on Leave.

4th January 1917 'D' Company supplied two parties of 20 at 8am for the C.R.E. Two Companies 'A' and 'C' (200 strong) working under the C.R.E. on Camp construction.
Draft of 4 other ranks joined the Battalion.
Working Party furnished by 'A' and 'C' Companies under the C.R.E.

Martin Body

5th January 1917 Battalion in Camp.
2/Lt. A.C.Bidgway, 'A' Company, and 2/Lt. F.R.Brooman proceeded to 8th Divisional School, AVESNE. Working Party of 200 other ranks furnished by 'A' and 'B' Companies. Enemy Artillery very busy all day, also German Aeroplanes very busy.

6th January 1917 Battalion left Y Camp at 3pm and marched by Companies as far as COMBLES, then by platoons to the lines. Ankle boots were changed for gum boots just beyond COMBLES. The following Officers accompanied the Battalion into action:-
Major   A.Tillet Commanding
Captain   H.Archer   'B' Company.   Second in Command.
2/Lt.   H.H.Jago   'A' Company.   Commanding
2/Lt.   J.L.H.Richards   'A' Company
2/Lt.   A.M.Taylor   'A' Company
Captain   H.Archer   'B' Company.   Commanding
2/Lt.   A.B.Kitson   'B' Company
2/Lt.   A.C.Faulkner   L.G.O. attached 'B' Company
2/Lt.   T.R.Johns   'C' Company.   Commanding
2/Lt.   E.L.Walters   'C' Company.
2/Lt.   P.Gay   'D' Company.   Commanding.
2/Lt.   A.E.Rutledge   'D' Company
2/Lt.   H.B.Brooman   'D' Company
Took over line opposite ST PIERRE VAAST WOOD. POLLUX SECTOR, from the 2nd West Yorkshire Regiment. The front line is almost the same as that taken over on 29/30th ultimo, with the exception of 9 and 10 posts being given up by us and four extra posts on the left added to our Sector.
During the night the enemy artillery was exceptionally quiet.

7th January 1917 Hostile aircraft very active during the morning. Enemy shelled the BAPAUME-PERONNE ROAD on both sides of Battalion HQ with 5.9 from 2.15pm to 10pm
2nd Scottish Rifles furnished a working party during the night to place wire in front of the Support line.
'B' Company were employed in carrying material to the front and support lines.
No casualties during the day.
Two new posts were begun in the Support line under R.E. supervision.
A patrol of 1 Officer, 2 NCOs and 5 men went out from No 8 Post and discovered that the enemy's wire immediately in front was from 3' to 3' 6" high and fairly deep.

8th January 1917 Hostile artillery fire was much below normal during the day, 2 salvoes of 4 shells of the 5.9 calibre fell near the Reserve line at 4.15pm.
'D' Company from the Support line and half of 'C' Company relieved the front line between 11.30pm and 12.30am on the night of 8/9th inst. 'A' Company coming back to the Support line and half Company of 'C' to the Reserve line.
No casualties occurred during the day.

The 2nd Devons War Diary

2/Lt. W.M.Thomson and 2/Lt. W.W.Drake returned from leave and joined the Details.
Draft of 105 other ranks joined the Battalion this day and taken on strength.

9th January 1917   At 1am a German came across "No Man's Land" and gave himself up at No 7 Post. He was marched to Battalion HQ and searched. The prisoner spoke English fluently and remarked that he saw our relief distinctly which took place an hour earlier. The captured man looked very fit and none the worse for his experience in the trenches. He was sent to Brigade HQ under escort.
Captain R.J.Andrews joined the Battalion from a Course at ALDERSHOT.
2/Lt. George Archer and 2/Lt. Maurice Gilbert Beck reported for duty this day.
A Working Party of 50 men from the Reserve Company were improving the front line posts during the night. A Forward Post, bomb store or ammunition dump was blown up by our artillery at U.20d.3.6 ½. at 11.25am.
Hostile artillery fire was below normal.

10th January 1917   The Battalion was relieved by the 2nd Battalion Irish Guards on the night of 10/11th instant. The Support and Reserve Companies were relieved between 4 and 5 pm and the front line later, having to proceed under cover of darkness.
During the four days in the POLLUX SECTOR one man was killed (attached T.M. Battery) and 1 wounded by shrapnel.
The Battalion marched to CRUCIFIX CORNER, MAUREPAS, independently by Companies and thence by lorry to No 14 Camp, leaving CRUCIFIX CORNER at 9.30pm and arriving at the Camp about 12 midnight.

There are no entries in the War Diary for the 11th and 12th January 1917.

13th January 1917   In Billets, usual working parties.
2/Lt. M.G.Beck and 32 other ranks proceeded to the Brigade Bomb School on a Course of Instruction in Bombing.
Between 1.30 and 2.30pm the enemy dropped about 20 shells of 8" calibre in different parts of BRAY. Several falling in the square near the Church, causing considerable damage.
No. 17900 Pte. C.Huxter, 'D' Company, was killed, No 33206 Pte. F.Radford, 'D' Company, wounded. About fifty casualties were caused to other troops in the Town, one shell falling in a billet occupied by the D.C.L.I.

14th January 1917   In Billets. Usual working parties.
2/Lt. T.R.Johns, 'C' Company, proceeded on a Lewis Gun Course at XV Corps School, BOUCHON.
Divine Service was held at 11am.   (Parade)

Martin Body

Holy Communion was held at 11.30am. (Voluntary)
Hostile shells were heard passing over BRAY between 8.30 and 9.30am in the direction of ETINEHEM.
The CO, Lt.Col. A.J.E.Sunderland rejoined the Battalion, having been absent owing to illness since 17/12/16.
The undermentioned Officers and NCO have been mentioned in Dispatches by Field Marshal Sir Douglas Haig, C-in-C. 13/11/16:-
Lt.Col. A.J.E. Sunderland
Captain F.R.Cobb, M.C.
Hon.Lt. & Quartermaster G.Palmer.
2/Lt. C.O.R.Jacob.
No 10832 Sgt. M.Reilly
Major A.Tillett has been awarded the MC 1/1/17.
Captain A.Tillett to be Acting Major, 25/11/16.

15th January 1917   In Billets. Working Parties as usual.
Lt.Col. A.J.E.Sunderland proceeded to Brigade HQ and is Acting Brigadier during Brigadier General Fagan's absence.
2/Lt. A.C.C.Pendrigh reported for duty this day.
2/Lt. P.J.Crang, 'D' Company, rejoined from 8th Divisional School, AVESNE, this day.

16th January 1917   In Billets. Working Parties as usual.
2/Lt. A.C.C.Pendrigh having joined the Battalion yesterday the 15th inst., is taken on strength and posted to 'B' Company.

17th January 1917   In Billets. Working Parties as usual.
The following Officers proceeded on Leave to the U.K. from 18th to 28th instant:-
2/Lt. A.E.Rutledge   'D' Company.
2/Lt. E.L.Walters   'C' Company.

18th January 1917   In Billets. Working Parties as usual.
A Battle Platoon has been formed and composed of the following Officers:-
2/Lt. G.Archer   'D' Company
2/Lt. R.Yandle   'B' Company
6 N.C.O's and 52 men.

20th January 1917   In Billets. Working Parties as usual.
The Battle Platoon move to B.T. Dump to do R.E. Fatigues.
Capt. A.Winch has returned from leave and takes over Temporary Command of 'D' Company from this day.
2/Lt. L.Pertwee, 'A' Company, returned from Leave.

21st January 1917   In Billets. Usual Working Parties.
Major A.Tillett, MC proceeded to FLIXECOURT to attend a Senior Officers' Conference.
Captain R.J.Andrews, MC will temporarily Command the Battalion from this date.
2/Lt. T.E.Johns, 'C' Company rejoined from XV Corps L.G. School BOUCHON, and will temporarily Command 'A' Company from this

date.
2/Lt. P.Gay 'D' Company and 25 other ranks proceeded this day to form part of the Divisional Composite Company.
2/Lt. W.M.Thomson 'D' Company and 3 other ranks proceeded to XV Corps School, BOUCHON, on a Course of Instruction in Stokes Mortar.

22nd January 1917 In Billets. Usual Working Parties.
2/Lt. G.Parker having rejoined the Battalion on 21st is taken on strength and posted to 'B' Company.
2/Lt. A.B.Kitson, 'B' Company, will be a Member of a F.G.C.M. on the 23rd inst. assembling at HQ 1st Home Counties Field Company. R.E. 2/Lt. J.D.Harcombe 'B' Company rejoined from Baggage Store, 8th Division BELLOY ST LEONARD on 21st instant.

23rd January 1917 In Billets. Usual Working Parties.
2/Lts. J.D.Harcombe, 'B' Company, and H.B.Brooman, 'D' Company, and 14 other ranks proceeded on leave to U.K.

24th January 1917 In Billets. Usual Working Parties.
The undermentioned officers having joined the Battalion this day are taken on strength and posted to Companies as under :-
2/Lt. J.L.Hiley   'C' Company.
2/Lt. D.V.M.Mansel-Carey 'D' Company
2/Lt. J.H.Willman   'D' Company
2/Lt. J.M.Haswell   'A' Company
2/Lt. J.L.Bowden   'B' Company
Captain E.D.Hill and 2/Lt. H.H.Goodman were granted Leave of Absence to proceed to PARIS from the 22nd to 24th instant inclusive.
On the night of 23/24th instant the enemy dropped bombs in and around BRAY causing some damage to property and killing 16 mules. They were driven off by our machines and gun fire.

25th January 1917 In Billets. Usual Working Parties.
On the night of 25/26th instant three bombs were dropped from a hostile aeroplane on BRAY at about 8.15pm killing one horse and wounding 7 others belonging to the Battalion Transport. The enemy machine was driven off by gun fire.

26th January 1917 In Billets. Usual Working Parties.
2/Lt. R.S.Holmes, 'C' Company, rejoined from 1st Corps HQ this day. Captain H.Archer, 'B' Company, took over the duties of Senior Major from 21st instant.

27th January 1917 Usual Working Parties during the morning. The Battalion proceeded to No 21 Camp at A.27.d.5.1. arriving about 4pm.
Enemy shells of 8" calibre were falling about 400 yards from B.T. Dump between 1 and 2.30pm.
The Battalion is now in Divisional Reserve.

28th January 1917 In Camp. Battalion Training.
Enemy aeroplanes very busy both day and night.
2/Lt. T.R.Johns 'C' Company took over the duties of Area Commandant, MARICOURT AREA, this day.
2/Lt. G.Parker 'B' Company took over Temporary Command of 'A' Company from this date.

29th January 1917 Battalion Training.
The BATTLE PLATOON were inspected by Brigadier General FAGAN and complimented on their smart appearance and general turnout.
2/Lt. M.G.Beck and 23 other ranks returned from a Course at the Brigade Bomb School.

30th January 1917 In Camp. Battalion Training.
2/Lt. C.W.White, 'A' Company reported to the A.P.M. Camp 17, this day for Traffic Control Duties.

31st January 1917 In Camp. Battalion Training.
Major A.Tillett rejoined the Battalion from the Senior Officer's Conference at FLIXECOURT.

The 2nd Devons War Diary

FEBRUARY 1917

1st February 1917 In Camp. Battalion Training. 2/Lt. W.M.Thomson, 'D' Company, rejoined the Battalion from a Stokes Mortar Course at XV. Corps School, BOUCHON.
2/Lt. F.R.Brooman, 'B' Company, and 2/Lt. A.C.Bidgway, 'A' Company, rejoined the Battalion from 8th Divisional School.

2nd February 1917 In Camp. C.of.E Parade Service in the Church Hut at 10am.

3rd February 1917 In Camp. Battalion Training.

4th February 1917 No.21 Camp. In Camp. Battalion Training.
2/Lt. V.C.Emery to the 8th Divisional School.

5th February 1917 In Camp. Battalion Training.

6th February 1917 In Camp. Battalion Training.

7th February 1917 In Camp. Battalion Training
Lt.Col. A.J.E.Sunderland rejoined the Battalion from Hospital and resumes Command of the Battalion.

8th February 1917 In Camp. Battalion Training.
Captain Archer proceeded on a Course of Instruction at the GHQ School, LE TOUQUET.

9th February 1917 In Camp. Battalion Training.
Lt. A.C.G.Roberts and 2/Lt. F.R.Brooman, 'B' Company, proceeded on leave to the U.K.

10th February 1917 The Battalion left Camp 21 and marched to Camp 112 being inspected by the Divisional General en route.

11th February 1917 The Battalion left 112 Camp and marched to CORBIE arriving about 2pm.

12th February 1917 In Billets. Battalion Training.
No. 8834 Sgt. J.H.Barrett to be 2/Lt. and posted to 9th Battalion 23/1/17.
No. 6588 Sgt. Major E.H.Littlewood to be 2/Lt. and posted to 8th Battalion 20/1/17.
Lt.Col. A.J.E.Sunderland proceeded on leave of absence to the U/K.

13th February 1917 In Billets. Battalion Training.
Lt. U.B.Burke joined the Battalion and posted to 'D' Company.
2/Lt.H.H.Jago, 'B' Company, rejoined from Musketry Course at CAMIERS.

14th February 1917 In Billets. Battalion on digging fatigue by SAILLY-LAURETTE MORLANCOURT Road - practice trenches.
2/Lt. E.L.Walters, 'C' Company, proceeded to R.F.C. HQ on probation as Observer.

15th February 1917 In Billets. Battalion Training.
Captain H.Archer, 'B' Company, rejoined from GHQ Lewis Gun School, LE TOUQUET.
2/Lt. A.C.C.Pendrigh, 'B' Company, returned from a Course of Musketry at PONT REMY.

16th February 1917 In Billets. Battalion Training.

17th February 1917 In Billets. Battalion Training.

18th February 1917 In Billets. Battalion Training. Divine Service C-of-E Parade for 23rd Infantry Brigade in the Square, CORBIE, at 10.30am. Divisional Band was present, Holy Communion at 11am in the Tivoli. Evening Service (Voluntary) in the Tivoli at 6pm.

19th February 1917 Battalion left CORBIE at 8.40am and marched to Camp 112 arriving about 1.15pm.
Capt. R.J.Andrews, MC proceeded for Duty at 8th Divisional HQ.

20th February 1917 Battalion left Camp 112 at 10am and marched to Camp 17, SUZANNE, arriving about 12 midday. Battalion was filmed en route. 200 yards interval was observed between Companies.
Capt. H.Archer, 'B' Company, is granted special Leave to the U/K from 20/2/17 to 1/3/17.

21st February 1917 Battalion left Camp 17 at 3pm and were conveyed from the Camp to MAUREPAS (Crucifix Corner) in motor lorries and marched from there to CRANIERES, arriving about 6 p.m.
The Battalion was in support and supplied a working party of all available men carrying ammunition, etc to the dumps immediately behind the front line. Gum Boots were drawn at ANDOVER en route.
2/Lt. J.H.Vincent relinquishes the Rank of Temporary Captain on ceasing to Command a Company.

22nd February 1917 Battalion in support. Supplied a working party of 300 other ranks carrying ammunition, etc. from ANDOVER to front line.
2/Lt. H.H.Goodman took over the duties of Camp Commandant at ANDOVER.
2/Lt. E.L.Walters and 2/Lt. W.L.Sparkes are both struck off strength of the Battalion.

The 2nd Devons War Diary

23rd February 1917 Battalion in support.
Supplied a working party of Officers and 263 other ranks carrying ammunition, etc. from ANDOVER to front line.
Major A.Tillett, MC proceeded on leave to U/K being granted leave of absence from 24/2/17 to 23/3/17.
Capt. R.J.Andrews, MC rejoined from Divisional HQ and took over Command of the Battalion.
2/Lt. C.E.Copleston rejoined from Hospital.

24th February 1917 Battalion in support. Supplied a working party of 9 Officers and 249 other ranks carrying ammunition, etc. from ANDOVER to front line.
The u/m Officers rejoined from Leave.
Lt.Col. A.J.E.Sunderland, Lt. A.C.G.Roberts, Lt. & Quartermaster G.Palmer, 2/Lt. F.R.Brooman.

25th February 1917 Battalion relieved 2nd Scottish Rifles.
'A' and 'D' Companies - AISNE DUMP.
'B' Company   - Front line. BOUCHAVESNES. N. Sector.
'C' Company   - Support line. LANGTON BARRACKS.
Battalion HQ (advanced) LANGTON BARRACKS.
Captain R.J.Andrews, MC, MO and L.G.Officer.
Battalion HQ, CO, Adjutant, OC Battle Platoon, Signalling Officer, Intelligence Officer.

26th February 1917 Disposition as 25th. Situation Normal. 3 Casualties.
2/Lt. J.L.Bowden, 'B' Company, having been invalided "sick" to England is struck off strength from 16/2/17.

27th February 1917 Disposition as 26th. Situation normal. One casualty. 'C' Company relieved 'B' Company on the night of the 27/28th inst.

28th February 1917 'C' Company in front line. 'B' in support. 'A' and 'D' Companies relieved 'C' and 'B' on the night of the 28/1st inst.

Martin Body

MARCH 1917

1st March 1917 Front Line - 'A' Company. Support Line - 'D' Company. 'B' and 'C' Companies - AISNE DUMP. HQ - YELLOW CAMP. 'B' and 'C' Companies and Battle Platoon supplied a working party carrying ammunition to the Front Line.
2/Lt. P.J.Crang, 'D' Company, having been invalided "sick" to England is struck off the strength from 21.2.17.
2/Lt. V.G.Emery, 'C' Company, took over the duties of Brigade Transport Officer on the 23rd ultimo.

2nd March 1917 HQ, 'B' and 'C' Companies left YELLOW CAMP and AISNE DUMP at 10am and marched to Camp 17 SUZANNE. 'A' and 'D' Companies were relieved on the night of 2/3rd inst by 1st Worcestershire Regiment.
2/Lt. H.H.Goodman having rejoined the Battalion this day resumes the duties of Bombing Officer.
'A' and 'D' Companies when relieved marched to 23 CAMP.

3rd March 1917 'A' and 'D' Companies joined the Battalion at CAMP 17 arriving about 3pm.
2/Lt. J.H.Willman 'D' Company having been invalided "sick" to England is struck off strength 23.2.17.
2/Lt. M.G.Beck   'B' Company proceeded to the 15th Corps Sniping School, BOUCHON.

4th March 1917 2/Lt.J.L.F.Hughes, 'C' Company proceeded to the 4th Army Telescopic Sight School, Pont NOYELLES.
The Battalion moved from Camp 17 at 4am on the morning of the 4th inst and marched to CRANIERES.
Captain R.J.Andrews MC, remained at Camp 17 in charge of details.
The Battalion was at the disposal of the 24th Brigade, and received orders about 4pm to proceed to the line to relieve the 2nd Battalion Northampton Regt. in the Sector newly captured east of BOUCHAVESNES.

The following Officers accompanied the battalion in action:-

Lt.Col. A.J.E.Sunderland   Commanding
Captain E.D.Hill   Adjutant
2/Lt. G.F.Thuiller   Commanding 'A' Company
2/Lt. H.H.Jago   Commanding 'B' Company
2/Lt. W.W.Drake   Commanding 'C' Company
2/Lt. U.B.Burke   Commanding 'D' Company
2/Lt. G.Archer   Officer Commanding Battle Platoon
2/Lt. J.D.Harcombe
2/Lt. J.L.H.Richards
2/Lt. A.C.C.Pendrigh
2/Lt. A.Bidgway
2/Lt. W.Tomson

The 2nd Devons War Diary

2/Lt. V.G.Emery
2/Lt. L.Pertwee
2/Lt. R.S.Holmes
2/Lt. A.B.Kitson
2/Lt. F.R.Brooman
2/Lt. D.V.M.Mansel-Carey
2/Lt. A.E.Rutledge
Other Ranks – 326.

During the relief enemy artillery opened a heavy barrage on our support line. Orders were received that FRITZ TRENCH (still in enemy hands) must be raided during the early morning of the 5th and the position captured during the day, consolidated.
'A' Company was allotted the triangle to consolidate where heavy fighting had taken place all the day. 'B' Company had the task of digging a new trench about 150 yards long to connect 'A' to 'C' Company. 'D' Company held the left of the Battalion Front. 'A' Company of the 2nd East Lancashire Regt attached to this Battalion, held the line dug across "NO MAN'S LAND" connecting our old line with the newly captured trench on the extreme left. Great difficulty was experienced during consolidation owing to intense barrages every half hour and little or no material to consolidate with. 'B' Company in consequence dug a new line almost entirely with entrenching tools, this trench in the morning was about 3 feet deep, which, under the circumstances, was a remarkable feat to the credit of the Company.

5th March 1917 Relief reported complete about 4.30am. The raid on FRITZ TRENCH took place about 3am by a small party of the Battle Platoon under 2/Lt. G.Archer. 3 dugouts were bombed but the order to destroy the dugouts was not carried out owing to the fact that Mobile Charges were not obtainable.
During the early morning 'A' Company did good work consolidating the triangle under very adverse conditions. They also put in a double Bombing Block in FRITZ TRENCH and wired round it. Other Companies also put in Bombing Blocks where necessary but were unable to wire them. About 5.30am the enemy delivered two feeble attacks against 'D' Company which were easily driven off. Consolidation was carried out during the day and parties sent from Companies to find wiring material to further consolidate during the night.
2/Lt. J.D.Harcombe made an effort to get 'A' Company in communication with Battalion HQ. The first line laid was cut in 8 places no sooner it was out. After persistent work communication was eventually obtained but was cut several times during the night and following day. In the evening the enemy opened several barrages at half hour intervals and bombarded with intensity about 11 o'clock. The "S.O.S" Signal was sent up by the Battalion on our right. Our artillery opened up an exceedingly intense barrage on the enemy's trenches.
Orders were received late in the evening that Mobile Charges

being obtainable, FRITZ TRENCH would be raided again in the early hours of the 6th. Dugouts were to be destroyed and the trench wrecked.
A party of 20 men including 6 sappers under 2/Lt. G.Archer carried out the raid. They proceeded along FRITZ TRENCH about 200 yards and saw none of the enemy. On the return journey the 3 dugouts bombed the previous evening were blown up, the explosion wrecking the trench in that vicinity.
Casualties during the 4/5th 17. Prisoners captured, wounded 2, unwounded 8.

6th March 1917 Enemy artillery was active throughout the day. Companies were engaged wiring during the night.
'D' Company's Covering Party had one man killed by an enemy sniper. Our artillery bombarded our own trenches doing considerable damage to our FRONT and SUPPORT Lines and buried a few men. Patrols went out from each Company. 'D' Company reported that the enemy were working a Bombing Block about 70 yards from our own block. 'C' Company patrolled as far as the Northern end of FRITZ TRENCH and reported that men were talking in the trench. The patrol was fired upon. The Company of Sherwoods attached to the Battalion were withdrawn from the line on the night of the 6/7th inst. Casualties – 4.

7th March 1917 2/Lt. Holmes and a party of 50 men were engaged clearing the battlefield. Enemy artillery was less active during the day.
During the afternoon enemy Trench Mortars and Rifle Grenades were active for the first time during these operations.
Light Mortars in the region opposite the triangle fired about 20 rounds and registered our wire.
An enemy aeroplane flew over our trench and fired on 'D' Company but did no damage.
'A' Company were relieved from the triangle by the 2nd Lincoln Regiment. After relief they withdrew to the Support Line, PALLAS TRENCH.
During the night wiring continued. The Company of 2nd East Lancs (attached) had one man killed whilst wiring.
Casualties 2.

8th March 1917 In the morning the Divisional General accompanied by the Brigadier General 24th Brigade visited the captured trenches and complimented the CO on the good work done by the Battalion in consolidating. In the evening the Battalion and the Company of East Lancs attached were relieved by the 2nd Worcester Regiment. Relief was reported complete about 9pm. The Battalion proceeded to Camp 163. Casualties 2.

9th March 1917 In Camp 163. Routine. The CO complimented Company Commanders upon the good work done in the trenches from the 4th to the 8th inst.

The 2nd Devons War Diary

10th March 1917 In Camp. Furnished Working Parties repairing screen on MAUREPAS – CURLU ROAD.

11th March 1917 In Camp. Furnished Working Parties repairing RANCOURT Road. 2/Lt. W.Thomson, 'D' Company, proceeded to the Brigade Grenade School.

12th March 1917 The Battalion relieved the 2nd Scottish Rifles in the RANCOURT Sector on the night on 12/13th inst. The line extended from C.9.b.8.4. to C.3.b.4.3.
Disposition: - 'C' and 'D' Companies FRONT LINE,
'A' Company SUPPORT
'B' and Battle Platoon RESERVE in dugouts.
Battalion HQ ARTHURS SEAT, C.8.a.0.7.
Guides met the Battalion at end of duck boards at ABODE LANE at 7.15pm. The following officers joined the Battalion yesterday: 2/Lts. A.M.Taylor, J.L.Farquharson, H.D.Gratwick, A.R.Newton, 10 other ranks also joined.

13th March 1917 Relief reported complete at 4am. Situation Normal during the day until 2pm when about 50 5.9 and 77mm. Shells fell near the Right Company HQ. Retaliation was asked for and our heavies replied about 4.30pm. Our patrols were active throughout the night. 2/Lt. J.F.L.Hughes, 'C' Company, rejoined from the 4th Army Telescopic Sight School.

14th March 1917 Enemy Artillery was active during the day. In the evening arrangements had been made for 'A' and 'B' Companies to relieve 'C' and 'D' Companies. Meanwhile, orders were received to cancel the relief and vigourous patrolling to take place throughout the night owing to the Division on our left reporting the enemy trenches in front of them had been vacated. The West Yorks on our left reported having occupied the enemy line. Consequently the CO issued orders about 10pm to enter the enemy trench. Strong patrols were out all the night and reported the enemy holding the line.

15th March 1917 At 4.15am 2 Platoons of 'C' Company entered the enemy trench without opposition, 2 platoons of 'D' Company following at 5.45am and took up their position on the right of 'C' Company. At 12 noon patrols went out from both front line Companies to the far end of ST PIERRE VAAST. The line reached was later taken up by the outposts. At 5pm we extended our line 500 yards to the right. The Battalion was relieved by the 2nd Scottish Rifles. Disposition being:-
Outpost Line   C.4.c.8.4 to C.10.d.5½.5.
Picquet Line   C.3.c.8.5½. to C.10.a.2.2.
Line of Resistance C.3.c.2.6. to C.9.b.8.4.
After Relief, HQ and 'A' and 'B' Companies proceeded to ANDOVER. 'C' and 'D' Companies to LANGTON BARRACKS.

16th March 1917 ROUTINE. 2/Lt. H.H.Jago rejoined from the 2nd Field Company R.E.
2/Lt. A.M.Taylor, 'A' Company, proceeded to PONT REMY on a Musketry Course.
Captain A.Winch, 'A' Company, rejoined from hospital.

17th March 1917 ROUTINE. 2/Lt. A.R.Newton, 'D' Company, proceeded to LE TOUQUET on a Lewis Gun Course.
2/Lt. G. Parker, 'B' Company, rejoined from a Course of General Instruction at the 4th Army School.
2/Lt. R.M.Haswell and 2/Lt. R.S.Holmes proceeded to the 8th Divisional School AVESNE.

18th March 1917 ROUTINE. 2/Lt. M.G.Beck, 'B' Company, rejoined from 15th Corps School, BOUCHON.

19th March 1917 ROUTINE. On the night of the 19th the Battalion was warned to hold itself in readiness to attack NURLU the following morning at 10am the 20th inst.

20th March 1917 The Battalion left Camp and marched to Canal Bank, MOISLAINS from where the attack was going to start.
'A' and 'B' Companies had been allotted VILLEWOOD and the factory respectively.
About 9.15am the OC Outposts reported to the Brigadier that NURLU had been vacated by the enemy. The attack was therefore not necessary and the Battalion was detailed to take over the Outpost Line from the 2nd West Yorks on the Divisional Front. In the afternoon this was again altered and the Outpost Line on the Divisional Front was held by 2nd West Yorks and 2nd Devons, Lt.Colonel A.J.E.Sunderland being OC Outposts.

21st March 1917 Day and Night – Quiet. Snow fell at intervals covering the ground.

22nd March 1917 Situation quiet, except for occasional shelling on the NURLU ROAD.
2/Lt. Pertwee and 12 men from the Battalion were sent to occupy AIZECOURT as an advanced post.
'C' Company were relieved by 'D' Company.

23rd March 1917 About 4.55am on the 23rd the advanced post in AIZECOURT was attacked by enemy Cavalry. 2 parties of about 50 approached the village from Right Left Flanks. After some shooting the enemy were dispersed. Casualties. 5 killed, 1 Officer and 6 other ranks wounded.
The Battalion were relieved by the 2 Scottish Rifles at 4pm. After relief the Battalion marched to Billets in MOISLAINS.

24th March 1917 In Billets. A working party of 200 were engaged on the New Line under R.E. Supervision.

The 2nd Devons War Diary

25th March 1917   In Billets. A working party of 200 proceeded to the New Line.
Meanwhile instructions were received that no work would be carried but the relief with the 2nd Scottish Rifles would take place and the Battalion would attack LIERAMONT that night. 'B' and 'C' Companies were detailed to do the attack. 'D' Company to act as Carrying Party and 'A' Company to hold the present Outpost Line with 1 Company of Scottish Rifles attached. Owing to extreme darkness the attacking Companies lost touch and were unable to carry out the operation.
The undermentioned officers joined the Battalion today:
Major   G.I.Watts
Lieut.   S.C.Clarke
2/Lt.   A.E.Titley
2/Lt.   W.E.H.Perry
2/Lt.   R.E.Burt
Received draft of 74 other ranks.

26th March 1917   Day and Night Quiet. Our Front Posts were pushed forward nearer LIERAMONT.

27th March 1917   It was reported by the R.C.D. that LIERAMONT had been vacated, consequently the CO immediately gave orders for 'A' Company to enter the village. Our troops occupied LIERAMONT at 11am and dug themselves in beyond the village. Enemy artillery was active during the day.
The Battalion were relieved in the afternoon by the 2nd Scottish Rifles and after relief proceeded to MOISLAINS.

28th March 1917   In Billets. Routine.

29th March 1917   Paraded for Trenches at 12 noon and completed relief of Scottish Rifles by 8pm. HQ were at AIZECOURT. At 6pm orders were received to hold ourselves in readiness to attack HEUDECOURT the following afternoon if the village had not fallen before then. Disposition of Battalion:- 'C' Company and half the Battle Platoon, Outpost Line, 'B' and 'D' in Support with 'A' in reserve.

30th March 1917   The Brigadier arrived at HQ about 9am and discussed plans for the attack. A Company Officers Conference was held at 'C' Company HQ at GUYENCOURT at 11am. 'A' Company was told off to attack the Right, 'D' Company to attack the Left of the village of HEUDECOURT, the Battle Platoon to "Mop Up" and 'B' Company to attack to the flank the village of REVELON, on right flank. The attack was launched at 4.15pm. 'D' Company went through without much resistance capturing only five prisoners. 'A' Company however, came under M.G. fire from the right flank and were temporarily held up. A platoon was thrown back to deal with the trouble, which it did very effectively, enabling the advance to go on. At 6.40pm our troops were

through the Village and on the way to the high ground, East and North of the Village. On reaching the far side of HEUDECOURT the Companies reorganised and pushed up the hill and dug themselves in clear of the captured village.
Casualties – 3 Killed and 22 Wounded.
'A' Company captured a Machine Gun.
'D' Company captured 5 prisoners, 3 of whom were wounded.

31st March 1917 Dispositions much the same as that of the 30th inst. 'D' Company withdrew from the Outpost line to trench rear of GUYENCOURT together with 'C' Company and the Battle Platoon.
2/Lt. A.M.Taylor, 'A' Company, rejoined from a Course of Instruction in Musketry at PONT REMY.
2/Lt. J.L.FARQUHARSON, 'C' Company, proceeded on a Course of Instruction in Signalling at the 4th Army School, LE QUESNOY.

The following is an extract from the 8th Divisional Commander's letter written on the 31st March 1917:-

"To take, during the 24 hours, in face of strong opposition, 1 large town, 2 villages, 1 hamlet, 1 railway station, 1 wood, and 3 copses, and to advance the line in places 6,000 yards, is a fine achievement.
Special credit is due to the 2nd Devon Regiment and 2nd Middlesex Regiment of 23rd Infantry Brigade and to the 1st Royal Irish Rifles and 2nd Rifle Brigade of the 25th Infantry Brigade".

The 2nd Devons War Diary

APRIL 1917

1st April 1917 'A' and 'B' Companies still holding the Outpost Line. GUYENCOURT shelled heavily by the enemy artillery but without damage. 2 German aeroplanes flew over our lines but were driven off by M.G. fire.
'A' Company captured a German M.G. in REVELON during attack on HEUDECOURT. 2nd Worcester Regiment relieved the Battalion at GUYENCOURT. One Company taking over the outpost line from 'B' Company. 'A' Company of the 2nd Northampton Regiment relieving 'A' Company.
2/Lt. H.D.Gratwick having been wounded in action on the 30th ultimo is struck off strength.
2/Lt. A.E.Rutledge, 'D' Company, rejoined from a Course of Instruction in Bayonet Fighting at the Divisional School, AVESNE.
2/Lt. A.Winch, 'B' Company, relinquishes the acting rank of Captain on ceasing to command a Company.

2nd April 1917 In billets. 'A' and 'B' Companies arrived from the line at 5.30am dead beat.

3rd April 1917 In billets. Battalion supplied working parties during the day. The Brigadier General inspected draft of 75 other ranks at Brigade HQ and expressed his opinion that they should all go before the A.D.M.S. Board.

4th April 1917 In billets. Battalion supplied working parties during the morning. The Battalion stood to from 2 to 7pm owing to an attack being carried out by the 25th Infantry Brigade.

5th April 1917 In billets. Battalion supplied working parties at MOISLAINS. The CO inspected the Battalion.
No. 15270 Pte. W.STEPHENS, 'D' Company, was awarded the Military Medal for gallantry in action at BOUCHAVESNES on the 6th March 1917.

6th April 1917 In billets. Brigadier inspected 'A' Company and expressed his entire satisfaction with the turnout of the men. After the inspection the Company formed up on the road and marched past.
The Battalion supplied working parties during the day.
Capt. E.D.Hill granted leave and handed over duties of Adjutant to Major Tillett MC.

7th April 1917 The Battalion moved from MOISLAINS to AIZENCOURT LE BAS.

8th April 1917 In billets. Working parties supplied during the day. The CO saw all platoon officers at 2pm.
The Brigadier, 23rd Infantry Brigade, interviewed all officers

and section commanders at AIZECOURT and spoke on the present situation and generally on the war. (6pm).
Captain R.J.Andrews MC proceeded to the 8th Divisional School for duty. Lt. S.V.Clarke, 'B' Company proceeded to the 23rd Brigade Bomb School. 2/Lt. R.E.Burt, 'C' Company was admitted to hospital from the 23rd Brigade Bomb School.

9th April 1917 In billets. Working parties supplied during the day.
Capt. H. Archer was a member of a Field General Court Martial at the Headquarters 2nd Middlesex Regiment at NURLU.
Lt.Col. A.J.E.SUNDERLAND was President of a F.G.C.M. at the 2nd West Yorks Regiment HQ at NURLU.
Lt. and Quartermaster G.Palmer proceeded on an Anti Gas Course at 4th Army School.
2/Lt. H.B.Brooman, 'D' Company, took over the duties of OC Battle Platoon.

10th April 1917 In billets. The Battalion marched from AIZECOURT to NURLU and was inspected by the Divisional Commander at Brigade Inspection. On completion of inspection he presented MM ribbon to No. 15270 Pte. W.Stephens, 'D' Company, for gallantry in action at BOUCHAVESNES. The Divisional Commander addressed the Battalion and congratulated the Battalion on their recent good work, also the above for his gallantry and devotion to duty. The Battalion then marched past the Divisional Commander in column of route.
Working parties were found by the Battalion in the afternoon.
2/Lts. H.D.Gratwick and L.Pertwee embarked for England (Invalid).

11th April 1917 The Battalion moved towards the line and billeted at GUYENCOURT, taking over from the Rifle Brigade. Captain P.Gay, 'D' Company, proceeded on a Lewis Gun Course at 15th Corps School.

12th April 1917 In billets. The Battalion was ordered to place 2 Companies in Defence Line, held by 2nd West Yorks Regiment, to be in position by evening. Companies to report at 2nd West Yorks HQ by 6pm. 'C' and 'D' Companies were detailed.
2/Lt. A.B.Kitson proceeded to 23rd Infantry Brigade as Liaison Officer.2/Lt. L.N.L.Tindal, 'C' Company, granted leave to the U.K. from 13/4/17 to 23/4/17.

13th April 1917 'C' and 'D' Companies still in main defence line. Hostile artillery actively shelled the Sunken Road and its vicinity from X.25.a.2.10 to X.19.c.6.5. from 6pm to 8pm and at intervals throughout the night 12/13th with 77mm shells and 4.2 shells. Otherwise situation normal. Battle Platoon sent to reinforce 'C' and 'D' Companies who were attached to 2nd West Yorks Regiment for the attack on VILLERS GUISLAINS on the morning of the 14th. 'C' and 'D' Companies to get in position

on the S. and S.E. of the village and attack at 5am on the 14th.
2/Lt. A.B.Kitson rejoined from duty as Liaison Officer at 23rd
Infantry Brigade HQ.
2/Lt. C.E.Coplestone, 'C' Company, proceeded for duty with
Prisoners of War Company, 8th Division.

14th April 1917   'A' and 'B' Companies in billets. 'C' and 'D'
Companies and Battle Platoon in front line around VILLERS
GUISLAINS.
The attack on VILLERS GUISLAINS was unsuccessful owing to strong
wire defences and heavy M.G. fire.
Casualties sustained by 2 companies and B.P.: 2/Lt. J.H.Vincent
wounded, 2/Lt. W.E.H.Perry reported "missing". 17 other ranks
killed, 26 other ranks wounded.
The following is a report of the action undertaken by 'C' and
'D' Companies and Battle Platoon on the attack on VILLERS
GUISLAINS. This report was rendered to 23rd Infantry Brigade HQ
by the 2nd West Yorks Regiment.

Report by Major R.J. McLaren, C.O. 2nd West Yorks:
"I have the honour to report that in accordance with 23rd
Infantry Brigade Operation Order No.38 I ordered 'D' and 'C'
Companies and Battle Platoon, 2nd Devon Regiment to be in
position ready to move forward at 4am behind posts of 2nd West
Yorks Regiment 'D' Company and ½ Battle Platoon on the right of
and including PEZIERE - VILLERS GUISLAIN road; 'C' Company on
left of same road. There was some delay in getting into
position and after giving officers information gained by patrols
of 2nd West Yorks Regiment I ordered them to move forward at
5am. 'C' Company, if finding difficulty on right and front, was
to push forward a strong patrol to get round to northern face of
village and then work inwards. Companies were to work in
patrols of six after getting through the wire and Battle Platoon
was to be used to form chain of posts around village as
Companies advanced through and around it.
2. The sky was just getting a bit light behind the village as
Companies advanced thus shewing up objective.
3. About 5.10am considerable M.G. fire and heavy sniping opened
from the S.E. of village, apparently two M.Guns were firing from
this face and one from about X.9.d.9.4. Most of this fire was
directed onto 'D' Company but one of these M.G. swept 'C'
Company as well. The fire against 'C' Company was not so heavy.
Machine guns were firing at them from about X.8.b.9.5. and
X.2.b.6.3. and considerable sniping. 'D' Company cut through
the wire and got inside but was held up by heavy M.G. fire from
a house heavily wired. Rifle grenade fire was opened on to this
but without effect and the Company Commander withdrew most of
his Company outside the wire and dug in. 'C' Company advanced
about 100 yards beyond posts of 2nd West Yorks and then came
under M.G. fire and heavy sniping and owing to this and the
formidable nature of the wire and to considerable casualties and

rather heavy shell fire, commenced to dig in. In this position he was about 100 yards from the wire with his centre about 40 yards from it. The OC 'C' Company directed the Stokes Gun attached to him to open fire on the M.G. in the southern face of the village, but before the gun could come into action all the team but one were casualties. 2/Lt. A.Ritchie, who was in command of this gun was himself acting as No.1 to the gun owing to casualties, and attempted with great energy to get into position but was shot through the thigh and chin just before he could open fire. The enemy sent up a light breaking into two green lights soon after the advance began and this resulted in artillery fire on the S.E., S. and S.W. faces of the wire round the village. A considerable number of Very lights were put up as the Companies were advancing.

I am of the opinion that the attack failed owing to the strong defences of the village:
(a) Machine guns - 5 in the village and one to the right flank, and one to the left.
(b) The heavy and continuous sniping, estimate 60 to 100 rifles.
(c) The wire.
(d) The enemy's artillery fire.
(e) Assaulting troops being seen by the use of Very Lights.

The troops acted well under trying conditions.
Captain J.H.Vincent led his Company well only failing at the last to gain his objective on account of the carefully protected M.G.
This officer was shot through the arm and another bullet through his field glasses, and another through his gas helmet." (Sd) R.J.McLaren, Major. 2nd West Yorks. Regiment

14th April 1917 cont'd.
'A' and 'B' Companies and H.Q. moved from GUYENCOURT at 6.30pm to relieve 2nd Scottish Rifles. Relief completed at 9pm. 'A' Company held east of GAUCHE WOOD, with posts. 'B' Company held line of resistance with 3 platoons and 2 Lewis Guns, the other platoon of 'B' Company relieving 2 platoons of 2nd Scottish Rifles at X.8.v.2.7. Night fairly quiet, only occasional shelling. Our own artillery very active.
2/Lt. V.G.Emery rejoined from hospital.

15th April 1917 'A' and 'B' Companies remained in same positions as 14th. 'C' and 'D' Companies and Battle Platoon at GUYENCOURT in billets.
Military Medals awarded to No.9336 L/Cpl. F.G.Redwood and No. 17292 Pte. H.L.Rogers for gallantry in action on 30/3/17, as follows:-
No. 9336 L/Cpl. F.Redwood. Whilst working through the village of HEUDECOURT he spotted a hostile M.Gun and engaged it in a duel with his Lewis Gun team, and directed his fire, with the effect that the hostile gun was knocked out and captured.
No. 17292 Pte. H.Rogers. For coolness during a duel with a hostile M.Gun which he quickly knocked out, causing the enemy to

abandon it after several attempts had been made to get it away.

16th April 1917 A new Brigade boundary was decided on and 'A' Company moved their posts north of GAUCHE WOOD. 'B' Company moving further to their right in main line of resistance. Details of new boundary reached us during the afternoon. 'C' and 'D' and Battle Platoon at GUYENCOURT in billets. Orders sent to these Companies to hold themselves in readiness to move at a moments notice.

17th April 1917 'A' and 'B' Companies position unchanged. 'C', 'D' and Battle Platoon at GUYENCOURT. Operation orders sent to these Companies to move up today and take over line held by 'B' Company. 'B' Company to move and dig themselves in to the N.W. end of the village of VILLERS GUISLAINS at a point X.2.c.4.5. approx. and act as inlying picquet, and as situation demands. 'A' Company to form a strong defensive flank to assist attack by 2nd West Yorks Regiment on VILLERS GUISLAINS on the morning of the 18th.

18th April 1917 'A' Company when in position were ordered to advance and establish themselves east of VILLERS GUISLAINS as soon as 2nd West Yorks Regiment had taken the village. 'B' Company dug themselves in west of VILLERS GUISLAINS and formed inlying picquet.
2nd Scottish Rifles relieved the Battalion in positions held by 'A' and 'B' Companies - relief completed at 3am. 'C', 'D' and Battle Platoon remained in brown line.
Wire received from Division that one Company of the Battalion to occupy permanently and construct line West of VILLERS GUISLAINS, which would be support line to main defence line. 'B' Company detailed to do this and start work by 10am on the 19th.
Captain R.J.Andrews MC appointed to Major on Headquarters, 17th battalion Welsh Regiment 40th Division. Capt. E.D.Hill rejoined from leave and resumed duties of Adjutant.

19th April 1917 'A', 'C', 'D' and Battle Platoon in main Defence Line (Reserve). 'B' Company working a new line west of VILLERS GUISLAINS in accordance with wire. Usual working parties supplied by 'C', 'D' and B.P. 'C' Company relieved by 'B' Company at 8pm.

20th April 1917 Usual working parties supplied. Day passed quiet. Disposition of Battalion same as on 19th, only 'D' Company relieved 'C' Company in new line west of VILLERS GUISLAINS.

21st April 1917 Disposition of Battalion unchanged. Usual working parties supplied.
Our artillery very active shelling GONNELIEU preparatory to attack on the village by the 25th Brigade. 'A' Company relieved

'D' Company in the line west of VILLERS GUISLAINS. Lt. S.V.Clarke rejoined from a course at Brigade Bomb School.

22nd April 1917 Disposition of Battalion unchanged. Operation orders received that the Battalion would relieve the 2nd Scottish Rifles in the left sub-sector in the evening, 'C', 'D' and Battle Platoon holding front line with 'B' Company in support. 'A' Company in reserve.
Orders received from Brigade that Company on the right ('C' Company) should push forward and occupy high ground X.4.b.9.5., X4.b.9.5., X.5.a.4.4., X.5.a.4.0. Sheet 57c.S.E. The night passed quiet.

23rd April 1917 The Battalion was relieved by 2nd Northampton Regiment and Royal Berkshire Regiment. Relief completed by 3am on 24th. Battalion withdrew to SOREL. Major G.I.Watts proceeded to England for duty.

24th April 1917 'A' and 'B' Companies arrived in billets at SOREL at 12.30am, 'C' Company, 'D' Company and Battle Platoon about 3am.
Baths were allotted the Battalion during the afternoon.

25th April 1917 Battalion in billets at SOREL. Working parties found by all Companies to work on roads at SOREL, LIERAMONT and HEUDECOURT.

26th April 1917 In billets. Usual working parties on roads.
2/Lt. W.M.Thomson, 'D' Company, proceeded to XV Corps School for duty as Instructor in Bombing.
Captain R.Yandle granted leave of absence to U.K. 26/4/17 to 6/5/17.
Baths allotted the Battalion at SOREL.

27th April 1917 Battalion in billets at SOREL-LE-GRAND.
Working parties of all available men in the Battalion to work on BROWN LINE running behind the village of VILLERS GUISLAINS.
2/Lt. V.G.Emery, 'C' Company, proceeded to Royal Flying Corps for duty and struck off strength.

28th April 1917 In billets. Working parties by all Companies to work on BROWN LINE.
Captain P.Gay rejoined from a course of instruction in Lewis Guns.
2/Lt. J.F.L.Hughes, 'C' Company admitted to hospital - sick.

29th April 1917 In billets. Working parties found by all Companies for work under R.E. on brown line.
2/Lt. W.H.Ivory and 40 other ranks joined the Battalion.

30th April 1917 In billets. Working parties found by all Companies and Battle Platoon for work under R.E. on brown line.
2/Lt. P.Gay took over the duties of Intelligence Officer.
2/Lt. W.W.Drake, 'C' Company, appointed Temp. Captain whilst Commanding Company - dated 26/1/17
2/Lt. G.F.Thullier, 'A' Company, appointed Temp. Captain whilst Commanding Company - dated 27/2/17
2/Lt. E.D.Hill and 2/Lt. P.Gay relinquish their rank of Acting Captain on ceasing to Command Companies.

Martin Body

MAY 1917

1st May 1917 Battalion in billets.
2/Lts. A.M.Taylor, A.C.C.Pendrigh and A.C.Bidgway leave for courses of instruction.
The Battalion left SOREL-LE-GRAND for the line and relieved the 2nd Royal Berks, 25th Brigade.
Battalion occupied outpost line, disposition as follows:-
Battalion HQ X.2.b.5.2. Ref. Map. 57C. S.E.
'A' Company in right sector of Front Line. 'B' Company - left (R.33.b.5.8. to R.34.d.5.9.)
'C' Company in support near Cemetery of VILLERS GUISLAINS.
'D' Company in Reserve with HQ on road X.2.a.1.55.
The relief was commenced at 9pm and completed at 11.15pm.
The enemy shelled GONNELIEU very heavily during the night.

2nd May 1917 Disposition the same.
Our artillery active bombarding the enemy line, cutting wire, principally in preparation for attack on LA VACQUERIE, SONNET FARM and Strong Post R.28.d.1/2.5. One man slightly wounded by shrapnel.

3rd May 1917 Disposition the same.
The night was quiet and patrols were sent out at 12 midnight by 'A' and 'B' Companies to examine the enemy wire. Both patrols returned at 1.30pm. One casualty in the afternoon ('B' Company) through a trench mortar exploding.
Captain J.H.Vincent, 'D' Company, embarked for England (wounded) 22/4/17.
2/Lt. F.R.Brooman, 'B' Company, is transferred to 'D' Company from 2/5/17.
2/Lt. J.L.H.Richards proceeds to England on leave.
Inter Company relief took place at 9pm. 'C' and 'D' Companies proceeded to the front line - 'A' and 'B' Companies occupy Support and Reserve trenches. 'C' and 'D' Companies sent out patrols. 'D' Company patrol sustained 2 casualties from enemy rifle fire.

4th May 1917 Practice bombardment carried out by our artillery at 4.5am. Enemy replied, but did no damage.
2/Lt. F.R.Brooman was slightly wounded in the hand. CO held a conference at Battalion HQ for Company Commanders on preparations for the forthcoming raid. The M.O. proceeded on leave, being relieved by Captain J.Hill. Captain M.R.McLeod of the 3rd Battalion was attached to the Battalion for 3 days from the 4th Army School of Instruction.
2/Lt. A.R.Newton, 'D' Company, granted permission to wear the badges of rank of Captain pending his appointment in the London Gazette.
At 9pm the Battle Platoon took over 7 posts on our left and relieved the 2nd Middlesex Regiment. Platoon held a frontage of 500 yards East of GONNELIEU R.27.d.4.4. to R.27.a.9.1.

The 2nd Devons War Diary

5th May 1917 Practice barrage by our artillery at 4.45am, practically no reply by the enemy. Disposition the same. Preparations were made to carry out a large raid on enemy trenches including SONNET FARM, the BARRACKS, LA VACQUERIE by the 23rd Brigade (2nd Scottish Rifles, 2nd Middlesex) and the 40th Division on our left flank. 'B' Company supplied a carrying party to carry T.M. Bombs. 16 HQ Stretcher Bearers attached to the 2nd Scottish Rifles. The attack commenced at 11pm and ended at 1am. At midnight extra stretcher bearers were asked for by the 2nd Scottish Rifles. Parties from 'A' and 'B' were sent. 'C' and 'D' Companies in the line also assisted. The enemy offered great resistance and inflicted many casualties by M.G. fire and shelling.

6th May 1917 Attack ended at 1am and the bombardment ended at 2am. Our bearers were busy with the wounded.
Lt. S.V.Clarke and 8 other ranks reported missing.
Letter received from the OC 2nd Scottish Rifles expressing his appreciation of the way in which our Stretcher Bearers and helpers worked to evacuate the wounded and dead from the raid area.
Captain M.R.McLeod returned to the 4th Army School of Instruction.
Battalion remained in the line in order to give another day's rest to the 2nd Scottish Rifles.
The Battle Platoon was relieved by the 2nd West Yorks and returned to its former position at Battalion HQ.
'A' and 'B' Companies relieved 'C' and 'D' Companies in front line. 'C' Company came back to support and 'D' to reserve.
2/Lt. F.R.Brooman, 'B' Company, rejoined Battalion from hospital.

7th May 1917 Disposition the same. Line very quiet. Lt. S.V.Clarke previously reported missing was now reported killed and 5 of his party wounded and one killed.
The Brigadier General and Brigade Major (23rd Brigade) called at HQ and visited the line.
We were relieved by the 2nd Scottish Rifles, relief was complete by 11.30pm.
The Battalion moved into Brigade Reserve and lived in Dug-outs and shelters in SUNKEN ROAD, W.6.d.6.0. to W.6.d.5.55. 'C' and 'D' Companies and Battle Platoon worked on GREEN LINE (Intermediate) from 9pm to 2am.
Captain R.J.Andrews MC was appointed 2nd in Command, 17th Battalion, Welsh Regiment on this date and struck off strength.
2/Lt. A.B.Kitson, 'B' Company, proceeded on a course of instruction at 23rd Brigade Bomb School.

8th May 1917 The Battalion was engaged in cleaning SUNKEN ROAD and building new shelters.
Except for occasional shelling, which did no damage, the day was

quiet.
Lt. and Quartermaster G.Palmer proceeded on leave to England.
2/Lt. W.W.Drake proceeded to take over duties of Quartermaster.
2/Lt. H.H.Goodman takes over Temp. Command of 'C' Company.
'A' and 'B' Companies formed a working party to dig trenches in front line R.27.a.5.10. to R.34.d.5.9.
'C' and 'D' Companies and Battle Platoon formed a working party to work on GREEN LINE (Intermediate) from R.26.c.10.10. to R.31.c.5.0.

9th May 1917 Dispositions same. Battalion constructed more shelters. Area very quiet.
At 9pm 'A' and 'B' Companies supplied working parties for GREEN LINE, 'C' and 'D' Companies and Battle Platoon for BLUE LINE.
2/Lt. H.H.Jago, 'B' Company, proceeded to the 4th Army School for a course of instruction.

10th May 1917 Disposition the same. Area quiet. The Battalion supplied working parties for GREEN AND BLUE LINES.
2/Lt. G.L.Hiley proceeded to LIERAMONT to take up the duties of Town Major. No. 8202 Pte. V.Harvey, 'C' Company (Stretcher Bearer), was awarded the Military Medal for Gallantry and Devotion to Duty when in action. Captain R.Yandle, 'C' Company, rejoined from leave to U.K.

11th May 1917 Disposition the same. Area quiet.
Lt. U.B.Burke and 20 men from 'A' Company proceeded to LIERAMONT as working party to erect tents there.
The Battalion relieved the 2nd Scottish Rifles in the line at dusk. Relief commenced at 9pm and finished at 11.30pm. Front fairly quiet.
Dispositions. GONNELIEU SECTOR (Map Reference 57c S.E. Edition 3). Battalion H.Q. X.2.b.7.4. VILLERS GUISLAINS 'C' and 'D' Companies in Front Line viz:- R.27.d.5.0. to R.34.d.6.8. 'A' Company in support X.2.b.75.15. 'B' Company in reserve X.2.a.5.55.
'A' and 'B' Companies found working parties for the GREEN LINE (Intermediate).

12th May 1917 Dispositions the same. Night fairly quiet except for a little shelling on Front. 1 other rank slightly wounded. VILLERS GUISLAINS was heavily shelled, otherwise a quiet day. The Battalion supplied working parties for the BLUE LINE. The Front Line Posts were connected and continuous trench made.

13th May 1917 Disposition the same. Lt.Col. A.J.E.Sunderland proceeded on leave to the U.K. from 14th to 24th May.
Major A.Tillett MC took over the Command of the Battalion.
The Battalion was to be relieved by the 14th H.L.I. 120th Brigade, 40th Division.
At 10.50pm the enemy opened a heavy barrage of 5 T.M.s and Shrapnel fire on our right Company frontage. At 1pm a party of

the enemy, about 40 strong, were seen moving towards No.2 Post, situated at R.34.b.3.1. from the direction of the Ravine. The garrison withheld their fire until the enemy were upon the wire. Rapid rifle and Lewis Gun fire was then opened upon them and several of the enemy were seen to fall and groans and cries were heard. The enemy replied with rifle fire but hastily retreated in disorder. A patrol was at once sent out to obtain any identification, meanwhile the 14th H.L.I. had arrived and relieved the post, they too, sending out a patrol. 2 enemy wounded were brought in. We suffered no casualties.
The relief commenced at 10.30pm and was completed by 12.30am.

14th May 1917 The Battalion proceeded to camp at AIZECOURT LE BAS. (Map reference FRANCE 62c.N.E. D.23.a.75.6.). The first party arrived at 2.30am. The rest of the Battalion were caught in a storm and arrived in camp drenched to the skin, but cheerful, about 5am. The men were busy all day cleaning kit, equipment etc. The CO and Adjutant attended a Brigade conference at HQ NURLU.

15th May 1917 Disposition the same. The Battalion commenced training according to Brigade programme.
2/Lt. G.L.Hiley, 'C' Company, rejoined from duty as Town Major of LIERAMONT.

16th May 1917 Battalion training. Bad weather prevented work in the afternoon.
The G.O.C. 8th Division, Major General W.C.G.Henneker DSO, ADC visited the Battalion.

17th May 1917 Battalion training. 2/Lt. P.Gay proceeded on leave to the U.K. Lt. U.B.Burke took over duties, temporarily, of Intelligence Officer during absence of 2/Lt. P.Gay on leave. The undermentioned officers joined the Battalion and were posted to Companies as shown:-
2/Lt. C.A.L.Briggs 'A' Company. 2/Lt. E.C.Luxon 'D' Company.
2/Lt. H.C.Squire 'B' Company.
2/Lt. J.L.H.Richards rejoined from leave to U.K.

18th May 1917 Battalion training. The officers attended a lecture on barrages by General Lloyd G.O.C. R.A. 8th Division at LIERAMONT during the afternoon.

19th May 1917 Battalion training. Captain Duncan MC, 23rd T.M.Battery lectured the officers and NCOs of the Battalion on the uses of Stokes Guns in attack.
The following officers proceeded to join the 1st Devonshire Regt:-
2/Lt. A.Winch 'B' Company. 2/Lt. J.L.H.Richards 'A' Company.
2/Lt. C.A.L.Briggs 'A' Company. 2/Lt. H.C.Squire 'B' Company
The Battalion played the 2nd Scottish Rifles at cricket in the afternoon and beat them by 22 runs.

20th May 1917 Church parade at 11.30am with the 2nd Scottish Rifles and 2nd Field Company R.E.
The Battle Platoon played the R.G.A. at football and won.

21st May 1917 In Camp. Battalion under training.

22nd May 1917 Battalion training. Major W.C.G.Henneker DSO, ADC, visited the camp.

23rd May 1917 Battalion training.

24th May 1917 Battalion training. A cricket match between Officers and NCOs resulted in favour of the NCOs.
Lt. G.A.W.Monk joined the Battalion and was posted to 'A' Company.

25th May 1917 Battalion training. Lt. Colonel A.J.E.Sunderland rejoined from leave to the U.K.

26th May 1917 The Regiment held Athletic Sports at AIZECOURT LE BAS. The Brigadier and his staff attended. Also many officers and other ranks of the Division.

27th May 1917 Church parade. Captain H.Archer proceeded on 1 month's leave to the U.K.

28th May 1917 Battalion training. 2/Lt. W.H.Radcliffe joined Battalion and was posted to 'B' Company.

29th May 1917 The Battalion struck camp at AIZECOURT LE BAS at 7.15am and paraded at 8.45am and marched to Camp 162 at CURLU, arriving at 1.30pm.

30th May 1917 Battalion training. 2/Lt. J.F.L.Hughes rejoined from hospital.

31st May 1917 Battalion training. In morning the Battalion practised the attack before the Divisional Commander and Brigadier General. During training in afternoon 1 Other Rank was badly wounded by stepping on an old bomb. The following officers rejoined the Battalion from courses:-
2/Lt. A.M.Taylor,   'A' Company
2/Lt. A.C.Bidgway,   'A' Company
2/Lt. A.C.C.Pendrigh,   'B' Company

The 2nd Devons War Diary

JUNE 1917

1st June 1917 Battalion left CURLU at 6.30am and marched to VILLE, arriving about 10.45am.

2nd June 1917 Battalion paraded at 10.50pm and marched to EDGEHILL Station where the Battalion entrained.
2/Lt. T.R.Johns, 'C' Company, embarked to England 'sick'.

3rd June 1917 Arrived at BAILLEUL at 1pm and marched to MERRIS, about 6 kilos.
Battalion billeted on outskirts of village of OUTTERSTEENE.
Captain G.F.Thullier, 'A' Company, proceeded on leave to U.K.

4th June 1917 General clean up in billets.
2/Lt. P.Gay, 'D' Company, returned from leave.

5th June 1917 Battalion in training.
2/Lt. J.H.Vincent to be temporary Captain whilst Commanding a Company from 12/4/17 to 14/4/17.
2/Lt. A.R.Newton to be temporary Captain whilst Commanding a Company from 29/4/17.

6th June 1917 Battalion in training.
C.O. inspected the Battalion. Draft of 15 other ranks joined from Base.
Cross country run of 3 miles in the evening, won by Pte. Gaylard, 'C' Company, time - 18 1/4 minutes.

7th June 1917 Battalion in training.
Cricket Match between Battalion and HQ of 1st Worcesters won by the latter by 8 wickets.

8th June 1917 Battalion in training. Draft of 15 other ranks joined from base.

9th June 1917 Battalion in training.
Brigadier-General G.W.St.G.Grogan CMG DSO inspected the new draft.
Cricket match between the Battalion and 1st Battalion Worcester Regiment resulted in a win for the Battalion as follows - 100 runs to 59 runs. The Divisional Band played during the afternoon.
Draft of 32 other ranks joined from Base.

10th June 1917 Battalion in training. Church parade held at OUTTERSTEENE at 11.30am.
Lt.Col. A.J.E.Sunderland was President of a F.G.C.M. at 2nd West York Regiment HQ.
Orders received from 23rd Infantry Brigade to prepare to move early the following morning.

Martin Body

11th June 1917 Battalion moved at 6.50am to BORRE area. Warning order received to prepare to move to area of Square G.11 Sheet 28 N.W.

12th June 1917 Battalion in training. Draft of 126 other ranks joined from Base.
Captain R.Yandle, 'C' Company, rejoined from course of instruction.
Battle Platoon abolished by Divisional order.
2/Lt. H.B.Brooman, 'D' Company, is attached to and takes over temporary Command of 'A' Company.

13th June 1917 Battalion moved at 2am to H.19 a. Sheet 28 N.W. arriving at 9am. Marched to DOMINION CAMP at 7pm.

14th June 1917 Preparations made to move to the line. All officers of the Brigade paraded on the Square at Dominion Camp to meet GOC 11 Corps to which the 8th Division is now attached. Lt.Gen. Sir Claude Jacob, KCB addressed those present and in a short speech welcomed the 8th Division to the Corps.
Battalion moved at 10pm and marched to the ECOLE at YPRES I.9.c and billeted for the night in cellars. Enemy shelling caused five casualties amongst our Lewis Gunners who were unloading a Lewis Gun Limber.
Major General L.J.Bols, CB, late of the Devon Regiment, Commanding 24th Division, visited the CO.
2/Lt. A.C.Bidgway proceeded to U.K. on leave.
2/Lt. H.H.Jago, 'B' Company, rejoined the Battalion from course at 4th Army School.

15th June 1917 The CO and Company Commanders went round the line in the morning. The Battalion moved up at 10pm and relieved the 2nd Northampton Regiment. The Battalion held the line from the Railway I.11.b.6.8. to BELLEWAARDE BEEK I.12.c.3.15. Reference Sheet 28 N.W. 1/20,000. Ed.5a.
'A' and 'D' Companies in the Front Line, 'B' Company in Support (Beck Trench), 'C' Company in reserve at the ECOLE-YPRES. I.9.6. HQ at I.11.b.55.20. Line fairly quiet, no casualties.

16th June 1917 Dispositions the same, night quiet. Enemy artillery very active on back area. Battalion employed on cleaning up the trenches which were badly hit about. The 1st North Lancashire Regiment on our left carried out a small raid on an enemy sap at 11.45pm covered by T.M. Barrage, otherwise the night was quiet.

17th June 1917 Disposition the same. The Brigadier, General G.W.St.G.Grogan CMG DSO visited the line in the evening. Captain Thullier rejoined from leave. A large party were sent out to dig a new trench from No.1 Crater to BELLEWARRDE BEEK (our right flank). Enemy were very active with rifle grenades and snipers. 5 casualties were sustained - 1 killed and 4

The 2nd Devons War Diary

wounded. The trench was half dug and two communication trenches begun and wired.

18th June 1917 Night quiet. Disposition the same. Enemy artillery was active. The work was continued on the new Front Trench and more wiring finished.
2/Lt.(A/Major) R.J.Andrews MC attached 17th Battalion Welsh Regiment was awarded the DSO for gallantry and devotion to duty in action.

19th June 1917 Dispositions the same. At 2am the enemy opened a barrage on our Front Line (right flank). We retaliated with rapid T.M. fire. The reserve Company moved from ECOLE to ESPLANADE - I.7.d.40.15.
Work on new Front Trench continued, revetting was commenced. Enemy artillery still very active. The CO attended a conference held at Brigade HQ at YPRES.

20th June 1917 Disposition the same. The Company Commanders attended a conference held at HQ by CO. The general outline of operations for the near future was brought forward.
The Battalion was relieved by the 2nd West Yorks Regiment and moved to ESPLANADE-YPRES. Relief commenced at 11pm and was completed by 1am 21st June, the enemy shelling YPRES during the move. 'A' Company had casualties passing through the town, 2/Lt. H.B.Brooman being wounded, 5 other ranks killed, 2 died of wounds and 9 wounded.
Captain R.Yandle proceeded on a course at 2nd Army School.

21st June 1917 The Battalion arrived at ESPLANADE at 4am. The enemy shelled the vicinity of billets and all troops had to remain in dugouts. The men were billeted in LONG TUNNEL under the Ramparts. Officers and HQ in shelters against Ramparts. The men rested and cleaned up.
The Brigadier General, 23rd Brigade, visited the Battalion. The enemy shelling was quieter during the evening.
Lt. U.B.Burke proceeded to Brigade as Brigade Observer. 2/Lt. A.E.Rutledge and 12 Other ranks proceeded to Second Army Summer Rest Camp, AMBLETEUSE.

22nd June 1917 Disposition the same. The enemy shelling continued but with less violence as previously. Battalion supplied working parties.

23rd June 1917 Disposition the same. Enemy artillery was still active, increasing towards evening.
Orders were received that the Battalion would relieve the 2nd Scottish Rifles on the night of 24/25th inst in the right Battalion sector. The bombardment of the Ramparts and vicinity was violent. All officers of HQ retired to Mined Passage under Ramparts, for the night. Battalion supplied working parties.

2/Lt. J.F.L.Hughes and 3 NCOs proceeded to BUSSEBOOM for course of instruction in Anti-Gas duties.

24th June 1917 The CO and Second in Command proceeded to the Front Line in the early morning to prepare for relief.
One Company to be left out of the line this tour and returned to Details Camp at HALIFAX CAMP. 'A' Company were detailed for this.
Company Commanders and Intelligence Officer moved to the Front Line in advance at 4pm. The Battalion relieved the 2nd Scottish Rifles at 10pm. Relief completed at 2am.

25th June 1917 Battalion in the line - Right Sector.
Dispositions. Reference ZILLEBEKE 1/10,000.
'C' Company Left Front-Line Company, HQ BIER CROSS ROADS - I.17.b.3.8.,
'B' Company Right Front Company,   HQ ZOUAVE WOOD I.18.c.4.5.,
'D' Company Support Company,   HQ RITZ TRENCH I.23.a.6.5.,
Battalion HQ I.17.c.25.55
'A' Company with Details at HALIFAX CAMP.
Night was fairly quiet. The enemy heavy artillery shelled YPRES.
2/Lt. J.D.Harcombe was granted leave to the U.K. from 25/6/17 to 25/7/17.

26th June 1917 Disposition the same. Enemy artillery was still active. The Battalion set out to dig a new trench in front of outpost line. About 60 yards of trench was dug about 3'6" deep and 2'6" wide. Battalion also repaired communication trenches.

27th June 1917 Disposition the same. Enemy artillery was still busy, especially during the night. The enemy aeroplanes was also very active. Work continued at night on the new front trench. 30 yards were dug by 'C' Company, making their trench 60 yards. 'B' Company lengthened theirs to 130 yards. More work was also carried out in communication trenches.

28th June 1917 Disposition the same. The enemy artillery was very active during the night, especially against our communication trenches. The Brigade Major, Captain F.C.Roberts, DSO visited the line.

29th June 1917 The morning was fairly quiet. The enemy opened a heavy barrage at 9am to 9.15am. No casualties. The Battalion prepared for relief by the 2nd East Lancs. Regiment. Company Commanders of the East Lancs. arrived in advance of the troops and took over. Relief commenced at 10pm and was completed by 2.30am (30th). The enemy it appears had planned a raid on the frontage of the Battalion on our right, a heavy barrage being put by them at 11pm. Some of which reached our right flank, causing 5 casualties in 'B' Company. The barrage finished at midnight, though no infantry attack materialised.

2/Lt. J.F.L.Hughes, 'C' Company, rejoined from Anti-Gas course.
Lt. U.B.Burke, 'D' Company, rejoined from duty with Brigade.

30th June 1917 The Battalion embussed at 6.30am at HALIFAX CAMP and journeyed to BLANC PIGNON and billets around. See HAZEBROUCK Map. (Near AUDRUICQ.), arriving at 2.30pm.
2/Lt. H.H.Jago took over Temp. Command of 'A' Company.

Martin Body

JULY 1917

1st July 1917 Dispositions the same. Voluntary Church parade - Army Chaplain visits and speaks to men.
Captain H.Archer rejoined from leave to U.K.

2nd July 1917 Battalion in training.
2/Lt. A.M.Taylor granted 10 days leave to U.K.
2/Lt. F.R.Brooman proceeded for attachment to 24th Infantry Brigade.
2/Lt. H.H.Goodman took over temporary Command of 'C' Company from 20/6/17.

3rd July 1917 Dispositions the same. Battalion in training.
Captain J.R.Cartwright has been awarded the DSO (Extract London Gazette No.30111 dated 4/6/17).
2/Lt. H.B.Brooman embarked to England 'wounded' on 24/6/17.
No.4761 Sgt. A.Wheaton, 'B' Company, and No.4812 L/Cpl. J.G.Dymond, 'B' Company, have been awarded medal for 'Long Service and Good Conduct'.
Temp. 2/Lt. A.B.Kitson to be Temporary Lt. from 24th July 1916 (but not to carry pay or allowances prior to 16th August 1916).
Temp. 2/Lt. J.H.Vincent and Temp. 2/Lt. R.S.Holmes to be Temp. Lts. from 22nd November 1916.
Concert given by the 'Detonators' at Scottish Churches hut, AUDRUICK, to the Battalion at 6.30pm.

4th July 1917 Dispositions the same. Battalion paraded at 8am and marched to new training ground at TOURNEHEM. Orders received to prepare to move tomorrow.
2/Lt. A.E.Rutledge rejoined the Battalion from Summer Rest Camp.
2/Lt. H.Edwards joined the Battalion and is posted to 'C' Company.

5th July 1917 Battalion paraded at 9am and proceeded to training ground at TOURNEHEM. After morning training Battalion moved to new billets at BONNINGUES, with the exception of 'B' Company who were billeted at HARICAT.

6th July 1917 Dispositions the same. Battalion training.
Captain T.Lawder, R.A.M.C. 24th Field Ambulance joined the Battalion for duty as Medical Officer, vice Captain D.Whyte who proceeded to England.

7th July 1917 Dispositions the same. Battalion in training.
2/Lt. J.L.Gregory joined the Battalion and is attached to 'D' Company. 2/Lt. W.W.Drake, 'C' Company, who proceeded to 23rd T.M.Battery for duty on 18/5/17 is struck off strength.
CO and 2nd in Command attended a Conference held at 23rd Infantry Brigade HQ at 4.30pm.
The Reverend C.F.Bateman joined the Battalion for duty as Chaplain.

The 2nd Devons War Diary

8th July 1917   Church parade held in field at village at 11am.

9th July 1917   Dispositions the same. Battalion in training.
Lt. A.B.Kitson proceeded to II. Corps Reinforcement Camp for duty as Platoon Commander.
Lt. R.S.Holmes proceeded to GHQ Lewis Gun School, LE TOUQUET, for a course of instruction.

10th July 1917   Dispositions the same.
Battalion paraded for demonstration in the 'Tanks in the attack'.
2/Lt. H.V.I.Watts joined the Battalion and posted to 'B' Company.
2/Lt. M.G.Beck, 'B' Company, proceeded for attachment to 24th Infantry Brigade.

11th July 1917   Battalion left BONNINGUES in buses at 10.30am for DELETTE, and arrived 3.30pm.

12th July 1917   Battalion paraded at 8.15am and marched to training ground to do the attack in conjunction with the other Battalions of the Brigade and returned to billets at 10.30am.

13th July 1917   Dispositions the same. Battalion paraded at 9.00am and marched to training ground where an attack was made by the Brigade. Colonel Campbell gave a lecture on Physical Training. 2/Lt. J.F.L.Hughes, 'C' Company, proceeded on leave to UK.
The Divisional Commanded awarded Parchment certificates to the u/m N.C.O. and men for gallantry and devotion to duty in action near Ypres between 10/6/17 and 21/6/17.
No. 8595 L/Cpl.H.R.Collins, 'A' Company. No. 18108 Pte.F.D.Lloyd, 'A' Company, No.8561 Pte. E.W.Fleming
2/Lt. F.R.Brooman rejoined from duty with 24th Infantry Brigade.

14th July 1917   The Battalion again practised the attack with the Brigade.

15th July 1917   2/Lt. V.T.J.Rainey joined the Battalion on the 11th inst. and was posted to 'B' Company.
The Battalion went out for the day and practised an attack with the Division.
Afterwards all officers of the Division assembled at COYECQUE and the Corps Commander gave a lecture on the forthcoming operations.

16th July 1917   Battalion had a rest, and general clean up. In the afternoon a Concert was held.
At 5pm all officers attended a lecture at COYECQUE. 2/Lt. A.C.Faulkner, 'B' Company, proceeded on leave to U.K.

Martin Body

17th July 1917 Lt. A.B.Kitson proceeded on leave to U.K. The Battalion practised the attack on the training ground with the Brigade. At 5.30pm a lecture was given by General Henneker to all officers at COYECQUE.

18th July 1917 The Battalion practised the attack in conjunction with the Division. Sir Douglas Haig was present. At 5.30pm a lecture was given to officers at COYECQUE.

19th July 1917 Battalion had a general clean up. A concert was held in the afternoon.

20th July 1917 The Battalion embussed at 9.30am and left DELETTE for BOESEGHEM, arriving at 12.30pm.

21st July 1917 Battalion in training. Embussed at 2.30pm and proceeded to STEENVOORDE, where a halt was made. Moved on at 9pm and arrived at destination at 11pm, which was a camp about 3 kilos behind POPERINGHE.

22nd July 1917 The Battalion rested, and paraded at 9.20pm and marched to VANCOUVER CAMP.

23rd July 1917 The Battalion moved from camp at 9.30am and took up its position in the RAMPARTS at YPRES. Details moved back to DOMINION CAMP.

24th July 1917 Dispositions the same. (Five men of the Battalion were killed in action on 24th July, during a retaliatory artillery barrage in the aftermath of a successful raid by the 2nd West Yorks, in which 2nd Devons Lewis Gunners had co-operated).

25th July 1917 The Battalion was shelled all day. Proceeded to take over from 2nd West Yorks in the RAILWAY WOOD sector. 'A' and 'D' Companies in the Front Line. 'B' Company and HQ in dugouts at Railway Wood. 'C' Company at MONTREAL CAMP. Casualties during the day were slight.

26th July 1917 Dispositions the same. At 5pm 12 men of 'A' Company under 2/Lt. A.E.Titley raided the enemy lines successfully. Our casualties were 2 men killed.
2/Lt. E.D.Hill proceeded to England to take up a Commission with the Indian Army Reserve of Officers.

<u>REPORT ON RAID BY 2nd DEVONSHIRE REGT.</u>
26/7/1917

The raiding party left our lines about MOMBER CRATER, proceeded to IDENTITY TRENCH, which was found to be empty.
The trench was entered from about I.12.a.0.4. - I.12.a.30.26.
The enemy was holding IDENTITY SUPPORT and rifle fire estimated at the strength of about 1 platoon was opened on our party.
The front line was found to be only 18" deep and much knocked

The 2nd Devons War Diary

about. There was an empty concrete M.G. emplacement at about I.12.c.42.92.
A hostile machine gun was in action at about I.12.a.9.4., and 4 or 5 snipers opened fire from some point about I.12. central. No prisoners were obtained.

<u>Herewith Report of Officer Commanding 2nd Devon.R. on raid carried out at 5 p.m. the 26th instant.</u>

1. <u>BARRAGES.</u> I watched the operation from our Front Line just N. of 2 A Crater.

The R.A. and Stokes Mortar Barrage appeared excellent. I thought the men got up rather too close to the barrage but none were hit by it.

A weak barrage opened on BEEK TRENCH about Zero plus 2.

The following are reported by other observers:-
Zero plus 3.   WEST LANE, CRATER TRENCH and RAILWAY.
Zero plus 9.   Junction of WEST LANE and front line.
Zero plus 17. RAILWAY, WEST LANE and BEEK TRENCH.

Barrage generally weak. Most shells fell in WEST LANE and Front Line. Shells came from N.E. and S.E. chiefly 77mm and 4.2" with a few 5.9's.

Zero plus 2.   The enemy sent up rockets which burst into two green stars.

2. <u>ENEMY ACTION.</u>
The Raid left our lines at Zero and proceeded as ordered. They met with no obstacle. The front line was only knee deep and was reported empty except by one man who stated that he was shot at from a dugout into which he threw six or seven bombs. I do not place much confidence in his statement.
There was an empty Concrete Machine Gun Emplacement at the South end of the trench.
2nd Lt. Titley reports enemy's second line held by about 20 men who opened on them with rifle fire.
A machine gun was in action about I.12.a.9.4. There were 4 or 5 snipers further South. Our men claim to have hit 4 or 5 Germans. Hostile Artillery ceased with ours.

3. <u>CASUALTIES.</u>
1 other rank killed
1 other rank missing believed killed.
Lt. U.B.Burke (observing) hit by splinter (At duty).

4. I regret that no prisoner was obtained, but consider that the party behaved very gallantly and did everything possible.

Martin Body

27th July 1917 Dispositions the same.

28th July 1917 'C' Company came up from MONTREAL CAMP and in the evening relieved 'D' Company. 'B' Company relieved 'A' Company. 'A' and 'D' Companies returned to Dugouts at RAILWAY WOOD.

29th July 1917 Dispositions the same.

30th July 1917 The day was rather wet. In the evening (10.30pm) 'A' and 'D' Companies moved from RAILWAY WOOD dugouts to take up their assembly positions for the attack.

31st July 1917 At ZERO hour, 3.50am, the attack was launched and the Battalion moved forward according to the programme. The 1st 3 lines of trenches were taken and the Battalion then moved forward to the BLUE LINE which was the final objective. Battalion HQ were established at LAKE FARM by 8am. The Companies then reorganised and at 10.50 moved forward to take up positions in support of the 25th Infantry Brigade. It was during this advance that our troops came under a heavy hostile shelling and machine gun fire from the right. Many casualties were sustained including Lt.Colonel A.J.E.Sunderland who was killed by rifle fire whilst leading the Battalion. The advance to the GREEN LINE had been held up owing to the troops on our right not gaining their objective. This brought enfilade fire upon our troops whilst in this vicinity. The Battalion finally took up a position approximately 200 yards East of South Station Buildings. The last part of the advance being by short rushes. About 2pm a message was received from the OC 2nd Rifle Brigade who were on our immediate front asking for reinforcements for his right flank as a hostile counter attack was expected. A platoon of 'B' Company was immediately sent forward. Defensive Flanks were then formed by the remainder of the Battalion. At 10pm the Battalion commenced to relieve the 2nd Rifle Brigade, our dispositions then being 2 Companies in the Front Line and 2 in support with Battalion HQ at SEXTON HOUSE. All night and early the next morning the Battalion was subjected to very heavy hostile shelling and machine gun fire.

The following officers accompanied the Battalion into action:-
Lt.Col. A.J.E.Sunderland
Captain H.Archer   2nd in Command
Lt.U.B.Burke   Intelligence Officer
Captain T.Lawder   R.A.M.C. Medical Officer
2/Lt.P.Gay   Acting Adjutant

'A' Company
2/Lt. H.H.Jago (Commanding Company)
2/Lt. A.M.Taylor
2/Lt. A.E.Titley
2/Lt. R.M.Haswell

'B' Company
2/Lt. G.Parker (Commanding Company)
2/Lt. A.C.C.Pendrigh
2/Lt. W.H.Radcliffe
2/Lt. H.V.I.Watts

'C' Company
2/Lt. H.H.Goodman (Commanding Company)
2/Lt. L.N.L.Tindall
2/Lt. G.L.Hiley
2/Lt.J.F.L.Hughes

'D' Company
Capt. A.R.Newton (Commanding Company)
2/Lt. F.R.Brooman   2/Lt. E.C.Luxon
2/Lt. W.H.Ivory

2/Lt. A.E.Rutledge Liaison Officer to Left Battalion
2/Lt. A.C.Bidgway Liaison Officer to right Battalion.

Martin Body

AUGUST 1917

1st August 1917   Battalion in the line near SOUTH STATION BUILDINGS, WEST OF BLACK LINE.
Enemy counter-attack withstood in the afternoon. Our casualties rather heavy.
Battalion relieved at night by the 8th South Lancashire Regiment (25th Division). Troops march to RAILWAY WOOD then to DOMINION CAMP AREA.
Officer casualties:-
Killed - Lt.Col. A.J.E.Sunderland, 2/Lt. A.M.Taylor.
Wounded - 2/Lt. W.H.Radcliffe, 2/Lt. G.Parker, Captain A.R.Newton,
2/Lt. A.C.Bidgway, 2/Lt. A.C.C.Pendrigh, 2/Lt. W.H.Ivory, Lt. U.B.Burke, 2/Lt. H.V.I.Watts, 2/Lt. R.M.Haswell, 2/Lt. J.F.L.Hughes.
Casualties to other ranks - 22 killed, 170 wounded, 37 missing, up to August 4th.

2nd August 1917   Battalion resting at DOMINION CAMP.
2/Lt. P.Gay ceases to do duty as A/Adjutant. 2/Lt. J.D.Harcombe takes up duties as A/Adjutant.

3rd August 1917   Battalion still at DOMINION CAMP but move in the evening to DEVONSHIRE CAMP, except 'A' and 'B' Companies. Major General Henneker, DSO G.O.C. 8th Division calls upon the officers of the Battalion to thank them and all ranks upon the splendid work done by the Battalion during the operations.

4th August 1917   Battalion in DOMINION and DEVONSHIRE CAMPS. The Corps Commander, Lt.General Sir Claude Jacob, KCB, visits the Battalion to thank the officers and men for the work done - especially in withstanding the enemy counter-attacks.
2/Lt. M.G.Beck, 'B' Company, proceeded to Fifth Army Summer Rest Camp.
2/Lt. F.A.F.Bone joined the Battalion and posted to 'B' Company.
Draft of 42 other ranks joined the Battalion.
Captain A.R.Newton, 'B' Company, relinquishes the acting rank of Captain on ceasing to Command a Company 1/8/17.

5th August 1917   Battalion in DEVONSHIRE CAMP re-organizing, refitting and training.
Lt. G.A.W.Monk and 2/Lt. V.T.J.Rainey rejoined from II.Corps Reinforcement Camp.

6th August 1917   Battalion in training. Divisional Band visits the Battalion.
Captain R.Yandle, 'C' Company, rejoined Battalion from II.Corps Reinforcement Camp.
2/Lt. H.H.Jago, 'A' Company, proceeded on leave to U.K.
Captain H.Archer took over duties of 2nd in Command from 31/7/17.

The 2nd Devons War Diary

2/Lt. H.H.Goodman took over Command of 'C' Company from 1/8/17.
Captain R.Yandle took over Command of 'D' Company from 1/8/17.
2/Lt. A.C.Faulkner, 'B' Company, took over Command of that Company from 31/7/17.
Draft of 10 Signallers joined the Battalion.

7th August 1917 Battalion in same camp. Parades under Company arrangements and training for specialists.
2/Lt. H.H.Jago (S.R.) to be Acting Captain whilst Commanding a Company.
2/Lt. G.F.Thullier, 'A' Company, relinquishes the Acting rank of Captain on ceasing to Command a Company, 25/6/17.

8th August 1917 Battalion in training.
2/Lt. P.Gay proceeded for duty with 23rd Infantry Brigade.
2/Lt. L.N.L.Tindall, 'C' Company, took over duties of Intelligence Officer, 7/8/17.
2/Lt. D.M.V.Mansel-Carey, 'D' Company, rejoined for duty from 490th Field Company, R.E.

9th August 1917 Battalion in same camp. Moved to RAILWAY WOOD. 'A' Company had about 10 casualties while on the WARRINGTON ROAD.

10th August 1917 Battalion returned to DOMINION CAMP.
2/Lt. A.R.Rutledge, 'D' Company, proceeded to Second Army School, WISQUES, for a course of instruction.

11th August 1917 Battalion moved up to SWAN CHATEAU. Lt. R.S.Holmes, 'C' Company, rejoined from leave to U.K.

12th August 1917 Battalion remained at SWAN CHATEAU until the afternoon when it moved forward to BELLEWAARDE RIDGE, with HQ in dug-outs in MUD LANE.
Dispositions - 'B' and 'C' in front line, 'A' and 'D' in second line with their left on the YPRES-ROULERS Railway.

13th August 1917 Battalion in same dispositions, except that 'A' Company had to move their two platoons on the right about 200 yards to the rear owing to heavy shelling. Casualties 10 other ranks.

14th August 1917 Same dispositions. 'A' and 'D' Companies found working parties in the evening carrying stores to make Brigade Dump.

15th August 1917 Battalion in same dispositions. At dusk HQ moved forward to Battle HQ in old German dug-out under YPRES-ROULERS Railway in WYLDE WOOD. 'B' and 'C' Companies moved into their assembly positions about midnight on WESTHOEK RIDGE. 'A' and 'D' Companies moved back to the vicinity of Brigade Dump ready to carry.

Martin Body

16th August 1917 2/Lt. J.L.Farquharson embarked for England 'sick' on the 5th inst.2/Lt. C.E.Coplestone, 'C' Company, struck off strength from this date.Captain A.R.Newton and 2/Lt. G.Parker embarked for England 'wounded' on the 4th inst. The following operations were carried out:-

'C' Company.
This Company was in support of the 2nd Middlesex Regiment and reached its objective. 3 strong points held up the advance. These were all in the railway. They were successfully cleared but resulted in the lines being about 600 yards in rear of the barrage. This enabled the hostile machine guns to come into action. Later the 2nd Middlesex Regiment had to withdraw. This Company assisted the withdrawal by hanging on to the positions as long as possible and opening a covering fire with rifles and Lewis guns. Large numbers of the enemy were killed including the enemy on the north side of the Railway.

'B' Company.
This Company was in support of the 2nd West Yorks Regiment and reached its objective with little difficulty, except for Sans Souci which contained 2 machine guns and about 12 men, and the HANNEBEKE WOOD which contained machine guns. These were successfully dealt with. The 2nd West Yorks had later to withdraw when this Company assisted by opening covering rifle and Lewis gun fire.

'A' Company and 'D' Company.
These Companies were employed as carriers. The first request was received about 2pm. Parties had to go to BIRR CROSS ROADS for water and S.O.S. rockets. The following is a list of stores sent forward:- 74 boxes S.A.A., 32 tins of water, 134 boxes of Rifle Grenades, 6 boxes rods for R.G.s, 88 boxes Very Lights, 2 boxes S.O.S. rockets, 50 shovels, 2 Lewis Guns, 60 L.G. magazines. All these were carried forward under heavy fire.

The following officers went into the attack:-
Lt.Col. A.Tillett, MC   Commanding
Captain R.Yandle   Acting 2nd in Command
2/Lt. J.D.Harcombe   Adjutant
2/Lt. L.N.L.Tindall   Intelligence Officer
Captain Lauder   Medical Officer
2/Lt. A.E.Titley and Lt. G.A.W.Monk   'A' Company
2/Lt. A.C.Faulkner and 2/Lt. V.T.J.Rainey   'B' Company
2/Lt. H.H.Goodman and Lt. R.S.Holmes   'C' Company
2/Lt. E.C.Luxon, 2/Lt. F.R.Brooman and
2/Lt. D.V.M. Mansel-Carey   'D' Company

17th August 1917 Headquarters in MUD LANE dug-outs. Remainder of Battalion in old trenches just outside, with the exception of 'A' and 'D' Companies who still held their positions on BELLEWAARDE RIDGE. After dark 'A' and 'D' were withdrawn to

The 2nd Devons War Diary

vicinity of MUD LANE.
2/Lt. A.C.Bidgway embarked for England 'wounded' 7/8/17.
2/Lt. H.V.I.Watts died of wounds 11/8/17.
2/Lt. M.G.Beck rejoined from 5th Army Summer Rest Camp.
The undermentioned NCOs and men were granted the MILITARY MEDAL for gallantry and devotion to duty 31/7/17 and 1/8/17:
No.6851 Pte. W.Fleming
No.9065 Pte.F.Edwards
No.7374 Sgt. W.Cockram
No.33101 Cpl. B.Kidger
No.8960 Pte. W.Hopkins
No.15402 L/Cpl. A.E.Shepherd
No.30443 Pte. S.O.Rundle
No.8595 Cpl. H.R.Collins
No.16709 Pte. J.Lock
No.14864 Pte. G.Rockley
No.8869 Sgt. E.Jordan
No.33233 Pte. W.Sandford
The following were awarded PARCHMENT CERTIFICATES:
2/Lt.C.E.White
No.4812 L/Cpl. J.Dymond

18th August 1917 Battalion remained at MUD LANE until the evening when they moved back to SWAN CHATEAU.
2/Lt. W.H.Ivory embarked for England 'wounded' 8/8/17
Captain H.H.Jago rejoined from leave to U.K. 17/8/17
Lt. A.B.Kitson rejoined from II Corps Reinforcement Camp.

19th August 1917 Battalion remained at SWAN CHATEAU until about 10.30pm when they were relieved by the 41st Division and moved to HALIFAX AREA.
The following were the casualties from 13/8/17 to 19/8/17:
Killed:- 2/Lt. H.H.Goodman, 16 other ranks.
Wounded:- 2/Lt. A.C.Faulkner, 67 other ranks.
Missing:- 7 other ranks.

20th August 1917 Battalion embussed at 2.30pm and proceeded to billets about 1 ½ miles N.W. of CAESTRE.
2/Lt. H.Edwards and 2/Lt. J.L.Gregory rejoined from II Corps Reinforcement Camp.
2/Lt. M.G.Beck and 2/Lt. G.L.Hiley were granted leave to U.K. from 20/8/17 to 30/8/17.
2/Lt. A.J.Snowden joined the Battalion and took over the duties of Lewis Gun Officer.
A draft of 314 other ranks joined the Battalion today.
2/Lt. A.C.C.Pendrigh died of wounds 19/8/17.

21st August 1917 Battalion paraded at 10.15am and marched to Divisional parade ground at LE BREARDE where the Division was inspected by Field Marshal SIR DOUGLAS HAIG at 12.30pm who complimented the Division on the excellent work done in the

recent attacks.
Lt. W.W.Drake, attached T.M.Battery, wounded 11/8/17.
Lt. F.A.F.Bone was admitted to hospital 12/8/17.
Hon.Lt. & Quartermaster G.Palmer to be Hon.Captain and Quartermaster (Extract London Gazette 3/6/17).
2/Lt. H.L.R.Baker rejoined the Battalion.
2/Lt. R.M.Haswell embarked for England 'wounded' 8/8/17. 2/Lt (A/Capt) H.H.Jago and 2/Lt. L.N.L.Tindal were awarded the Military Cross.
No.8005 CSM (A/RSM) F.H.Radford, No.8826 Sgt. L.Crispin and No.8915 Sgt. A.H.Partridge were awarded the Distinguished Conduct Medal.
2/Lt. (A/Captain) A.R.Newton and 2/Lt. G.Parker mentioned in despatches.

22nd August 1917 Battalion in same billets. A memorial for those killed in the late fighting round YPRES was held in the field at Battalion HQ. About 100 men from each Battalion in the Brigade attended.
Lt. W.W.Drake died of wounds 16/8/17.

23rd August 1917 Battalion in same billets. Company training 8.30am to 12.30pm and 2 to 2.45pm.
2/Lt. W.H.Radcliffe rejoined the Battalion from the Base. A draft of 4 other ranks joined this day.

24th August 1917 Battalion in same billets and carried on with Company training.
The Divisional Commander visited the Battalion about 3pm.
The following officers joined the Battalion this day:-
2/Lt. L.M.Easterbrook, 2/Lt. G.D.Ferard, 2/Lt. L.Lacey-Smith, 2/Lt. T.H.Haine, 2/Lt. H.S.Heard, 2/Lt. S.T.Mears.

25th August 1917 Battalion in same billets and carrying on with Company training.
Lt.(A/Capt.) H.Archer awarded the DSO, and Lt. H.K.Williams (attached 8th Divisional Signal Company) awarded MC for gallantry and devotion to duty East of Ypres on 31/7/17 - 1/8/17.

26th August 1917 Battalion in same billets. There was a service for R.C.s in CAESTRE Church at 9am and for C.of E.s in the field at Headquarters at 10am.

27th August 1917 Battalion paraded at 4am and marched to camp opposite The Custom House about a mile S. of NEUVE EGLISE.
2/Lt. A.R.Newton relinquishes the rank of Captain on ceasing to Command a Company 31/7/17.
2/Lt. W.W.Drake to be Act.Lt. whilst in Command of 23rd T.M.Battery 1/6/17.
2/Lt. H.S.Heard proceeded to 23rd T.M.Battery and is struck off the strength of Battalion.

The 2nd Devons War Diary

28th August 1917 Battalion in same camp. The weather was bad, high wind and rain all day and training had to be carried out in the huts. The CO went up to see the line which the Battalion is to take over.
2/Lt. J.H.C.Willy and 2/Lt. B.W.Jeffery joined the Battalion.
2/Lt. F.R.Brooman and 2/Lt. D.V.M.Mansel-Carey proceeded on 10 days leave to the U.K.
The following are awarded PARCHMENT CERTIFICATES for gallantry and devotion to duty east of YPRES between 31/7/17 and 16/8/17:
Lt. A.C.G.Roberts, No. 8648 Sgt. F.E.Way, No. 4761 Sgt. A.Wheaton, No. 8990 Pte. J.Prince, No.10829 Pte. S.Gale, No.16442 Pte. D.J.Rees, No.13185 Pte. H.Downey, No.13099 Pte. A.J.Davies, No.11478 Pte. G.Pugsley, No. 8208 L/Cpl. V.Harvey

29th August 1917 Dispositions the same. Company Commanders went up to see the new line.
Lt. U.B.Burke rejoined the Battalion from the Base and drafts of 7 other ranks and 16 other ranks joined the Battalion.

30th August 1917 Battalion in same camp. There was a voluntary Church Service and Holy Communion held in the Y.M.C.A. hut at 12 noon.
2/Lt. S.T.Mears proceeded on a course of instruction in observation and sniping at the Second Army School, DE SEULE.

31st August 1917 Battalion moved up to the trenches in PLOEGSTEERT WOOD sector.
Dispositions:-
Front Line, Right   'C' Company
Front Line, Left   'A' Company
Support Company   'B' Company
Reserve Company   'D' Company
2/Lt. G.D.Ferard proceeded to ETAPLES, on a tour of duty.

Martin Body

SEPTEMBER 1917

1st September 1917   In trenches. Dispositions unchanged.
2/Lt. B.W.Jeffery, 'B' Company, proceeded to 23rd Brigade Bomb School near NIEPPE.
Lt. A.C.C.Roberts and Lt. U.B.Burke proceeded to U.K. on 10 days leave.

2nd September 1917   Dispositions unchanged.
2/Lt. T.Keiller joined Battalion on 1st inst.
2/Lt. M.G.Beck and 2/Lt. G.L.Hiley returned from leave to U.K.

3rd September 1917   Dispositions unchanged. Casualties – 2 killed, 3 wounded. Draft of 17 other ranks joined Battalion yesterday.

4th September 1917   Dispositions unchanged. Casualties – 2 killed, 3 wounded.
Lt.Col. H.St.J.Jefferies, 2nd West Yorks Regiment (Acting Brigadier) visited the line.

5th September 1917   Dispositions the same. Casualties – 3 killed, 2 wounded.

6th September 1917   Dispositions the same.
The Corps Commander, Major General (temp.Lt.Gen) Sir A.G.Hunter-Weston, KCB, DSO, visited the Battalion.
About 10pm Battalion was relieved by 2nd West York Regiment and moved back to billets in LE ROSSIGNOL area, with the exception of 'B' Company who stayed in SUPPORT FARM, C.1.b.7.4. S.E. of PLOEGSTEERT.
The following officers joined the Battalion. They were taken on strength and posted to Companies as shewn:-
2/Lt. J.Geddes 'A' Company   2/Lt. G.E.Baxter 'B' Company
2/Lt. E.T.Sandford 'D' Company
4 other ranks joined Battalion.

7th September 1917   Companies proceeded to Divisional Baths at PAPOT. The remainder of the day was spent in cleaning up.
2/Lt. L.Corry joined Battalion and posted to 'C' Company.
2/Lt.(A/Capt) G.F.Thullier took over Command of 'C' Company.
Captain T.A.Lawder, M.O., R.A.M.C., returned from leave to U.K.
The Rev. G.Bateman, Chaplain, proceeded on leave to U.K.
A draft of 17 other ranks joined Battalion.

8th September 1917   In billets at LE ROSSIGNOL.
The following officers proceeded on leave to U.K. :-
Lt.Col. A.Tillett, MC   2/Lt. L.N.L.Tindall, MC   2/Lt. A.E.Titley, 'A' Company.

The 2nd Devons War Diary

9th September 1917 There was a voluntary C. of E. service at Battalion HQ at 11.30am.
A football match between the Officers and Sergeants of the Battalion resulted in a win for the latter by 3 goals to 2.

10th September 1917 2/Lt. D.V.M.Mansel-Carey, 'D' Company, returned from leave to U.K. and proceeded for duty as Right Brigade Tramways Officer.
A football match between the Battalion and 249th M.G.Company resulted in a win for the latter by 5 goals to nil.

11th September 1917 2/Lt. F.R.Brooman, 'C' Company, returned from leave to U.K.
A football match between HQ and 'A' Company resulted in a draw of 1 goal each.

12th September 1917 2/Lt. G.L.Hiley, 'C' Company, proceeded for duty with 15th Field Company, R.E.
The Battalion relieved the 2nd West York Regiment in the PLOEGSTEERT sector. Dispositions as follows:-
Front Line, Right — 'B' Company
Front Line, Left   — 'D' Company
Support Company   — 'C' Company
Reserve Company   — 'A' Company
Battalion HQ at the CONVENT.

13th September 1917 Dispositions the same.
The undermentioned officer and NCO were awarded decorations as follows for gallantry and devotion to duty East of YPRES between 15th – 17th August 1917:-
The Military Cross – 2/Lt. A.C.Faulkner, 'B' Company.
The Distinguished Conduct Medal – No.8595 Cpl. H.R.Collins, 'A' Company. (Collins had been killed in action on 4th September 1917).
The following officers returned from leave to U.K. :-
Lt. U.B.Burke and Lt. A.C.G.Roberts.

14th September 1917 Dispositions the same.
Lt. F.A.F.Bone, 'B' Company, having embarked for England 'sick' was struck off strength.

15th September 1917 Dispositions the same.
Lt. G.A.W.Monk, 'A' Company, and 2/Lt. H.Parker, 'B' Company, proceeded on leave to U.K.

16th September 1917 Dispositions the same.
2/Lt. A.E.Rutledge, 'D' Company, rejoined from course of instruction at 2nd Army School.

17th September 1917 Dispositions the same.

18th September 1917 Dispositions the same.
The Battalion was relieved by 2nd West Yorks Regiment in the evening and returned to the billets they had vacated.

19th September 1917 In billets. Interior economy.
In the evening there was a football match between 'A' and 'B' Companies. The latter Company won by 2 goals to 1.
A draft of 10 other ranks joined the Battalion.

20th September 1917 Company training. A practice Rugby match was played in the evening.

21st September 1917 Company training. In the afternoon all available officers witnessed an exhibition in bayonet fighting by a party of men under the Brigade P.T. Staff Sgt.Major. At 9pm all officers and senior NCOs practised marching on a Compass.
The final of the Inter-Platoon Football Competition was played at 5pm between HQ and 'B' Company, resulting in a win for HQ by 3 goals to nil.
A concert was held at HQ at 6pm.
Lt.(A/Major) A.Tillett MC to be Acting Lt.Col. whilst commanding a Battalion, 15th August 1917.
Lt.(A/Capt.) H.Archer DSO to be Acting Major whilst employed as Major on HQ 15/8/17.
2/Lt. A.C.Faulkner MC and 2/Lt. H.H.Goodman to be Acting Captains from 15/8/17 to 16/8/17, whilst Commanding Companies.
The following NCOs and men were awarded the MILITARY MEDAL for gallantry and devotion to duty East of YPRES between 15th to 17th August:-
No. 9040 Sgt. E.S.AYRE, 'B' Company. No. 20540 L/Sgt. H.UNSWORTH , 'B' Company. No. 11333 L/Cpl. J.K.HOSKINS, 'A' Company. No. 6710 Sgt. A.F.R.SUTTON 'C' Company. No. 8953 Sgt. P.H.COX, 'C' Company. No. 9522 Sgt W.T.PILE, 'C' Company. No. 204881 Pte. A.WEARY, 'C' Company. No. 30813 Pte J. SMALE "C" Company. Captain R.YANDLE, 'D' Company proceeded to UK on 10 days leave. 2/Lt. A.E.TITLEY and 2/Lt. L.N.L.TINDALL, M.C. returned from leave 20/9/17.

22nd September 1917 Dispositions the same.
At 5pm a football match between the Lewis Gunners and 2nd West Yorks Regiment drummers was won by the latter.
At 6pm there was a Battalion run - Course 2 miles.
Won by Sgt. Gill, 'A' Company. 2nd - 2/Lt. E.T.Sandford,'D' Company. 3rd - 2/Lt. J.P.Tucker,'D' Company.
4th - L/Cpl. Jousiffe,'D' Company.
Lt.Col. A.Tillett M.C., rejoined from leave to U.K.
2/Lt. A.E.Rutledge, 'D' Company, proceeded on leave to U.K.

23rd September 1917 Dispositions the same.
Voluntary Church Parade at 11am at HQ. R.C.s and Nonconformists had a service at NIEPPE. Battalion played 25th Field Ambulance

The 2nd Devons War Diary

at Rugby at 5pm resulting in a win for the latter by 8 points to 6.
2/Lt. H.S.Heard, 'C' Company (attached 23rd M.G. Company) was wounded on 21st inst.
No.8876 Pte. M.Bond (attached 23rd M.G.Company) awarded the MM for gallantry and devotion to duty East of Ypres between 15th and 17th August 1917.

24th September 1917 .There was a lecture by the Brigadier to all officers at NIEPPE at 11am on Defence Scheme.
The Battalion moved up to take over the line from 2nd West Yorks Regiment at 8.30pm.
'A' Left Front Company; 'C' Right Front Company; 'B' in Support; 'D' in Reserve.
Casualties - 8 wounded, 1 missing believed killed.   (SDGW does not record a fatality on this day).

25th September 1917 In the trenches. The Brigadier visited HQ about 12.30pm. A quiet day. Our patrols were busy all night.
Casualties - 1 wounded.
Captain and Quartermaster G.Palmer proceeded on leave to U.K.

26th September 1917 In the trenches. The Brigadier visited LAURA and LILLIAN Posts at about 10.30pm. The Brigade Major and an R.E. Officer went out and patrolled bridges over River LYS.
Special Company, R.E., fired gas bombs on enemy trenches.
Casualties - 2 killed and 4 wounded.
A draft of 10 other ranks joined the Battalion.

27th September 1917 In trenches. No casualties. 2/Lt. H.Parker, 'B' Company, rejoined from leave to U.K.

28th September 1917 In trenches. Casualties - 1 other rank gassed.

29th September 1917 In trenches. Casualties - 1 wounded, 2 shell shock.
5 other ranks joined the Battalion from Base.
2/Lt. L.M.Easterbrook, 'A' Company, proceeded to 4th Army School of Instruction.
2/Lt. S.P.Tozer and 15 other ranks joined the Battalion.
2/Lt.(A/Capt.) G.F.Thullier, 'C' Company, was admitted to hospital 'sick'.

30th September 1917 The Battalion was relieved by 2nd West Yorks Regiment at 9.30pm and moved back to LE ROSSIGNOL area in billets.
'A' Company to PONT DE NIEPPE.
Casualties - 1 wounded. 2/Lt. V.T.J.Rainey, 'B' Company, killed.

Martin Body

OCTOBER 1917

1st October 1917 Battalion resting. Draft of 10 other ranks joined.
2/Lt. G.D.Ferard rejoined from tour of duty at ETAPLES.
A rugby match between the officers and the remainder of the Battalion was won by the latter by 21 points to nil.

2nd October 1917 Battalion training. The Divisional Commander presented Medal Ribbons at 11.30am.
2/Lt. A.E.Titley, 'A' Company, and 4 other ranks proceeded to Summer Rest Camp, WIMEREAUX.
A football match between the Battalion and 26th Field Ambulance resulted in a win for the Ambulance by 2 goals to 1.

3rd October 1917 Battalion training. Draft of 14 other ranks joined.
Captain R.Yandle, 'D' Company, rejoined from leave to U.K.
A soccer match between HQ and 2nd West Yorks Drummers resulted in a win for HQ by 5 goals to 2.

4th October 1917 Battalion training.
2/Lt. J.L.Gregory 'D' Company, proceeded to Brigade Bomb School for a course of instruction.
2/Lt. M.G.Beck proceeded for duty with 23rd Brigade Bomb School.
2/Lt. T.Keiller, 'C' Company, reported to 23rd T.M.Battery for duty.
Lt. G.A.W.Monk, 'A' Company, granted extension of leave until 6th October.
A rugby match PROBABLES versus POSSIBLES resulted in a draw of 6 points each.

5th October 1917 Battalion training.
2/Lt. S.H.Heard, 'C' Company, attached 23rd T.M.Battery embarked for England wounded.
2/Lt. A.E.Rutledge, 'D' Company, rejoined from leave to U.K.
Captain T.Lawder, MO, proceeded to 24th Field Ambulance for duty.
Lt. H.F.Kane, U.S.A.M.C. joined for duty.

6th October 1917 Battalion training.
2/Lt. E.C.Luxon, 'D' Company, proceeded on leave to U.K.
2/Lt. J.J.Huntingford joined the Battalion and posted to 'C' Company.
Battalion run resulted as follows:- 1st 2/Lt. Baxter 'B' Company, 2nd Pte. Pitts 'A' Company, 3rd Sgt. Seery 'C' Company.

7th October 1917 Battalion training.
Lt. L.N.L.Tindal MC proceeded for duty with 23rd Infantry Brigade.

The 2nd Devons War Diary

8th October 1917   2/Lt. D.V.M.Mansel-Carey, 'D' Company, rejoined from duty as Tramway Control Officer.
Battalion relieved the 2nd West Yorks Regiment in the line.

9th October 1917   In the trenches. Captain G.A.W.Monk, 'A' Company, rejoined from leave.

10th October 1917   In the trenches.
Lt. W.H.Radcliffe, 'B' Company, proceeded on leave to the U.K.
2/Lt. B.W.Jeffery, 'B' Company, proceeded to Corps Reinforcement Camp for duty as Bombing Instructor.

11th October 1917   In the trenches.
Lt. A.B.Kitson, 'B' Company, appointed Acting Captain whilst Commanding a Company.

12th October 1917   In the trenches.

13th October 1917   In the trenches.
2/Lt. L.Corry, 'C' Company, admitted to hospital 'sick'.

14th October 1917   In the trenches. 2/Lt. A.E.Titley, 'A' Company, rejoined from Summer Rest Camp, WIMEREAUX.

15th October 1917   In the trenches.

16th October 1917   Battalion was relieved by 2nd West Yorks Regiment.

17th October 1917   Interior Economy.
2/Lt. L.Corry, 'C' Company, proceeded on leave to U.K.
Major H.Archer DSO granted leave to the U.K.
Lt. R.S.Holmes appointed Acting Captain whilst Commanding a Company from 31/8/17 to 7/9/17.

18th October 1917   Battalion training.
2/Lt. A.C.Faulkner MC embarked for England 'wounded'.
2/Lt. M.G.Beck rejoined from duty at 23rd Brigade Bomb School.
2/Lt. E.C.Luxon, 'D' Company, rejoined from leave.
A rugby match between 'B' and 'D' Companies resulted in a win for 'D'
Company by 21 points to nil.

19th October 1917   Battalion training.
2/Lt. S.P.Tozer to be T/Lt. from 1/7/17.
A soccer match between Battalion and 5th Black Watch Labour Battalion resulted as follows:-
Battalion 3 goals, Black Watch nil.

20th October 1917   Battalion training.
2/Lt. E.E.Beare joined the Battalion and posted to 'C' Company. A rugby match played between the Battalion and Rifle Brigade, resulted as follows:-
Battalion 23 points, Rifle Brigade nil. A very successful concert was held in the evening.

21st October 1917   Divine Service.

22nd October 1917   Battalion training.
A football match between HQ and 2nd West Yorks Drummers resulted in a win for the former by 2 goals to nil.
A soccer match between 'D' Company and 3rd Canadian Light Railway was won by the former by 3 goals to 1.

23rd October 1917   Battalion training. Lt. W.H.Radcliffe, 'B' Company, rejoined from leave to U.K.
A Brigade boxing tournament was held in the afternoon.

24th October 1917   Battalion training.
2/Lt. S.T.Mears, 'D' Company, proceeded on a course of instruction at the II Corps Infantry School, MILLAM.
In the evening the Battalion relieved the 2nd West Yorks Regiment.

25th October 1917   In the trenches. Lt. R.S.Holmes, 'C' Company and 2/Lt. G.E.Baxter, 'B' Company, proceeded on a course of instruction at X Corps Infantry School, BOESCHEPE.

26th October 1917   In the trenches.

27th October 1917   In the trenches. 2/Lt. W.H.Edwards, 'C' Company, proceeded on leave to U.K. from 28/10/17 to 7/11/17.

28th October 1917   In the trenches. Casualties 3 other ranks killed, 1 other rank wounded.

29th October 1917   In the trenches. Casualties 3 other ranks wounded.

30th October 1917   In the trenches. The G.O.C. 23rd Infantry Brigade visited the Battalion. Casualties 1 other rank killed.

31st October 1917   In the trenches.

The 2nd Devons War Diary

NOVEMBER 1917

1st November 1917 In the trenches. On the night 1/2nd the Battalion was relieved in the line by the 2nd West Yorks Regiment, and proceeded to billets - HQ, 'A' and 'D' Companies at LE ROSSIGNOL, 'C' Company at PONT DE NIEPPE, 'B' Company in HUNTERS AVENUE, PLOEGSTEERT WOOD at disposal of OC 2nd West Yorks Regiment.

2nd November 1917 Company training was carried out. 2/Lt. G.L.Hiley rejoined from duty with 15th Field Company R.E.

3rd November 1917 Battalion in training.
Major H.Archer DSO rejoined from leave. 2/Lt. J.L.Gregory proceeded to U.K. on leave.
A Rugby Football match between the Regimental Team and 24th Field Ambulance resulted in a win for the latter by 12 points to 3.

4th November 1917 Divine Service. 2/Lt. A.J.Snowden proceeded for duty at 23rd Brigade School.
'B' Company moved from HUNTERS AVENUE to billets in NIEPPE.

5th November 1917 Battalion in training.
2/Lt. E.E.Beare proceeded to U.K. on leave.
A Rugby Football match was played between 'A' and 'D' Companies and resulted in a win for the former by 14 points to 3.

6th November 1917 Battalion in training.
2/Lt. M.G.Beck proceeded to VIII Corps School, TERDEGHEM, for duty as Bombing Instructor.
2/Lt. L.Mc.I.Easterbrook rejoined from a course at 4th Army Infantry School.
At 6pm the Battalion relieved the 2nd West Yorks Regiment in Support in PONT DE NIEPPE, 1 Company in RESERVE AVENUE, 1 Company FUSILIER TERRACE, 1 Company in HUNTERS AVENUE, 1 Company PONT DE NIEPPE.

7th November 1917 Same dispositions.

8th November 1917 Captain J.Moyle joined the Battalion.
In the evening the Battalion took over the left sector of the line. HQ the Convent, 'C' and D' Companies in the front line, 'B' Company in Support and 'A' in reserve. Casualties 3 wounded.

9th November 1917 Same dispositions. During the night of 8/9th our Standing Patrol at MOAT FARM was attacked at 1am and 1.20am. In the first case they were driven off with rifle and L.G. fire. The second time the enemy returned about 60 strong and attacked from all sides, but were eventually driven off. Our casualties

were 17 wounded and 5 missing.
The Brigadier visited the Battalion during the morning and again at night when he went round our Standing Patrols himself. Lt. L.N.L.Tindal MC rejoined from duty with 23rd Infantry Brigade. 2/Lt. E.C.Luxon wounded.

10th November 1917 Same dispositions. A quiet day, no casualties. Captain J.D.Harcombe proceeded on 14 days leave to U.K.

11th November 1917 The Battalion was visited by G.O.C. 4th Australian Infantry Brigade.
The Battalion was relieved at about 7pm by 2nd West Yorks Regiment and moved back to LE ROSSIGNOL Camp. Casualties 1 killed, 1 wounded.

12th November 1917 The Battalion marched to billets in the BERQUIN Area and was temporarily under the orders of 25th Infantry Brigade.

13th November 1917 Same dispositions. Day of rest and Interior Economy.
Lt. S.P.Tozer, 2/Lt. J.Geddes, 2/Lt. L.Mc.I.Easterbrook and 2/Lt. T.H.Haine proceeded to the 9th Battalion Devonshire Regiment.
Lt. A.J.Snowden rejoined from duty with the 23rd Brigade School.
2/Lt. H.L.R.Baker rejoined from hospital on 11th inst.

14th November 1917 Company training. Draft of 9 other ranks joined the Battalion.

15th November 1917 Training continued. Battalion again under the Command of 23rd Infantry Brigade.

16th November 1917 Training continued. A Battalion run in the afternoon resulted as follows:-
1st, Pte. Selley, 2nd Pte. Stephens, 3rd Pte. Barrow.

17th November 1917 Battalion paraded at 12.30pm and marched to new billets in the MERRIS Area.

18th November 1917 Battalion paraded at 1.30pm and marched to CAESTRE where they entrained at 4.30pm for BRANDHOEK, detraining at 6pm and moved into Camp 'B'.

19th November 1917 Battalion paraded at 1pm and marched to 'A' Camp at WIELTJE. Lt. L.L.Smith was admitted to hospital.

20th November 1917 Same disposition. Battalion furnished working parties. Casualties 4 wounded.

The 2nd Devons War Diary

21st November 1917 Same disposition. Working parties as usual.
2/Lt. P.Gay struck off the strength having been ordered a Medical Board whilst on leave to the U.K.
2/Lt. J.L.Gregory rejoined from leave to U.K. on the 19th inst.
Captain G.Palmer admitted to hospital 'sick'.

22nd November 1917 Same disposition. The CO, Second in Command and Company Commanders visited the line.
2/Lts. L.Corry and E.T.Sandford proceeded to VIII Corps School for a course of instruction.
2/Lt. E.E.Beare rejoined from leave to the U.K.

On 22nd November 1917, Private Ernest Lawrence, 3/20272, aged 21, faced a firing squad in the prison at Ypres, having been found guilty on three counts of desertion and awarded the death sentence.

23rd November 1917 The Battalion moved up to the line N. of PASSCHENDAELE by Platoons, the leading Platoon starting at 3pm. Battalion HQ at METCHEELE.
Casualties - 1 killed, 10 wounded.
2/Lt.E.E.Beare admitted to hospital on 22nd inst.
2/Lt.H.Parker rejoined from a P.T. course at Second Army School.
(SDGW does not record a 2nd Devon being killed on 23rd November 1917).

24th November 1917 'A' and 'B' Companies in the front line, 'C' and 'D' Companies in Support.
Casualties - 2 killed, 13 wounded.

25th November 1917 At 12.20am the front line was advanced about 150 yards. The following is a report of the operations -
On the night of the 23/24th extensive patrolling was carried out with a view to locating exact positions of enemy's outpost line and how far the advancement of our line would be interfered with by enemy activity. Patrols reported that many Germans were occupying shell holes and retired on patrols approaching. The supposed strong point at W.25.c.15.40. and M.G. at W.25.c.4.3. were confirmed. Arrangements were made with the OC 'B' Company, 2nd West York Regiment, who were advancing on our right. Particular attention was paid to visual reconnaissance by day on the 24th and favourable landmarks etc were pointed out to the men. By 12.20am the 25th Platoons were ready to advance in columns of sections under their section commanders at 28 yards interval.
At 12.30am the platoons on the left advanced to their new position and dug in, at the same time a platoon under 2/Lt.Titley advanced against the strong point. This was taken with very little difficulty and the platoon dug in on their new position.
The right platoon was not so fortunate at first although they ultimately gained their position. Delay in starting was due to the fact that both the Officer and NCO detailed to advance on

the Machine gun were killed just previous to the advance. On hearing of this Captain H.H.Jago MC took charge of this party under orders from Major H.Archer DSO. Owing to the bright moonlight the M.G. crew easily spotted our right post and within 10 minutes another four men were killed or wounded. This made a direct advance on the gun out of the question. Arrangements were then made with the 2nd West Yorks Regt, for them to detail some men especially to work round the back of the gun while the party covered their advance by occupying the enemy Machine Gun's attention from the front. This was successful and by an advance from two directions at once the enemy machine gun was forced to retire and evacuate the post. The right platoon were then able to make good their ground and dig in on the new line. Owing to not being able to gain touch with the West Yorks, our right flank was thrown back as a defensive flank.
The following night patrols were out and succeeded in locating the West Yorks. Information was passed on to the relieving Unit as to how to establish connection and maintain the line.
The morning of the 25th saw us in our correct position on the crest with an uninterrupted view for about 400 yards with no dead ground between. Many Germans were killed and wounded as several stretcher parties were out next morning and picked up their casualties. 5 prisoners were taken for identification purposes and passed on. The enemy was obviously very disorganised as next day a lot of running about between shell holes was observed. Our men made good use of their rifles. No resistance of any strength was encountered. The enemy retired, in some cases leaving rations, etc. behind. The enemy sent out patrols during the night subsequent to our advance but they showed no inclination to fight. Our positions were very alert and any hostile movement was at once checked by accurate rifle and M.G. fire. Our men showed great determination, and their use of the rifle and bayonet showed they are realising its possibilities.

The Battalion was relieved by 2nd Scottish Rifles about 8pm and moved back into dugouts and shelters at CAPRICORN, close to SPREE FARM (Sheet 28 N.E. 1/20,000). Casualties - 3 killed, 14 wounded.
Major H.Archer, DSO killed.
2/Lt. J.H.C.Willy killed.
2/Lt. J.L.Gregory missing.

26th November 1917 Day spent in cleaning up and reorganising. One carrying party furnished for front line. Casualties - 3 wounded. 2/Lt. D.V.M.Mansel-Carey, and 2/Lt. T.Keiller embarked for England on the 18th 'sick'.

27th November 1917 Still at CAPRICORN supplying working parties to carry to front line.
Captain H.H.Jago MC, assumed duties of Second in Command.

28th November 1917 Battalion moved off by Companies to relieve 2nd Scottish Rifles in the front line North of PASSCHENDAELE at 5pm.
Dispositions - 'A' Company - Right Support. 'B' Company - Left Front. 'C' Company - Left Support.
'D' Company - Right Front.
Casualties - 1 killed, 16 wounded.
Captain J.D.Harcombe rejoined from leave to U.K.

29th November 1917 Still in line. Casualties - 3 killed, 8 wounded.
Captain R.Yandle, wounded (at duty). Lt.Col. A.Tillett, MC, wounded.
Captain H.H.Jago took over Command of the Battalion.
Lt. R.S.Holmes and 2/Lt. G.E.Baxter rejoined from X. Corps School. 2/Lt. S.T.Mears rejoined from II. Corps School.

30th November 1917 Still in the line. About 8am the enemy attempted an attack against our positions but was repulsed by rifle and L.G. fire with heavy losses. Our S.O.S. Barrage came down just as he was getting back to his trenches and did great damage.
After dark the Battalion was relieved by the 2nd Royal Irish Rifles and moved back to 'E' Camp, St.JEAN.

Casualties - 7 killed, 12 wounded.
Captain A.B.Kitson wounded.
Captain G.A.W.Monk wounded.
2/Lt. A.E.Rutledge wounded.

Martin Body

DECEMBER 1917

1st December 1917 Battalion remained in 'E' Camp cleaning up.

2nd December 1917 Entrained at St.JEAN Station at 8am. Detrained at WIZERNES and marched into billets at SETQUES.

3rd December 1917 Interior Economy and general clean up.
Lt.Col. C.H.M.Imbert-Terry, DSO, took over Command of the Battalion.
A congratulatory message was received from the Army Commander, Lt.General Sir H.Rawlinson, KCB, on the behaviour of the Battalion in recent operations.
Lt.Col. A.Tillett, MC, died of wounds.

The recent spells of activity in the Ypres Salient had resulted in a substantial number of casualties and had also taken its toll of the battalion's senior officers. On 1st August 1917, the C.O., Lieutenant-Colonel A.J.E. Sunderland, was killed in action and was replaced by Lieutenant-Colonel A. Tillett. On 3rd December, Tillett died of wounds suffered on the 29th November, upon which Captain H.H. Jago took temporary command, until the new C.O., Lieutenant-Colonel C.H.M. Imbert-Terry was appointed on 3rd December. In addition, the second-in-command, Major H. Archer was killed in action on 25th November, Captain H.H. Jago taking over as second-in-command on 27th November.

4th December 1917 Continued Interior Economy.

5th December 1917 The Divisional General inspected the Officers and NCOs of the Battalion at 10.35am and congratulated the Battalion on the good work done by them on the PASSCHENDAELE front.
The Lord Lieutenant of Devon, Earl Fortesque, KCB, lunched with the Battalion and afterwards inspected the men on parade.
Captain H.H.Jago, MC, temporarily took over the duties of Second in Command on 28/11/17
2/Lt. A.E.Titley temporarily took over Command of 'A' Company, 28/11/17.
2/Lt. F.R.Brooman temporarily took over Command of 'B' Company, 30/11/17.
Lt. A.J.Snowden temporarily took over the duties of Quartermaster on 28/11/17.
Captain J.Moyle proceeded on leave to U.K.
Rest of Battalion beat Officers, WOs and Sgts, in a football match by 3 goals to 2.

6th December 1917 Training continued.
2/Lt. E.T.Sandford rejoined from course at VIII.Corps School 5/12/17.
Lt. A.J.Snowden resumed the duties of L.G.O. (Lewis Gun Officer).
No.8565 R.Q.M. Sgt. W.Moyser took over duties of Quartermaster.

The 2nd Devons War Diary

7th December 1917   Lt. U.B.Burke granted permission to wear the Badges of Rank of Captain pending the announcement of promotion in 'London Gazette'.
2/Lt. J.J.Huntingford, 'C' Company, rejoined from hospital on 4th inst.
Lt. G.D.Ferard, 'B' Company, rejoined from duty with 23rd Infantry Brigade.
'C' Company defeated 'B' Company in a rugby football match by 10 points to nil.

8th December 1917   Training continued.

9th December 1917   The Chaplain held services at the following times - 8.30am, 10am, and 5pm.
Captain and Quartermaster G.Palmer struck off strength from 28/11/17.
1/Lt. H.F.Kane, Medical Officer, proceeded on leave to U.K.
Parchment Certificate awarded by G.O.C. Division to No.30560 Pte. J.E.Hamley, 'A' Company, for gallantry and devotion to duty near PASSCHENDAELE on 24-25/12/17.
2/Lt. G.Thullier relinquished the acting rank of Captain on 29/9/17.

10th December 1917   No.8140 C.Q.M.S., S.W.J.Cox appointed R.Q.M.S. from 6/12/17.
1/Lt. L.B.Faulk, M.O.R.C, U.S.A. attached to the Battalion as MO.

11th December 1917   2/Lt. A.E.Rutledge, 'D' Company, rejoined the Battalion and taken on strength.
Lt. L.N.L.Tindal, MC, proceeded on Intelligence Course at VIII.Corps School, TERDEGHEM.
The following were awarded the Military Medal for gallantry and devotion to duty near PASSCHENDAELE between 25th and 30th November 1917 -

No.8648	Sgt. F.Way	'D' Company
No.15596	Pte. W.J.Pike	'A' Company
No.16709	Pte. W.Lock	'C' Company
No.15320	Cpl. T.G.Upshall	'C' Company
No.11319	Pte. J.G.Browning	'A' Company
No.9835	Pte. T.Casey	'A' Company
No.12753	Pte. D.Williams	'C' Company

'D' Company defeated 'C' Company in an Inter-Company rugby match by 3 points to nil.

12th December 1917   Training continued. A rugby football match between 'Possibles' and 'Probables' resulted in a win for the former by 3 points to nil.

13th December 1917   Training continued. A football match (Soccer) played between the Battalion and 12th Divisional

Martin Body

Signals was won by the latter by 4 goals to nil.

14th December 1917 Training continued. Result of Inter-Company Soccer Knock-out – Left half 'A' Company, 8 goals, 'C' Company, nil.

15th December 1917 Training continued. Inter-Company Soccer Knock-out resulted in a win for Right half 'D' versus Left half 'B' by 2 goals to 1.

16th December 1917 Chaplain held Divine Services at 8.30am, 10am, and 5.30pm. Captain A.B.Kitson embarked for England 'wounded' on 6/12/17.

17th December 1917 Captain H.H.Jago MC, proceeded on leave to U.K. from 17/12/17 to 2/1/18.
1/Lt. L.B.Faulk, MO, proceeded on leave to Paris.
1/Lt. C.W.Maxson, M.O.R.C., U.S.A., temporarily attached to Battalion as Medical Officer.

18th December 1917 Lt. K.Gatey, MC, and Lt. A.L.Noon joined the Battalion and posted to 'A' Company.

19th December 1917 2/Lt. B.W.Jeffery, 'B' Company, rejoined from duty at Corps reinforcement Camp.
2/Lt. H.L.R.Baker, 'A' Company, proceeded to U.K. on leave from 19/12/17 to 2/1/18. Training continued.

20th December 1917 Training continued.

21st December 1917 Training continued. Captain J.Moyle, 'D' Company, rejoined from leave to U.K.
The following decorations were awarded for gallantry and devotion to duty near PASSCHENDAELE between 18th November and 2nd December 1917.
Captain H.H.Jago, MC - Bar to MC, 2/Lt. A.E.Titley - MC
The undermentioned were mentioned in Sir Douglas Haig's Dispatch of November 7th.
Temp.2/Lt.(Act.Major) R.J.Andrews, DSO MC
Lt.(Act.Captain) H.Archer, DSO
2/Lt.(Act.Captain) A.R.Newton
2/Lt. G.Parker
2/Lt. H.Parker
Major(Temp.Lt.Col.) A.J.E.Sunderland
Lt.(Act.Lt.Col.) A.Tillett, MC
No.7673 CSM J.H.Bauer
No.7296 CQMS S.G.Carthew
No.8140 CQMS S.W.J.Cox
RSM Radford won semi-final of the Divisional Boxing Competition held at QUELMES.

The 2nd Devons War Diary

22nd December 1917 Training continued.
2/Lt. M.G.Beck seconded for duty as Instructor at VIII.Corps School 6th November 1917.
Lt. U.B.Burke to be Acting Captain whilst Commanding a Company from 13/10/17.
Temp.Lt. J.D.Harcombe to be Adjutant and Acting Captain whilst so employed from 3/8/17.
Lt.(Temp.Captain) A.Tillett, MC, ceased to hold the appointment of Adjutant, 25/11/16.
Captain G.A.W.Monk proceeded on 14 days sick leave to U.K. 12/12/17.
2/Lt. H.Edwards and 2/Lt. J.P.Tucker rejoined from Second Army School on 15/12/17.

23rd December 1917 Usual services held by the Chaplain.
Draft of 25 other ranks joined the Battalion.
No.16709 Pte. J.Lock was awarded a bar to the MM for gallantry and devotion to duty near PASSCHENDAELE between 20th November and 30th November 1917.
No.8258 CSM Hobbs awarded the DCM for gallantry and devotion to duty near PASSCHENDAELE.

24th December 1917 Battalion carried out Field Firing Competition which resulted in a win for 'C' Company.
Captain W.L.Clegg and 2/Lt. J.C.Holberton joined the Battalion.
A concert was held in the evening at 8pm.

25th December 1917 Church of England service at 9am
CO visited men's dinners at 12.45pm.
The Divisional Commander and Brigadier visited the Battalion at 3pm.
The final of half Company Football Competition resulted in a win for 'D' Company versus 'B' Company by 4 goals to 2.

26th December 1917 Cleaning up and preparing to move.
2/Lt. R.C.A.Cardew joined the Battalion on 24/12/17.
Lieut. L.N.L.Tindal MC rejoined from Course of Intelligence at VIII Corps School on 24/12/17.
2/Lt. G.E.Baxter 'B' Company, admitted to hospital 'sick' 25/12/17.
Lt. A.J.Snowden and Lt. R.S.Holmes proceeded on leave to U.K.
Lt. J.C.Holberton proceeded for temporary duty with 23rd T.M.B.

27th December 1917 Battalion paraded at 4.30am and marched to WIZERNES where it entrained for BRANDHOEK arriving at 10.30am and moved into 'B' Camp.

28th December 1917 Still at 'B' Camp. Lt. G.D.Ferard temporarily took over duties of L.G.O.

29th December 1917 Battalion was visited at 12 noon by the Corps Commander who watched a demonstration of bayonet fighting.
2/Lt. F.R.Brooman, 'B' Company, proceeded on a course of instruction at Fourth Army School, FLIXECOURT.
2/Lt. H.Parker temporarily took over the Command of 'B' Company.

30th December 1917 Two Companies went to Divisional Baths at VLAMERTINGHE.
Battalion moved off at 2.15pm by Companies to JUNCTION CAMP, St.JEAN.
2/Lt. G.F.Thullier and 2/Lt. L.L.Smith rejoined from hospital.
Drafts of 16 other ranks and 46 other ranks joined the Battalion.
Captain J.Moyle, 'D' Company, proceeded on a Lewis Gun Course at Brigade School.
2/Lt. J.J.Tall, 'B' Company, proceeded on a Bombing and Rifle Bombing Course at Brigade School.

31st December 1917 Same camp. The Commanding Officer attended a conference at Brigade HQ.
2/Lt. G.L.Hiley proceeded on a Gas Course at VIII.Corps School, STEENVOORDE.

The 2nd Devons War Diary

JANUARY 1918

1st January 1918 Battalion at 'B' Camp BRANDHOEK.

2nd January 1918 Same camp. 2/Lt. H.Leach joined Battalion.
Lt. G.F.Thullier granted 14 days leave to U.K.

3rd January 1918 Battalion moved off at 5.45pm by Platoons to reserve position at BELLEVUE.
Lt. C.F.Chapman joined the Battalion. Details at Brake Camp.

4th January 1918 Same dispositions.
2/Lt. E.E.Davis, 2/Lt. W.J.Hannam, 2/Lt. R.Tadman and 2/Lt. F.W.W.McCrea joined the Battalion.
2/Lt. H.L.R.Baker rejoined from leave to U.K.
Lt. W.L.Clegg proceeded for attachment to 57th Battery R.F.A.

5th January 1918 Still at Bellevue. At 7pm moved off by Companies to relieve the 2nd Middlesex Regiment in left sector front line.
Dispositions -
'B' Company right front
'C' Company centre front
'D' Company left front
Captain Burke appointed Second in Command and was in charge of front line.
Battalion HQ 1500 yards in rear at Pill Box 83. Only communication with front line by runner.

6th January 1918 Same dispositions. Quiet day. Lt. G.D.Ferard and 2/Lt. S.T.Mears granted 14 days leave to U.K. Major H.H.Jago MC, rejoined from leave to U.K.

7th January 1918 Battalion relieved about 5.30pm by the 1st Sherwood Foresters. Marched back to WIELTJE and entrained on a light railway and were conveyed to 'B' Camp, BRANDHOEK.

8th January 1918 Same camp. Day spent in cleaning up.
2/Lt. F.W.W.McCrea admitted to hospital.
2/Lt. E.E.Beare proceeded for duty with 8th Division HQ.

9th January 1918 Same camp. Day spent in improving and repairing huts.

10th January 1918 More work on huts. CO attended a conference at Brigade HQ.
2/Lt. H.L.R.Baker rejoined from duty with 21st Squadron R.F.C.
Lt. R.S.Holmes and Lt. A.J.Snowden rejoined from leave to U.K.
2/Lt. G.Parker to be Lt. 24/7/17 2/Lt. G.F.Thullier to be Lt. 1/7/17. 2/Lt. W.H.Radcliffe to be Lt. 1/7/17. 2/Lt. R.A.Wykes to be Lt. 1/7/17. 2/Lt. G.D.Ferard to be Lt. 14/1/17. 2/Lt. A.R.Newton to be Lt. 1/7/17

Martin Body

11th January 1918   Same camp.   12.30pm Battalion paraded and entrained in light railway at Haslar Siding for WIELTJE. Tea at WIELTJE and marched into left Battalion Sector of Divisional front North of PASSCHENDAELE. 'A', 'B' and 'C' Companies in front line, 'D' Company in close support.

12th January 1918   Still in the line.

13th January 1918   Still in the line.
Night of 13/14th relieved by 2nd Middlesex Regiment and moved into Brigade Reserve at BELLEVUE. During the tour in the front line 'C' Company captured 2 prisoners and 'D' Company 1. 2/Lt. J.J.Huntingford admitted to hospital 12/1/18.

14th January 1918   Still at BELLEVUE.

15th January 1918   Same dispositions.
Night of 15/16th Battalion was relieved by 2/Rifle Brigade, marched back to WIELTJE and entrained in light railway for BRANDHOEK and thence into 'B' Camp. Lt. K.Gatey, MC, admitted to hospital.
2/Lt. E.D.Davis and 2/Lt. W.J.Hannam proceeded for a course of instruction at VIII Corps School.
Lt. A.J.Snowden proceeded for a course of instruction in Lewis Guns at GHQ School, LE TOUQUET.

16th January 1918   Parade at 10am and entrained at BRANDHOEK at 11am.
Detrained at GODEWAERSVELDE and marched to billets in the WINNEZEELE area.
2/Lt. E.E.Beare rejoined from duty at 8th Divisional HQ.
2/Lt. J.J.Huntingford rejoined from hospital.

17th January 1918   Reorganising and interior economy.
Captain U.B.Burke, 2/Lt. G.L.Hiley, 2/Lt. B.W.Jeffery, 2/Lt. E.T.Sandford and 2/Lt. J.P.Tucker proceeded on 14 days leave to U.K., yesterday.
Lt. R.S.Holmes took over temporary command of 'C' Company during absence of Captain U.B.Burke, on leave.

18th January 1918   Interior economy and cleaning up billets.
Lt. G.F.Thullier, MC, takes over Command of 'B' Company.
2/Lt. R.C.A.Cardew proceeded on a course of instruction in signalling at the X Corps School.

19th January 1918   Company training.

20th January 1918   Lt. G.D.Ferard and 2/Lt. S.T.Mears rejoined from leave to U.K.

21st January 1918   Company training.

The 2nd Devons War Diary

22nd January 1918 Company training.
Lt.Col. C.H.M.Imbert-Terry DSO proceeded on 14 days leave to U.K.
2/Lt.(A.Capt.) G.F.Thullier awarded the MC.
Lt.(A/Lt.Col.) A. Tillett MC awarded the DSO.
Captain J.Moyle proceeded on a course of instruction in L.G.
2/Lt. J.J.Tall proceeded on a course of bombing.

23rd January 1918 Specialists training.
Lt. L.N.L.Tindal MC and 2/Lt. A.E.Titley MC proceeded to U.K. on 14 days leave. Lt. A.C.G.Roberts proceeded to U.K. on one months leave. Lt. K.Gatey MC temporarily takes over command of 'A' Company. 2/Lt. J.J.Huntingford was admitted to hospital, yesterday. Lt. K.Gatey MC rejoined from hospital, yesterday. 2/Lt. A.E.Titley MC is granted permission to wear badges of rank of Captain.

24th January 1918 Battalion route march.

25th January 1918 Specialists training.

26th January 1918 Battalion paraded at 9.15am and marched to WINNEZEELE to entrain for POPERINGHE where they were billeted at the CLOISTERS.
Lt. A.L.Noon temporarily takes over duties of Quartermaster.

27th January 1918 Three Companies supplied working parties at WIELTJE.
Lt.Col. G.F.Green joined the Battalion and took over Command.
Lt. A.L.Noon and 2/Lt. H.Leach granted leave to PARIS.
2/Lt. A.E.Titley MC and 2/Lt. F.R.Brooman to be acting Captains while Commanding a Company.Temp.Lt.(A/Capt) A.B.Kitson relinquishes the pay of acting rank on ceasing to command a Company.CSM Bauer is appointed Acting RSM.

28th January 1918 Three Companies supplied working parties to WIELTJE.

29th January 1918 Three Companies supplied working parties to WIELTJE.

30th January 1918 Three Companies supplied working parties to WIELTJE.Lt. L.L.Smith and 2/Lt. A.E.Rutledge proceeded to U.K. on 14 days leave.2/Lt. E.E.Beare proceeded to 8th Divisional HQ for Intelligence duties.

31st January 1918 Three Companies supplied working parties to WIELTJE.

Martin Body

FEBRUARY 1918

1st February 1918 RSM Radford rejoined the Battalion from hospital on 31/1/18.
2/Lt. G.E.Baxter having embarked for England on 20/1/18 is struck off strength.
A rugby match between the Battalion and the 25th Field Ambulance on 31/1/18 resulted in a win for the former by 11 points to 6.

2nd February 1918 Lt. C.F.Chapman, 'B' Company, proceeded to the Fourth Army Musketry School on a course of instruction.
Captain U.B.Burke and 2/Lt. B.W.Jeffery MM rejoined from leave to the U.K.

3rd February 1918 The Battalion moved from the Cloisters, POPERINGHE, to billets in the WINNEZEELE area.
The following officers rejoined from leave to the U.K. on the 2nd inst.
2/Lt. G.L.Hiley, 2/Lt. J.P.Tucker, 2/Lt. E.T.Sandford
Lt. A.J.Snowden rejoined from a course of instruction at GHQ School.
2/Lt. E.D.Davis rejoined from a course of instruction at the VIII Corps School, TERDEGHEM.

4th February 1918 No.8910 Cpl. A.J.Bowden was granted a permanent commission in the Regular Army and posted to 'A' Company.
No.9415 Sgt. W.Maunder MM was granted a permanent commission in the Regular Army and posted to 'C' Company.
No.7673 CSM J.H.Bauer was awarded the Belgian Croix de Guerre.
Lt. W.L.Clegg and 2/Lt. R.Tadman proceeded to 23rd Brigade School for courses of instruction.

5th February 1918 Lt. A.J.Snowden proceeded to 23rd Brigade School for duty.
2/Lt. A.E.Rutledge proceeded to England for a six months tour of duty.

6th February 1918 Captain R.Yandle and Lt.W.H.Radcliffe granted 14 days leave to U.K.Captain J.Moyle temporarily took over command of 'D' Company during the absence of Captain Yandle.

7th February 1918 Battalion route march.
2/Lt. M.G.Beck having been taken on the strength of VIII Corps School is struck off the strength of the Battalion.
2/Lt. H.L.R.Baker was admitted to hospital.
Lt. K.Gatey MC proceeded on a course of instruction at the Fourth Army Infantry School, FLIXECOURT.

8th February 1918 Captain A.E.Titley MC and Lt. L.N.L.Tindal MC rejoined from leave.2/Lt.H.Parker proceeded for a 6 months tour of duty in England.

The 2nd Devons War Diary

9th February 1918 The officers and NCOs of the Battalion went to a demonstration in consolidating shell holes.

10th February 1918 Battalion paraded at 6.15am and marched to GODEWAERSVELDT where they entrained for St.Jean Station and marched from there to camp at Irish Farm.
On arrival officers from the Battalion went forward to see the COs of Battalions holding the line.
Captain A.E.Titley resumed command of 'A' Company 8/2/18.
2/Lt. R.Tadman proceeded for duty with the 23rd T.M.Battery.

11th February 1918 Battalion moved off at 4pm by Companies to front line.'D' Company took over right front and 'C' and 'A' Companies from support Company of 1st Border Regiment. 'B' Company took over from left front Company of 1st Lancs Fusiliers. Battalion HQ at Bellevue.Front line N.W. of PASSCHENDAELE.Support on the GOUDEBERG SPUR.Captain A.H.Cope taken on strength of the Battalion.

12th February 1918 'D' Company spread out and took over 3 posts to their left from the 1st Worcestershire Regiment.
Major H.H.Jago MC relinquishes the acting rank of Major and resumes his acting rank of Acting Captain.
Captain A.E.Titley MC relinquishes the acting rank of Captain.
Captain H.H.Jago MC took over Command of 'A' Company.
2/Lieuts. F.R.Brooman and J.J.Huntingford proceeded on 14 days leave to the U.K.
Lt. W.L.Clegg and 2/Lt. R.Tadman rejoined from courses of instruction at the 23rd Brigade School.
Lt.Col. B.C.James DSO taken on strength of the Battalion.

13th February 1918 'D' Company again spread out and took over 5 more posts from 1st Worcestershire Regiment.
'B' Company took over 3 posts from right of 'D' Company.

14th February 1918 Still in same position in line.
2/Lt. S.T.Mears proceeded to England for six months tour of duty and is struck off strength.
2/Lt. J.L.Gregory previously reported 'missing', officially accepted as Prisoner of War 1/1/18.

15th February 1918 Battalion was relieved by 2nd Rifle Brigade and moved back to 'B' Camp BRANDHOEK, by road as far as WIELTJE and thence by light railway to Haslar Siding.
Lt. L.L.Smith rejoined from 14 days leave to U.K.

16th February 1918 Interior economy.

17th February 1918 Church service at 11am. 60 men per Company attended.Brigadier inspected the Battalion at 'B' Camp at 11.30am.Captain J.Moyle was admitted to hospital 'sick'.

2/Lt. J.P.Tucker temporarily took over command of 'D' Company.
2/Lt. E.E.Beare rejoined from duty at 8th Divisional HQ.
Captain A.H.Cope assumed the duties of Second in Command on 12th inst.
Battalion bathed at VLAMERTINGHE between 9am and 3pm.

18th February 1918 Draft of 1 NCO and 5 men joined the Battalion.

19th February 1918 Battalion moved off at 12.30pm and proceeded by light railway to St.Jean.
Tea on the road and marched to BELLE VUE by Platoons at 500 yards interval to relieve 2nd Royal Berks Regiment, in reserve.

20th February 1918 Bellevue was subjected to considerable gas shelling during day and the Battalion had 8 casualties from gas.

21st February 1918 Same dispositions.

22nd February 1918 Lt. R.S.Holmes proceeded on Instructors course in Lewis Guns at GHQ School.
Lt. W.H.Radcliffe rejoined from leave to the U.K.
Lt. A.L.Noon, 2/Lt. H.Leach and 2/Lt. G.L.Hiley detailed to proceed to Infantry Wing, VIII Corps School, TERDEGHEM and 23rd inst.

23rd February 1918 Battalion was relieved in Bellevue positions at 5pm by the 2nd East Lancs Regiment and returned to 'B' Camp BRANDHOEK by light railway from WIELTJE.

24th February 1918 Battalion resting and cleaning up. The Chaplain held services in the camp at 8am and 10.30am also 6.30 and 7.30pm.

25th February 1918 Interior economy.

26th February 1918 The Brigadier wrote complimenting the Battalion on the good work done during the tour at Bellevue.
Captain J.D.Harcombe, 2/Lt. W.Maunder MM, and 2/Lt. A.J.Bowden granted 14 days leave to the U.K.
Captain R.Yandle resumed Command of 'D' Company on the 23rd inst.
2/Lt. B.W.Jeffery MM proceeded for a course of instruction at 4th Army School.

27th February 1918 Battalion moved off by light railway from Hagle Siding at 1.45pm to Junction Camp.
From there they proceeded by road to relieve the 2/Royal Berks. Regiment in the PASSCHENDAELE sector.
'A' and 'C' Companies in the front line.
'B' and 'D' Companies on the GOUDBERG SPUR.
Battalion HQ at BELLEVUE.

The 2nd Devons War Diary

Lt.Col. B.C.James DSO proceeded for duty at the 23rd Brigade School.

28th February 1918   2/Lt. F.R.Brooman and 2/Lt. J.J.Huntingford rejoined from leave to the U.K.

Martin Body

MARCH 1918

1st March 1918 Battalion in the line. 2/Lt. E.E.Beare was wounded.
The Brigadier General visited the Battalion in the line.

2nd March 1918 Battalion in the line. 2/Lt. H.L.R.Baker rejoined from hospital.

3rd March 1918 At 6pm 'A' and 'C' Companies assisted the 2nd Middlesex Regiment in a raid on TEAL COTTS by a dummy raid on their right. The operation was very successful and 'A' and 'C' Companies were thanked for their help by Lt.Col. Page MC, Commanding 2nd Middlesex Regiment.

4th March 1918 The Battalion was relieved by 2nd Royal Berkshire Regiment at 12.30am and returned to 'B' Camp, BRANDHOEK, by usual route.

5th March 1918 Interior economy.
Lt. A.J.Snowden rejoined from 23rd Brigade School.

6th March 1918 Battalion furnished a working party of approx. 300 men to work on the defences round WIELTJE. Remainder of the Battalion marched to POPERINGHE and took over new billets. The working party was brought back by train and rejoined the Battalion same night.

7th March 1918 A working party of approx. 450 supplied for same work.
Draft of 58 other ranks joined the Battalion. 30 other ranks proceeded for duty with 8th Divisional M.G. Battalion.

8th March 1918 2/Lt. H.Edwards proceeded on 14 days leave to U.K.
Lt.Col. G.F.Green proceeded to U.K. on leave.
Working party supplied as on 7th inst.

9th March 1918 Working party again.
Lt. L.N.L.Tindal MC and Battalion Observers proceeded to STEENVOORDE on a course of instruction under Brigade I.O.

10th March 1918 Working party again. Lt.Col. B.C.James DSO rejoined from duty with 23rd Brigade School.

11th March 1918 Working party again.
The following is an extract from a letter from the Brigadier:-
"The Brigadier General wishes to congratulate all ranks for the good name the Battalion received for work in the forward area, and also to thank Commanding Officers for the great trouble they took to make ceremonial parades in POPERINGHE a success and credit to the Brigade."

The 2nd Devons War Diary

12th March 1918 Battalion entrained at HOPOUTRE, detrained at LUMBRES and marched into billets at SETQUES.
No.7296 CQMS S.G.Carthew granted a commission in the Regular Army and posted to 'D' Company.
Lt. R.S.Holmes rejoined from a course of instruction at GHQ Small Arms School 11/3/18.
2/Lt. E.D.Davis proceeded for duty with 23rd Infantry Brigade.

13th March 1918 Interior economy.
Lt. L.N.L.Tindal MC and Battalion Observers rejoined from course at STEENVOORDE.
Lt. H.G.Morrison proceeded on a course of instruction in Trench Mortars at VIII Corps School.

14th March 1918 Training. Draft of 7 other ranks joined the Battalion.

15th March 1918 Training and baths.
The Divisional General and Brigadier inspected the Battalion at their training and expressed great satisfaction with the turn out, keenness and training of all ranks.
No.8021 A/CQMS F.Lethbridge granted a commission in the Regular Army and posted to 'B' Company.
Lt. A.L.Noon, 2/Lt. G.L.Hiley and 2/Lt. H.Leach rejoined from VIII Corps School.
Captain J.D.Harcombe and 2/Lt. W.Maunder rejoined from leave to U.K.

16th March 1918 Training.

17th March 1918 Sunday, was observed as a holiday with voluntary church parades.
Captain J.D.Harcombe, 2/Lieuts. F.R.Brooman, G.L.Hiley and J.P.Tucker proceeded to England on a six month s tour of duty.
2/Lt. A.J.Bowden rejoined from leave to U.K.

18th March 1918 Training continued.
Lt.K.Gatey MC rejoined from Fourth Army School.

19th March 1918 Training continued. A demonstration was given by a platoon from the Fourth Army School.Lt. W.L.Clegg was admitted to hospital sick.

20th March 1918 Training.

21st March 1918 2/Lt. B.W.Jeffery rejoined from Fourth Army School.

At 5.00am on 21st March 1918, the Germans commenced their long-expected Spring Offensive with a terrific bombardment along sixty miles of the front line, from a point just south of Arras down to, and including, La Fere. The main focus of the attack was to the right of St. Quentin, their first objective being Amiens. The German numbers had swelled enormously following the cessation of fighting against Russia, and their offensive was, in effect, a 'last roll of the dice' to destroy the weakened British and French Armies before the fresh soldiers of the American Expeditionary Force (A.E.F.) could appear on the Western Front in meaningful numbers. They believed that when that happened, the last chance of victory would be over. It is also possible that they considered that if they damaged the Allies badly enough before the A.E.F.'s arrival, a cessation of hostilities might be negotiated on favourable terms.

Further north, in the vicinity of Ypres, the 2nd Devons were not immediately affected by the 'Kaiserschlacht', but events to the south would soon draw them in.

The War Diary entries in the ensuing period are mostly very brief and somewhat lacking in detail. This was because of the desperate situation encountered by the battalion and it is no surprise that keeping the diary up to date, under the prevailing conditions, was of secondary importance.

22nd March 1918 2/Lt. A.E.Titley MC proceeded on a course of instruction at the Fourth Army School, FLIXECOURT.
2/Lt. H.Leach proceeded on a course of instruction in musketry at Fourth Army School, NORTBECOURT.
The Battalion marched to WIZERNES and entrained for the south.

23rd March 1918 The Battalion detrained at CHAULNES and was immediately rushed into the line in front of VILLERS CARBONNEL about K.2.80.40. Sheet Amiens 17.

At about 1.00pm the 2nd Devons tramped into Villers-Carbonnel. Some of the 50th Division were already trickling back across the Somme, with the enemy reported to be in hot pursuit. In great haste, the 2nd Devons occupied St. Christ Bridge and a length of river bank stretching nearly two miles to Happlincourt, a vast distance compared to the 1st July 1916 at Ovillers, when the battalion's frontage was just 200 yards.

Just as the Devons took up their positions, the cavalry, who had been covering the Fiftieth Division's retirement, fell back through them from the far side of the river. The battalion's position was reasonably strong, with three spurs running down to the Somme, where trenches from which good fields of fire could be dug and some flanking support given by each company to its neighbours. 'C' Company, commanded by Captain Ulick Burke was on the right, covering St. Christ Bridge, while 'B', commanded by Captain Thullier and 'A', under Captain Titley, continued the line north to Happlincourt. 'D' Company, commanded by Captain Yandle, was in close support behind 'C' Company.

Towards evening the Germans began to advance towards the bridge, first with patrols and then in stronger units. They were beaten back and a counter-attack by a platoon of 'C' Company, led by 2nd Lieut. Maunder, met the enemy on the bridge each time they tried to cross, killing many and driving the rest back. Although the position was successfully defended up to this point, arrangements for demolishing the bridge had gone awry, and its destruction was incomplete.

24th March 1918 In line. Beat off several attacks.

The 2nd Devons War Diary

23rd March may have been taxing for the 2nd Devons, but the 24th was to prove far harder as, along the entire length of the 8th Division's front, the Germans repeatedly attacked in force. On the Division's right flank, the 25th Brigade had not been able to reach their position in time to prevent the enemy crossing the river, enabling the enemy to drive back the screen formed by the depleted remains of the 20th Division. This made it necessary for the 8th Division's reserves to be rushed to this flank, which left the 24th Division inadequately supported.

The 24th Division's right flank was then driven back and it was only through the courage and tenacity of the 1st Sherwood Foresters that a disaster was averted. However, with their flank now effectively covered by the Sherwood Foresters, the 2nd Devons could concentrate on their own stretch of the front, which was coming under increasing pressure. Three times the enemy attacked, but after severe fighting were they held off.

At one point a strong party of Germans waded across the river just up from the bridge, in an attempt to outflank the defenders, but once again 2nd Lieut. Maunder's platoon met them, charged across the road and up the river embankment, and went in with the bayonet. Supported by 2nd Lieut. Huntingford and another platoon, between them they drove off the attackers, who were then caught by the Foresters as they tried to get away, nearly 20 prisoners being taken. Casualties among the defenders had been heavy, but far less than the German's losses. So it was that the day ended with the position intact, although the Battalion's troops were exhausted.

25th March 1918 Withdrew to line in front of ESTREES.

25th March saw a renewal of enemy attacks. On the right flank things were not going well for the Germans were already west of the Somme, having crossed the river at Berthencourt, worked forward towards Licourt and continued their advance. To add to the problems, news from the left flank was received that the enemy had also crossed the river north of Eterpigny, and although the 2nd West Yorks, who had been relieved by the 2nd Middlesex, desperately tried to cover the Brigade's exposed flank, they could only check the enemy's progress, not push them back.

Meanwhile, although attacked repeatedly, the 2nd Devons clung on to their position and, at 1514, the 23rd Brigade informed 8th Division HQ that its line was still intact. However, their successful defence seemed more than likely to lead to the battalion being outflanked and surrounded, so orders were issued for them to withdraw. This retirement was not commenced immediately, but by about 1800 Colonel Cope had to send Brigade HQ a message to the effect that, as both of his flanks were unprotected, he was about to pull back to a line between Misery and Villers-Carbonnel. 'C' Company withdrew first, covered by 'D' Company, which maintained a position near Misery until most of 'C' Company had got away. One platoon of 'C', however, despite being surrounded, remained near the bridge and made a determined fight to the last. When 'D' Company started their withdrawal they found the enemy already behind them, but a resolute attack with fixed bayonets cleared a way through, and, helped by the HQ Company, led by Lieut. Tindal, and two platoons of 'B' Company, 'D' got away safely, while the remainder of 'B' Company and most of 'A' also got back. Captain Thullier was killed during this withdrawal but, overall, the difficult operation was successfully completed.

From the unfortunately named Misery, the 2nd Devons drew back through Horgny, where they halted for four hours, before moving on to Estrees, to rejoin the 23rd Brigade in front of

Soyecourt. Here they took the right of the Brigade's position, with the heavily depleted 2nd Middlesex in the centre, and the 2nd West Yorkshires on the left.

Information regarding casualties in the 2nd Devons was hard to attain, but Captain Thullier, 2nd Lieut. Davis and 2nd Lieut. Carthew were known to have been killed, 2nd Lieut. Hannam was missing, and Lieut. Gatey and 2nd Lieut. Sandford were wounded. The men were tired, exhausted and short of food, but nevertheless, set to work to dig in for the night. 'C' Company, who done such sterling work at St. Christ Bridge, were placed in reserve, and even managed to find an old French trench in good condition with excellent dug-outs. By dawn 'C's survivors were rested and had even put up some wire defences.

26th March 1918 A general line was to be held running North and South of ROSIERES. Battalion was in Brigade Support.

The morning of the 26th March dawned fine and quiet, but it wasn't long before the enemy renewed the attack. Against the 8th Division they made little headway, but on the left had more success, and it soon became evident that the Division's position was compromised. About 1000, on orders from Corps HQ, a withdrawal to a line between Rouvroy – Proyart was begun. The 23rd Brigade led the way, followed by the 24th, both being covered by the 25th, which was in position near Lihons.

In the 23rd Brigade the 2nd Middlesex was detailed to retire first, covered by the 2nd Devons but, just as the move was starting the enemy attacked in force. The Divisional artillery was ready for them, however, and helped the 2nd Devons to bring the attackers to a halt. This enabled the 2nd Middlesex to retire in relative safety, followed by the 2nd Devons.

In anticipation of the withdrawal, Lieut. Lacy-Smith had been sent back to reconnoitre the line of retirement to Rosieres, about eight miles to the south west, a precaution which proved timely for the direction of the move took the battalion across the front of the enemy. Nevertheless, forewarned is forearmed, and it was a relatively successful move, in the process of which the battalion managed to inflict heavy casualties on Germans advancing from Bovent. Unfortunately, 'C' Company, who were the last to go, lost a lot of men who were cut off and taken prisoner. By 1600, the weary battalion had retired through Rosieres and bivouacked in a quarry behind the village. Rations and hot tea were waiting for them and the exhausted men had their first real night's rest since leaving Flanders.

27th March 1918 Battalion was called upon to counter-attack through HARBONNIERES which they did with great success. Details which were left behind were also called out and successfully beat back an attack just North of ROSIERES.
2/Lt. H.Edwards rejoined from leave and from a Composite Battalion.

Early on the morning of 27th March, while the hungry men of the Battalion were at breakfast, German shells started falling in the area of the front line. More shells, mostly 5.9s, very soon started falling in the village and it wasn't very long before the Germans resumed their attacks. Against the 8th Division they were again checked, but further north, where the line was very weakly held, they made progress. At 1100 an urgent message reached 23rd Brigade HQ to send the reserve battalion to make a counter-attack near Proyart, where the enemy had broken through. Colonel Cope immediately got the Devons moving and at about 1300 reached Harbonnieres. Here was utter confusion, with guns and limbers falling rapidly back and men straggling around in disorder. The situation was quite obviously precarious, and the situation needed to be taken in hand without delay, but Colonel Cope could get no precise information as to where he would find the right flank of the 39th Division, who were evidently holding on north of the gap. In addition, he had not been given a definite objective, and as Proyart was not visible from Harbonnieres, keeping direction was not easy.

However, the counter-attack was promptly launched with whatever men were to hand: the 22nd battalion, Durham Light Infantry and the Divisional Pioneers on the right, a mixed detachment on the left, and the 2nd Devons pushed forward in two lines. The first line comprised 'A' and 'B' Companies, the second line 'D' Company, with the remnants of 'C' Company held in reserve.

The strength of the German forces ahead was unknown, but as they crested the rise north-east of Harbonnieres, they were raked by machine-gun fire and artillery shells and suffered heavy losses. The battalion was without any artillery support of its own but, nevertheless, the men forged ahead in extended order, dashing in short rushes, throwing themselves to the ground and firing their rifles before dashing forward again, taking advantage of being able to hide in the unkempt long grass. The down-side of the long grass was that they could not see very far forward and eventually came to a thick belt of barbed wire. There were a few gaps in this, which they thought the Germans would have covered but, surprisingly, they got through without too much trouble and engaged in hand-to-hand fighting with the German defenders in some old trenches. In short order, the 2nd Devons put many of the enemy to the bayonet and took the trench and some buildings along the Amiens – Peronne road. They also took a number of prisoners and captured five field guns.

To the right of the Devon's new position there were some burning coal heaps, a light railway and a couple of steam locomotives. These were still in German hands, and enemy soldiers were machine-gunning from a position by one of the locos, causing a worrying amount of damage. Colonel Cope sent a platoon to eliminate it, and the problematic machine gun was duly silenced.

The 22nd D.L.I. had kept up with the 2nd Devons, and the intensity of their counter-attack was instrumental in holding the Germans at bay. Colonel Cope, who kept a firm control of the attack, did not press their success too far, and halted his men just short of the Amiens high road, where they dug in. That evening the Germans gathered for another attack, but were repulsed, after which the 2nd Devons and 22nd D.L.I. remained in position until 0400 the next morning, when they received orders to retire once more.

When the battalion moved off to Harbonnieres, certain details, mainly shoe-makers, tailors and other "employed" men, had been left at Rosieres with the transport under Lieuts. Holmes and Snowden. During the afternoon an especially vigorous German attack broke through near Rosieres Station, and this party, less than 40 strong, was thrown in along with a few R.E. and 2nd West Yorks to recover the lost ground. So energetically and gallantly did this handful counter-attack, that the enemy was thrust back and the line restored, as many as 80 prisoners and two machine-guns being captured. One Lance-Corporal distinguished himself by working round the Germans flank and capturing a machine-gun and six men single-handed. However, in spite of this success and that near Harbonnieres, the pressure on the left flank necessitated another retirement.

28th March 1918 In line at CAIX. 2/Lt. A.E.Titley MC rejoined from Fourth Army School.

At 0800 on the 28th March, a further retirement was begun to the line Vrely – Caix, and by mid-day the 8th Division was in its new position. The 2nd Devons were placed in reserve near

Beaucourt, south west of Caix, where a fresh stand was made, but at about 3.00pm the 8th Division received orders to fall back to Moreuil to cover a retirement over the River Avre, as the divisions on both flanks had been driven back, in which circumstances the 8th also had to retire.

The 2nd Devons accomplished this latest retirement in good order, but the other two battalions of the Brigade had great difficulty in getting away, being closely engaged and almost surrounded, with most of the 2nd West Yorks and the left company of the 2nd Middlesex being cut off for a while. At Moreuil the battalion found billets, but its night's rest was disrupted in the small hours of 29th March, by orders to move at once back to Jumel, where the 8th Division was to concentrate and be held in reserve.

29th March 1918 Marched back to JUMEL. In billets.

Other British units were now covering Amiens, and the exhausted remnants of the 8th Division managed to spend the day at rest, but in the evening a report came through that the line had broken near Moreuil, and the 23rd Brigade, now reduced to less than 500 men of the 2nd Devons and some details of the 2nd West Yorks and 2nd Middlesex, dejectedly turned out and tramped eastward, only to be met half-way along the road by news that the situation had been restored and that they could return to Jumel.

30th March 1918 Battalion moved up to hold line on east side of river at CASTEL.

At 4.30am on the 30th March, in response to the latest orders, the Battalion left the billets at Jumel and marched in a north-easterly direction towards Berteaucourt. Yet again, when they were half-way to their destination, fresh orders were received and now, instead of going to Berteaucourt, they took up positions on high ground overlooking Castel, with the River Avre and the railway in front of them.

In the evening, what was left of the 23rd Brigade was ordered to move past Sencat Wood and form a line running north to south from the corner of Moreuil Wood to the bridge over the River Avre, at Castel.

In the morning of 30th March, orders were received to move again, this time northwards nearer to Amiens, but en route the Brigade was diverted to support the 2nd Cavalry Division, who were attempting to clear Moreuil Wood, which the Germans had just taken. This involved the battalion manning and entrenching a position just east of the River Avre, but in the evening came fresh orders to relieve the cavalry in Moreuil Wood.

31st March 1918 Enemy attacked heavily and we withdrew in order to conform with movements of unit on left flank.
Casualties:-
Capt. G.F.Thullier MC killed 25/3/18
2/Lt. E.D.Davis   killed 25/3/18
2/Lt. S.G.Carthew   killed 25/3/18
2/Lt. W.J.Hannam   missing 25/3/18
Lt.   A.L.Noon   died of wounds 02/4/18

The following were wounded:-
2/Lt. E.T.Sandford 25/3/18
2/Lt. J.J.Huntingford 27/3/18

The 2nd Devons War Diary

```
Lt.     K.Gatey MC 25/3/18
Lt.     A.J.Snowden 27/3/18
Lt.     C.F.Chapman 27/3/18
Lt.     L.N.L.Tindal MC 31/3/18
Lt.     L.L.Smith 27/3/18
2/Lt.   A.J.Bowden 27/3/18
Capt.   R.Yandle 27/3/18

Total:- Officers - 14.   Other Ranks - 304.
```

The relief of the cavalry was difficult in the extreme dark, with rain pelting down, but before dawn the 2nd Devons were in position, with the remains of the 2nd Middlesex on their left and a few 2nd West Yorks and Royal Engineers on their right. Patrols went out and discovered German troops advancing.

A tremendous bombardment heralded an enemy attack, for the Germans had managed to bring up some 5.9's and a few larger guns, with which they poured shells into the wood. The 2nd Devons rapidly found themselves hard pressed, the 2nd Middlesex party was overcome, and the enemy, still moving forward, outflanked the battalion and forced it to retire.

Captain Burke and some of 'C' Company valiantly helped to get a few British guns away, and the 2nd Royal Berkshires counter-attacked and stalled the enemy attack, enabling the 23rd Brigade to make a stand astride a little neck of wood connecting the main wood to a large copse to the north-west. Orders were received that evening to co-operate with the Second Cavalry Division in a counter-attack the following morning.

Martin Body

APRIL 1918

1st April 1918 Formed line outside wood which we successfully held.

An attack, delivered about 9.00am on April 1st, did not involve the exhausted survivors of the 23rd Brigade in any heavy fighting but, being successful, allowed them to advance their left a little. That night they were relieved by French troops and the battalion was sent on its way to a rest area. On the evening of the 2nd April they thankfully set off for Ailly-sur-Somme in motor-lorries. Their ordeal was over, for the time being.

2nd April 1918 Relieved by the French and came out at DUMMARTIN. Embussed at SAINS-EN-AMIENOIS at 11am and debussed at AILLY-SUR-SOMME.
Marched to billets at BREILLY.

3rd April 1918 Major G.F.Green struck off strength.
Captain J.Moyle struck off strength.
2/Lieuts. P.Gay, A.L.Noon and A.J.Snowden to be Lieuts. 1/7/17
There was a special order in R.O.s in which the Divisional Commander expressed his sincere gratitude to all ranks for the splendid work they had done. The Commanding Officer also thanked the Battalion for the manner in which they had supported him.
The following officers (attached 23rd T.M.Battery) became casualties on the dates shewn:-
Lt. J.C.Holberton 28/3/18 (Wounded)   2/Lt. R.Tadman 24/3/18 (missing)   Men rested.

4th April 1918 2/Lt. H.L.R.Baker, 'A' Company, took over Command of 'D' Company from this date. Men rested.

5th April 1918 Lt.Col. B.C.James DSO proceeded to take Command of 22nd D.L.I. and was struck off strength. Training carried on.

6th April 1918 Lt.Col. C.H.M.Imbert-Terry DSO struck off the strength of Battalion. Training.

7th April 1918 The Battalion was inspected by the Divisional Commander who expressed his thanks and admiration to the officers and men of the Battalion for what he described as "a great achievement".
Lt.Col. R.H.Anderson-Morshead DSO joined Battalion and took over Command from this day.
2/Lt. H.Leach rejoined from course of instruction in musketry at Fourth Army School, NORTBECOURT on 5th inst.
Major A.H.Cope assumed the duties of Senior Major.
Captain H.H.Jago MC took over Command of 'D' Company.
2/Lt. B.W.Jeffery MM took over Command of 'B' Company from 26th ult. Training.

The 2nd Devons War Diary

8th April 1918   Captain M.R.M.McLeod was attached to Battalion for duty from Fourth Army School.

9th April 1918   Training.   Lt. F.E.Harris and 2/Lt. W.E.Dyson joined Battalion.
2/Lt. R.C.A.Cardew rejoined from a course of instruction in signalling at X Corps School and assumed duties of Signalling Officer.
Lt. W.L.Clegg rejoined from hospital.
Lt. H.G.Morrison rejoined from course of instruction at VIII Corps School.

10th April 1918   Training.   Lt. H.G.Morrison proceeded for duty with 23rd T.M.Battery.

11th April 1918   Battalion marched 20 kilos to WARLUS and billeted there for the night.

12th April 1918   Battalion marched to HANGEST-SUR-SOMME and bivouaced there for night.

13th April 1918 Battalion entrained at HANGEST and detrained at DREUIL-LES-AMIENS, marching from there to billets in SALEUX.

14th April 1918   Voluntary church parade at 6.30pm.
2/Lt. F.W.W.McCrea having embarked for U.K. on 25/3/18 is struck off strength.
Lt. A.L.Noon died of wounds on 2/4/18
Lt. W.H.Radcliffe to be A/Captain with pay and allowance of Lt. whilst employed as Acting Adjutant.
Major A.F.Northcote joined Battalion and temporarily assumed duties of Quartermaster.

15th April 1918   The undermentioned to be Lieuts. 1st July 1917:
2/Lt. H.H.Jago MC,   2/Lt. L.N.L.Tindal MC.
Captain M.R.M.McLeod ceased to be attached to Battalion.

16th April 1918   Battalion training.

17th April 1918   Draft of 75 other ranks joined Battalion.
The undermentioned were awarded Parchment Certificates by Divisional Commander for gallantry and devotion to duty west of the SOMME between 22nd March and 2nd April.
2/Lt   J.J.Huntingford
8510 CSM S.H.Taylor
9328 Sgt.J.T.Bowden
30929 Pte. W.Devine
25650 Pte. E.W.Sizer
8427 A/CSM A.G.Small
8255 Pte. W.J.Manley
8648 Sgt. F.Way MM
Continued training.

18th April 1918 Battalion training.

19th April 1918 The following awarded Parchment Certificates by Divisional Commander for gallantry and devotion to duty west of SOMME between 22nd March and 2nd April.
Lt.(A/Capt) W.H.Radcliffe
2/Lt.(A/Capt) A.E.Titley MC
33124   L/Cpl. L.Bryan
204358 Pte.   H.C.Gaskill
89003   Pte.   S.Bonetta
69037   Pte.   L.V.Smith
7113   CSM   H.W.Garnham
267262 Pte.   J.Harper
33140   Pte.   C.H.Knuckey
31822   Pte.   P.Joy
9792   Pte.   J.T.Dunmall
20390   Sgt.   C.Smith
Battalion marched to billets in BLANGY TRONVILLE. Battalion details remained at CAMON.

Following the casualties incurred during the March retreat on the Somme, the Eighth Division could have done with more than a bare fortnight, which was all the time it was given, to absorb the large drafts which had sent to replenish its depleted battalions. Even the 2nd Devons, who had emerged as almost the strongest battalion in the division required 230 reinforcements to bring it up to something approaching full establishment.

20th April 1918 Moved into line and took over VILLERS BRETTONEUX defence line.

21st April 1918 Captain A.H.Cope to be A/Major whilst so employed 26/2/18.
Battalion still in line.

22nd April 1918 Battalion relieved by 2nd East Lancs Regiment and moved back to billets in BLANGY TRONVILLE.

23rd April 1918 Battalion moved into line and took over the CACHY SWITCH S.W. of VILLERS BRETTONEUX. Details moved to RIVERY on account of shelling.
Disposition. Night 23/24th.
Battalion HQ - U.4.a. (cent) - 2 Companies U.3.b. - 2 Companies 35.C. (Very scattered position)

24th April 1918 3.00am
Heavy enemy barrage, at first chiefly gas but gradually thickened up with H.E. and some shrapnel.
7am Hostile barrage still on - a good deal of rifle and M.G. fire to front - whole front covered in smoke. (Impossible to see men at 150 yards).
7.30am No news of an attack except from 2 CSMs of a London Regiment saying their front had been forced by 15 tanks and the

The 2nd Devons War Diary

Right was coming back.
7.40am Tank appeared and passed through Battalion HQ posts U.4.a. - Runner for 2 left Companies reported 4 tanks in O.35.c. advancing N.W. down valley.
8.30am At this time various small parties of enemy were observed approaching my centre and right - engaged with rifle fire and no organised attack came off, although small parties were continually dribbling up and M.G. fire on our position increased.
9.00am Battalion HQ re-occupied their original posts after tank had passed through. Battalion Command Post established at O.3.b.9.3. - completely out of touch with two left Companies and half Battalion HQ having become casualties - no reports from Brigade or 2 Front Battalions.
10.00am Boche seen dribbling down from Railway Cutting O.34.b. - small squads 3 - 6. This continued till 2.30 p.m. when at least 150 enemy and numerous M.G.s had entered BOIS d' AQUENNE in O.34.a. and ever increasing M.G. fire was coming from this wood then in rear of CACHY SWITCH.
1.00pm Enemy attempted to advance on our front but were easily kept off, no enemy getting within 100 yards of our line of posts.
2.30pm Enemy working West in BOIS d' AQUENNE were gradually cutting off my 2 Right Companies and also firing heavily with M.G.s into rear of Devon trenches.
3.00pm Accompanied by Adjutant I left Command Post for Brigade HQ and reported situation there.
5.00pm Collected stray Devon Parties in BOIS L' ABBEE. These were from 2 Left Companies. With this force about 40 strong garrisoned reserve line and on orders of Brigade established 3 standing patrols in O.33.a. (West Edge)
25/4/18 Dawn. On orders of Brigade cleared E. edge of wood from O.34.a.8.8. (House in wood) to O.34.b.2.9. CACHY-VILLERS ROAD. The enemy abandoned numerous M.G., Light M.G. and a few L.T.M.s and on emerging into the open crossed up on to the spur in U.4.a. and O.34.d. and were well caught in so doing by rifle fire from Devon line U.3.b. This wood-clearing party started digging in on the E. of the wood, but about 8am after meeting Brigade Major and O.C. West Yorks ordered party to cross valley at E. edge of wood and dig in afresh on line O.34.a.9.0. to U.4.b.0.4. - 200 yards - 400 yards clear of wood. This was done with practically no casualties and I placed the wood-clearing party of Devons on the left flank of the 2 Companies of Devons that had held their ground in U.3.b. This left the Devons in a long thin line about 1200 (at least) garrisoned by 4 officers and about 280 other ranks.
10am. New line well dug in and no change in positions took place till relief by 48 A.I.F. on night 27/28th.

25th April 1918 The undermentioned awarded the MM for gallantry and devotion to duty West of SOMME between 22nd March and 2nd April.
44137 Pte. H.F.Marshall
14860 Sgt. H.W.Gill
26061 Sgt. J.S.Seldon
33172 Cpl. C.Greenslade
22128 L/Cpl. E.J.Lear
68798 Pte. A.E.Street
33155 Pte. E.Henson
31038 Pte. W.Young
15000 Cpl. T.H.Grainger
8868 L/Cpl.C.W.Wakeham
8553 Sgt. W.Goodyear

The undermentioned officers joined Battalion:
Lt. L.N.L.Tindal MC
Lt. S.H.Cox
Lt. W.L.Barrett
2/Lt. L.D.Heppenstall
2/Lt. C.Wreford
2/Lt. A.E.Upperton
2/Lt. W.T.Cross
2/Lt. S.J.Cussell
2/Lt. R.Lambert
2/Lt. C.A.Hillier
2/Lt. C.H.Deeks
2/Lt. R.J.Matthews
2/Lt. C.E.Pells
2/Lt. F.Malkin

26th April 1918 Battalion still in line. 2/Lt. F.D.Clarke joined Battalion.

27th April 1918 Battalion was relieved by 48th A.I.F. and marched back to billets in BLANGY TRONVILLE.

28th April 1918 Battalion moved to PONT NOYELLES and joined details there.
Captain U.B.Burke assumed the duties of A/Adjutant.
Lt. L.N.L.Tindal MC assumed the duties of A/Adjutant and Intelligence Officer.
2/Lt. H.Edwards took over Command of 'A' Company, Lt. S.H.Cox 'B' Company, Lt. W.L.Clegg 'C' Company,
2/Lt. H.L.R.Baker 'D' Company.

29th April 1918 Interior economy.
2/Lt. F.D.Clarke takes over Command of Scouts Platoon.

30th April 1918 Interior economy and reorganisation.

One of the men of the 2nd Devons who fell on 27th April 1918 was 8376 Cpl. Ernest Comer, whose 1914 Star, British Medal and Victory Medal trio are pictured below (author's collection). Cpl. Comer served with the 2nd Devons in Cyprus and Egypt before the war, and sailed to France with the battalion on 6th November 1914.

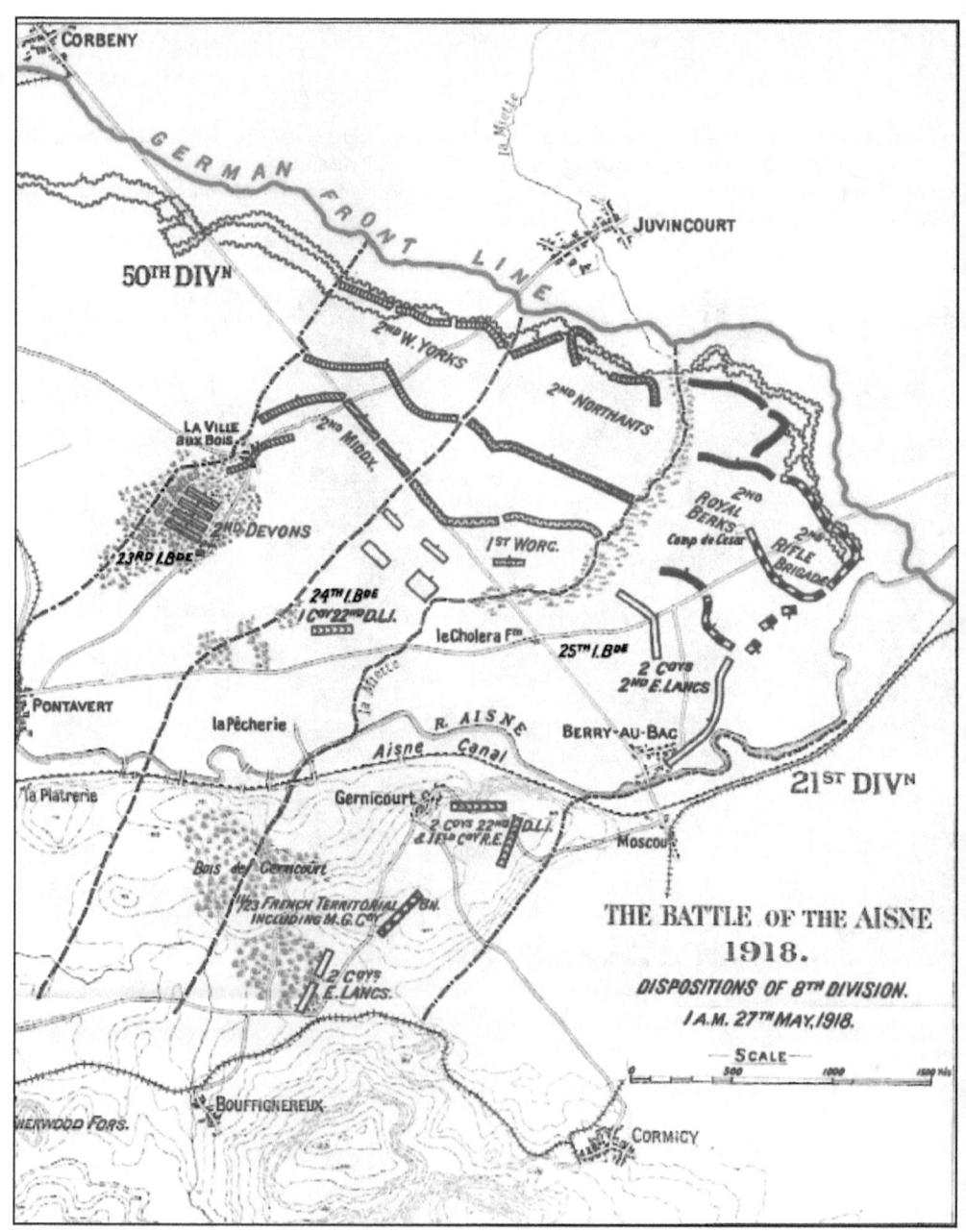

The 2nd Devons War Diary

THE 1918 BATTLE OF THE AISNE –
THE 2nd DEVON'S STAND AT THE BOIS DES BUTTES

MAY 1918

1st May 1918 Billets. Under orders to move to ABBEVILLE AREA by bus from AMIENS. Transport moved to LE MESGES – SOUES area. Orders were cancelled. Battalion to move on 2nd May.

2nd May 1918 Orders again cancelled. Transport rejoined Battalion from SOUES area.
Captain C.T.Openshaw, Captain J.Milner MC, Captain E.A.Miller and Captain S.H.Parsloe joined Battalion.

3rd May 1918 In billets. Orders received to move early next morning.

4th May 1918 On the move. Battalion entrained at SALEUX for new area.

The Spring of 1918 had been cruel to the 8th Division, but more bad fortune was to head its way before the month of May ended. Between 21st March and 30th April 1918, the Division had suffered almost 9,000 casualties, and two of its battalions: the 2nd West Yorkshires and the 2nd Middlesex had, to all intents and purposes, been wiped out twice. The 2nd Devons had not fared very much better and there was not a unit in the Division which was not made up of new drafts, mostly comprising partly trained lads of 18.

It was too much to expect so shattered a division to immediately go back into the front line and expect it to perform with any degree of success. What was required was for it to be transferred to a quiet sector where the exhausted survivors could rest, integrate and train the large drafts of reinforcements. However, along the entire British front line, there were no 'quiet' sectors where heavily damaged units could regroup, train and hold the line at the same time. Such sectors were only to be found further south, in French territory.

So it was that the 8th, 21st, 25th and 50th Divisions were formed into the IXth Corps under the recently assimilated Allied High Command, led by Field Marshal Foch, and effectively became part of General Duchene's French 6th Army. As such, they were sent south to take over a quiet section of the French front line, fifteen miles in length, between the Chemin des Dames and Rheims, on the River Aisne. As troops were in short supply, the Divisions could not be entirely taken out of the line to train the newly arrived recruits and men transferred from the Army Service Corps, but the move to this quiet sector to reorganise was the best that could be achieved under the circumstances

5th May 1918 (Sunday) Battalion detrained at LA FERE EN TARDENOIS and marched to billets in DRAVEGNY.

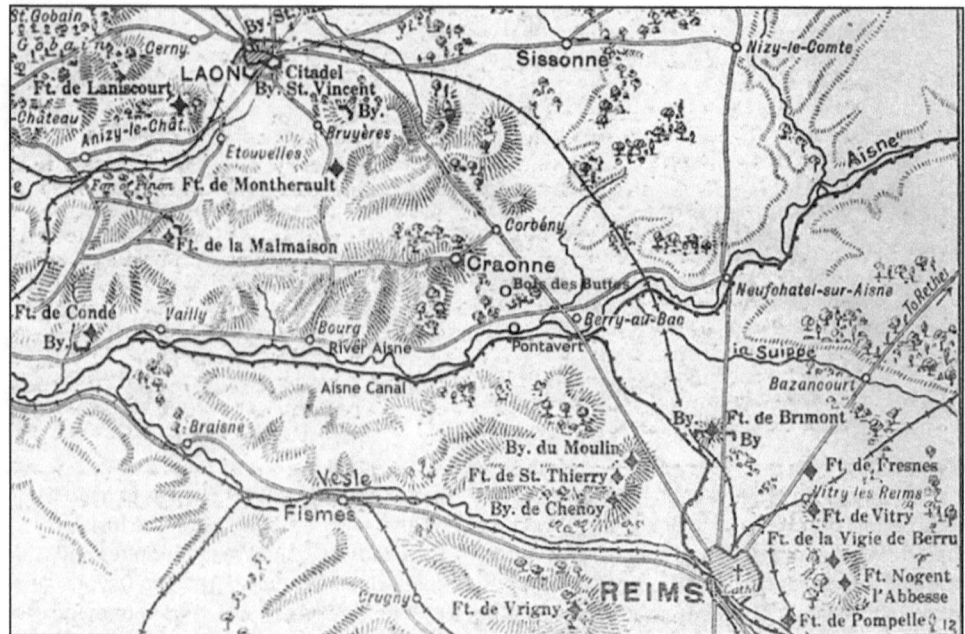

To the battle-weary survivors of the 8th Division, most of whose only experiences of the Western Front were in the battered, muddy, depressing horrors of Ypres and the Somme, the Champagne region in spring was like a dream. Here was peace and sunshine. Rolling hills topped by unshelled woods, lush meadows, lazy streams, vineyards and fields of corn, with the civilian population living unconcernedly as close as two miles to the front line. There had in fact been considerable fighting along the local front line as recently as 1917, but the appearance of the many shell-holes, dug-outs and disused trenches was softened by a growth of new grass, weeds and shrubbery. The only obvious signs of the vicious fighting that had taken place were the rusty remains of seven or eight burnt-out French tanks, some massive tangles of rust-red barbed wire and numerous concrete pill-boxes, large and small, heavily pockmarked by shell-fire. In this now quiet landscape, the 8th Division was assigned a front of six miles, stretching from Berry-au-Bac to Juvincourt.

The 2nd Devons War Diary

6th May 1918 In billets. Day spent in cleaning up etc. Very wet at night.

7th May 1918 Training commenced.

8th May 1918 In training. A demonstration in Signal Rockets and bombs given by French officer.

9th May 1918 Training carried on. Massed drums of the Brigade played retreat. A Brigade Concert was held in the evening.

10th May 1918 ROMAIN. Battalion marched to billets at ROMAIN starting 7.30am and arriving 12.30pm. Day very hot.
Major A.F.Northcote departed for duty at III Corps HQ.
Lt. J.Orton, Lt. J.C.Stands, Captain A. Fergusson, 2/Lieuts. R.Hill, C.H.Repton and P.R.Adams joined Battalion.

11th May 1918 Battalion marched from ROMAIN to CONCEVREUX QUARRY (near ROUCY).
Weather still hot. CO with Brigadier and remaining COs made a reconnaissance of the line.

12th May 1918 Day very wet. 23rd Brigade relieved 217th French Regiment of 71st Division in the left sub-sector (JUVINCOURT SECTOR), the Battalion taking over the Front Line trenches. Captain E.A.Miller granted leave to PARIS.

The new sector which the British IXth Corps was to occupy lay between Bermicourt and Bouconville, north-west of Rheims, and was where shattered French Divisions had often been sent to recuperate. It appeared that fighting the Germans had been the last thing on their minds, as rumour had it that the French troops who the 8th Division relieved had been there for a year without firing a shot and were, apparently, surprised and indignant when asked to point out the fighting positions.

The 8th Division's sector formed a salient which pushed out into the German lines, and the trenches the Division inherited were strange to say the least. Some were ten feet deep and of no use whatsoever as fighting trenches, while others were so shallow as to afford no real protection. There was also what appeared to be a veritable and unplanned maze of these trenches, making defence a headache. There were, however, many deep dug-outs, well-constructed, but built with comfort rather than defence in mind.

On 12th May, the 23rd Brigade took over the left of the 8th Division's allotted sector from the French 71st Division. This was in the centre of the IX Corps frontage, and stretched from Berry au Bac to Juvincourt. On the 23rd Brigade's immediate right was the 24th Brigade, with the 25th Brigade occupying the ground on the extreme right. Next to them was the 21st Division, while on the 23rd Brigade's immediate left was the 50th Division. The frontage of the 8th Division was about 10,000 yards, which was quite a long stretch for its three brigades, totalling nine battalions, bearing in mind that all of those units had recently been cut to pieces. All three battalions of the 23rd Brigade were required in the line at the same time to cover so long a sector, which did not allow for any rotation of units, however, the front was so quiet, and the likelihood of an enemy attack so remote, that it was felt that the much needed training could continue while they were in the line. Unfortunately, a shortage of experienced NCOs made it almost impossible to turn the reinforced battalions into cohesive fighting units. Another unfortunate factor was the positioning of the Brigade's front line, which had the River Aisne and the Aisne Canal to its rear, in a shallow swampy valley.

The officers, NCOs and men of the 8th Division were, of course, completely unaware that this apparent 'rest camp' in which they found themselves, was to be the epicentre of a forthcoming German offensive.

13th May 1918   In the trenches. Day very quiet. The Brigadier visited the line.

14th May 1918   Re-arrangement of Companies. 3 Companies in Front Line and one in support. Enemy heavily shelled batteries.

15th May 1918   Day very quiet. Enemy inactive. Weather still very hot. Batteries were again shelled.

16th May 1918   In the trenches. Still very quiet and hot. Major A.H.Cope DSO proceeded for duty as Commandant of IX Corps School.

17th May 1918   Day quiet. Counter battery work continued. Captain E.A.Miller rejoined from leave to PARIS.

18th May 1918   The enemy attempted to rush posts held by the Battalion. A few bombs were thrown. No men missing.

19th May 1918   Weather still warm. Day quiet.

20th May 1918   The Battalion was relieved at dusk by 2nd West Yorks Regiment. Battalion also carried out a raid on enemy line which proved abortive – no prisoners or identifications.

This tour of duty in the front line had largely proved to be as quiet and restful as promised. The damage to the surrounding countryside was minimal and there were still peasants working in the fields close to the line. There had been some minor counter-battery shelling, but the only infantry activity had been on the 18th, when the enemy tried to rush a post and were beaten off, and on the 20th, when the German front line was raided at a junction with a communication trench named Boyau Baltique, but this was deserted and no contact was made.

Once in reserve at Roucy, the 2nd Devons started a demanding training programme. In the meantime, it had become apparent to the senior British officers that a major German attack was being planned, and they felt that the current dispositions would not be able to stand up to a strong enemy attack. They proposed that a lightly held out-post line should be made north of the Aisne, with the main defence line south of the river. This would make it possible for British artillery and machine guns on the south bank to bombard the forward area in depth, over which the German attack would have to pass to engage the main defence line along the river. It would also allow time to destroy the bridges necessary to supply the thinly held outpost line north of the river. Field Marshal Foch had previously instructed his local French Commanders to heed the experience of the British IX Corps Commanders, but they ignored the warning and overruled the British suggestions, with dire consequences.

21st May 1918 ROUCY. Relief completed by 12.50am. Battalion in billets in ROUCY. 2/Lt. H.L.R.Baker MC admitted to hospital.

22nd May 1918 In billets. Battalion training.

23rd May 1918 Training carried on.

24th May 1918 Training as usual. 2/Lt. C.A.Hillier admitted to hospital.

25th May 1918 Training. Captain J.H.Millman joined Battalion. 2/Lt. A.E.Rutledge rejoined Battalion from 6 months tour of duty.

By this time the Battalion was virtually up to establishment in officers, 28 having joined since Villers-Brettoneux, but its complement of NCOs and men was less than 800 and, as stated earlier, far too many of them had no experience of soldiering on the Western Front. As a result, a larger number of them than usual were away at training schools or on courses.

While in billets at Roucy, there had been rumours of a possible German offensive but, up to May 25th, General Denis Duchene and his French Headquarters staff refused to accept the likelihood of such a thing.

Despite this, some discerning 8th Division officers could see ominous signs that all was not well, and they were perfectly correctbecause a large-scale attack was about to be launched on the Chemin des Dames Ridge. The German plan was for the attack to be vigorous enough to convince the Allies that this was the 'main event', and was intended to draw their forces away from the real area of their main offensive, codenamed Operation Hagen, which was planned to take place in Flanders in July and end the war with a great German victory.

The attack on the Chemin des Dames would be become known as 'The Battle of the Aisne' and, violent and costly though it proved to be to the 2nd Devons, among others, it was a side show. However, matters did not go well for the Germans in the summer of 1918, and despite their success on the Aisne, Operation Hagen never took place.

However, prior to the German offensive, there had been signs that all was not well. The Germans were quiet, which was often a bad sign. They weren't making any patrols. When a German artillery shell landed anywhere near a British battery they would cease firing, which meant that they had got the range. An observation balloon was also very active behind the German lines beyond Juvincourt. All in all it was obvious that the enemy was up to something, although nobody probably wanted to believe it.

26th May 1918 Sunday. Divine Services.
Battalion was ordered to move into Support at BOIS DES BUTTES. Enemy expected to attack.

(Extract from 2/Lt. King's report, detailing the events between 26th May and 2nd June 1918).
"The Battalion moved up into close support to the other two Battalions of the 23rd Infantry Brigade at 9pm in LA VILLE-AUX-BOIS."

Two German prisoners, from a unit not previously seen in the area, were captured on the

26th May and brought the startling news that thirty-five enemy divisions were going to attack early the next morning. This was dismissed in many Allied quarters because German security had been so tight that the preparations had gone largely unnoticed, and the general concensus was that an attack, if one took place, would be small. Despite this, some preparations for an enemy attack were begun, and General Grogan visited the 2nd Devons HQ at Roucy and ordered them to move north of both the Aisne Canal and Aisne River lines, to occupy some dug-outs on a sandstone hill known as the Bois des Buttes. In this position they were to act as Brigade Reserve, 1,200 metres behind the first line of defence. This was an out-post Line, manned by the 2nd West Yorks, about half a mile west of the junction of the Rheims-Laon and Juvincourt-Pontavert roads. Just in front of the 2nd Devons lay La Ville au Bois, on the other side of which lay the aforementioned 'first line of defence' and beyond that the Main Defence Line, manned by the 2nd Middlesex, deployed along the Corbeny – Berry-au-Bac road. The 2nd Devon's four and a half mile march to the Bois des Buttes was made after sundown, their way illuminated by the flashes of British and French artillery, which started a harassing barrage of the German positions just as the 2nd Devons left Roucy. Shortly before midnight the battalion reported to Brigade HQ that they were holding their reserve position on the Bois des Buttes.

The Bois des Buttes is a twin-topped hillock, about thirty metres high, five hundred metres across and lightly wooded. Heavy fighting had previously taken place there in 1916 and early 1917 and it was criss-crossed with numerous old trenches, mostly too deep to be of any use, which the Devons unfortunately had little opportunity to investigate. There were a number of large, deep tunnels dug through the hill, which were dry and timber-lined, where the entire battalion could shelter in company-sized dug-outs. Inside there was electric lighting, provisions for Company and Regimental Aid Posts, and ammunition stores, but the battalion had only been there for about an hour before massed German artillery opened up in a single devastating roar.

27th May 1918 1am. Bombardment commenced followed later by enemy attack. Battalion with remainder of Brigade were forced to retire under heavy shelling and M.G. fire. Lt.Col. R.H.Anderson-Morshead DSO missing. Major A.H.Cope DSO was put in Command of Brigade troops. Many rearguard actions were fought.

The brevity of the War Diary entry for 27th May 1918, barely gives a clue to the horrendous and costly day that the Battalion endured, but 2nd Lieutenant King's report serves to put some flesh on the bones of the story. With the help of eye-witness accounts and other historical records the events of the day can be outlined.

'The Devonshire Regiment 1914-1918, vol.1' compiled by C.T.Atkinson:
"...at 1 o'clock the bombardment suddenly opened in tremendous force, deluging the position with a flood of H.E. and gas shell, which compelled everybody for miles back to put on gas masks. In no previous attack had the Germans concentrated such a force of artillery, and the bombardment surpassed all hitherto experienced. The battalions in the outpost zone suffered terribly, but the Devons, in their underground shelters, escaped almost entirely, though despite the masks some men were gassed."

The 2nd Devons War Diary

Extract from 2/Lt. King's report:
Monday 27th May "At 1am an intense enemy barrage of gas and high explosive shells was effected against the front and support lines, followed at 4.0am by an attack in considerable force. Almost immediately the Battalion found itself surrounded, the enemy having forced both flanks, and the result was that practically every man including the personnel of Battalion Headquarters was either killed or taken prisoner. About 80 only escaped, and the party rallied in a line of trenches in a field on the right hand side of the LA VILLE-AUX-BOIS - PONTAVERT road.
A successful withdrawal was then made to some rising ground immediately due South of the canal south of PONTAVERT, which was held until about 6am. This party next fell back to the trench running north of and parallel to the CONCEVREUX - CORMICY road, and in conjunction with the surviving members of other units successfully stemmed the enemy's advance until 2pm, effecting great casualties on him. It was then necessary expeditiously to withdraw the party once more, owing to the fact that enemy patrols were reported to be in ROUCY, and a detour around the town was made to the high ground to the South and the enemy were further kept in check until nearly midnight."

Tuesday 28th May "Early in the morning the Devons took up a new position on high ground between VENTELAY and MONTIGNY when they were compelled by renewed enemy attacks to withdraw to the river in front of JONCHERY at about 10am. This position was held for over two hours until the left flank was forced to give way. Reinforcements of the Devons for this left flank successfully held the enemy for a further two hours.
Later a stand was made between JONCHERY and BRANSCOURT, where the unit in co-operation with others held a strong point on the main JONCHERY - BRANSCOURT road until about 4 o'clock in the afternoon. Weight of numbers necessitated a further withdrawal to a high plateau north of SAVIGNY and here throughout the night a determined and effective resistance was maintained."

The German attack on the Aisne was codenamed 'Operation Blucher' and employed the same initially successful tactics used in 'Operation Michael' on the Somme in March 1918. British fears regarding the attack were fully realised and the out-post Line and Main Defence Lines were subjected to a massed trench mortar bombardment. At a range of fifty to three hundred metres, the 2nd West Yorks, who were manning the vulnerable out-post Line, suffered appalling losses. Trenches were blown in, dug-outs collapsed and their defensive wire was cut. Besides the 2nd West Yorks, the 2nd Middlesex, 2nd Devons and the British artillery, mostly north of the River Aisne, were subjected to a concentrated bombardment of gas shells for ten minutes.

As suspected, the positions had all been plotted by the German Batteries, under the command of Colonel Bruchmuller, and gas shells were fired to explode as far back as Divisional HQ at Roucy, and in the Transport Lines. Bruchmuller claimed he had used mathematical calculations to register the 6,000 guns at his disposal, which helped the Germans to keep their intentions secret.

German field and medium gun batteries concentrated their fire on the British positions in turn, in addition to a heavy gun battery being assigned to every known British position throughout the entire length of the bombardment. The precise time that the maelstrom of fire fell on the 2nd Devons, the majority of whom were sheltering underground at the Bois des Buttes, is not recorded by the battalion, but 'its intensity passed all hitherto experienced'. Although casualties among the Devons were light, it was impossible for anyone to leave the underground dug-outs, and additional ammunition could not be collected from a dump south of the river.

5 Field Battery, Royal Artillery, was positioned just to the rear of the 2nd Devons, and received the systematic massed attentions of the German artillery at 0335 for only five minutes, but was left with heavy casualties and only four guns serviceable.

Captain Ulick Burke:
"…..we had lots of Middlesex wounded coming back through us. They got over the river, back over the Pontavert Bridge behind us. Then the West Yorks who were in support started coming back and they went through us. The order was to stay put as long as we could – we were not to retire! We stayed where we were. We were on two small hills. We shot and shot and shot till the fellows in the trenches could hardly hold their rifles. They killed thousands; I have never seen so many dead in front of our trenches. We were shooting at their artillery that was coming down, because they didn't stop – they went through us."
('Forgotten Voices of the Great War', by Max Arthur).

Eventually, between 0400 and 0500, after what must have seemed like ages to the officers and men sheltering in the tunnels, orders were given to occupy the trenches. Three companies took up their positions in the firing line, with the fourth and Battalion Headquarters to their rear on what the Official History describes as a "pimple," in support.

The time of the first German infantry advance is not certain, but it is thought that the 25th Division, holding the Division's left side, was attacked at 0345 hours. By the use of box barrages and tear gas, German storm-troopers searched for gaps in the line caused by the barrage and stole through, leaving the more strongly defended pockets of resistance isolated. Behind the storm-troopers came four pioneer companies, a machine gun section, and flame thrower and trench mortar detachments. This 'attack by means of infiltration' was followed up by normal infantry regiments, who advanced behind a creeping barrage at the rate of one kilometre in forty minutes. Their role was to mop up the remaining British positions, after which reserves were sent in to support successful attacks, thereby deepening and widening the penetration.

The 2nd West Yorks, positioned roughly between La Ville au Bois and Juvincourt, were rapidly overcome, and the enemy penetrated the battle zone, in spite of the best efforts of the 2nd Middlesex, who were outnumbered and overwhelmed. Consequently, the 2nd Devons were heavily engaged as soon as they emerged from the tunnels. One platoon, on reaching its allotted trench, found enemy machine-gunners already behind it.

"We obliterated these before they knew what had happened," wrote the platoon commander, "and this cheered up the troops, who were young and rather demoralized by the shelling and the general uncertainty."

But the position was not good. The troops were unfamiliar with the ground, which was wooded and confusing, and the trenches were too deep to be defended. It was also misty, which helped mask the enemy's approach and made it impossible for the British artillery to pick out targets. Retreating men of the 2nd West Yorks and the 2nd Middlesex were pouring back from the front with the Germans hard on their heels, but the Devons made a terrific stand along the northern edge of the Bois des Buttes. The enemy soldiers unlucky enough to be detailed to advance against them were easily held off, even though the young and inexperienced soldiers defending the position could not wipe out as many of their opponents as the '15-aimed-rounds-a-minute' men of 1914 would have done. Nevertheless, at about 0515, 8th Division HQ received a message that the battalion was holding off repeated attacks and was confident of retaining its position.

An eye-witness described the 2nd Devons at this time as:

"......an island in the midst of an innumerable and determined foe, fighting with perfect discipline, and, by the steadiness of their fire, mowing down the enemy in large numbers."

At dawn, approximately 0400 hours, Lieutenant Colonel Rupert Henry Anderson-Morshead had ordered his battalion to deploy to its battle positions. In the growing daylight, the Aisne valley was shrouded in mist and little could be seen of the open ground immediately in front, although the high ground at Roucy to their rear stood out above the mist, as did the Chemin des Dames in front. As the men of the Battalion made their way forward they found that many of the trenches had been smashed to shallow hollows. Although casualties among the Devons had been light thus far, from now on they would suffer an increasing flow of casualties from the continual shell fire.

On the left, 'B' Company occupied a line of partially blown-in trenches facing north-west towards Corbeny. In similarly damaged trenches, 'D' Company was positioned overlooking the ruins of La Ville-aux-Bois. 'C' Company, to the right of 'D', was occupying the flat marshy ground to the north-east, while 'A' Company remained with Anderson-Morshead, in the trenches surrounding the top of the Bois des Buttes. Once he had sent out his companies, Anderson-Morshead lost all communication with them, because shell fire continually destroyed the telephone wires and runners quickly became casualties when running in the open from shell hole to shell hole. Because of the shape of the ground, mist, smoke, dust and foliage, Anderson-Morshead could not see his three forward Company positions, so right from the start, the Company Commanders, all lieutenants, were left on their own to carry out the 6th Army order that 'not an inch of sacred French soil was to be surrendered'.

Almost immediately after the Devons took up their battle positions, 'B' Company was attacked from the left by troops of the German 50th Division, who had advanced rapidly through the British 50th Division's position and approached the Bois des Buttes under cover of the mist. The first wave of attackers that appeared were storm-troopers of the 158th Infantry Regiment, but they were forced to take cover from the rapid rifle fire and the fire of the two Lewis guns of 'B' Company. To counter this, the Germans fired dozens of rifle grenades, which caused many casualties among the men sheltering in the trenches. Shortly afterwards, under covering fire, German storm-troopers who had been lying in dead ground, rushed forward, determined to take 'B' Company's trench. This attack was beaten off with heavy casualties, as was a third wave of Germans throwing stick bombs. Following this setback, the enemy resumed his artillery barrage, which further depleted the ranks of the Devons. The Devon's deployment under fire and 'B' Company's achievements in beating off repeated and powerful enemy attacks were the first instances of the determined defence against overwhelming odds which was to characterise the battle.

The British 25th Brigade, in the Berry-au-Bac salient on the 8th Division's right, was rapidly broken by the German attack, and a similar attack on the 50th Division, on the 2nd Devon's left flank, quickly followed. Meanwhile, German storm-troopers worked their way from Berry-au-Bac down to the La Miette stream and into the rear of the 23rd and 24th Brigades who, by 5.30am, still managed to prevent an enemy breakthrough on their front, in spite of heavy casualties. However, attacked from both front and rear, the British troops remaining in the Battle Zone were overrun by the German 52nd Division, 7th Reserve Division and part of the German 50th Division. The only cohesive British unit now left north of the River Aisne was the 2nd Devons.

Unfortunately, the Germans had progressed faster against the 50th Division than they had against the 8th. Outflanked early on by the enemy's rapid advance against the French further to the west, the 50th were thrown back, leaving the flank of the 8th's battle zone exposed. Although the 2nd Devons held back their immediate attackers, substantial numbers of the enemy began to appear on their left flank and to their rear, followed at around 7.00am by a turning movement between the Bois des Buttes and the Bois de l'Edmond, which cut off their direct line of retreat. Exact details of what happened are hard to find as the survivors were, for the most part, left with confused and incoherent memories of the dire circumstances in which the battalion fought and died.

Subsequent attacks on 'B', 'C' and 'D' Companies followed the same pattern, although, when the mist dispersed as the sun rose, more of the enemy were mowed down by the Lewis gun teams. Visibility being clearer meant that the Devons were able to disrupt the forward movement of the German artillery and the fetching up of stores to re-supply the attacking troops. The stubborn resistance of the Devons on the Bois des Buttes was obviously of concern to the Germans, and a number of enemy aircraft strafed, bombed and dropped smoke markers at the edge of the wood to aid their artillery. The Devons on the ground quickly learned to move after a German aircraft had flown over their heads, because a burst of accurate shell fire was likely to follow. Another method of German artillery spotting employed was the use of observation balloons tethered to tanks, which followed the infantry at a safe distance.

Anderson-Morshead, concerned at the apparent loss of his runners and without telephone communication to his Company Commanders, sent L/Cpl. Jordan, his batman, to get information, and, hearing the attack on his left, sent Lt. Maunder and the HQ Company to reinforce 'B' Company. However, they were met by groups of men coming back who said that there was no longer a front line, the enemy were close behind, and they had been ordered to retire. Lt. Maunder had these men join his HQ Company, and they established a rudimentary line on the side of the hill, in old trenches and shell holes, from which they were able to hold up the advancing Germans who appeared shortly afterwards.

Out-flanked on the left and seriously depleted in numbers, 'C' and 'D' Companies were forced to retire into the wood. Bearing in mind that most of the 2nd Devons were young and inexperienced, many in their first battle, having endured heavy shelling and seen so many of their comrades and officers killed and wounded, it is surprising that they did not just run away, but they didn't, and with their help the Devons made the Germans fight for every inch of the wood.

On the right, the remnants of 'C' Company were forced to move when it was seen that the 24th Brigade was no longer protecting its right flank, and that a German force was approaching them from the east. Lieutenant Tindal made the decision that as no order to retire had been received, 'C' Company would defend its corner of the wood. The surviving officers and NCOs agreed, if required, to fight to the last man. The new position ran parallel with the La Ville-aux-Bois to Pontavert road, facing Berry-au-Bac. Although by this time 'C' Company was only about forty strong, Lt. Tindal split the Company into two, one half to give covering fire, while the other, led by Tindal himself, would charge the enemy, as this appeared to be the only action that might break up the enemy attack. The Germans were getting close to the trenches when Tindal ordered his twenty-odd men to attack. With a wild yell they charged the entire German battalion, but before hand-to-hand fighting could be joined they became entangled in old barbed wire, hidden by long grass and bushes. Instead they took what cover they could and continued to fire at the enemy, who retaliated with hand grenades, rifle and machine gun fire. More casualties ensued before Sgt. Cosway carried out a fighting withdrawal with eight survivors.

While deploying, 'D' Company found that a group of German storm-troopers was already in the trench system. Sgt. Hooper DCM led a party of men against them, hurling hand grenades, and they drove the enemy out with their bayonets, however, the storm-troopers counter attacked with stick grenades, causing the Devons to withdraw once again. Yet again, the twelve survivors of Sgt. Hooper's platoon drove the Germans out, but were themselves soon driven back before attacking for an incredible third time and again driving the enemy out. However, the few remaining Devons of this party were then forced to scatter to escape more waves of stick grenades, machine gun fire and strafing from the air. Lt. Cyril Elmore Pells, leading another party of 'D' Company, coached his inexperienced troops in field craft, while using his rifle to good effect. Lt. Pells, whose only child had been killed when a German submarine sank the Lusitania, nursed a bitter hatred of the enemy. He was killed during this action.

The three forward companies were, by this stage of the battle, reduced to small groups of men surrounded by large numbers of Germans. In an instance typical of many brave efforts that day, Pte. Knight and five other men from 'C' Company found themselves in a short stretch of old trench with enemy soldiers all around them. Instead of surrendering, they formed a rough circle and blazed away at their enemies until an opportunity arose for them to break out and occupy another trench further back, from where they continued to shoot at the advancing Germans. Doubtless there were many such acts of bravery that day, but unfortunately there were often no survivors to relate their stories.

In addition to the use of highly trained, heavily armed storm-troopers, the Germans also made use of twenty-five captured Allied tanks of various types and around 15 forty ton German A7Vs, armed with a 6-pdr (57mm) gun and six machine guns. At least two tanks were deployed against 'D' Company, where they helped to drive the British back from the edge of the wood. Unfortunately the Devons could do little to counter the tanks, although their mobility was seriously hampered by the heavily shelled ground in the wooded areas.

L/Cpl. Jordan and Pte. Staddon reported back to Anderson-Morshead to inform him that 'B' Company had been virtually wiped out and that 'C' and 'D' could not last very much longer. By 0700 hours, and only six hours after the fighting started, the C.O. knew that he and the remains of the Battalion were virtually surrounded. They were being attacked from the front, left and right, and the Germans were working their way southwards along both flanks of the wood. Captain Ulick Burke made a reconnaissance of the rear and saw that formations of German infantry were marching along the road from Berry-au-Bac to Pontavert and had set up machine guns which were firing upon groups of British walking wounded and other stragglers.

At 0830 hours, Anderson-Morshead moved to the reverse slope of the Bois des Buttes, where he divided the remnants of HQ and 'A' Companies into three groups and allocated positions to them.

Anderson-Morshead spoke the following words to his remaining soldiers:

'Your job for England, men, is to hold the blighters up as much as you can, to give our troops a chance on the other side of the river. There is no hope of relief and we have to fight to the last.' (The Keep Military Museum, Dorchester).

One group, led by Captain Burke, held the trenches on the forward slope, Anderson-Morshead and a second group held the right flank, while Lt. Barrett and the third group held the left flank. These new positions were an improvement, each with a good field of fire and plenty of targets and, while the largely inexperienced troops could not fire their SMLE rifles very quickly, they still inflicted a great deal of damage on the advancing Germans. In the words of one survivor, 'there were so many of the enemy, everywhere, by this time that it would have been difficult to fire in any direction without hitting them'.

At approximately 0930 hours, L/Cpl. Jordan spotted German troops, guns and transport moving along the road from Juvincourt towards Pontavert, on the south side of the Bois des Buttes. Anderson-Morshead, who was with Jordan, took his pipe from his pocket and calmly remarked as he filled it with tobacco, 'Ah well, Jordan, we shall have to make the best of it!'

The fifty or so men of the 2nd Devons who remained on the hill were now divided into two groups, one led by Anderson-Morshead, the other by Captain Burke. The plan was to slow down the German advance along the road by withdrawing, in contact with the enemy, towards the river line at Pontavert, during which time they hoped to pick up parties of stragglers from other regiments to boost their strength.

The two groups moved down the easterly slope of the Bois des Buttes, towards the Juvincourt – Pontavert road. Anderson-Morshead took his party across the road onto the right flank, while Captain Burke's party stayed on the left. The unexpected movement of these parties of Devons threw the Germans into confusion and they halted, having been under the impression that all resistance had been eliminated. In short order the Devons opened fire and destroyed a German artillery team with rifles and Lewis guns. Cautiously at first, the enemy fought back, and the Devons were eventually driven back in short bounds, turning after each bound to fire and knock down more of the enemy. Anderson-Morshead saw a group of Germans coming down the slope from the Bois des Buttes which they had so recently occupied, and sent a Captain and six men to fight them off, but it was a hopeless task and they quickly became casualties. Meanwhile, as he directed the fire of his troops, pistol in one hand, riding crop in the other, Anderson-Morshead was shot and killed. So ended the life of a very brave man.

Captain Ulick Burke:
"About five to twelve the Regimental Sergeant Major came to me and said he couldn't locate any of the other companies. As far as we were concerned there were twenty-three of us; we had just about 200 rounds of ammunition left. They were coming on: I said 'Right, three men go out and strip any of the dead you can find of their ammunition!' We went on firing until all the ammunition was gone. We held on till about half past twelve when the only ammunition left was 6 rounds in my revolver. Suddenly I said, 'Charge!' I was wounded in the legs – about nine machine-gun bullets up my legs – and they charged with the Sergeant Major. Twenty-three men charged against nearly 10,000 Germans. That finished us. We were soon picked up by the Germans and our wounds were dressed."
('Forgotten Voices of the Great War', by Max Arthur).

The 2nd Devons War Diary

The stand of the Devons was over and the few men left of the HQ and 'A' Company, started back towards the river. Large numbers of German troops were also moving towards the Aisne River and Canal crossings and these had to be avoided. Some of the badly wounded, such as Lieutenant Clegg, dragged themselves as far as the river, only to be taken prisoner there. Some of the unwounded men, including Lieutenant Hill of 5 Platoon, 'B' Company, fought their way back to the river bank where, out of ammunition, they too were captured. Others swam the river to the supposedly safe side, only to be captured by Germans who had already crossed the river and driven the British defenders back across the Aisne Canal.

Some remnants of 'B' Company, led by 2nd Lieutenant Clarke of 6 Platoon, after fighting off strong attacks soon discovered that they were all but surrounded. He led the platoon through the maze of trenches on the Bois des Buttes until they encountered more enemy troops. They managed to fight them off and tried to escape in the opposite direction, but ran into some Germans. Thes they also fought off, and escaped to the top of the hill from where they made their way out through the tunnels to the southern side in a hail of bullets. Clarke then led the survivors through the wood towards Pontavert, evaded the Germans, crossed both the Aisne River and the Canal and joined General Grogan and a mixed group of soldiers at La Platerie

Approximately forty men escaped to safety and, together with men from the transport lines and Captain Cope's Lewis gun school, continued to help delay the German breakthrough, which was eventually halted five days later on the River Marne, forty miles from Paris.

After all resistance had been overcome on the north side of the river, the only 2nd Devons left were 2nd Lieut. Clarke's party, the transport men and other details back at Ventelay, men under instruction at Divisional Schools, and a few employed by the 23rd Brigade and the 8th Division. But these men were Devons and were themselves inspired by the spirit and determination exhibited by their comrades at the Bois des Buttes. Once back across the River Aisne and the Aisne Canal, 2nd Lieut. Clarke's party had been positioned by General Grogan in some old trenches west of the Pontavert-Roucy road. From this position, the advance of the Germans directly towards them was checked, but on the right, near Gernicourt, they were already through where bridges had, unfortunately, been left standing. This made a retirement to Roucy necessary.

At Roucy, a little before noon, the remnants of the 8th Division joined up with a brigade of the 25th Division and for several hours the Germans were again held up. Unfortunately, nearly all of the Division's guns had been lost because they had been kept north of the Aisne and could not be got away. Without artillery support, of course, the task of defending their position was made considerably more difficult. Throughout the early afternoon the Germans were creeping forward, protected by folds in the ground from the Lewis guns and rifles which was virtually all that the defenders could use. Despite getting within a couple of hundred yards, the British held the enemy there until, late in the afternoon, they gained enough ground on the left to outflank the small British force and make them retreat. By nightfall the British were withdrawing back down the slopes leading to Ventelay.

The stand had been greatly aided by a scratch reinforcement under Major Cope, mainly men under instruction at the Lewis gun and other Schools, which included about 40 Devons. At Ventelay, the parties led by 2nd Lieut. and Major Cope joined forces, and took up a line on high ground, with the Vesle to the rear.

Only 4 NCOs and 13 men are listed as being killed in action on 27th May - there were in fact many more of course and these are recorded on the entry for 31st May. The specific date that some of these men fell is, not surprisingly, uncertain.

28th May 1918 Fighting continued. Battalion again retired.

Early on 28th May, the Germans once again advanced in force, necessitating a retirement across the River Vesle, where General Grogan organised a determined stand. As the remnants of the 8th, 25th and 50th Divisions poured across Jonchery bridge, he rallied them to a good position along the railway embankment, which ran parallel to the left bank of the river. There was a wide stretch of marshy ground between the railway embankment and the river, and the defenders began to hope that, this time, they would be able to stop the enemy, who repeatedly pressed forward, taking many casualties as a result. Unfortunately, although checked at Jonchery, the Germans had better luck against the French further to the west and before long had crossed the river and were, once more, menacing their flank.

As luck would have it, there was a canteen located in Jonchery and rather than let its contents fall into enemy hands, the men were told to help themselves, which bolstered up their flagging spirits.

"There was one mad rush and scramble and men returned with their packs filled with useless stuff, tooth-brushes, razors, boxes of soap, in fact anything they could lay their hands on, and for the next day or so they were all smoking cigars," one officer later wrote.

Major Cope formed a defensive flank facing to the west and covered General Grogan's men while they vacated Jonchery. This flank guard held on for some time in the village, until they discovered that the enemy was already to their rear, forcing a hasty retirement. Once more halting and facing the enemy, they took up a position between Vandeuil and Branscourt.

The stand at Branscourt followed what was now becoming a normal course of events: the position was outflanked, causing Major Cope's men to be driven back to some high ground in the rear, where a fresh stand was made. This checked the Germans until about 8pm, at which point they advanced in force from some woods on the left and pushed the British off the top of the ridge, also capturing a farm about 2,000 yards to the north of Savigny sur Ardre. The 2nd Devons now totalled about 140, more details having come up from the transport lines, and they were supported by a handful of men of other units but, despite their overall paucity of numbers, they dashed forward resolutely in response to the Brigadier's order to counter-attack and forced the enemy back, retaking the farm and securing the dominating ground around it.

"Fighting became very monotonous now," wrote a survivor, *"We would hold a position until we were outflanked, when we withdrew to the next ridge, and the same thing happened again. Our left flank was in the air the whole time and he* (the Germans) *always concentrated upon it."*

29th May 1918 Fighting still in progress. Elements of Brigade troops still in line.

Extract from 2/Lt. King's report:
Wednesday 29th May
"In the early hours of the morning it was necessary to withdraw from the plateau, as the enemy again threatened the left flank, and a new position was consolidated just north-east of FAVERELLE. This was held till about 4pm when a ridge north-east of TRAMERY was lined. Later a strong position was occupied immediately south of CHAMBRECY and maintained until the night of 31st May/1st June.

The 2nd Devons War Diary

Meanwhile another party of Devons and stragglers from all units of the Division concentrated on CHAMPLAT and re-organised and formed into the 1st-8th Divisional Composite Battalion. The Devons were about 40 strong and composed mainly of Regimentally employed men (tailors, shoemakers etc.) and the drums. This Battalion moved up about mid-day to SARCY where it received orders to make a counter attack on LHERY. When just about to carry out the attack at 4pm the order was cancelled, and an alternative position was taken up on the ridge north of BOULEUSE. Throughout the night a successful stand was made."

There were only a handful of senior officers left standing: General Grogan; his Brigade staff-officers; Smythe, GSO 111 8th Division; Major Cope, 2nd Devons; Colonel Moore, 1st Sherwood Foresters; and two 50th Division colonels. There was also a machine gun team with an inoperative gun and a scattering of men from the constituent units of the 8th, 25th and 50th Divisions, making a grand total of around two hundred and fifty hungry, dirty, tired men, many of whom were wounded, together with a number of French colonial troops who had come up as reinforcements.

The position to the north of Savigny was held until well into next morning, 29th May. But by 11am, a French withdrawal on the left flank forced a retirement to a plateau just to the north of Treslon. At this point a line was taken on a reverse slope, hidden from direct enemy observation. When the Germans appeared over the crest of the hill, they received so hot a reception that, for several hours, they could not make any progress. However, enemy aeroplanes spotted the exact line held by the British, after which the attackers brought up trench mortars, which they used to great effect. Eventually, between 5.30 and 6 pm, a determined attack pushed General Grogan's remaining forces out and drove them down into the valley.

As the men retired, French reinforcements began appearing, too late to be of help. If they had arrived ten minutes earlier they could have saved the situation but, under the circumstances, a withdrawal to a ridge north of Bouleuse was necessary. Here the 6th Wiltshires, of the newly-arrived 19th Division, were already in position, and General Grogan rallied his exhausted men on them for yet another stand. It was a miracle that they had the strength to respond, but Grogan's personal bravery held them firm. The line was not a good one, sitting on a forward slope under observation from the previous position, now held by the enemy, while thickets and woods spoiled their field of fire and covered the German's advance. Twice the enemy nearly broke through, but on each occasion a batch of reinforcements arrived, making counter-attacks possible, which saved the situation. At about 9pm the Germans relaxed their pressure and drew back.

One of the reinforcements which arrived was an 8th Division Composite Battalion, which had been organised at Champlat mostly from stragglers, but included about 40 Devons, bandsmen and regimentally employed men. This unit did good service in the fight on Bouleuse ridge.

30th May 1918 Transport moved to BOIS DU BOURSAULT. Elements of Brigade troops collected at NANTEUIL.

Extract from 2/Lt. King's report:
Thursday 30th May "At mid-day the Battalion was forced to withdraw from the ridge, owing to the fact that the enemy was

working around the right flank and commencing an enfilading movement. The Platoon of Devons which was sent up to the right flank, in conjunction with units of the 19th Division successfully withdrew with very few casualties, and the whole force placed itself in the ARDRE Valley and effectively withheld all enemy thrusts until midnight."

On 30th May General Grogan handed over command of the 8th Division to a Brigadier from the Nineteenth Division, and orders were issued to withdraw the Division behind the River Marne. The 23rd Brigade established its headquarters at Etrechy, where the transport and other details were gathered, but the detachments which had fought the rear-guard action from Pontavert to Bouleuse could not yet be spared from the line and were being pushed further back to the Champlat-Chambrecy-Bligny line. The 1st Composite Battalion, including a number of 2nd Devons, occupied Bligny Hill, against which the Germans made repeated but unsuccessful attacks.

"This was as far as the enemy got," a survivor of the Devons wrote later.

31st May 1918 Transport and men from Battalion in line moved to GOINGES. Brigade troops still in line.

Extract from 2/Lt. King's report:
Friday 31st May "About 12.30am the Battalion was ordered to move to the rear and the day was spent on reorganisation and rest."

'The Devonshire Regiment 1914-1918, vol.1' compiled by C.T.Atkinson:
'……an eye-witness, a Major of the Royal Artillery, happened to catch a glimpse of Colonel Anderson-Morshead's last stand. "At a late hour of the morning," he writes, "I, with those of my men who had escaped the enemy's ring of machine-guns and his fearful barrage, found the C.O. of the 2nd Devons and a handful of men holding the last trench North of the Canal. The C.O. was calmly writing his orders with a perfect hell of H.E. all round him. I spoke to him, and he told me that nothing could be done. He refused all offers of help from my artillerymen, who were unarmed, and sent them off to get through if they could. His magnificent and dauntless courage and determination to carry on to the end moved one's emotion."

Colonel Anderson-Morshead had not commanded the 2nd Battalion for very long, but his name is inextricably linked both with its stubborn defence at Villers-Bretonneux and the heroic stand at the Bois des Buttes. It seems unjust that he was not awarded a Victoria Cross for his bravery and determination on the Bois des Buttes, which equals the deeds of Colonel Wilfrith Elstob, VC, at Manchester Hill on the Somme on 21st March 1918.

The 2nd Devons War Diary

JUNE 1918

1st June 1918 In the field. Transport at GOINGES. Day spent in cleaning up. Element of Brigade troops in line. Lt. and Quartermaster F.Gunn MC joined Battalion.

From 2/Lt. King's report:
Saturday 1st June "The Battalion moved up to the BOIS D'ECLISSE where it was joined by a party of about 30 Devons, which had been holding the position immediately south of CHAMBRECY since 29th May."

Although the 8th Division had been withdrawn from the fighting on 30th May, the Composite Battalion, which included a number of 2nd Devons, was still engaged.

2nd June 1918 Lt. D.M.Atkinson proceeded to line as OC Brigade Composite Company.
Orders were received late, to move early tomorrow to ETRECHY. Brigade troops still in line. Draft of 62 other ranks joined Battalion.

23rd Brigade Headquarters had relocated to the Bois de Boursault, in the forest of Enghien, where stragglers dribbling back from the front were gathering. After transport men, drivers, servants, stretcher-bearers, bandsmen were weeded out, the five hundred or so remaining combatant men of the 23rd Brigade were formed up and sent to join the approximately seven hundred and fifty other survivors of the 8th Division in the firing-line, which now ran through the Bois de Courton. This force was split into two composite battalions, the 1st-8th and 2nd-8th, commanded by Lt.Col.E.M.Beale of the Machine Gun Corps, and Lt.Col.D.Mitchell of the Durham Light Infantry (Pioneers), who were the 8th Division's only Lieutenant Colonels left.

Meanwhile, information was received that the Germans had continued to forge ahead and had reached the Marne, at Chateau Theirry which, if they managed to cross the river in force, would threaten the Allied concentration in the Bois de Boursault. As a result the composite battalions were ordered to move.

Extract from 2/Lt.King's report: "Sunday 2nd June to night of Tuesday/Wednesday 11th/12th June, the 1st-8th and 2nd-8th Divisional Composite Battalions held the BOIS D'ECLISSE and the BOIS DE COURTON until relieved.

3rd June 1918 Details and Transport moved to ETRECHY at 6am. Brigadier inspected the Transport. Brigade troops still in line.

4th June 1918 Brigade troops still in line. Nothing of interest. Fine day.

5th June 1918 Brigade troops still in line. Very hot. 8005 A/RSM F.Radford awarded Bar to DCM.

6th June 1918 Brigade troops still in line. Very hot.

Day by day it became evident that the front had become stationary and apart from two attacks on Montagne de Bligny on June 6th, which were repulsed by the Composite Battalions, no more enemy attacks were made. Their advance had ground to a halt.

7th June 1918 Brigade troops still in line. Training. Very hot.

8th June 1918 Brigade troops still in line. Training. Very hot.

9th June 1918 Brigade troops still in line. Training. Very hot. Battalion moved from ETRECHY to billets at BROUSSY starting at 8.45am and arriving at about mid-day.

10th June 1918 In the field. In billets at BROUSSY. Battalion training.

11th June 1918 In billets. Battalion training. Weather hot.

12th June 1918 In billets. Battalion training. 2/Lt. F.D.Clarke, 2/Lt. J.N.King and 90 other ranks rejoined from Divisional Composite Battalion. Orders received to move on morning of 14th.

13th June 1918 In billets. Men resting.

14th June 1918 Battalion paraded at 1.30pm and marched to FERE CHAMPENOIS entraining at 5am.
The 8th Division's attachment to the French 6th Army came to an end on this day.

15th June 1918 Battalion detrained at 1.30am HANGEST-SUR-SOMME and marched to ETREJUST arriving at 9.30am.

16th June1918 Battalion training.

17th June1918 Battalion training.
Major G.E.R.Prior MC joined and took over Command of the Battalion.

18th June 1918 Battalion training.
Battalion HQ, 'A' and 'B' Companies moved to AVESNE. 'C' and 'D' Companies remaining at ETREJUST.
Draft of 14 officers and 74 other ranks joined. Names of officers as follows:-
Lt. R.W.Bowen   Lt. P.A.Osborne   Lt. W.C.D.Taylor
Lt. P.J.Bretherton   Lt. W.H.Simmonds   2/Lt. L.G.Holloway
2/Lt. J.N.E.Crucefix   2/Lt. C.H.Townsend   2/Lt. S.Groves
2/Lt. A.G.Sandwell   2/Lt. J.H.Hicks   2/Lt. A.R.Williams

The 2nd Devons War Diary

2/Lt. R.J.E.Hall   2/Lt. J.D.James

19th June 1918   In the field. In billets. Battalion training. 52 other ranks rejoined from 2/8th Divisional Composite Battalion.
Also 2/Lt. C.H.Deeks.

20th June 1918   In billets. Battalion training. G.O.C. 8th Division inspected and addressed the Battalion. Draft of 100 other ranks joined as draft.

21st June 1918   In billets. Battalion training. Draft of 254 other ranks joined.

22nd June 1918   Battalion moved from AVESNE to CITERNE by march route, arriving at about 1pm.
The undermentioned were awarded Military Medals for gallantry and devotion to duty between the AISNE and the MARNE from 27th May to 2nd June 1918:-
 6947 Pte. R.Taylor   attached 23rd Infantry Brigade.
26135 Pte. G.Gregory attached 23rd Infantry Brigade.
45514 Sgt. A.G.Smith   8255 Pte. W.G.Manley   74004 Pte. A.Dunn

23rd June 1918   Battalion moved from CITERNE to MONTIERES CAMP by march route, starting at 8.30am and arriving at about 4pm. Dinners served on march.

24th June 1918   In camp. Battalion training and re-organising.

25th June 1918   In camp. Battalion training.

26th June 1918   In camp. Battalion training.
The following officers joined from England:-
Lt. R.L.Brokenshire   Lt. L.Elliott   Lt. W.H.Byrde
Lt. G.J.Martin   2/Lt. G.W.V.Ladds

27th June 1918   In camp at MONTIERES. In the field. Battalion training (Musketry on open range).
The undermentioned were awarded Parchment Certificates for gallantry and devotion to duty between the AISNE and the MARNE from 27th May to 2nd June 1918:- 11391 L/Cpl. F.G.Smart
15817 Cpl. G.H.Robbins attached 23rd T.M. Battery.

28th June 1918   Battalion training. Captain F.A.F.Bone joined from England and 39 other ranks as draft.
The undermentioned were awarded Military Medals for gallantry and devotion to duty between the AISNE and the MARNE from 27th May to 2nd June 1918:-
15527 Sgt. W.G.Taylor   74050 Pte. W.G.Hand
290807 Pte. T.Hulks (handwriting indistinct)
Lt. A.C.G.Roberts awarded the Military Cross, vide second supp

to London Gazette No.30716 of 31/5/18.

29th June 1918 Battalion training at MONTIERES. Brigade Commander addressed the Battalion at training area.
The following decorations were awarded to the undermentioned for gallantry and devotion to duty between the AISNE and the MARNE from 27th May to 2nd June 1918:-
The Military Cross   2/Lt. C.H.Repton
The Distinguished Conduct Medal   33172 Cpl. C.Greenslade MM

30th June 1918 Battalion in camp. Divine services.

The 2nd Devons War Diary

JULY 1918

1st July 1918 Battalion training as before.
2/Lt. L.Elliott admitted to hospital.

2nd July 1918 Battalion training.

3rd July 1918 Battalion training.
Lt. W.H.BYRDE took over duties of Signalling Officer as from 1/7/18.

4th July 1918 Battalion training.

5th July 1918 Battalion training - Company in attack.
Captain T.Bell joined for attachment.
2/Lt. D.M.Atkinson joined for duty and posted to 'B' Company.
Draft of 31 other ranks arrived.

6th July 1918 Battalion training - Range.
Captain E.W.Horne joined from 1st Devons and took over duties of Adjutant as from 6/7/18.

7th July 1918 Divine service.

8th July 1918 Battalion in attack towards TILLOY-FLORIVILLE - semi-open warfare. (Training).

9th July 1918 Battalion training.
2/Lt. F.D.Clarke awarded MC and 9328 A/RSM Bowden, 28796 Pte. E.Stockman, the DCM for gallantry and devotion to duty between the AISNE and MARNE.
2/Lt. A.E.Upperton proceeded to XXII Corps Signal School.

10th July 1918 Battalion training.
A.R.A. Competition for selection of best platoon in Companies.
Brigade Boxing Tournament held.
Captain T.Bell proceeded to join 1/7th Battalion D.L.I.

11th July 1918 Draft of 22 other ranks joined from base.
Training in the morning.
Battalion sports held in afternoon, in field between MONTIERES and MONCHAUX. Weather wet.

12th July 1918 Battalion engaged in Brigade attack towards GAMACHES (training).

13th July 1918 Battalion training.
A.R.A. Competition on Range. No.2 platoon 'A' Company winners and 15 platoon 'D' Company runners up.

14th July 1918 Divine service. Billeting party proceeded to BOURSEVILLE.
Lt. P.A.Osborn and 2/Lt. F.D.Clarke MC proceeded to PARIS PLAGE for rest camp.

15th July 1918 Battalion left MONTIERES and marched to BOURSEVILLE. In billets by 1.15pm.
Captain F.A.F.Bone left for U.K. on special leave.
2/Lt. T.N.King rejoined from PARIS PLAGE.
The following officers joined from base:-
2/Lieuts. A.T.Bush, F.D.Thronton, J.Sayes, G.M.Young, B.R.Brown, W.H.Millard, G.R.Taylor, S.J.Williams, W.Exton.

16th July 1918 Battalion training in new area.
2/Lt. E.A.Collier joined from base.
5231 Pte. E. Bond and 8213 Cpl. F.Aggett awarded the Meritorious Service Medal.
Lt. S.H.Cox reported as a Prisoner of War in GERMANY.
Divisional Commander addressed all officers of Brigade at HAUTEBUT.

17th July 1918 CO held kit inspection. Company training at BOURSEVILLE.

18th July 1918 2/Lt. C.A.Hellier and 17 other ranks joined from base.
Battalion carried out Field Training Scheme on Training Area.
Divisional Sports held at WOINCOURT.
2/Lt. C.A.Kendall joined from base.

19th July 1918 Warning order to move at 5.30pm.
Battalion in training.

20th July 1918 Battalion left billets at BOURSEVILLE at 12.50am and marched to EU and entrained for new area.
Arrived at SAVY at 4.30pm and marched to camp at MONT ST.ELOY, arriving at 8.15pm.

21st July 1918 Battalion relieved 1/7th Royal Scots in ACHEVILLE SECTOR. Battalion conveyed to Canadian Monument by motor lorries leaving at 3pm. Took up position, on a four Company frontage, of Right Battalion of Right section. Canadians on the right, 2nd Middlesex Regiment on the left, 2nd West Yorks Regiment in support.

22nd July 1918 Captain J.Wells MC joined the Battalion.

23rd July 1918 Battalion in line. Lt. P.A.Osborn and 2/Lt. F.D.Clarke MC rejoined from PARIS PLAGE.
2/Lt. J.Drummond joined the Battalion. 1 other rank joined.
Casualties - 1 other rank wounded.

The 2nd Devons War Diary

24th July 1918 Captain J.Wells MC took over Command of 'C' Company.
Same dispositions.
A patrol under command of 2/Lt. E.A.Collier engaged an enemy patrol a few yards outside MONTREAL TRENCH. Enemy made off leaving in our hands 1 UNTER-OFFIZIER killed. No casualties to our patrol.
Other casualties - 1 other rank wounded.

25th July 1918 2/Lt. A.E.Upperton granted leave to U.K. from 22/7/18 to 5/8/18. 2/Lt. J.Drummond posted to 'D' Company.
Casualties - 1 other rank wounded.
A.R.A. Competition. 'A' Company No.2 platoon, won 23rd Infantry Brigade competition.

26th July 1918 Same dispositions.

27th July 1918 Same dispositions. Sgt. McCormack proceeded to England for temporary Commission. Casualties - 2 other ranks wounded.

28th July 1918 Same dispositions.
2/Lt. W.Exton, 'D' Company, and 2 other ranks proceeded to VIII Corps School for a course of instruction in Anti-Gas.

29th July 1918 Same dispositions.

30th July 1918 Battalion still in line. Same dispositions.

31st July 1918 The Battalion was relieved by 2nd Middlesex Regiment, relief commencing at 3.30pm. Battalion now in support and holding the BROWN LINE. 'B' Company on R.E. Working Party with 185th Tunnelling Company, in camp near NEUVILLE ST. VAAST.
Lt.(A/Captain) U.B.Burke MC officially accepted as prisoner of war in Germany (W.O.List of 10/7/18).
Lt. A.E.Rutledge reported missing 27-31/5/18, officially accepted as prisoner of war in Germany (W.O.List of 2/7/18).

Martin Body

AUGUST 1918

1st August 1918   Battalion still in BROWN LINE.

2nd August 1918   Same dispositions. Enemy aeroplane brought down behind our lines. Our Lewis gunners took active part in the operation and claim to have brought it down.
1,000 drums of gas discharged into MERICOURT from Brigade front.

3rd August 1918   Lt. P.A.Osborne proceeded to Base and is struck off strength of Battalion.
No.2 Platoon 'A' Company won Divisional A.R.A. competition.

4th August 1918   Nine other ranks joined Battalion and taken on strength.

5th August 1918   Battalion relieved by 2nd Battalion Rifle Brigade. Relief commencing at 6.30pm. Battalion less 'B' Company proceeded to Hills Camp in NEUVILLE ST. VAAST in huts. 'B' Company proceeded to Cinema Camp.Cpl. G.Budd awarded DCM on 24/3/18.

6th August 1918   2/Lt. G.E.Baxter joined Battalion.

7th August 1918   Lecture by Divisional Gas Officer in Y.M.C.A. Hut to Battalion.2/Lt. G.E.Baxter taken on strength and posted to 'C' Company.
Extract from appointments 4/8/18, "Lt. E.W.Horne to be Acting Major."

8th August 1918   HQ Company and Transport proceeded to BERTHONVAL Farm for baths during the course of the day.

9th August 1918   Captain R.J.Matthews having been taken on strength of L.T.M. Battery is struck off strength of Battalion.

10th August 1918   A football match was played against the 7th D.L.I. in the afternoon. Result – Devons 4 goals – D.L.I. 1 goal.

11th August 1918   Battalion training.

12th August 1918   Concert given in the Y.M.C.A. by the Battalion concert party at 6pm.

13th August 1918   Training carried on at NEUVILLE ST VAAST.

14th August 1918   Battalion proceeded to the trenches in a new sector at WILLERVAL and relieved the 5th Royal Scots Fusiliers, 52nd Division. Battalion disposed in depth on a one company front.

The 2nd Devons War Diary

15th August 1918 Holding the line. Sector very quiet.

16th August 1918 Same dispositions.

17th August 1918 Dispositions of Battalion changed. 'A' Company still in BROWN LINE. Remainder on a 3 company front. Companies disposed in depth. Front extended North to WILLERVAL ROAD. Casualties 1 other rank wounded.
Captain W.H.Simmonds proceeded to First Army Infantry School on course of instruction. Major E.W.Horne proceeded on leave to U.K.

18th August 1918 A patrol under 2/Lt. G.N.Kendall consisting of 1 platoon succeeded in passing enemy Observation line and entering ARLEUX through which it proceeded. No enemy were encountered. Casualties nil.
2/Lt. L.D.Heppenstall proceeded on Gas Course to VIII Corps School.

19th August 1918 Projector and gas born attack on enemy from our sector.
2nd Middlesex Regiment relieved by 2nd West Yorks Regiment on our left.
2/Lt. A.T.Bush posted to 23rd T.M. Battery and struck off strength.
Captain E.H.Saville joined Battalion and took over command of 'B' Company.

20th August 1918 Another patrol under 2/Lt. B.R.Brown entered ARLEUX without encountering enemy.
New post taped in rear of BLACK LINE.

21st August 1918 Patrol was sent out at 8pm under 2/Lt. A.R.Williams. Entered ARLEUX and successfully engaged the enemy, the effects of 2 dead Germans being brought back and identification (69th Res. Inf. Regiment) obtained. Patrol Commander congratulated by G.O.C.
A.R.A. competition again won by No.2 Platoon, 'A' Company –v– 2nd Scottish Rifles. (Corps competition).
2/Lt. E.A.Collier proceeded to Army Musketry Camp, MATRINGHEM.

22nd August 1918 3am. Heavy gas shelling in neighbourhood of BLUE LINE. 2/Lt. C.A.Hellier and 15 other ranks gassed.
Corps Commander and Divisional General visited the line.
Captain F.J.Bretherton proceeded on a Bye-products course.
2/Lt. A.E.Upperton rejoined from XXII Corps School.
Casualties – 2 other ranks wounded.

23rd August 1918 Construction of 2 new posts outside Observation line commenced.

24th August 1918 Battalion relieved by 2nd Middlesex Regiment and moved into Hills Camp, NEUVILLE ST VAAST.
Casualties - 2 other ranks wounded.

25th August 1918 2/Lt. A.E.Upperton granted leave to U.K. from 22/7/18 to 5/8/18. 2/Lt. J.Drummond posted to 'D' Company.
Casualties - 1 other rank wounded.
A.R.A. Competition. 'A' Company No.2 platoon, won 23rd Infantry Brigade competition.

26th August 1918 Camp inspected by Corps Commander (VIII Corps). Battalion at half hours notice to proceed to trenches owing to operations re advancing front line.

27th August 1918 Officers football match -v- D.L.I. Result 2nd Devons 11 - D.L.I. nil.
24th Division Concert Party at Y.M.C.A.
Captain F.A.F.Bone pronounced B 11 and struck off strength of Battalion.

28th August 1918 Battalion medically inspected.
2/Lt. W.Exton and 36 other ranks proceeded to Army Musketry Camp, HEZECQYES.
Battalion at 1 hours notice to move. Lt. G.T.Martin MC to Brigade (temporarily) as Brigade Intelligence Officer.
23rd Infantry Brigade G.28/120.
23rd Brigade Northern Boundary:- T.30.d.6.9. - T.30.c.75.75 - T.29.D.1.5. thence along WESTERN ROAD to T.27.c.0.0. - T.26.d.2.0. - B.1.d.6.9. - A.12.a.8.5. - thence westwards.
23rd Brigade Southern Boundary. C.7.a.0.4. - B.12.a.0.4. - along MACHINE GUN TRENCH (inclusive to Left Brigade) to B.11.a.5.3. - B.10.a.6.3. - B.10.a.0.0. - along TIRED ALLEY (inclusive to Left Brigade).
The main line of resistance of the 23rd Infantry Brigade is the old BLACK LINE.
The main line of resistance of the 24rd Infantry Brigade on the right is BON SUPPORT.
Following information obtained from prisoners:- Enemy main line of resistance is along FRESNOY Trench with 3 Companies in line and 1 Company in support in FLANGE and UNIFORM TRENCH.
Battalion HQ U.19.b.4.8. Battalion were expecting relief either on the night 26th/27th or 27th/28th.
Sentry group posted in TORTOISE Trench.

29th August 1918 3 Platoon of 'A' Company required in line tonight for carrying Trench Mortars. To remain in BROWN LINE after work pending further orders.

30th August 1918 Relieving 2nd West Yorks Regiment in left sub-sector of Brigade Front on September 1st.
1 Platoon of 'A' Company returning tonight from carrying party.

The 2nd Devons War Diary

Instructions received from Brigade to leave "Battle Surplus" out of line.
Remaining 2 platoons of 'A' Company returned from line tonight.
11 other ranks more or less gassed last night.
Lt.Col. G.E.R.Prior MC and Captain R.L.Brokenshire visited West Yorks in line this afternoon.
2/Lt. R.H.Hobern and 2/Lt. F.R.Folkes joined Battalion and posted temporarily to 'D' Company.

31st August 1918 Extract from List No.102 "Appointments, Commissions" Lt. R.W.B??? 5/Gloucester Regiment to be Acting Captain whilst employed as Acting Adjutant, with pay and allowances of Lt.
The undermentioned to be acting Captains whilst commanding Companies:-
Lt. R.L.Brokenshire (S.R.) 29/6/18.
Lt. W.H.Simmonds 4th Gloucester Regiment 19/6/18.
Operation Orders for relief of 2nd West Yorks Regiment issued tonight.
2/Lt. W.H.Millard rejoined from a Course of Instruction at VIII Corps School.

Martin Body

SEPTEMBER 1918

1st September 1918 Battalion relieved 2nd West Yorks Regiment in left sector. Relief complete at about 7.15pm.
'A' Company in OAK VALLEY forming outposts in newly captured trench. 'B' Company in ARLEUX also newly captured. Other Companies in BLACK Line.
Enemy twice attempted to bomb 'A' Company post in OAK VALLEY but were driven off with bombs on both occasions. Groans heard indicating enemy casualties.
Casualties nil. 2/Lt. H.Parker joined Battalion and posted to 'C' Company.

2nd September 1918 2nd Battalion Devonshire granted the French Distinction "CITATION" in recognition of the great stand on the MARNE, May 1918. The first Infantry Regiment in the British Army to be granted this very rare distinction.
Posts of 'A' Company bombed, 3 men being wounded, enemy driven off with bombs.
Patrol under 2/Lt. J.Drummond engaged enemy patrol. Our casualties 2 wounded. Enemy reported to leave 3 dead which they fetched in later, seen by man who became entangled in wire, returning later.
Casualties 5 wounded.
CROIX de GUERRE conferred on Battalion by the French.

3rd September 1918 Holding ARLEUX LOOP. Some slight changes in dispositions of posts, 'A' Company pushing 2 posts out into ARLEUX village. Casualties 50 other ranks (49 gassed, 1 wounded)
2/Lt. W.Exton, 'D' Company, admitted to 51 C.C.S. from 1st Army Musketry Camp.

4th September 1918 Holding the line. Work on trenches. Casualties 4 other ranks wounded. Major E.W.Horne rejoined from leave to U.K.

5th September 1918 Holding the line, work on trenches etc. Casualties nil.
The following awarded Parchment Certificates by Divisional Commander for gallantry and devotion to duty in the field:-
2/Lt. A.R.Williams, 32059 Pte. D.Fullerton, 32055 Pte. C.Caines, of 'B' Company.

6th September 1918 Holding the line, work on trenches etc. 3 other ranks gassed.

7th September 1918 Same dispositions. 1 other rank wounded.

8th September 1918 Enemy patrol bombed 'C' Company post wounding 2 other ranks, driven off with Lewis Gun.

The 2nd Devons War Diary

9th September 1918 Holding the line. Weather wet and trenches very muddy.

10th September 1918 Holding the line. Very wet and muddy.

11th September 1918 Lt. W.L.Clegg, reported missing 27/5/18, officially accepted as Prisoner of War.
14864 Pte. G.Rockley reported missing 25/3/18 escaped from territory occupied by enemy, arrived in U.K. 22/8/18.

12th September 1918 Wet and muddy. Holding the line.

13th September 1918 Wet and muddy. Holding the line. 2/Lt. G.F.Thomas joined Battalion and posted to 'A' Company.

14th September 1918 Same dispositions. 2/Lt. A.R.Williams rejoined from leave in France.

15th September 1918 Holding the line. Normal.

16th September 1918 Holding the line. Normal day.

17th September 1918 Battalion relieved in the trenches by 2nd Middlesex Regiment and proceeded to HILLS CAMP, NEUVILLE ST VAAST.

18th September 1918 Day spent in cleaning up and baths. Divisional Guard found by Battalion in honour of "CITATION". Mess meeting in afternoon. New "War Bond" lottery started.

19th September 1918 Battalion proceeded for the day to VILLERS AU BOIS to take part in Tank demonstration. No tanks turned up so Battalion did an attack.

20th September 1918 Visited by the Brigadier General about noon who lunched in the mess. Platoon football in the afternoon.

21st September 1918 Resting at NEUVILLE ST VAAST. Inter platoon football. Show in evening at Y.M.C.A. by "The Dumplings".

22nd September 1918 Training. Inter platoon football.

23rd September 1918 Battalion proceeded to MONT ST. ELOY where it was inspected by the Divisional Commander. Medals presented. Inter platoon football.

24th September 1918 Resting Hills Camp. Lt. (A/Captain) W.H.Radcliffe joined Battalion for duty and took over 2nd in Command 'B' Company.

25th September 1918 Final - Platoon football competition. No.6 Platoon -v- Signallers and Runners. Result a draw. Match to be played again.
Funeral of Lt.Col. Lowry 2nd West Yorks Regiment. Officers of Battalion attended.

26th September 1918 Final Platoon football - Winners, Signallers and Runners, score 1 - 0.
Battalion relieved 2nd West Yorks Regiment in Left Sector.
The following is an extract from "Special Order of the Day", published on 26th September 1918.

"The following citation which appeared in the Orders of the Day, No.371 of the 5th French Army, on August 20th 1918, on behalf of 2nd Battalion Devonshire Regiment, is published for the information of all ranks:-
'On the 27th May 1918, at a time when the British Trenches were subjected to fierce attacks, the 2nd Battalion the Devonshire Regiment repelled successive enemy assaults with gallantry and determination and maintained an unbroken front till a late hour. The staunchness of this Battalion permitted defences South of A. to be organised and their occupation by reinforcements to be completed.
Inspired by the sangfroid of their gallant Commander, in the face of an intense bombardment, the few survivors of the Battalion, though isolated and without hope of assistance, held on to the trenches north of the river and fought to the last with an unhesitating obedience to orders. Thus the whole Battalion - Colonel, 28 Officers, and 552 Non-commissioned Officers and men - responded with one accord and offered their lives in ungrudging sacrifice to the scared cause of the Allies'".

Night of 26/27th. Battalion attacked enemy's Outpost system in conjunction with 2nd Middlesex Regiment on the Right and 7th D.C.L.I. (20th Division) on the Left. We captured BRITANNIA and BRANDY trenches on both sides of the ARLEUX-FRESNOY Road, killing large numbers of the enemy and holding our gains. Full report attached.
Casualties 15 killed and 15 wounded, including HQ Signallers and Runners who were shelled moving up to the position - also includes 1 Officer wounded, 2/Lt. G.F.Thomas, 'A' Company.

OPERATIONS.

On the night of the 26th/27th September 1918 the Battalion carried out a successful attack in conjunction with the 2nd Battalion MIDDLESEX REGIMENT and the 7th Duke of Cornwall's Light Infantry.
The objectives for this Battalion were BRITTANIA and BRANDY Trenches east of ARLEUX-EN-GOHILLE (North East of ARRAS).
'A', 'D', and 2 Platoons of 'C' Company were the assaulting troops advancing in two waves to the assault. The Barrage was

provided by Field Guns, Howitzers and Machine Guns and was excellent. ZERO hour was at midnight and within ¾ of an hour of this time the objectives had been taken all along the line. Seven prisoners were taken and a number of the enemy were found dead in the captured trenches. Two Light Machine guns and One Automatic Pistol of a new type were also captured together with numerous documents. Prisoners belonged to the 25th and 69th R.I.R. (Reserve Infantry Regiment)

Our casualties during the operation were 9 killed and 1 officer and 11 other ranks wounded.

Two Sections of 'A' Company advanced beyond the objective and eventually reached FRESNOY PARK, they were forced to return owing to our own barrage and captured three prisoners (including the above).

The operation was entirely successful and the following wire was received from General Headquarters:- 'Congratulations to Battalion on successful operations'.

On the afternoon of the 27th September 1918 a patrol of six other ranks under 2/Lt. W.H.MILLARD was sent to ascertain whether the enemy held the FRESNOY LINE as it was reported that the enemy had evacuated this trench. This patrol did exceedingly good work and returned with 2 prisoners which they captured in daylight from the enemy lines.

27th September 1918 Battalion consolidated new positions – congratulated by GHQ on successful show. Pushed out patrols – One under command of 2/Lt. W.H.Millard bringing in 2 prisoners. This officer was congratulated by the Brigade Commander.

Despite the low key War Diary entry for 27th September, 16 men and an officer, Lt. Charles Wilfred Eales, are recorded as having been killed in action. The Operations Report for the day states that 9 men and 1 officer were killed.

28th September 1918 Battalion holding whole of Brigade Outpost line. Enemy counter-attacked at 2am but was repulsed. Casualties 2/Lt. A.R.Collier wounded. 1 other rank killed, 3 other ranks wounded.

29th September 1918 Battalion holding Brigade Outpost Line. Much rain has fallen within the last two days and line in consequence is in a bad condition. Casualties nil.

30th September 1918 Battalion still holding Outpost Line – day very quiet – strong northerly wind but no rain – Line still very wet and dirty.

Martin Body

OCTOBER 1918

1st October 1918 Battalion holding Outpost Line.

2nd October 1918 Battalion relieved by D.C.L.I. and went out to STIRLING CAMP, east of ST. LAURENT BLANGY near ARRAS. 'C' and 'D' Companies in reserve forward near ATHIES.

3rd October 1918 Battalion at STIRLING CAMP.

4th October 1918 STIRLING CAMP. 'A' and 'B' Companies relieved 'C' and 'D' Companies at ATHIES.

5th October 1918 At STIRLING CAMP.

6th October 1918 Battalion relieved 6th Gordon Highlanders, 51st Division, in the line in front of FAMPOUX. Battalion to attack FRESNES-ROUVROY Line in support to 2nd Middlesex Regiment and 2nd West Yorks Regiment tomorrow morning. 'B' and 'C' Companies to be under orders of above Battalions.
Zero hour fixed for dawn, 5am, morning of 11th. 8 platoon 'B' Company to form Right Defensive Flank at BIACHES ST. VAAST.

7th October 1918 At 5am this morning 2nd West Yorks and 2nd Middlesex Regiment supported by 'C' and 'D' Companies 2nd Devons attacked the FRESNES-ROUVROY Line on a 1000 yard front and succeeded in taking all objectives. 1 platoon 'B' Company under 2/Lt. J.Sayes successfully established a defensive post on the right flank of the Right Battalion beyond the Electric Power Station, BIACHE ST. VAAST taking several prisoners and a M.G. About 80 prisoners were taken by the Brigade.
In the evening the new line of the 2nd West Yorks Regiment was taken by the 2nd Devons.

8th October 1918 Late last night and early this morning our patrols cleared the village of FRESNES-LEZ-MONTAUBAN and GLOUCESTER WOOD taking a few prisoners and establishing posts to the east.

9th October 1918 Active Patrolling and advancing posts in front.
A shell burst outside 'C' Company HQ killing 2/Lt. G.E.Baxter and 2 other ranks, and wounding 2/Lt. G.M.Young and several other ranks.

10th October 1918 'C' and 'D' Companies relieved in the front line by 'A' and 'B' Companies. Post pushed out further and contact with enemy maintained. Patrol Encounters etc.

The 2nd Devons War Diary

11th October 1918 At dawn (5.15am) this morning the 2nd Devons and 2nd Middlesex Regiment attacked QUEANT-DROCOURT LINE (WOTAN LINE) just N. of VITRY-EN-ARTOIS on a front of 1000 yards. No resistance on the part of the enemy who had retired an hour or so previously. A few prisoners were captured and all objectives taken. About 20 casualties from our own barrage.
2nd West Yorks Regiment pushed on forward and established posts E. of QUEANT-DROCOURT Line.
2/Lt. Folkes and 2/Lt. Williams wounded.

12th October 1918 In support holding QUEANT-DROCOURT Line. Excellent dug-out accommodation.
Mines and booby-traps successfully removed.

13th October 1918 Battalion took over outpost line from 2nd West Yorks Regiment extending from CORBEHEM to LA BRAVELLE FARM on a front of 5000 yards. Enemy holding E. bank of deviation of the SCARPE with M.G. posts on W. bank.
Our positions very heavily shelled and a lot of accurate M.G. fire. Ground around our left post flooded by enemy opening canal sluice and post compelled to withdraw about 600 yards. Our line runs roughly 2000 yards W. of DOUAI.

14th October 1918 Relieved from outpost line by 2nd Battalion Middlesex Regiment and returned to support in QUEANT-DROCOURT Line.
Relief completed at about 11 tonight.

15th October 1918 Cleaning up and resting in QUEANT-DROCOURT Line.
News of proposed armistice has come through but very little details.

16th October 1918 Resting in QUEANT-DROCOURT Line. Raining and ground muddy.

17th October 1918 'A' Company practised crossing the SCARPE in pontoon boats made by the Field Company.
The undermentioned officers joined the Battalion for duty:-
2/Lt. A.M.Harvey, 2/Lt. D.J.Tuckett, 2/Lt. A.Willis, Lt. R.C.D.Napier, Lt. B.A.Schooling, 2/Lt. S.T.Mears.

18th October 1918 Battalion working on roads in vicinity of billeting area and towards QUIERRY-LA-MOTTE.

19th October 1918 Work carried out on roads. 2/Lt. R.R.Folkes embarked for England.

20th October 1918 Battalion marched to village of RACHES via DOUAI. Good billets in village. A few civilians returned having been released by the Boche who had deported them several days before. Battalion HQ in CHATEAU PLAISANT.

21st October 1918 Cleaning up and working parties on roads. All Companies working 6 hours.
Village structurally intact but a great deal of damage to furniture was done by the Huns. All windows and most of the ornaments were broken and village looted from end to end.

22nd October 1918 All Companies working 6 hours on roads towards MONTREUIL and FLINES. Many pianos found in the village added to the amusement of the men. Billets cleaned up and made very comfortable.

23rd October 1918 The Battalion marched to MARCHIENNES and occupied billets in the town. Many civilians living in the town and considerably less damage done by the Hun. News received that during their retirement the Huns deposited as many civilians as the town would hold in ST. AMAND and then proceeded to heavily shell the place.

24th October 1918 Battalion parade in the morning. Football indulged in during the afternoon.
2/Lt. A.R.Williams proceeded on leave to the U.K.

25th October 1918 One hours notice at 1400 hours to move to ST.AMAND.
Battalion moved at 1310 hours. Whole Battalion in large hospital. Town not badly damaged. No civilians in town.

26th October 1918 Battalion relieved the 2nd Northamptonshire Regiment in ODENEZ village and posts touching River Escaut. Captain J.Wells MC assumed duties of 2nd in Command of 1st Battalion Sherwood Foresters.

27th October 1918 'A', 'C' and 'D' Companies, with 'B' Company in support, attempted to cross RIVER ESCAUT and Canal JARD with object to establish posts to enable the success to be exploited.
'A' Company on right flank effected a crossing by 0230 over the R.ESCAUT, one platoon and one M.G. section establishing post between River and Canal.
'D' Company, central Company, were able to get 1 officer and 2 other ranks across the river but remainder of Company were met with heavy shelling and M.G. fire. The Brigadier ordered their withdrawal. 2/Lt. W.Exton and 2 other ranks got back by swimming River.
'C' Company, left Company, effected a crossing but were ordered to withdraw.
Casualties 28 other ranks.

28th October 1918 'A' Company's platoon that had effected a crossing of the river and the M.G. section, were captured by the enemy at 1100 hours. L/Cpl. Marchment and 2 men escaped. The 2 men were wounded. They reported that 2/Lt. Harvey and the

The 2nd Devons War Diary

remainder had been captured, all being wounded except 2/Lt. Harvey and 1 other rank.
Casualties 1 officer and 18 other ranks.
Very little shelling.
1 man of 'A' Company killed on patrol.
Lt.Col. G.E.R.Prior MC rejoined Battalion from French leave.
Lt. G.T.Martin MC admitted to Casualty Clearing Station.

At about 1100, an enemy counter-attack delivered from two sides, overwhelmed the post and captured nearly the whole platoon of 'A' Company who had crossed the river, only three men escaping at the time, although two days later four machine-gunners managed to return to our lines. As a result, 'C' Company's post also had to be withdrawn. The battalion's casualties in this unfortunate episode came to nearly fifty.

29th October 1918   Very quiet all night.

30th October 1918   Four Machine Gunners supposed captured on the 28th effected a safe crossing to our lines.
The Corps, Divisional and Brigade Generals visited the Battalion HQ.
Battalion HQ moved into village of ODENEZ.
River L'Escaut bridged by R.E.s at 2100 hours but it gave way.
'A', 'B' and 'D' Companies effected a crossing by Jerusalem Rafts - no casualties in crossing.
R.E.s built a Jerusalem Pontoon Bridge.
'B' Company were heavily shelled at 2330 hours.

<u>Diary of operations during the forcing of the passage of the RIVER L'ESCAUT Night of 30/31st October 1918</u>

1820 hours.   Battalion HQ opened at Q4d90.60.
1935 hours.   Jerusalem Pontoons arrived. 'C' Company left to take up position as covering party.
Intermittent M.G. Fire.
2000 hours.   Two first platoons ('A' and 'D' Companies) of Bridgehead crossing by pontoon. Message received that R.E. are already throwing Bridge across.
2010 hours.   Message received from 'B' Company that they are moving to Assembly position.
2020 hours.   1 bridge in position. 'A' and 'D' Companies instructed to cross immediately.
2045 hours.   'B' Company ordered to move up to garden wall ready to cross on 'D' Company reaching objective.
2115 hours.   Message received that all 'C' Company are in position on Tow Path. Crossing by Bridge proceeding very slowly as end has collapsed. More Jerusalems arriving.
2315 hours.   14 more Jerusalems arrived. 3 platoons across, remainder crossing by pontoons now fairly quickly.
2320 hours.   Bosche patrol reported approaching copse about Q.5.a.90.50. to Q.5.a.&C.
2350 hours.   Crossing proceeding with very little opposition.

Martin Body

Message received from 23rd Infantry Brigade to effect the crossing of the CANAL DU JARD tonight by any means possible, making Bridgehead east of CANAL when 2nd West Yorks will push through us. 2nd Middlesex at one hours notice to move.

31/10/18

0030 hours. 'B' Company commencing crossing of River. 'A' and 'D' Companies across and Bridgehead established.

0100 hours. Fairly heavy shelling just N.E. of River Bank and in village. Retaliation called for. 3 Platoons of 'B' Company across.

0150 hours. R.E. Officer wounded in hand. 1 prisoner (wounded) captured by 'A' Company belonging to 451 Regiment states 20 Bosche this side of CANAL, remainder have gone back distance of 2 and a half miles. Appears unreliable.

0230 hours. Message received from 'A' Company that Bosche are massing on right for counter attack. Information confirmed by B.I.O. (Battalion Intelligence Officer?). 'A' Company have had several casualties. 'C' Company ordered to send up platoon to 'A' Company. 'D' Company to hold their reserve platoon in readiness to reinforce.

0310 hours. 2 M.G. ordered to report to 'A' Company.

0330 hours. 'B' Company report to Company HQ at Fosse Amoury and no possible crossing of CANAL DU JARD. M.G. fire from opposite side of CANAL, direction of K.34.b.1.3.

0415 hours. Bridge reported now fully repaired and dry crossing possible. Considerable gas shelling about FOSSE AMOURY.

0650 hours. Dispositions are as follows:- 'A' Company HQ Q5e40.90 with two weak platoons near wood and two platoons pushed forward to Q5a80.50 and Q5b2.0. with orders to push forward to PONT JOLLY.

'D' Company:- 1 Platoon at Q5.a.??.?? with Company HQ at Q.4.b.9.6. Remaining Platoons around Island at D.4.b.8.6.

'B' Company HQ at K.34.d.5.0. 4 Platoons around debris. Orders given to push 1 platoon to K.34.8.8. towards bridge and 1 platoon to work N. along Canal.

0605 hours. Message from 'D' Company. 4 other ranks wounded.

0815 hours. GOC Brigade congratulated Battalion on successful operation last night.

0830 hours. Canadians reported Bosche massing for counter attack at Q.5.b.6.7. and on road running N.E. from there. Artillery and Brigade informed. 2nd West Yorks relieving us tonight. Casualties 12 other ranks wounded (through R.A.F.) 1 killed. Probably incomplete.

0850 hours. Heavy shelling of Battalion HQ. S.O.S. sent up from Right Front. Brigade and Artillery informed.

0910 hours. Cpl. Pope and 2 men reported at Battalion HQ. 'A' Company less about 5 men and Captain Brokenshire, back across the river. Casualties heavy. Under pressure from exceedingly heavy barrage, 'A' Company withdrew across the river, leaving Captain Brokenshire, Lt. Napier and 4 men behind who held on to bank with 6 Lewis Guns.

1145 hours. 1 platoon of 'C' Company to reinforce Captain

Brokenshire on bank. Lt. Napier carried wounded man on his back across the bridge, under the bombardment.
'A' Company's casualties caused chiefly in street adjacent to Battalion HQ.
1100 hours. Report through from OC 'B' Company on FOSSE ARMOURY. Runner swam river and arrived minus his boots, coats etc. OC Company reports 2/Lt. Sayes killed and casualties very heavy. Out of touch with 'D' Company and unable to evacuate wounded. Previous runner drowned in attempt to get message through. Reply sent to "hold on", relief being sent tonight.
1510 hours. Fairly frequent heavy bursts of shellfire. Total casualties estimated about 80. O.O. 297 (**operation order?**) received for relief tonight.
1640 hours. Orders received to withdraw posts immediately and proceed to billets. Situation on flanks responsible.
1730 hours. Report received from Captain Taylor that bridge has been broken. More pontoons due from R.E. Crossing progressing slowly.
1830 hours. 'A' and 'C' Companies clear.
1915 hours. 'B' Company all clear and all wounded across.
1930 hours. 490th Company R.E. arrived with more Jerusalems.
1950 hours. Last of 'D' Company across and Brigade wired to this effect.

The man mentioned in the 11.00 entry above as, "Runner swam river and arrived minus his boots, coats etc."was 32273 Pte. G.Hawley, who was awarded the DCM for his efforts.

The attack of the night of 30th-31st October was the last time that the 2nd Devons were to strike against the enemy in the Great War. Unfortunately, because the attempt had been brought forward two days to occupy the German artillery while another Division advanced on Valenciennes, it left insufficient preparation time for the immediate objective to be attained. This was no fault of the officers and men of the 2nd Devons, whose courage and skill was, as usual, beyond reproach. In its other aims the operation succeeded in as much as the German artillery was prevented from being moved to assist with the defence of Valenciennes, which duly fell to the British.

Although men of the 2nd Devons would continue to die of wounds and sickness, this was the last day in the Great War that any would be recorded as 'Killed in Action'. Sadly, 1 officer and 12 men of the battalion were killed in action on that night, so heartbreakingly close to the end of the war. One of those unfortunate men was 3/6834 Lance-Corporal George Pearson, from Edmonton, Middlesex, who had served in France with the 2nd Devons since 3rd December 1914. Another was 32186 Corporal Robert Whitlock, MM, from Woodstock, Oxfordshire, who joined the BEF on 24th July 1915, originally as 14892 of the Somerset Light Infantry.

31st October 1918 See diary of operations attached. (Above)

Martin Body

NOVEMBER 1918

1st November 1918 Battalion took billets in ST.AMAND. Cleaning up billets during the day. At 1700 hours shelling near 'A' Company's billets. No casualties. CSM J.Radford appointed Acting RSM.

2nd November 1918 Parades by Companies. Wet day. Concert in the evening. ST.AMAND shelled at 1600 hours.
Captain P.J.Bretherton awarded the MC.
10027 Cpl. C.Spurway awarded the DCM.
69282 Cpl. H.May MM awarded bar to MM.
The undermentioned were awarded the Military Medal:-
8859 Sgt. J.Lorey   9273 Pte. E.Coles   69327 Pte. J.Watkins
74093 Pte. A.Powell   49009 Pte. H.Cooper   32121 Pte. T.Midlane

3rd November 1918 Battalion parade for Church Service at 1000 hours. Fine day.
ST.AMAND shelled at 1730 hours. Captain and Adjutant R.W.Bowen granted leave to U.K. 5-19/11/18.

4th November 1918 Battalion moved at 1300 hours to WARLAING. Fine day. Men in good billets.

5th November 1918 Very wet day, seriously hampered training. 2/Lt. F.D.Clarke MC rejoined from First Army School.

6th November 1918 Very wet day. Interfered with training.

7th November 1918 Very wet day. 2/Lt. S.J.Williams embarked for U.K. wounded.
Lt.W.H.Simmonds struck off and taken on establishment of 1st Army School.

8th November 1918 Very wet day. Battalion Parade - Organisation.
Divisional Commander's Inspection postponed.

9th November 1918 Battalion moved from WARLAING to ESCAUPONT. Good billets. No civilians in the town. Town not badly damaged. 2/Lt. F.D.Clarke MC proceeded on leave to U.K. Captain and Adjutant R.W.Bowen granted 2 days extension of leave.

10th November 1918 Fine day. Church Service at 1100 hours. Battalion moved at 1400 to QUIVERCHAIN.

11th November 1918 Battalion moved at 0700 hours to TERTRE. News of the armistice received by Battalion whilst on march. Civilians shewed great pleasure on entry of Battalion. TERTRE full of troops. Lt. R.H.Cummings joined Battalion and posted to 'D' Company.

The 2nd Devons War Diary

The 2nd Devons reached Tertre on the morning of the 11th November, and were moving forward to support the other battalions of the 23rd Brigade, who were within 1,000 yards of the Mons-Jurbise road, when 1100 struck and the Armistice came into force, upon which the brigade was detailed to occupy the Ghlin-Maisieres area. The fighting war was over.

12th November 1918 Battalion moved to GHLIN. Civil population shewed great enthusiasm at Battalion entry. Good billets.

13th November 1918 Battalion Concert Party "DUMPLINGS" gave a performance. Major E.W.Horne granted local leave from 13 to 24/11/18.

14th November 1918 Battalion parades.

15th November 1918 Battalion lined the streets of MONS for the formal entry of General Horne and were the first Infantry Regiment to march past. Battalion congratulated by Divisional Commander on its smart turn-out.

16th November 1918 Battalion moved in buses from GHLIN to RUMES near TOURNAI. Billets not good.

17th November 1918 Divine Services. 2/Lt. W.Exton proceeded to 23rd Infantry Brigade as Education Officer.
Lt. G.L.Hiley joined the Battalion and posted to 'C' Company.
Captain E.H.Saville MC awarded Parchment Certificate for Devotion to Duty in FRESNES-ROUVROY and QUENT-DROCOURT attack.

18th November 1918 Battalion moved to LA GLANERIE. Billets not good.
2/Lieuts. A.G.Sandwell and G.N.Kendall rejoined from course.

19th November 1918 Lt. G.T.Martin MC struck off strength from 5th inst.
2/Lt. J.D.Harcombe joined Battalion and posted to 'B' Company.
2/Lt. C.H.Townsend proceeded on leave to U.K.

20th November 1918 Company parades. Reading and writing room opened for Battalion. "DUMPLINGS" gave a performance.
2/Lt. A.P.Tucker joined Battalion and posted to 'B' Company.

21st November 1918 Captain P.J.Bretherton MC rejoined from leave to U.K.

22nd November 1918 2/Lt. J.D.Harcombe admitted to hospital.

23rd November 1918 2/Lt. R.J.Cock joined Battalion and posted to 'B' Company. Captain and Adjutant R.W.Bowen rejoined from leave to U.K.

Martin Body

24th November 1918 Major E.W.Horne rejoined from leave in France.

25th November 1918 Battalion moved from billets in LA GLANERIE to Infantry Barracks, TOURNAI.

26th November 1918 Battalion under Major E.W.Horne practised Battalion parade with a view to Brigade parade.
Lt.Col. G.E.R.Prior MC rejoined from 23rd Brigade HQ.

27th November 1918 Battalion marched to TAIGNTINIES for Brigade parade under Brigadier General G.W.St.G.Grogan VC, CMG, DSO.

28th November 1918 Battalion parades. 2/Lt. C.Luffman proceeded for duty as Area Commandant, ATH.

29th November 1918 Battalion parades.

30th November 1918 2/Lt. F.D.Clarke MC rejoined from leave to U.K.

The 2nd Devons War Diary

DECEMBER 1918

1st December 1918   Divine Services.

2nd December 1918   Battalion parades. A concert was given by the Battalion Concert Party "The Dumplings" in the Y.M.C.A. 2/Lt. A.R.Williams struck off strength whilst on leave (Medical Board).

3rd December 1918   Battalion parades. A repatriated prisoner taken by the enemy near CONDE on the 28th October, visited the Battalion on his return from LIEGE.

4th December 1918   Battalion parades.

5th December 1918   Great Ceremonial Parade on CHAMP DE MANOEUVRES, when the CROIX DE GUERRE was presented to the Battalion by the French General de Division De La Guiche.

6th December 1918   Battalion parades.

7th December 1918   H.M. The King accompanied by the Prince of Wales and Prince Albert visited TOURNAI. The Battalion massed in the BOULEVARD, N. of the CHAMP DE MANOEUVRES.

8th December 1918   Divine Service in PALACE OF JUSTICE. Lt. D.M.Atkinson rejoined from leave at PARIS PLAGE. 2/Lt. C.H.Townsend rejoined from leave to U.K.

9th December 1918   Battalion parades. Battalion played the 24th Field Ambulance at Rugby and were beaten by 15 points to 8. 2/Lieuts. D.E.Baker and A.G.Sandwell granted leave to U.K.

10th December 1918   Battalion parades. Concert given by the "Dumplings".

11th December 1918   Battalion parades. Compulsory Education started by authorities. Wet day.
2/Lt. F.D.Thornton granted leave to U.K. 2/Lieuts. B.R.Brown MM, G.N.Kendall, J.Drummond granted leave to U.K.
Colour Party proceeded to U.K. for Battalion Colours. Party consisted of 2/Lt. J.J.Marchant, 2/Lt. H.Parker, CSM J.Bourne, Sgt. J.Lorey and L/Cpl. E.Searl.

12th December 1918   Battalion parades. Captain W.C.D.Taylor rejoined from leave to U.K.

13th December 1918   Presentation by the G.O.C. 8th Division of Medal Ribbons and Parchment Certificates to 23rd Infantry Brigade, at TAINTIGNIES.

14th December 1918   Battalion parades. Draft of 19 other ranks joined.

15th December 1918 Divine Service in CINEMA. Lt.Col. G.E.R.Prior MC granted leave to the U.K.

16th December 1918 Battalion parades. 2/Lt. R.H.Hobern rejoined from course.

17th December 1918 Battalion moved by march route to billets at BARRY.

18th December 1918 2/Lt. E.A.Collier rejoined from Base. Battalion marched to billets at ATH.

19th December 1918 Inspection of Billets by G.O.C. 23rd Infantry Brigade.

20th December 1918 Battalion training.
Military Medals awarded to 290153 Cpl.(now Sgt.) G.White, 292047 Pte. T.Wickham, 71214 Pte. V.G.Hutt,
Bar to Military Medal awarded to 74004 Pte. A.Dunn.

21st December 1918 Battalion training. Tables and forms procured for seating accommodation for Christmas Dinners. "Dumplings" gave a performance in Y.M.C.A. ATH.

22nd December 1918 Divine Service.

23rd December 1918 Colour Party rejoined from U.K. with Colours.
Captain E.H.Saville MC and Lt. and Quartermaster F.Gunn MC granted leave to U.K.

24th December 1918 Battalion parades. Preparation for Christmas Day.

25th December 1918 XMAS DAY. Battalion had dinners in Company Messes. CO visited each Company at dinner.
Church service at 1115 hours.

26th December 1918 BOXING DAY. No parades. Inter Company football matches arranged.

27th December 1918 Battalion training. Football matches in the afternoon.

28th December 1918 Battalion training. Games and recreational training in afternoon.

29th December 1918 Divine Service. 2/Lieuts. D.E.Baker and A.G.Sandwell rejoined from leave to U.K.

30th December 1918 Battalion training. Football matches in afternoon. 2/Lieuts. B.R.Brown MM, G.N.Kendall and J.Drummond rejoined from leave to U.K.

The 2nd Devons War Diary

31st December 1918   Adjutant's and Commanding Officer's Parades. Football in the afternoon.

JANUARY 1919

1st January 1919   Battalion parades.
2nd January 1919   Battalion training.
3rd January 1919   Battalion training. Captain Brokenshire and Lt. W.H.Radcliffe rejoined from base. 2/Lt. F.D.Thornton rejoined from leave to leave to U.K.
4th January 1919   Battalion training. Football - 2nd Devons 3 .v. 2nd Middlesex Reg. 1.
5th January 1919   Church parades in Salle des Concert, ATH.
6th January 1919   Battalion training. Lt.Col. G.E.R.Prior MC rejoined from leave to U.K.
7th January 1919   Battalion training.
8th January 1919   Battalion training. The undermentioned proceeded to the U.K. as conducting officers for demobilisation parties :- 2/Lt. A.Willis, 2/Lt. L.D.Heppenstall. 2/Lt. R.S.Minton evacuated to U.K. 'sick' and struck off strength.
9th January 1919   Battalion training.
10th January 1919   Battalion training. Lt. and Quartermaster F.Gunn MC rejoined from leave to U.K.
Lt.R.C.D.Napier proceeded on leave to U.K.
11th January 1919   Battalion training. 2/Lt. J.D.Harcombe struck off strength.
12th January 1919   Sunday. Services in the Halle des Concerts, Ath.
13th January 1919   Battalion training.
14th January 1919   Battalion training.
Lt.J.J.Marchant proceeded to U.K. as Conducting Officer for demobilisation parties.

   The 8th Division was not one of those selected for the Army of Occupation and demobilization was soon to start in earnest, batches of men to be dispatched at short intervals, generally to the U.K. to resume their civilian occupations. Later on, a number of men not demobilized in the initial batches, were unlucky enough to be retained and drafted to units in the Army of Occupation.

15th January 1919   Battalion training.
Sgt. W.Gorman, 'C' Company, awarded the Chevalier de L'Ordre Leopold II.
16th January 1919   Battalion training.
17th January 1919   Battalion training.
18th January 1919   Battalion training. Ceremonial Parade. Reception of the King's and Regimental Colours into the Battalion.
19th January 1919   Divine Service at 10.30am.

20th January 1919 Battalion parades. Concert by the Regimental Concert Party "The Dumplings" in the Halle des Concert, Ath. Captain W.C.D.Taylor proceeded to U.K. for demobilisation.
21st January 1919 Battalion training.

22nd January 1919 Battalion training.
Lt. A.C.G.Roberts MC appointed Acting Captain 31/12/18 vide London Gazette.
2/Lt. B.R.Brown appointed Education Officer.
2/Lt. C.Luffman proceeded to U.K. for demobilisation.
23rd January 1919 Battalion training.
24th January 1919 Battalion training.
25th January 1919 Battalion training.
26th January 1919 Divine Service in the Halle des Concert, ATH.
27th January 1919 Battalion training.
28th January 1919 Battalion training.
29th January 1919 Battalion training.
30th January 1919 Battalion training.
31st January 1919 Battalion training. 2/Lt. A.Willis rejoined from leave to U.K.

FEBRUARY 1919

1st February 1919 Battalion training. 2/Lt. A.Willis admitted to hospital.
2nd February 1919 Divine Service in Y.M.C.A., ATH.
3rd February 1919 Battalion training. Lt. H.W.Byrde proceeded to U.K. for demobilisation.
4th February 1919 Battalion training.
Captain S.H.Parsloe (Transport Officer, 23rd Infantry Brigade) taken on strength from 29/1/19.
5th February 1919 Battalion training.
6th February 1919 Battalion training.
2/Lt. J.J.Huntingford granted permission to wear badges of rank of Lt. pending announcement appearing in London Gazette.
7th February 1919 Battalion training. 2/Lt. A.G.Sandwell proceeded to U.K. for demobilisation.
8th February 1919 Battalion training.
9th February 1919 Divine Services in Y.M.C.A., ATH.
10th February 1919 Battalion training.
11th February 1919 Battalion training.
12th February 1919 Battalion training.
Lt. C.W.White (attached 8th Division) demobilised and struck off strength. Lt. J.J.Marchant rejoined from leave to U.K.
13th February 1919 Battalion training.
Lt. R.C.D.Napier MC proceeded to U.K. for demobilisation.
14th February 1919 Battalion training.
Captain A.G.C.Roberts MC proceeded to U.K. for demobilisation.
Lt. R.H.Cumming MC rejoined from leave to U.K.

The 2nd Devons War Diary

15th February 1919 Battalion training.
2/Lt. A.Willis rejoined from hospital.
2/Lt. A.S.Watkins proceeded to U.K. as Conducting Officer for demobilisation party.
2/Lt. C.H.Townsend took over duties of Transport Officer.
16th February 1919 Church parade.
17th February 1919 Battalion training. 2/Lt. L.D.Heppenstall proceeded to U.K. for demobilisation.
18th February 1919 Battalion training. Captain R.L.Brokenshire MC proceeded on special leave to U.K.
19th February 1919 Battalion training.
20th February 1919 Battalion training.
2/Lt. R.J.Shutter rejoined from leave to U.K.
Lt. S.T.Mears proceeded to U.K. for demobilisation.
21st February 1919 Battalion training. 2/Lt. A.E.Collier proceeded to U.K. as Conducting Officer for demobilisation party.
22nd February 1919 Battalion training.
23rd February 1919 Divine Services. 2/Lt. S.Groves proceeded to U.K. as Conducting Officer for demobilisation party.
24th February 1919 Battalion training.
25th February 1919 Battalion training.
26th February 1919 Battalion training.
27th February 1919 Battalion training.
28th February 1919 Battalion training.
2/Lt. B.R.Brown proceeded on leave to U.K.
2/Lt. R.J.Shutter proceeded for duty with D.A.D.R.T. Dunkirk and is struck off strength.

MARCH 1919

1st March 1919 Orders received that draft of 150 other ranks would be required from men retained for the Army of Occupation, to proceed to 2/8th Worcesters at CHERBOURG.

These men's turn for demobilization had not yet arrived, and what they thought about being posted to the Army of Occupation in Germany instead of leaving the army and returning home is open to conjecture. One can only hope they volunteered.

2nd March 1919 Divine Service.
3rd March 1919 Captain P.J.Bretherton MC demobilised on leave.
4th March 1919 Nothing of interest.
5th March 1919 Captain M.R.M.McLeod rejoined from Fourth Army School.
6th March 1919 Nothing of interest.
7th March 1919 Nothing of interest.
8th March 1919 Nothing of interest.
9th March 1919 Nothing of interest.
10th March 1919 Nothing of interest.

Martin Body

11th March 1919 Captain F.H.Saville MC and Lt.B.M.Schooling demobilised whilst on leave.
Major E.W.Horne proceeded to U.K. for 2 month's leave prior to assuming duties of Adjutant at Depot, Devon Regiment.
12th March 1919 Nothing of interest.
13th March 1919 2/Lt. F.D.Clarke MC granted 2 month's leave to England.
14th March 1919 Nothing of interest.
15th March 1919 Nothing of interest.
16th March 1919 Lt. D.M.Atkinson, Lt. J.P.Tucker and 126 other ranks proceeded to join 2/8th Worcesters at CHERBOURG to form part of Army of Occupation.
17th March 1919 Nothing of interest.
18th March 1919 7810 CSM J.J.Lane awarded the "Medaille Barbetie Si Credinta - 1st Class".
19th March 1919 Nothing of interest.
20th March 1919 24 other ranks (balance of draft of 150 other ranks ordered) proceeded to join 2/8th Worcester Regiment at CHERBOURG. 2/Lt. G.R.Taylor proceeded for duty with Chinese Labour Corps.
21st March 1919 Nothing of interest.
22nd March 1919 Nothing of interest.
23rd March 1919 Nothing of interest.
24th March 1919 Nothing of interest.
25th March 1919 Captain S.H.Parsloe proceeded to U.K. for demobilisation.
26th March 1919 Nothing of interest.
27th March 1919 2/Lt. G.N.Kendall granted 14 days leave to U.K.
28th March 1919 Captain W.Exton MC demobilised.
29th March 1919 Nothing of interest.

30th March 1919 Lt.Col. G.E.R.Prior DSO, MC proceeded on leave to U.K. prior to joining 51st Devon Regiment with the Army of Occupation in Germany, as Second in Command.
31st March 1919 Lt. R.H.Cumming demobilised.
1/1st Hereford Regiment arrived at ATH for the purpose of relieving the Battalion.

APRIL 1919

1st April 1919 2/Lieuts. D.E.Baker and C.H.Townsend departed for the U.K. and are struck off strength.
2nd April 1919 Nothing of interest.
3rd April 1919 Nothing of interest.
4th April 1919 Nothing of interest.
5th April 1919 2/Lt. A.Willis admitted to hospital.
6th April 1919 Band Boys visited BRUSSELS.
7th April 1919 Nothing of interest.
8th April 1919 Nothing of interest.
9th April 1919 Nothing of interest.
10th April 1919 Lt. H.Parker MC rejoined from Conducting Duty

The 2nd Devons War Diary

to the U.K.
11th April 1919 Nothing of interest.
12th April 1919 Nothing of interest.
13th April 1919 Lt. F.R.Brooman. 2/Lieuts. J.Drummond, S.Groves, B.R.Brown MM, A.S.Watkins, F.D.Thornton, R.H.Hobern proceeded to Prisoners of War Companies and are struck off strength.
14th April 1919 Nothing of interest.
15th April 1919 2/Lt. R.J.Cock departed for demobilisation. Orders received for the Cadre to entrain on the 16th.
16th April 1919 Cadre and Band entrained at 1700 hours for Dunkirk.
17th April 1919 Cadre and Band arrived at 1400 hours. Marched to Delousing Camp for Bath etc, afterwards proceeding to No.2 Embarkation Camp.
18th April 1919 In Camp. Orders received for embarkation on 19th at 1100 hours.
19th April 1919 Cadre left DUNKIRK on SS 'ANTRIM' for England.

On 19th April 1919, the 2nd Devons sailed away from France and the final entry was made in the War Diary.

On 28th June 1919, the signing of the Treaty of Versailles officially brought the Great War to an end.

Martin Body

The 2nd Devons War Diary

PART 2

THE LOST MEN

A CHRONOLOGICAL LIST OF THE 2nd DEVONS WHO DIED IN THE GREAT WAR

KIA = Killed in action   DoW = Died of wounds

NOVEMBER 1914

19th November 1914
Lance-Sergeant John Hole 6940 KIA
born: St.Thomas's, Exeter   enlisted: Exeter
No known grave. Name recorded on Le Touret Memorial, panel 8 and 9. Age 30.
'Soldiers Died in the Great War' (SDGW) records him as KIA on 20/10/14, when the battalion was still in England. His Medal Card records that he joined the BEF on 06/11/14. The correct date is 19/11/14, when the War Diary records an unnamed fatality, but no death is recorded in SDGW. 1901 Census: general carrier, son of David Hole, general labourer, and Eliza Hole, Park Street, Crediton, Devon. 1911 Census: Lance-Corporal 2/Devons, St. George's Barracks, Malta.

20th November 1914
Pte. William Sinclair 8841 KIA
born: Ayr, Ayrshire   enlisted: Devonport
Buried: Guards Cemetery, Windy Corner, Cuinchy, grave IX.J.19. Age 27.
Joined BEF: 06/11/14 with original cadre. 1901 Census: boarder at Dunnichen Road, Woodville Coty, Forfar, Angus, Scotland. 1911 Census: 2/Devons, St. George's Barracks, Malta.

Pte. Frank Michelmore Stevens 3/5264 KIA
born: Plymouth   enlisted: Plymouth
Buried: Aubers Ridge British Cemetery, grave VII.A.6. Age 25.
Joined BEF: 06/11/14 with original cadre. 1901 Census: son of John Stevens, coal merchant, and Harriet F. Stevens, 5 Penrose Villas, Elmswood Terrace, Bradley Road, Plymouth, Devon. 1911 Census: draper's assistant, living with parents, at same address.

21st November 1914
Pte. Leonard George Potter 8711 KIA
born: Plymouth enlisted: Exeter   residence: Plymouth
No known grave. Le Touret Memorial, panel 8 and 9. Age 26. 'C' Company.
Joined BEF: 06/11/14 with original cadre. No Medal Card . 1901 Census: son of Thomas C. Potter, widower, labourer in ship yard, 34 Millbay Road, Millbay, Plymouth. 1911 Census:

2/Devons, St. George's Barracks, Malta. CWGC: brother of Alfred E. Potter, of 61 St. Leonards Road, Prince Rock, Plymouth.
Pte. George White 6819 DoW
born: London   enlisted: London
Buried: La Gorgue Communal Cemetery, grave I.I.1. Joined BEF: 06/11/14 with original cadre.

24th November 1914
Pte. Charles Appleton 9195 Died
born: Pamber, Hants.   enlisted: Aldershot   residence: Farnborough
Buried: Merville Communal Cemetery, grave I.L.34. Age 22.
Joined BEF: 06/11/14 with original cadre. 1901 Census: son of George Appleton, bricklayer, and Jane Appleton, Prospect Lane, Cove, Hartley Wintney, Hants. 1911 Census: 1/Devons, Mooltan and Lucknow Barracks, Uttar Pradesh, India. CWGC: family address: Stack Farm, Prospect Road, Cove, Farnborough, Hants.

25th November 1914
Pte. Edward Charles Connolly 9097 DoW
born: Curragh, Co. Kildare, Ireland   enlisted: Perham Down, Hants   residence: Plymouth
Buried: Merville Communal Cemetery, grave I.L.39. Age 21. Joined BEF: 06/11/14 with original cadre. 1911 Census: 1/Devons, Mooltan and Lucknow Barracks, Uttar Pradesh, India. CWGC: son of Mr. and Mrs. J. Connolly, 15 Hoe Street, Plymouth. Native of Curragh Camp, Co. Kildare, Ireland.

26th November 1914
Pte. John Furneaux 9120 DoW
born: Newton Abbot   enlisted: Newton Abbot   residence: Kinkerwell, Devon
Buried: Aubers Ridge British Cemetery, grave VII.A.5. Age 24. Joined BEF: 06/11/14 with original cadre. 1911 Census: house painter/decorator, boarder 3 Pennsylvania Road, Torquay, Devon.

27th November 1914
Pte. John Butt 4328 KIA
born: Pinhoe, Devon   enlisted: Exeter   residence: Pinhoe   No known grave. Le Touret Memorial, panel 8 and 9. Age 39.
Joined BEF: 06/11/14 with original cadre. 1911 Census: 2/Devons, St. George's Barracks, Malta. CWGC: son of the late John Butt and Eliza Butt, Pinhoe, Exeter. Served in South African Campaign.
Pte. Alfred Quick 8601 KIA
born: Tiverton, Devon   enlisted: Exeter   residence: Wellington, Somerset
Buried: Aubers Ridge British Cemetery, grave VII.A.4. Age 25. Joined BEF: 06/11/14 with original cadre. 1901 Census: son of William Quick, road contractor, and Selina Quick, 2 Northend Cottages, Culmstock, Tiverton, Devon. 1911 Census: 2/Devons, St. George's Barracks, Malta.
Pte. Herbert George Riggs 8126 KIA
born: Sidmouth, Devon   enlisted: Exeter   residence: Colaton Raleigh, Devon
Buried: Aubers Ridge British Cemetery, grave VII.A.3. Age 28. Joined BEF: 06/11/14 with original cadre. 1901 Census: son of John Gibson Riggs, carter on farm, and Louisa Riggs, 2 Whiles Cottages, Colaton Raleigh, Honiton, Devon. 1911 Census: 2/Devons , St. George's

Barracks, Malta. CWGC: family address: Pikes Cottage, Colaton Raleigh, Devon .
28th November 1914
Pte. Thomas Brown 8286 DoW
born: Lambeth, Surrey   enlisted: Exeter   residence: Hampton Hill, Middx.
Buried: Merville Communal Cemetery, grave I.K.41. Age 27. Joined BEF: 06/11/14 with original cadre. CWGC: son of Mrs. Emma Brown, 5A Jubilee Buildings, Tower Street, Waterloo Road, London.

30th November 1914
Pte. William Alfred Edwards 8898 KIA
born: Bideford, Devon   enlisted: Bideford
Buried: Aubers Ridge British Cemetery, grave VII.B.31. Age 22. Joined BEF: 06/11/14 with original cadre. 1901 Census: son of Frederick O. Edwards, mason's labourer, and Harriet Edwards, collar button-holer, 4 Union Street, Bideford, Devon. 1911 Census: 2/Devons, St. George's Barracks, Malta. CWGC: records Harriet Edwards as deceased, Frederick Edwards 5 Lamerton Place, Gunstone Street, Bideford, Devon.
Pte. Ernest Bradford 8320 DoW
born: Exeter   enlisted: Exeter
Buried: Merville Communal Cemetery, grave I.K.37. Age 26. Joined BEF: 06/11/14 with original cadre. 1911 Census: 2/Devons, St. George's Barracks, Malta. CWGC: son of Ellen Bradford, 1 Ida Cottages, Paris Street, Exeter.

Martin Body

DECEMBER 1914

1st December 1914
Pte. Frederick James Leworthy 9446 DoW
born: South Molton, Devon   enlisted: Exeter   residence: South Molton
Buried: Merville Communal Cemetery, grave I.K.20. Age 17. Joined BEF: 06/11/14 with original cadre. 1911 Census: schoolboy, son of William Leworthy, chimney sweep, and Annie Leworthy, 16 North Street, South Molton, Devon. CWGC: family address: Mockham Cottage, Charles, South Molton, Devon. An older brother, William James Leworthy, 9462, also with the 2/Devons , DoW on 07/09/1916. A third brother, Herbert N. Leworthy also served in the Army but survived.

12th December 1914
Pte. Henry Coome 9104 DoW (home)
born: Exeter   enlisted: Bulford, Hants.   residence: Exeter
Buried: Brompton Cemetery, grave N.172756. Age 23. Joined BEF: 06/11/14 with original cadre. CWGC: son of Henry and Eliza Coome, 5 Church Street, Heavitree, Exeter. Name on Combs-Coomb & C. Research Group web site, British World War 1 Dead 1914-1918.

14th December 1914
Pte. Thomas Charles Widdicombe 9870 DoW
born: Torquay, Devon   enlisted: Exeter   residence: Torquay
Buried: Aubers Ridge British Cemetery, grave VII.B.8. Age 19. Joined BEF: 06/11/14 with original cadre. 1901 Census: son of Thomas Widdicombe, mason's labourer, and Annie Widdicombe, 2 Laburnum Cottage, Tormoham, Torquay, Devon. 1911 Census records him as a servant engaged in 'General Dairy Work', at 12 Sherwill Hill, Chelston, Torquay, Devon. CWGC: family address: 28 Magdalene, Torquay, Devon.

16th December 1914
Pte. Walter Burston 8741 KIA
born: Wiveliscombe   enlisted: Exeter   residence: Wellington, Somerset
No known grave. Le Touret Memorial, panel 8 and 9. Age 25. Joined BEF: 06/11/14 with original cadre. 1901 Census: son of Walter Burston, farm carter, and Elizabeth Burston, Kerswell Cottage, Hockworth, Tiverton, Devon. 1911 Census: 2/Devons, St. George's Barracks, Malta. CWGC: family address: Hams Cottage, Petton, Bampton, Devon.

17th December 1914
Pte. Frank Bovin 9209 KIA
born: St.Peter's Port, C.I.   enlisted: Fort George, C.I.
Buried: Aubers Ridge British Cemetery, grave IV.D.13. Age 23. Joined BEF: 06/11/14 with original cadre. CWGC: son of Mr. and Mrs. P. Bovin, North Side, Momains Vale, Guernsey.

18th December 1914
Captain Reginald Benjamin Featherstone KIA
Born: Annerley, Surrey
No known grave. Le Touret Memorial, panel 8 and 9. Age 30. 'C' Company. Joined BEF: 06/11/14 with original cadre. 1911 Census: Grammar School, Plympton, Devon.CWGC: son of the late Benjamin Featherstone, and husband of Anna Elizabeth Featherstone, Ruffold, Colyford, Devon.

The 2nd Devons War Diary

Captain Charles James Spencer KIA
Born: Leicester, Leicestershire
Buried: Aubers Ridge British Cemetery, grave IV.F.3. Age 35. Joined BEF: 06/11/14 with original cadre. 1911 Census: Captain Spencer and wife had a son aged under 4 months, Charles R. Spencer. The Elms, Wonford, Exeter, Devon.CWGC: son of Mr. A. Spencer, Leicester, and husband of Katharine Margaret Spencer, of Crapstone House, Yelverton, Devon.

Captain Ronald George Legge KIA
Born: Southgate, London
No known grave. Le Touret Memorial, panel 8 and 9. Age 36. Born: 4th July 1878. Joined BEF: 06/11/14 with original cadre. 1911 Census: Officer in the Army (serving) Infantry of the Line, Adjutant Territorials. Mrs. Legge applied for her husband's 1914 Star 29/11/17. CWGC: son of Hon. Charles Gounter Legge and Mary Garnier. Married Phyllis Mildred Harriet Ford (now Mrs. Roger Baggallay) on 19th November 1910. Fought in the Boer War 1900–1901 with the Imperial Yeomanry. Grandson of 4th Earl of Dartmouth.

Pte. James Baker 3/5778 KIA
born: Tiverton   enlisted: Tiverton
No known grave. Le Touret Memorial, panel 8 and 9. Age 21. Joined BEF: 04/11/14, with original cadre.1911: mason's labourer, living with his family at 18 Chapel Street, Tiverton.CWGC: son of Charles Baker and Jane Baker, Allshire Cottage, Dulverton, Somerset.

Pte. Henry Beer 3/7318 KIA
born: Totnes, Devon   enlisted: Exeter   residence: Ivybridge, Dev.
No known grave. Le Touret Memorial, panel 8 and 9. Age 45. Joined BEF: joined BEF: 04/11/14, with original cadre. 1911 Census: agricultural labourer, boarding at Leigh Hill, Harberton. CWGC: son of Mrs. Sarah Ann Binmore (formerly Beer), Harberton, Totnes, Devon.

Pte. Walter Robert Bidder 3/6464 KIA
born: Braunton, Devon   enlisted: Barnstaple   residence: Braunton
No known grave. Le Touret Memorial, panel 8 and 9. Age 19. Joined BEF: 06/11/14 with original cadre. 1901 Census: son of John Bidder, farmer, and Eliza Jane Bidder, Lower Winsham, Braunton, Devon. 1911 Census: farmer's son working on farm, at Winsham, Braunton, Devon

Pte. Walter James Biggs 9798 KIA
born: Camberwell   enlisted: Stratford, Essex   residence: Camberwell
No known grave. Le Touret Memorial, panel 8 and 9. Age 33. Joined BEF: 06/11/14 with original cadre. 1901 Census: husband of Emily L. Biggs, father of Walter J. Biggs, 25 Gloucester Road, Camberwell.

Pte. William Henry Blake 9351 KIA
born: Brixham, Devon   enlisted: Brixham   residence: Churston, Devon
No known grave. Le Touret Memorial, panel 8 and 9. Age 21. Joined BEF: 06/11/14 with original cadre. 1911 Census: 3/Devons, Howell Road, Exeter. CWGC: son of Mr. and Mrs. W. H. Blake, 37 Stanley Gardens, Marldon Hill, Paignton, Devon.

Pte. William Ernest Braund 9277 KIA
born: Bow, Devon   enlisted: Crediton, Devon   residence: Exeter
Buried: Bailleul Road East Cemetery, Saint Laurent Blangy. Grave II.C.5. Age 25. Joined BEF: 06/11/14 with original cadre. 1911 Census 3/Devons, Howell Road, Exeter. CWGC: son of the late James and Annie Braund.

Pte. Francis William Buttle 8756 KIA
born: Woodbury, Devon   enlisted: Exeter   residence: Exmouth
No known grave. Le Touret Memorial, panel 8 and 9. Age 25. Joined BEF: not recorded on

Medal Card. 1911 Census: 2/Devons, St. George's Barracks, Malta. CWGC: son of Francis William and Lydia Buttle, 19 Woodland Terrace, Cefn Rogerstone, Newport, Mon.

Pte. Alfred Chudley 3/7248 KIA
born: Morchard Bishop   enlisted: Llanelly
No known grave. Le Touret Memorial, panel 8 and 9. Joined BEF: 06/11/14 with original cadre. 1901 Census: son of John Chudley, farm labourer, and Mary Chudley, East of Green, Morchard Bishop, Devon.

Pte. John Collins 6410 KIA
born: Jersey C.I.   enlisted: Jersey
No known grave. Le Touret Memorial, panel 8 and 9. Age 34. Joined BEF: 06/11/14 with original cadre. CWGC: son of Richard Collins, Pier Road, St. Helier, Jersey.

Sgt. Ernest John Court 5897 KIA
born: Westminster   enlisted: London S.W.
No known grave. Le Touret Memorial, panel 8 and 9. Age 31. 'C' Company. Joined BEF: 05/11/14, with original cadre. 1911 Census: Soldier (Lance-Sergeant) Devon Regiment, 45 Paris Street, Exeter. CWGC: son of George Court and Mary Court, 159 Hartfield Road, Wimbledon, London, and husband of Bessie Cecelia White (formerly Court), 128 Chapel Street, Tiverton, Devon.

Pte. Archelaus Curtis 8541 KIA
born: Exeter   enlisted: Bideford
No known grave. Le Touret Memorial, panel 8 and 9. Born March 1890. Age 24. Joined BEF: 05/11/14, with original cadre. 1901 Census: son of Archelaus Curtis, domestic, and Ellen Curtis, No. 1 Cottage, Mill Lane, Woolwich, London. 1911 Census: 2/Devons, St. George's Barracks, Malta.

Pte. Sidney James Davis 9327 KIA
born: Plymouth   enlisted: Devonport
Buried: Cabaret-Rouge British Cemetery, Souchez. Grave XXIX.C.6. Age 23. Joined BEF: not recorded on Medal Card. 1911 Census: gardener, nephew of Sarah Ann Davis, 12 Somerset Place, Stoke, Devonport. CWGC: son of Mrs. Bessie J. Davis, 6 Edgecombe Place, West Hoe, Plymouth.

Cpl. Fred Dowell 8463 KIA
born: Exeter   enlisted: Exeter
No known grave. Le Touret Memorial, panel 8 and 9. Age 24. Joined BEF: 06/11/14, with original cadre. CWGC: son of Frederick and Ellen Dowell, 12 Poltimore Square, Exeter.

Pte. William Henry Elson 8406 KIA
born: Northampton   enlisted: Plymouth
No known grave. Le Touret Memorial, panel 8 and 9. Age 27. Joined BEF: 06/11/14 with original cadre. 1911 Census: 2/Devons, St. George's Barracks, Malta. CWGC: son of the late George and Maria Elson, 12 Summerland Place, Plymouth.

Pte. Frank Charles Evans 6916 KIA
born: London   enlisted: London S.W.
No known grave. Le Touret Memorial, panel 8 and 9. Age 31. Joined BEF: 06/11/14 with original cadre. CWGC: husband of the late Elizabeth Evans.

Pte. Frederick Gooding 8515 KIA
born: Bideford   enlisted: Bideford
No known grave. Le Touret Memorial, panel 8 and 9. Age 24. Joined BEF: 05/11/14 with original cadre. 1911 Census: 2/Devons, St. George's Barracks, Malta. CWGC: son of George and Sarah Gooding, Moreton Lodge, Bideford, Devon.

Pte. James Gooding 9622 KIA
born: Barnstaple   enlisted: Exeter   residence: Chittlehampton
No known grave. Le Touret Memorial, panel 8 and 9. Age 20. Joined BEF: 05/11/14 with original cadre. 1901 Census: son of John Gooding, horseman on farm, and Hannah Gooding, Chittlehampton, Devon.

Pte. Harry James Harding 3/6830 KIA
born: London   enlisted: Stratford
No known grave. Le Touret Memorial, panel 8 and 9. Age 25. Joined BEF: 28/09/14. 1901 Census: eldest child of Harry Harding, farrier, and Elizabeth Harding. Mrs. Harding applied for son's 1914/15 Star 27/03/19.

Pte. William Hearn 8860 KIA
born: Launceston, Cornwall   enlisted: Exeter   residence: Launceston
No known grave. Le Touret Memorial, panel 8 and 9. Age 24. Joined BEF: 06/11/14 with original cadre. 1911 Census: 1/Devons, North Tidworth, Andover, Hants. CWGC: son of Mrs. Emily Penrose, Western Terrace, Launceston, Cornwall.

L/Cpl. Ralph Hewitt 9212 KIA
born: Exmouth   enlisted: Exeter   residence: Exmouth
No known grave. Le Touret Memorial, panel 8 and 9. Joined BEF: 06/11/14 with original cadre. 1911 Census: 1/Devons, North Tidworth, Andover, Hants.

Pte. William James Highland 8927 KIA
born: Penzance, Cornwall   enlisted: Devonport   residence: Liskeard, Corn.
No known grave. Le Touret Memorial, panel 8 and 9. Age 24. Joined BEF: 06/11/14 with original cadre. 1901 Census: son of Stephen Highland, picture-framer, and Elizabeth Ann Highland, of Elvington Street, Kingsbridge, Devon. 1911 Census: 1/Devons, North Tidworth, Andover, Hants.

Pte. William Edward Holmes 3/5827 KIA
born: Okehampton   enlisted: Exeter   residence: Okehampton
Buried: Cabaret-Rouge British Cemetery, Souchez. Grave XVI.AA.47. Age 22. No Medal Card. 1911 Census: 1/Devons, North Tidworth, Andover, Hants. CWGC: son of Mrs. E. Wills, Mount View, Borleigh, North Tawton, Devon.

Pte. Stephen Hooper 9447 KIA
born: Brixham   enlisted: Exeter   residence: Brixham
No known grave. Le Touret Memorial, panel 8 and 9. Age 21.
Date joined BEF: 06/11/14 with original cadre. 1901 Census: son of Susan Hooper, laundress, Mill Street, Brixham, Devon. CWGC: son of the late William Hooper, and husband of Susan Day (formerly Hooper), 23 Prospect Road, Brixham, Devon.

Pte. William Frederick Horsam 3/7325 KIA
born: Teignmouth   enlisted: Exeter   residence: Teignmouth
No known grave. Le Touret Memorial, panel 8 and 9. Age 42. Joined BEF: 27/10/14. 1901 Census: general labourer, son of Emily Atkinson, laundress, of 11 Mulberry Street, West Teignmouth, Devon. 1911 Census: farm labourer, Middle Street, Shaldon, with wife and 5 children. CWGC: son of William F. Horsam, and husband of Elizabeth Ellen Horsam, 22 Willow Street, Teignmouth, Devon.

Pte. William Johnson 3/6130 KIA
born: Brixham   enlisted: Brixham
No known grave. Le Touret Memorial, panel 8 and 9. Age 25. Joined BEF: not recorded on Medal Card. 1901 Census: son of Samuel Johnson, fish salesman/smack owner, and Susan Johnson, Melbourne, Brixham, Devon.

Pte. George Frederick Knapman 3/6520 KIA
born: Ashburton   enlisted: Exeter   residence: Kingsteignton
No known grave. Le Touret Memorial, panel 8 and 9. Age 32. Joined BEF: 06/11/14 with original cadre. 1911 Census: quarryman in stone quarry, husband of one year of Edith Knapman, living at Ware Cross, Kingsteignton. CWGC: son of William and Mary Ann Knapman. Name recorded on Kingsteignton War Memorial, Sandpath Road, Kingsteignton.

Pte. Albert Edward Knight 3/6617 KIA
born: Truro, Cornwall   enlisted: Truro
No known grave. Le Touret Memorial, panel 8 and 9. Age 17. Joined BEF: 06/11/14 with original cadre. 1901 Census: son of Joseph Knight, general labourer, and Sarah Jane Knight, 20 Calewick Street (Rose and Crown), Kenwyn, Truro, Cornwall. 1911 Census: errand boy, with parents at Moresk Place, Truro.

Pte. Percy Thomas Lang 9528 KIA
born: Braunton   enlisted: Exeter   residence: Braunton
Buried: Cabaret-Rouge British Cemetery, Souchez. Grave XXIX.C.7. Age 23. Joined BEF: 06/11/14 with original cadre. 1901 Census: stepson of Thomas Physick, farm labourer, and Elizabeth Physick, Georgeham, Barnstaple, Devon.

Pte. Frederick John Little 9766 KIA
born: London   enlisted: London
No known grave. Le Touret Memorial, panel 8 and 9. No Medal Card.

Pte. Thomas Arthur Luxton 8551 KIA
born: Bideford   enlisted: Bideford
No known grave. Le Touret Memorial, panel 8 and 9. Age 23. Joined BEF: 06/11/14 with original cadre. 1901 Census: son of William H. Luxton, greengrocer, and Mary Grace Luxton, 50a Meddon Street, Bideford, Devon. 1911 Census: 2/Devons, St. George's Barracks, Malta. CWGC: family address: 35 Meddon Street, Bideford, Devon.

Pte. Joseph Marks 5290 KIA
born: Birr, Ireland   enlisted: London   residence: Portsmouth
No known grave. Le Touret Memorial, panel 8 and 9. Age 29. Joined BEF: 06/11/14 with original cadre. 1911 Census: 2/Devons, St. George's Barracks, Malta.

Pte. George Monk 9257 KIA
born: London   enlisted: Exeter
Buried: Cabaret-Rouge British Cemetery, Souchez. Grave XXIX.C.11. Age 23. Joined BEF: 06/11/14 with original cadre. 1911 Census: boot maker, 99 Glenarm Road, Clapton, London, living with wife, Florence Monk, and 5 week old son George James Monk.CWGC: son of Mrs. Daisy Monk, 40 Great Eastern Road, Stratford, London.

Pte. William James Moore 3/6569 KIA
born: Exeter   enlisted: Okehampton
No known grave. Le Touret Memorial, panel 8 and 9. Age 19. Joined BEF: 04/11/14.1911 Census: horse driver, son of William Edward Moore, widower, Carter, 5 St. David's Place, Red Cow Village, Exeter.CWGC: son of Mrs. Mary Moore, High Street, North Tawton, Devon.

Pte. George Morrell 5886 KIA
born: London   enlisted: London S.E.
No known grave. Le Touret Memorial, panel 8 and 9. Age 31. Joined BEF: 06/11/14 with original cadre. 1911 Census: engineer's labourer, living with wife and 2 month old daughter Hilda Louise Morrell, 150 Blackfriars Road, Southwark. CWGC: son of Amelia Morrell, 72A Barkham Terrace, Lambeth Road, London, and the late George Morrell. Husband of Charlotte Louise Jane Morrell, 7 Malmsey Place, Vauxhall Street, Lambeth. Served in Boer War.

The 2nd Devons War Diary

Pte. Thomas Morris 3/6515 KIA
born: Torquay   enlisted: Torquay
No known grave. Age 19. Le Touret Memorial, panel 8 and 9. Age 19. Joined BEF: 06/11/14 with original cadre. 1901 Census: son of Eliza Morris, no occupation, Tormoham, Torquay, Devon. 1911 Census: errand boy, stepson of Harry Alford and Eliza Alford.

Pte. John Nickols 9401 KIA
born: Moretonhampstead   enlisted: Newton Abbot
No known grave. Le Touret Memorial, panel 8 and 9. Age 20. 'A' Company. Joined BEF: 06/11/14 with original cadre. CWGC: son of George and Florence Nickols, East Ogwill, Newton Abbot, Devon.

Pte. Sydney George Norman 9640 KIA
born: Combe Martin   enlisted: Barnstaple   residence: Combe Martin
No known grave. Le Touret Memorial, panel 8 and 9. Age 21. Joined BEF: 06/11/14 with original cadre. 1901 Census: son of Richard Norman, ordinary agricultural labourer, and Elizabeth Ann Norman, Cutcliffe's, Combe Martin, Devon. CWGC: family address: 3 Church Street, Combe Martin, Devon.

Cpl. Charles Osborn 8121 KIA
born: Twickenham   enlisted: Exeter   residence: Exmouth
Buried: Cabaret-Rouge British Cemetery, Souchez. Grave XVI.AA.48. Joined BEF: 06/11/14 with original cadre. 1911 Census: 2/Devons, St. George's Barracks, Malta.

Pte. Daniel Passmore 9585 KIA
born: Crediton   enlisted: Exeter   residence: Crediton
No known grave. Le Touret Memorial, panel 8 and 9. Age 20. Joined BEF: 06/11/14 with original cadre. Also on Medal Card as 9586. 1901 Census: son of William Passmore, tanner's labourer, and Lydia Passmore, Paradise, Crediton, Devon. 1911 Census: waggoner on farm, living with his family at 8 Cockwell, Crediton. CWGC: family address: 8 Kiddicott, The Green, Crediton, Devon.

Sgt. John Reynolds 8273 KIA
born: Okehampton   enlisted: Exeter   residence: Hatherleigh
No known grave. Le Touret Memorial, panel 8 and 9. Age 24.
No Medal Card . 1901 Census: 11 year old servant, 'cattle boy on farm', employed by Samuel Daniel, farmer, Speares Fishleigh, Hatherleigh, Devon. 1911 Census: 2/Devons, St. George's Barracks, Malta. CWGC: son of John Reynolds and Mary Jane Reynolds, Hatherleigh, Devon.

Pte. William Reynolds 7274 KIA
born: Gibraltar   enlisted: Exeter
No known grave. Le Touret Memorial, panel 8 and 9. Age 37. Joined BEF: 06/11/14 with original cadre. 1911 Census: Carter to Haulier, husband of Florence Mabel Reynolds, 6 Tucketts Square, Summerland Street, Exeter. CWGC: husband of Florence Mabel Reynolds, 4 Parsonage Place, St. Sidwells, Exeter.

Pte. William John Rogers 933 KIA
born: Saltash, Cornwall   enlisted: Plymouth
No known grave. Le Touret Memorial, panel 8 and 9. Age 22. Joined BEF: 06/11/14 with original cadre. 1901 Census: only son of William Ingles Rogers, journalist/reporter, and Emma Jane Rogers, Lambhay Hill, Plymouth, Devon. 1911 Census: with the 3/Devons at Howell Road, Exeter. CWGC: family address: 8 Finewell Street, Plymouth.

Pte. Walter Rowe 8863 KIA
born: Exeter   enlisted: Exeter
No known grave. Le Touret Memorial, panel 8 and 9. Age 26. Joined BEF: 06/11/14 with

original cadre. 1891 Census: James Rowe, engine fitter, and Bessie Rowe, Commercial Road, St. Mary Steps, Exeter, Devon. 1901 Census: Victoria Cottages, Exeter, mother not recorded. 1911 Census: 2/Devons, St. George's Barracks, Malta. CWGC: family address: 1 Northernhay Street, Exeter. Brother John, two years older, also killed with 2/Devons.

Pte. Stanley Jerome Seldon 9030 KIA
born: Exeter   enlisted: Devonport
No known grave. Le Touret Memorial, panel 8 and 9. Joined BEF: 06/11/14 with original cadre. 1911 Census: with the 1/Devons at North Tidworth, Andover, Hants.

Pte. John William Skinner 8790 KIA
born: Exmouth   enlisted: Exeter   residence: Exmouth
Buried: Cabaret-Rouge British Cemetery, Souchez. Grave XVI.AA.46. Age 30. Joined BEF: 06/11/14 with original cadre. 1911 Census: 2/Devons, St. George's Barracks, Malta. CWGC: son of Mrs. W. J. Skinner, 4 Meadow Street, Exmouth, Devon.

Pte. Lewis James Smith 7106 KIA
born: Plymouth   enlisted: Battersea, Surrey   residence: Ilfracombe
No known grave. Le Touret Memorial, panel 8 and 9. Age 34. 'C' Company. Joined BEF: 06/11/14 with original cadre. 1911 Census: Army Reservist/Draper's Assistant, boarder 15 Claremont Street, Plymouth. CWGC: son of the late Captain James Smith and Elizabeth Ellen Smith. Served in the Boer War.

Pte. John Westaway 9440 KIA
born: Newton Abbot   enlisted: Exeter   residence: Newton Abbot
No known grave. Le Touret Memorial, panel 8 and 9. Age 18. Joined BEF: 06/11/14 with original cadre. 1901 Census: son of James Westaway, labourer at clay works, and Mary Westaway, 2 Court, East Street, Wolborough, Newton Abbot, Devon. 1911 Census: general labourer, 4 Fisher Court, Paignton, Devon.

Pte. Charles George Westcott 8655 KIA
born: Exeter   enlisted: Exeter
No known grave. Le Touret Memorial, panel 8 and 9. Age 26. Joined BEF: 19/01/15. 1911 Census: 2/Devons, St. George's Barracks, Malta. CWGC: son of John Westcott and Bessie Westcott, Ratisloe, Poltimore, Exeter.

Pte. Ernest John Weston 8891 KIA
born: Colyton, Devon   enlisted: Exeter   residence: Colyton
No known grave. Le Touret Memorial, panel 8 and 9. Joined BEF: 06/11/14 with original cadre. 1911 Census: 2/Devons, St. George's Barracks, Malta.

Pte. George Wheaton 8770 KIA
born: Crediton   enlisted: Exeter   residence: Broadwood Kelly
No known grave. Le Touret Memorial, panel 8 and 9. Age 22. Joined BEF: 06/11/14 with original cadre. Medal Card annotation: *'A. Wheaton makes application for 1914 Star in respect of the services of the late Private G. Wheaton. 03/11/19'*. 1911 Census: 2/Devons, St. George's Barracks, Malta. CWGC: only son of Archelaus John Wheaton and Mary Jane Wheaton, 166 Sewell Street, East Fremantle, Western Australia.

Pte. Frederick George White 8545 KIA
born: Axminster   enlisted: Exeter   residence: Axminster
Buried: Pont-Du-Hem Military Cemetery, La Gorgue. Grave IV.A.7. Joined BEF: 06/11/14 with original cadre. 1911 Census: 2/Devons, St. George's Barracks, Malta.

Pte. Frederick James Wilkey 9518 KIA
born: Totnes   enlisted: Newton Abbot   residence: Totnes
No known grave. Le Touret Memorial, panel 8 and 9. Age 20.

Joined BEF: 06/11/14 with original cadre. CWGC: son of the late Mr. and Mrs. E. Wilkey.
Sgt. William Woolacott 4884 KIA
born: North Tawton   enlisted: Exeter   residence: Bondleigh, Devon
Buried: Bailleul Road East Cemetery, St.Laurent-Blangy. Grave II.C.4. Joined BEF: 06/11/14 with original cadre.
Pte. Alfred Wooldridge 10146 KIA
born: Plymouth   enlisted: Haverfordwest   residence: Plymouth
No known grave. Le Touret Memorial, panel 8 and 9. Age 25. 'A' Company. Joined BEF: not recorded on Medal Card. CWGC: son of John Albert Wooldridge and Elizabeth Ann Wooldridge, 50 Mainstone Avenue, Cattedown, Plymouth.
Pte. Arthur Worth 8788 KIA
born: Lydford   enlisted: Devonport   residence: Tavistock
No known grave. Le Touret Memorial, panel 8 and 9. Age 22. Joined BEF: 06/11/14 with original cadre. CWGC: son of William Worth and Eliza Worth, Ivy Cottage, Peter Tavy, Tavistock, Devon.
Pte. Walter Harvey 9250 DoW
born: Colyton, Devon   enlisted: Honiton, Devon   residence: Musbury, Devon
No known grave. Le Touret Memorial, panel 8 and 9. Age 22. 'D' Company. Joined BEF: 06/11/14 with original cadre. CWGC: son of Mr. and Mrs. J. Harvey, Rosemary Cottage, Musbury, Axminster, Devon.   Enlisted March, 1911.
Pte. Robert Mitchell 9444 DoW
born: Sheerness   enlisted: Exeter   residence: Portsmouth
No known grave. Le Touret Memorial, panel 8 and 9. Age 22. Joined BEF: 06/11/14 with original cadre.
Pte. Henry Sercombe 8903 DoW
born: Exeter   enlisted: Exeter
No known grave. Le Touret Memorial, panel 8 and 9. Age 17.
Joined BEF: 06/11/14 with original cadre. 1901 Census: Son of Henry C. Sercombe, bank manager, and Alice L. Sercombe, Broadgate, Exeter.

19th December 1914
Pte. George Crout 9783 KIA
born: Manaton, Devon   enlisted: Exeter   residence: Manaton
No known grave. Le Touret Memorial, panel 8 and 9. Age 18. Date joined BEF: 05/11/14 with original cadre. 1911 Census: butcher, 2 Cross Street, Moretonhampstead, Devon. CWGC: son of Herbert and Eliza Crout, 2 Cross Street, Moretonhampstead, Devon.

20th December 1914
Pte. Archibald Charles John Chase 8274 DoW
born: Suffolk   enlisted: Aldershot
Buried: Estaires Communal Cemetery and Extension. Grave I.D.10. Age 24. Joined BEF: 06/11/14 with original cadre. 1911 Census: 2/Devons, St. George's Barracks, Malta. CWGC: son of William Dermis Chase and Elizabeth Chase.

21st December 1914
Sgt. Wilfred Bagwell 7537 DoW
born: Kinkerswell   enlisted: Exeter   residence: Torquay
Buried: Boulogne Eastern Cemetery. Grave III.B.71. Age 29.

Joined BEF: 06/11/14 with original cadre. 1901 Census: brickyard labourer, boarding at 46 Osborn Street, Wolborough, Newton Abbot, Devon. 1911 Census: 2/Devons, St. George's Barracks, Malta. CWGC: native of Torquay, husband of Alice Bagwell, 3 Higher Brunswick Place, Paris Street, Exeter.

24th December 1914
Pte. William Widger 9502 DoW
born: Totnes   enlisted: Exeter   residence: Totnes
Buried: Estaires Communal Cemetery and Extension. Grave I.D.6. Age 24.
Joined BEF: 06/11/14 with original cadre. Medal card annotation reads: *'Mrs. A. Widger makes app: for 1914 Star in respect of the services of her son the late Pte. W. Widger. Further letter from A. Widger re. Victory Medal in respect of services of the late Pte. W. Widger'*.1901 Census: son of George Widger, horseman on farm, and Annie Widger, Borestonfoot Cottage, Halwell, Totnes, Devon. CWGC: family address: Harberton, Totnes, Devon.
Pte. Reginald William Giles 3/6194 Died
born: Wellington, Somerset   enlisted: Taunton, Somerset
Buried: Boulogne Eastern Cemetery. Grave III.A.80. Age 22. Joined BEF: 07/11/14 with original cadre. 1891 Census: son of William Giles, house painter, and Mary E. Giles, Court No. 3, Back of Cheapside, Taunton, Somerset. 1911 Census: 3/Devons, Higher Barracks, Howell Road, Exeter, Devon. CWGC: Wellington, Somerset.

25th December 1914
Pte. Richard Gregory 8316 KIA
born: Devonport   enlisted: Devonport
No known grave. Le Touret Memorial, panel 8 and 9. Age 26. Joined BEF: 06/11/14 with original cadre. 1911 Census: 2/Devons, St. George's Barracks, Malta. CWGC: brother of Mrs. R. Beaumont, 20 Stanley Street, Devonport.

27th December 1914
Pte. John Bailey 8602 DoW
born: Holsworthy, Cornwall   enlisted: Exeter   residence: Bude, Cornwall
Buried: Boulogne Eastern Cemetery. Grave III.A.79. Age 30. Joined BEF: not recorded on Medal Card. 1901 Census: servant, farm hand, employed by the Dymond family, Clevendon Farm, Bradworthy, Holsworthy, Cornwall. 1911 Census: 2/Devons, St. George's Barracks, Malta.

29th December 1914
Pte. Henry Phillips 3/6480 DoW
born: Exeter   enlisted: Exeter
Buried: Exeter Higher Cemetery. Grave B.D.28.14. Joined BEF: 06/11/14 with original cadre.

The 2nd Devons War Diary

JANUARY 1915

1st January 1915
Pte. Fred Bishop 8837 KIA
born: Tiverton   enlisted: Tiverton
No known grave. Le Touret Memorial, panel 8 and 9. Age 24. Joined BEF: 06/11/14 with original cadre. 1901 Census: son of John Bishop, carter on farm, and Sarah Jane Bishop, Meadhayes Cottage, Tiverton, Devon. 1911 Census: 2/Devons, St. George's Barracks, Malta. CWGC: Sarah Jane Bishop's address: Ducksdale Cottage, Washfield, Tiverton, Devon.
Pte. William Rolston 3/7145 DoW
born: Newton Abbot   enlisted: Exeter   residence: Kingsteignton
Buried: Boulogne Eastern Cemetery. Grave III.A.81. Age 44. Joined BEF: 06/11/14 with original cadre. CWGC: son of Samuel Rolston and Mary Rolston, 49, Barton Avenue, Keyham, Devonport. Native of Kingsteignton, Newton Abbot.

3rd January 1915
Pte. Harry Ridges 8795 DoW (home)
born: Kingsbridge   enlisted: Torquay   residence: Dartmouth
Buried: Dartmouth (Longcross) Cemetery. Grave 253. Age 23. Joined BEF: 06/11/14 with original cadre. 1901 Census: son of John E. Ridges, ordinary farm labourer, and Florence Ridges, 7 Towns Lane, Loddiswell, Kingsbridge, Devon. 1911 Census: 2/Devons, St. George's Barracks, Malta. CWGC: family address: 2 Oakford Terrace, Dartmouth, Devon.

4th January 1915
Pte. Ernest Edwin Sampson 9641 DoW
born: South Molton   enlisted: South Molton
No known grave. Le Touret Memorial, panel 8 and 9. Age 22. No Medal Card . 1901 Census: John Sampson, carter, and Bessie Sampson, Yard Wells Cottage, South Molton, Devon. CWGC: family address: 36 South Street, South Molton, Devon.

6th January 1915
L/Cpl. Ernest Edward Twitchett 8623 KIA
born: Clare, Suffolk   enlisted: Haverhill   residence: Clare
No known grave. Le Touret Memorial, panel 8 and 9. Age 24. Joined BEF: 06/11/14 with original cadre. 1911 Census: 2/Devons, St. George's Barracks, Malta. CWGC: son of Thomas Twitchett and Emma Twitchett, Ashen, Essex.
Pte. Albert David Rees 7381 DoW
born: Newcastle, Glam.   enlisted: Bridgend   residence: Cardiff
Buried: Lille Southern Cemetery. Grave III.A.25. Age 36. Joined BEF: 06/11/14 with original cadre. Medal Card records Army Number as 3/7381. 1901 Census: draper's assistant, son of David R. Rees, mason, and Elizabeth Rees, 25 Alfred Street, Roath, Cardiff, Wales. 1911 Census: draper/dealer, husband of Muriel Rees, 3 Amesbury Road, Cardiff. CWGC: son of Elizabeth Rees, of Cardiff, husband of Muriel Rees, I Primrose Villas, Portfield Street, Hereford.

9th January 1915
Pte. James Rowe 3/7131 DoW
born: Norwich   enlisted: Norwich
Buried: St.Sever Cemetery, Rouen. Grave A.3.1. Age 28. Joined BEF: 17/12/14. 1901 Census:

printer (letterpress), son of Nathaniel Rowe, general labourer, 2 Pages Yard, Norwich, Norfolk.

12th January 1915
Pte. Charles Hayter 9406 KIA
born: Plymouth   enlisted: Devonport
No known grave. Le Touret Memorial, panel 8 and 9. Age 20. Joined BEF: not on Medal Card. 1901 Census: son of George Hayter, general labourer, and Mary Jane Hayter, laundress, 44 Claremont Street, Plymouth.

13th January 1915
Sgt. Samuel John Ford 8811 KIA
born: Plymouth   enlisted: Devonport
Buried: Aubers Ridge British Cemetery. Grave VII.A.14. Age 23. Joined BEF: not recorded on Medal Card. 1911 Census: serving 2/Devons, St. George's Barracks, Malta. CWGC: son of Mr. R. and P. J. Whitfield, Cove Cottage, 5 West Hoe Road, Millbay, Plymouth.
Pte. John Froom 3/7846 KIA
born: Axminster   enlisted: Exeter   residence: Axminster
No known grave. Le Touret Memorial, panel 8 and 9. Joined BEF: 27/12/14.
Pte. Alfred Hodson 9130 KIA
born: Cheltenham   enlisted: Exeter
No known grave. Le Touret Memorial, panel 8 and 9. Age 22. Joined BEF: 06/11/14 with original cadre. CWGC: adopted son of Charles John Denner and Bessie Denner, Upper High Street, Sidmouth, Devon.

14th January 1915
Sgt. James Hogg 7062 KIA
born: Peebles N.B.   enlisted: Devonport
Buried: Aubers Ridge British Cemetery. Grave VII.A.1. Joined BEF: 06/11/14 with original cadre.

16th January 1915
Pte. Edward Samuel Woolf 3/7082 DoW
born: Mauritius (Hastlington, Cheshire)   enlisted: London
Buried: Boulogne Eastern Cemetery. Grave III.C.46. Age 45. Joined BEF: 27/12/14. 1911 Census: living on independent means, visiting 1 Westbourne Street, Sloane Square, London. CWGC: son of Edward Samuel and Mary Woolf, Abbeyfield, Sandbach, Cheshire and Haslington Hall, Crewe, Cheshire.

17th January 1915
Pte. Wilfred Grayer 8189 KIA
born: Brighton, Sussex   enlisted: Shepton Mallett
No known grave. Le Touret Memorial, panel 8 and 9. Age 20. Joined BEF: 27/12/14. 1901 Census: son of Josiah Grayer, coachman/domestic, and Sarah Grayer, 6 Victoria Mews, Second Avenue, Hove, Sussex. 1911 Census: Page/Domestic, son of Josiah Grayer, Coachman/Domestic, and Sarah Grayer, address as 1901. CWGC: family address as 1901 Census.

The 2nd Devons War Diary

18th January 1915
Pte. Percy Fricker Allen 8557 KIA
born: Exeter   enlisted: Exeter
No known grave. Le Touret Memorial, panel 8 and 9. Age 24. Joined BEF: 06/11/14 with original cadre. 1901 Census: boarder, age 10, St. John's Hospital (School), Exeter. 1911 Census: with the 1/Devons, Mooltan and Lucknow Barracks, Uttar Pradesh, India.

23rd January 1915
Pte. Frank Gilbert 3/6934 KIA
Born: London   enlisted: London   residence: Stratford, Essex
No known grave: Le Touret Memorial, panel 8 and 9. Age 21. No Medal Card. CWGC: son of George and Mary Ann Gilbert, 33 Candy Street, Parnell Road, Old Ford, Bow, London.

24th January 1915
Pte. Thomas Lake 8543 DoW sustained on 23rd January
born: Exeter   enlisted: Exeter   residence: Bath, Somerset
Buried: Aubers Ridge British Cemetery. Grave VII.A.13. Age 25. Joined BEF: 06/11/14 with original cadre. 1911 Census: 2/Devons, St. George's Barracks, Malta.
Pte. William Richard Edwards King 9275 KIA
born: Totnes   enlisted: Exeter   residence: Totnes
Buried: Aubers Ridge British Cemetery. Grave VII.B.14. Age 22. Joined BEF: 06/11/14 with original cadre. 1901 Census: 3/Devons, Higher Barracks, Howell Road, Exeter, Devon. CWGC: son of James J. E. King, 18 Leechwell Street, Totnes, Devon.

25th January 1915
Pte. William Henry Edwards 3/6867 KIA
born: Canning Town   enlisted: Stratford
No known grave. Le Touret Memorial, panel 8 and 9. Joined BEF: 06/11/14 with original cadre.
Pte. Charles Leaman 8820 KIA
born: Ashburton   enlisted: Exeter   residence: Ashburton
No known grave. Le Touret Memorial, panel 8 and 9. Age 30. Joined BEF: 06/11/14 with original cadre. 1911 Census: 'Groom, Private In The Devonshire Regiment, Servant To Staff Officer', Mount Cottage, Longbrook Street, Exeter, Devon, with wife Sarah Leaman and daughter Lilian Gladys Leaman.
Pte. Arthur Courtenay Warren 3/6496 KIA
born: Plymouth   enlisted: Devonport
No known grave. Le Touret Memorial, panel 8 and 9. Age 35. 'C' Company. Joined BEF: 06/11/14 with original cadre. 1901 Census: son of Henry Warren, hotel proprieter (pub), and Elizabeth Warren, 19 Tavistock Road, Plymouth, Devon. 1911 Census: coal dealer, son of Henry Warren, coal dealer, and Elizabeth Warren, 9 Rowe Street, Plymouth, Devon. CWGC: Elizabeth Warren, 9 Rowe Street, Plymouth.
Pte. William Edward James 14220 DoW
born: Swansea   enlisted: Swansea
No known grave. Le Touret Memorial, panel 8 and 9. Age 25. Joined BEF: 27/12/14. 1901 Census: son of William A. James, bonded merchant, and Eliza A. James, 23 Promenade, Swansea.

Pte. Samuel Moulson 8450 DoW
born: Devonport   enlisted: Devonport
Buried: Boulogne Eastern Cemetery. Grave III.C.43. Joined BEF: 04/11/14 with original cadre.
1911 Census: 2/Devons, St. George's Barracks, Malta.

26th January 1915
Pte. Frederick George Hamlyn 8916 DoW
born: Christow, Devon   enlisted: Exeter   residence: Christow
Buried: Merville Communal Cemetery. Grave I.K.6. Age 21.
Joined BEF: 06/11/14 with original cadre. Medal Card annotation: *'Mrs. C. Hamlyn makes application for 1914 Star Clasp in respect of the services of her two late sons. 18/01/20'.*
1901 Census: son of George Hamlyn, farm labourer, and Caroline Hamlyn, Court Cottage, Christow, Exeter. 1911 Census: 2/Devons, St. George's Barracks, Malta.

30th January 1915
Sgt. Sidney Alfred Blake 7129 KIA
born: Charleton, Devon   enlisted: Exeter   residence: Charleton
Buried: Aubers Ridge British Cemetery. Grave V.F.5. Age 32. Joined BEF: 06/11/14 with original cadre. 1901 Census: son of Alfred Blake, builder/stone mason, and Annie Blake, West Charleton, Kingsbridge, Devon. 1911 Census: 2/Devons, St. George's Barracks, Malta. CWGC: family address: "The Laurels," Kingsbridge, Devon; husband of Florence Mary Wade (formerly Blake), I Lutton Cottages, South Brent, Devon.

31st January 1915
Captain Eustace Arundel De St Barbe Sladen Watkins (3/Devons, attached 2/Devons).
DoW Buried: Merville Communal Cemetery. Grave I.L.2. Age 25. Joined BEF: 07/11/14 with original cadre. Medal Card annotation: *'R.G. Watkins Esq. applies for 1914 Star in respect of his late son. 23/03/18'.* 1901 Census: Eastman's boarding school, Portsmouth. 1911 Census: Army Lieutenant, 3/Devons, son of Robert Arundel Watkins, Estate Agent, and Mary Etheldesh Watkins, Castle Combe, Chippenham, Wiltshire. Born 1889, Chippenham, Wiltshire.
L/Cpl. Christopher George Dunsford 9499 KIA
born: Sidmouth   enlisted: Exeter   residence: Sidford
No known grave. Le Touret Memorial, panel 8 and 9. Joined BEF: 06/11/14 with original cadre. 'B' Company. Age 19. 1901 Census: son of George Dunsford, carter on farm, and Alice Dunsford, Turnpike Cottage, Sidbury, Devon. 1911 Census: gardener/domestic, son of George Dunsford, waggoner on farm, and Alice Dunsford, Sidford, Devon.

The 2nd Devons War Diary

FEBRUARY 1915

1st February 1915
Pte. Harold Lionel Salter 8569 DoW
born: Ottery St. Mary   enlisted: Exeter
Buried: Aubers Ridge British Cemetery. Grave V.F.4. Age 22. Joined BEF: 06/11/1914 with original cadre. 1910 Census: son of Henry Salter, labourer, and Bessie Salter, of Castle Farm, Ottery St. Mary, Devon. 1911 Census: 2/Devons, St. George's Barracks, Malta.
Pte. James Bowden 3/7266 DoW
born: North Molton   enlisted: Exeter   residence: Port Talbot
Buried: Aubers Ridge British Cemetery. Grave V.F.1. Joined BEF: 07/11/14 with original cadre.

5th February 1915
Pte. Robert Horwood Darke 14216 KIA
born: Sturminster, Dorset   enlisted: Exeter   residence: Sturminster
Buried: Aubers Ridge British Cemetery. Grave VII.A.12. Age 34. Joined BEF: 27/12/14. 1901 Census: son of James Edward Darke, widower. James Edward Darke and his sons, Robert and Tom, were boarders 17 Grove Estate, Grove Road, Portland, Dorset. 1911 Census: Vegetable Cook at Restaurant, step-grandson of Emma Congdon, Lodging House Keeper, 44 New King Street, Bath, Somerset. CWGC: son of James Edward Darke and Harriet Darke, I Moorside, Sturminster Newton, Dorset.
Pte. Walter George Alsop 9044 DoW
born: Crediton   enlisted: Exeter
Buried: Estaires Communal cemetery and Extension. Grave II.D.1. Age 22. Joined BEF: 06/11/14 with original cadre. CWGC: son of Thomas and Harriett Alsop, Poughill, Crediton, Devon.
Pte. John Green 3/8191 KIA
Born: Swansea   enlisted: Swansea
No known grave. Le Touret Memorial, panel 8 and 9. Joined BEF: 04/01/1915.

6th February 1915
Pte. Arthur Horrell 9714 KIA
born: Barnstaple   enlisted: Exeter   residence: Barnstaple
No known grave. Le Touret Memorial, panel 8 and 9. Age 20. Joined BEF: 22/08/14 with 1/Devons. 1911 Census: working for a coal merchant, son of Samuel Horrell, general labourer, 3 Fry's Court, Fore Street, Ilfracombe, Devon. CWGC: adopted son of Mrs. F. Mansfield, 7 Fore Street, Ilfracombe, Devon.

7th February 1915
Pte. Frederick William Boon 9308 KIA
born: Sheffield   enlisted: Exeter   residence: Lyme Regis
No known grave. Le Touret Memorial, panel 8 and 9. Age 22. Joined BEF: 06/11/14 with original cadre. Medal Card annotation: *'Mrs. F. L. Baker applies for 1914 Star in respect of her late son.'* 1901 Census: son of Fanny L. Boon, widow, charwoman, Silver Street, Lyme Regis, Dorset.

Pte. James Bray 8883 KIA
born: Kingsteignton   enlisted: Exeter   residence: Kingsteignton
No known grave. Le Touret Memorial, panel 8 and 9. Age 25. Joined BEF: 06/11/14 with original cadre. 1901 Census: son of James Bray, clay cutter/labourer, and Agnes Bray, Greenhill Lane, Kingsteignton, Devon. 1911 Census: 2/Devons, St. George's Barracks, Malta. CWGC: family address: 2 Woolaton Terrace, Kingsteignton, Newton Abbot, Devon.

Pte. Evan Stanley Evans 8176 KIA
born: Lampeter, Cardigan   enlisted: Swansea
Buried: Aubers Ridge British Cemetery. Grave VII.A.11. Age 24. Joined BEF: 04/01/15. On Medal Card as 'Stanley Evans'. 1901 Census: son of Evan Evans, farmer, and Mary Evans, Bridie, Lampeter, Cardiganshire, Wales. CWGC: family address: 51 Woodville Road, Mumbles, near Swansea, Wales.

Pte. Albert Isaacs 8698 KIA
born: Totnes   enlisted: Plymouth   residence: Torquay
Buried: Aubers Ridge British Cemetery. Grave V.F.3. Joined BEF: 06/11/14 with original cadre. Age 29. 1911 Census: 2/Devons, St. George's Barracks, Malta.

Pte. Richard Milton 3/7533 KIA
born: Torrington   enlisted: Exeter   residence: Ashburton
Buried: Aubers Ridge British Cemetery. Grave IV.F.8. Age 34.
Joined BEF: 12/12/14. CWGC: son of James Milton and Mary Milton, Ashburton, Devon; husband of Alethea E. R. Hannaford (formerly Milton), West Street, Ashburton, Devon.

9th February 1915
Pte. Hedley John Harvey 8276 DoW
born: Truro, Cornwall   enlisted: Devonport
Buried: Wimereux Communal Cemetery. Grave I.C.30. Age 28.
Joined BEF: 06/11/14 with original cadre. 1911 Census: general farm labourer, nephew of Frances Harvey, West Bradley, Glastonbury, Somerset. CWGC: stepson of Jessie Harvey, 32 Exeter Street, Plymouth.

10th February 1915
Pte. George Baglow 9534 DoW
born: Bideford   enlisted: Exeter   residence: Barnstaple
Buried: Merville Communal Cemetery. Grave I.J.1. Age 21. 'A' Company. Joined BEF: 06/11/14 with original cadre. 1901 Census: son of Percival J. Baglow, general labourer, and Fanny Baglow, laundress, 35 Hardaway Head, Barnstaple, Devon. 1911 Census: servant, Horseman on Farm, Blakewell Mills, Marwood, Barnstaple, Devon. CWGC: family address: 21 Hardaway Head, Barnstaple.

11th February 1915
Pte. Joseph Campbell 8889 KIA
born: Southport, Cheshire   enlisted: Barnstaple
Buried: Aubers Ridge British Cemetery. Grave VI.A.8. Joined BEF: 17/12/14.
Pte. Alfred George Edwards 9574 DoW
born: Axminster   enlisted: Exeter   residence: Broadwinsor, Dorset
Buried: Merville Communal Cemetery. Grave I.H.4. Age 21. Date joined BEF: 06/11/14 with original cadre. 1901 Census: records him as George A. Edwards, son of Lucy J. Edwards, living on parish relief, Back Lane, Broadwinsor, Beaminster, Dorset. 1911 Census: Law Clerk,

grandson of Alfred Edwards, widower, LSWR pensioner, 4 South View Terrace, Exeter, Devon. CWGC: son of Frederick Charles Edwards and Lucy Jane Edwards, Trustams, Broadwinsor, Beaminster, Dorset.

12th February 1915
Pte. James Hall 9231 DoW
born: Exeter   enlisted: Exeter
Joined BEF: 06/11/14 with original cadre. CWGC: no grave or memorial reference.

13th February 1915
Pte. Stanley Bulford 9832 DoW
born: Walthamstow   enlisted: Stratford   residence: Walthamstow
Buried: Le Treport Military Cemetery. Plot 1. Row B. Grave 2. Age 18. Joined BEF: 06/11/14 with original cadre. 1901 Census: son of John Charles Bulford, house painter, and Elizabeth Bulford, 8 Arkley Crescent, Walthamstow. 1911 Census: Shop Boy, son of Elizabeth Bulford, domestic, 211 Blackhorse Road, Walthamstow, Essex. CWGC: son of the late John Charles and Elizabeth Bulford, of Walthamstow.

16th February 1915
Pte. Alfred May 7471 DoW sustained 15th February
born: Exeter   enlisted: Exeter
No known grave. Le Touret Memorial, panel 8 and 9. Age 42. Joined BEF: 17/12/14. Army number 3/7471 on Medal Card. 1911 Census: Waggoner on Farm, husband of Elizabeth Ann May, father of Edward May and daughters Eula May, Ivy May and Laura May, Bridge Cottages, Pinhoe, Exeter, Devon. CWGC: records him as the son of William May. Served in India and in Boer War.

18th February 1915
Pte. Ernest Mills 1263 KIA
born: Tiverton   enlisted: Cardiff
Buried: Aubers Ridge British Cemetery. Grave V.E.1. Joined BEF: 04/01/15. Army number 12637 on Medal Card.
Pte. John Gordon Willcocks 3/6199 KIA
born: Totnes   enlisted: Newton Abbot   residence: Totnes
Buried: Aubers Ridge British Cemetery. Grave V.F.2. Age 21. 'D' Company. Joined BEF: 12/09/14 with 1/Devons. 1901 Census: son of J. C. Willcocks, mason's labourer, and Kate Willcocks, Behind Bull Inn, Totnes, Devon. 1911 Census: with 3/Devons, Higher Barracks, Howell Road, Exeter, Devon. CWGC: husband of Edith Mary Watts (formerly Willcocks), 2 Heals Cottages, Fore Street, Totnes, Devon.

20th February 1915
Pte. James Curtis 8572 Died
born: Appledore, Devon   enlisted: Bideford
Buried: Vielle-Chapelle New Military Cemetery, Lacouture. Grave IX.B.17. Age 28. Joined BEF: 05/11/14 with original cadre. 1901 Census: son of Francis Curtis, mariner seas, and Elizabeth Curtis, 3 Church Fields, Northam, Appledore, Devon. 1911 Census: 2/Devons, St. George's Barracks, Malta.

23rd February 1915
Pte. Arthur Young 8833 KIA
born: Ottery St.Mary   enlisted: Exeter   residence: Ottery St.Mary
No known grave. Le Touret Memorial, panel 8 and 9. Age 26. Joined BEF: 06/11/14 with original cadre. 1901 Census: son of James Young, farm labourer, and Margaret Young, Talewater Farm, Talaton, Honiton, Devon. 1911 Census: with the 2/Devons, St. George's Barracks, Malta.
Pte. Bert Walters 11089 DoW
born: Exeter   enlisted: Exeter   residence: Exmouth
Buried: Estaires Communal Cemetery and Extension. Grave I.E.11. Joined BEF: 20/01/15.
Pte. William Williams 12875 DoW
born: Brecon   enlisted: Ferndale, Glam.
No known grave. Estaires Communal Cemetery and Extension. Sp. Mem. B.5. Joined BEF: not on Medal Card.

24th February 1915
Pte. John Herbert Parker 11916 KIA
born: Swansea   enlisted: Swansea
No known grave. Le Touret Memorial, panel 8 and 9. Joined BEF: 04/01/15.

25th February 1915
Pte. Albert Edward Clark 3/7080   KIA
born: Exeter   enlisted: Exeter
No known grave. Le Touret Memorial, panel 8 and 9. Age 36. Joined BEF: 17/12/14. 1911 Census: House Painter, grandson of Charles Henry Clark, widower, Commercial Traveller, 10 Salem Place, Exeter, Devon. CWGC: son of Mrs. Kate Clark; husband of Eva Mary Clark, 18 Clifton Street, Newtown, Exeter.
26th February 1915
Pte. Bernard F. McCarthy 8514 DoW
born: Plymouth   enlisted: Plymouth
No known grave. Estaires Communal Cemetery and Extension. Sp. Mem. B.4. Age 26. 'B' Company. Joined BEF: not on Medal Card. 1901 Census: son of John McCarthy, beerhouse keeper, and Margaret McCarthy, 19 Granby Street, Plymouth, Devon. 1911 Census: 2/Devons, St. George's Barracks, Malta.

28th February 1915
Pte. Walter Thomas Pike 9066 DoW
born: Guernsey, C. I.   enlisted: Exeter   residence: Plymouth
Buried: Merville Communal Cemetery. Grave I.E.2. Age 22. Joined BEF: 06/11/14 with original cadre. 1901 Census: son of Walter Pike, gardener, and Amelia Pike, Les Pointes, Guernsey, Channel Islands. 1911 Census: with the 1/Devons, Mooltan and Lucknow Barracks, Uttar Pradesh, India.

The 2nd Devons War Diary

MARCH 1915

1st March 1915
Pte. John Rice 3/6484 Died
born: Exeter   enlisted: Exeter
Buried: Ste. Marie Cemetery, Le Havre. Grave Div.19.A.3. Age 21. Joined BEF: 06/11/14 with original cadre. 1911 Census: general labourer, son of John Rice, hawker, and Eva Rice, 5 West Street, Exeter. CWGC: family address as above.

10th March 1915
Lt. Reginald Plumtre Bates KIA
Buried: Royal Irish Rifles Graveyard, Laventie. Grave IV.D.3. Age 25. Joined BEF: 06/11/14 with original cadre. Medal Card records him as Raymond Plumtre Bates. 1911 Census: 2/Lt. Raymond Plumptre Bates, 2/Devons, St. George's Barracks, Malta. Son of Philip Bates and Ada Bates, Edgbaston, Warwickshire.
Lt. Robert Owen Bristowe KIA
Buried: Royal Irish Rifles Graveyard, Laventie. Grave IV.D.4. Age 26. Joined BEF: 06/11/14 with original cadre. Mentioned in despatches. Medal Card annotation: *'Mrs. E. Harrison makes application for 1914 Star in respect of the services of her son, the late R. O. Bristowe. 18/05/19.'* 1911 Census: 2/Lt. Bristowe, 2/Devons, St. George's Barracks, Malta. CWGC: son of Ethel Harrison (formerly Bristowe), 13 Oakley Street, Chelsea, London, and the late Stanley Bristowe.
2/Lt. Mark Gilham Windsor KIA
Buried: Vielle-Chapelle New Military Cemetery, Lacouture. Grave VII.C.5. Age 24. Joined BEF: 26/10/14 as Pte. M.G.Windsor, 28th London Regiment. Commissioned 2/Lt. 2/Devons 14/02/15. CWGC: son of Eleanor Wynne Windsor, 28 Windsor Road, Palmers Green, London, and the late Herbert Bolten Windsor.
2/Lt. George Clinton Wright KIA
Buried: Guards Cemetery, Windy Corner, Cuinchy. Grave IX.D.41. Age 24. Joined BEF: 22/08/14 with 1/Devons as 9678 Cpl. George C. Wright, before commission as 2/Lt. Mentioned in despatches. Annotation to Medal Card: *'G. Wright Esq. applies for 1914 Star in respect of the services of his late son. 04/12/17.'* *'Inf. Recs. Exeter return for disposal 1914 Star 26/05/20.'* CWGC: son of George and Agnes Wright, "Penlee," 7 St. George's Street, Mountfields, Shrewsbury.
Cpl. Frank Bond 8415 KIA
born: Topsham, Devon   enlisted: Exeter   residence: Topsham
No known grave. Le Touret Memorial, panel 8 and 9. Age 22. Joined BEF: 06/11/14 with original cadre. 1911 Census: 2/Devons, St. George's Barracks, Malta.
Pte. Sydney Bowden 11273 KIA
born: Ashburton   enlisted: Exeter   residence: Torquay
No known grave. Le Touret Memorial, panel 8 and 9. Age 19. Joined BEF: 19/01/15. Medal Card and 1901 Census record him as Sidney Bowden. 1901 Census: grandson of Susan Bowden, widow, Globe Arch, Ashburton, Devon.
Pte. Cyril Vivian Brice 3/7604 KIA
born: Falmouth   enlisted: Devonport
No known grave. Le Touret Memorial, panel 8 and 9. Joined BEF: 11/12/14.

Pte. George Burnham 8497 KIA
born: Cork, Ireland   enlisted: Aldershot
No known grave. Le Touret Memorial, panel 8 and 9. Age 24. Joined BEF: 06/11/14 with original cadre. 1901 Census: visitor, son of Kate Burnham, also listed as visitor (husband soldier in South Africa), 1 Finity Cottage, West End Lane, Aldershot, Hants. 1911 Census: 2/Devons, St. George's Barracks, Malta. CWGC: son of the late Mr. and Mrs. Burnham.

Pte. Simon Chivall 9561 KIA
born: Buckfastleigh   enlisted: Exeter   residence: Ashburton
No known grave. Le Touret Memorial, panel 8 and 9. Age about 18. Joined BEF: 22/08/14 with 1/Devons . 1901 Census: recorded Horace S. Chivall, son of William Chivall, dyer's labourer in woollen mills, and Rosina Chivall, woollen weaver, Buckfast Cottages, Buckfastleigh, Devon.

A/Cpl. William Michael Curran 8498 KIA
born: Aldershot   enlisted: Colchester
No known grave. Le Touret Memorial, panel 8 and 9. Age 28. Date joined BEF: 05/11/14, according to Medal Card, with original cadre. 1901 Census: son of Thomas Curran, waiter and Army pensioner, and Catherine Curran, 24 Myrtle Grove, Colchester, Essex. 1911 Census: 2/Devons, St. George's Barracks, Malta. CWGC: son the late Thomas Curran and Catherine Curran, 13 Myrtle Grove, Colchester. His brother Francis John Curran also died in the war.

Sgt. Wilfred Henry Denham 8315 KIA
born: Bideford   enlisted: Exeter   residence: Teignmouth
No known grave. Le Touret Memorial, panel 8 and 9. Age 26. Joined BEF: 06/11/14 with original cadre. 1901 Census: son of Francis Denham, butcher's foreman, and Elizabeth Denham, 11 Chelsea Place, Teignmouth, Devon. 1911 Census: 2/Devons, St. George's Barracks, Malta. CWGC: Francis Denham's address: Bridge Cottage, Norton Fitzwarren, Taunton, Somerset.

Sgt. John Dixon 4348 KIA
born: Camberwell   enlisted: London
No known grave. Le Touret Memorial, panel 8 and 9. Age 51. Joined BEF: 06/11/14 with original cadre. 1901 Census: 'fitter/joiner, 55 Northcote Street, Newcastle-Upon-Tyne, husband of Emily Dixon, father of Alfreda E. Dixon and Helen S. Dixon.

Pte. Fred Drew 3/8083 KIA
born: Crediton   enlisted: Exeter   residence: Lapford
No known grave. Le Touret Memorial, panel 8 and 9. Joined BEF: 17/12/14.

Pte. Harry Fisher 13363 KIA
born: Falmouth   enlisted: Exeter   residence: Falmouth
No known grave. Le Touret Memorial, panel 8 and 9. Joined BEF: 27/12/14. Medal Card annotation: *'Presumed dead'*.

Pte. Edward Frederick Hawkins 9009 KIA
born: Newton Abbot   enlisted: Exeter   residence: Newton Abbot
Buried: Aubers Ridge British Cemetery. Grave V.E.8. Age 26. Joined BEF: 06/11/14 with original cadre. Son of Harry Hawkins, stone quarryman, and Harriett Hawkins, Rock Cottage, Abbotskerwell, Newton Abbot, Devon. CWGC: family address: 3 Hillside Cottages, Abbotskerswell, Newton Abbot.

Pte. Albert Kingdom 7024 KIA
born: Tiverton   enlisted: Exeter   residence: Tiverton
No known grave. Le Touret Memorial, panel 8 and 9. Age 28. Joined BEF: 17/12/14. Medal card annotation: *'Regarded dead'*. 1901 Census: 'servant/stock boy of cattle', Waterhouse

Farm, Bampton, Devon.
Pte. Edwin Miller 11617 KIA
born: Stockport, Cheshire   enlisted: Blackburn, Lancs.   residence: Stockport
No known grave. Le Touret Memorial, panel 8 and 9. Age 35. Joined BEF: 02/02/15. 1901 Census: 'textile machine erector/fitter', son of William Miller, Cotton Mill Manager, 134 Carrington Road, Stockport. 1911 Census: 'spinning mule erector', husband of Mary Miller, father of Charles Edwin Miller, 49 Aberdeen Crescent, Stockport, Cheshire.
Pte. George Nicholls 8428 KIA
born: Plymouth   enlisted: Plymouth
No known grave. Le Touret Memorial, panel 8 and 9. Age 28. Joined BEF: 06/11/14 with original cadre. 1901 Census: 'inmate' in an unspecified institution. 1911 Census: 2/Devons, St. George's Barracks, Malta.
Pte. Thomas Oliver 12867 KIA
born: Treorchy, Glam.   enlisted: Pentre, Glam.   residence: Treorchy
No known grave. Le Touret Memorial, panel 8 and 9. Age 29. Joined BEF: 09/02/15. 'B' Company. 1901 Census: son of William Oliver, coal hewer, and Ann Oliver, 16 Park Road, Ystrady Fodwy, Cwmpark, Rhondda, Glamorgan, Wales.
L/Cpl. Horace Leonard Paddon 7315 KIA
born: Exeter   enlisted: Exeter
No known grave. Le Touret Memorial, panel 8 and 9. Age 28. Joined BEF: 06/11/14 with original cadre. 1901 Census: son of Edward Paddon, bootmaker and dealer, and Mary A. Paddon, Fore Street, Kingsteignton, Devon. 1911 Census: 2/Devons, St. George's Barracks, Malta. CWGC: son of Mrs. Mary A. Paddon, Cowick Cottage, Exeter. Mrs. Paddon applied for 1914 Star due to her son, 19/10/19.
Sgt. George Sanders 8598 KIA
born: London   enlisted: Ilfracombe
Buried: Guards Cemetery, Windy Corner, Cuinchy. Grave IX.C.29. Joined BEF: 06/11/14 with original cadre.
Pte. Henry Smith 7605 KIA
born: Bath   enlisted: Bath
No known grave. Le Touret Memorial, panel 8 and 9. Age 28. No Medal Card. CWGC: son of Thomas Smith and Fanny Smith.
Pte. Henry Trace 9003 KIA
born: Bideford   enlisted: Exeter   residence: Monkleigh
No known grave. Le Touret Memorial, panel 8 and 9. Age 24. Joined BEF: 06/11/14 with original cadre. 1911 Census: 1/Devons, Mooltan and Lucknow Barracks, Uttar Pradesh, India. CWGC: son of John Trace, 14 Dugdale Street, Minehead, Somerset.
Pte. Brinley Vanstone 3/8310 KIA
born: Swansea   enlisted: Swansea
No known grave. Le Touret Memorial, panel 8 and 9. Joined BEF: 04/01/15. Age 22. 1901 Census: Brinley Geo. Vanstone, son of Charles Vanstone, worker steelworks, and Elizabeth Vanstone, 28 Brunswick Street, Swansea. 1911 Census: general labourer, boarding at 14 Pegler Street, Brynhyrfryd.
Pte. David John Watkins 12864 KIA
born: Tredegar, Mon.   enlisted: Pontypridd, Glam.   residence: Treforest
No known grave. Le Touret Memorial, panel 8 and 9. Age 20. Joined BEF: 09/02/15. 1901 Census: recorded as born 1898, so may have lied about his age when he enlisted. Son of David Watkins, collier, and Mary Ann Watkins, 8 Tramroad Side, Merthyr Tydfil, Wales. CWGC: son

of Mrs. Mary Ann Watkins, 5 Egypt Street, Pontypridd, Glam.
L/Cpl. Joseph Wedge 14607 KIA
born: Cannock, Staffs.   enlisted: Walsall, Staffs.
No known grave. Le Touret Memorial, panel 8 and 9. Age 29. Joined BEF: 09/02/15. Medal card annotation reads, *'Death regarded 10/03/15'*. 1901 Census: son of Henry Wedge, navvy, and Alice Wedge, 6 Whitehall Road, Walsall, Staffs. CWGC: son of Henry Wedge, 15 Tantarra Street, Walsall, Staffs; husband of Elsie Melita Wedge, 131 Embankment Road, Plymouth.
A/Cpl. Walter John Wilson 6977 KIA
born: Leyton   enlisted: Stratford
No known grave. Le Touret Memorial, panel 8 and 9. Age 28. Joined BEF: 06/11/14 with original cadre. 1911 Census: 2/Devons, St. George's Barracks, Malta. CWGC: son of Mrs. Mary Ann Swift, 110 Vansittart Road, Forest Gate, Essex.
Pte. Sidney Francis Harry Gigg 8705 DoW
born: Honiton   enlisted: Exeter   residence: Seaton
No known grave. Le Touret Memorial, panel 8 and 9. Age 26. Joined BEF: 06/11/14 with original cadre. 1911 Census: 2/Devons, St. George's Barracks, Malta. CWGC: son of Sidney Gigg and Elizabeth Ann Gigg, 12 Summerland Place, Seaton, Devon.

11th March 1915
Pte. John James Choak 9383 KIA
born: Helston, Cornwall   enlisted: Newton Abbot   residence: Bovey Tracey
No known grave. Le Touret Memorial, panel 8 and 9. Age 21. Joined BEF: 16/02/15. 1911 Census: 'Soldier 3/Devons '. CWGC: son of George A. M. Choak and Louisa Choak, 17 South View, Bovey Tracey, Devon.
Pte. Sidney Herman Farley 9579 KIA
born: Totnes   enlisted: Exeter   residence: Totnes
No known grave. Le Touret Memorial, panel 8 and 9. Age 24. Joined BEF: 06/11/14 with original cadre.
Pte. John William Jones 12754 KIA
born: Pontardulais   enlisted: Swansea   residence: Pontardulais
No known grave. Le Touret Memorial, panel 8 and 9. Age 19. Joined BEF: 04/01/15. CWGC and Medal Card record him as William John Jones.
Pte. James Lenihan 5116 KIA
born: London   enlisted: London
No known grave. Le Touret Memorial, panel 8 and 9. Joined BEF: 06/11/14 with original cadre. 1911 Census: 2/Devons, St. George's Barracks, Malta.
Cpl. William Henry Margetts 9335 KIA
born: Exeter   enlisted: Hele, Devon
No known grave. Le Touret Memorial, panel 8 and 9. Age 22. Joined BEF: 06/11/14 with original cadre. 1901 Census: son of Henry Edward Margetts, railway station master, and Eva Florence Margetts, 10 Summerland Villas, Minehead, Somerset. 1911 Census: Paper Maker, living with his parents. CWGC: son of Eva Florence Margetts, 12 Stanley Terrace, Bristol Road, Bridgwater, Somerset, and the late Henry Edward Margetts. SDGW records his name as Oxford Margetts. 'Oxford' may have been a nickname because the entry stating that he was born in Exeter is incorrect, as the 1901 and 1911 Census' both record that he was born in Bletchingdon, Oxfordshire. Presumably his father moved to Devon with his job on the railway.

Pte. John Parker 9180 KIA
born: Tiverton   enlisted: Tiverton   residence: Halberton
No known grave. Le Touret Memorial, panel 8 and 9. Age 22. Joined BEF: 06/11/14 with original cadre.CWGC: brother of Mrs. B. Pinn, Canns Cottage, Beaford, Devon.

Pte. James Pearce 3/7062 KIA
born: Cholsey   enlisted: Reading   residence: Finchampstead
No known grave. Le Touret Memorial, panel 8 and 9. Joined BEF: 17/12/14.

Pte. John W. Perryman 8968 KIA
born: Leytonstone, London   enlisted: Exeter   residence: Ottery St.Mary
No known grave. Le Touret Memorial, panel 8 and 9. Age 22. Joined BEF: 06/11/14 with original cadre. 1911 Census: working in a grocery, son of Thomas Perryman, insurance agent, and Lizzie Perryman, 10 Candler Street, Tottenham, Middlesex. CWGC: Thomas W. Perryman, auctioneer, Lizzie Perryman and family, 25 High Street, Ilfracombe, Devon.

Pte. James Randall 6692 KIA
born: Crediton   enlisted: Exeter   residence: Crediton
No known grave. Le Touret Memorial, panel 8 and 9. Age 32. Joined BEF: 06/11/14 with original cadre. 1911 Census: 2/Devons, St. George's Barracks, Malta. CWGC: brother of Mr. A. G. Randall, The Black Dog, Crediton, Devon.

Pte. Charles Shute 8800 KIA
born: Torquay   enlisted: Torquay
No known grave. Le Touret Memorial, panel 8 and 9. Age 26. Joined BEF: 06/11/14 with original cadre. 1901 Census: son of the late James Albert Shute, stone quarryman, and Sarah Ann Shute, 18 Church Lane, Tormoham, Torquay, Devon. 1911 Census: 2/Devons, St. George's Barracks, Malta. CWGC: son of the late James Albert Shute and Sarah Ann Shute; husband of Mabel Florence Shute, 4 Carlton Road, Ellacombe, Torquay.

A/Cpl. William John Simpson 8713 KIA
born: Manchester   enlisted: Portsmouth   residence: Portsmouth
No known grave. Le Touret Memorial, panel 8 and 9. Joined BEF: 06/11/14 with original cadre. 1911 Census: 2/Devons, St. George's Barracks, Malta.

Pte. James Smith 8735 KIA
born: Plymouth   enlisted: Plymouth
No known grave. Le Touret Memorial, panel 8 and 9. Age 33. Joined BEF: 06/11/14 with original cadre. 1901 Census: farm wagon driver, son of Emma Smith, widow, 42 High Street, Plymouth, Devon.

Pte. John William Turner 11222 KIA
born: Chulmleigh   enlisted: Barnstaple
No known grave. Le Touret Memorial, panel 8 and 9. Age 21. Joined BEF: 22/02/15.1901 Census: son of John William Turner, agricultural labourer, and Mary J. Turner, Grosvenor Street, Barnstaple, Devon. 1911 Census: grocer's assistant, son of John William Turner, mason's labourer, and Mary Jane Turner, 2 Alma Place, Pilton Street, Barnstaple, Devon.

Pte. John Yeo 3/7088 KIA
born: Exeter   enlisted: Exeter
No known grave. Le Touret Memorial, panel 8 and 9. Age 29. Joined BEF: 06/11/14 with original cadre. Son of Thomas Yeo, railway clerk, and Mary J. Yeo, 36 Paris Street, Exeter, Devon.

Pte. Lancelot Beynon 12632 DoW
born: Neath, Glam.   enlisted: Aberavon, Glam.
Buried: Merville Communal Cemetery. Grave I.D.2. Age 39. Joined BEF: 02/02/15.CWGC: son

of William Beynon and Mary Beynon, 42 Wern Road, Skewen, Neath.
Pte. Harry Green 10118 DoW
born: Shepton Mallett   enlisted: Cardiff   residence: Pilton
Buried: Estaires Communal Cemetery and Extension. Grave II.R.2. Joined BEF: 16/12/14. CWGC: son of Mr. H. T. Green, Lower Street, Pilton, Shepton Mallet.
Pte. John Joseph Munro 3/7629 DoW
born: London   enlisted: London
No known grave. Le Touret Memorial, panel 8 and 9. Age 32. Joined BEF: 11/12/14. 1911 Census: tin-plate worker (general), living with his mother and daughter, 40 Wade Street, Poplar, London. CWGC: husband of Adelaide Emily Munro, 128 Kerbey Street, Poplar, London.
Pte. Richard Selley 10016 DoW
born: Newton Abbot   enlisted: Newton Abbot
Buried: Estaires Communal Cemetery and Extension. Grave III.C.8. Age 18. Joined BEF: 16/12/15. 1901 Census: son of Richard Selley, urban council labourer, and Caroline Selley, No. 4 Court, Marlborough Street, Newton Abbot, Devon. 1911 Census: errand boy, living with parents at 41 Hilton Road, Newton Abbot, Devon.

12th March 1915
Captain Claude Alexander Lafone, DSO KIA
Buried: Royal Irish Rifles Graveyard, Laventie. Grave IV.D.6. Age 38. 'D' Company. Joined BEF: 06/11/14 with original cadre. CWGC: son of Alfred William Lafone and Harriet Lafone, Springfield, Walton-on-Thames, Surrey. A. W. Lafone applied for his son's 1914 Star, 26/11/17.
Pte. William Brooks 8077 KIA
born: Tiverton   enlisted: Tiverton
No known grave. Le Touret Memorial, panel 8 and 9. Joined BEF: 06/11/14 with original cadre. CWGC: son of James Brooks and Ellen Brooks, Knowle, Bawdrip, Bridgwater, Somerset.
Pte. Alfred John Brown 13139 KIA
born: Torquay   enlisted: Porth, Glam.   residence: Torquay
No known grave. Le Touret Memorial, panel 8 and 9. Age 29. 'B' Company. Joined BEF: 17/02/15. 1901 Census: bootmaker's assistant, son of Elizabeth Brown, widow, 8 Madrepere Road, Tormoham, Torquay, Devon. CWGC: Elizabeth Brown's address 3 Temperance Place, Union Street, Torquay.
A/Cpl. Ernest Daniel Eva 8850 KIA
born: Plymouth   enlisted: Devonport
No known grave. Le Touret Memorial, panel 8 and 9. Age 23. Joined BEF: 06/11/14 with original cadre. Medal card annotation reads: *'B. Eva applies for 1914 Star due to late son'*. 1901 Census: son of Daniel Eva, labourer, and Bessie Eva, wash works, of 2 Parade, Plymouth, Devon. 1911 Census: 2/Devons, St. George's Barracks, Malta.
Pte. Nathaniel Gibson 8694 KIA
born: Devonport   enlisted: Exeter   residence: Devonport
No known grave. Le Touret Memorial, panel 8 and 9. Age 26. Date joined BEF: 06/11/14 with original cadre. 1901 Census: 'inmate' at the Shaftesbury School, Bisley, Surrey. 1911 Census: 2/Devons, St. George's Barracks, Malta. CWGC: the son of the late John Gibson and Mary Gibson.
Pte. Bertram George Gillard 9637 KIA
born: Kingsbridge   enlisted: Kingsbridge
No known grave. Le Touret Memorial, panel 8 and 9. Age 19. 'B' Company. Joined BEF:

06/11/14 with original cadre. 1901 Census: son of John Thomas Gillard, house painter, and Susan Gillard, of Church Street, Kingsbridge, Devon. CWGC: family address: Kent Cottage, Fore Street, Kingsbridge, Devon.

Pte. Giles Glanfield 8555 KIA
born: Tiverton   enlisted: Tiverton
No known grave. Le Touret Memorial, panel 8 and 9. Age 30. Joined BEF: 05/11/14 with original cadre. Has a second Medal Card with name spelt 'Glandfield'. 1901 Census: son of John Glanfield, gardener, and Sarah Glanfield, Garden Cottage, Loxbeare, Tiverton, Devon.

Pte. Percy Henry Gribble 8534 KIA
born: Axminster   enlisted: Axminster
No known grave. Le Touret Memorial, panel 8 and 9. Joined BEF: 06/11/14 with original cadre. 1911 Census: 2/Devons, St. George's Barracks, Malta.

Pte. Fearnley Hare 9121 KIA
born: Totnes   enlisted: Exeter   residence: Buckfastleigh
No known grave. Le Touret Memorial, panel 8 and 9. Age 22. Joined BEF: 06/11/14 with original cadre. 1901 Census: son of Emma Hare, widow, engine cleaner at woollen mill, Buckfast Cottage, Buckfastleigh, Devon.

L/Cpl. Samuel Haskings 85071 KIA
born: Tiverton   enlisted: Tiverton
No known grave. Le Touret Memorial, panel 8 and 9. Age 23. Joined BEF: 06/11/14 with original cadre. 1911 Census: 2/Devons, St. George's Barracks, Malta. CWGC: son of the late Mrs. Leah Haskings, 6 Rudd's Buildings, Melbourne Street, Tiverton, Devon.

Pte. Charles Henry Hodson 11293 KIA
born: Brixham   enlisted: Exeter   residence: Brixham
No known grave. Le Touret Memorial, panel 8 and 9. Age 21.
No Medal Card. 1901 Census: son of Charles Edward Hodson, grocer (shopkeeper) and Fanny Green Hodson, 10 Brach, Brixham, Devon. CWGC: family address: Avon House, Brixham, Devon.

Pte. William Samuel James 12913 KIA
born: Siftney, Cornwall   enlisted: Caerphilly, Glam.
No known grave. Le Touret Memorial, panel 8 and 9. Age 36. Joined BEF: 04/01/15. CWGC: son of Elizabeth James, 29 Mid Road, Caerphilly, Cardiff, and the late William James.

Pte. Charles Keefe Masey 11526 KIA
born: Dawlish   enlisted: Barnstaple   residence: Saltash
No known grave. Le Touret Memorial, panel 8 and 9. Age 23. Joined BEF: 09/02/15. 1901 Census: son of James G. J. H. Masey, chief boatman for coast guard, and Elizabeth C. Masey, Higher Town, St. Martins, Scilly Isles. 1911 Census: apprentice printer, son of James Masey, naval pensioner, and Elizabeth C. Masey, 118 Fore Street, Saltash, Cornwall. CWGC: son of Elizabeth Clements Masey, Bethel, St. Austell, Cornwall, and the late James Masey.

Pte. Frederick Charles Pearce 3/6757 KIA
born: Honiton   enlisted: Exeter   residence: Honiton
Buried: Royal Irish Rifles Graveyard Cemetery, Laventie. Grave VI.A.18. Age 20. Joined BEF: 06/11/14 with original cadre. 1911 Census: 'assistant on road and farm', son of William Pearce, road contractor, and Susan Pearce, Shortmoor, Stockland, Honiton, Devon. CWGC: son of William Pearce and Susan Pearce, 95 High Street, Pontypool, Monmouthshire. Native of Combe Raleigh, Devon.

Sgt. James Madick Moses Tuckerman 8459 KIA
born: Kingsbridge   enlisted: Dartmouth
No known grave. Le Touret Memorial, panel 8 and 9. Age 25. Joined BEF: 06/11/14 with original cadre. 1901 Census: son of Robert H. Tuckerman, timber haulier/carter, and Fanny S. Tuckerman, Smith Street, Dartmouth, Devon. 1911 Census: 2/Devons, St. George's Barracks, Malta.

Pte. Walter Willis 12888 KIA
born: Caerphilly, Glam.   enlisted: Caerphilly
Buried: Vielle-Chapelle New Military Cemetery, Lacouture. Grave VIII.C.2. No Medal Card. CWGC: brother of Mrs. S. A. Davies, 7 Inverness Place, Roath Park, Cardiff.

Pte. William Evans 3/8177 DoW
born: Swansea   enlisted: Swansea
Buried: Boulogne Eastern Cemetery. Grave III.D.6. Joined BEF: 04/01/15.

Pte. Arthur Horton 8367 DoW
born: Plymouth   enlisted: Plymouth
Buried: Boulogne Eastern Cemetery. Grave III.D.8. Age 25. 'A' Company. Joined BEF: 06/11/14 with original cadre. 1911 Census: 2/Devons, St. George's Barracks, Malta. CWGC: son of Phillip Horton and Elizabeth Horton, 11 Belmont Road, Ivybridge, Devon.

Pte. Ernest Smith 11196 DoW
born: Budleigh Salterton   enlisted: Exeter   residence: Budleigh Salterton
No known grave. Le Touret Memorial, panel 8 and 9. Age 21. Joined BEF: 19/01/15. 1911 Census: farm labourer, son of Charles Smith, agricultural implement maker machinist wood work, and Mary Smith, Milltown, Marwood, Devon. CWGC: brother of Fredrick W. Smith, Cromley Cottage, East Budleigh, Devon.

Pte. Richard Warren 8720 DoW
born: Bow, Devon   enlisted: Exeter   residence: Copplestone, Devon
Buried: Boulogne Eastern Cemetery. Grave III.D.8. Age 23. Joined BEF: 06/11/14 with original cadre. 1901 Census: son of John Warren, horseman on farm, and Mary Warren, Marshall Cottage, Ide, Tiverton, Devon. 1911 Census: 2/Devons, St. George's Barracks, Malta. CWGC: son of Mary Jane Warren, of Bagborough, Taunton, and the late John Warren.

Pte. John Weeks 11205 DoW
born: Torrington   enlisted: Exeter   residence: Torrington
Buried: Estaires Communal Cemetery and Extension. Grave III.B.5. Age 33. Joined BEF: 02/02/15. 1901 Census: navvy, son of George Weeks, carpenter, and Elizabeth Weeks, 119 New Street, Great Torrington, Devon. CWGC: son of George Weeks and the late Elizabeth Weeks.

13th March 1915
Pte. Vincent Cahill 3/7535 KIA
born: Torquay   enlisted: Exeter   residence: Torquay
No known grave. Le Touret Memorial, panel 8 and 9. Age 40. Joined BEF: 12/12/14. 1891 Census: son of William Cahill, labourer, of 20 Melville Street, Tormoham, Torquay, Devon. 1911 Census: general labourer, husband of Elizabeth Cahill, laundry woman, 12 Alexandra Road, Ellacombe, Torquay, Devon. It is possible that Vincent Cahill had served with the 2/Devons for an unknown period between 1892 and 1910 and, as a reservist, was recalled to the colours in 1914. CWGC: son of William Cahill and Mary Cahill, husband of Elizabeth Jane Cahill, 32 Queen's Street, Torquay.

Pte. William Lewis Gratton 3/7817 KIA
born: Aberdare, Glam.   enlisted: Exeter   residence: Tedburn St.Mary
No known grave. Le Touret Memorial, panel 8 and 9. Age 40. Joined BEF: 09/02/15. Medal card annotation: *'died on or since 13/05/15'*. 1891 Census: agricultural labourer, son of William Henry Gratton, agricultural labourer, and Thirza Gratton, domestic, of Dennington Road, Swimbridge, Devon. 1901 Census: navvy, husband of Annie E. Gratton, 17 Adelaide Cottages, Hanwell, Middlesex (son Sidney was born in Hanwell in 1901). 1911 Census: farm labourer, husband of Annie Gratton, Wrafton R.S.O. Devon. CWGC: son of William Henry and Thirza Gratton, Landkey Newland, Barnstaple, Devon, husband of Annie Elizabeth Gratton, 4 Bradiford Pilton, Barnstaple, Devon. His brothers Alfred Frank Gratton (2/Devons 06/10/16), Thomas John Gratton and Sydney James Gratton also died in the war.

Pte. Tom Hughes 12874 KIA
born: Pontardulais   enlisted: Swansea   residence: Pontardulais
No known grave. Le Touret Memorial, panel 8 and 9. Age 22. Joined BEF: 04/01/15. CWGC: son of Thomas and Frances Hughes, Myrtle House, Mynyddllno, Pontardulais, Glam.

Pte. George Reed 8493 KIA
born: Havant, Hants.   enlisted: Gosport, Hants.   residence: Fareham, Hants.
No known grave. Le Touret Memorial, panel 8 and 9. Age 25. Joined BEF: 06/11/14 with original cadre. 'B' Company. 1911 Census: 2/Devons, St. George's Barracks, Malta. CWGC: son of Mrs. G. Reed, 67 Kent Street, Portsea, Portsmouth.

Pte. George Robert Russell 3/6979 KIA
born: London   enlisted: London
No known grave. Le Touret Memorial, panel 8 and 9. Joined BEF: 06/11/14 with original cadre. Medal card annotation: *'Mrs. Russell makes application for clasp in respect of the services of her late son, G. R. Russell'*. 1911 Census: draper's assistant, son of George Thomas Russell, coachman, and Miriam Russell, 55 Canton Street, Poplar, London.

Pte. Albert Smith 12650 KIA
born: Plymouth   enlisted: Devonport   residence: Ivybridge
No known grave. Le Touret Memorial, panel 8 and 9. Joined BEF: 02/02/15. Medal card annotation:*'Death regarded' 13/03/15.*

Cpl. Walter Frank Sparrow 8293 KIA
born: Barnstaple   enlisted: Exeter
No known grave. Le Touret Memorial, panel 8 and 9. Age 25. Joined BEF: 05/11/14 with original cadre. 1891 Census: son of Charles A. Sparrow, railway porter, and Susanna Sparrow, Newport Road, Barnstaple, Devon. 1911 Census: 2/Devons, St. George's Barracks, Malta. CWGC: son of Mrs. Susanna Sparrow, 2 Higher Church, Barnstaple, and the late Mr. Sparrow.

Pte. Walter Stoyles 8319 KIA
born: Dawlish   enlisted: Exeter   residence: Dawlish
No known grave. Le Touret Memorial, panel 8 and 9. Age 26. Joined BEF: 06/11/14 with original cadre. 1911 Census: 2/Devons, St. George's Barracks, Malta.

Pte. Henry Wallser 8854 KIA
born: Jersey C.I.   enlisted: Devonport
No known grave. Le Touret Memorial, panel 8 and 9. Age 23. 'B' Company. Date joined BEF: 06/11/14 with original cadre. 1911 Census: 2/Devons, St. George's Barracks, Malta. CWGC: son of the late John Wallser and Isabelle Wallser, 10 Wotten Cottage, Rendle Street, Plymouth.

Pte. William David Warren 9681 KIA
born: Plymouth   enlisted: Exeter   residence: Kingsbridge
No known grave. Le Touret Memorial, panel 8 and 9. Age 20. Joined BEF: 06/11/14 with

original cadre. 1901 Census: son of Henry J. Warren, ordinary agricultural labourer, and Alice Warren, Cricket Field, Aldeburgh, Suffolk.

Pte. Alfred Hugh Badcock 12787 DoW
born: Exeter   enlisted: Caerphilly
Buried: Estaires Communal Cemetery and Extension. Grave II.P.3. Age 34. Joined BEF: 17/2/15. 1901 Census: 'general porter', son of Hugh Badcock and Elizabeth Badcock, dressmaker, 61 Exe Street, Exeter, Devon. 1911 Census: 'skilled labourer', husband of Ellen Badcock, 2 Trinity Place, Exeter.

Pte. Owen Evans 13204 DoW
born: Llangeinwen, Anglesey   enlisted: Tonyrefail, Glam.
Buried: Merville Communal Cemetery. Grave I.M.7. Joined BEF: 02/02/15.

Pte. Albert Henry Lomas 9891 DoW
born: Aldershot   enlisted: Woolwich   residence: Charlton
Buried: Merville Communal Cemetery. Grave II.A.9. Age 22. Joined BEF: 06/11/14 with original cadre. 1901 Census: son of Joseph Lomas, dockyard labourer, and Mary Louisa Lomas, 38 Cedar Grove, Charlton, Greenwich. 1911 Census: shop assistant, living with parents, 13 Church Lane, New Charlton, Kent. CWGC: family address: 16 Lydenburg Street, Charlton, London.

Pte. Levi Taylor 3/7783 DoW
born: Birmingham   enlisted: Birmingham
Buried: Le Touquet-Paris Plage Communal Cemetery. Grave I.B.5. Joined BEF: 27/12/14. Record in SDGW stating that he died at 'home' is suspect, as he is buried in France.

14th March 1915

L/Cpl. William Harrild 8787 KIA
born: Deptford   enlisted: Devonport   residence: Deptford
No known grave. Le Touret Memorial, panel 8 and 9. Age 23. Joined BEF: 06/11/14 with original cadre. 1901 Census: son of Henry Harrild, carpenter, and Esther Harrild, 47 Creek Street, Deptford. 1911 Census: 2/Devons, St. George's Barracks, Malta. CWGC: family address: 12 Bolton Road, Edmonton, London.

Pte. James Parr 8881 DoW
born: Crediton   enlisted: Exeter   residence: Crediton
Buried: Merville Communal Cemetery. Grave II.D.5. Age 24. Joined BEF: 22/08/14 with 1st Battalion. 1901 Census: son of James Parr, mason's labourer, and Bessie Parr, Lees Court, High Street, Crediton, Devon. CWGC: son of Mrs. B. Parr, of "Kiddicott," High Street, Crediton, Devon. CWGC lists his death as 10th March 1915.

Pte. Reginald Hawkin Purchase 8610 DoW
born: Cullompton   enlisted: Exeter   residence: Cullompton
Buried: St. Sever Cemetery, Rouen. Grave A.5.16. Age 32. 'B' Company. Joined BEF: 06/11/14 with original cadre. 1901 Census: shop assistant, son of Agnes Purchase, shopkeeper, Fore Street, Cullompton, Devon. 1911 Census: 2/Devons, St. George's Barracks, Malta. CWGC: son of late Mr. and Mrs. T. H. Purchase, Cullompton, Devon.

Pte. George Edwin Weeks 8641 DoW
born: Plymouth   enlisted: Exeter   residence: Plymouth
Buried: Estaires Communal Cemetery and Extension. Age 25. Joint Grave III.B.19. Joined BEF: 16/02/15. 1911 Census: 2/Devons, patient at Military Hospital, Cottonera, Strada Mercanti, Valletta, Malta.

The 2nd Devons War Diary

15th March 1915
Pte. William Henry Bagwell 11244 DoW
born: Torquay   enlisted: Exeter   residence: Torquay
Buried: Wimereux Communal Cemetery. Grave I.E.3. Age 19. Joined BEF: 02/02/15. 1901 Census: son of William Bagwell, general labourer, and Lucy Bagwell, 8 Higher Terrace Mews, Torquay, Devon.
Pte. Albert George Berry 11839 DoW
born: Ottery St.Mary   enlisted: Exeter   residence: Ottery St.Mary
Buried: Longuenesse (St. Omer) Souvenir Cemetery. Grave I.A.60. Age 31. Joined BEF: 06/11/14. 1901 Census: son of William Berry, and Mary Berry, lace maker, 35 Sandhill Street, Ottery St. Mary, Devon. 1911 Census: bricklayer, husband of Maud Mary Berry, father of three children, 46 Sandhill Street, Ottery St. Mary, Devon.

16th March 1915
Pte. Herbert William Godfrey 11508 DoW
born: Ottery St.Mary   enlisted: Exeter   residence: Ottery St.Mary
Buried: Estaires Communal Cemetery and Extension. Grave III.H.1. Age 20. Joined BEF: 19/01/15. 1901 Census: son of Mr. Herbert J. Godfrey, bricklayer's labourer, and Harriet J. Godfrey, Broad Lane, Winkfield, Surrey. 1911 Census: servant, 11 Yonder Street, Ottery St. Mary, Devon. CWGC: family address: Little Silver, Exminster, Devon.
Pte. Harry Stoneman 9591 DoW
born: Exeter   enlisted: Exeter
Buried: Estaires Communal Cemetery and Extension. Grave III.H.2. Age 19. Joined BEF: 06/11/14 with original cadre. 1901 Census: son of Harry Stoneman, market tolls collector, and Emily Mary Stoneman, 11 Cottons Buildings, Exeter, Devon. 1911 Census: 'wellwright' (wheelwright?), son of Harry Stoneman, marine pensioner, and Emily M. Stoneman, 36 St. Leonards Avenue, Exeter.

17th March 1915
Pte. Clarence Henry Crook 3/6616 KIA
born: Dawlish   enlisted Exeter   residence: Dawlish
No known grave. Le Touret Memorial, panel 8 and 9. Age 19. Joined BEF: 05/11/14 with original cadre. 1901 Census: son of James Crook, mason, and Alma Crook, Manor Row, Dawlish, Devon. 1911 Census: telegraph messenger, son of James Henry Crook, bricklayer, stepson of Louisa Crook, Golden Terrace, Dawlish, Devon.
Pte. William John Boyland 3/6824 DoW
born: Tallaton, Devon   enlisted: Exeter
Buried: Aubers Ridge British Cemetery. Grave V.C.12. Age 18. Joined BEF: 19/01/15. 1901 Census: son of John Thomas Boyland, ordinary agricultural labourer, and Selina Boyland, High Story, Blackthorne Lane, Pinhoe, Devon. 1911 Census: green grocer's errand boy, son of John Thomas Boyland, carter, and Selina Boyland, 18 Roseberry Road, Exmouth, Devon.
Pte. Albert Edward Spicer 9077 DoW
born: Exeter   enlisted: Exeter   residence: Plymouth
Buried: Boulogne Eastern Cemetery. Grave III.D.35. Age 24. Joined BEF: 05/11/14 with original cadre.

18th March 1915
Pte. Reggie Harding 3/8200 DoW
born: Swansea   enlisted: Swansea
Buried: Aubers Ridge British Cemetery. Grave V.B.11. Age 19. No Medal Card . CWGC: son of Thomas James Harding and Grace Harding, 35 Pentreguinea Road, St. Thomas, Swansea.

19th March 1915
Pte. William Henry Beer 9399 KIA
born: Kenn   enlisted: Exeter   residence: Dawlish
No known grave. Le Touret Memorial, panel 8 and 9. Age 23. Joined BEF: 06/11/14 with original cadre. CWGC: son of Walter Beer and Maria Beer, Tucker's Cottage, Ide, Exeter.
Pte. Henry Gooding 8776 KIA
born: Sidmouth   enlisted: Exeter   residence: Sidmouth
No known grave. Le Touret Memorial, panel 8 and 9. Age 25. Joined BEF: 05/11/14 with original cadre. 1901 Census: son of Arthur Gooding, labourer, and Alice Gooding, lace maker, Sidbury, Honiton, Devon.

20th March 1915
Pte. Stanley John Foster 8038 DoW
born: Plymouth   enlisted: Devonport
Buried: Boulogne Eastern Cemetery. Grave III.D.46. Age 27. Joined BEF: 06/11/14 with original cadre. 1911 Census: 2/Devons, St. George's Barracks, Malta. CWGC: brother of Percy S. Foster, 28 Harbour View, Devonport, Devonshire.

25th March 1915
Pte. Arthur Turner (home) 8999 DoW
Born: Bideford, Devon   enlisted: Exeter, Devon   residence: Barnstaple, Devon
Buried: Barnstaple Cemetery. Grave A.247. Age 26. 'B' Company. Joined BEF: 22/08/14 with original cadre of 1/Devons .*Mrs. Isabella Turner makes application for Mons Star due to her late son, Pte A. Turner.* 1901 Census: son of John Turner, bootmaker, and Emma Turner, London Street, Barnstaple, Devon. CWGC: son of Mr. and Mrs. J. B. Turner, 8 Loverings Place, Barnstaple.

26th March 1915
Pte. William Henry Hill 3/7068 DoW
Born: Stockport, Cheshire   enlisted: Plymouth, Devon
Buried: Boulogne Eastern Cemetery. Grave III.D.63. Age 17. Joined BEF: 16/02/15. 1901 Census: son of Henry Hill, bricklayer, and Bertha Hill, cotton reeler and spinner, 18 Ducie Street, Stockport, Cheshire. 1911 Census: schoolboy, son of Henry Hill, bricklayer, and Bertha Hill, 3 Cobury Street, Plymouth, Devon. CWGC: son of Henry and Bertha Hill, 28 St. Andrew's Street, Plymouth, Devon.

28th March 1915
Pte. Albert George Gudge 9083 DoW
Born: Lyme Regis, Dorset   enlisted: Exeter, Devon   residence: Uplyme, Devon
Buried: Sailly-Sur-La-Lys Canadian Cemetery. Grave II.A.6. Age 21. 'D' Company. Joined BEF: 06/11/14 with original cadre of 2/Devons . 1911 Census: 1/Devons, Mooltan and Lucknow Barracks, Uttar Pradesh, India. CWGC: son of Joseph and Ellen Gudge, The Haven, Harcombe,

Uplyme, Devon.
Pte. William Richard Hughes 14219 DoW
Born: Porth, Glam.   enlisted: Mardy, Glam.
Buried: St. Sever Cemetery, Rouen. Grave A.7.3. Age 19. Joined BEF: 27/12/14. 1911 Census: coal miner/hewer, son of Thomas Hughes, colliery fireman, and Elizabeth Ann Hughes, 66 James Street, Mardy, Glam. CWGC: son of Thomas and E. Ann Hughes, address as 1911.

Martin Body

APRIL 1915

1st April 1915
Pte. Edward Thomas Foster 11777 KIA
born: Devonport   enlisted: Exeter   residence: Tiverton
No known grave. Ploegsteert Memorial, panel 3. Age 29. Joined BEF: 11/12/14. 1901 Census: apprentice French polisher, son of John Foster, Naval fireman, retired, and Susan Foster, 64 Alexandra Road, Devonport, Devon. 1911 Census: French polisher and cabinet maker, husband of Dorothy Foster, father of two, 8 William Street, Plymouth, Devon.

13th April 1915
Pte. George Edward Simpkins 9688 KIA
born: Gloucester   enlisted: Gloucester
Buried: Ration Farm Military Cemetery, La Chapelle-D'Armentieres. Grave VI.B.3. Age 19. Joined BEF: 22/08/14 with 1/Devons . 1901 Census: son of Albert Edward Simpkins, engine fitter, and Alberta Simpkins, 68 Gloucester Street, Devonport. 1911 Census: engine fitter's assistant, son of Albert E. Simpkins, engine fitter, and Alberta Simpkins, 114a Charlotte Street, Morice Town, Devonport.   CWGC: family address: 114a Charlotte Street, Devonport.

15th April 1915
Pte. Robert Richard Williams 3/6855 KIA
born: Plymouth   enlisted: London
Buried: Ration Farm Military Cemetery, La Chapelle-D'Armentieres. Grave VI.K.2. Age 18. Joined BEF: 06/11/14 with original cadre. CWGC: youngest son of Ralph Abercrombie Williams and Mary Ann Williams, 1 River Street, Essex Road, Islington, London.

The 2nd Devons War Diary

MAY 1915

4th May 1915
Pte. John Tarr 15096 KIA
Born: West Knowle, Somerset   enlisted: Taunton, Somerset   residence: Dulverton
Buried: Le Trou Aid Post Cemetery, Fleurbaix. Grave D,8. Age 36. Joined BEF: 17/03/15. 1911 Census: farm labourer, husband of Frances Tarr, father of three, Marsh Bridge, Dulverton, Somerset. CWGC: husband of Frances Tarr, 2 Weir Head, Dulverton, Somerset.

7th May 1915
Sgt. George Taylor Randle 7742 DoW
Born: Kingsbridge, Devon   enlisted: Kingsbridge, Devon
Buried: Sailly-Sur-La-Lys Canadian Cemetery. Grave II.E.106. Age 29. Joined BEF: 06/11/14 with original cadre as a Private. Medal card indicates that at the time of his death he had transferred to the Army Cyclist Corps, promoted to Sergeant, serial no. 1485. 1911 Census: 2/Devons, St. George's Barracks, Malta. CWGC: brother of Samuel Randle, Plymouth Road, South Brent, Devon.

9th May 1915
2/Lt. Frederick Cecil Banes Walker KIA
Buried: Le Trou Aid Post Cemetery, Fleurbaix. Grave F.1. Age 26. Joined BEF: not on Medal Card. Formerly Pte. Walker, 4th Gloucestershire Regiment, commissioned in 3/Devons, attached to 2/Devons. CWGC: son of Harry and Mary Alexandra Banes Walker, "Verriers," North Petherton, Bridgwater, Somerset.
Lt. Charles Alan Ramsay (Bunny) Tennant KIA
Buried: Le Trou Aid Post Cemetery, Fleurbaix. Grave C.5. Age 26. Joined BEF: not on Medal Card. Formerly Pte. Tennant, 2742, 14th London Regiment, commissioned as 2/Lt. in the Dorsetshire Regiment and attached to the 2/Devons. 1901 Census: born at Broxbourne, Hertfordshire, boarder at Grove House (private school), Guildford, Surrey. CWGC: son of William A. Tennant and Agnes Tennant, Orford House, Ugley, Essex.
Pte. Charles John Bowden 9075 KIA
born: Newton Abbot, Devon   enlisted: Totnes
No known grave. Ploegsteert Memorial, panel 3. Age 25. Joined BEF: 06/11/14 with original cadre. 1901 Census: son of John Jeffery Bowden, carter on farm, and Mary Jane Bowden, Gappah, Chudleigh Knighton, Newton Abbot, Devon. CWGC: family address: 27 Bridgetown, Totnes, Devon.
Pte. David John Bowden 3/7321 KIA
born: Ashburton, Devon   enlisted: Newton Abbot   residence: Ashburton
No known grave. Ploegsteert Memorial, panel 3. Age 31. 'C' Company. Joined BEF: 24/03/15. 1901 Census: son of John Bowden, general labourer, and Bessie Bowden, North Street, Ashburton, Devon. 1911 Census: general labourer, son of Bessie Bowden, charwoman, North Street, Ashburton, Devon.
Pte. John Burge 9404 KIA
born: Exmouth, Devon   enlisted: Devonport
Buried: Le Trou Aid Post Cemetery, Fleurbaix. Grave M.3. Joined BEF: 23/02/15. CWGC: son of Mrs. Jane Burge, 13 Waterloo Street, Stonehouse, Plymouth.

Pte. Edward James Carpenter 6950 KIA
born: Ashford, Middlesex   enlisted: London
No known grave. Ploegsteert Memorial, panel 3. Age 33. Joined BEF: 06/11/14 with original cadre. 1901 Census: boarder, nephew of Walter E. Warters and Celia E. Warters, Ashford House Stables, Sunbury, Staines, Middlesex. 1911 Census: 2/Devons, St. George's Barracks, Malta.

Pte. John Carreau 9475 KIA
born: Jersey, Channel Islands   enlisted: Jersey
No known grave. Ploegsteert Memorial, panel 3. Age 22. Joined BEF: 06/11/14 with original cadre. The best match in the 1901 Census is for a Jean Carreau, 'inmate' at Jersey Industrial School, Jersey, Channel Islands.

Pte. Ernest William Davey 8781 KIA
born: Tiverton, Devon   enlisted: Exeter
No known grave. Ploegsteert Memorial, panel 3. Age 23. Joined BEF: 06/11/14 with original cadre. 1901 Census: son of Sidney John Davey, lace hand (?), and Emma E. Davey, 56 St. Andrews Street, Tiverton, Devon. 1911 Census: 2/Devons, St. George's Barracks, Malta. CWGC: brother of Mr. F. Davey, Shircombe Farm, Hawkridge, Dulverton, Somerset. (1901 Census lists a brother named Frederick).

Pte. Arthur Dicker 3/6993 KIA
born: Tiverton, Devon   enlisted: Exeter   residence: Tiverton
No known grave. Ploegsteert Memorial, panel 3. Age 22. Joined BEF: 17/12/14. 1901 Census: son of Samuel Dicker, general labourer, and Emily Dicker, Tiverton, Devon (address unreadable). CWGC: son of Mrs. E. Dicker, 4 Steer's Court, Westexe South, Tiverton, Devon.

Pte. Clifford Dowden 8900 KIA
born: Stonehouse, Devon   enlisted: Exeter   residence: Stonehouse
No known grave. Ploegsteert Memorial, panel 3. Age 24. No Medal Card. 1901 Census: son of Albert H. Dowden, navvy, and Charlotte Dowden, 15 Waterloo Street, Stonehouse, Devon.

Pte. Bert Fred Dymond 3/7124 KIA
born: Stonehouse, Devon   enlisted: Exeter
No known grave. Ploegsteert Memorial, panel 3. Age 18. Joined BEF: 19/01/15. 1911 Census: named Bertie Dymond, tailor, son of Fred Dymond, dockyard labourer, and Laura Dymond, 48 Pembroke Street, Devonport, Devon. CWGC: son of Mrs. Laura Dymond, 6 Cumberland Street, Devonport, Devon.

Sgt. George Elsworthy 8917 KIA
born: Exeter, Devon   enlisted: Exeter
No known grave. Ploegsteert Memorial, panel 3. Age 18. Joined BEF: 06/11/14 with original cadre. 1901 Census: son of Caroline Elsworthy, 15 Fore Street, Torpoint, St. German's, Cornwall. 1911 Census: with brother Frederick at grandparents address: Thomas Hall, bricklayer, and Emily Hall, 13 Coronation Road, South Wonford, Heavitree, Devon.

Pte. John Evans 12710 KIA
born: Llandilos, Montgomery   enlisted: Tonypandy, Glam.   residence: LLwynpia, Glam.
No known grave. Ploegsteert Memorial, panel 3. Age 34. Joined BEF: 04/01/15. CWGC: son of John Evans and Margaret Evans, 6 Glamorgan Terrace, Llwynypia (Rhondda), Glam.

Pte. Walter Friend 6863 KIA
born: Exeter, Devon   enlisted: Exeter
No known grave. Ploegsteert Memorial, panel 3. Age 29. Joined BEF: 01/09/14 with 1st Battalion. 1901 Census: porter (grocer), son of Clement Friend, supervisor Singer Sewing Machine Co., and Anna Friend, 13 Summerland Street, Exeter. 1911 Census: 2/Devons, St.

George's Barracks, Malta.

Pte. Edward Fryer 3/8119 KIA
born: Coaley, Glos.   enlisted: Mardy, Glos.   residence: Waley, Glos.
No known grave. Ploegsteert Memorial, panel 3. Age 24. Joined BEF: 04/01/15. 1901 Census: son of Charles Fryer, general labourer, and Harriett Fryer, Elmcote Lane, Coaley, Dursley, Glos.

Pte. George Dilwyn Gillard 3/8185 DoW
Born: Swansea   enlisted: Swansea
No known grave. Ploergsteert Memorial, panel 3. Age 19. Joined BEF: 04/01/1915.

Pte. Harold Arthur Hames 14299 KIA
born: Dorchester, Dorset   enlisted: Exeter   residence: Dorchester
No known grave. Ploegsteert Memorial, panel 3. Age 20. Joined BEF: 27/12/14. 1901 Census: boarder (age 6) at 28 Princes Street, Dorchester, Dorset. 1911 Census: recorded as Harry Hames, schoolboy, son of Edwin Hames, fruit grower, and Eliza Hames, Sandy Lane, Ferndown, Wimborne, Dorset.

Cpl. Herbert Harris 8525 KIA
born: London   enlisted: Barnstaple
No known grave. Ploegsteert Memorial, panel 3. Age 24. Joined BEF: 06/11/14 with original cadre. 1911 Census: 2/Devons, St. George's Barracks, Malta. CWGC: son of Emily Ida Harris, 2 Cavendish Square, Lynton, Devon, and the late Harry Herbert Harris. Mrs. Harris applied for her late son's medals, 21/12/19.

Pte. George Haywood 14782 KIA
born: Audley, Staffs.   enlisted: Pentre, Glam.
No known grave. Ploegsteert Memorial, panel 3. No Medal Card.

Pte. Joseph George Hoare 11348 KIA
born: Axminster   enlisted: Axminster
No known grave. Ploegsteert Memorial, panel 3. Age 20. Joined BEF: 24/01/15. 1901 Census: son of Joseph George Hoare, ordinary agricultural, labourer, and Harriet Maria Hoare, Church Hill, Musbury, Axminster, Somerset.

Pte. Wilfred George Hodges 9241 KIA
born: Chard, Somerset   enlisted: Taunton   residence: Chard
No known grave. Ploegsteert Memorial, panel 3. Age 20. Joined BEF: 06/11/14 with original cadre. 1901 Census: son of Samuel Hodges, thatcher, and Mary Jane Hodges, Chard, Somerset. CWGC: family address: Lower Coombes, Chard, Somerset. CWGC records death as 9th May 1917 – name on Ploegsteert Memorial suggests that 9th May 1915 is more likely to be correct. Medal Card does not state the date of death but records him as DoW.

Pte. William Arthur Hunt 7517 KIA
born: Tiverton, Devon   enlisted: Cardiff
Buried: Le Trou Aid Post Cemetery, Fleurbaix. Grave C.11. Joined BEF: 04/01/15.

Pte. Stanley Thomas Jenkins 12922 KIA
born: Swansea   enlisted: Swansea
No known grave. Ploegsteert Memorial, panel 3. Joined BEF: 09/02/15. CWGC: son of Mrs. Annie Jenkins, 37 Hoskins Terrace, Pentregethin Road, Swansea, and husband of Beatrice Fielding (formerly Jenkins), 52 Brynmelin Street, Swansea.

Pte. Idris Jones 12752 KIA
born: Pontardulais, Glam.   enlisted: Swansea   residence: Pontardulais
No known grave. Ploegsteert Memorial, panel 3. Joined BEF: 19/01/15.

Pte. Albert Edward Ladd 9947 KIA
born: Homerton, Middx.   enlisted: Stratford   residence: Homerton
No known grave. Ploegsteert Memorial, panel 3. Age 18. Joined BEF: 11/12/14. 1911 Census: errand boy, son of Charles William Ladd, mercurial gilder, and Mary Ann Ladd, 12 Marlow Road, Homerton, Hackney.

Pte. Fred Meers 6564 KIA
born: Exeter, Devon   enlisted: Exeter
No known grave. Ploegsteert Memorial, panel 3. Also recorded as 'Fred Mears' on medal card. Joined BEF: 06/11/14 with original cadre. 1911 Census: one of several 'music hall artistes', visiting Eduard and Ellen Fanny Bursill, 37 New North Road, Exeter, Devon. The other artistes were: Alfred Meers, age 42 (father?) born Cheltenham; Florence Elizabeth Francis Clare, age 28, born Birmingham; Walter Winter, age 27, born Leipzig, Saxony, Germany; and Alfred Griffiths, age 43, born Somerset, stage manager, Hippodrome.

Pte. Thomas Michael Newton 3/6577 KIA
born: Dublin, Ireland   enlisted: Devonport
No known grave. Ploegsteert Memorial, panel 3. Joined BEF: 06/11/14 with original cadre.

Pte. Harry Parsons 11347 KIA
born: Tiverton, Devon   enlisted: Exeter
No known grave. Ploegsteert Memorial, panel 3. Age 18. Joined BEF: 24/03/15. 1901 Census: son of Harry Parsons, general labourer, and Lucy Parsons, Kingdom, Broadhembury, Tiverton, Devon. CWGC: family address: Woodbeare Cottage, Plymtree, Cullompton, Devon.

Pte. Herbert Perryman 7467 KIA
born: Barnstaple, Devon   enlisted: Ilfracombe
No known grave. Ploegsteert Memorial, panel 3. Age 30. Joined BEF: 22/08/14 with 1st Battalion. 1901 Census: servant/horseman on farm, employed by Benjamin Richmond, 'Chichesters', Berrynarbor, Barnstaple, Devon. 1911 Census: farm labourer, husband of Ella Perryman, Little Shelfin, Westdown.

L/Cpl. Albert Pine 8411 KIA
born: Exeter, Devon   enlisted: Exeter
Buried: Le Trou Aid Post Cemetery, Fleurbaix. Grave M.2. Age 28. Joined BEF: 06/11/14 with original cadre. 1901 Census: son of Joseph Pine, labourer, and Charlotte Pine, laundress, 14 Oakfield Street, Heavitree, Exeter. 1911 Census: 2/Devons, St. George's Barracks, Malta. CWGC: son of the late Joseph Pine, brother of Mrs N. Knight, 91 Mincing Lake Road, Stoke Hill, Exeter.

Pte. Frederick James Roberts 9582 KIA
born: Stonehouse, Devon   enlisted: Devonport
Buried: Bailleul Road East Cemetery, St. Laurent-Blangy. Grave IV.E.12. Age 20. 'B' Company. Joined BEF: 22/08/14 with 1/Devons. 1901 Census: son of Mary Roberts, widow, charwoman, High Street, East Stonehouse. CWGC: son of the late John Brown Edward Roberts and Mary Roberts, 5 Waterloo Street, Stonehouse, Plymouth.

L/Cpl. Samuel Roberts 3/6924 KIA
born: London   enlisted: Stratford, Essex
No known grave. Ploegsteert Memorial. Age 23. Joined BEF: 06/11/14 with original cadre. 1901 Census: son of Stephen Freshney, furniture dealer, and Elizabeth Freshney, 56 Ben Jonson Road, Stepney, London. 1911 Census: waiter, living with his parents and siblings at 35 Ben Johnson Road. His brother, Robert Samuel Freshney, 3/6913, age 20, 56 Ben Jonson Road, was KIA on 23rd May 1915, also with the 2/Devons.CWGC: records 'Samuel Roberts' as an 'alias', real name Stephen Arthur Freshney. Awarded Cross of St. George 4th Class (Russia).

The 2nd Devons War Diary

Pte. Samuel Salter 3/6990 KIA
born: Ottery St. Mary   enlisted: Exeter
No known grave. Ploegsteert Memorial, panel 3. Age 17. No Medal Card . 1901 Census: son of William Salter, agricultural labourer, and Caroline Salter, Wiggaton, Ottery St. Mary, Devon. 1911 Census: schoolboy, son of William Salter, labourer, and Caroline Salter, Wiggaton, Ottery St. Mary, Devon. CWGC: son of Mrs. C. Salter, Bridge Cottage, Wiggaton, Ottery St. Mary, Devon.

Pte. Edgar James Sellek 11349 KIA
born: Exmouth, Devon   enlisted: Exmouth   residence: Exmouth
No known grave. Ploegsteert Memorial, panel 3. Age 21. 'D' Company. Joined BEF: 24/03/15. 1901 Census: son of Thomas Henry Sellek, bricklayer, and Emily Sellek, 5 Little Albion Place, Withycombe Raleigh, Exmouth, Devon. 1911 Census: farm labourer, address as above.

Pte. George Skinner 7895 KIA
born: South Molton, Devon   enlisted: South Molton   residence: Chittlehampton
Buried: Le Trou Aid Post Cemetery, Fleurbaix. Grave M.5. Age 29. No Medal Card . 1901 Census: son of John Baker Skinner, carpenter/wheelwright, and Grace Skinner, Blenwell, Chittlehampton, South Molton, Devon. 1911 Census: 2/Devons, St. George's Barracks, Malta.

L/Cpl. Charles Frederick Sprague 8760 KIA
born: Axminster, Devon   enlisted: Axminster
No known grave. Ploegsteert Memorial, panel 3. Age 25. Joined BEF: 05/11/14 with original cadre. 1911 Census: 2/Devons, St. George's Barracks, Malta.

Pte. Henry James Thomas 8425 KIA
born: Plymouth, Devon   enlisted: Exeter   residence: Plymouth
No known grave. Ploegsteert Memorial, panel 3. Age 27. 'B' Company. Joined BEF: 06/11/14 with original cadre. 1901 Census: son of Henry Thomas, clerk (shipping), and Minnie Thomas, 6 Morley Road, Plymouth, Devon. 1911 Census: 2/Devon , St. George's Barracks, Malta. CWGC: family address: 38 Harwell Street, Plymouth.

Pte. Sidney Amos Trout 10125 KIA
born: Exeter, Devon   enlisted: Exeter
No known grave. Ploegsteert Memorial, panel 3. Age 19. 'C' Company. Joined BEF: 16/02/15. Medal Card annotation: *'Death regarded 9/5/15'*. 1911 Census: 'gardener assistant', son of John Trout, jobbing gardener, and Elizabeth Trout, High Street, Topsham, Devon. CWGC: son of John V. Trout, Trees Court, Fore Street, Topsham, Exeter.

Pte. John Twigg 14175 KIA
born: Haverfordwest, Pembs.   enlisted: Pentre, Glam.
No known grave. Ploegsteert Memorial, panel 3. Age 32. Joined BEF: 24/03/15. 1901 Census: son of William Twigg, coal miner/hewer, and Ann Twigg, 7 Union Street, Ystradfodwg, Rhondda, Glamorgan. 1911 Census: 'collier, coal hewer', with parents, 7 Union Street, Gelly, Rhondda, Glamorgan.

Pte. Samuel Walker 10127 KIA
born: Plymouth, Devon   enlisted: Exeter   residence: Plymouth
No known grave. Ploegsteert Memorial, panel 3. Joined BEF: 03/12/14.

Pte. James Ward 11169 KIA
born: Marylebone   enlisted: Fulham   residence: Marylebone
No known grave. Ploegsteert Memorial, panel 3. Age 25. Joined BEF: 24/03/15. 1901 Census: born 1890, Marylebone, grandson of James Ward and Jane Ward, 39 Paxton Road, Chiswick, London. 1911 Census: son of James Ward, general labourer, and Harriet Ward,

launderess, 10 Watson's Mews, Marylebone, Middx. James Ward volunteered for the Army at Fulham on the 6th September 1914, the same day as Charlie Yates and the Ranelagh Rovers football team.

Cpl. Jack Edward Watts 8313 KIA
born: Torquay, Devon   enlisted: Exeter   residence: Torquay
No known grave. Ploegsteert Memorial, panel 3. Age 27. Joined BEF: 06/11/14 with original cadre. 1911 Census: 2/Devons, St. George's Barracks, Malta. CWGC: son of Mrs. Clara Watts, of 37 Church Lane, Torre, Torquay.

L/Sgt. George Webster 3/7039 KIA
born: Bideford, Devon   enlisted: Swansea
Buried: Le Trou Aid Post Cemetery, Fleurbaix. Grave M.4. Joined BEF: 27/12/14.

Pte. Sidney Whitty 9649 KIA
born: Birmingham   enlisted: Exeter
Buried: Le Trou Aid Post Cemetery, Fleurbaix. Grave M.1. Age 30. Joined BEF: 22/08/14 with 1/Devons . 1901 Census: son of Alfred John Whitty, gardener, and Mary Jane Whitty, Billesley House Lodge, Stoney Lane, Yardley, Worcestershire.

L/Cpl. David Howells 9549 DoW
born: Neath, Glam.   enlisted: Exeter   residence: Newton Abbot
No known grave. Ploegsteert Memorial, panel 3. Age 22. Joined BEF: 06/11/14 with original cadre. CWGC: son of David Howells, 25 Pendrill Street, Neath, Glam.

Pte. Arthur John Bennett 11408 DoW
born: Chagford, Devon   enlisted: Exeter   residence: Chagford
No known grave. Ploegsteert Memorial, panel 3. Age 19. Joined BEF: 24/03/15. CWGC: son of Mrs. H. Bennett, Lower Street, Chagford, Devon.

Pte. Harry Nicholls 11221 DoW
born: Torrington, Devon   enlisted: Torrington
Buried: Merville Communal Cemetery. Grave II.R.7. Age 24. Joined BEF: 24/03/15. 1901 Census: son of Thomas Nicholls, carpenter, and Mary Nicholls, silk glove machinist, I Calf Street, Great Torrington, Devon. 1911 Census: recorded as Henry Nicholls, 'school and chemist's errand boy', living with parents, address as above.

10th May 1915
Pte. William Ellis 11224 KIA
born: Kingsteignton   enlisted: Newton Abbot   residence: Kingsteignton
No known grave. Ploegsteert Memorial, panel 3. Joined BEF: 24/03/15.

Pte. Frederick Josiah Squire 11263 KIA
born: Torquay   enlisted: Exeter   residence: Torquay
No known grave. Ploegsteert Memorial, panel 3. Age 21. Joined BEF: 02/02/15. 1901 Census: son of Josiah John Squire, general labourer, and Elizabeth Jane Squire, 12 Princes Road, Tormoham, Torquay, Devon. 1911 Census: servant 'working horse' at James Skinner's farm at Tattiscombe, Parracombe, Devon. CWGC: family address, 49 Princes Road, Ellacombe, Torquay.

Pte. Charles Walker 11283 KIA
born: Plymouth   enlisted: Exeter   residence: Plymouth
No known grave. Ploegsteert Memorial, panel 3. Joined BEF: 02/02/15. CWGC: records Army number as R/283.

Sgt. John Henry Bulley 8372 DoW
born: Plymouth   enlisted: Plymouth
Buried: Merville Communal Cemetery. Grave II.S.1. Age 26. Joined BEF: 06/11/14 with original cadre. 1911 Census: 2/Devons, St. George's Barracks, Malta. CWGC: son of Mrs. Bessie Stapleton, 2 Cromatie Road, Prince Rock, Plymouth.

L/Cpl. Henry Francis Caseley 14184 DoW
born: Dawlish   enlisted: Swansea   residence: Newton Abbot
No known grave. Ploegsteert Memorial, panel 3. Age 19. 'A' Company. Joined BEF: 04/01/15. 1911 Census: saddler, son of Henry Caseley, gardener domestic, and Joanna Caseley, 26 Halcyon Road, Newton Abbot, Devon. Later joined the Great Western Railway. Name recorded on the GWR Roll of Honour, the only GWR footplate man to lose his life serving with 2/Devons in WW1. Started as an Engine Cleaner at Newton Abbot, moved to Swansea in 1913, where he enlisted. Name recorded on the War Memorial at All Saints Church, Highweek, Newton Abbot, Devon.

Pte. William Henry Edwards 13224 DoW
born: Tonyrefail, Glam.   enlisted: Tonyrefail
Buried: Sailly-Sur-La-Lys Canadian Cemetery. Grave II.C.70. Age 34. Joined BEF: 06/11/14 with original cadre. CWGC: son of Morgan Edwards and Elizabeth Edwards, Lerry View, Elerch, Talybont, Cardiganshire.

11th May 1915
Pte. Albert James Gollop 3/6803 DoW
born: Exeter   enlisted: Exeter
Buried: Merville Communal Cemetery. Grave II.S.7. age 17. Joined BEF: 19/01/15. 1911 Census: son of Richard Gollop, 'formerly a stone mason', and Mary Ann Gollop, 71 Okehampton Street, Exeter, Devon. Mrs E. Hoare applied for medals for her deceased brother 01/11/20.

12th May 1915
Drummer Ernest Victor Copsey 7756 DoW
born: Colchester, Essex   enlisted: Warrington   residence: Marylebone
Buried: Merville Communal Cemetery. Grave III.B.4. Age 27. 'A' Company. Rank 'Private' when died. Joined BEF: 06/11/14 with original cadre. 1901 Census: son of Francis Benjamin Copsey, cab driver/groom, and Alice Copsey, 6 Courtnell Street, Paddington, Middlesex. 1911 Census: 2/Devons, St. George's Barracks, Malta. Born at Chaletindy, Kent.

Pte. Frank Robert Johnston 10024 DoW
born: Bridgwater, Somerset   enlisted: Exeter   residence: Bridgewater
Buried: Merville Communal Cemetery. Grave III.A.2. Age 28. No Medal Card. CWGC: son of Benjamin Johnston, Whittes, North Newton, Bridgwater, Somerset, and the late Jane Johnston. Native of Combwich, Bridgwater.

13th May 1915
Pte. Arthur Tarr 8925 DoW
Born: Exeter, Devon   enlisted: Exeter, Devon
Buried: Exeter (Exwick or St. Thomas) Cemetery. Grave X.438. Age 24. Joined BEF: 06/11/14 with original cadre. 1901 Census: son of George Tarr, labourer/sawyer in sawmill, and Ellen Tarr, 3 Oxford Street, St. Thomas, Exeter, Devon. 1911 Census: 2/Devons, St. George's Barracks, Malta. CWGC: son of Mrs. Ellen Tarr, 55 Oxford Street, St. Thomas, Exeter.

15th May 1915
Pte. William Charles Pope 3/6422 Died
Born: Tiverton, Devon   enlisted: Exeter, Devon   residence: Tiverton, Devon
Buried: Longuenesse (St. Omer) Souvenir Cemetery. Grave I.A.112. Age 35. 'B' Company. 1911 Census: maltster's labourer, husband of Florence Pope, 13 Seward's Court, Leat Street, Tiverton, Devon. CWGC: son of Mr. and Mrs. J. Pope, Uplowman, Tiverton, husband of Mrs. Florence Pope, 13 Seward's Court, Leat Street, Tiverton, Devon. Served in Boer War.

16th May 1915
Pte. William John Roach 9349 DoW
Born: India   enlisted: India   residence: Devonport, Devon
Buried: Wimereux Communal Cemetery. Grave I.G.31A. Age 22. Joined BEF: not on medal card.

17th May 1915
L/Cpl. Frederick James Braund 9158 KIA
born: Bow, Devon   enlisted: Exeter   residence: Bow, Devon
Buried: Le Trou Aid Post Cemetery, Fleurbaix. Grave C.6. Age 22. Joined BEF: 06/11/14 with original cadre. 1901 Census: son of James Braund, horseman on farm, and Sarah Braund, Ford, Colebrook, Crediton, Devon. 1911 Census: with 1/Devons, Mooltan and Lucknow Barracks, Uttar Pradesh, India.

Pte. Thomas Bicknell 6732 DoW
born: Chelsea, Middx.   enlisted: London   residence: London S.W.
Buried: Le Trou Aid Post Cemetery, Fleurbaix. Grave C.4. Age 34. Joined BEF: 04/11/14 with original cadre. 1911 Census: general labourer, married to Ethel Beatrice Bicknell, 37 Rotherwood Road, Putney, London. CWGC: son of Henry Bicknell and Minnie Bicknell, of Kensington, London; husband of Ethel Beatrice Macer (formerly Bicknell), 43 Milman Road, Kilburn, London.

Pte. Lionel Howard 11310 DoW (home)
born: Dartmouth   enlisted: Exeter   residence: Dartmouth
Buried: Dartmouth (Longcross) Cemetery. Grave 153. Age 26. Joined BEF: 09/02/15. 1901 Census: stepson of John Perring, 'sailor seas', of Fishmonger's Lane, Dartmouth. 1911 Census: stepson of John Perring, seaman, son of Annie Perring, of Rovingsea, Bayards Cove, Dartmouth, Devon. CWGC: son of Mrs. A. I. Perring, 21 Clarence Street, Dartmouth.

21st May 1915
Pte. Harry Ernest Clarke 3/6937 DoW
born: Wood Green, Middx.   enlisted: Stratford, Essex
Buried: Merville Communal Cemetery. Grave III.F.5. Age 20. 'D' Company. Joined BEF: not on Medal Card. CWGC: son of Mrs. E. Moseley, 20 Stromness Road, Southchurch, Southend-on-Sea.

23rd May 1915
Pte. Robert Samuel Freshney 3/6913 KIA
born: Stepney, Middx.   enlisted: Stratford, Essex
Buried: Le Trou Aid Post Cemetery, Fleurbaix. Grave C.3. Age 20. Joined BEF: 17/12/14. Recorded as Samuel Freshney on Medal Card.   1901 Census: son of Stephen Freshney, furniture dealer, and Elizabeth Freshney, 35 Ben Jonson Road, Stepney, London. 1911 Census:

errand boy, son of Stephen Freshney, labourer, and Elizabeth Freshney, furniture dealer, 35 Ben Jonson Road, Stepney, London. Robert Freshney's elder brother, Pte. Stephen Arthur Freshney, 3/6924, (alias Samuel Roberts), was KIA on 9th May 1915, also with 2/Devons.

25th May 1915
Pte. William Alfred Northcott 9639 KIA
born: Plymouth, Devon   enlisted: Plymouth
Buried: Rue-Petillon Military Cemetery, Fleurbaix. Grave I.F.16. Age 21. Joined BEF: 06/11/14 with original cadre. CWGC: son of Mrs. Elizabeth Northcott, 7 Jubilee Place, Plymouth.

30th May 1915
Pte. Jack Roberts 11889 DoW
born: Tiverton, Devon   enlisted: Tiverton
Buried: Boulogne Eastern Cemetery. Grave VIII.A.55. Age 21. Joined BEF: 09/02/15. 1901 Census: recorded as John Roberts, son of Samuel Roberts, agricultural labourer, and Maria Roberts, Edburies, Poughill, Crediton, Devon. 1911 Census: servant, 'game boy' on Harry Herbert Pearcey's farm, Lower Ford, Cullompton, Devon. CWGC: family address: Pages, Cruwys Morchard, Tiverton, Devon.

31st May 1915
L/Cpl. William Fuller 8128 KIA
born: Torquay, Devon   enlisted: Exeter
Buried: Royal Irish Rifles Graveyard, Laventie. Grave IV.F.12. Age 25. Joined BEF: 06/11/14 with original cadre. 1911 Census: 2/Devons, St. George's Barracks, Malta. CWGC: son of Harry Fuller and Ada Fuller, 2 Teignmouth Road, Upton, Torquay.

JUNE 1915

2nd June 1915
L/Cpl. Charles Frederick Cann 8626 Died
born: Chagford, Devon   enlisted: Exeter
Buried: Merville Communal Cemetery. Grave III.H.8. Age 25. Joined BEF: 06/11/14 with original cadre. 1891 Census: son of George Cann, coachman, and Alice Cann, Avalon House, Lower Street, Chagford, Devon. 1901 Census: son of George Cann, cab proprietor, 18 Okehampton Street, St. Thomas, Devon. 1911 Census: 2/Devons, St. George's Barracks, Malta. CWGC: son of Alice Cann, 18 Okehampton Street, St. Thomas', Exeter.

Pte. John Hill 7853 KIA
born: Barnstaple, Devon   enlisted: Barnstaple
Buried: Pont-Du-Hem Military Cemetery, La Gorgue. Grave V.B.25. Age 30. Joined BEF: 06/11/14 with original cadre. 1911 Census: 2/Devons, St. George's Barracks, Malta.

7th June 1915
Pte. Henry Charles Jacob Belsham 3/6975 KIA
born: Leytonstone, Essex   enlisted: Stratford, Essex
Buried: Rue-Du-Bacquerot (13th London) Graveyard, Laventie. Grave D.10. Age 18. 'B' Company. Joined BEF: 23/02/15. 1911 Census: schoolboy, son of Henry Frederick Belsham, Navvy, and Alice Belsham, 28 Byron Road, Leyton, Essex. CWGC: son of Henry F. and Alice Belsham, 6 Edith Road, Stratford New Town, Essex.

Pte. Edward Alec Reeves 9563 KIA
born: Southampton, Hants.   enlisted: Exeter   residence: Southampton
Buried: Rue-Du-Bacquerot (13th London) Graveyard, Laventie. Grave D.11. Age 20. Joined BEF: 22/08/14 with 1/Devons . 1911 Census: grocer's porter, son of Edward J. Reeves, police constable, and Annie E. Reeves, 53 MacNaughten Road, Southampton, Hants. CWGC: son of Edward J. Reeves, police constable, and Annie E. Reeves, 10 Harcourt Road, Portswood, Southampton.

9th June 1915
Pte. Harold John Bristow 9864 DoW
born: Silvertown, Essex   enlisted: Stratford, Essex   residence: Plaistow
Buried: Sailly-Sur-La-Lys Canadian Cemetery. Grave III.B.13. Age 18. Joined BEF: not recorded on Medal Card. 1901 Census: son of Robert Bristow and Mary Bristow, Ketous Docks, Essex. 1911 Census: errand boy, son of Mary Bristow, widow, 37 Arragon Road, East Ham, Essex.

18th June 1915
Pte. Arthur Endacott 11339 KIA
born: Chagford, Devon   enlisted: Exeter   residence: Chagford
No known grave. Ploegsteert Memorial, panel 3. Age 19. Date joined BEF: 24/03/15. 'Arthur Endicott' on Medal Card. 1901 Census: son of James Endacott, general labourer, and Elizabeth Endacott, New Street, Chagford, Devon. 1911 Census: general labourer, son of James Endacott, general labourer, and Elizabeth Endacott, New Street, Chagford, Devon.

Pte. Thomas Jackson 15282 KIA
born: Walsden, Lancs.   enlisted: Rochdale
Buried: Rue-Du-Bacquerot (13th London) Graveyard, Laventie. Grave G.8. Age 22. Joined BEF: 18/05/15. 1901 Census: son of Abraham Jackson, cotton weaver, and Emma Jackson, 2

Elm Street, Todmorden, Walsden, Lancs. CWGC: family address: 687 Rochdale Road, Todmorden, Walsden.

21st June 1915
Pte. Thomas Carroll 9173 DoW
born: Middlesborough   enlisted: Stratford, Essex   residence: Middlesborough
Buried: Rue-Du-Bacquerot (13th London) Graveyard, Laventie. Grave G.7. Age 20. Joined BEF: 06/11/14 with original cadre. 1911 Census: unemployed, son of Thomas Carroll, general labourer Electric Lights, and Kate Carroll, 90 Richmond Street, Middlesborough, Yorkshire. CWGC: son of Mrs. Margaret Carroll, 35 Kendell Street, Middlesbrough.

30th June 1915
Pte. William Kelly Hall 9970 DoW (home)
born: Brixham, Devon   enlisted: Devonport
Buried: Shorncliffe Military Cemetery. Grave C.117. Age 19. Joined BEF: 11/12/14. 1901 Census: son of Kate Hall, tobacconist, 92 Market Street, Eastleigh, Hampshire. 1911 Census: boy, 43rd Brigade Royal Field Artillery, Royal Artillery Barracks West Side And Other Buildings On West Side Of Common, Royal Artillery Barracks (West Side). CWGC: son of Captain William Hall (Royal Artillery) and Mrs. Kate Hall, 29 Clarence Street, Penzance, Cornwall.

JULY 1915

5th July 1915
Pte. Thomas Augustine Edwards 11317 KIA
born: Exeter   enlisted: Exeter
Buried: Y Farm Military Cemetery, Bois Grenier. Grave D.50. Age 19. 'D' Company. Joined BEF: 25/05/15. 1911 Census: errand boy, son of Thomas Edwards, labourer, and Alice Edwards, domestic, 5 Hicks Place, Bartholomew Street East, Exeter, Devon. CWGC: son of Mr. and Mrs. T. A. Edwards, address as above.

7th July 1915
Cpl. Julius Englebert Spoerry 8057 DoW
born: St. Pancras, London   enlisted: London
Buried: Kensal Green (All Soul's) Cemetery. Grave 213.8.4. (Screen Wall). Died in England. Age 28. Joined BEF: 05/11/14 with original cadre. 1901 Census: recorded as Englebert J. Spoerry, son of Jules Spoerry, hotel porter, and Emily Spoerry, 104 Stibbington Street, St. Pancras, London. 1911 Census: 2/Devons, St. George's Barracks, Malta. CWGC: son of Julius Spoerry and his wife Emily Higgins, 34 Pancras Square, London.
Pte. Frederick Arthur Mitchell 3/8063 DoW
born: London   enlisted: Stratford, Essex
Buried: Bailleul Communal Cemetery Extension (Nord). Grave I.D.91. Joined BEF: 26/01/15.

15th July 1915
Pte. George Westcott 11509 DoW
born: Dowland, Devon   enlisted: Exeter   residence: Dowland
Buried: Bailleul Communal Cemetery Extension (Nord). Grave I.D.116. Age 21. Joined BEF: 19/01/15. 1901 Census: son of Samuel Westcott, carpenter, and Sarah Westcott, Vanstone Cottage, Dowland, Torrington, Devon. 1911 Census: farmer's son working on farm, son of Samuel Westcott, farmer, and Sarah Westcott, Dowland, Torrington, Devon.

19th July 1915
Pte. Cecil Priddle 8570 KIA
born: Taunton   enlisted: Exeter   residence: Tiverton
Buried: Y Farm Military Cemetery, Bois Grenier. Grave D.31. Age 25. Joined BEF: 04/11/14 with first cadre. 1901 Census: born in Curry Mallet, Somerset, son of Cornelius W. Priddle, labourer in garden, and Rebecca Priddle, The Rectory, Thorn Falcon, Taunton. 1911 Census: 2/Devons, St. George's Barracks, Malta.

The 2nd Devons War Diary

AUGUST 1915

5th August 1915
Pte. Samuel Pearse 9007 DoW
born: Okehampton, Devon   enlisted: Exeter   residence: Teignmouth
Buried: Sailly-Sur-La-Lys Canadian Cemetery. Grave III.A.6. Joined BEF: 06/11/14 with original cadre. Age 24. 1911 Census: 2/Devons, St. George's Barracks, Malta.

22nd August 1915
Pte. William Vaughan 12735 DoW
born: Llanelli, Carmarthen   enlisted: Caerphilly, Glam.   residence: Llanbradach, Glam.
Buried: Y Farm Military Cemetery, Bois Grenier. Grave D.32. Age 30. Joined BEF: 24/03/15.CWGC: husband of Leah Vaughan, 50 School Street, Llanbradach, Cardiff. CWGC records death on 28/08/17, but Medal Card and SDGW record 22/08/15.

26th August 1915
Pte. Percy Shaxton 11359 KIA
born: Exmouth, Devon   enlisted: Exeter
Buried: Rue Petillon Military Cemetery, Fleurbaix. Grave I.F.29. Age 27. Joined BEF: 24/03/15. 1901 Census: son of Thomas Shaxton, gardener/domestic, and Mary Shaxton, The Village, Bideford, Devon. 1911 Census: General Servant Agricultural, Venn Mills, East Putford, Devon.
Pte. Frederick Maurice White 3/6874 Died
born: London   enlisted: London
Buried: Sailly-Sur-La-Lys Canadian Cemetery. Grave II.B.46. Age 20. 'B' Company. Joined BEF: 03/12/14. CWGC: son of George White and Charlotte White, 51 Northbank Road, Walthamstow, London.

27th August 1915
Pte. William Henry Newcombe 11501 KIA
born: Chulmleigh, Devon   enlisted: Exeter   residence: Chulmleigh
Buried: Rue Petillon Military Cemetery, Fleurbaix. Grave I.F.30. Age 24.   Joined BEF: 19/01/15. 1911 Census: 2/Devons, St. George's Barracks, Malta.

28th August 1915
Pte. Robert George Heaman 15510 DoW
born: Burrington, Devon   enlisted: Exeter   residence: Crediton
Buried: Merville Communal Cemetery. Grave III.U.3. Age 39. Joined BEF: 25/05/15. 1901 Census: farmer, son of Robert Heaman, retired farmer, and Eliza Amelia Heaman, of Burrington, Devon. 1911 Census: farmer, son of Robert Heaman, retired farmer, and Eliza Amelia Heaman, of Hayne Farm, Burrington, Chulmleigh, Devon. CWGC: husband of F. J. Heaman, 1 Spinning Path, Bath Road, Exeter.

SEPTEMBER 1915

26th September 1915
Pte. David Thomas Price 3/8271 KIA
born: Pontrhydyfen, Glam. enlisted: Porth, Glam.
Buried: Y Farm Military Cemetery, Bois-Grenier. Grave G.15. Age 21. Joined BEF: 27/12/14. 1901 Census: son of Charles Price, coal hewer, and Catherine Price, Station Terrace, Victoria Road, Michaelston, Neath, Glamorgan. 1911 Census: Coal Miner Hewer, son of Catherine Price, 7 Upper Fforchdwm Street, Pontrhydyfen, Port Talbot, Glamorgan, Wales. CWGC: son of Mrs. Catherine Price, 31 Jestyn Street, Porth (Rhondda), Glamorgan.

OCTOBER 1915

2nd October 1915
L/Cpl. Charles Mitchell 9356 KIA
born: Truro, Cornwall enlisted: Exeter residence: Truro
Buried: Rue David Military Cemetery, Fleurbaix. Grave I.C.18. Age 22. Joined BEF: 06/11/14 with original cadre. CWGC: son of Frederick Mitchell and Mary Jane Mitchell, 3 Boscawen Row, Truro, Cornwall.

Pte. Richard Henry Warne 8739 KIA
born: Guernsey, Channel Is. enlisted: Exeter residence: Plymouth
Buried: Rue David Military Cemetery, Fleurbaix. Grave I.B.27. Age 24. Joined BEF: 06/11/14 with original cadre. 1901 Census: son of Simeon P. Warne, general labourer, and Caroline Warne, 32 Clarence Street, Plymouth, Devon. 1911 Census: 2/Devons, St. George's Barracks, Malta. CWGC: family address: 3 Eton Terrace, Ilbert Street, Plymouth.

7th October 1915
Pte. Charles Henry Reekes 15514 DoW
born: Brighouse, Lancs. enlisted: Halifax residence: Todmorden
Buried: Merville Communal Cemetery. Grave IV.H.2. Age 18. Joined BEF: 22/05/15. 1901 Census: son of Henry Reekes, railway tunnel miner, and Mary Reekes, 20 Russell Street, Todmorden, Lancs. 1911 Census: warehouse (worker), son of Henry Reekes, tunnel miner, and Mary Reekes, 733 Rochdale Road, Walsden, Lancs. CWGC: son of Henry Reekes, 733 Rochdale Road, Walsden, Todmorden, Lancs and the late Mary Reekes. Pte Reekes DoW suffered on 2nd October (see War Diary transcription).

30th October 1915
Pte. William Charles Densham 3/6654 KIA
born: Honiton, Devon enlisted: Honiton
Buried: White City Cemetery, Bois-Grenier. Grave A.6. Age 20. Joined BEF: 20/09/14 with 1/Devons. 1901 Census: son of William H. Densham, builder's carter, and Sarah A. Densham, Lust Buildings, Honiton, Devon.

The 2nd Devons War Diary

NOVEMBER 1915

13th November 1915
Pte. Charles Martin 11419 KIA
born: unknown   enlisted: 'In the field'   residence: Torquay
Buried: Rue-David Military Cemetery, Fleurbaix. Grave I.C.19. Joined BEF: 04/01/15.

23rd November 1915
Sgt. Ernest James Dawe 8728 KIA
born: Plymouth, Devon   enlisted: Exeter   residence: Plymouth
Buried: Y Farm Military Cemetery, Bois-Grenier. Grave K.24. Age 28. Joined BEF: 06/11/14 with original cadre. 1911 Census: 2/Devons, St. George's Barracks, Malta. CWGC: son of Mary Holman (formerly Dawe), 3 Wentworth Place, Embankment Road, Plymouth, and the late William Dawe.

DECEMBER 1915

11th December 1915
Pte. Sidney Gillard 9185 Died
born: Crediton, Devon   enlisted: Exeter   residence: Crediton
Buried: Aire Communal Cemetery. Grave I.C.13. Joined BEF: 06/11/14 with original cadre.

JANUARY 1916

11th January 1916
Temp. Capt. Thomas Cyril Bruce Joy KIA
Born: Kensington, London
Buried: Kut War Cemetery. Grave K.25. Age 29. Medal Card records Captain Joy as being KIA on 11/12/15. Joined BEF: 06/11/14 with original cadre, was serving on attachment with the Dorset Regiment at the time of his death. Gazetted to 1st Battalion Devonshire Regiment, from Oxford, in 1911. 1901 Census: son of George W. Joy, artist/painter/sculptor, and Florence I. M. Joy, Woodside, Purbrook, Hants. 1911 Census: Army Student, son of George William Joy, Artist Painter in Oils, and Florence Isabel Mary Joy, 51 Palace Court, Bayswater, London.

23rd January 1916
Cpl. Charles Buckingham 7393 KIA
born: Launceston, Cornwall   enlisted: Plymouth
Buried: Y Farm Military Cemetery, Bois-Grenier. Grave J.9. Age 32. Joined BEF: 22/08/14 with 1/Devons. 1901 Census: 'farm servant/agricultural worker', St. Mellion Village, Launceston, Cornwall.

31st January 1916
Pte. Samuel Stacey 15162 KIA
born: Tavistock, Devon   enlisted: Liverpool   residence: Tavistock
Buried: Y Farm Military Cemetery, Bois-Grenier. Grave J.5. Age 32. Joined BEF: 31/05/15.

Martin Body

1901 Census: Tin Miner, son of Elizabeth Stacey, widow, Trewin, Calstock, Launceston, Cornwall. 1911 Census: butcher, at the time a patient at Newton Abbot Hospital and Dispensary, Newton Abbot, Devon.

FEBRUARY 1916

18th February 1916
Pte. Harry Mayle 8930 Died (home)
born: Plymouth, Devon   enlisted: Exeter   residence: Torpoint, Cornwall
Buried: Leeds (Lawns Wood) Cemetery. Grave: Screen Wall.W.447. Age 25. Joined BEF: 06/11/14 with original cadre. 1911 Census: 1/Devons, Mooltan and Lucknow Barracks, Uttar Pradesh, India. CWGC: son of Mrs. A. Mayle, of Merrifield, Devon.

MARCH 1916

22nd March 1916
Pte. John Shepherd 3/7113 KIA
born: Colyford, Devon   enlisted: Hounslow, Middx.   residence: Southleigh, Devon
Buried: Rue-Du-Bacquerot (13th London) Graveyard, Laventie. Grave B.12. Age 35. Joined BEF: 17/12/14. Medal Card and CWGC record number as 3/7114. CWGC: son of the late William and Sarah Shepherd.

APRIL 1916

22nd April 1916
L/Cpl. James Howard 8914 KIA
born: Exeter, Devon   enlisted: Exeter
Buried: Aveluy Communal Cemetery Extension. Grave D.28. Age 24. Joined BEF: 06/11/14 with original cadre. CWGC: son of John Howard, of Exeter, husband of Elsie Maria Howard, 5 Market Street, Exeter.
Cpl. Frederick William Sussex 8540 KIA
born: Torrington, Devon   enlisted: Bideford
Buried: Aveluy Communal Cemetery Extension. Grave D.29. Age 24. Joined BEF: 06/11/14 with original cadre. Medal Card annotation reads: *F. Sussex Esq. makes application for clasp in respect of the services of his late son Cpl. F. W. Sussex. 8-12-19.*   1901 Census: son of Frederick Sussex, shoemaker, and Elizabeth Sussex, Cross Street, Northam, Devon. 1911 Census: 2/Devons, St. George's Barracks, Malta.
Pte. James Johnson 14980 DoW
born: Longton, Staffs.   Enlisted: Longton
CWGC does not list a grave or memorial reference for this man. Age 32. Joined BEF: 18/05/15. 1901 Census: potter's kilnman, son of Thomas Johnson, potter's kilnman, and Alice Johnson, potter's gilder, 1 Hawkin's Yard, Normacot Road, Longton, Staffs.

The 2nd Devons War Diary

30th April 1916
Pte. John William Kelley 17659 DoW
born: Oldham, Lancs.   enlisted: Manchester   residence: Rochdale
Buried: St. Sever Cemetery, Rouen. Grave A.20.17. Age 22. Joined BEF: 31/12/15. CWGC: son of John Thomas Kelley and Susan Jane Kelley, 3 Ivor Street, Newtown, Rochdale, Lancs. 1911 Census: labourer, son of Susan Jane Kelley, widow, domestic, 14 George Street, Castleford, Lancs.

MAY 1916

5th May 1916
Sgt. John Kearns 7443 DoW
born: Preston, Lancs.   enlisted: Preston
Buried: Millencourt Communal Cemetery Extension. Grave A.4. Age 35. Joined BEF: 06/11/14 with original cadre. 1901 Census: son of Patrick Kearns and Ellen Kearns, of 1 Purle Lane, Preston, Lancs. John Kearns, his parents and his sister, Mary E. Kearns, worked in the cotton industry. (Sgt. Kearns died of wounds suffered in an accident with a bomb at 23rd Infantry Brigade bomb school).

11th May 1916
Cpl. Frank Dear 7560 KIA
born: Plymouth, Devon   enlisted: Exeter   residence: Plymouth
Buried: Aveluy Communal Cemetery Extension. Grave D.33. Joined BEF: 22/08/14 with original cadre of 1/Devons.

14th May 1916
Pte. George Soper 3/5165 KIA (by a canister)
born: Chudleigh, Devon   enlisted: Plymouth   residence: Horrabridge, Devon
Buried: Aveluy Communal Cemetery Extension. Grave D.34. Age 30. Joined BEF: 07/11/14 with original cadre. Number on Medal Card: 5165. 1901 Census: butcher's boy, son of William Soper, jobbing gardener, and Mary Ann Soper, 3 Higher Town Cottages, Whitchurch, Tavistock. CWGC: family address: Horrabridge, Devon.

18th May 1916
Pte. Bertram John Armstrong 15487 Died
born: Woolwich, Kent   enlisted: Woolwich
Buried: Ste. Marie Cemetery, Le Havre. Grave Div.19.CC.2. Age 23. Joined BEF: 25/05/15. 1911 Census: writer, son of John Henry Armstrong, Driller, and Annie Charlotte Armstrong, 75 Samuel Street, Woolwich, London.

26th May 1916
Pte. Albert John Langdon 3/5789 DoW
Born: Paignton, Devon   enlisted: Torquay, Devon
Buried: Estaires Communal Cemetery and Extension. Grave 1.H.11. Age unknown. Joined BEF: 06/11/14 with original cadre.

Martin Body

JUNE 1916

5th June 1916
2/Lt. Harold Edgar Marchant KIA
born: Chippenham, Wilts.
Buried: Aveluy Communal Cemetery Extension. Grave C.39. Age 19. Joined BEF: not recorded on Medal card. Annotation on Medal card reads: *Mr. E. M. Marchant (father) applies for late son's medals 11.5.21.* 1901 Census: son of Edward M. Marchant, General Draper, and Jane Marchant, 4 Alma Place, Plymouth. At the time of his death the family address was 82 Kenwyn Road, Torquay. 1911 Census: schoolboy, son of Edward M. Marchant, draper, and Jane Marchant, 21 St. Budeaux Terrace, Devonport, Devon.
Pte. George Marchant 9182 KIA
born: Taunton, Somerset   enlisted: Taunton
Buried: Aveluy Communal Cemetery Extension. Grave C.38. Age 21. Joined BEF: 06/11/14 with original cadre. 1901 Census: son of Mr. Sidney H. Marchant, hospital porter, and Sarah J. Marchant, 2 Lower Queen Street, Taunton, Somerset. Family address: 37 St. Augustine St. North, Taunton, Somerset.
L/Cpl. William Lee 3/8231 KIA
born: London   enlisted: Tonypandy, Glam.   residence: Porth, Glam.
Buried: Aveluy Communal Cemetery Extension. Grave D. 35. Joined BEF: 27/12/14.
Pte. Archibald Harry Phillips 9294 KIA
born: Exeter, Devon   enlisted: Exeter
Buried: Aveluy Communal Cemetery Extension. Grave D.36. Age 23. Joined BEF: 06/11/14 with original cadre. 1901 Census: living with his 29 year old sister, shopkeeper/general dealer, in Plymouth. 1911 Census: tailor, grandson of Mary Ann Phillips, 3 Haldon View Terrace, Heavitree, Exeter.

8th June 1916
Pte. James Bertram Offord 20508 KIA
born: Rochdale, Lancs.   enlisted: Rochdale
Buried: Aveluy Communal Cemetery Extension. Grave 40. Age 23. Joined BEF: not recorded on Medal Card. 1901 Census: son of James E. Offord, mason/manager of marble works, and Edith Offord, 64 Boundary Street, Rochdale. 1911 Census: assistant clerk, James Edward Offord, marble merchant, and Edith Offorf, 44 Castlemere Street, Rochdale, Lancs. CWGC: family address: 12 Bramhall Street, Rochdale.

17th June 1916
Sgt. George Webber 7410 KIA
born: Teignmouth, Devon   enlisted: Teignmouth
Buried: Aveluy Communal Cemetery Extension. Grave C.41. Age 31. Joined BEF: 06/11/14 with original cadre. Medal Card records Army number as 7310. 1901 Census: ironmonger's errand boy, son of William Webber, house painter, and Eliza Webber. George Webber was the eldest of 9 living children. 1911 Census: 2/Devons, St. George's Barracks, Malta.

19th June 1916
Pte. George Henry Gilbert 18859 Died
born: Devonport, Devon   enlisted: Plymouth
Buried: Aveluy Communal Cemetery Extension. Grave C.42. Age 42. Joined BEF: not recorded

on Medal card. CWGC: son of Mrs. A. Gilbert, of Plymouth; husband of Mary Ann Street (formerly Gilbert), 21 Clowance Lane, Devonport. Private Gilbert was probably a man 'accidentally killed in the trenches' recorded in War Diary on 19th June 1916.

24th June 1916
Pte. Edward Thomas Pannell 8793 DoW
born: London   enlisted: Exeter   residence: Exmouth
Buried: Heilly Station Cemetery, Mericourt-L'Abbe. Grave I.C.5. Age 33. Joined BEF: 06/11/14 with original cadre. 1901 Census: servant to a baker, 10 Strand, Littleham, Exmouth. 1911 Census: 2/Devons, St. George's Barracks, Malta.

30th June 1916
CSM Mark Turner 7293 KIA
Born: Crediton, Devon   enlisted: Exeter   residence: Crediton, Devon
No known grave. Name inscribed on the Thiepval Memorial, Pier and Face 1.C. Age 30. Joined BEF: 06/11/14 with original cadre. 1891 Census: son of Lewis Turner, shepherd, and Grace Turner, Uton Farm, Crediton, Devon. 1901 Census: 'Cattle Boy on Farm' at Westwood Village, Crediton, Devon. 1911 Census: 'Corporal 2/Devonshire Regiment', with parents in Uton Village, Crediton, Devon. CSM Turner was killed by shell fire.

Martin Body

JULY 1916

1st July 1916
Capt. James Alfrey Andrews KIA
Officer commanding the front line. He was killed while leading the attack.
Buried: Serre Road Cemetery No.2. Grave XV.B.14. Born 20th April 1890. Age 26. Son of the late Lt. Col. J. W. Andrews, and of Emily Andrews, of "Bantony," Robertsbridge, Sussex. He is commemorated on the war memorials at Robertsbridge and Salehurst, Sussex. 1901 Census: pupil at Sandhurst, Berkshire, in 'Eagle' House. 1911 Census: 2nd/Lt. 1/Devons, Mooltan and Lucknow Barracks, India.

2/Lt. Cecil Victor Beddow KIA
Buried: Serre Road Cemetery No.2. Grave XV.A.5. Age 19. Born 25 September 1896.
Joined BEF: 20/05/16. Address on Medal Card: "Mascotte", Imber Park Road, Esher, Surrey. 1901 Census: son of Josiah Beddow, 'Medical Practitioner', age 43, mother, Grace Mary Beddow, age 31, also Leslie Towne Beddow, age 11 and Muriel Grace Beddow, age 8. 89 Cazenove Road, Hackney, Middlesex. 1911 Census: schoolboy at King's School, Castle House, College Green, Worcester.
Later attended Blundell's School as a 'Day Boy', from the age of 15 years 8 months (May 1912 to Summer 1913). 6'1.5" tall, 37.5" chest, 6/6 vision, in good health, unmarried.
Named on Blundell's School Memorial and in the stained glass memorial, 'King's School Cloister Window', in Worcester Cathedral. Joined 'F' Company, Inns of Court OTC (Officer Training Corps) on 10 December 1914 and remained with them until 26 March 1915, during which time he was promoted to L/Cpl. Discharged from OTC to take a commission in the Devonshire Regiment in March 1915.
Sent to the 2/Devons in France on 20 May 1916. His brother, Leslie Beddow, joined the 9th Devons, rose to the rank of Captain, and also served in the RAF. He survived the war and in 1920 was working in Shanghai, China, for Harrison's, King and Irwin. For Cecil Beddow's gravestone the family chose the inscription: 'And they rise to their feet as he passes by gentlemen unafraid'. Family addresses at the time of his death: Pynes House, Thorverton, Devon, and "Mullion", Ballard Estate, Swanage, Dorset.

2/Lt. Leonard Arthur Carey KIA
No known grave. Thiepval Memorial, Pier and Face 1.C. Age 24. Joined BEF: 23/04/16 as 1288 of King Edwards Light Infantry. Commissioned 23/4/16 in 2/Devons. 1901 Census: family as son of Ernest Edward Carey, shipping broker, aged 43 and Mary, aged 41, 73 Lichfield Grove, Finchley, Middlesex. Youngest of the four children: Mansel Carey, aged 15 (in 1901), Gladys May Carey, aged 14, and Phillip Dudley Carey, aged 12.

2/Lt. George Sholto Douglas Carver KIA
Officer commanding 'C' Company Attached from 3/Devons .No known grave. Thiepval Memorial, Pier and Face 1.C. Age 29. Joined BEF: not recorded on Medal Card. Annotation on Medal Card reads: 'App. For War Medal by Lt. Col. E. Carver 14/06/21.'1891 Census: son of William Edward and Beatrice Enuna Elizabeth Carver, "Southstoke," Exmouth, Devon. The family also resided in Westward Ho! Road, Northam, Devon.

2/Lt. Francis Baker Coldwells KIA
Attached from 3rd Battalion. Formerly PS/4685 Sgt. F.B.Coldwells, Royal Fusiliers.
No known grave. Thiepval Memorial, Pier and Face 1.C. Age 26. Born December 1891 at Purley, Surrey.Joined BEF: not on Medal Card. Son of Joseph George Coldwells (born 1864, Croydon) and Elizabeth Baker (born 1869, Barnstaple, died 1901). 1901 Census: son of Joseph George Coldwells (widower) company secretary, aged 37, Rochfort Villa, Brighton Road,

Purley, Surrey, with his four sons.
1911 Census: scholar undergraduate, 16 Lennard Road, West Croydon, Surrey. Francis Baker Coldwells was the eldest of four brothers: Pte. Leonard George Coldwells, born 1893, KIA 31/10/14, age 22, London Regiment, 14th (County of London) Battalion (London Scottish). 2/Lt. Charles Albert Coldwells, born 1895, KIA 28/9/15, age 20, RHA and RFA. Captain Edward Greenwood Coldwells, born 1897, Leinster Regiment, survived.

2/Lt. Eric Melville Gould KIA
Bombing officer. Attached from 3/Devons. No known grave. Thiepval Memorial, Pier and Face 1.C. Age 23. Joined BEF: 13/5/16. Son of Claude W. D. and Elizabeth S. C. Gould, of Pilton Abbey, Barnstaple, Devon. 1901 Census: son of Claude Gould, 39, 'Builder's Merchant and Solicitor', and Elizabeth Gould, 40, Park Lane, Barnstaple.

2/Lt. Edward Arthur Jago KIA
Attached from 3rd Battalion. No known grave. Thiepval Memorial, Pier and Face 1.C. Age 19. Joined BEF: 22/05/16. 1901 Census: son of W.H. Jago, of Haye, Plympton, Devon, 'Eglinton', Mannamead, Plymouth. Brother of Captain Henry Harris Jago DSO MC, 2/Devons, KIA 24 April 1918, near Villers Bretonneux. Edward Arthur Jago and Henry Harris Jago are commemorated on a memorial in a window at Emmanuel Church, Compton Gifford, Plymouth. A chapel in the church was dedicated to their memory in 1919.

2/Lt. Maurice Carew Ley KIA
Born: Fulham
Formerly with 17th Battalion, Royal Fusiliers. Buried: Ovillers Military Cemetery. Grave III.Y.1. Age 20. Joined BEF: 24/11/15. 1911 Census: schoolboy, son of Arthur Henry Ley, banker's clerk, widower, 77 Comeragh Road, West Kensington, London. CWGC: son of Arthur Henry Ley and Violet Ley, address as above.

2/Lt. John Spence McGowan KIA
Attached from 3rd Battalion. No known grave. Thiepval Memorial, Pier and Face 1.C. Age 19. Joined BEF: 19/05/16. Medal Card annotations: *'Mother entitled to all medals.' 'Alice C. McGowan applies for medals due to her late son. 29/10/19.'* 1911 Census: schoolboy at The School, Rottingdean, Sussex. Educated at Sherborne. CWGC: son of Alice Clara McGowan, "Ao Tea Roa", Dormans Land, Lingfield, Surrey, and the late Robert Smith McGowan.

Capt. Alban Preedy KIA
'B' Company CO. No known grave. Thiepval Memorial, Pier and Face 1.C. Age 23. Joined BEF: 18/05/15. Born Sept. 1892, birth registered in Plymouth. Medal Card records father's address as 3 Albert Terrace, Torpoint, Cornwall. Son of the Rev. Canon Arthur Preedy, 43, and Beatrice J. Preedy, 43, of Saltash, Cornwall. 1901 Census: The Vicarage in Saltash, where Arthur Preedy was a 'Church of England Clergyman'.

Pte. Francis William George Andrews 17814 KIA
born: London   enlisted: Walthamstow
No known grave. Thiepval Memorial, Pier and Face 1.C. Age 25. Joined BEF: not on Medal Card. 1911 Census: 'bookseller, street', son of Eleanor Emily Andrews, widow, 37 Percival Street, Clerkenwell, London. CWGC: son of Eleanor Emily Andrews, 2 Quakers Lane, Potters Bar, Middx, and the late Richard George Andrews. Husband of Mabel Emily Grace Good (formerly Andrews), 113 Hoe Street, Walthamstow, Essex.

Pte. Frank Andrews 12718 KIA
born: Sherborne, Dorset   enlisted: Abercynon, Glam.
No known grave. Thiepval Memorial, Pier and Face 1.C. Joined BEF: 16/2/15.

Pte. George Henry Avery 11301 KIA
born: Barnstaple, Devon   enlisted: Barnstaple
Buried: Ovillers Military Cemetery. Grave VI.M.1/3. Joined BEF: 24/03/15.

Pte. Samuel James Bailey 8235 KIA
born: Hayle, Cornwall   enlisted: Dartmouth   residence: Hayle
No known grave. Thiepval Memorial, Pier and Face 1.C. Age 29. Joined BEF: 06/11/14 with original cadre. 1901 Census: grandson of Joseph Northey, retired engine fitter, son of Samuel J. Bailey, engine fitter, and Kate Bailey, 27 Mount Pleasant, Hayle, Cornwall. 1911 Census: 2/Devons, St. George's Barracks, Malta.

Pte. George Henry Baldwin 9929 KIA
born: Boxmoor, Herts   enlisted: Hertford   residence: Boxmoor
No known grave. Thiepval Memorial, Pier and Face 1.C. Age 32. Joined BEF: 03/12/14. 1901 Census: labourer, son of Sarah Baldwin, widow 'supported by sons', Mission House Farm, Abbots Langley, Herts.

Sgt. James Banks 8590 KIA
born: Deptford, London   enlisted: London   residence: Reading
No known grave. Thiepval Memorial, Pier and Face 1.C. Age 24. Joined BEF: 06/11/1914 with original cadre. Medal Card records him as Drummer, later as Corporal. 1911 Census: 2/Devons, St. George's Barracks, Malta. CWGC: brother of Mrs. J. M. Hedgecock, 6 Lindfield Terrace, Wick, Littlehampton, Sussex.

Pte. Thomas Roger Barnes 9839 KIA
born: Whitechapel, London   enlisted: London
No known grave. Thiepval Memorial, Pier and Face 1.C. Age 21. No Medal Card . 1901 Census: son of William J. Barnes, railway checker, and Elizabeth Barnes, 32 Mitford Road, Islington, London. 1911 Census: GPO engraver, son of William Thomas Barnes, railway porter, and Elizabeth Barnes, address as above.

Cpl. William James Barrett 7989 KIA
born: Ottery St.Mary, Devon   enlisted: Exeter   residence: Ottery St.Mary
No known grave. Thiepval Memorial, Pier and Face 1.C. Age 28. 'D' Company. Joined BEF:26/02/15. 1901 Census: son of James Barrett, brick maker, and Ellen Barrett, Yonder Street, Ottery St. Mary, Devon. 1911 Census: soldier, son of James Barrett, general labourer, and Ellen Barrett, Mill Street, Ottery St. Mary, Devon.

Pte. Herbert James Bates 16172 KIA
born: Fulham, London   enlisted: Southwark   residence: Sunbury
Buried: Ovillers Military Cemetery. Grave VII.M.6. Joined BEF: not on Medal Card. Age 18. 1901 Census: son of Eva M. Bates, widow, worker in lodging house – char, 13 Crookham, Fulham, Middlesex.

Cpl. Edgar Boam, MM 14569 KIA
born: Matlock, Derbyshire   enlisted: Rochdale
No known grave. Thiepval Memorial, Pier and Face 1.C. Age 19. Joined BEF: 15/12/15. No reference to Military Medal award on Medal Card. 1901 Census: son of Margaret Ellen Walton, of 31 Belfield Road, Rochdale, Lancs, and Henry Walton (stepfather), out-door worker, 81 Worsley Street, Rochdale, Lancs. 1911 Census: apprentice, stepson of Henry Walton, general labourer, son of Margaret Ellen Walton, nee Boam, 15 Belfield Road, Rochdale, Lancs.

L/Cpl. Ernest John Bowden 8687 KIA
born: Kenton, Devon   enlisted: Teignmouth   residence: Dawlish
No known grave. Thiepval Memorial, Pier and Face 1.C. Age 23. Joined BEF: 24/03/15. 1901 Census: son of James Bowden and Elizabeth Bowden, 63 Manor Row, Brook Street, Dawlish,

Devon.
Pte. Albert Bowles 9148 KIA
born: Broadhembury, Devon   enlisted: Exeter   residence: Honiton
Buried: Serre Road Cemetery No.2. Grave XV.A.8. Age 24. Date joined BEF: 06/11/14 with original cadre. 1901 Census: son of Samuel Bowles, labourer/carter, and Sarah Ann Bowles, Hembercombe, Broadhembury, Devon. CWGC: family address: The Village, Broadhembury.
Pte. Montague Thomas Brittain 15119 KIA
born: Barnstaple, Devon   enlisted: Neath, Glam.
No known grave. Thiepval Memorial, Pier and Face 1.C. Age 20. Joined BEF: 20/06/15. 1901 Census: recorded as Monty Thomas Brittain, son of Ebenezer Brittain, circular sawyer, and Ellen Brittain, 16 Zion's Place, Barnstaple.
Sgt. John Henry Burgoyne 7978 KIA
born: Kingsbridge, Devon   enlisted: Kingsbridge
No known grave. Thiepval Memorial, Pier and Face 1.C. Age 29. Joined BEF: 06/11/14 with original cadre. 1901 Census: son of George G. A. Burgoyne, agricultural labourer, and Lavinia Burgoyne, Aveton Gifford, Kingsbridge, Devon. 1911 Census: 2/Devons, St. George's Barracks, Malta.
Pte. John Henry Burrell 19005 KIA
born: Woolwich, London   enlisted: Woolwich
No known grave. Thiepval Memorial, Pier and Face 1.C. Age 18. Joined BEF: not on Medal Card. CWGC: son of Mrs. F. G. Burrell, 4 Siemens Road, Woolwich, London.
Pte. Henry Butler 14135 KIA
born: Rhondda, Glam.   enlisted: Pentre, Glam.   residence: Campark
No known grave. Thiepval Memorial, Pier and Face 1.C. Age 23. Date joined BEF: 21/09/15. Medal Card annotations: *'Presumed dead 1/7/16. App. For 1914-15 Star from Mrs. Butler in respect of the services of her son the late Pte. H. Butler. 16/1/19. Reply on form 8 from Mrs. Butler.'* CWGC: son of Ann Butler, 283 Park Road, Cwmparc, Treorchy (Rhondda), Glamorgan, and the late Thomas Butler.
Pte. Frederick Cann 8974 KIA
born: Crediton, Devon   enlisted: Exeter   residence: Crediton
No known grave. Thiepval Memorial, Pier and Face 1.C. Age 23. Joined BEF: 06/11/14 with original cadre. 1901 Census: son of Samuel Cann, labourer in farm yard, and Mary Cann, Sandford Village, Crediton, Devon. 1911 Census: 1/Devons, Mooltan and Lucknow Barracks, India.CWGC: family address: 3 East Street, Crediton, Devon.
L/Cpl. William Cann 7772 KIA
born: Exeter, Devon   enlisted: Exeter   residence: Thorverton
No known grave. Thiepval Memorial, Pier and Face 1.C. Age 30. Joined BEF: 22/08/14 with 1/Devons. CWGC: son of Mrs. Emma Cann, East Raddon, Thorverton, Exeter.
Pte. Leslie George Carder 20160 KIA
born: Exmouth, Devon   enlisted: Exeter   residence: Exmouth
No known grave. Thiepval Memorial, Pier and Face 1.C. Age 26. Joined BEF: not on Medal card. 1901 Census: son of Charles Carder, sailor/seas, and Mary Carder, 45 Bicton Street, Littleham, Exmouth, Devon. CWGC: parent's address; 3 Duck Cottages, Exmouth, Devon, husband of Bessie Gertrude Barlow (formerly Carder), 21 Scowcroft Lane, Shaw, Oldham, Lancs.
Pte. Thomas Carney 15017 KIA
born: Liverpool   enlisted: Liverpool
No known grave. Thiepval Memorial, Pier and Face 1.C. Age 19. Joined BEF: 29/06/15. 1901

Census: son of David Carney, labourer, and Julia Carney, 2 Court 3 House, Liverpool, Lancashire. CWGC: mother Julia Hardiman, 12 Pollard Street North, Charlestown Road, Halifax, Yorkshire.

L/Cpl. Arthur Charles Carpenter 9147 KIA
born: Exeter, Devon   enlisted: Exeter
No known grave. Thiepval Memorial, Pier and Face 1.C.   Joined BEF: not on Medal Card.

Pte. Henry Carpenter 15478 KIA
born: Todmorden, Lancs.   enlisted: Halifax   residence: Todmorden
No known grave. Thiepval Memorial, Pier and Face 1.C. Age 30. Joined BEF: 21/09/15. Medal Card note: *'Presumed dead 1/7/16'*. 1901 Census: son of William H. Carpenter, mule skinner, and Clara Carpenter, weaver, 8 Back Bank View, Todmorden, Yorkshire. CWGC: husband of Betsy Carpenter, 21 Market Street, Shade, Todmorden.

Drummer Walter Frederick James Carr 9150 KIA
born: Exeter, Devon   enlisted: Dover   residence: Exeter
Buried: Ovillers Military Cemetery. Grave VIII.I.4. Age 19. Joined BEF: 06/11/14 with original cadre. CWGC: son of Jessie Ellen Carr, 61 Parr Street, Exeter, and the late Sergeant A.E. Carr (Devonshire Regiment – died prior to WW1).

Pte. Charles Carter 9674 KIA
born: Woodbury, Devon   enlisted: Exeter   residence: Woodbury
No known grave. Thiepval Memorial, Pier and Face 1.C. Age 21. Joined BEF: 17/12/14. CWGC: son of William John Carter and Mary Carter, Cottles Cottage, Woodbury, Exeter.

L/Cpl. Walter Henry Carter 9991 KIA
born: Barnet, London   enlisted: Stratford, Essex   residence: Barnet
No known grave. Thiepval Memorial, Pier and Face 1.C. Age 18. Date joined BEF: 09/11/14 with 1/Devons. 1901 Census: youngest of five children of Georgina Carter, widow, newsagent/shopkeeper, 168 High Street, Hadley, Barnet, Middlesex. CWGC: mother's address: High Road, Whetstone, London.

Pte. William George Challis 11136 KIA
born: Knightsbridge, London   enlisted: Marylebone
No known grave. Thiepval Memorial, Pier and Face 1.C. Age 24. Joined BEF:24/03/15. 1911 Census: warehouseman, son of Alice Challis, widow, 5 Ann's Place, Kinnerton Street, London S.W. CWGC: son of Mrs. A. Challis, 2 Stewarts Grove, Fulham, London; husband of M. A. Challis, 10 "S" Peabody Avenue, Ebury Bridge, London. Volunteered on 6th September 1914 at Marylebone.

Pte. Thomas J. Clark 14211 KIA
born: Carmarthen, Wales   enlisted: Swansea
No known grave. Thiepval Memorial, Pier and Face 1.C. Age 21. Joined BEF: 27/12/14. CWGC: son of Henry Clarke, 12A Rock Street, Waun Wen, Swansea, Glam, and the late Sarah Ann Clarke.

Pte. Jonas Clegg 15113 KIA
born: Waterfoot, Lancs.   enlisted: Rochdale
Buried: Ovillers Military Cemetery. Grave VI.E.8. Age 38. Joined BEF: 18/05/15. 1911 Census: coal miner/hewer, husband of Nellie Clegg, 27 Hanover Street, Rochdale, Lancs.

Pte. Kingsley Cody 19149 KIA
born: Norton, Worcs.   enlisted: Exeter
Buried: Serre Road Cemetery No.2. Grave XV.B.11. Age 29. Joined BEF: not on Medal Card. 1901 Census: son of Edward Cody, magician, and Anna Cody, of Tidcombe Cottages, Tiverton, Devon. 1911 Census: 'jobbing wood sawyer for carpenter', husband of Mary Cody,

Stoneyford, Colaton Raleigh, Ottery St. Mary, Devon. CWGC: husband of Mary Louisa Cody, 16 Yonder Street, Ottery St. Mary, Devon.

Pte. Francis E. Collings 16940 KIA
born: Totnes, Devon   enlisted: Totnes
No known grave. Thiepval Memorial, Pier and Face 1.C. Age 25. Joined BEF: not on Medal Card. 1911 Census: stone carter, son of James G. Collings, road contractor, and Helen Collings, Stoke Gabriel, Totnes, Devon.

Pte. Ernest Cook 14602 KIA
born: Brook, Isle of Wight   enlisted: Kingston-on Thames   residence: Epsom, Surrey
Buried: Ovillers Military Cemetery. Grave VIII.Q.7. Joined BEF: 24/03/15.

Pte. Sidney Archibald Copp 20042 KIA
born: Silverton, Devon   enlisted: Cullompton   residence: Bradninch, Devon
No known grave. Thiepval Memorial, Pier and Face 1.C. Age 22. Joined BEF: not on Medal Card. 1901 Census: son of William Copp, 'ordinary agricultural labourer', and Polly Copp, charwoman, Mount Pleasant, Cullompton Hill, Bradninch, Devon. 1911 Census: servant/cowman, on the farm of Albert Hussey, Lower Weaver, Plymtree, Cullompton, Devon. Sidney Copp's 32 year old brother, Thomas, was also killed in action on 1st July 1916, with 7/Devons.

L/Cpl. John Cornish 8384 KIA
born: Fremington, Devon   enlisted: Exeter   residence: Fremington
No known grave. Thiepval Memorial, Pier and Face 1.C. Age 25. Joined BEF: 05/11/14 with original cadre. Also noted on Medal Card as 8284. 1901 Census: son of Samuel Cornish, coal humper, and Fanny Cornish, Muddlebridge, Fremington, Devon. CWGC: family address: Muddlebridge, Fremington, Devon.

L/Cpl. Charles Edward Cox 8767 KIA
born: Kasauli, India   enlisted: Exeter
Buried: Ovillers Military Cemetery. Grave VIII.I.6. Age 25. 'B' Company. Joined BEF: 05/11/14 with original cadre. 1911 Census: 2/Devons, St. George's Barracks, Malta. CWGC: son of William Samuel Cox and Theresa Cox, 45 Howell Road, Exeter, Devon.

Pte. Ernest Charles Stephen Cox 14744 KIA
born: Sidmouth, Devon   enlisted: Exeter   residence: Sidmouth
No known grave. Thiepval Memorial, Pier and Face 1.C. Age 18. Joined BEF: 25/07/15. 1901 Census: son of Charles Cox, agricultural labourer, and Elizabeth Cox laundress, Cheese Lane, Sidmouth, Devon. 1911 Census: schoolboy, son of Charles Cox, farm labourer, and Elizabeth Ann Cox, laundress, Cotmaton, Cheese Lane, Sidmouth, Devon.

Pte. John Jonas Curd 11168 KIA
born: Willesden, London   enlisted: Fulham   residence: Isleworth
Buried: Ovillers Military Cemetery. Grave VI.I.3. Age 19. Joined BEF: 24/03/15. Medal card annotation: *'Pres. dead'*.1911 Census: errand boy, son of Joseph Curd, farrier, and Martha Eliza Curd, 104 Linkfield Road, Isleworth, Middlesex. CWGC: family address as above. John Curd volunteered for the Army at Fulham on 6 Sept 1914.

Pte. William John Daniel 3/8117 KIA
born: Newbridge-on-Wye   enlisted: Aberavon
No known grave. Thiepval Memorial, Pier and Face 1.C. Age 24. Joined BEF: 04/01/15. 1911 Census: 'cold rolls roller – tinplate works', son of William Thomas Daniel, blacksmith, and Annie Daniel, 1 Avon Street, Velindre, Aberavon, Glam. CWGC: son of William Thomas Daniel and Annie Daniel, 17 Avon Street, Velindre, Aberavon, Glam.

Pte. Edgar Dart 16768 KIA
born: Devonport, Devon   enlisted: Plymouth
Buried: Ovillers Military Cemetery. Grave VII.T.1. Age 23. Joined BEF: not on Medal Card. Medal Card records him as Alfred E. Dart. 1901 Census: son of Theodore Dart, labourer, and Amelia Dart, Clayton Place, Plymouth.

Cpl. Ernest John Davey 14130 KIA
born: Barnstaple, Devon   enlisted: Tavistock   residence: Exeter
No known grave. Thiepval Memorial, Pier and Face 1.C. Age 20. Joined BEF: 14/03/15. Medal Card annotation reads: *Application for 1914-15 Star from Mr. A. Bizley on behalf of Miss E. M. Paget, sole legatee of the late Cpl. E. J. Davey. 22/12/18.* 1911 Census: 'merchant clerk', son of Robert Davey, cellarman, and Louisa Davey, 32 Roberts road, Exeter, Devon.

Pte. Brinley Davies 11919 KIA
born: Swansea   enlisted: Swansea
No known grave. Thiepval Memorial, Pier and Face 1.C. Joined BEF: not on Medal Card.

Pte. George Davies 12064 KIA
born: Swansea   enlisted: Swansea
No known grave. Thiepval Memorial, Pier and Face 1.C. Age 19. Joined BEF: 24/03/15. 1901 Census: son of William Davies, watchman at copper works, and Eliza Davies, 2 Port Tennant Court, Port Tennant Road, Swansea, Glam. CWGC: family address as 1901.

Pte. Thomas Henry Davies 16974 KIA
born: Camborne, Cornwall   enlisted: Plymouth   residence: Camborne
No known grave. Thiepval Memorial, Pier and Face 1.C. Age 20. Date joined BEF: not on Medal Card. CWGC: son of the late Richard Davies.

Pte. Albert John Deveney 10910 KIA
born: Plymouth, Devon   enlisted: Devonport
Buried: Ovillers Military Cemetery. Grave IX.C.3. Age 24.Joined BEF: 07/07/15 with 1/Devons. 1911 Census: recorded as Bert Deveney, 'hawker, general', boarding at 13 Octagon Street, Plymouth, Devon. CWGC: son of Mrs. Elizabeth K. Blake, 26 Bath Street, Plymouth.

Pte. Frederick William Dodd 15365 KIA
born: Lustleigh, Devon   enlisted: London
No known grave. Arras Memorial, Bay 4. Joined BEF: 07/07/15 with 1/Devons . Medal Card records number as No. 15635, annotated *'Pres. Dead'.* 1901 Census: son of Jessie Dodd, 'wife of copper miner', 44 Exeter Street, Tavistock, Devon. 1911 Census: 'school and laundry errand boy', son of Jessie Dodd, widow, 'wool comber', 19 Exeter Street, Tavistock, Devon.

Pte. Leonard Willie Dorey 8645 KIA
born: Chichester, Sussex   enlisted: Petersfield   residence: Stoten, Hants
Buried: Ovillers Military Cemetery. Grave XVI.C.5. Age 25. Joined BEF: 22/08/14, with original cadre of 1/Devons . 1901 Census: son of William Dorey, labourer on farm, and Elizabeth Dorey, Fern Beds, Up Marden, Chichester, Sussex. 1911 Census: 1/Devons, Mooltan and Lucknow Barracks, Uttar Pradesh, India.

Pte. Walter Doxey 15160 KIA
born: Chequerbert, Lancs.   enlisted: Horwich   residence: Chequerbert
No known grave. Thiepval Memorial, Pier and Face 1.C. Age 30. Joined BEF: 18/05/15. 1901 Census: 19 year old hemp rope maker, son of Jane Doxey, widow, 675 Manchester Road, Westhoughton, Bolton, Lancs. CWGC: son of James and Jane Doxey, 723 Manchester Road, Chequerbert, Bolton, husband of Annie Wood (formerly Doxey), 3 Lorensen Avenue, Merlynston, North Coburn, Victoria, Australia.

Pte. Frederick Drew 8269 KIA
born: Crediton, Devon   enlisted: Exeter   residence: Crediton
No known grave. Thiepval Memorial, Pier and Face 1.C. Age 27. Joined BEF: 06/11/14 with original cadre. 1901 Census: son of James Drew, horseman on farm, and Isabella Drew, Smith's Cottage, Sandford, Crediton, Devon. 1911 Census: 2/Devons, St. George's Barracks, Malta.

Pte. Arthur Dunham 16968 KIA
born: no record   enlisted: Rochdale
No known grave. Thiepval Memorial, Pier and Face 1.C. Joined BEF: not on Medal Card.

A/Cpl. Samuel Mark Ebdon 8747 KIA
born: Exeter, Devon   enlisted: Exeter
Buried: Ovillers Military Cemetery. Mash Valley Memorial. 27. Age 26. Joined BEF: 06/11/16 with original cadre. 1911 Census: servant/butcher, Chapel Street, Exmouth, Devon. CWGC: son of John Ebdon and Bessie Ebdon, 33 Summerland Street, Exeter.

Pte. Ernest Edworthy 16941 KIA
born: Zeal, Devon   enlisted: Exeter   residence: Boe, Devon
Buried: Serre Road Cemetery No.2. Grave XV.B.7. Age 26. Joined BEF: not recorded on Medal Card. 1901 Census: son of John Edworthy, 'ordinary agricultural labourer', and Grace Edworthy, Knowle, Crediton, Devon. 1911 Census: farm labourer, brother of John Edworthy, farm labourer, Waterlane Cottage, Bow, Devon.

Pte. Charles Elliott 10338 KIA
born: Ivybridge, Devon   enlisted: Devonport
No known grave. Thiepval Memorial, Pier and Face 1.C. Age 22. Joined BEF: 02/05/15. 1901 Census: son of Thomas Elliott, navvy, and Catherine Elliott, 12 Renown Street, Devonport, Devon. 1911 Census: general labourer, son of Catherine Elliott, widow, fish hawker, 3 Batter Street, Plymouth, Devon. CWGC: son of Mrs. Kate Elliott.

Pte. John Elston 15101 KIA
born: Crediton, Devon   enlisted: Exeter   residence: Crediton
No known grave. Thiepval Memorial, Pier and Face 1.C. Age 41. Joined BEF: not recorded on Medal Card. 1901 Census: ship maker riveter, son of Louise Elston, widow, Exeter Road, Crediton, Devon, husband of Mrs. John Elston, 4 Southwoods Buildings, Cowick Street, St. Thomas, Exeter, Devon. 1911 Census: shoemaker, son of Louisa Elston, widow, 10 Cherry Gardens, Crediton, Devon. Veteran of Boer War and North West Frontier of India, Punjab and Tirah Expeditions, 1897-8.

Pte. John Evans 8768 KIA
born: Crediton, Devon   enlisted: Exeter   residence: Wonford
No known grave. Thiepval Memorial, Pier and Face 1.C. Joined BEF: 06/11/16 with original cadre.

Pte. Frederick William Farley 18942 KIA
born: Kennford, Devon   enlisted: Exeter   residence: Kennford
No known grave. Thiepval Memorial, Pier and Face 1.C. Age 18. Joined BEF: 21/12/15. 1901 Census: son of William Farley, agricultural labourer, and May A. Farley, Bampfield Cottage, Kenn, Tiverton, Devon. It is likely that Frederick Farley and the next entry, George Farley, could have been related, maybe nephew and uncle.

Pte. George Farley 8871 KIA
born: Kennford, Devon   enlisted: Exeter   residence: Kennford
No known grave. Thiepval Memorial, Pier and Face 1.C. Age 48. Joined BEF: 07/01/15. 1901 Census: son of Richard Farley, agricultural labourer, and Martha Farley, Westes, Kenn,

Tiverton, Devon.
Pte. John Fitzgerald 9869 KIA
born: Canterbury, Kent   enlisted: London   residence: Plumstead
Buried: Serre Road Cemetery No.2. Grave III.B.26. Age 22. Joined BEF: 17/12/14. CWGC: son of Mrs. Fitzgerald, 9 Alabama Street, Plumstead, London; husband of Edith Ellen Fitzgerald, of 5 Summerland Terrace, Summerland Street, Exeter.
Pte. Arthur Flowers 12711 KIA
born: Rhondda, Glam.   enlisted: Tonypandy, Glam.
No known grave. Thiepval Memorial, Pier and Face 1.C. Joined BEF: 09/02/12.
Sgt. Horace George Fogg 9961 KIA
born: Ongar, Essex   enlisted: Stratford, Essex   residence: Ongar
Buried: Serre Road Cemetery No.2. Grave II.B.27. Age 21. Joined BEF: 02/05/15. Recorded on Medal Card as *'died'*. 1901 Census: son of William Fogg, hay binder, and Sarah Fogg, School House, Fyfield Street, Fyfield, Ongar, Essex. 1911 Census: farm labourer, son of William Fogg, hay binder, widower, Fyfield, Ongar, Essex. William Fogg passed away before his son died.
L/Cpl. Thomas Foster 8465 KIA
born: Exeter, Devon   enlisted: Exeter
No known grave. Thiepval Memorial, Pier and Face 1.C. Age 28. Joined BEF: 06/11/14 with original cadre. 1911 Census: 2/Devons, St. George's Barracks, Malta. CWGC: son of Mrs. Alice Tarr, 4 Red Cow Village, St. Davids, Exeter.
Pte. Richard Gidley 15432 KIA
born: Okehampton, Devon   enlisted: Exeter   residence: Okehampton
No known grave. Thiepval Memorial, Pier and Face 1.C. Age 17. Joined BEF: 18/05/15. Medal Card annotation reads, *'Regarded dead 1/7/16'*. 1911 Census: schoolboy, boarding at the home of William Moore, farm labourer, Well Farm, Throwleigh, Okehampton, Devon.
Pte. Ralph James Gifford 3/6297 KIA
born: Brixham, Devon   enlisted: Exeter   residence: Brixham
No known grave. Thiepval Memorial, Pier and Face 1.C. Age 23. Joined BEF: 17/12/14. Medal Card records him with 9/Devons. CWGC: son of Charles Albert Gifford and Keturah Gifford, Union Lane, Brixham, Devon. Enlisted August, 1914.
Pte. William Peter Northey Gilbert 3/7135 KIA
born: Camborne, Cornwall   enlisted: Devonpoint   residence: Torpoint, Cornwall
No known grave. Thiepval Memorial, Pier and Face 1.C. Age 26. Joined BEF: 29/06/15. 1901 Census: tin dresser, son of William Gilbert, tin miner, and Susan A. Gilbert, charwoman, Rescadinnick, Camborne.
Sgt. William Albert Golding MM 8502 KIA
born: Exeter, Devon   enlisted: Exeter
No known grave. Thiepval Memorial, Pier and Face 1.C. Age 27. Joined BEF: 05/11/14 with original cadre. 1901 Census: son of Daisy S. Golding, widow, laundry maid, of East Wonford, Heavitree, Devon. 1911 Census: 'sugar boiler', brother of Joshua Golding, 'van man fruit merchant', 19 Richmond Street, Plymouth, Devon.
Pte. Frederick Charles Victor Govus 7146 KIA
born: London   enlisted: London   residence: London S.W.
No known grave. Thiepval Memorial, Pier and Face 1.C. Age 34. Joined BEF: 22/08/14 with original cadre of 1/Devons. 1911 Census: carman, brother of Arthur F. Govus, 36a Priory Grove, Lambeth, London. CWGC: son of the late Frederick Govus; husband of Edith Grace Govus, 9 Clifton Road, Kingston Hill, Kingston-on-Thames, Surrey. Served in Boer War.

Pte. Alfred Lewis Green 8408 KIA
born: Worcester, Worcs.   enlisted: Plymouth
No known grave. Thiepval Memorial, Pier and Face 1.C. Age 28. 'A' Company. Joined BEF: 06/11/14 with original cadre. 1901 Census: son of John Green, general labourer, and Elizabeth Ann Green, Upper Park Street, Worcester. CWGC: family address: 1 Sanders Place, Plymouth, Devon.

Pte. John Green 3/6875 KIA
born: London   enlisted: Stratford, Essex
No known grave. Thiepval Memorial, Pier and Face 1.C. Age 20. Joined BEF: 13/11/14 with 1/Devons. CWGC: son of William Green and Lilian Green, 18 Elmsdale Road, Walthamstow, Essex.

Pte. Arthur Greenbank 15612 KIA
born: Todmorden, Lancs.   enlisted: Rochdale   residence: Littleborough
No known grave. Thiepval Memorial, Pier and Face 1.C. Age 20. Joined BEF: 01/06/15. Medal Card annotation: *'Regarded dead 1/7/16'*. 1901 Census: son of Thomas Greenbank, coachman/domestic, and Clara Greenbank, Coachman's House, Castle Lodge, Todmorden, Lancashire.

Pte. David Daniel Griffiths 3/8194 KIA
born: Swansea   enlisted: Crediton   residence: Swansea
No known grave. Thiepval Memorial, Pier and Face 1.C. Age 21. No Medal Card. 1911 Census: 'tin plate trade tender', son of David Griffiths, police pensioner, and Sarah Ann Griffiths, 50 Iorweth Street, Swansea, Glam. CWGC: son the late D. Griffiths, police inspector, and Mrs. D. Griffiths, Manselton, Swansea, Glam.

Pte. William George Grigg 11123 KIA
born: Camberwell, Surrey   enlisted: London S.E.
No known grave. Thiepval Memorial, Pier and Face 1.C. Age 39. Joined BEF: not on Medal Card. 1911 Census: wood sawyer, married 16 years to Emily Charlotte Grigg, 52 Lonecroft Road, Camberwell. Father of 8.

Pte. Henry John Hall 15022 KIA
born: Wokingham, Berks.   enlisted: Tiverton
No known grave. Thiepval Memorial, Pier and Face 1.C. Age 21 (SDGW), 19 (1901 Census). Joined BEFF: 02/05/15. Medal Card annotation: *'Regarded dead 1/7/16'*. 1901 Census: son of Arthur John Hale, coachman, and Mary Ann Hale, Forest Road, Wokingham, Berks. CWGC: family address: Froghall Green, Wokingham, Berks.

Pte. Henry Thomas Hamlyn 14349 KIA
born: Teignmouth, Devon   enlisted: Exeter   residence: Teignmouth
No known grave. Thiepval Memorial, Pier and Face 1.C. Age 23. Joined BEF: 27/12/14. 1901 Census: son of Thomas W. Hamlyn, dock labourer, and Emma Hamlyn, West Teignmouth, Devon. 1911 Census: recorded as Harry Hamlyn, Army private, son of Thomas William Hamlyn, dock labourer, and Emma Hamlyn, 26 Bitton Road, Teignmouth, Devon.
Pte. Hamlyn was 2/Lt. Eric Melville Gould's batman. An eye witness, Pte. Cyril Jose, who was badly wounded later in the day, later wrote that Hamlyn and Gould were killed side by side.

Pte. John Courtney Hancock 15142 KIA
born: Torrington, Devon   enlisted: Exeter   residence: High Bickington
Buried: Serre Road Cemetery No.2. Grave XV.C.5. Age 22. Joined BEF: 18/05/15. 1911 Census: 'servant, cowboy' on farm of James Tapper Badcock, Coombe, Roborough, Beaford, Devon. CWGC: son of Mrs. Mary Hancock.

Pte. Augustine Hannaford 3/7532 KIA
born: Torquay, Devon   enlisted: Exeter   residence: Torquay
No known grave. Thiepval Memorial, Pier and Face 1.C. Joined BEF: 27/12/14. 1911 Census: 'fireman' on the vessel/ship 'Cherrybrook', at port of Hull Road, River Humber, Yorkshire.

Pte. Arthur Harding 3/8199 KIA
born: Barnstaple, Devon   enlisted: Swansea   residence: Barnstaple
No known grave. Thiepval Memorial, Pier and Face 1.C. Age 19. Joined BEF: 24/03/15. 1901 Census: son of William Harding, navvy, and Ellen Harding, 8 Ages Lane, Barnstaple, Devon. 1911 Census: general labourer, son of William Harding, general labourer, and Ellen Harding, 49 Azes Lane, Barnstaple, Devon. CWGC: family address: 11 Hardaway Head, Queen Street, Barnstaple.

Pte. William James Harris 15957 KIA
born: Chittlehampton, Devon   enlisted: South Molton   residence: Chittlehampton
No known grave. Thiepval Memorial, Pier and Face 1.C. Age 17. Joined BEF: not on Medal Card. 1901 Census: son of Frederick J. Harris, butcher, and Mary E. Harris, Chittlehampton, Devon. 1911 Census: schoolboy, son of Frederick James Harris, butcher, and Mary Elizabeth Harris, Ambow, Chittlehampton, Devon.

Sgt. Ernest John Hatton 3/5673 KIA
born: Torquay, Devon   enlisted: Newton Abbot   residence: Torquay
No known grave. Thiepval Memorial, Pier and Face 1.C. Age 27. Joined BEF: not on medal card. 1901 Census: son of Frederick Hatton, house painter, and Henrietta Hatton, 14 Dunmere Road, Tormoham, Torquay, Devon. 1911 Census: saw yard labourer, son of Frederick Hatton, house painter, and Henrietta Hatton, 58 East Street, Newton Abbot, Devon. Before Sgt. Hatton's death, his father passed away. CWGC: husband of Florence Annie Hatton, 11 Warbro' Road, Babbacombe, Torquay, Devon.

Pte. Alfred Helsdon 21010 KIA
born: Greenwich, London   enlisted: London S.E.
No known grave. Thiepval Memorial, Pier and Face 1.C. Joined BEF: not on medal card.

Cpl. Henry William Hemborough 9047 KIA
born: Wellington, Somerset   enlisted: Exeter
Buried: Ovillers Military Cemetery. Grave XV.I.4. Age 23. Joined BEF: 06/11/14 with original cadre. 1911 Census: 1/Devons, Mooltan and Lucknow Barracks, Uttar Pradesh, India.

Sgt. Norman Hamilton Herring 9325 KIA
born: Belfast, Ireland   enlisted: Devonport
No known grave. Thiepval Memorial, Pier and Face 1.C. Age 27. Joined BEF: 06/11/14 with original cadre. 1901 Census: son of Mary A. Herring, widow, teacher (music/piano), 23 Albert Terrace, Plymouth, Devon.

Pte. Ernest Heyworth 15613 KIA
born: Littleborough, Lancs.   enlisted: Rochdale   residence: Littleborough
No known grave. Thiepval Memorial, Pier and Face 1.C. Age 17. Joined BEF: 01/05/15. 1901 Census: grandson of Betty Heyworth, widow, 70 Todmorden Road, Littleborough, Lancs. 1911 Census: 'doffer at cotton manufacturer – school part time', son of Barker Heyworth, weaver, and Maria Heyworth, 12 Greenvale, Littleborough, Lancs.

Pte. Archie Hill 16195 KIA
born: Princetown, Devon   enlisted: Exeter   residence: Beaworthy
Buried: Serre Road Cemetery No.2. Grave XV.B.8. Age 19. Joined BEF: not on Medal card. 1911 Census: 'servant – cowboy', on farm of Peter Spry, Bangors, Bratton, Clovelly, Devon. CWGC: son of Robert and Elizabeth Hill, Keeper's Cottage, Lydford.

The 2nd Devons War Diary

Pte. William Henry Hobbs 3/7137 KIA
born: Plymouth, Devon   enlisted: Devonport
No known grave. Thiepval Memorial, Pier and Face 1.C. Joined BEF: 17/02/15. Medal Card annotation: *'Regarded dead 1/7/17'*.

Pte. William George Horwood 3/6843 KIA
born: London   enlisted: London
No known grave. Thiepval Memorial, Pier and Face 1.C. Joined BEF: 02/05/15.

Pte. William Henry Hunt 20041 KIA
born: Sandford, Devon   enlisted: Exeter   residence: Exminster
Buried: Serre Road Cemetery No.2. Grave XV.B.10. Date joined BEF: not on Medal Card.

Pte. Alfred William Hutcheson 15587 KIA
born: Cambridge, Cambs.   enlisted: Exeter   residence: Lew Down
No known grave. Thiepval Memorial, Pier and Face 1.C. Age 36. Joined BEF: 01/06/15. Medal Card annotation: *'Regarded dead 1/7/16'*. 1911 Census: under gardener, husband of Alice Hutcheson, Chester Moor Cottages, Bratton, Clovelly, Devon. CWGC: father of W. A. Hutcheson, "Clovelly," Shenley Road, Far Bletchley, Bucks.

Sgt. Bernard Hutchinson 7228 KIA
born: Sheffield, Yorks.   enlisted: Sheffield
No known grave. Thiepval Memorial, Pier and Face 1.C. Age 30. 'F' Company. Joined BEF: 06/11/14 with original cadre. 1901 Census: son of Harry R. Hutchinson, table knife cutler, and Charlotte Reaney Hutchinson, 115 Lansdowne Road, Sheffield. 1911 Census: 2/Devons, St. George's Barracks, Malta. CWGC: family address: 28 Club Street, Club Garden Road, Sheffield.

Pte. David John Jones 13056 KIA
born: Rhymney, Monmouth   enlisted: Ferndale, Glam.
No known grave. Thiepval Memorial, Pier and Face 1.C. Joined BEF: 04/01/15.

Pte. Frederick Thomas Jones 15391 KIA
born: Pancraswick, Devon   enlisted: Holsworthy   residence: Pancraswick
No known grave. Thiepval Memorial, Pier and Face 1.C. Age 21. Joined BEF: 18/05/15. Medal Card annotation reads *'Regarded dead 1/7/16'*. CWGC: son of William Jones and Hannah Jones, Woodsdown, Pancraswick, Holsworthy, Devon.

Pte. William Jones 14258 KIA
born: Exeter, Devon   enlisted: Exeter
Buried: Serre Road Cemetery No.2. Grave XV.A.11. Age 42. Joined BEF: 24/03/15. CWGC: records husband of Mary Ann Way (formerly Jones), 9 Victoria Road, Exmouth.

Pte. William Henry Jones 14154 KIA
born: Tonypandy, Wales   enlisted: Pentre, Glam.   residence: Rhondda, Glam.
Buried: Serre Road Cemetery No.2. Grave XV.C.7. Joined BEF: 24/03/15.

Pte. Lewis Albert Keen 9131 KIA
born: Crediton, Devon   enlisted: Exeter   residence: Crediton
No known grave. Thiepval Memorial, Pier and Face 1.C. Age 24. Date joined BEF: 06/11/14 with original cadre. CWGC: son of Humphrey Keen and Mary Ann Keen, 18 Dean Street, Crediton, Devon.

Pte. Alfred George Keens 13149 KIA
born: Milton Ernest, Beds.   enlisted: Porth , Glam.   residence: Kempston Hardwick, Beds.
Buried: Ovillers Military Cemetery. Grave XVI.A.3. Age 31. Joined BEF: 02/02/15. 1911 Census: railway guard, visiting David Bryant, railway signalman, 24 Mill Lane, Hampstead, London. CWGC: husband of Annie Keens, 301 Humberstone Road, Leicester.

L/Cpl. Gordon Kingdom 8207 KIA
born: Tiverton, Devon   enlisted: Exeter   residence: Tiverton
Buried: Ovillers Military Cemetery. Grave VI.E.3. Age 25. Joined BEF: 06/11/14 with original cadre. 1901 Census: son of William Kingdom, chimney sweep, and Janet Kingdom, Tiverton, Devon. 1911 Census: 2/Devons, St. George's Barracks, Malta. CWGC: family address: North Cottage, Howden, Tiverton, Devon.

Pte. William Henry Lambell 9350 KIA
born: Newton Abbot, Devon   enlisted: Newton Abbot   residence: Bickington
No known grave. Thiepval Memorial, Pier and Face 1.C. Age 32. Joined BEF: 06/11/14 with original cadre. 1901 Census: son of William Lambell, general labourer, and Emma Lambell, No. 3 Court, Woodway, Chudleigh, Newton Abbot, Devon. CWGC: family address: Court House, St. Laurence Road, Ashburton, Devon.

Pte. Leo Jacob Langwasser 3/6829 KIA
born: Newton Abbot, Devon   enlisted: Exeter   residence: Torquay
No known grave. Thiepval Memorial, Pier and Face 1.C. Age 19. Joined BEF: 03/12/14. 1901 Census: son of Jacob A. Langwasser, shed labourer on Great Western Railway, and Sarah Ann Langwasser, 11 Quay Road, Wolborough, Newton Abbot, Devon. 1911 Census: chemist's errand boy, son of Jacob Langwasser, general labourer, and Sarah Ann Langwasser, 9 Warberry Vale, Tormoham, Newton Abbot, Devon. CWGC: family address: Skew Cottages, Station Road, Cullompton, Devon. Jacob Langwasser originally came from Relsburg, Bavaria, Germany, but by 1901 was a British subject.

Pte. Herbert Loveridge 20601 KIA
born: Stockland, Devon   enlisted: Exeter   residence: Axminster
No known grave. Thiepval Memorial, Pier and Face 1.C. Age 29. No Medal Card . 1901 Census: son of John Loveridge, blacksmith, and Catherine Loveridge, Myrtle Cottage, Ham, Stockland, Axminster, Devon.

Sgt. George Luxton 6779 KIA
born: Hatherleigh, Devon   enlisted: Exeter   residence: Hatherleigh
No known grave. Thiepval Memorial, Pier and Face 1.C. Age 37. Joined BEF: 22/08/14 with original cadre of 1/Devons . 1901 Census: 'horseman on farm', at Tavistock, Devon. 1911 Census: recorded as L/Cpl. Luxton, 2/Devons, St. George's Barracks, Malta. CWGC: son of the late G. and M. Luxton.

Pte. Herbert Martin 9162 KIA
born: Southampton, Hants.   enlisted: Southampton
No known grave. Thiepval Memorial, Pier and Face 1.C. Age 28. Date joined BEF: not on Medal card. 1901 Census: son of John Martin, India rubber factor agent, and Fanny Martha Martin, 40 Bernard Street, St. Mary's, Southampton, Hants.

Pte. David Matthews 12963 KIA
born: Pontardulais, Glam.   enlisted: Swansea   residence: Pontardulais
No known grave. Thiepval Memorial, Pier and Face 1.C. Age 26. 'A' Company. Joined BEF: 04/01/15. 1911 Census: underground haulier (coal mine), son of David Matthews, general haulier, and Ann Matthews, Ynysletty, Pontardulais, Glamorgan. CWGC: son of Ann Matthews, Craig Fawr, Pontardulais. Glamorgan, and the late David Matthews.

Sgt. Thomas Henry May 9734 KIA
born: Chulmleigh, Devon   enlisted: Exeter   residence: Crediton
No known grave. Thiepval Memorial, Pier and Face 1.C. Age 19. Joined BEF: 09/02/15. 1901 Census: son of William May, farm labourer, and Mary Ann May, Chudleigh, Crediton, Devon. 1911 Census: servant on farm, son of William May, farm labourer, and Mary Ann May,

Barnson's Cottage, Canesmill, Thelbridge, Morchard Bishop, Devon. CWGC: Mary Ann May, at Allerdown Cottage, Sandford, Crediton, Devon, at time of son's death.

Pte. Francis Mitchell 3/5311 KIA
born: Plymouth, Devon   enlisted: Plymouth
Buried: Serre Road Cemetery No.2. Grave XV.B.12. Age 34. Joined BEF: 06/11/14 with original cadre. 5311 on Medal Card. 1901 Census: Army private at Bulford Camp, Amesbury, Wiltshire.

Pte. Frederick George Moody 11151 KIA
born: London   enlisted: Marylebone
No known grave. Thiepval Memorial, Pier and Face 1.C. Age 19. Joined BEF: 24/03/15. 1911 Census: clerk (country house), son of Edwin Moody, lamplighter, and Mary Moody, 10 Dudley Place, Paddington. Frederick Moody was one of the two members of the Ranelagh Rovers football team who were KIA during the war. His friend Charles Hulbert Yates, 11187, also died on this day.

Cpl. Bryson Roy Murray MM 9184 KIA
born: Newport, IOW   enlisted: Portsmouth   residence: Shovwell, IoW
No known grave. Thiepval Memorial, Pier and Face 1.C. Age 22. Joined BEF: 06/11/14 with original cadre. CWGC: son of Mary Lydia Barton, of Rose Cottage, Shovwell, Isle of Wight.

Pte. Frank Leonard Northcott 16805 KIA
born: Plymouth, Devon   enlisted: Devonport
No known grave. Thiepval Memorial, Pier and Face 1.C. Joined BEF: not on medal card.

Pte. Frank Taylor Ogden 15504 KIA
born: Rochdale, Lancs.   enlisted: Rochdale
Buried: Ovillers Military Cemetery. Grave VII.G.9. Age 20. Joined BEF: 25/05/15. 1901 Census: son of Edmund Ogden, grocer/shopkeeper, and Sarah Jane Ogden, 79 South Street, Rochdale, Lancashire. 1911 Census: errand boy, son of Edmund Ogden, grocer and confectioner, and Sarah Jane Ogden, address as above. CWGC: family address: 218 Yorkshire Street, Rochdale, Lancashire.

Pte. Edgar Lytton Older 15528 KIA
born: London   enlisted: London
No known grave. Thiepval Memorial, Pier and Face 1.C. Age 24. Joined BEF: 25/05/15. 1901 Census: son of Edgar Older, stoker (electric light), and Alice Older, 283 Railton Road, Lambeth, London. 1911 Census: messenger, son of Edgar Older, stoker at Mansions, Whitehall (Government), and Alice Older, 283 Railton Road, Herne Hill, London SE.

Pte. Harry Orchard 11111 KIA
born: Stonehouse, Devon   enlisted: Devonport
No known grave. Thiepval Memorial, Pier and Face 1.C. Age 33. Joined BEF: 02/02/15. Medal Card annotation: *'Pres dead 1/7/16'*. 1901 Census: son of John Orchard, engine driver stationary, and Harriet Orchard, Brownshill, Chalford, Gloucestershire. 1911 Census: grocers assistant, son of Harriett Orchard, widow, Brownshill, Gloucestershire.

L/Cpl. Frank Ernest Osborn 8355 KIA
born : Newton Abbot, Devon   enlisted: Tavistock   residence: Newton Abbot
No known grave. Thiepval Memorial, Pier and Face 1.C. Age 27. Joined BEF: 06/11/14 with original cadre. 1911 Census: 2/Devons, St. George's Barracks, Malta. CWGC: son of John Osborn and Sarah Osborn, East Street, Denbury, Newton Abbot, Devon.

Pte. William Page 11326 KIA
born: Barnstaple, Devon   enlisted: Barnstaple
Buried: Serre Road Cemetery No.2. Grave III.A.1. Age 23. Joined BEF: 24/03/15. 1901

Census: son of Henry Page, gardener, and Edith Page, Barton Cottages, Newton Tracey, Devon. 1911 Census: gardener/domestic, son of Henry Page, gardener/domestic, widower, address as above.

Pte. David Palmer 3/8265 KIA
born: Swansea, Wales   enlisted: Swansea
No known grave. Thiepval Memorial, Pier and Face 1.C. Age 18. Joined BEF: 27/12/14. Medal Card records him with 6/Devons. 1911 Census: schoolboy, son of Owen Palmer, coal hewer, and Gwenllian Owen, Mynddgarnlwyd, Landore, Glamorganshire.

Pte. Christopher Payne 11269 KIA
born: Honiton, Devon   enlisted: Exeter   residence: Honiton
No known grave. Thiepval Memorial, Pier and Face 1.C. Age 24. Joined BEF: 19/01/15. 1911 Census: garden worker/domestic, son of Samuel Payne, coachman/domestic, and Mary Payne, The Stables, Wiscombe Park, Southleigh, Colaton, Devon. Samuel and Mary Payne were Irish, from Kildare and Tipperary respectively, although only child Christopher Payne was born in Devon.

Pte. William Henry Peckins 1504 KIA
born: Newton Abbot, Devon   enlisted: Paignton
No known grave. Thiepval Memorial, Pier and Face 1.C. Age 19. Joined BEF: 29/06/15. Medal card number 15043. 1901 Census: nephew of Samuel Gifford, fisherman, and Emily Gifford, North Furzeham Road, Brixham, Devon. 1911 Census: errand boy, still with aunt and uncle, Higher Street, Brixham, Devon.

Pte. Alexander Peers 8527 KIA
born: Liverpool, Cheshire   enlisted: Warrington   residence: Liverpool
Buried: Ovillers Military Cemetery. Grave XII.C.5. Age 26. Joined BEF: 06/11/14 with original cadre. 1901 Census: son of William Peers, bricklayer, and Elizabeth Peers, 10 Bective Street, West Derby, Edge Hill, Liverpool. 1911 Census: 2/Devons, St. George's Barracks, Malta.

Pte. Arthur Petherick 15451 KIA
born: Stratton, Cornwall   enlisted: Holsworthy   residence: Bridgerule
No known grave. Thiepval Memorial, Pier and Face 1.C. Age 33. Joined BEF: 21/09/14. 1911 Census: farm labourer, husband of Salena Petherick, Kingsford Cottage, Pancrasweek, Holsworthy, Devon.

Pte. Charles Henry Preece 20170 KIA
born: Presteigne, Radnorshire   enlisted: Pontypridd   residence: Treforest
No known grave. Thiepval Memorial, Pier and Face 1.C. Age 23. Joined BEF: not on Medal Card. 1901 Census: son of Edwin Preece, foreman platelayer Great Western Railway, and Martha Preece, Hereford Street, Presteigne, Radnorshire. 1911 Census: Charles Leonard Preece, railway porter, son of Martha Preece, widow, retired sick nurse, Green End, Presteign, Radnorshire.

L/Cpl. George Henry Prout 8921 KIA
born: Devonport, Devon   enlisted: Devonport
Buried: Ovillers Military Cemetery. Grave VIII.I.6. Age 22. Joined BEF: 06/11/14 with original cadre. 1901 Census: son of Jane Prout, 39a James Street, Devonport. 1911 Census: 2/Devons, St. George's Barracks, Malta.

L/Cpl. Charles Prowse 15075 KIA
born: Hartland, Devon   enlisted: Exeter   residence: Hartland
No known grave. Thiepval Memorial, Pier and Face 1.C. Age 29. Joined BEF: 29/06/15. Medal Card and CWGC spelling is Prouse. 1911 Census: schoolboy at boarding school, 26 College Road, Clifton, Bristol, Glos.

Pte. William George Pugsley 19103 KIA
born: South Molton, Devon   enlisted: Exeter   residence: Lapford
No known grave. Thiepval Memorial, Pier and Face 1.C. Age 17. Joined BEF: not on Medal Card, but names him William J. Pugsley. 1901 Census: son of Frank Pugsley, of West Farm, Lapford, Devon. 1911 Census: recorded as Willam John Pugsley, son of Frank Pugsley, farm labourer, and stepmother Emma Pugsley, West Lapford, Morchard Bishop, Devon.

Pte. Frederick Leonard Purvey 9804 KIA
born: London   enlisted: Stratford, Essex
No known grave. Thiepval Memorial, Pier and Face 1.C. Age 22. Joined BEF: 03/12/14 with 1/Devons . 1911 Census: messenger, son of George William Purvey, printer's warehouseman, and Ellen Margaret Purvey, 60 Cromwell Road, Islington, London. CWGC: son of George William and Ellen Margaret Purvey, address as above.

Cpl. William Reed 8280 KIA
born: Tiverton, Devon   enlisted: Tiverton
No known grave. Thiepval Memorial, Pier and Face 1.C. Age 27. Joined BEF: 22/08/14 with original cadre of 1/Devons. CWGC: son of Charles Reed and Eliza Ann Reed, Champles Farm, Stoodleigh, Tiverton, Devon.

Pte. Kenneth William Reeves 17793 KIA
born: Chelsea, London   enlisted: Fulham
No known grave. Thiepval Memorial, Pier and Face 1.C. Age 16. Joined BEF: not on Medal Card, but records number as 17792. 1901 Census: son of Harry Reeves, omnibus traffic supervisor, and Caroline M. Reeves (who was born in Canada), 37 Delview Road, Fulham. CWGC: mother at 7 Dolby Road, Hurlingham, London.

Pte. Mark Rice 3/6730 KIA
born: Liverpool, Cheshire   enlisted: Exeter   residence: Seacombe
No known grave. Thiepval Memorial, Pier and Face 1.C. Age 20. Joined BEF: 11/12/14. Medal Card annotation: *'death accepted 1/7/16'*. 1901 Census: son of Thomas Rice, road labourer, and Mary Rice, 4 Mersey Street, Seacombe, Wallasey, Cheshire. 1911 Census: 'assistant', son of Thomas Rice, dock labourer, and Mary Rice, 8 Victoria Grove, Seacombe, Cheshire. CWGC: family address: 8 Victoria Grove, Seacombe.

Pte. Reginald George Richards 3/6783 KIA
born: Barnstaple, Devon   enlisted: Barnstaple
No known grave. Thiepval Memorial, Pier and Face 1.C. Age 18. 'B' Company. Joined BEF: 03/12/14 with 1/Devons . 1901 Census: son on Edith Richards, charwoman, of 15 Hardaway Head, Barnstaple. 1911 Census: railway contractor/labourer, son of Thomas Henry Richards, mason labourer, and Adill Richards (married for 25 years), 36 Hardaway Head, Barnstaple, Devon.CWGC: son of Thomas Henry Richards and Edith Richards, 36 Hardaway Head, Barnstaple, Devon.

Pte. Ernest Ridgeway 18701 KIA
born: Exeter, Devon   enlisted: Newton Poppleford
No known grave. Thiepval Memorial, Pier and Face 1.C. Age 19. Joined BEF: 21/12/15. 1901 Census: son of Sarah Ridgeway, widow, Millhayes, Hemyock, Devon. 1911 Census: recorded as Ernest Tom Ridgeway, shoemaker's apprentice, boarder 1 Cox's Court Park, Tiverton, Devon.

Pte. Phillip Roberts 3/8283 KIA
born: Swansea, Wales   enlisted: Swansea
Buried: Ovillers Military Cemetery. Grave VIII.Y.4. Age 23. Joined BEF: 27/12/14. Medal card annotation: *'death regarded 1/7/16'*. 1901 Census: son of Hopkin Roberts, starter stationary engine tinworks, and Gwenllian Roberts, 28 Lynn Street, Swansea. 1911 Census:

tinworker/greaser, son of Hopkin Roberts, general labourer, and Gwenllian Roberts, 28 Lynn Street, Cwmbwrla, Swansea.

Pte. Ernest Alfred Rogers 18652 KIA
born: Portlemouth, Devon   enlisted: Kingsbridge
Buried: Ovillers Military Cemetery. Grave IX.N.8. Age 29. Joined BEF: 15/12/15. 1901 Census: 'tea maker on farm', son of John Adams Rogers, widower, horseman at Rickham Farm, East Portlemouth, Kingsbridge, Devon. 1911 Census: farm labourer/servant, Higher Borough, Prawle, Kingsbridge, Devon. CWGC: brother Mr. W. H. Rogers, East Prawle, Salcombe, Kingsbridge, Devon.

Pte. John Rowe 8468 KIA
born: Exeter, Devon   enlisted: Exeter
Buried: Ovillers Military Cemetery. Grave XIII.C.1. Age 27. Joined BEF: 06/11/14 with original cadre. 1911 Census: 2/Devons, St. George's Barracks, Malta.

Cpl. Thomas Rowe 7000 KIA
born: Birmingham, Worcs.   enlisted: Plymouth
No known grave. Thiepval Memorial, Pier and Face 1.C. Age 43. Joined BEF: 06/11/14 with original cadre. CWGC: son of the late George Albert Rowe, 67 Agathas Road, Ward End, Birmingham.

Pte. Charles Saunders 11219 KIA
born: Barnstaple, Devon   enlisted: Barnstaple
Buried: Aveluy Communal Cemetery Extension. Grave F.28. Date joined BEF: 24/03/15.

Pte. William Searson 13371 KIA
born: Manchester, Lancs.   enlisted: Rochdale
No known grave. Thiepval Memorial, Pier and Face 1.C. Age 28. No Medal Card. 1911 Census: general labourer, lodging at Manchester Workhouse, New Bridge Street, Manchester, Lancashire.

Sgt. William Shaxon MM 8029 KIA
born: Bideford, Devon   enlisted: Exeter   residence: Bideford
Buried: Ovillers Military Cemetery. Grave VI.S.3. Age 28. Joined BEF: 06/11/14 with original cadre. 1901 Census: 'cow boy on farm', employed by Robert Harris, farmer, of Buckland Brewer, Bideford, Devon. 1911 Census: 2/Devons, St. George's Barracks, Malta.

Pte. Stanley Skelley 16956 KIA
born: Cornwood, Devon   enlisted: Plymouth   residence: Cornwood
No known grave. Thiepval Memorial, Pier and Face 1.C. Age 27. No Medal Card. 1901 Census: son of Uriah Skelley, stone mason, and Thirza Skelley, Sutton, Cornwood, Totnes, Devon. CWGC lists death 15th July 1916.

Pte. Frederick James Skinner 9361 KIA
born: Colaton Raleigh, Devon   enlisted: Exeter   residence: Colaton Raleigh
No known grave. Thiepval Memorial, Pier and Face 1.C. Age 24. 'A' Company.Joined BEF: 06/11/14 with original cadre. 1901 Census: son of George Henry Skinner, horseman (on estate), and Louisa Annie Troke Skinner, Quashbrook Cottage (3), Colaton Raleigh, Sidmouth, Devon. 1911 Census: 3/Devons, Higher Barracks, Howell Road, Exeter, Devon.

Pte. Harry Smith 17562 KIA
born: Todmorden Lancs.   enlisted: Halifax, Yorks.   residence: Todmorden
No known grave. Thiepval Memorial, Pier and Face 1.C. Age 19. Joined BEF: not on Medal Card. 1901 Census: son of James Smith, carpenter and joiner, and Fanny Smith, 243 Halifax Road, Todmorden. Fanny Smith was born in Redruth, Cornwall. 1911 Census: cotton weaver, son of James Smith, joiner, and Fanny Smith, address as above.

The 2nd Devons War Diary

Pte. Harry Stamp 15590 KIA
born: Tooting, London   enlisted: Battersea   residence: Balham
No known grave. Thiepval Memorial, Pier and Face 1.C. Age 32. Joined BEF: 01/06/15. 1901 Census: only child of Lucy Stamp, widow, laundress, 119 Graveney Road, Streatham, Wandsworth, Surrey. 1911 Census: bricklayer, husband of Florence Stamp, address as above. Widowed mother and 2 children recorded at same address.

Sgt. Harry Thomas Stone 10195 KIA
born: Jalapahur, India   enlisted: Cork, Ireland
Buried: Ovillers Military Cemetery. Grave XIII.Y.2. Age 19. 'D' Company. Joined BEF: 18/05/15. CWGC: son of Mabel P. Stone, 85 Standard Road, Hounslow, Middx. and the late George Stone.

Cpl. William Henry Strawbridge 9550 KIA
born: Ashburton, Devon   enlisted: Exeter   residence: Sidford, Devon
Buried: Ovillers Military Cemetery. Grave VIII.G.5. Age 21. Joined BEF: 06/11/14 with original cadre. 1901 Census: son of William Henry Strawbridge, 'ordinary agricultural labourer', and Elizabeth Amanda Strawbridge, Landscove Cottage, Haverton, Totnes, Devon. 1911 Census: cattle man on farm/servant, at Brook Farm, Buckfastleigh, Devon. CWGC: family addres: 49 Yonder Street, Ottery St. Mary, Devon.

Pte. Joseph Tanner 6402 KIA
born: Torquay, Devon   enlisted: Torquay
No known grave. Thiepval Memorial, Pier and Face 1.C. Age 43. Joined BEF: 22/08/14 with original cadre of 1/Devons . Medal Card annotation: *Application from Mrs. A. Tanner for medals awarded to the late Pte J. Tanner 20.4.20.* CWGC: son of Mrs. Harriett Tanner, 19 Stentsford Hill, Torquay.

Pte. Frank Hamlet Tattersall 18739 KIA
born: Coalbrookdale, Shropshire   enlisted: Rochdale
No known grave. Thiepval Memorial, Pier and Face 1.C. Age 18. Joined BEF: not on Medal Card. 1901 Census: son of Hamlet Tattersall, carter for the Lancashire and Yorkshire Railway, and Charlotte Tattersall, 21 Rowland Street, Rochdale, Lancs. Frank Hamlet Tattersall was 3 years old in 1901, the second youngest of ten children, despite his mother being only 36. Hamlet Tattersall was 40. 1911 Census: apprentice machine fitter, sister of Charlotte Tattersall, head of family, card-room hand/cotton, 14 John Street, Castleton, Lancashire.

Pte. Charles Taylor 3/6854 KIA
born: London   enlisted: London   residence: Eastbourne
Buried: Serre Road Cemetery No.2. Grave III.C.5. Age 19. Joined BEF: 17/03/15. Medal Card annotation: *'death regarded 1/7/16.'* 1911 Census: van boy, son of Henry James Taylor, shoe black, and Sarah Ann Taylor, 7 Turin Street, Bethnal Green, London. CWGC: son of Henry James Taylor and Sarah Taylor, 8 Cymon Street, Bethnal Green, London.

Pte. George James Thomas 14174 KIA
born: Abergavenny, Wales   enlisted: Honiton   residence: Swansea
No known grave. Thiepval Memorial, Pier and Face 1.C. Age 32. Joined BEF:02/05/15. CWGC: son of Peter Thomas, 20 Oakwood Road, Brynmill, Swansea, and the late Harriet Thomas.

Pte. George Edward Thompson 15240 KIA
born: Burnley, Lancs.   enlisted: Colne, Lancs.
No known grave. Thiepval Memorial, Pier and Face 1.C. Date joined BEF: 18/05/15.

Pte. Charles Victor Triggs 20582 KIA
born: Kingston, Devon   enlisted: Kingsbridge
No known grave. Thiepval Memorial, Pier and Face 1.C. Age 29. Joined BEF: not on Medal Card. 1901 Census: son of Bessie Triggs, widow, 31 Kingston Villas, Kingston, Devon. 1911 Census: wall mason, son of Bessie Triggs, widow, Kingston, near Kingsbridge, Devon. CWGC: son of Charles Triggs and Bessie Triggs, Yealmpton, Plymouth, and husband of the late Janet Triggs.

Pte. Ernest George Vass 11491 KIA
born: Brixham, Devon   enlisted: Exeter   residence: Brixham
Buried: Serre Road Cemetery No.2. Grave XV.A.7. Age 23. Joined BEF: 04/01/15. 1911 Census: apprentice painter and decorator, son of Maria Vass, married, 51 King Street, Brixham, Devon. CWGC: son of Arthur James Vass and Maria Vass, 17 Belle Vue Terrace, Ranscombe Road, Brixham, Devon.

Pte. James Vile 9056 KIA
born: Ilminster, Somerset   enlisted: Exeter   residence: Ilminster
No known grave. Thiepval Memorial, Pier and Face 1.C. Age 23. Joined BEF: 06/11/14 with original cadre. 1901 Census: son of Albert Vile, general labourer, and Sarah Ann Vile, 7 Prospect Buildings, Cross, Ilminster, Somerset. 1911 Census: 2/Devons, St. George's Barracks, Malta.

Pte. Frederick Joseph Vincent 15606 KIA
born: London   enlisted: Exeter   residence: London S.W.
Buried: Ovillers Military Cemetery. Grave XVI.A.3. Age 18. Joined BEF: 01/06/15. Medal Card annotation, '*death regarded 1/7/16*'. 1901 Census: son of Ernest Vincent, railway porter, and Mary Vincent, coffee shop proprioter, 37 Wick Road (coffee shop), Hackney, Middlesex.

Pte. Richard Lloyd Wade 3/8311 KIA
born: Swansea, Wales   enlisted: Swansea
Buried: Ovillers Military Cemetery. Grave VI.M.1/3. Age 20. Joined BEF: 04/01/15. 1901 Census: son of Richard L. Wade, coal tipper, and Margaret Wade, 8 Paxton Terrace, Swansea. 1911 Census: errand boy, son of Richard Lloyd Wade, dock labourer, and Margaret Wade, 44 Wellington Street, Swansea, Glam.

Pte. Charles James Wakeham 20787 KIA
born: Paignton, Devon   enlisted: Newton Abbot   residence: Brixham
Buried: Ovillers Military Cemetery. Grave XV1.E.3. Age 32. 'C' Company. Joined BEF: not on Medal Card. 1901 Census: son of Susan Wakeham, Brixham, Devon. 1911 Census: gardener, stepson of E.G. Norris, diver, and Susan Elizabeth Norris (mother), Overgang Road, Brixham, Devon. CWGC: son of Mrs. S. E. Norris, 42 Garlic-Rea, Brixham, Devon, and incorrectly records his surname as Wakeman.

Pte. William James Walker 13547 KIA
born: Somerton, Somerset   enlisted: Yeovil   residence: Somerton
Buried: Serre Road Cemetery No.2. Grave XV.C.13 (Sp. Mem.) Age 36. Joined BEF: 10/08/15. 1901 Census: 'ordinary agricultural labourer, son of James Walker, 'cattleman on farm', and Fanny Walker, 5 Church Lane, East Lydford, Shepton Mallet, Somerset. 1911 Census: farm labourer, boarding at West Lydford, Taunton, Somerset.

Pte. Arthur Walton 15272 KIA
born: Hebden Bridge, Yorks.   enlisted: Halifax   residence: Todmorden
No known grave. Thiepval Memorial, Pier and Face 1.C. Age 23. Joined BEF: 18/05/15. 1911 Census: cotton weaver, son of William Walton, cotton weaver, and Ada Walton, 657 Robertshaw Terrace, Cornholme, Todmorden, Yorkshire. CWGC: son of Willie Walton, 3

Wickenbury Clough, Todmorden.

Pte. Arthur Francis Watts 3/6202 KIA
born: Totnes, Devon enlisted: Exeter residence: Totnes
Buried: Serre Road Cemetery No.2. Grave XV.C.8. Age 25. 'C' Company. Joined BEF: 06/11/14 with original cadre. 1911 Census: 3/Devons, Higher Barracks, Howell Road, Exeter, Devon. CWGC: son of Sarah Mary Watts, 45 High Street, Totnes, Devon, and the late Alfred Watts.

Pte. Alfred George Webber 3/831 KIA
born: Highbridge, Somerset enlisted: Taunton residence: Highbridge
No known grave. Thiepval Memorial, Pier and Face 1.C. 27/12/14. Age 29. Joined BEF: not on Medal Card. Medal Card annotation: *'death regarded 1/7/16'*. 1901 Census: son of William Webber, general labourer, and Emily Webber, Elm Cottage, Brent Knoll, Axbridge, Somerset. 1911 Census: gardener/groom, son of William Webber, jobbing gardener, and Emily Webber, Brent Street, near Brent Knoll, Somerset.

Pte. Thomas Weeks 17542 KIA
born: London enlisted: London
No known grave. Thiepval Memorial, Pier and Face 1.C. Age 35. Joined BEF: 31/12/15. 1911 Census: cooper, husband of Mary Weeks, 66 Henshaw Street, Southwark, London. CWGC: husband of Mary Symmons (formerly Weeks), address as above.

Pte. William Westlake 12595 KIA
born: Hatherleigh, Devon enlisted: Exeter residence: Hatherleigh
No known grave. Thiepval Memorial, Pier and Face 1.C. Age 24. Joined BEF: 09/02/15. 1901 Census: son of William Westlake, general farm labourer, and Emily Westlake, South Street, Hatherleigh, Devon. 1911 Census: horseman, Lower Upcott Farm, Hatherleigh, Devon. CWGC names father as the late William Westlake.

L/Cpl. Charles Henry White 15086 KIA
born: Plympton, Devon enlisted: Plymouth
Buried: Serre Road Cemetery No.2. Grave XV.A.10. Age 32. Date joined BEF: 29/06/15.

Pte. John White 8146 KIA
born: Porth, Glamorgan enlisted: Porth residence: Rhondda
Buried: Ovillers Military Cemetery. Grave IX.Q.10. Age 31. Joined BEF: 27/12/14. CWGC and Medal Card record his Army number as 3/8146. CWGC: son of George White, 13 Tram Road, Dinas, husband of Elizabeth Maud White, 11 Tram Road, Dinas, (Rhondda), Glam.

Pte. Thomas Wicks 9821 KIA
born: Saffron Walden, Essex enlisted: Stratford, Essex
No known grave. Thiepval Memorial, Pier and Face 1.C. Age 22. Joined BEF: 02/12/14 with 1/Devons. Medal Card annotation: *'pres. Dead'*. CWGC: son of George Wicks and Ellen Wicks.

Pte. William Currey Wilson 16879 KIA
born: Wembury, Devon enlisted: Plymouth
No known grave. Thiepval Memorial, Pier and Face 1.C. Age 39. Joined BEF: not on Medal Card. 1901 Census: 'farmer's son', son of William Wilson, farmer, Elburton Village, Plymstock, Plympton, Devon. CWGC: son of the late William and Emma Wilson.

Pte. Herbert Woolacott 9084 KIA
born: Barnstaple, Devon enlisted: Exeter residence: Barnstaple
Buried: Ovillers Military Cemetery. Grave IX.C.4. Age 21. Joined BEF: 06/11/14 with original cadre. 1901 Census: son of John Woolacott, labourer in nursery, and Thirza Woolacott, Newland, Landkey, Barnstaple.

Pte. Thomas Woolway 15220 KIA
born: no record   enlisted: Merthyr, Glam.
No known grave. Thiepval Memorial, Pier and Face 1.C. Joined BEF: 18/05/15. Medal Card annotation: *'death regarded 1/7/16'*.

Pte. Charles Hulbert Yates 11187 KIA
born: Paddington, London   enlisted: Marylebone   residence: Paddington
No known grave. Thiepval Memorial, Pier and Face 1.C. Age 22. Joined BEF: 24/03/15. Born 12th November 1893. 1901 Census: son of Charles Henry Yates, assistant in stationer's shop, and Maria Yates, nee Hulbert, 108 Seymour Road, Marylebone, London. 1911 Census records him as 'errand boy (shop)', eldest child of Charles Henry Yates, house painter (unemployed), formerly stationery assistant, and Marie Yates, 126 Clarendon Street, Paddington, Middlesex. Had also worked as a plumber's mate for his uncle, Alexander Smith, during which time he worked on the construction of the White City Stadium, for the 1908 Olympic Games. Enlisted 6th November 1914 at Marylebone with the rest of the Ranelagh Rovers football team. Charles Yates was great uncle of Martin Body, the author of this book, and his sister, the late Janice Body.

Pte. Edward Bickford 15376 DoW
born: Millbrook, Cornwall   enlisted: Plymouth   residence: Millbrook
No known grave. Thiepval Memorial, Pier and Face 1.C. Age 22. Joined BEF: 18/05/15. 1911 Census: recorded as Ed Bickford, servant on farm, Tre Rule Farm, St. Germans, Cornwall. CWGC: brother of Mrs. Alice Page, 12 Cornwall Street, Devonport.

Pte. William Sidney Bolton 9862 DoW
born: Bath, Somerset   enlisted: Bath
Buried: Ribemont Communal Cemetery Extension. Grave II.J.6. Age 20. Joined BEF: 06/11/14 with original cadre. 1911 Census: son of John William Bolton, stone mason, and Clara Louisa Bolton, 5 and 6 Lucklom Buildings, Tyning Lane, Bath, Somerset. CWGC: son of Clara L. Bolton, 14 Clements Street, Walcot, Bath.

Pte. William Dibble 7729 DoW
born: Barnstaple, Devon   enlisted: Barnstaple
No known grave. Thiepval Memorial, Pier and Face 1.C. Age 32. Joined BEF: 22/08/14 with 1/Devons. 1901 Census: stone breaker/labourer, son of George Dibble, stone breaker/labourer, and Elizabeth Dibble, charwoman, 5 Green Lane, Barnstaple, Devon.

Sgt. John Lurburam Gilliland 9261 DoW
born: Exmouth, Devon   enlisted: Exmouth
No known grave. Thiepval Memorial, Pier and Face 1.C. Date joined BEF: 22/08/14/with 1/Devons.

L/Cpl. Robert David Jones 12920 DoW
born: Swansea   enlisted: Swansea
No known grave. Thiepval Memorial, Pier and Face 1.C. Age 23. Joined BEF: 16/02/15. CWGC: brother of Mrs. Davidge, 1 Barnfield Street, Heywood, Lancs.

Pte. Alfred Mitchell 11323 DoW
born: Axminster, Devon   enlisted: Axminster
No known grave. Thiepval Memorial, Pier and Face 1.C. Joined BEF: 10/08/15.

Pte. James Saunders 10015 DoW
born: Watford, Herts.   enlisted: Hertford   residence: Watford
No known grave. Thiepval Memorial, Pier and Face 1.C. No Medal Card.

The 2nd Devons War Diary

2nd July 1916
Pte. Ernest Hawkins 15592 DoW
Born: London   enlisted: London   residence: Hammersmith
Buried: Warloy-Baillon Communal Cemetery Extension. Grave I.B.23. No Medal Card.
L/Cpl. John Lee 8302 DoW
Born: Holsworthy, Devon   enlisted: Exeter, Devon   residence: Honicknowle, Devon
Buried: Puchevillers British Cemetery. Grave I.A.14. Age 31. Joined BEF: 06/11/14 with original cadre. 1911 Census: 2/Devons, St. George's Barracks, Malta.

3rd July 1916
Pte. George Frederick Wilson 8714 DoW
born: Bracknell, Berks.   enlisted: Portsmouth
Buried: Puchevillers British Cemetery. Grave I.B.47. Age 26. Joined BEF: 06/11/14 with original cadre. 1911 Census: 2/Devons, St. George's Barracks, Malta. CWGC: brother of Charles W. Wilson, Bowood, Calne, Wilts.

4th July 1916
Pte. Joshua Fielden 15591 DoW
born: Littleborough, Lancs.   enlisted: Rochdale   residence: Littleborough
Buried: Puchevillers British Cemetery. Grave I.C.2. Age 22. Joined BEF: 01/06/15. 1911 Census: 'Labour Operative Cotton Carrier', son of Cyril Fielden, Dairy Farmer, and Eliza Jane Fielden, Deanhurst, Littleborough, Lancs. CWGC: son of Cyril Fielden and Eliza Jane Fielden, Littleborough, Lancs.
Pte. Robert Phillips 16889 DoW
born: Paignton, Devon   enlisted: Newton Abbot   residence: Paignton
Buried: Heilly Station Cemetery, Mericourt-L'Abbe. Grave I.C.24. Joined BEF: not on Medal Card.

5th July 1916
Pte. William James Lewis 3/8327 DoW
born: Swansea   enlisted: Swansea
Buried: Boulogne Eastern Cemetery. Grave VIII.C.93. Age 23. Joined BEF: 27/12/14. 1911 Census: 'Coal Rolls Roller', son of David Lewis, Engineman Stationery, and Margaret Lewis, 23 Lynn Street, Cwmbwrla, Swansea. CWGC: son of David Lewis and Margaret Lewis, 23 Lynn Street, Cwmbwrla, Swansea.

6th July 1916
Pte. Frederick John Beer 20349 DoW
born: no record   enlisted: Exeter   residence: Newton Abbot
Buried: Daours Communal Cemetery Extension. Grave I.A.18. Age 39. Joined BEF: not on Medal Card. 1911 Census: general farm labourer, husband of Sarah Jane Beer, father of 4 daughters aged between 1 and 5, Lower Bowden Cottage, Totnes, Devon. CWGC: son of John Beer, Merrit Flats, Totnes Rd., Paignton, Devon, husband of Sarah Jane Beer, South Street, Tenbury, Newton Abbot. Devon.
Pte. John Teague 10220 DoW
born: Truro, Cornwall   enlisted: Truro
Buried: Heilly Station Cemetery, Mericourt-L'Abbe. Grave I.A.26. Joined BEF: 25/07/15.

7th July 1916
Pte. Thomas Laurence Ash 16955 DoW
born: Portsmouth, Hants.   enlisted: Plymouth
Buried: Boulogne Eastern Cemetery. Grave VIII.C.105. Age 26. Joined BEF: not on Medal Card. 1911 Census: nephew of William Dart, Naval Pensioner, Cambridge Villa, West Street, Havant, Hampshire. CWGC: son of Thomas Ash, husband of Ellen Ash.

8th July 1916
Pte. Robert May 3/6737 DoW
born: Paignton, Devon   enlisted: Torquay   residence: Paignton
Buried: Warloy-Baillon Communal Cemetery Extension. Grave III.C.1. Age 18. No Medal Card. 1901 Census: son of Edwin May, gardener, and Annie May, 7 Ebenezer Road, Paignton, Devon.

11th July 1916
Pte. Francis Watkins 13072 DoW
born: Pontypridd, Glam.   enlisted: Pontypridd
Buried: Boulogne Eastern Cemetery. Grave VIII.D.98. Joined BEF: 04/01/15.

13th July 1916
Pte. Thomas May 15520 DoW
born: Wallsden, Lancs.   enlisted: Halifax   residence: Littleborough
Buried: Boulogne Eastern Cemetery. Grave VIII.D.112. Joined BEF: 25/05/15. Named Tom May on Medal card.
Pte. John Thresher 8688 DoW (home)
born: Taunton, Devon   enlisted: Taunton
Buried: Salisbury (Devizes Road) Cemetery. Grave 3.400. Age 27. Joined BEF: 06/11/14 with original cadre. 1911 Census: 2/Devons, St. George's Barracks, Malta.

14th July 1916
L/Cpl. Frederick George Collins 9538 DoW
born: Truro   enlisted: Exeter   residence: Barnstaple
Buried: Boulogne Eastern Cemetery. Grave VIII.D.118. Age 25. No Medal Card. CWGC: son of Mr. and Mrs. Skerry, 11 South Street, Newport, Barnstaple, Devon.

16th July 1916
Pte. Frank David Kitchener 17615 KIA
born: Edmonton, London   enlisted: Mill Hill   residence: Edmonton
Buried: Cambrin Churchyard Extension. Grave O.36. Age 36. Joined BEF: not on Medal Card. 1901 Census: 'pattern maker', son of charwoman, Mary Kitchener, widow, 1 Pleasant Cottages, Edmonton, Enfield, London. 1911 Census: 'advertising and business manager' (newspapers), 25 Boileau Road, Ealing, Middlesex.
Pte. Dudley Charles Clift 3/7122 KIA
born: Plymouth, Devon   enlisted: Devonport
Buried: Cambrin Churchyard Extension. Grave O.35. Age 17 (also recorded as being 20 years old, which may mean he gave a false age on enlistment). Joined BEF: 02/05/15. 1901 Census: son of Samuel Clift, coal dealer, and Eda Elizabeth Clift, 7 St. Leonard's Road, Plymouth. 1911 Census: schoolboy, son of Eda Clift, 18 Laira Street, Plymouth. Family address: II Morley Street, Plymouth, at time of death.

The 2nd Devons War Diary

17th July 1916
Pte. Alfred William Broderick 18328 KIA
born: Shoreditch, Middx.   enlisted: Shoreditch   residence: Spitalfields
Buried: Cambrin Churchyard Extension. Grave O.39. Age 21. 'A' Company. Joined BEF: not on Medal Card. 1901 and 1911 Census record him as the son of Alfred Walter Broderick, 'beer retailer, pub.', and Sarah Jane Broderick, 271, Brick Lane, Bethnal Green, London. CWGC: family address as above.

Pte. Ernest George Poolman 18572   KIA
born: Codford St. Mary, Wilts.   enlisted: Newton Abbot, Devon   residence: Ashburton
Buried: Cambrin Churchyard Extension. Grave O.47. Age 22. Joined BEF: not on Medal Card. 1901 Census: son of Walter Poolman, rural postman, and Elizabeth Poolman, 3 Bank Lane, Totnes, Devon.

18th July 1916
2/Lt. Alfred Morris Rogers KIA
Attached from 15th Battalion, Gloucestershire Regiment. With 2/Devons from 12th July 1916. Buried: Cambrin Churchyard Extension. Grave O.45. Age 23. Joined BEF: 17/03/15. Formerly 2502 Pte. A. M. Rogers, 15th Battalion, London Regiment. Commissioned in the 15th Gloucestershire Regiment 24/12/15. 1911 Census: schoolboy, son of Alfred George Rogers, commercial clerk, and Anna Olivia Rogers, 7 Fairlawn Road, Montpelier, Bristol. Before joining the Army 2/Lt. Rogers was a Civil Servant with the Ministry of Labour in London, and resided at 63 Chelverton Road, Putney.

Pte. Alfred George Edwards 19037 KIA
born: Buckerell, Devon   enlisted: Exeter   residence: Cullompton
No known grave. Loos Memorial, Panel 35 to 37. Age 20. Joined BEF: not on Medal Card. 1911 Census: assistant to his father, John Robert Edwards, 'manager to the wheelwritey and general engineering and barley milling', and Amy Georgina Edwards, Hackpen Mills, Craddock, Cullompton, Devon. CWGC: son of Mr. J. R. and Mrs. A. G. Edwards, Fore Street, Uffculme, Devon.

Pte. Fred England 16684 KIA
born: Torquay, Devon   enlisted: Torquay
Buried: Cambrin Churchyard Extension. Grave O.46. Age 21. Joined BEF: not on Medal Card. 1901 Census: son of William Henry England, plasterer, and Emily England, 5 Prospect Place, Torquay. 1911 Census: 'errand boy, chemist', son of William Henry England, plasterer, and Emily England, 37 Westbourne Road, Torquay, where they lived at the time of his death.

Pte. Sidney Charles Nile 3/6216 KIA
born: Plymouth, Devon   enlisted: Plymouth
No known grave. Loos Memorial, Panel 35 to 37. Age 25. 'A' Company. Joined BEF: 06/11/14 with original cadre. CWGC: son of William Nile and Emily Nile, 9 Clifton Street, Plymouth.

Pte. David John Owen 7606 KIA
born: Pontardulais, Glam.   enlisted: Swansea   residence: Pontardulais
No known grave. Loos Memorial, Panel 35 to 37. Age 24. No Medal Card. CWGC: son of Mrs. Harris, Arasfan, Loughon Road, Pontardulais, Glam.

Pte. Charles Spiller 11232 KIA
born: Axminster, Devon   enlisted: Axminster   residence: no record
No known grave. Loos Memorial, Panel 35 to 37. Age 28. 'A' Company. Joined BEF: 24/03/15. Number on Medal Card is 11332. 1911 Census: 'carter on farm', son of William Spiller, farm labourer, and Ann Spiller, Castle Hawkchurch, Axminster, Devon. CWGC: son of

William Spiller and Ann Spiller, Courshay, Hawkchurch, Axminster, Devon.
L/Cpl. Arthur John Arberry 11429 DoW (home)
born: Stonehouse, Devon   enlisted: Devonport
Buried: Ford Park Cemetery (Formerly Plymouth Old cemetery)(Pennycomequick). Grave General C.12.11. Age 25. Joined BEF: 19/01/15. 1901 Census: son of John J. Arberry, painter, and Annie Arberry, dressmaker, 44 Emma Road, Stonehouse, Somerset. 1911 Census: 'white-smith', son of Mary Ann Arberry, widow, dressmaker, Mountway Cottages, Bishops Hull, Taunton.

22nd July 1916
Pte. William Stephens 18507 DoW
born: Birmingham   enlisted: Fulham, Middx.
Buried: St. Sever Cemetery, Rouen. Grave A.32.19. Age 21. Joined BEF: not on Medal Card. CWGC: nephew of Mrs. Ellen Deadman, 45 Sedlescombe Road, Fulham, London.

25th July 1916
2/Lt. John Archibald Rennie Attached from3/Devons DoW
Buried: Camelon Cemetery. Grave E.496. AGE 29. Joined BEF: 20/05/16. CWGC: son of Archibald Cochran Rennie and Mary Walker Gillies Rennie, 'Maryville' 14 Hodge Street, Falkirk, Stirlingshire, Scotland.

27th July 1916
Pte. Harold Willie 11536 DoW
born: London enlisted: Exeter
Buried: Brixham (St. Mary) Churchyard. Grave S.E.14.12. Age 22. No Medal Card. 1901 Census: boarding pupil at St. Marylebone School. Annotation for place of birth of the 25 pupils on the relevant page reads: *"No information – presumably in Marylebone"*. 1911 Census: apprentice trawlerman, living in the home of Samuel Partridge, fisherman trawler, 10 Mount Pleasant Road, Brixham, Devon.

30th July 1916
Pte. Bertie George Chipperfield 12241 KIA
born: Mutford, Suffolk   enlisted: London N.
Buried: Cambrin Churchyard Extension. Grave P.7. Age 36. Joined BEF: 27/07/15. 1901 Census: 'railway servant', son of George Chipperfield, butcher's assistant, and Rosalie M. Chipperfield, 31 Warren Street, Clerkenwell, Middlesex. 1911 Census: railwayman, boarder at home of Alfred Mason, locomotive driver, 74 St. Augustine's Road, Camden Town, London.
Pte. Thomas Henry Hobbs 20792 KIA
born: Thorpe, Suffolk   enlisted: Plymouth
Buried: Bethune Town Cemetery. Grave V.G.47. Age 24. Joined BEF: not recorded on Medal Card. 1901 Census: son of Charles Hobbs, boatman H.M. Coastguard, and Annie Hobbs, Church Road, West Mersea, Essex. 1911 Census: 'brick maker brick works', son of Charles Hobbs, H.M. Coastguard, and Annie Hobbs, Coast Guard Station, Battery Green, Lowestoft, Suffolk. CWGC: family address: 43 Durnford Street, Stonehouse, Plymouth.

The 2nd Devons War Diary

AUGUST 1916

3rd August 1916
Pte. Charles Donald Smale 7457 DoW (home)
born: Ottery St. Mary, Devon   enlisted: Ottery St. Mary
Buried: Newton Poppleford Cemetery. Grave: Near North West Corner. Age 29. Joined BEF: 22/08/14 with 1/Devons. 1901 Census: pupil 'Wallingbrook' boarding school, Leigh Road, Chulmleigh, Devon.

11th August 1916
Pte. William John Hodge 3/6561 KIA
born: Totnes, Devon   enlisted: Totnes   residence: Blackawton
Buried: Vermelles Military Cemetery. Grave III.N.5. Age 28. Joined BEF: 20/09/14 with 1/Devons . 1911 Census: 2/Devons, St. George's Barracks, Malta.

13th August 1916
Pte. Ernest Heath 16665 KIA
born: Totnes, Devon   enlisted: Newton Abbot   residence: Totnes
Buried: Vermelles Military Cemetery. Grave III.N.6. Age 22. Joined BEF: not on Medal card. 1901 Census: son of Frederick Heath, grocer's porter, and Dinah Heath, 4 Cistern Street, Totnes, Devon. 1911 Census: errand boy, son of Frederick Heath, grocer's warehouseman, and Dinah Heath, 4 Cistern Street, Totnes, Devon.

14th August 1916
2/Lt. William Herbert Lesley Vesey-Fitzgerald KIA
Buried: Vermelles Military Cemetery. Grave III.N.9. Age 29. No Medal Card. CWGC: son of Gerald and Emma Vesey Fitzgerald, 15 Nevern Place, London, S.W.5.
Pte. John Phillips Linton 16937 DoW
born: Plymouth, Devon   enlisted: Torquay
Buried: Choques Military Cemetery. Grave I.J.51. Age 28. Joined BEF: not on Medal card. CWGC: son of Betsy Linton, 39 Cornwall Street, Devonport.

15th August 1916
Pte. George William Stanley Read 1015 KIA
born: Plymouth, Devon   enlisted: Plymouth
Buried: Vermelles Military Cemetery. Grave III.N.23. Age 18. No Medal Card. Attached to 2/Devons from 1st/7th Devons. CWGC: son of Job Read and Florence L. Read, 8 Cleveland Road, St. Judes, Plymouth.

20th August 1916
Pte. George James Baker 9141 KIA
born: Starcross, Devon   enlisted: Exeter   residence: Starcross
Buried: Vermelles Military Cemetery. Grave III.O.12. Age 24. Joined BEF: 06/11/14 with original cadre. 1901 Census: son of Amos Baker, farm worker, and Jane Baker, Welcombe Cottage, Kenton, Devon. CWGC: family address: New Road, Starcross, Exeter.

21st August 1916
2/Lt Horace Acomb KIA
Buried: Vermelles Military Cemetery. Grave VI.D.29. Age 23. Attached from 11th Yorkshire Regiment. No Medal Card. 1901 Census: son of William Acomb, railway engine driver, and Elizabeth Acomb, 3 South Parade, York. CWGC: family address: 3 South Parade, York.
Pte. Edward Patrick Kellehar 6464 KIA
born: Marylebone, Middx. enlisted: London
Joined BEF: 27/08/14 with 1/Devons.
Pte. John Kershaw 15266 KIA
born: Rochdale, Lancs. enlisted: Rochdale
Buried: Vermelles Military Cemetery. Grave VI.D.30. Age 36. Joined BEF: 21/09/15.
Pte. Mark Skinner 19229 KIA
born: Bovey Tracey, Devon   enlisted: Exeter   residence: Bovey Tracey
Buried: Vermelles Military Cemetery. Grave VI.D.28. Age 27.
No Medal Card. 1901 Census: son of Thomas L. Skinner, clay miner, and Elizabeth A. Skinner, Whitehall Cottages, Highweek, Newton Abbot. 1911 Census: servant/cattle man, on farm of Marshall Gilbert, South Filham, Ugborough, Ivybridge, Devon. CWGC: family address: 13 Exeter Road, Newton Abbot, Devon.
Pte. John Webb 19236 KIA
born: Lydford, Devon   enlisted: Exeter   residence: Princetown
Buried: Vermelles Military Cemetery. Grave VI.D.26. Age 39.
Joined BEF: not on Medal Card. 1911 Census: tin miner, underground, 4 Caunter's Row, Princetown, Devon.CWGC: son of Elizabeth Webb and the late Thomas Webb, Postbridge, Dartmoor, Devon; husband of Elizabeth J. Webb, New London, Princetown, Dartmoor, Devon.

22nd August 1916
Pte. William Henry Darch 9763 DoW
born: Abbotsham, Devon   enlisted: Barnstaple
Buried: Vermelles Military Cemetery. Grave III.O.13. Age 28. Joined BEF: 22/08/14 with 1/Devons. CWGC: son of Thomas Darch, Lovacott, Newton Tracey, Barnstaple, Devon.
Pte. Harold James Parsons 16914 DoW
born: Truro, Cornwall   enlisted: Plymouth
Buried: Boulogne Eastern Cemetery. Grave VIII.B.153. Age 24.
Joined BEF: not on Medal card. 1911 Census: shop assistant, son of Frederick Parsons, waiter, and stepson of Beatrice Parsons, 2 St. Aubyns Road, Truro, Cornwall. CWGC: son of Frederick Parsons, 2 St. Aubyns Road, Truro, Cornwall, and the late Sarah Parsons.
Pte. Robert Yeo 9453 DoW
born: Barnstaple, Devon   enlisted: Exeter
Buried: Vermelles Military Cemetery. Grave III.O.11. Age 22.
Joined BEF: 22/08/14 with 1/Devons. 1901 Census: son of William J. Yeo, gardener, and Jane Yeo, 4 Sunnybank, Barnstaple.
1911 Census: stable lad, son of William Yeo, gardener/domestic, and Jane Yeo, Hawley Cottage, Barnstaple, Devon. CWGC: family address: 13 Trinity Street, Barnstaple, Devon.

25th August 1916
L/Cpl Stanley Harvey 9191 KIA
born: Truro, Cornwall   enlisted: Devonport
Buried: Vermelles Military Cemetery. Grave VI.A.13. Age 26.

Joined BEF: 06/11/14 with original cadre. 1911 Census: engineer fitter, son of Thomas Harvey, engineer fitter, and Sarah Harvey, 8 Trelawney Cottages, Falmouth, Cornwall. L/Cpl Harvey was killed while on a 'spoils party'.

SEPTEMBER 1916

3rd September 1916
Pte. Frederick John Knapman 9837 KIA
born: Newton Abbot, Devon   enlisted: Exeter   residence: Dawlish
Buried: Lonsdale Cemetery, Authuile. Grave III.H.4. Age 22. Joined BEF: 28/04/14 with 1/Devons. 1911 Census: farm labourer, lodging at home, son of John Thomas Knapman, farm labourer, stepson of Florence Knapman, 2 Pulsford Cottage, Denbury, Newton Abbot, Devon. CWGC: son of John Knapman; husband of Maud E. Collins (formerly Knapman), 6 Stockton Road, Dawlish, Devon.

5th September 1916
Pte. Thomas Dimond 19041 KIA
born: Broadclyst, Devon   enlisted: Axminster
Buried: Vermelles Military Cemetery. Grave V.B.6. Age 36. Joined BEF: not on Medal Card. 1911 Census: farmer's son, working on farm, son of Jane Dimond, widow, farmer, Abbey Mill, Dunkeswell Abbey, Honiton, Devon. CWGC: records Army number as 3/19041, son of J. H. Dimond, 2 Sunny Side, Payhembury, Ottery St. Mary, Devon; husband of Mrs. Murray (formerly Dimond), Broadhempston Village, Totnes.

7th September 1916
Pte. Richard Henry Hobbs 21649 KIA
born: Tavistock, Devon   enlisted: Plymouth   residence: Yealmpton
Buried: Vermelles Military Cemetery. Grave V.B.11. Age 27. Joined BEF: not on Medal Card. 1901 Census: son of William Hobbs, 'ordinary agricultural labourer', and Mary Hobbs, of Underhill, Whitchurch, Tavistock, Devon. 1911 Census: 'son assisting in the business of market gardening', son of Mary Hobbs, widow, market gardener, Underhill Cottage, Whitchurch, Tavistock, Devon. CWGC: family address: Moorshop, Tavistock, Devon, and husband of Louisa Mary Hobbs, Lydford Station, Bridestowe, Devon.
Pte. William James Leworthy 9462 DoW
born: Barnstaple, Devon   enlisted: South Molton
Buried: Bethune Town Cemetery. Grave V.H.55. Age 24. Joined BEF: not on Medal Card. CWGC and Medal Card name him William Henry Leworthy. 1901 Census: son of Noah Leworthy, farm labourer, and Mary Jane Leworthy, Knackershole, Stoke Rivers, Barnstaple, Devon. 1911 Census: recorded as William H. Leworthy, farm labourer, son of Noah Leworthy, farm labourer, and Mary Jane Leworthy, Thorne Park, Charles, South Molton, Devon. CWGC: family address: Mockham Cottage, Charles, South Molton, Devon. A younger brother, Frederick James Leworthy, 9442, also of the 2/Devons, was KIA on 01/12/1914.

8th September 1916
Pte. John Thomas Walker 15404 KIA
born: Holme, Lancs.   enlisted: Halifax   residence: Todmorden
Buried: Vermelles Military Cemetery. Grave V.B.12. Age 27. Joined BEF: 18/05/15. CWGC: son of Lawrence Walker and Harriet Walker, 4 Mount Pleasant, Cornholme, Todmorden. Native of Portsmouth, Todmorden.

The 2nd Devons War Diary

9th September 1916
L/Cpl. John Francis Roberts 8885 KIA
born: Witheridge, Devon   enlisted: Exeter   residence: Rackenford, Devon
Buried: Vermelles Military Cemetery. Grave V.B.16. Age 29. Joined BEF: 06/11/14 with original cadre. CWGC: son of Mrs Elizabeth Roberts, Blindwill Cottage, Rackenford, Morchard Bishop, Devon.

10th September 1916
2/Lt. Gilbert L. Hosegood KIA
Buried: Vermelles Military Cemetery. Grave II.D.22. Age 20. Joined BEF: 16/01/15. Formerly a Red Cross orderly. Commissioned in September 1915 in the 3/Devons, attached to 2/Devons 26/07/16. 1901 Census: son of Henry Hosegood, corn merchant, and Ellen S. Hosegood, 26 Clarendon Road, Bristol, Gloucestershire. 1911 Census: 'at school', son of Henry Hosegood, corn merchant, and Ellen Sarah Hosegood, 6 Downleaze, Sneyd Park, Bristol, Gloucestershire. CWGC: family: 6 Downleaze, Bristol, Gloucestershire.

13th September 1916
Pte. Alfred Rider 6757 KIA
born: Homerton, London   enlisted: Dalston
Buried: Vermelles Military Cemetery. Grave V.C.5. Age 31. Joined BEF: 27/08/14 with 1/Devons . CWGC: eldest son of Alfred and Rosetta Rider.
Sgt. William Cornish DCM 8588 DoW
born: Bridford, Devon   enlisted: Exeter
Buried: La Neuville British cemetery, Corbie. Grave II.D.49. Age 26. Joined BEF: 22/08/14 with original cadre of 1/Devons . 1901 Census: stepson of William Harding, carter at quarry, and Mary Grace Harding (mother) Bell Lane, Hennock, Newton Abbot. CWGC: son of William and Mary Grace Cornish, Bishopsteignton, Devon.
The citation for the award of Sgt. Cornish's DCM reads as follows:
"For conspicuous gallantry. He held up, under heavy fire from machine guns and rifles, the frame work of a shelter, where men had been buried by a shell explosion. Later he went out twice, under fire, and over very exposed ground, with messages to a neighbouring trench."

15th September 1916
Pte. Charles Enos Sanders 16788 KIA
born: Frithelstock, Devon   enlisted: Torrington
Buried: Vermelles Military Cemetery. Grave V.C.7. Age 21. No Medal Card. 1901 Census: son of John Sanders, cattleman on farm, and Rosa Sanders, Milton Damerell, Holsworthy, Devon. 1911 Census: horseman, son of John Sanders, farm labourer, and Rosa Sanders, Higher House, Kingscott, St. Giles, Torrington, Devon. CWGC: family address: St. Giles-in-the-Wood, Torrington, Devon.

16th September 1916
L/Cpl. Arthur George Gilbert Cox 11648 KIA
born: Eversholt, Beds.   enlisted: Devonport   residence: Eversholt
Buried: Vermelles Military Cemetery. Grave V.C.6. Age 26. Joined BEF: 19/01/15. 1901 Census: son of Frederick Cox, park labourer, and Alice Mary Cox, Tearls End, Eversholt, Beds. CWGC: family address: Eversholt, Woburn, Beds.

L/Cpl. John Parker Hannaford MM 15493 KIA
born: South Pool, Devon   enlisted: Kingsbridge   residence: Salcombe
Buried: Vermelles Military Cemetery. Grave V.C.8. Age 20. Joined BEF: 25/05/15. 1901 Census: son of James Hannaford, horseman on farm, and Elizabeth Jane Hannaford, 'Harland', East Portlemouth, Kingsbridge, Devon.

Pte. Albert Edward Crossley 16216 DoW
born: Clapton, London   enlisted: Walthamstow
Buried: Vermelles Military Cemetery. Grave V.C.9. Age 19. Joined BEF: not on Medal Card. 1901 Census: son of Frederick Crossley, greengrocer/shopkeeper, and Ellen Crossley, 1 High Road, Leyton, Walthamstow. CWGC: mother's address: 33 West Street, Grove Road, Walthamstow, London.

22nd September 1916

Pte. Horace Cecil Palmer 33192 DoW
born: Topsham, Devon   enlisted: Exeter   residence: Topsham
Buried: Longuenesse (St. Omer) Souvenir Cemetery. Grave IV.A.56. Age 22. Joined BEF: not on Medal Card. 1901 Census: son of Alfred William Gidley Palmer, rural postman, and Eliza Ann Palmer, Fore Street, Topsham, Devon. Recorded as Cecil Palmer. 1911 Census: assistant postman, son of Alfred William Gidley Palmer, gardener/domestic, and Eliza Ann Palmer, Fore Street, Topsham, Devon. CWGC: husband of Frances Palmer, 1 Marine Villas, Beer, Devon.

Pte. Percy Harold Rowe 25313 DoW
born: London   enlisted: London
Buried: Bethune Town Cemetery. Grave V.H.66. Date joined BEF: not on Medal Card.

23rd September 1916

Pte. William Greenaway 15602 DoW
born: Holsworthy, Devon   enlisted: Exeter   residence: Rockbeare
Buried: Choques Military Cemetery. Grave I.J.106. Age 35. Joined BEF: 01/06/15. 1911 Census: 'horseman on farm, husband of Katie Greenaway, father of five, Woodley Cottages, Newton St. Cyres, Devon.CWGC: husband of Katie Elizabeth Greenaway, Rockbeare, Exeter.

28th September 1916

2/Lt. Charles William Cooper Hannah Attached from 3/Devons . KIA
Born: Calcutta, India
Buried: Philosophe British Cemetery, Mazingarbe. Grave I.G.7. Age 22. No Medal Card. 1911 Census: boarder at Exeter School, Exeter, Devon. CWGC: son of Garlies Stuart Hannah and Lilian Esther Hannah, 43 Lancaster Park, Richmond, Surrey.

30th September 1916

Pte. Frederick James Parsons 33209 DoW (home)
born: Cullompton, Devon   enlisted: Cullompton
Buried: Cullompton Cemetery. Grave 13.3. Age 21. Joined BEF: not on Medal Card. 1901 Census: son of Richard Parsons, bricklayer's labourer, and Mary Ann Parsons, 'College', Cullompton, Devon. 1911 Census: bricklayer, son of Richard Parsons, Army pensioner, and Mary Ann Parsons, Duke Street, Cullompton, Devon. CWGC: family address: 15 New Street, Cullompton, Devon.

The 2nd Devons War Diary

OCTOBER 1916

3rd October 1916
2/Lt. Francis Burrows Lloyd Formerly 28th Battalion, London Regiment KIA
Buried: Philosophe British Cemetery, Mazingarbe. Grave I.G.8. Age 21. Joined BEF: 26/10/14 possibly with 28th London Regiment. 1911 Census: pupil, boarding at the Grammar School, Worcester Street, Bromsgrove, Worcestershire. CWGC: native of Shipston-on-Stour, son of The Rev. D. Lloyd and Margaret A. Lloyd, of Shipston-on-Stour, Worcs.

5th October 1916
Capt . Arthur Herbert Smith KIA
No known grave. Loos Memorial, Panel 35 to 37. 'C' Company. No Medal Card. CWGC: son of Thomas J. Smith and Hannah Ellen Smith, 312 Priory Road, St. Deny's, Southampton.
L/Cpl. William James Avery 18768 KIA
born: Alphington, Devon   enlisted: Exeter
Buried: Philosophe British Cemetery, Mazingarbe. Grave I.V.14. Age 23. No Medal Card. 1911 Census: farm labourer, son of William James Avery, gas stoker, and Annie Avery, 3 Elm Place, St. Thomas, Exeter, Devon. CWGC: son of William James Avery, 32 Fords Road, St. Thomas, Exeter.
Sgt. Frederick George Bayliss 8143 KIA
born: Bristol, Somerset   enlisted: Exeter   residence: Bristol
Buried: Philosophe British Cemetery, Mazingarbe. Grave I.G.13. Age 26. Joined BEF: 06/11/14 with original cadre. 1911 Census: bandsman, 2/Devons, St. George's Barracks, Malta. CWGC: son of John and Hannah Bayliss, of Bristol.
Pte. Alfred Frank Gratton 3/6619 KIA
born: Barnstaple   enlisted: Barnstaple
Buried: Philosophe British Cemetery, Mazingarbe. Grave I.G.11. Age 22. Joined BEF: 16/02/15. 1901 Census: son of William Henry Gratton and Thirza Gratton, Landkey, Barnstaple, Devon. 1911 Census: thatcher, son of William Henry Gratton, thatcher, and Thirza Gratton, Newland, Landkey, Barnstaple, Devon. His brothers Sydney James Gratton, Thomas John Gratton and William Lewis Gratton (2/Devons, 13/03/15) were also killed during the war.
L/Cpl. William Heath 15285 KIA
born: Manchester, Lancs.   enlisted: Rochdale
No known grave. Loos Memorial, Panel 35 to 37. Age 22. Joined BEF: 18/05/15. 1911 Census: working in a 'wash house', son of Charles Heath, widower, window cleaner, grandson of William Heath, carter, 24 Morris Road, Ancoats, Manchester, Lancashire.
Pte. John Hegson 15128 KIA
born: Colne, Lancs.   enlisted: Colne
No known grave. Loos Memorial, Panel 35 to 37. Joined BEF: 18/05/15.
L/Cpl. Edwin Charles Hicks 8554 KIA
born: St. Austell, Cornwall   enlisted: Plymouth   residence: St. Austell
No known grave. Loos Memorial, Panel 35 to 37. Joined BEF: 06/11/14 with original cadre. 1901 Census: son of Edwin Hicks, Coast Guard, and Elizabeth Hicks, Coast Guard Buildings, Talland, Liskeard, Cornwall. 1911 Census: 2/Devons, St. George's Barracks, Malta.
Pte. William Henry Sheldon 10983 KIA
born: Glyn-Neath, Glam.   enlisted: Neath   residence: Cwmargoed, Monmouth
CWGC does not list a grave or memorial reference for this man. Age 25. Joined BEF: 24/03/15. 1911 Census: coal hewer, boarding at 4 Penygraig Row, Pontlottyn, Glamorgan. (As

there is an eleven year old girl named Rose Sheldon living at this address and listed as 'daughter', it appears that William Sheldon's mother had remarried and was now Margaret Dole, five years the wife of John Dole, coal miner hewer).
L/Cpl. Frank Snell 9160 KIA
born: Whimple, Devon   enlisted: Exeter   residence: Allercombe, Devon
No known grave. Loos Memorial, Panel 35 to 37. Age 24. Joined BEF: 06/11/14 with original cadre. CWGC: son of the late Amos Snell; husband of Mary J. Snell, Lawn Cottage, Strete Raleigh, Whimple, Exeter.
Pte. Alfred Stringer 17100 KIA
born: Walworth, Surrey   enlisted: London S.E.
No known grave. Loos Memorial, Panel 35 to 37. Joined BEF: not on Medal Card.
Pte. John Edward Viney 18965 KIA
born: Holloway, Middx.   enlisted: London
No known grave. Loos Memorial, Panel 35 to 37. Age 21. Joined BEF: not on Medal Card. 1911 Census: fishmonger's assistant, son of G.W. Viney, motor driver, 6 Victor Road, Finsbury Park, London. CWGC: son of George W. and Helen Viney, 50 Grafton Road, Holloway, London.
L/Cpl. William Joseph Walsh 8402 KIA
born: Plymouth, Devon   enlisted: Plymouth
No known grave. Loos Memorial, Panel 35 to 37. Age 26. Joined BEF: 06/11/14 with original cadre. 1911 Census: 2/Devons, St. George's Barracks, Malta.

5th and 6th October 1916
Pte. Arthur Carpenter 19063 DoW
born: Marwood, Devon   enlisted: Exeter   residence: Barnstaple
Buried: Philosophe British Cemetery, Mazingarbe. Grave I.G.10. Age 25. Joined BEF: 21/12/15. 1901 Census and CWGC record him as the son of Charity Emily Carpenter, shirt maker, of Guineaford Village, Marwood, Barnstaple. 1911 Census: 'postman and boot repairer', living with mother in Guineaford Village.
Pte. Thomas George Kerswill 25781 DoW
born: Plymouth, Devon   enlisted: Plymouth   residence: no record
Buried: St. Sever Cemetery, Rouen. Grave B.14.46. Age 29. Joined BEF: not on Medal Card. 1901 Census: 'assistant boat manufacturer', son of Frederick J Kerswill, boat manufacturer, and Bessie E. B. Kerswill, 14 Portland Villas, Plymouth. 1911 Census: 'leather merchant', husband of Eliza louise Kerswill, 18 Greenbank Avenue, Plymouth, Devon.
Pte. William Henry Parnell 20788 DoW
born: Ashburton, Devon   enlisted: Newton Abbot
Buried: Bethune Town Cemetery. Grave V.H.82. Age 36. Joined BEF: not on Medal Card. 1911 Census: general labourer, son of John Parnell, general labourer, and Ann Maria Parnell, 88 North Street, Ashburton, Devon. CWGC records same information.
Pte. Robert Henry Roberts 33576 DoW
born: Islington, London   enlisted: London
Buried: Bethune Town Cemetery. Grave V.H.83. Age 30. No Medal Card. 1911 Census: draper's packer, husband of Bertha Roberts, father of two small children, 51 Cornwallis Road, Edmonton, London.
Pte. William Taylor 11393 KIA
born: Newton Abbott   enlisted: Newton Abbott
No known grave. Loos Memorial, panel 35 to 37. Age 23. Joined BEF: 19/01/1915.

15th October 1916
L/Cpl. Christopher Mann 9318 DoW
born: Exeter, Devon   enlisted: Exeter
Buried: Longuenesse (St. Omer) Souvenir Cemetery. Grave IV.A.66. Age 27. Joined BEF: 06/11/14 with original cadre. 1901 Census: son of James Mann, mortar mason, and Jessie Mann, Seaford Street, Exeter. 1911 Census: 3/Devons, Higher Barracks, Howell Road, Exeter, Devon. CWGC: family address: 2 Gill's Cottages, Cheeke Street, Exeter.

19th October 1916
Pte. William Charles Webber MM 9347 DoW
born: Dartmouth, Devon   enlisted: Dartmouth
Buried: Longuenesse (St. Omer) Souvenir Cemetery. Grave IV.A.68. Age 23. Joined BEF: 06/11/14 with original cadre. CWGC: son of Charlie Webber and Sarah Webber, Newcomin Cottages, Dartmouth.

22nd October 1916
Pte. Frank Hilton Blunt 8346 DoW
born: Torquay, Devon   enlisted: Devonport   residence: Torquay
Buried: Longueval Road cemetery. Grave G.1. Age 28. Joined BEF: 06/11/14 with original cadre. 1901 Census: son of Edward James Blunt, clerk, and Fanny Blunt, dressmaker, 37 Abbey Road, Torquay. 1911 Census: 2/Devons, St. George's Barracks, Malta.
Pte. William Parker 26141 DoW
born: Bovey Tracey, Devon   enlisted: Newton Abbot   residence: North Bovey
Buried: Longuenesse (St. Omer) Souvenir Cemetery. Grave IV.A.67. Age 35. Joined BEF: not on Medal Card. 1901 Census: servant/carter on farm, Westacott, Ashreigney, South Molton, Devon. 1911 Census: 'gardener domestic', son of John Parker, farm labourer, and Charlotte Parker, North Bovey, Moretonhampstead, Devon. CWGC: husband of Violet C. Parker, "Haytor View," Chudleigh Knighton, Newton Abbot.

24th October 1916
Pte. James Tope Poole 3/6878 DoW
born: Brixham, Devon   enlisted: Paignton   residence: Brixham
Buried: Grove Town Cemetery, Meaulte. Grave I.P.29. Age recorded by CWGC: 22. Joined BEF: 02/05/15. 1901 Census: born in 1897, making real age around 19. Son of James Poole, fisherman, and Eliza Poole, Milton Street, Brixham, Devon. 1911 Census: butcher, living with parents, May Flower Cottages, 60 Drew Street, Brixham, Devon. CWGC: family address: Baker's Hill, Brixham.

25th October 1916
Sgt. Joseph Henry Penwarn 8480 KIA
born: Devonport   enlisted: Plymouth
No known grave. Thiepval Memorial, Pier and Face I.C. Age 26 Joined BEF: 06/11/14 with original cadre. 1901 Census: son of Richard Henry Penwarn, dockyard labourer, and Caroline Penwarn, 21 Ferndale Avenue, Devonport, Devon. 1911 Census: 2/Devons, St. George's Barracks, Malta.

27th October 1916
Pte. Ernest Beazley 3/7100 KIA
born: Torquay, Devon   enlisted: Exeter   residence: Torquay
Buried: Guard's Cemetery, Lesboeufs. Grave IX.J.4. Age 22. Joined BEF: 17/02/15. 1911 Census: grocer's assistant, patient in Torbay Hospital on census day.
Pte. Frank Humphreys 11170 KIA
born: London   enlisted: Fulham
Buried: Guard's Cemetery, Lesboeufs. Grave X.A.10. Age 16. Joined BEF: 24/03/15. 1901 Census: son of Henry J. Humphreys, iron worker, and Agnes Humphreys, 2 Britannia Court, Hammersmith. 1911 Census: at 74 Grosvenor Road, Hanwell. Volunteered for the Army on 6th September 1914 at Fulham.
Pte. Harry Charles Norman 32096 KIA
born: Yarlington, Somerset   enlisted: Oxford
Buried: Valenciennes (St. Roch) Communal Cemetery. Grave II.D.16. Formerly 30373 Ox and Bucks Light Infantry. Joined BEF: not on Medal Card. Age 16. 1901 Census: grandson of Charles Hill and Mary J. Hill, Pins Lane, Yarlington, Somerset.
Pte. Herbert James Spiller 15052 KIA
born: Wandsworth, London   enlisted: Cullompton
Buried: Guard's Cemetery, Lesboeufs. Grave X.I.6. Joined BEF: 28/04/15.

29th October 1916
Pte. George Cole 26146 KIA
born: Stoke Fleming, Devon   enlisted: Newton Abbot   residence: Totnes
No known grave. Thiepval Memorial, Pier and Face I.C. No Medal Card.
Cpl. James Foxwell 14783 KIA
born: Croscombe, Somerset   enlisted: Pentre, Glam.   residence: Wells, Somerset
No known grave. Thiepval Memorial, Pier and Face I.C. Age 28. Joined BEF: 24/03/15. CWGC: son of Obed and Elizabeth Foxwell, Long Street, Croscombe, Wells, Somerset.
Pte. Samuel John Hawkes 25943 KIA
born: Ilsington, Devon   enlisted: Newton Abbot   residence: Bovey Tracey
Buried: Thiepval Anglo-French Cemetery, Authuile. Grave I.F.1. Age 32. Joined BEF: not on Medal card. 1901 Census: general carter, corn, son of George Hawkes, shoe and boot maker, and Caroline Hawkes, Mount Pleasant, Mary Street, Bovey Tracey. 1911 Census: carter, husband of Amelia Hawkes, St. Mary Street, Bovey Tracey, Devon. CWGC: husband of Amelia Bessie Hawkes, 2 White Heather Terrace, Bovey Tracey.
Pte. John Philip Murphy 9851 KIA
born: Weymouth, Dorset   enlisted: Exeter   residence: Plymouth
Buried: Guard's Cemetery, Lesboeufs. Grave VIII.B.1. Age 21. Joined BEF: 06/11/14 with original cadre. 1901 Census: 'pauper', son of Kate Murphy, widow, pauper. 1911 Census: printer's apprentice, boarding at St. Philip, Teignmouth Road, Torquay, Devon.
Pte. Thomas Henry Richards 11395 KIA
born: Exeter, Devon   enlisted: Exeter
No known grave. Thiepval Memorial, Pier and Face I.C. Joined BEF: 17/12/14.
Pte. Albert West 3/8316 KIA
born: London   enlisted: Bristol
No known grave. Thiepval Memorial, Pier and Face I.C. Age 28. Joined BEF: 27/12/14. CWGC: son of George West.

The 2nd Devons War Diary

30th October 1916
2/Lt. Charles Bouchier Rodd KIA
No known grave. Thiepval Memorial, Pier and Face I.C. Age 18. Joined BEF: 10/09/16. 1901 Census: son of Richard R. Rodd, solicitor, and Mary Rodd, 80 Durnford Street, East Stonehouse, Devon. 1911 Census: pupil at Boy's School, Prolens School, Prolens, Cornwall.
Pte. Frederick Youlden Reed 11516 KIA
born: Okehampton, Devon   enlisted: Exeter   residence: Highampton, Devon
No known grave. Thiepval Memorial, Pier and Face I.C. Age 27. Joined BEF: 04/01/15. 1901 Census: 12 year old 'servant/cattleman on farm', employed by Edwin Hill, farmer, Westacott, Sampford Courtenay, Devon. 1911 Census: waggoner on farm, employed by Stephen George Quick, farmer, Crockers Hill, Meeth, Hatherleigh, Devon. CWGC: son of Charity Reed, Town Farm, Highampton, Devon, and the late John Reed.
Pte. Robert Simmonds 11321 KIA
born: Cullompton, Devon   enlisted: Exeter   residence: Cullompton
No known grave. Thiepval Memorial, Pier and Face I.C. Joined BEF: 19/01/15.
Pte. Robert Luke Joslin 7492 DoW
born: Exeter, Devon   enlisted: Exeter
Buried: Grove Town Cemetery, Meaulte. Grave II.D.10. Age 34. No Medal Card. 1911 Census: general labourer, son of Richard Joslin, wood sawyer, and Maria Joslin, 36 Azes Lane, Barnstaple.
Pte. William John Knapman 8972 DoW
born: Crediton, Devon   enlisted: Exeter   residence: Thorverton
Buried: Grove Town Cemetery, Meaulte. Grave II.A.17. Age 25. Joined BEF: 06/11/14 with original cadre. 1911 Census: 1/Devons, Mooltan and Lucknow Barracks. CWGC: son of Richard Henry and Emma Knapman, of Thorverton, Devon; husband of Alice Knapman, Winscott Cottages, Newton St. Cyres, Exeter.
Pte. William John Rookes 33161 DoW
born: Silverton, Devon   enlisted: Silverton
Buried: Grove Town Cemetery, Meaulte. Grave II.A.7. Age 31. 'A' Company. Formerly No. 558, Devonshire Regiment. Joined BEF: not on Medal card. CWGC: son of Samuel Rookes and Elizabeth Ann Rookes; husband of Ellen Rookes, Church Terrace, Silverton, Exeter.

31st October 1916
Pte. Frederick George Cole 9132 KIA
born: Christow, Devon   enlisted: Exeter
Buried: London Cemetery and Extension, Longueval. Grave 9.H.42. Age 27. Joined BEF: 06/11/14 with original cadre. CWGC: son of Alfred Cole and Emma Cole, Humber Cottage, Bishopsteignton, Devons.
L/Cpl. William Dodds 9800 KIA
born: Walker, Northumberland   enlisted: Newcastle-On-Tyne
Buried: Guard's Cemetery, Lesboeufs. Grave III.X.2. Age 22. No Medal Card. CWGC: son of John Dodds and Ann Ellison Dodds, 13 Prospect Buildings, Walker-on-Tyne, Newcastle-on-Tyne.
Pte. Douglas William Lavers 3/7285 DoW
born: Newton Abbot, Devon   enlisted: Exeter   residence: Torquay
Buried: Grove Town Cemetery, Meaulte. Grave II.A.16. Age 45. Joined BEF: 04/01/15. Named William Lavers on Medal Card. CWGC: son of George and Elizabeth Ann Lavers, 62 East

Street, Newton Abbot, Devon.
Pte. Frederick John Narracott 15576 DoW
born: Stoke Gabriel, Devon   enlisted: Paignton   residence: Stoke Gabriel
Buried: Grove Town Cemetery, Meaulte. Grave II.A.18. Age 32. Joined BEF: 01/06/15. CWGC: husband of Elizabeth S. Narracott, 12 Oxford Terrace, Mill Street, Crediton, Devon.

The 2nd Devons War Diary

NOVEMBER 1916

6th November 1916
Pte. George Chapman 12719 DoW
Born: Cardiff, Glamorgan   enlisted: Abercynon, Glam.
Buried: St. Sever Cemetery Extension, Rouen. Grave O.I.F.4. Age 32. Joined BEF: 02/02/15. 1901 Census: railway engine cleaner, son of Charles Chapman (born in Canada), retired engine driver, and Emma Chapman, 8 Heath Villa, Glancynon Terrace, Llanwonno, Rhondda Valley, Abercynon, Glam. 1911 Census: railway porter, son of Charles Chapman, retired railway guard, and Emma Chapman, 27 Gertrude Street, Abercynon, Glam. CWGC: son of Charles and Emma Chapman, 27 Gertrude Street, Abercynon, Glam.

7th November 1916
Pte. Albert Annenberg 3/6916 KIA
born: York   enlisted: Stratford, Essex
No known grave. Thiepval Memorial, Pier and Face I.C. Joined BEF: 15/12/15.
Pte. Bertie John James Ball 33563 KIA
born: Frithelstock, Devon   enlisted: Durham   residence: Darlington
No known grave. Thiepval Memorial, Pier and Face I.C. Age 28. No Medal Card. 1901 Census: son of Thomas Ball, road contractor, and Mary Ann Ball, Frithelstock, Devon.
Pte. William Smith 33125 listed as 'missing'
born: Dartmouth   enlisted: Dartmouth
No known grave. Name recorded on the Thiepval Memorial, Pier and Face I.C., but Medal Card records him as being discharged on 03/01/19. Joined BEF: not on Medal Card. He is also shown on Medal Card as 1083, Devonshire Regiment. CWGC has no record of his death. No doubt the name 'Smith' has contributed to the confusion.

9th November 1916
Pte. Fred Carpenter 11320 KIA
born: Exeter   enlisted: Exeter   residence: Silverton
Buried: Caterpillar Valley Cemetery, Longueval. Grave XXVII.F.7. Age 19. Joined BEF: 15/12/15. 1911 Census: named Frederick Thomas Carpenter, farm servant, son of Richard Carpenter, labourer at paper mill, and Jessie Carpenter, Park View, Hele, Collumpton, Devon (parish of Silverton).
Pte. Charles Lawry 6400 KIA
born: Plymouth   enlisted: Bodmin
No known grave. Thiepval Memorial, Pier and Face I.C. Joined BEF: 06/11/14 with original cadre.

10th November 1916
A/Cpl. Rowland Prior 8440 KIA
born: Crediton   enlisted: Exeter   residence: Crediton
No known grave. Thiepval Memorial, Pier and Face I.C. Age 28. Joined BEF: 06/11/14 with original cadre. 1901 Census: son of Edwin Prior, farmer and builder, and Mary Prior, Cheriton Fitzpaine, Crediton, Devon. Grandson of James Prior, mason, of the same address. 1911 Census: 2/Devons, St. George's Barrack, Malta. CWGC: family address: 3 Parliament Street, Crediton, Devon.

Pte. Frederick Jarrett 8667 KIA
born: Bridgwater   enlisted: Bridgwater
No known grave. Thiepval Memorial, Pier and Face I.C. Age 27. Joined BEF: 06/11/14 with original cadre. 1901 Census: only child of Ellen Jarrett, widow, laundress, No.7 Court, West Street, Bridgwater, Somerset. 1911 Census: 2/Devons, St. George's Barrack, Malta.

11th November 1916
Pte. Henry John Crate 3/6302 KIA
born: Chard   enlisted: Exeter
No known grave. Thiepval Memorial, Pier and Face I.C. Age 25. Joined BEF: 05/11/14 with original cadre. 1901 Census: son of Job Crate, agricultural labourer, and Elizabeth Crate, Barn Cottages, Wayford, Chard, Somerset.

12th November 1916
Sgt. Harry Tancock 8804 DoW
born: Okehampton   enlisted: Okehampton
Buried: Etaples Military Cemetery. Grave XII.D.7A. Age 27. Joined BEF: 06/11/14 with original cadre. 1901 Census: son of Harry Tancock, horseman on farm, and Mary Tancock, Broadmoor Cottage, Drewsteignton, Okehampton, Devon. Native of Jacobstow, Devon. 1911 Census: 2/Devons, St. George's Barracks, Malta.

13th November 1916
Pte. William Davey 7070 Died
born: Exeter   enlisted: Exeter
Buried: Soues Churchyard. Grave: Near North West Angle of Church. Joined BEF: 17/12/14. Medal Card number 3/7070.

21st November 1916
Pte. William Henry Smith 25707 Died
born: Trull, Somerset   enlisted: Tiverton   residence: Cullompton
Buried: Mont Huon Military Cemetery, Le Treport. Grave I.K.7. Age 29. 'B' Company. Joined BEF: not on Medal Card. CWGC: son of G. and P. Smith, of Taunton, Somerset; husband of D. J. Smith, Liskeard, Cornwall.

25th November 1916
Pte. Henry Reuben Reeves 205046 KIA
born: Portsmouth   enlisted: Portsmouth
No known grave. Tyne Cot memorial, Panel 38 to 40. Age 38. Formerly 203187 of the Dorset Regiment. CWGC records the date of death as 25/11/1917 – late series Army number suggests this is probably correct. Joined BEF: not on Medal Card. 1901 Census: cycle assembler, son of John Reuben Reeves, electrical fitter and Emma Reeves, 73 Cornwall Road, Portsmouth, Hants. 1911 Census: 'cycle enameller', son of John Reuben Reeves, electrical fitter, and Emma Reeves, address as above. By the time of Henry Reeves' death, John Reuben Reeves had died.

The 2nd Devons War Diary

DECEMBER 1916

12th December 1916
Pte. Thomas Louis Willshire 10985 DoW
born: Exeter   enlisted: Neath, Glam.
Buried: St. Pierre Cemetery, Amiens. Grave VII.A.6. Age 26. Joined BEF: 24/03/15. Named Thomas Wiltshire on Medal card. 1911 Census: construction labourer, lodging at Red Jacket Huts, Skewen, Neath, Glam. CWGC: son of Lewis Willshire, Hollobury, Bude, Cornwall; husband of Ethel K. Johns (formerly Willshire), 10 Bethlehem Road, Neath, Glam.

30th December 1916
Pte. Thomas John Hodge 8467 KIA
born: Plymouth   enlisted: Plymouth
Sailly-Saillisel British Cemetery. Special Memorial 8. Age 26. Joined BEF: 06/11/14 with original cadre. 1901 Census: son of Elizabeth M. Hodge, charwoman, 43 St. Leonards Road, Plymouth.

31st December 1916
Pte. George John Ascott 17560 KIA
born: Marylebone   enlisted: Marylebone
No known grave. Thiepval Memorial, Pier and Face I.C. Age 24. Joined BEF: 11/10/15. 1901 Census: son of Henry Ascott, poulterer's assistant, and Charlotte Ascott, 31 Paddington Street, St. Marylebone.
Pte. William Henry Clatworthy 17530 KIA
born: Plymouth   enlisted: Canning Town   residence: Poplar
No known grave. Thiepval Memorial, Pier and Face I.C. Age 31. Joined BEF: 01/10/15. 1911 Census: railway clerk, husband of Maud Louisa Clatworthy, father of three, 31 Susannah Street, Poplar, London. CWGC: husband of Maud Louisa Rens (formerly Clatworthy), 303 Grosvenor Buildings, Manisty Street, Poplar, London.
Pte. Bernard Walter Way 11946 DoW
born: Crediton   enlisted: Cardiff   residence: Crediton
Buried: Grove Town Cemetery, Meaulte. Grave II.J.23. Age 23. Joined BEF: 02/02/15. 1901 Census: son of Emma White, widow, Park View, Union Road, Crediton, Devon. 1911 Census: 'sugar grinder', son of Emma Elizabeth Galsworthy, widow, 2 Queen's Court East, Crediton, Devon.
Pte. Josiah Henry Auton 16928 Died
born: Woodbury   enlisted: Exeter   residence: Woodbury
Buried: Grove Town Cemetery, Meaulte. Grave II.F.43. Age 18. Joined BEF: not on Medal Card. Age at death recorded in SDGW is 24, so he may have added six years to his real age on enlistment. 1911 Census: errand boy, son of Josiah Auton snr., builder's labourer, and Fanny Auton, 5 Nosworthy Row, Cheeke Street, Exeter, Devon. CWGC: youngest son of William John Auton, Cross Hill Cottage, Woodbury Salterton, Exeter, Devon.

JANUARY 1917

7th January 1917
Pte. Francis Ange Pommerett 16858 DoW
born: Jersey C.I.   enlisted: Plymouth
Buried: Bois Guillaume Communal cemetery. Grave II.C.6A. Age 24. Joined BEF: not on Medal Card. CWGC: son of Emily Pommerett and the late Eugene Pommeret, St. Heliers, Jersey, C.I.

8th January 1917
Pte. Walter Williams 8949 KIA
born: Devonport   enlisted: Devonport
Sailly-Saillisel British Cemetery. Special Memorial 7. Joined BEF: 06/11/14 with original cadre. 1911 Census: 2/Devons, St. George's Barracks, Malta.

13th January 191
Pte. Charles Huxter 17900 KIA
born: Bridport, Dorset   enlisted: Exeter   residence: Bridport
Buried: Bray Military Cementery. Grave I.D.40. Age 18. Joined BEF: not on Medal Card. 1911 Census: named Charles Reginald Huxter, schoolboy, son of Albert Edward Huxter, general engineer/smith, and Amelia Elizabeth Huxter, 1 Keyford Place, Frome, Somerset.

18th January 1917
L/Cpl. John Bridgeman 16229 Died
born: Launceston   enlisted: Exeter   residence: Christow, Cornwall
Buried: Neufchatel-Hardelot (Neufchatel) Churchyard. Grave 18. Age 31. Joined BEF: 11/10/15. 1891 Census: with his mother at Tower Street, Launceston, his grandfather's house. 1901 Census: draper's errand boy, son of Sarah Bridgeman, Tower Street, Launceston, Cornwall. CWGC: son of William Bridgeman and Sarah Bridgeman, Tower Street, Launceston.

30th January 1917
Pte. Reginald Gilbert Garland 23172 KIA
born: Barnstaple   enlisted: Barnstaple
Buried: Hooge Crater Cemetery. Grave III.J.13. Age 23. Joined BEF: not on Medal Card. 1901 Census: son of George Garland, builder's contractor, and Annie Garland, 12 New Buildings, Barnstaple, Devon. 1911 Census: apprentice carpenter, son of George Garland, builder, and Annie Garland, 15 Vicarage Lawn, Barnstaple, Devon.

The 2nd Devons War Diary

FEBRUARY 1917

5th February 1917
Pte. William Bowden 28992 Died
born: Filleigh, Devon   enlisted: Barnstaple   residence: Ilfracombe
Buried: Bray Military Cementery. Grave I.D.12. No Medal Card.
Pte. Albert Ernest Squires 26282 Died
born: Shaugh Prior, Devon   enlisted: Plymouth   residence: Plympton
Buried: St. Sever Cemetery Extension, Rouen. Grave O.IV.R.7. Age 32. Date joined BEF: not on Medal Card. 1891 Census: son of John Squires, clay labourer, and Charlotte E. Squires, Tory Coombe Cottage, Shaugh Prior, Tavistock, Devon. 1911 Census: china clay labourer, son of John Squires, china clay labourer, Lower Lee, Lee Moor, Roborough, Devon. CWGC: husband of Edith E. Squires, 4 Long Row, Lee Moor, Roborough, Devon.

9th February 1917
Cpl. Edmund Alfred Hayman 11060 DoW
born: Bridgwater   enlisted: Exeter   residence: Exmouth
Buried: St. Sever Cemetery Extension, Rouen. Grave O.V.F.10. Age 32. Joined BEF: 27/07/15. 1891 Census: son of Edmund A. Hayman, tile maker, and Sarah K. Hayman, Withycombe Cottage, Withycombe Raleigh, Devon. 1901 Census: son of Edmund Alfred Hayman, clay tile moulder, and Sarah Kelly Hayman, Brickyard Cottage, Withycombe Raleigh, Exmouth, Devon. 1911 Census: brick machinist/labourer, son of Edmund A. Hayman, clay tile moulder, and Sarah K. Hayman, 83 Withycombe Village, Exmouth, Devon. CWGC: family address: 83 Withycombe Raleigh, Exmouth.

24th February 1917
Pte. Albert Adey 45524 Died
born: Bransgore, Hants.   enlisted: Bournemouth
Buried: La Neuville Communal Cemetery, Corbie. Grave B.77. Age 39. 'B' Company. Joined BEF: not on Medal Card. CWGC records him as the son of Sidney Adey and Sarah Adey, Bransgore, nr. Christchurch. 1891 Census: son of Sarah Adey, widow, charwoman, Christchurch, Bransgore, Hampshire. 1901 Census: baker, husband of Margaret Adey, 26 Hannington Road, Pokesdown, Hampshire. 1911 Census: carman, husband of Margaret Adey, father of one, 116 Wolverton Road, Boscombe, Hants. CWGC: family address: 51 Wolverton Road, Boscombe, Hampshire.

25th February 1917
Pte. Albert Grabham 33204 (872 on medal card) Died
Born: Cullompton, Devon   enlisted: Cullompton, Devon
Buried: La Neuville Communal Cemetery, Corbie. Grave B.80. Age 19. Joined BEF: not on medal card. 1911 Census: schoolboy, nephew of Robert Sellick, estate mason, and Emma Sellick, of Bradfield, Uffculme, Devon. Possibly the illegitimate son of Bessie Grabham, who was living at Higher Weaver, Cullompton, Devon, with her parents, John Grabham, farmer, and Keziah Grabham. CWGC: records him as the son of Bessie Moore, 31 Rockwell Green, Wellington, Somerset.

MARCH 1917

7th March 1917
Pte. Richard Ernest Gill 26096 DoW
born: Bishopsteignton   enlisted: Newton Abbot
Buried: Bray Military Cemetery. Grave II.D.44. Age 33. Joined BEF: not on Medal Card. 1911 Census: general labourer, husband of Elizabeth Anne Gill, The Terrace, Bishopsteignton, Teignmouth. CWGC: husband of the late Elizabeth Anne Gill, Bishopsteignton, Teignmouth Devon.

8th March 1917
Pte. Frederick Hayward 27671 KIA
born: Redcliffe   enlisted: Bristol   residence: Bedminster
No known grave. Thiepval Memorial, Pier and Face 1C. Joined BEF: not on Medal Card.
Pte. Sydney Daniel Sheppard 3/6773 KIA
born: Bideford   enlisted: Bideford
No known grave. Thiepval Memorial, Pier and Face 1C. Joined BEF: 20/09/14 probably with 1/Devons.
Cpl. Robert Venn 33171 KIA
born: Bickleigh   enlisted: Cullompton   residence: Bickleigh
No known grave. Thiepval Memorial, Pier and Face 1C. Age 25. Joined BEF: not on Medal Card. 1911 Census: paper maker, boarding at Fore Street, Bradninch, Devon.
Pte. Richard Henry Radmore 16945 KIA
born: Plymouth   enlisted: Plymouth
Buried: Fins New British Cemetery, Sorel-Le-Grand. Grave VII.E.25. Age 27. Joined BEF: not on Medal Card. 1891 Census: son of George Radmore, mason's labourer, and Sarah J. Radmore, 7 Nicholls Court, Plymouth, Devon. 1901 Census: son of George Radmore, fish hawker, and Sarah Radmore, 11 Castle Street, Plymouth, Devon.
Pte. John Henry Manning 3/7187 DoW
born: London   enlisted: London
Buried: Fins New British Cemetery, Sorel-Le-Grand. Grave VII.G.4. Age 42. Joined BEF: 17/12/14. 1911 Census: coal waggoner, husband of Edith Manning, 16 Laburnum Street, Torquay, Devon. CWGC: son of the late Edward Manning and Emily Manning. Served in the Boer War.

14th March 1917
Pte. Herbert Felix Bryant 17039 KIA
born: Plymouth   enlisted: Exeter   residence: Plymouth
Buried: Sailly-Saillisel British Cemetery. Grave III.I.4. Age 29. Joined BEF: not on Medal Card. 1901 Census: son of Richard Bryant, engraver, steel and copper plate, and Ellen Bryant, 8 Raleigh Street, Plymouth, Devon. 1911 Census: dock labourer, son of Ellen Elizabeth Bryant, widow, 16 Anson Place, Plymouth, Devon.
Pte. Harold Wild 15389 KIA
born: Rochdale   enlisted: Crewe
No known grave. Thiepval Memorial , Pier and Face 1C. Date joined BEF: 18/05/15.

16th March 1917
Pte. Ernest Charles Millman 3/6526 KIA
born: Newton Abbot enlisted: Newton Abbot
No known grave. Thiepval Memorial, Pier and Face 1C. Age 22. Joined BEF: 04/11/14 with original cadre. 1901 Census: son of Charles Millman, clay miner, and Sibella Millman, 11 East Street, Wolborough, Devon. 1911 Census: scholar at Devon and Exeter Boys Industrial School.

20th March 1917
Pte. Arthur Tom White 33238 DoW
born: Crediton enlisted: Crediton
Buried: Bray Military Cemetery. Grave II.D.12. Age 20. Joined BEF: not recorded on Medal Card. 1901 Census: son of John White, cabinet maker, and Charlotte White, 71 High Street, Crediton, Devon. 1911 Census: schoolboy, son of John White, carpenter, and Charlotte White, 48 High Street, Crediton, Devon. CWGC: family address: 56 High Street, Crediton, Devon.

23rd March 1917
Pte. Montague William Anning 18950 KIA
born: Dalwood, Devon enlisted: Exeter residence: Okehampton
Buried: Peronne Communal Cemetery Extension. Grave III.F.8. Age 29. Joined BEF: 21/12/15. 1901 Census: living at home of Abraham Anning (relationship unreadable on Census), carter/miller, West Street, Okehampton, Devon. 1911 Census: at the house of his brother-in-law, John Harris, carter, and sister Annie Harris, Kempley Road, Okehampton, Devon.

Pte. William Chard 20035 KIA
born: Plymouth enlisted: Exeter residence: Exbourne
Buried: Peronne Communal Cemetery Extension. Grave V.H.10. Age 37. Joined BEF: not on Medal Card. 1901 Census: general labourer, eldest child of Susan Chard, widow, 173 Florence Terrace, Plymouth, Devon. 1911 Census: stepson of Septomous Spear, living on private means, and his mother Susan Spears, Birchwood, Exbourne, Devon.

Pte. John Henry Green 29683 KIA
born: Torquay enlisted: Torquay
Buried: Peronne Communal Cemetery Extension. Grave V.F.2. Joined BEF: not on Medal Card.

Pte. Henry William Innus 17160 KIA
born: Camden Town enlisted: London
Buried: Peronne Communal Cemetery Extension. Grave III.F.6. Joined BEF: not on Medal Card.

Pte. Walter Rowland 12757 KIA
born: Taunton enlisted: Caerphilly residence: Huish, Somerset
Buried: Peronne Communal Cemetery Extension. Grave V.I.9. Joined BEF: 03/12/14.

A/L/Cpl. William Thomas Mudge Truman 21023 KIA
born: Devonport enlisted: Devonport
Buried: Peronne Communal Cemetery Extension. Grave III.F.7. Age 17. Joined BEF: not on Medal Card. 1911 Census: son of William Thomas Mudge Truman, dockyard boilermaker, and Primrose Elizabeth Truman, 39 Cecil Street, Plymouth, Devon.

27th March 1917
Cpl. Albert Edward Holmes 12608 KIA
born: Battersea   enlisted: Kingston-on-Thames
Buried: Peronne Communal Cemetery Extension. Grave III.J.17. Joined BEF: 24/03/15.
Pte. Robert Hall 8528 KIA
born: no record   enlisted: London
Buried: Peronne Communal Cemetery Extension. Grave III.J.16. Joined BEF: 06/11/16 with original cadre.

30th March 1917
A/Cpl. Francis George Larcombe 26094 KIA
born: Williton, Somerset   enlisted: Newton Abbott   residence: Dawlish, Devon
Buried: Heudicourt Communal Cemetery. Grave 1. Age 33. Joined BEF: not on Medal Card. 1891 Census: son of John C. Larcombe, gamekeeper, and Georgiana Larcombe, certificated school mistress, of Pitminster, Lowton, Somerset. 1901 Census: cattleboy on farm/servant, Slade Farm, Dulverton, Somerset. 1911 Census: recorded as George Larcombe, head gamekeeper, wife of Ellen Larcombe, father of Ellen, age 6, Beech Grove Lodge, Dawlish.
Pte. William Neville Joyce Pinson 14451 KIA
born: Plymouth   enlisted: Liverpool   residence: Brixham
Buried: Tincourt New British Cemetery. Grave IX.A.19. Age 21. Joined BEF: 24/03/15. 1911 Census: errand boy, son of Richard Pinson, warehouseman, and Elizabeth Pinson, 55 Paris Street, Exeter, Devon.
Pte. Sydney Joseph Samuels 44148 KIA
born: Plymouth   enlisted: Plymouth
No known grave. Thiepval Memorial, Pier and Face 1C. Joined BEF: not on Medal Card.
Pte. William Benjamin Warne 7430 KIA
born: Totnes   enlisted: Totnes
Buried: Peronne Communal Cemetery Extension. Grave III.L.11. Age 31. Joined BEF: 06/11/14 with original cadre. 1891 Census: son of James Warne, general labourer, R.N. Reserve, and Mary Warne, 47 High Street, Totnes, Devon. 1901 Census: son of James Warne, general labourer and widower, Cottage Behind 47 High Street, Totnes, Devon. 1911 Census: 2/Devons, St. George's Barracks, Malta. CWGC: step-son of Mrs. Mary J. Warne, Steps Cottage, South Street, Totnes, Devon.

The 2nd Devons War Diary

APRIL 1917

2nd April 1917
Pte. Thomas Henry Down 30553 DoW
born: Devonport   enlisted: Plymouth
Buried: Bray Military Cemetery. Grave II.E.59. Age 25. Joined BEF: not on Medal Card. Formerly 1699 of the Devonshire Regiment. 1901 Census: son of Harry Down, skilled labourer in arsenal at Bull Point, and Elizabeth Down, 4 Taylor Cottages, Riverside, Devonport, Devon. 1911 Census: dockyard painter, son of Harry Down, skilled labourer at Naval Ordnance Depot, and Elizabeth Down, 1 Taylor Place, St. Budeaux, Devonport, Devon. CWGC: family address: 6 Tamer Place, St. Budeaux, Devonport, Devon.

10th April 1917
Pte. Charles Lewis Williams 42693 DoW
born: Bideford, Devon   enlisted: Exeter   residence: Torquay
Buried: Bray Military Cemetery. Grave II.G.44. Age 29. Joined BEF: not on Medal Card. 1901 Census: son of John M. Williams, mason's labourer, and Elizabeth Williams, 14 Honistone Street, Bideford, Devon. 1911 Census: 'waiter at boarding house', 9 Beacon Terrace, Torquay, Devon.

14th April 1917
2/Lt. William Everard Hill Perry KIA
Buried: Villers Hill British Cemetery, Villers-Guislain. Grave VI.C.20. Age possibly 19. Joined BEF: 12/03/17, (possibly date of joining BEF as an officer). Formerly Pte. 27308 of the Ox and Bucks Light Infantry. Date of commission not recorded on Medal Card. 1901 Census: son of Thomas Wallis Perry, elementary schoolmaster, and Bessie Perry, Down End, St. Kinnow, Cornwall. 1911 Census: schoolboy, son of Thomas Wallis Perry, head teacher, widower, School House, Whimple, Devon. Commemorated on Hele's School War Memorial, Exeter, and Whimple War Memorial.
Pte. James Baker 26245 KIA
born: Exminster   enlisted: Exeter
No known grave. Thiepval Memorial, Pier and Face 1C. Age 35. Joined BEF: not on Medal Card. 1901 Census: farm labourer, son of James Baker, general labourer, and Annie Baker, 29 King Street, Exeter, Devon.
L/Cpl. Joseph Knox Birkett 27607 KIA
born: Birmingham   enlisted: Birmingham
Buried: Villers Hill British Cemetery, Villers-Guislain. Grave VI.C.31. Age 20. Joined BEF: not on Medal Card. 1901 Census: son of John Adam Birkett, elementary schoolmaster, and Hannah Birkett, 11 Bankes Road, Aston, Birmingham. 1911 Census: 'office boy wholesale drapery' son of John A. Birkett, schoolmaster assistant, and Hannah Birkett, 148 Kenelm Road, Birmingham, Warwickshire. CWGC: family address: Manor Road, Stratford-on-Avon.
Pte. Robert Broadway 26122 KIA
Born: Redruth, Cornwall   enlisted: Plymouth
Buried: Villers Hill British Cemetery, Villers-Guislain. Grave VI.C.7. Age 34. Joined BEF: not on Medal Card. 1911 Census: licensed hawker, married to Sara Broadway, also licensed hawker, father of 4 children, living in a tent and living waggon, address: Ivybridge GPO, Devon.

Sgt. Sidney Callaghan 9378 KIA
born: St. Germans, Cornwall   enlisted: Devonport
Buried: Villers Hill British Cemetery, Villers-Guislain. Grave VI.C.29. Age 23. Joined BEF: 06/11/14 with original cadre. 1901 Census: son of John H. Callaghan, railway labourer, and Mary E. Callaghan, St. Stephens, Burraton Cross, Cornwall.

Pte. Albert Diccox 22313 KIA
born: Hillmarton, Wilts.   enlisted: Marlborough   residence: Lower Uppam
No known grave. Thiepval Memorial, Pier and Face 1C. Age 26. Joined BEF: not on Medal Card. 1901 Census: son of John Diccox, carter on farm, and Sarah Diccox, Wanboro' Plain, Wanborough, Wiltshire. CWGC: family address: Idstone Ashbury, Wilts.

Pte. Herbert Eller 13180 KIA
born: Hackney   enlisted: Abertrydwr
Buried: Arras Memorial, Bay 4. Age 26. Joined BEF: 09/02/15. Attached to 23rd Brigade Trench Mortar Battery. Enlisted August 1914. 1901 Census: son of Carl Herman Eller, pastry cook – bread, and Sarah Eller, Goodleigh Road, Barnstaple, Devon. 1911 Census: baker, boarding at Bude Street, Appledore, Devon. CWGC: family address: 16 Bicton Street, Barnstaple.

Pte. Albert Gill 21647 KIA
born: St.Mabyn, Cornwall   enlisted: Devonport   residence: Washaway, Cornwall
Buried: Villers Hill British Cemetery, Villers-Guislain. Grave VI.C.23. Age 26. Joined BEF: not on Medal Card. 1911 Census: gardener domestic, boarding at 3 Fistral Place, Newquay, Cornwall.

Pte. John Haydon 7606 KIA
born: Cullompton   enlisted: Exeter   residence: Bradninch
Buried: Villers Hill British Cemetery, Villers-Guislain. Grave VI.C.30. Age 32. Joined BEF: 22/08/14 with original cadre of 1/Devons. 1901 Census: son of John Haydon, mill labourer, and Margaret Jane Haydon, Hence Street, Bradninch, Cullompton. 1911 Census: paper sorter, husband of Kate Haydon, Westend, Bradninch. CWGC: husband of Kate Haydon, Kentisbeare, Cullompton, Devon.

Pte. Alfred Fredrick Hedges 45533 KIA
born: Havant, Hants.   enlisted: Havant
CWGC: no record. Joined BEF: not on Medal Card.

Pte. Richard Wallace Jackson 16579 KIA
born: Bere Alston, Devon   enlisted: Plymouth   residence: Bere Alston
No known grave. Thiepval Memorial, Pier and Face 1C. Age 22. Joined BEF: not on Medal Card. CWGC: son of the late Septimus Oliver Jackson and Annie Grace Jackson, "Clamoak," Bere Alston, Devon.

Pte. William Hubert Lamble 21288 KIA
born: Charleton, Devon   enlisted: Newton Abbot   residence: Kingsbridge
Buried: Villers Hill British Cemetery, Villers-Guislain. Grave VI.C.18. Age 19. Joined BEF: not on Medal Card. 1911 Census: servant, farm boy, boarding at Edward Stooke's farm, Coleridge, Chillington, Kingsbridge, Devon.

Pte. Donald Colway Larcombe 15988 KIA
born: Exeter   enlisted: Exeter Buried: Villers Hill British Cemetery, Villers-Guislain. Grave VI.C.24. Age 27. Joined BEF: 14/07/15 with 1/Devons. 1891 Census: son of James C. Larcombe, railway guard, and Alice M. Larcombe, Rose Cottage, St. Daniel, Exeter, Devon. 1901 Census: 3 Manor Road, St. Thomas, Exeter, Devon. 1911 Census: porter, son of Alice Mary Larcombe, widow, 35 Howell Road, Exeter.

Pte. William James Priddis 25869 KIA
born: Exmouth   enlisted: Exeter   residence: Ebbw Vale, Mon.
Buried: Villers Hill British Cemetery, Villers-Guislain. Grave VI.C.21. Age 33. Joined BEF: not on Medal Card. 1891 Census: son of James Priddis, mason, and Mary Priddis, Woods Cottages, Littleham, Devon. 1901 Census: stationer's errand boy, son of James Priddis, bricklayer, and Mary Priddis, Tower Street, Littleham, Devon. 1911 Census: bricklayer's labourer, husband of Francis Minnie Priddis, father of Frederick, age 5, 11 Meadow Street, Exmouth, Devon. CWGC: husband of Frances Minnie Priddis, 99 Egremont Road, Exmouth.

Pte. Sidney Albert Rowe 33215 KIA
born: Topsham, Devon   enlisted: Topsham
Buried: Villers Hill British Cemetery, Villers-Guislain. Grave VI.C.25. Age 19. Joined BEF: not on Medal Card. Formerly 916, Devonshire Regiment. 1901 Census: son of Walter John Rowe, farm labourer, and Elizabeth Ann Rowe, Red Cow, Topsham, Devon. 1911 Census: son of Walter John Rowe, cowman on farm, and Elizabeth Ann Rowe, High Street, Topsham, Devon. CWGC: family address: 59 High Street, Topsham, Devon.

Pte. Reginald Sanders 3/6797 KIA
born: Bideford   enlisted: Barnstaple
Buried: Villers Hill British Cemetery, Villers-Guislain. Grave VI.C.19. Age 21. Joined BEF: not recorded on Medal Card. 1901 Census: son of John William Sanders, mason, and Lydia Grace Sanders, 27 Belle Meadow, Barnstaple, Devon. 1911 Census: son of John William Sanders, bricklayer, and Lydia Grace Sanders, 18 Zions Cottages, Barnstaple, Devon. CWGC: Lydia Sanders, widow, 34 Ages Lane, Barnstaple, Devon.

Pte. Charles Edward Schofield 19070 KIA
born: St.Luke's, Middx.   enlisted: Finsbury
No known grave. Thiepval Memorial, Pier and Face 1C. Age 19. No Medal Card. 1911 Census: office boy, son of Charles Schofield, upholsterer, and Emma Schofield, 31 Hollybush Gardens, Bethnal Green, London.

Sgt. Henry Lyman Sohier 9848 KIA
born: St.Helier, Jersey   enlisted: St.Helier
Buried: Villers Hill British Cemetery, Villers-Guislain. Grave VI.C.6. Age 20. Joined BEF: 24/08/15. 1901 Census: son of Mr. Lyman J. Sohier, tobacconist/shopkeeper, and Florence Sohier, 35 Queen Street, St. Helier, Jersey, Channel Islands. 1911 Census: schoolboy, son of Lyman Sohier, hotel keeper, and Florence Sohier, Victoria Hotel, St. Peter's Valley, Jersey. CWGC: L. J. Sohier at Victoria Hotel, St. Peter's Valley, Jersey.

Pte. Charles Henry Weeks 3/6362 KIA
born: Torquay   enlisted: Torquay
No known grave. Thiepval Memorial, Pier and Face 1C. Age 24. Joined BEF: 12/09/14 with original cadre of 1/Devons. 1901 Census: of Charles Weeks, retail coal dealer, and Mary Weeks, 1 Church Street, Tormoham, Torquay, Devon. 1911 Census: son of Mary Weeks, widow, laundress, 43 Victoria Road, Tormoham, Torquay, Devon. CWGC: son of Mary Ann Bonning (formerly Weeks), and the late Charles Henry Weeks, husband of Beatrice Weeks, Silver Street, Honiton, Devon.

16th April 1917
Pte. Albert John Baker 25081 DoW
born: Ottery St.Mary   enlisted: Exeter   residence: Ottery St.Mary
Buried: Lapugnoy Military Cemetery. Grave III.C.12. Age 33. Joined BEF: not on Medal Card. 1891 Census: son of John Baker, agricultural labourer, and Fanny Baker, West Hill, Ottery St.

Mary, Devon. CWGC: 1/Devons, husband of Edith Baker, Dogs Lane, Ottery St. Mary, Devon.

18th April 1917
Pte. James Warren 16884 KIA
born: Crediton   enlisted: Pangbourne, Berks.   residence: Crediton
No known grave. Thiepval Memorial, Pier and Face 1C. Age 24. Joined BEF: not on Medal Card. 1901 Census: son of James Warren, widower, mason's labourer, Paradise, Crediton, Devon. 1911 Census: mason's labourer, son of James Warren, widower, mason's labourer, 3 Paradise, Crediton, Devon.

19th April 1917
Sgt. Alfred John Irwin 8032 DoW
born: Combe Martin   enlisted: Combe Martin
Buried: Bray Military Cemetery. Grave II.H.25. Age 30. Joined BEF: 06/11/14 with original cadre. Formerly 9032, Devonshire Regiment. 1911 Census: 2/Devons, St. George's Barracks, Malta.

20th April 1917
Pte. Harry Robert Prigg 21718 DoW
born: Ottery St.Mary   enlisted: Ottery St.Mary
Buried: Bray Military Cemetery. Grave II.H.27. Age 27. Joined BEF: not on Medal Card. 1911 Census: baker, son of George Prigg, general labourer, and Phoebe Prigg, 7 Yonder Street, Ottery St. Mary, Devon. CWGC: son of George Prigg and Phoebe Prigg, 7 Yonder Street, Ottery St. Mary, Devon.

22nd April 1917
L/Cpl. Norman Horsham 33197 DoW
born: Cullompton   enlisted: Cullompton
Buried: St. Sever Cemetery Extension, Rouen. O.IX.G.5. Age 20. Joined BEF: not on Medal Card. 1911 Census: son of John Horsham, cattle man, and Emma Horsham, of Trumps, Clyst Hydon, Whimple, Devon. CWGC records: son of the late John Horsham and Emma Horsham. Native of Clyst Hydon, Exeter.

The 2nd Devons War Diary

MAY 1917

4th May 1917
L/Sgt. Reginald Louis Roberts, M.M. 9987 DoW
born: Watford   enlisted: Hatfield   residence: Watford
Buried: La Chapelette British and Indian Cemetery, Peronne. Grave I.C.5. Age 23. Joined BEF: not on Medal Card. 1901 Census: Louis Roberts, son of Charles Roberts, electrical engineer, and Mary E. Roberts, 38 Brightwell Road, Watford, Herts.

6th May 1917
Lt. Stanley Vingoe Clarke KIA
Buried: Villers Hill British Cemetery, Villers-Guislains. Grave IV.D.14. Age 28. Joined BEF: not on Medal Card. Attached from 5th (Prince of Wales) Battalion (Territorial). Medal Card records him with Devonshire Regiment Territorial Force. Resided at Kingsbridge, Devon.
Pte. Francis William Gough 23163 KIA
born: South Molton   enlisted: Tiverton   residence: South Molton
Buried: Villers Hill British Cemetery, Villers-Guislains. Grave IV.D.12. Age 19. Joined BEF: not on Medal Card. 1901 Census: son of Richard Gough, coachman not domestic, and Mary Ann Gough, 10 Thorne's Court, South Molton, Devon. 1911 Census: schoolboy, son of Richard Gough, general labourer, and Mary Ann Gough, 1 Thorne Court, South Molton, Devon. CWGC: family address: 1 Thorne Terrace, Barnstaple Street, South Molton, Devon.
Pte. Bertie Moore 6962 KIA
born: Torquay   enlisted: Exeter   residence: Barnstaple
Buried: Villers Hill British Cemetery, Villers-Guislains. Grave IV.D.8. Joined BEF: 06/11/15 with original cadre.
Cpl. Alfred Richard Pears 16512 KIA
born: Twickenham   enlisted: London   residence: Twickenham
CWGC does not list a grave or memorial reference for this man. Age 27. Joined BEF: 01/10/15. 1891 Census: son of Richard Pears, labourer, and Ellen Pears, 1 Oak Cottage, Twickenham, Middlesex. 1901 Census: son of Richard Pears, widower, general labourer, 4 The Embankment, Twickenham. 1911 Census: 'waterman', living at home of sister, Ellen Floyd, and husband James Floyd, house painter, 4 The Embankment, Twickenham, Middlesex.
Pte. Henry Wilcocks 26117 KIA
born: Devonport   enlisted: Devonport
No known grave. Thiepval Memorial, Pier and Face 1C. Age 24. Joined BEF: not on Medal Card. 1911 Census: recorded as Henry Carbery Wilcocks, farmer, son of Henry Madgwick Dansey Wilcocks, tin mine manager, and Julia Cecilia Wilcocks, Challacombe, nr. Princetown, Dartmoor, Devon.

10th May 1917
Pte. Frederick Thomas Hitchcock Webber 33189 DoW
born: Clyst Hydon, Devon   enlisted: Cullompton
Buried: St. Sever Cemetery Extension, Rouen. Grave P.II.L.14A. Age 23. 'A' Company. Joined BEF: not on Medal Card. Formerly 805 of the Devonshire Regiment. 1901 Census: son of Edwin John Webber, mason, and Mary Ann Webber, Reach Cottages, Clyst Hydon, Devon. 1911 Census: servant/boy on farm, Broad Oak, Clyst Hydon, nr. Whimple, Devon. CWGC: family address: Andrew's Cottage, Clyst Hydon, Exeter.

15th May 1917
Pte. Edgar James Hamlyn 6871 DoW
born: Plymouth enlisted: Plymouth
Buried: St. Marie Cemetery, Le Havre. Grave Div.62.I.C.10. Age 37. Joined BEF: 06/11/14 with original cadre. 1911 Census: casual labourer, boarding at 10 and 11 Octagon Street, Plymouth, Devon. CWGC: son of James Hamlyn and Emma Hamlyn, Plymouth.

17th May 1917
Pte. Robert James Wallington 12194 DoW
born: Islington enlisted: Islington
Buried: La Chapelette British and Indian Cemetery, Peronne. Grave II.E.7. Age 19. Joined BEF: 27/07/15. 1901 Census: son of Frederick Charles Wallington, builder's labourer, 83 Elthorne Road, Islington, London. CWGC: son of Frederick Charles Wallington and Ellen Wallington, 78 Hazellville Road, Hornsey Rise, London. Enlisted in Duke of Cornwall's Light Infantry in 1914.

27th May 1917
Pte. Arthur Henry Litton 11340 Died
born: Exmouth enlisted: Exmouth
Buried: Cologne Southern Cemetery, Germany. Grave XIV.D.12. Age 28. Joined BEF: 02/05/15. 1911 Census: merchant tailor, son of Henry Litton, mason/labourer, and Emma Litton, 32 New Street, Exmouth, Devon.

The 2nd Devons War Diary

JUNE 1917

9th June 1917
Sgt. Sidney George White 8485 Died
born: Ottery St.Mary   enlisted: Exeter   residence: Ottery St.Mary
Buried: Cerisy-Gailly Military Cemetery. Grave I.C.16. Joined BEF: 06/11/14 with original cadre. 1911 Census: 2/Devons, St. George's Barracks, Malta.

18th June 1917
Cpl. Walter Gill 20067 KIA
born: Malborough, Devon   enlisted: Cardiff   residence: Kingsbridge
Buried: Menin Road South Military Cemetery. Grave I.S.1. Age 21. Joined BEF: not on Medal Card. 1901 Census: son of William Luckham Gill, carter on farm, and Elizabeth Ann Gill, Coombe Cottage, Malborough, Devon. 1911 census: 'assistant in business', nephew of Albert Henry Gill, boarding house keeper, Rock House, Thurlestone Sands, nr. Kingsbridge, Devon. CWGC: family address: Heycourt, Malborough, Kingsbridge, Devon. Cpl. Gill's death is alluded to, anonymously, in the War Diary on 17th June.

19th June 1917
Pte. William Henry Weeks 18151 Died
born: Paignton   enlisted: Plymouth
Buried: Lijssenthoek Military Cemetery,Ypres. Grave XIV.E.17. Age 23. Joined BEF: not on Medal Card. 1901 Census: son of Thomas Weeks, blacksmith, and Hannah Weeks, Torquay, Devon. 1911 Census: servant/waggoner on farm, Wollaton, Brixton, nr. Plymouth, Devon.

20th June 1917
Pte. Albert Emmanuel Daniels 33169 DoW
born: Bradninch   enlisted: Bradninch
Buried: Belgian Battery Corner Cemetery. Grave I.A.6. Age 25. Joined BEF: not recorded on Medal Card. Formerly 663, Devonshire Regiment. 'A' Company. 1901 Census: of Francis Daniels, wheelwright, and Fanny Daniels, Hence Street, Bradninch, Devon. CWGC: husband of Rose Ellen Daniels, 2 Culme View, Exeter Road, Cullompton, Devon.

21st June 1917
L/Cpl. Frederick Herbert Dorrington 16112 KIA
born: Romford, Essex   enlisted: Holloway,Middx.
Buried: Belgian Battery Corner Cemetery. Grave I.A.2. Age 28. Joined BEF: 28/07/15 with 1/Devons . 1891 Census: son of Frederick Dorrington, house painter, and Rose Dorrington, 3 Monks Road, Romford, Essex. 1901 Census: with parents, 45 Monks Road, Romford. 1911 Census: 'wine and spirit merchant/barman', husband of Grace Dorrington, 'sewing machinist/furs', 24 Prebend Street, Islington, London. CWGC: husband of Grace Alice Dorrington, 69 Albany Cottages, Popham Street, Islington, London. L/Cpl Dorrington had been wounded in September 1916.
Pte. Fred Marwood 11560 KIA
born: Exeter   enlisted: Exeter
Buried: Belgian Battery Corner Cemetery. Grave I.A.5. Age 25. Joined BEF: 09/02/15. 1901 Census: son of John Marwood, electrical engineer, and Louisa Marwood, 1 Perkins Village, Farringdon, Devon. 1911 Census: servant/butcher, 6 Rosemouth Cottages, Pinhoe, Devon.

CWGC: family address: Mill House, Farringdon, Exeter. Husband of Eveline Marwood, Birchy Barton Cottage, Heavitree, Exeter.
Pte. Frederick Thomas Peters 203283 KIA
born: Torquay, Devon   enlisted: Newton Abbot   residence: Torquay
Buried: Belgian Battery Corner Cemetery. Grave I.A.4. Age 19. Joined BEF: not on Medal Card. 1901 Census: son of William H. Peters, general labourer, and Jessie M. L. Peters, laundress, 1 Chester Row, Tormoham, Torquay, Devon. 1911 Census: schoolboy, grandson of Mary Holmes, widow/laundress, 3 Bronshill Terrace, Torquay, Devon. CWGC: family address: 50 Victoria Park Road, Torquay.
Pte. George Southcott 26767 KIA
born: Egham, Surrey   enlisted: Exeter   residence: Budleigh Salterton
Buried: Belgian Battery Corner Cemetery. Grave I.A.1. Age 34. Joined BEF: not on Medal Card. 1891 Census: son of James Southcott, police constable, and Caroline Southcott, High Street, Oxted, Surrey. 1901 Census: carpenter, son of James Southcott, police sergeant, and Caroline Southcott, Police Station, Godstone, Surrey. 1911 Census: carpenter, husband of Fan Southcott, Colaton Raleigh, Devon. CWGC: family address: Newton Poppleford, Devon. Husband of Jean Southcott, Mount Pleasant Cottage, Knowle, Budleigh Salterton, Devon.
Pte. Albert Waldron 203594 KIA
born: Barnstaple   enlisted: Barnstaple
Buried: Belgian Battery Corner Cemetery. Grave I.A.3. Age 19. Joined BEF: not on Medal Card. 1901 Census: grandson of Samuel Waldron, woodman on estate, and Mary Ann Waldron, Loits Houses, Chittlehampton, South Molton, Devon. 1911 Census: schoolboy, inmate, Barnstaple Union Workhouse and Cottage Homes, Barnstaple, Devon.

22nd June 1917
Pte. William Charles Hamilton Geake 26133 DoW
born: Truro, Cornwall   enlisted: Plymouth
Buried: Mendinghem Military Cemetery. Grave II.E.4. Age 18. Joined BEF: not on Medal Card. Pte. Geake DoW suffered on 20th June.

25th June 1917
Pte. John Brown 44263 KIA
born: Manchester   enlisted: Manchester
Buried: Perth Cemetery (China Wall). Grave I.A.14. Age 39. Joined BEF: not on Medal Card. CWGC: husband of Eliza Mary Brown, 10 Chatsworth Street, Chorlton-on-Medlock, Manchester.
Pte. William Burley 5234 KIA
born: Plymouth   enlisted: Plymouth
Buried: Barlin Communal Cemetery Extension. Grave I.A.40. Joined BEF: 06/11/14 with original cadre. CWGC: named W.F.G. Burley.

27th June 1917
Pte. Fred Norman 45537 KIA
born: no record   enlisted: Christchurch, Hants.
Buried: Perth Cemetery (China Wall). Grave I.B.10. Joined BEF: not on Medal Card.

30th June 1917
Pte. Charles Edward Reading 43173 DoW
born: Birmingham   enlisted: Birmingham
No known grave. Ypres (Menin Gate) Memorial, Panel 21. Age 33. Joined BEF: not on Medal Card. 1891 Census: son of Charles Reading, joiner, and Elizabeth Reading, 4 Water Lane, Aston, Birmingham, Warwickshire. 1901 Census: joiner, 63 Hayle Road, Aston, Birmingham. 1911 Census: carpenter, son of Charles Reading snr., carpenter, and Elizabeth Reading, 473 Green Lane, Birmingham, Warwickshire. CWGC: son of Elizabeth Reading, 473 Green Lane, Small Heath, Birmingham, and the late Charles Reading.

JULY 1917

23rd July 1917
Pte. Jack Steer 8802 Died
born: Ashburton, Devon   enlisted: Devonport
Buried: Longuenesse (St. Omer) Souvenir Cemetery. Grave I.C.63. Age 27. 'C' Company. Joined BEF: 06/11/14 with original cadre. 1891 Census: named as John Steer, son of George Steer, tanner's labourer, and Susan Steer, Market Street, Buckfastleigh, Devon. 1901 Census: son of George Steer, navvy on extension works, and Susan Steer, 27 Elliott Street, Devonport, Devon. 1911 Census: 2/Devons, St. George's Barracks, Malta. CWGC: family address: 64 Notte Street, Plymouth, Devon.

24th July 1917
Pte. John Butler 30882 KIA
born: London   enlisted: Kennington   residence: Walworth
Buried: Perth Cemetery (China Wall). Grave I.D.5. Joined BEF: not on Medal Card. Formerly 27028, Dorsetshire Regiment. CWGC: named A. J. Butler.
Pte. Albert Gloyne 30859 KIA
born: Hennock, Devon   enlisted: Exeter   residence: Hennock
Buried: Perth Cemetery (China Wall). Grave I.D.5. Age 26. Date joined BEF: 19/01/15, with 1/Devons . 1901 Census: son of John Gloyne, gamekeeper, and Louisa Gloyne, The Village, Hennock, Devon. 1911 Census: 'labourer in stone quarry', son of John Henry Gloyne, 'miner in ore mine', and Louisa Gloyne, Hennock, Bovey Trecay, Devon. CWGC: son of Louisa Gloyne, Hennock, Bovey Tracey, Devon, and the late John Henry Gloyne.
Pte. Frank Henderson 10998 KIA
born: West Ham, London   enlisted: Exeter   residence: Kenton, Devon
Buried: Perth Cemetery (China Wall). Grave I.D.5. Age 21. Joined BEF: 02/09/15. 1911 Census: scholar, inmate, Devon and Exeter Boys Industrial School, Exeter, Devon. CWGC: shows number 10996, ward of William Heppell, Church Stile House, Industrial School, Exminster, Exeter. Name recorded on Kenton War Memorial, Devon.
Pte. Charles Hamlet Smith 204848 KIA
born: no record   enlisted: Woolwich, Kent
Buried: Perth Cemetery (China Wall). Grave I.D.5. Joined BEF: not on Medal Card. Formerly 8401 of 21st London Regiment.
Pte. John White 35585 KIA
born: Kidderminster, Worcs.   enlisted: Worcester   residence: Kidderminster
Buried: Perth Cemetery (China Wall). Grave I.D.5. Age 21. Joined BEF: not on Medal Card. 1901 Census: son of Dorcas White, threader, grandson of Mary A. White, 1 Court, Churchfield, Kidderminster, Worcestershire. CWGC: son of Dorcas Evans, 12 Paddock Court, Dudley Street, Kidderminster, Worcs.

25th July 1917
Pte. John Carmody 18073 KIA
born: Somers Town, Middx.   enlisted: St.Pancras
Buried: Belgian Battery Corner Cemetery. Grave I.G.9. Date joined BEF: not on Medal Card.

Pte. Frederick Gidley 26291 DoW
born: Stonehouse   enlisted: Plymouth
Buried: Belgian Battery Corner Cemetery. Grave I.G.8. Age 33. 1891 Census: son of Thomas Gidley, foreman to general carrier, and Elizabeth Gidley, 28 Hobart Street, East Stonehouse, Devon. 1901 Census: grocer's assistant, son of Thomas Gidley, foreman general carrier, and Elizabeth Gidley, 62 Wolsdon Street, Plymouth, Devon. 1911 Census: grocery warehouseman, husband of Edith Marion Gidley, 210 Beaumont Road, Plymouth. CWGC: husband of Edith Marion Pethick (formerly Gidley), 7 Glendower Road, Peverell, Plymouth.

27th July 1917
Pte. Charles Derry 267370 KIA
born: Stonehouse   enlisted: Bodmin
No known grave. Ypres (Menin Gate) Memorial, Panel 21. Age 30. No Medal Card. CWGC: husband of Edith A. Derry, St. Nicholas Street, Bodmin, Cornwall.
Pte. Albert Stanley Goodwin 30807 KIA
born: Birmingham   enlisted: Dorchester   residence: Portland
Buried: Hooge Crater Cemetery. Grave III.I.3. Age 19. Joined BEF: not on Medal Card. Formerly 18816, Dorsetshire Regiment. 1901 Census: son of William E. Goodwin, pipe salesman, and Sarah J. Goodwin, 152 Gooch Street, Birmingham. 1911 Census: son of William E. Goodwin, grocer, and Sarah J. Goodwin, 58 Wakeham Road, Portland, Dorset.
Pte. William Thomas Leslie 204888 KIA
born: Bedminster   enlisted: Bristol
Buried: Hooge Crater Cemetery. Grave III.I.6. Age 31. Joined BEF: not on Medal Card. Formerly 203207, Dorsetshire Regiment. 1911 Census: miner/labourer underground, son of James Leslie, general labourer, and Martha Leslie, 35 Jasper Street, Bedminster, Bristol, Gloucestershire.
Pte. Daniel Patrick Mulcahy 204889 KIA
born: Bristol   enlisted: Bristol
No known grave. Ypres (Menin Gate) Memorial, Panel 21. Age 20. Joined BEF: not on Medal Card. Formerly 203210, Dorsetshire Regiment. 1901 Census: son of William Mulcahy, empty packing case dealer, and Bridget Mulcahy, 36 Heyward Road, Bristol, Somerset. 1911 Census: schoolboy, son of Patrick Mulcahy, railway porter, and Bridget Mulcahy, 12 Heber Street, Redfield, Bristol, Gloucestershire. CWGC: son of Mrs B. Mulcahy, 18 Morse Road, Bristol.
Pte. James Garfield Stevens 30775 KIA
born: Camborne, Cornwall   enlisted: Redruth   residence: Camborne
No known grave. Ypres (Menin Gate) Memorial, Panel 21. Age 19. Joined BEF: not on Medal Card. Formerly 34859, Duke of Cornwall's Light Infantry. 1911 Census: schoolboy, son of John Stevens, widower/tin miner, Belman's Row, Camborne, Cornwall. CWGC: son of J. Stevens and Annie Stevens, 31 Redbrooke Road, Stray Park, Camborne, Cornwall.

28th July 1917
Pte. Charles John Blake 30810 KIA
born: Crichel, Dorset   enlisted: Shaftesbury
No known grave. Ypres (Menin Gate) Memorial, Panel 21. Joined BEF: not on Medal Card. Formerly 18972, Dorsetshire Regiment.
Pte. Ernest Charles Sutton 30797 KIA
born: Chelsea   enlisted: Camberwell
No known grave. Ypres (Menin Gate) Memorial, Panel 21. Joined BEF: not on Medal Card.

Formerly 28144, Dorsetshire Regiment.
Pte. Alfred John Bingle 33554 DoW
born: Middle Lypiatt, Glos.   enlisted: Stroud, Glos.
No known grave. Ypres (Menin Gate) Memorial, Panel 21. Age 28. Joined BEF: not on Medal Card. Formerly 4865, Gloucestershire Regiment. 1891 Census: son of Alfred J. Bingle, porter wholesale clothing, heavy, and Margaret E. Bingle, Lime Kilns, Stroud, Gloucestershire. 1911 Census: assistant porter to a general outfitters, son of Alfred John Bingle, porter to general outfitters, and stepson of Elizabeth Bingle, Limekilns, Stroud, Gloucestershire.
Pte. Edwin Stacey 30841 DoW
born: Nether Stowey, Som.   enlisted: Taunton   residence: Bridgwater
No known grave. Ypres (Menin Gate) Memorial, Panel 21. Age 25. Joined BEF: 02/06/15. Formerly 16683, Somerset Light Infantry. 1901 Census: son of Frederick Stacey, coachman domestic, and Eliza Stacey, Mary Street, Nether Stowey, Somerset. 1911 Census: farm labourer, son of Frederick Stacey, hotel ostler, and Eliza Stacey, Castle Street, Nether Stowey, Bridgwater, Somerset.

29th July 1917
Pte. Reginald Herbert Billing 30848 KIA
born: East Pennard, Somerset   enlisted: Stone, Somerset
Buried: Tyne Cot Cemetery, nr. Ypres. Grave LXVII.F.22. Age 21. Joined BEF: not on Medal Card. Formerly 1144, West Somerset Light Infantry, and 27688, Somerset Light Infantry. 1901 Census: son of Herbert W. Billing, general labourer on farm, and Jane Ann Billing, Stone, East Pennard, Shepton Mallet, Somerset. 1911 Census: general farm labourer, son of William Herbert Billing, cow man on farm, and Jane Ann Billing, Stone, East Pennard, Shepton Mallett, Devon.
Pte. Frederick David Lloyd 18108 KIA
born: Great Torrington, Devon   enlisted: London
Buried: Lijssenthoek Military Cemetery, Ypres. Grave XIV.I.16. Age 30. Joined BEF: not on Medal Card. 1891 Census: son of Robert Lloyd, licensed victualler, maltster and brewer, and Eliza Lloyd, 'New Inn', 14 Well Street, Great Torrington, Devon. CWGC: family address: 516 Jefferson Avenue, West Kildonan, Manitoba, Canada.
Pte. George Brice 8151 DoW
born: Brixham   enlisted: Exeter   residence: Brixham
Buried: Tyne Cot Cemetery, nr. Ypres. Grave LXVI.F.15. Age 29. Joined BEF: 22/08/14 with original cadre of 1/Devons. 1891 Census: son of William Brice, fisherman, and Mary E Brice, Broad Steps, Brixham, Devon. 1901 Census: does not name parents, eldest in household Minnie Brice, general domestic servant, age 19, Market Alley, Brixham. 1911 Census: 2/Devons, St. George's Barracks, Malta. CWGC: family address: Paradise Place, Brixham, Devon. Husband of Mrs. S. Brice.

31st July 1917
Lieutenant-Colonel Alfred Joseph Elton Sunderland KIA
Buried: Belgian Battery Corner Cemetery. Grave I.F.2. Age 42. Joined BEF: 03/11/14, three days before original cadre. Three times mentioned in despatches. Annotation to Medal Card reads: *J. Sunderland Esq. applies for 1914 Star in respect of his late son Lt. Col. Sunderland. 28/11/17.* 1881 Census: son of James Sunderland, vicar of Egginton, and Florence Margaret Sunderland, Egginton Vicarage, Leighton Buzzard, Bedfordshire. 1891 Census: scholar at Marlborough College. 1911 Census: Captain Sunderland, 2/Devons, St. George's Barracks,

Malta.
L/Cpl. Charles Andrew 14193 KIA
born: Sirhowy, Monmouthshire   enlisted: Merthyr, Glam.   residence: Abergam, Glam.
Buried: Tyne Cot Cemetery, nr. Ypres. Grave XXIX.C.3. Age 26. Joined BEF: 04/01/15. CWGC: son of Thomas Andrew and Fanny Andrew, 11 The Grove, Aberfan, Glamorgan.

Pte. Cornelius Joseph Bartlett 26866 KIA
born: no record   enlisted: Dorchester   residence: Bridport
No known grave. Ypres (Menin Gate) Memorial, Panel 21. Joined BEF: not on Medal Card. Formerly 268626, Dorsetshire Regiment.

Pte. William John Farrow Bates 26524 KIA
born: Dartmouth   enlisted: Newton Abbot   residence: Dartmouth
No known grave. Ypres (Menin Gate) Memorial, Panel 21. Age 36. Joined BEF: not on Medal Card. 1891 Census: son of David Bates, builder, and Louisa Bates, innkeeper, Steam Packet Inn, Duck Street, Dartmouth, Devon.

Sgt. Norman John Batters 7642 KIA
born: Devonport   enlisted: London   residence: Devonport
No known grave. Ypres (Menin Gate) Memorial, Panel 21. Age 21. Joined BEF: 06/11/14 withoriginal cadre. 'B' Company. CWGC: son of Joseph Batters and Elizabeth Ann Batters.

Pte. Herbert Stanley Behenna 27615 KIA
born: Chasewater, Cornwall   enlisted: Truro   residence: Chasewater
No known grave. Ypres (Menin Gate) Memorial, Panel 21. Age 21. Joined BEF: not on Medal Card. 1901 Census: son of Thomas Behenna, tin miner captain, and Eliza Reed Behenna, Creeg Browse, Kenwyn, Chasewater, Cornwall. 1911 Census: student, son of Thomas Behenna, tin dresser, and E.R. Behenna, Unity Wood, Cox Hill, Chasewater, Cornwall.

Pte. John Bolt 203383 KIA
born: North Tawton, Devon   enlisted: Okehampton   residence: Spreyton, Devon
Buried: Bedford House cemetery, Ypres. Grave: Enclosure No.4.IV.D.7. Age 20. Joined BEF: not on Medal Card. 1901 Census: son of Henry Bolt, ordinary agricultural labourer, and Sarah Bolt, charwoman, of High Street, North Tawton, Devon.

Cpl. James Frederick Bourhill 33173 KIA
born: Edmonton   enlisted: Torquay
Buried: Tyne Cot Cemetery, nr. Ypres. Grave XXIX.C.4. Age 21. Joined BEF: not on Medal Card. Formerly 710, Devonshire Regiment. 1911 Census: carpenter's apprentice, son of David Bourhill, nurseryman's foreman, widower, 4 Mallock Road, Cheldton, Torquay, Devon. CWGC: son of David Bourhill and Kate Bourhill, "Fairlight," Sherwell Lane, Chelston, Torquay, Devon.

Pte. Ernest Edward Brant 29704 KIA
born: Exeter   enlisted: Exeter
No known grave. Ypres (Menin Gate) Memorial, Panel 21. Age 21. Joined BEF: not on Medal Card. 1891 Census: son of Frederick Brant, waggoner, and Anna Brant, Southwoods Buildings, St. Thomas, Exeter, Devon.

Pte. George Henry Brogan 19184 KIA
born: St.Helier C.I.   enlisted: Jersey C.I.
No known grave. Ypres (Menin Gate) Memorial, Panel 21. Age 33. Joined BEF: not on Medal Card. 1891 Census: son of William Brogan, gas fitter, and Louisa Ann Brogan, book keeper, 2 Providence Square, St. Helier, Jersey, Channel Islands. 1911 Census: general labourer, son of Louisa Ann Brogan, 2 Cambridge Cottages, Oxford Road, Jersey.

Pte. Thomas Brooks 5839 KIA
born: Spreyton, Devon   enlisted: Okehampton
No known grave. Ypres (Menin Gate) Memorial, Panel 21. Age 34. Joined BEF: 12/09/14 with 1/Devons. CWGC: son of Philip James Brooks, Falkadon Cottages, Spreyton, Bow, Devon.

Pte. James Henry Burt 203644 KIA
born: Buckfastleigh   enlisted: Newton Abbot   residence: Buckfastleigh
Buried: Tyne Cot Cemetery, nr. Ypres. Grave XLV.B.14. Age 26. Joined BEF: not on Medal Card. 1891 Census: son of Richard Burt, farm labourer, and Elizabeth Burt, Cottage,Buckfast,Buckfastleigh, Devon. 1901 Census: father 'labourer in woollen factory', mother'serge weaver',Buckfast Institute Cottage, Buckfastleigh, Devon. 1911 Census: 'labourer weaver woollen factory', son of Richard Burt, farm labourer, and Elizabeth J. Burt, serge weaver, Buckfastleigh, Devon. CWGC: husband of Maude Hayman(formerly Burt), Eliott Plain, Buckfastleigh, Devon.

Pte. Thomas Percival Buscombe 30823 KIA
born: Helston, Cornwall   enlisted: St.Austell   residence: Par
No known grave. Ypres (Menin Gate) Memorial, Panel 21. Age 21. Joined BEF: not on Medal Card. Formerly 34871, Duke of Cornwall's Light Infantry. 1901 Census: son of Montague Buscombe, saddle harness maker, and Katie Buscombe, 14 Meneage Street, Helston, Cornwall. 1911 Census: apprentice harness maker, other details as in 1901 Census. CWGC: family address: 19 West Park, St. Columb, Cornwall.

Pte. Charles James Carey 43324 KIA
born: Devonport   enlisted: Plymouth
Buried: Perth Cemetery (China Wall). Grave III.L.20. Age 40. Joined BEF: not on Medal Card. 1881 Census: son of Joseph Carey, painter, and Eliza Ann Carey, tailoress, 1 Prospect Row, Stoke Damerell, Devonport, Devon.

Pte. William John Chick 30846 KIA
born: Bridgwater   enlisted: Bridgwater
No known grave. Ypres (Menin Gate) Memorial, Panel 21. Age 21. Joined BEF: not on Medal Card. Formerly 20175, Somerset Light Infantry. 1901 Census: son of William Chick, gardener domestic, and Alice Chick, Queen Street, Bridgwater, Somerset. 1911 Census: apprentice hairdresser, details as 1901 Census.

Pte. Frederick Edwin James Clarke 12737 KIA
born: Bristol   enlisted: Caerphilly   residence: Bristol
No known grave. Ypres (Menin Gate) Memorial, Panel 21. Age 37. Joined BEF: 02/02/15. 1911 Census: engineer, husband of Amy Clarke, 49 Montague Street, St. James, Bristol, Glos. CWGC: son of the late Edwin Clarke and Sarah Ann Clarke, husband of Amy Maria Clarke, II Regent Street, Spring Street, Bedminster, Bristol, Glos.

Cpl. Joseph Corby 26735 KIA
born: Margate   enlisted: Reading
No known grave. Ypres (Menin Gate) Memorial, Panel 21. Age 31. Joined BEF: not on Medal Card. 1901 Census: son of Ebenezer J. Corby, hotel porter, and Susan Corby,Rye, Sussex. 1911 Census: 'agent', boarding at 90 Brighton Road, Reading, Berkshire. CWGC:husband of Lillian Beatrice Corby, Brighton Road, Reading. Father inDover, Kent.

Pte. Albertus Hamilton Davis 204875 KIA
born: no record   enlisted: Bodmin   residence: St.Austell
No known grave. Ypres (Menin Gate) Memorial, Panel 21. Age 31. Joined BEF: not on Medal Card. Formerly 201440, Somerset Light Infantry. 1911 Census: 'tailor maker', husband of Mabel Davis, Aylmer Place, St. Austell, Cornwall. CWGC: son of Solomon Palmer Davis and

JessieDavis, 41 Carclew Street, Truro, husband of Mabel Davis, 18 Richmond Hill, Truro, Cornwall.

Pte. Percy William Day 43802 KIA
born: Sunningdale, Berkshire   enlisted: Reading   residence: Sunningdale
No known grave. Ypres (Menin Gate) Memorial, Panel 21. Age 32. Joined BEF: not recorded on Medal Card. 1891 Census: son of Charles Day, general labourer, and Elizabeth Day, Sunninghill Road, Old Windsor, Berkshire. 1901 Census: 'working in garden'. 1911 Census: gardener domestic, son of Charles Day, gardener domestic, and C. Day, Church Road, Sunningdale, Berkshire.

L/Sgt. Denis Donoghue 49039 KIA
born: Westbourne Park, London   enlisted: London S.E.
Buried: Bedford House Cemetery, Ypres. Grave: Enclosure No.4.IV.H.19. Age 33. Joined BEF: not on Medal Card. 1891 Census: son of Joseph P. O. Donoghue, railway accountant, and Elizabeth Donoghue, 14 Keith Gardens, Hammersmith, London.

Pte. David Dun 267960 KIA
born: Bristol   enlisted: Bristol
No known grave. Ypres (Menin Gate) Memorial, Panel 21. Age 32. Joined BEF: not on Medal Card. 1891 Census: son of John N. Dun, carpenter, and Charlotte Dun, 35 Temple Street, Temple, Bristol, Somerset. 1901 Census: telegraph messenger. 1911 Census: 'town postman', husband of Kate Dun, 47 Victoria Road, Redfield, Bristol, Glos. CWGC: husband of KateDun, 25 Stanley Park, Easton, Bristol.

Pte. Samuel John Emmett 26082 KIA
born: Harberton, Devon   enlisted: Newton Abbot   residence: Totnes
No known grave. Ypres (Menin Gate) Memorial, Panel 21. Age 34. Joined BEF: not on Medal Card. 1891 Census: son of Samuel James Emmett, edge tool grinder, and MariaEmmett, Leigh,Harberton, Devon. CWGC: husband of Annie Winter Emmett, 19 Leechwell, Street, Totnes,Devon.

Cpl. James Coverdale English 3/8168 KIA
born: Hartlepool, Durham   enlisted: Hartlepool
No known grave. Ypres (Menin Gate) Memorial, Panel 21. Age 24. Joined BEF: 27/12/14. 1901 Census: son of John English, clerk in wood yard, and Agnes English, 207 Beaconsfield Terrace, West Hartlepool, Durham. 1911 Census: apprentice joiner, son of John English, widower, joiner, 12 Caledonian Road, West Hartlepool, Yorkshire. CWGC: son of the late John English and father of Agnes English, West Hartlepool.

L/Cpl. Charles Abraham Farmer 15593 KIA
born: Kings-Brompton   enlisted: Taunton   residence: Dulverton
No known grave. Ypres (Menin Gate) Memorial, Panel 21. Age 26. Joined BEF: 01/06/15. 1901 Census: son of Henry B. Farmer, police inspector, and Ann Grigg Farmer, 25 Beatrice Avenue, Plymouth, Devon.

Pte. William John Franklin 27079 KIA
born: Warminster, Wiltshire   enlisted: Warminster
No known grave. Ypres (Menin Gate) Memorial, Panel 21. Age 41. Joined BEF: not on Medal Card. 1881 Census: son of William Franklin, mason, and Elizabeth Franklin, West Street, Warminster, Wilts. 1901 Census: son of William Franklin, bricklayer, and Elizabeth Franklin, 68 Pound Street, Warminster, Wilts. 1911 Census: bricklayer, husband of Minnie Franklin, 78 Pound Street, Warminster, Wilts. CWGC: family address: Victoria Road, Warminster, Wiltshire, husband of Minnie F. Hemmings (formerly Franklin), 26 Worcester Buildings, Larkhall, Bath.

Pte. Richard Ernest William French 30381 KIA
born: Lydford   enlisted: Plymouth
Buried: Tyne Cot Cemetery, nr. Ypres. Grave XXVI.H.12. Age 30. Joined BEF: not on Medal Card. Formerly 34972, Duke of Cornwall's Light Infantry. 1891 Census: son of John French, farmer, and Ann S. French, Lydford, Devon. 1901 Census: employed by Richard Coates, farmer, as servant/cattleman, Runnage Farm, Lydford, Devon. 1911 Census: tin miner, under ground, husband of Jessie French, Middle Merripitt, Postbridge, near Princetown, Devon.

Pte. Charles Gaylard 11826 KIA
born: Cardiff   enlisted: Caerphilly
No known grave. Ypres (Menin Gate) Memorial, Panel 21. Age 27. No Medal Card. 1901 Census: son of Byron Gaylard, blacksmith, and Louie Gaylard, 29 Theodora Street, Roath, Cardiff, Glamorgan. 1911 Census: labourer, visiting David Walters' family, 6 Emerald Street, Cardiff, with brothers Philip and Giles Gaylard.

Sgt. William John Gollop 8621 KIA
born: Exeter   enlisted: Exeter
No known grave. Ypres (Menin Gate) Memorial, Panel 21. Age 26. Joined BEF: 05/11/14 with original cadre. 1901 Census: stepson of John Ash, labourer (brickmakers), and Louisa M. Ash (mother), George's Square, Exeter, Devon. 1911 Census: 2/Devons, St. George's Barracks, Malta.

Pte. William Ernest Percy Gower 30821 KIA
born: Camberwell   enlisted: Camberwell
No known grave. Ypres (Menin Gate) Memorial, Panel 21. Joined BEF: not on Medal Card. Formerly 2779, Dorsetshire Regiment.

Pte. George Harvey 17881 KIA
born: Holloway, London   enlisted: Holloway
Buried: Ypres Town Cemetery Extension. Grave II.G.16. Joined BEF: not on Medal Card.

L/Sgt. George Hendrie 20072 KIA
born: Westminster   enlisted: Finsbury
No known grave. Ypres (Menin Gate) Memorial, Panel 21. Age 31. Joined BEF: not on Medal Card. 1901 Census: merchant's clerk, stepson of William J. Mathieson, shipping clerk, and Maud Mathieson (mother), 55 Seventh Avenue, East Ham, Essex.

Pte. Charles Frederick Hubbard 52849 KIA
born: Canterbury, Kent   enlisted: Birmingham   residence: West Croydon
No known grave. Ypres (Menin Gate) Memorial, Panel 21. Age 24. Joined BEF: not on Medal Card. Son of George Hubbard, general blacksmith, and Charlotte M. Hubbard, 36 Grafton Road, Croydon, Kent. 1911 Census: drapery assistant, boarding at 107 Clarendon Street, Dover, Kent. CWGC: family address: Angel Hill, Stonham, Stowmarket, Suffolk.

Pte. Percy Hurrell 44096 KIA
born: Plympton   enlisted: Plymouth   residence: Plympton
No known grave. Ypres (Menin Gate) Memorial, Panel 21. Joined BEF: not on Medal Card.

Pte. Frederick Charles Jones 47597 KIA
born: Belbroughton Worcs.   enlisted: Bromsgrove
No known grave. Ypres (Menin Gate) Memorial, Panel 21. Age 20. Joined BEF: not on Medal Card. 1901 Census: son of Charles H. Jones, market gardener, and Agnes Jones, Bournheath, Bromsgrove, Worcestershire.

L/Cpl. John Robert Jordan 20382 KIA
born: London   enlisted: Cardiff   residence: Rhymney
No known grave. Ypres (Menin Gate) Memorial, Panel 21. Joined BEF: not on Medal Card.

Pte. Wilfred Keates 30795 KIA
born: Sherborne   enlisted: Sherborne
No known grave. Ypres (Menin Gate) Memorial, Panel 21. Age 24. Joined BEF: not on Medal Card. 1901 Census: son of William Keates, mason's labourer and Annie Keates, Newland, Sherborne, Dorset. 1911 Census: baker journeyman, son of William Keates, builder's labourer, and Annie Keates, Newland, Sherborne, Dorset. CWGC: son of the late William Keates and Annie Keates, of Sherborne, Dorset, husband of Eva H. Godsell (formerly Keates), 49 Vaughan Street, Pwllgwaun, Pontypridd, Glam.

Pte. William Kemp 30789 KIA
born: no record   enlisted: Bermondsey
No known grave. Ypres (Menin Gate) Memorial, Panel 21. Age 37. Joined BEF: not on Medal Card. Formerly 27026, Dorsetshire Regiment. CWGC: son of the late William George Kemp and Elizabeth Jane Kemp, husband of Florence Kemp, 16 Frean Street, Bermondsey, London.

Pte. Charles William Lawrence 204880 KIA
born: Lambeth, Surrey   enlisted: Bodmin   residence: Amesbury
No known grave. Ypres (Menin Gate) Memorial, Panel 21. Age 38. Joined BEF: not on Medal Card. 1911 Census: employed at Whitesmith (Balloon Factory, Government), visiting Henry Mortimer, Yew Tree Laundry, Salisbury Street, Amesbury, Wiltshire.

Pte. William Henry Martyn 203574 KIA
born: Plymouth   enlisted: Plymouth
No known grave. Ypres (Menin Gate) Memorial, Panel 21. Age 37. Joined BEF: not on Medal Card. Formerly 30473, Devonshire Regiment. 1911 Census: assisting in the family dairy business, son of Elizabeth Martyn, widow, dairy business, 23 Waterloo Street, Devonport, Plymouth. CWGC: brother of Miss K. Martyn (probably Catherine Amelia Martyn), 23 Waterloo Street, Devonport, Plymouth.

Cpl. Roy Alexander McMorran 20514 KIA
born: Torquay, Devon   enlisted: Torquay
No known grave. Ypres (Menin Gate) Memorial, Panel 21. Age 20. Joined BEF: not on Medal Card. 1901 Census: son of William McMorran and Caroline McMorran, Tormoham, Torquay, Devon. 1911 Census: schoolboy, son of William McMorran, carriage proprietor, and Caroline McMorran, 2 Megla Villas, Torquay, Devon. CWGC: family address: 'Alderbury', Warberry Road West, Torquay, Devon.

Pte. John Middleton 26333 KIA
born: Wastfield, Devon   enlisted: Newbury   residence: Beenham
No known grave. Ypres (Menin Gate) Memorial, Panel 21. Age 34. Joined BEF: not on Medal Card. 1911 Census: servant, stock man on the farm of John Copp, Gogwell Farm, Tiverton, Devon. CWGC: son of E. Middleton, Middle Hill Farm, Knowstone, Barnstaple, Devon.

Pte. Frederick Charles Miller 15698 KIA
born: Highweek, Devon   enlisted: Newton Abbot
No known grave. Ypres (Menin Gate) Memorial, Panel 21. Age 31. Joined BEF: not on Medal Card. 1911 Census: shop assistant ironmonger, son of Frank Miller, draper's warehouseman, and Mary Jane Miller, 51 Emmanuel Road, St. Thomas, Exeter, Devon.

Pte. William Thomas Monday 3/6888 KIA
born: Yarmouth I.O.W.   enlisted: Stratford Essex
No known grave. Ypres (Menin Gate) Memorial, Panel 21. Age 21. Born Dec. 1895. Joined BEF: 24/03/15. 1901 Census: names him Thomas Monday, son of William Thomas Monday, police constable, and Annie Monday, 14 Chesterton Terrace, West Ham, London. CWGC: family address: 29 Abbey Road, West Ham, London.

Cpl. William Newcombe 8912 KIA
born: Exmouth   enlisted: Exeter   residence: Exmouth
No known grave. Ypres (Menin Gate) Memorial, Panel 21. Age 29. Joined BEF: 06/11/14 with original cadre. CWGC: son of Mrs. Ellen Pengilley, 47 Roseberry Road, Exmouth, Devon.

Pte. Walter Henry Palmer 45962 KIA
born: Bridgwater   enlisted: Taunton
No known grave. Ypres (Menin Gate) Memorial, Panel 21. Age 34. Joined BEF: not on Medal Card. 1901 Census: bricklayer's labourer, son of Walter Palmer, bricklayer's labourer, and Susan Palmer, Mount, Bridgwater, Somerset. 1911 Census: farm labourer, husband of Christinna Palmer, 13 Mount Terrace, Bridgwater, Somerset. CWGC: family address: "Horsepond," Friarn Street, Bridgwater, husband of Christina Louisa Caller (formerly Palmer), Chilton Trinity, Bridgwater, Somerset.

Pte. John Perry 30786 KIA
born: Lyme Regis   enlisted: Dorchester   residence: Lyme Regis
No known grave. Ypres (Menin Gate) Memorial, Panel 21. Age probably 40. Joined BEF: not on Medal Card. Formerly 18752, Dorsetshire Regiment. 1881 Census: son of William Perry, mariner, Mill Green, Lyme Regis, Dorset. 1901 Census: coachbuilder's labourer, husband of Bessie Perry, Midford, Dorset. 1911 Census: employed in 'net dying and farring', husband of Bessie Perry, twine net maker, South Street, Bridport, Dorset.

Pte. Cyril Ernest Prynn 44099 KIA
born: East Looe, Cornwall   enlisted: Plymouth
No known grave. Ypres (Menin Gate) Memorial, Panel 21. Age 32. Joined BEF: not on Medal Card. 1891 Census: son of Robert Prynn, fish merchant, and Eliza Ann Prynn, Fore Street, East Looe, Cornwall. 1901 Census: fish curer, living with his parents, Shutta Lane, East Looe. 1911 Census: 'stoker in fat factory', at home of brother, John Rundle Prynn, manufacturer's agent, and Margaret Jane Prynn, 2 St. Andrew's Place, Plymouth, Devon.

Pte. George Sharratt 23885 KIA
born: no record   enlisted: Coventry
Buried: Tyne Cot Cemetery, nr. Ypres. Grave XXVI.H.23. Age 22. Joined BEF: not on Medal Card. 1911 Census: grocer's assistant, son of Arthur Sharratt, horse keeper, and Annie Sharratt, 100 Radford Road, Coventry, Warwickshire. CWGC: son of Mrs. Annie Agnes Sharratt, 8 Court, 2 House, New Buildings, Coventry, Warwickshire.

Pte. Mia Smith 47713 KIA
born: Hill Croome, Worcs.   enlisted: Worcester
No known grave. Ypres (Menin Gate) Memorial, Panel 21. Age 32. Joined BEF: not on Medal Card. 1891 Census: son of Frederick Smith, general labourer, and Ann Smith, Baughton Hill, Hill Croome, Worcestershire. 1911 Census: farm labourer, son of Frederick Smith, farm labourer, and Anna Smith, Baughton Hill, Earls Croome, Worcestershire.

Pte. Alfred Samuel Tapscott 30541 KIA
born: Exeter   enlisted: Exeter
No known grave. Ypres (Menin Gate) Memorial, Panel 21. Age 20. 'C' Company. Joined BEF: not on Medal Card. 1901 Census: son of Edward Thomas Tapscott, tradesman's porter, and Ada Jane Tapscott, 7 Richmond Place, Exeter, Devon. 1911 Census: schoolboy, son of Ada Jane Tapscott, widow, 'sextoness', 7 Richmond Place, Paul Street, Exeter, Devon. CWGC: son of Mrs. Ada Jane Tapscott, 16 Pancras Lane, Paul Street, Exeter.

Sgt. James Albert Vernon 8317 KIA
born: Plymouth   enlisted: Plymouth
No known grave. Ypres (Menin Gate) Memorial, Panel 21. Age 28. Joined BEF: 06/11/14 with

original cadre. 1911 Census: 2/Devons, St. George's Barracks, Malta. CWGC: son of the late Mr. and Mrs. Walter Vernon, husband of Mrs. T. Gilbert (formerly Vernon), 4 Ashley Place, North Road, Plymouth.

Pte. Alfred White 30791 KIA
born: Church Knowle, Dorset   enlisted: Poole   residence: Parkstone
Buried: Tyne Cot Cemetery, nr. Ypres. Grave XLV.B.16. Age 38. Joined BEF: not on Medal Card. Formerly 27195, Dorsetshire Regiment. 1891 Census: son of William White, labourer, and Maria White, Ashley Road, Kinson, Dorset. 1911 Census: dairyman, milk vendor, husband of Annie White, Westwick, Upper Road, Parkstone, Dorset. CWGC: husband of Annie Harriett White, "Hill Croft," Bournemouth Road, Parkstone, Dorset.

Pte. Frederick Charles Willey 5013 KIA
born: Axminster   enlisted: Honiton   residence: Axminster
No known grave. Ypres (Menin Gate) Memorial, Panel 21. Age 25. Joined BEF: 06/11/14 with original cadre. 1911 Census: cook, son of Thomas Willey, gardener domestic, Hambridge, Taunton, Somerset.

Pte. Edwin Woolfries 30843 KIA
born: no record   enlisted: Portsea, Hants
No known grave. Ypres (Menin Gate) Memorial, Panel 21. Age 26. Joined BEF: not on Medal Card. 1911 Census: inmate at H.M. Prison, Longport Street, Canterbury, Kent, formerly employed as a 'general hawker'. CWGC: son of Mr. and Mrs. E. Woolfries, 4 Prosperous Street, Poole, Dorset.

Pte. William James Wright 27954 KIA
born: Worcester   enlisted: Worcester
No known grave. Ypres (Menin Gate) Memorial, Panel 21. Joined BEF: not on Medal Card. CWGC: husband of Edith Mabel Merchant (formerly Wright), Back Field, New Street, Upton-on-Severn, Worcester.

Martin Body

AUGUST 1917

1st August 1917
2/Lt. Arthur Martin Taylor KIA
No known grave. Ypres (Menin Gate) Memorial, Panel 21. Age 23.
No Medal Card. 1911 Census: son of Martin Church Taylor, congregational minister, and Sarah Hester Taylor, Daisy Bank, Egerton Road, Whitefield, nr. Manchester, Lancashire. CWGC: son of the Rev. Martin C. Taylor and Sarah H. Taylor, 9 Westminster Terrace, Douglas, Isle of Man.

Pte. Albert Conway 16347 KIA
born: Whimple, Devon   enlisted: Christow, Devon
No known grave. Ypres (Menin Gate) Memorial, Panel 21. Age 20. Joined BEF: 31/12/15. 1901 Census: son of Charles Conway, serving in Army in South Africa, and Emily Conway, Green, Whimple, Devon. 1911 Census: 'yard boy', son of Charles Conway, farm labourer, and Emily Conway, Stevens Cottages, Days Lane, Exminster, Devon. CWGC: family address: 9 Cross View, Alphington, Exeter.

Pte. Charles Thomas Harris 33182 KIA
born: Topsham   enlisted: Exeter   residence: Topsham
No known grave. Ypres (Menin Gate) Memorial, Panel 21. Age 21. Joined BEF: not on Medal Card. Formerly 777, Devonshire Regiment. 1911 Census: servant, 'cowboy', on the farm of Robert Pyne, Shepherd's Farm, Clyst St. Mary, Exeter, Devon.

Pte. William Ings 30798 KIA
born: Fordingbridge   enlisted: Dorchester   residence: Poole
Buried: Tyne Cot Cemetery, nr. Ypres. Grave XLIV.A.38. Age 22. Joined BEF: not on Medal Card. Formerly 27438, Dorsetshire Regiment. 1911 Census: dairyman, son of Alfred Ings, carter on farm, and Jane Ings, Old Wareham Road, Longfleet, Poole Dorset. CWGC: son of Alfred Ings and Jane Ings, 5 Oakdale, Longfleet, Poole, Dorset.

Pte. Frank Saddler 203419 KIA
born: no record   enlisted: Birmingham
No Medal Card found or Census records identified.

L/Cpl. Joseph Charles Sando 204874 KIA
born: Redruth   enlisted: Redruth
Buried: Tyne Cot Cemetery, nr. Ypres. Grave XLIV.A.38. Age 23. Joined BEF: not on Medal Card. Formerly 202192, Duke of Cornwall's Light Infantry. 1901 Census: son of Joseph Sando, wall maker, and Elizabeth Grace Sando, Channel View Terrace, Redruth, Cornwall. 1911 Census: stone mason, son of Joseph Sando, stone mason, and Elizabeth Grace Sando, 3 Channel View Terrace, Redruth, Cornwall. CWGC: family address: Higher Raymond Road, Redruth, Cornwall.

Pte. Charles Toms 30811 KIA
born: Exeter   enlisted: Exeter
Buried: Tyne Cot Cemetery, nr. Ypres. Grave XLIV.A.38. Age 32. Formerly 24220, Dorsetshire Regiment. Joined BEF: not on Medal Card. 1911 Census: 'maltster's labourer', husband of Lilian Toms, cigar maker, 14 Chamberlain Road, Willeys Avenue, St. Thomas, Exeter, Devon. CWGC: husband of Mrs. L. Toms, 59 Clifton Road, Newtown, Exeter.

Pte. James Treays 44126 KIA
born: Plymouth   enlisted: Plymouth
Buried: Tyne Cot Cemetery, nr. Ypres. Grave XLIV.A.38. Age 30. Joined BEF: not on Medal Card. 1911 Census: general labourer, son of Samuel Treays, general labourer, and Mary Treays, 8 Rodney Street, St. Budeaux, Devonport, Devon.

Pte. Ralph Washington Williams 16949 KIA
born: Plymouth   enlisted: Plymouth
Buried: Tyne Cot Cemetery, nr. Ypres. Grave XLIV.A.38. Age 26. Joined BEF: not on Medal Card. 1901 Census: son of Thomas Williams, foreman limestone quarry and Justice of the Peace, and Emma Jane Williams, 37 Mainstone Terrace, Plymouth, Devon. 1911 Census: carpenter, son of Thomas Williams, 'disabled by blasting at quarries', and Emma Jane Williams, 31 Staddon View Terrace, Pomphlett, Plymouth. CWGC: family address: 31 Staddon View Terrace, Pomphlett, Plymouth.

A/Cpl. Alfred Samuel Crimp 20523 DoW
born: Kingsbridge   enlisted: Plymouth
Buried: Ljissenthoek Military Cemetery. Grave XVI.J.8A. Age 21. Joined BEF: not on Medal Card. 1901 Census: son of Jane Crimp (widow), 37 Northumberland Street, Devonport, Devon. 1911 Census: errand boy, stepson Albert E. Taylor, Seaman Petty Officer 1st Class, and son of Jane Taylor nee Crimp, 83 Duke Street, Devonport, Devon. CWGC: son of Jane Taylor (formerly Crimp), Kingsbridge, Devon, and the late William John Crimp.

2nd August 1917
Pte. Harry Neve 45536 DoW
born: Hemblington, Norfolk   enlisted: Alton, Hants.
Buried: Mendinghem Military Cemetery. Grave III.E.22. Age 41. Joined BEF: not on Medal Card. 1891 Census: gamekeeper, son of George Neve, gamekeeper, and Mary Ann Neve, Pedham, Ranworth, Norfolk. 1901 Census: gamekeeper at New Foundout Farm, Horsham, Sussex. CWGC: husband of Emily E. Neve, Burkham Lodge, Alton, Hants.

3rd August 1917
Pte. Arthur Samuel Charles Ashton 17166 DoW
born: Plymouth   enlisted: Devonport
Buried: The Huts cemetery, West-Vlaanderen, Ypres. Grave I.C.2. Age 26. Joined BEF: not on Medal Card. 'D' Company. 1901 Census: son of William Ashton, stock cutter woollen goods, and Ellen Ashton, 7 Baring Street, Plymouth, Devon. 1911 Census: 'clerk in coachbuilder's office', son of William Ashton, cutter in clothing factory, and Ellen Ashton, 22 Prospect Street, Plymouth, Devon. CWGC: names him Arthur Samuel Jewett Ashton, son of W. and E. Ashton, of Plymouth, husband of Elizabeth Mary Manley (formerly Ashton), 162 Swanwick Avenue, Toronto, Canada.

4th August 1917
L/Cpl. John Richard Gilpin 26684 DoW
born: Hastings   enlisted: Plymouth
Buried: Mendinghem Military Cemetery. Grave III.B.38. Age 36. Joined BEF: not on Medal Card. 1901 Census: general labourer, son of Francis H. Gilpin, general labourer, and Esther A. Gilpin, Kellys Cottages, Plymstock, Devon.

Pte. Samuel Williams 3/6821 DoW
born: Wiveliscombe   enlisted: Exeter
Buried: Brandhoek New Military Cemetery. Grave IV.D.10. Joined BEF: 17/02/15, 1/Devons.

5th August 1917
L/Cpl. Frederick Perkin 9068 DoW
born: Tavistock   enlisted: Exeter   residence: Tavistock
Buried: Brandhoek New Military Cemetery. Grave VI.E.11. Age 29. Joined BEF: 06/11/14 with original cadre. 1901 Census: son of James Perkin, railway platelayer, and Emma J. Perkin, 4 Madge Hill, Tavistock, Devon. CWGC: son of Mrs. E. Perkin, I Vigo Bridge Road, Tavistock, Devon.

6th August 1917
Pte. Horace Tomkins 47702 DoW
born: Bretforton, Worcs.   enlisted: Evesham
Buried: Etaples Military Cemetery. Grave XXV.L.5A. Age 36. Joined BEF: not on Medal Card. 1911 Census: metal stamper, husband of Rose Tomkins, father of one, 28 Brantley Road, Witton, Birmingham, Worcestershire. CWGC: son of Frederick Tomkins and Eliza Tomkins, Lower End, Bretforton, Honeybourne, Worcestershire.

7th August 1917
Sgt. Ernest Edwin Drewe 3/7772 DoW
born: Exeter   enlisted: Stoke-On-Trent
Buried: Boulogne Eastern Cemetery. Grave IV.C.53. Age 38. Joined BEF: not on Medal Card. 1911 Census: 'labourer of gas works', husband of Harriett Drewe, father of two, 14 Toby's Buildings, Lower Street, Exeter, Devon.

10th August 1917
A/Cpl. John Henry Harris 9219 KIA
born: Exeter   enlisted: Exeter
No known grave. Ypres (Menin Gate) Memorial, Panel 21. Age 24. Joined BEF: 04/01/15. Annotation to Medal Card: *Reverted for misconduct* (to L/Cpl. from Cpl.).1901 Census: son of George Harris, bricklayer's labourer, and Eliza Jane Harris, 12a King Street, Exeter, Devon. 1911 Census: 2/Devons, St. George's Barracks, Malta. CWGC: family address: 4 Ewings Lane, West Street, Exeter.
Pte. Alfred C. H. Manning 15274 KIA
born: Torquay   enlisted: Exeter   residence: Torquay
No known grave. Ypres (Menin Gate) Memorial, Panel 21. Age 19. Joined BEF: 18/05/15. 1911 Census: schoolboy, son of John Henry Manning, coal waggoner, and Edith Manning, 16 Laburnam Street, Torquay, Devon. CWGC: son of John Henry Manning and Edith Emily Manning, 16 Laburnum Street, Torre, Torquay.
Pte. Frank Stentiford 15494 KIA
born: Morchard Bishop   enlisted: Exeter   residence: Crediton
No known grave. Ypres (Menin Gate) Memorial, Panel 21. Age 27. Joined BEF: 25/05/15. 1901 Census: son of James Stentiford, agricultural labourer, and Lucy Stentiford, of Wood End, Morchard Bishop, Devon. 1911 Census: farm labourer, living with his sister, Annie Stentiford, house keeper, The Village, Morchard Bishop, Devon. CWGC: family address: Fore Street, Morchard Bishop, Devon. Husband of Florence Stentiford, 8 Stanbury Place, High Street, Crediton, Devon.
Pte. John Thomas Sampson 20944 DoW
born: Penally, Pembrokeshire   enlisted: Exeter
Buried: Boulogne Eastern Cemetery. Grave VIII.I.1. Age 20. 'C' Company. Joined BEF: not on

Medal Card. 1901 Census: son of John Sampson, Sergeant Infantry, and Alice Beatrice Sampson, Town Barracks, Exeter, Devon. CWGC: family address: 23 St. Sidwells Avenue, Exeter.

11th August 1917
2/Lt. Harold Vaughan Iremonger Watts Attached from 7th (Cyclist) Battalion. DoW
Formerly with Devonshire Regiment Territorial Force. Buried: Mendinghem Military Cemetery. Grave IV.B.35. Age 27. Joined BEF: 08/07/17. Medal Card records rank of Captain. 1901 Census: undergraduate at Oxford, guest student at the Royal Military College, Sandhurst, Berkshire. CWGC: son of Francis Watts and Edith Ursula Watts, of Newton Abbot, husband of Helen M. Watts, Chine House, Boscombe, Bournemouth. 2/Lt. Watts died of wounds suffered on 31st July 1917.
Pte. Fred Burgess 3/7063 DoW
born: London   enlisted: Exeter
Buried: Mont Huon Military Cemetery, Le Treport. Grave III.A.4B. Age 19. Joined BEF: 16/02/15.
Pte. George Frederick Kettlewell 11148 DoW
born: Holloway   enlisted: Marylebone   residence: Camberwell
Buried: Brandhoek New Military Cemetery. Grave V.B.10. Age 24. No Medal Card. 1901 Census: son of Thomas Kettlewell, carter/carrier, and Phoebe Kettlewell, 10 Sarsden Buildings, Marylebone, Middlesex. 1911 Census: clerk, son of Thomas Kettlewell, carman, and Phoebe Kettlewell, 6 Vestry Mews, Vestry Road, Camberwell, London. George Kettlewell must have stood in line with Charlie Yates, Fred Moody and the Ranelagh Rovers when he enlisted at Marylebone on 6th September 1914.

12th August 1917
L/Cpl. Thomas Henry Lodge 8529 DoW
born: Exeter   enlisted: Exeter
Buried: Mendinghem Military Cemetery. Grave IV.E.8. Age 28. Joined BEF: 06/11/14 with original cadre. 1891 Census: son of William Charles Lodge, shoring smith, and Gertrude Lodge, Shapter Street, Topsham, Devon. 1901 Census: son of William Charles Lodge, farrier/blacksmith, and Gertrude Lodge, 19 Rosebery Road, Elm Side, Exeter. 1911 Census: 2/Devons, St. George's Barracks, Malta.

13th August 1917
Pte. Frederick Nott 16191 DoW
Born: no record   enlisted: no record   residence: Barnstaple, Devon
Buried: Calais Southern Cemetery. Grave: Plot H, Row 2, Grave 10. Age 29. Joined BEF: 09/12/15. CWGC: son of Thomas and Mary Ann Nott, 41, Aze Lane, Barnstaple, Devon.

14th August 1917
Pte. John Henry Fishlock 5578 KIA
born: Pewsey, Wiltshire   enlisted: Swindon   residence: Highworth, Wilts.
Buried: Bedford House Cemetery, Ypres. Grave: Enclosure No.4. IV.F.1. Age 25. Formerly 34603, Dorsetshire Regiment. Joined BEF: not on Medal Card. 1901 Census: son of William Fishlock, carter on farm, and Sarah Fishlock, Cripps Field Cottage, Pewsey, Wiltshire. 1911 Census: 'under carter on farm', son of William Fishlock, carter on farm, and Sarah Fishlock, Lower Upham, Aldbourne, Wiltshire.

Pte. Joseph Sanders 30784 KIA
born: Winterslow, Wiltshire   enlisted: Winchester
No known grave. Ypres (Menin Gate) Memorial, Panel 21. Age 24. Joined BEF: not on Medal Card. Formerly 18604, Dorsetshire Regiment. CWGC: son of Sydney Sanders and Emma Sanders, South Wanston Downs, Sutton Scotney, Hampshire, husband of Sarah Ann Jane Langstone (formerly Sanders), 17 South Road, Horsell, Woking, Surrey.

Pte. John James Knapman 19021 DoW
born: Bow, Devon   enlisted: Exeter   residence: Exminster
Buried: Ljissenthoek Military Cemetery. Grave XVII.F.17. Age 29. Joined BEF: not on Medal Card. 1891 Census: son of John Knapman, agricultural labourer, and Jane Knapman, Wood House, Spreyton, Devon. 1911 Census: watch repairer, son of Jane Knapman, widow, Badlake Cottage, Badlake Hill, Newton Abbot, Devon.

15th August 1917
2/Lt. Harold Henry Goodman KIA
Attached from 3rd Battalion. No known grave. Tyne Cot Memorial, Panel 38 to 40. Age 27. CWGC records rank of Captain. Joined BEF: not on Medal Card. Formerly Private 4886, 20th Royal Fusiliers. 1901 Census: son of Mr. Albert V. Goodman, grocer's assistant, and Bessie Goodman, 26 West Bridge Cottages, Tavistock, Devon. 1911 Census: student, visiting Arthur Smith Graham, Ambrook House, Ipplepen, nr Totnes, Devon.

Sgt. Robert John Algate 8282 KIA
born: Plymouth   enlisted: Devonport
No known grave. Tyne Cot Memorial, Panel 38 to 40. Age 28. Joined BEF: 07/11/14 with original cadre. 1911 Census: 2/Devons, St. George's Barracks, Malta. CWGC: husband of Laura Victoria Salter (formerly Algate), 61 Barton Avenue, Keyham, Devonport, Devon.

Pte. Frederick Charles Batten 203255 KIA
born: Shute, Devon   enlisted: Axminster   residence: Honiton
No known grave. Tyne Cot Memorial, Panel 38 to 40. Age 22. Joined BEF: not on Medal Card. 1911 Census: 'farmer's son working on farm', son of Samuel Batten, farmer, and Sarah Batten, Aplins farm, Monkton, nr. Honiton, Devon.

Pte. Sidney Blight 14295 KIA
born: Torrington   enlisted: Bargoed, Glam.   residence: Shebbear
No known grave. Tyne Cot Memorial, Panel 38 to 40. Age 33. Joined BEF: 24/03/15. 1901 Census: groom (not domestic), son of Richard Blight, farm labourer, and Fanny Blight, Shebbear Village, Devon.

Pte. Walter Charles Butler 26466 KIA
born: Exeter   enlisted: Exeter
No known grave. Tyne Cot Memorial, Panel 38 to 40. Age 36. Joined BEF: not on Medal Card. 1901 Census: town postman, son of John Butler, town postman, and Ellen Butler, 7 North Tower, Exeter, Devon. 1911 Census: postman, son of Ellen Butler, widow, 49 Bonhay Road, Exeter, Devon.

Pte. Albert William Cose 25859 KIA
born: Holsworthy   enlisted: Exeter
No known grave. Tyne Cot Memorial, Panel 38 to 40. Age 38. Joined BEF: not on Medal Card. 1911 Census: engine shed labourer, husband of Ellen Cose and father of five children, 8 Turks Head Court, Cowick Street, St. Thomas, Exeter.

Cpl. William Charles Couling 6737 KIA
born: Oxford   enlisted: Devonport
No known grave. Tyne Cot Memorial, Panel 38 to 40. Age 33. Joined BEF: 05/11/14 with original cadre. 1911 Census: 2/Devons, St. Georges Barracks, Malta.
Pte. Maurice Harry Davis 203373 KIA
born: Stoke Fleming, Devon   enlisted: Newton Abbot   residence: Woodbury
No known grave. Tyne Cot Memorial, Panel 38 to 40. Age 25. Joined BEF: not on Medal Card. 1911 Census: working at farm, son of Richard Hinley Truby Davis, farmer, and Sophia Emily Davis, Strete, Dartmouth, Devon. CWGC: son of Mrs S. E. Davis, "California," Modbury, Devon, and the late Mr. R. H. Davis.
Pte. Alfred Edwin Evans 30771 KIA
born: Birmingham   enlisted: Birmingham
No known grave. Tyne Cot Memorial, Panel 38 to 40. Age 19. Joined BEF: not recorded on Medal Card. Formerly 27952, Duke of Cornwall's Light Infantry. 1901 Census: son of Henry J. Evans, baker, and Elizabeth Annie Evans, 43 Garrison Lane, Aston, Birmingham, Warwickshire. 1911 Census: son of Henry James Evans, retired baker, and Eliza Evans, 171 Coventry Road, Aston, Birmingham, Warwickshire. CWGC: records the family address as 145 Tame Road, Witton, Birmingham.
Pte. Frank Burnett Hall 30845 KIA
born: Mempnett, Somerset   enlisted: Chewstoke, Somerset
No known grave. Tyne Cot Memorial, Panel 38 to 40. Age 23. Joined BEF: not on Medal Card. Formerly 26248, Somerset Light Infantry. 1901 Census: son of Francis Hall, carpenter/joiner, and Frances Hall, 3 Blenheim Terrace, Minehead, Somerset.
Pte. John Abner Oliver 26019 KIA
born: no record   enlisted: Trowbridge
No known grave. Tyne Cot Memorial, Panel 38 to 40. Joined BEF: not on Medal Card.
Pte. Frederick John Pitt 45122 KIA
born: Barton-St-David, Som.   enlisted: Castle Cary   residence: Barton-St-David
Buried: Buttes New British Cemetery, Polygon Wood. Grave XXIX.A.8. Age 22. Joined BEF: not on Medal Card. 1901 Census: eldest son of William Henry Pitt, stone quarry man, and Martha Pitt, Chislett's Garden, Barton St. David, Taunton, Somerset. 1911 Census: ironmonger's porter, boarding at the house of Susan George, 14 Benedict Street, Glastonbury, Somerset.
Pte. John Smale MM 30813 KIA
born: Torrington   enlisted: Barnstaple   residence: Torrington
No known grave. Tyne Cot Memorial, Panel 38 to 40. Age 31. Joined BEF: not on Medal Card. Formerly 24305, Devonshire Regiment. 1891 Census: son of Richard Smale, agricultural labourer, and Mary Ann Smale, Blagadon, Coombe Cross, Torrington. 1901 Census: servant/cattle lad, Maggadon, Huntshaw, Devon. 1911 Census: 'waggoner laundry', lodging at the home of John Ley, Abbotsham, Devon. CWGC: husband of Mary Jane Smale, 99 New Street, Great Torrington, Devon.
Pte. Ernest Frederick Thorne 25876 KIA
born: Exeter   enlisted: Exeter
No known grave. Tyne Cot Memorial, Panel 38 to 40. Joined BEF: not on Medal Card.
Pte. Edward Albert Warfield 205161 KIA
born: London   enlisted: Barnstaple
No known grave. Tyne Cot Memorial, Panel 38 to 40. Age 31. Joined BEF: not on Medal Card. 1901 Census: son of Edward Warfield, publican, and Annie Warfield, of the William IV pub, Harrow Road, Willesden, Middlesex. 1911 Census: licensed victualler, husband of Phyllis May

Warfield, The Hoops Inn, Horns Cross, Parkham, Devon. CWGC: son of the late Edward Warfield, of Kensal Green, London, and husband of Phyllis May Warfield, George Hotel, Odiham, Hants.

Pte. Archibald Walter Webber 205164 KIA
born: Ashreigney, Devon   enlisted: Barnstaple   residence: Burrington
No known grave. Tyne Cot Memorial, Panel 38 to 40. Age 23. Joined BEF: not on Medal Card. 1901 Census: son of John Webber, farmer and Lydia Webber, Winswood Faran, Burrington, Umberleigh, Devon.

Pte. Arthur Winn 290394 KIA
born: Helston   enlisted: Helston
No known grave. Tyne Cot Memorial, Panel 38 to 40. Age 22. Joined BEF: not on Medal Card. 1901 Census: son of William John Winn, wheelwright, and Kate Winn, near Almshouses Hill, Helston, Cornwall. 1911 Census: outfitter's assistant, son of W.J. Winn, wheelwright, and Kate Winn, Gwealhellis, Wendron, Helston, Cornwall.

2/Lt. Wilfred Wallace Drake DoW
Buried: Brandhoek New Military Cemetery No.3. Grave I.A.12. Age 34. Joined BEF: 22/07/16. Attached to 23rd Brigade Trench Mortar Battery. 1901 Census: pupil/teacher at boarding school, son of William Drake, baker, and Louise M. Drake, High Street, Stalham, Norfolk. 1911 Census: certificated teacher, boarder: 13 Waylen Street, Reading, Berkshire. CWGC: husband of Gladys Drake, Reading, Berks.

Pte. Harry Gray 30809 DoW
born: Shaftesbury   enlisted: Shaftesbury
Buried: Ljissenthoek Military Cemetery. Grave XVII.AA.12A. Age 19. Joined BEF: not on Medal Card. Formerly 18971, Devonshire Regiment. 1901 Census: son of John Gray, coal carrier, and Lynda Louisa Gray, Brickhill, Motcombe, Shaftesbury, Dorset. CWGC: family address, St. John's Hill, Shaftesbury, Dorset.

Sgt. Albert William Hebdon 15097 DoW
born: London   enlisted: Mill Hill
Buried: Brandhoek New Military Cemetery. I.AA.11. Age 20. 'D' Company. Joined BEF: 18/05/15. 1911 Census: leather trunk maker, son of Albert Hebdon, chairmaker, and Ada Hebdon, 9d Broad Street, Station Dwellings, Finsbury, London. CWGC: son of Albert Hebdon and Ada Hebdon, Finsbury, London.

Pte. Arthur George Shelley 204882 DoW
born: Exbury, Hants.   enlisted: Brockenhurst   residence: Fawley, Hants.
CWGC does not list a grave or memorial reference for this man. Age 41. Joined BEF: not on Medal Card. 1891 Census: agricultural labourer, son of Joseph Shelley, agricultural labourer, and Jane Shelley, Cottage No 2, Exbury Village, Hampshire. 1901 Census: coachman/domestic, husband of Ethel Shelley, Solent Cottages, Exbury, Hampshire. 1911 Census: 'coachman at present', husband of Ethel Shelley, 'out of a situation', King's Copse, Fawley, Hampshire.

16th August 1917
Pte. Walter Radford 30865 KIA
Born: Cheddington, Dorset.   enlisted: Charlton, Somerset.   Residence: Ilminster
No known grave. Tyne Cot Memorial, panel 38 to 40. Age 23. Joined BEF: not on Medal Card. 1901 Census: son of John Radford, shepherd on farm, and Hannah Radford, of Charleton Horethorne, Dorset. 1911 Census: farm hand/horseman, living with parents at Charleton Horethorne.

17th August 1917
2/Lt. Alexander Conrad Cuthbertson Pendrigh Attached from 6th Devons (Territorials). DoW Buried: St. Sever Cemetery, Rouen. Grave: Officers, B.10.3. Age 19. (DoW sustained 31st July 1917). 'B' Company. Joined BEF: not on Medal Card. Formerly Private 7113, Inns of Court O.T.C. Commissioned 2/Lt. in the Devonshire Regiment T.F. (Territorial Force). Son of David Croll Pendrigh and Valentine Marie Wilhelmine Pendrigh, nee Weissenborn, 1 Fell Road, Croydon, Surrey. Educated at Whitgift Grammar School, Croydon, where he was distinguished as a scholar and athlete. Volunteered for service in 1915. 1911 Census: schoolboy, son of David Croll Pendrigh, editor, and Valentine Marie Wilhelmine Pendrigh, 5 The Waldrons, Croydon, Surrey. Valentine Pendrigh was a native of Cassell, Germany.
A/Cpl. Frederick William Harris 8520 DoW
born: Bideford   enlisted: Exeter   residence: Bideford
Buried: Mendinghem Military Cemetery. Grave III.F.5. Age 27. Joined BEF: 06/11/14 with original cadre. 1911 Census: 2/Devons, St. George's Barracks, Malta.
Pte. John Thomas Pickett 51556 DoW
born: Chatham, Kent   enlisted: Birmingham
Buried: Menin Road South Military Cemetery. II.E.28. Age 21. Joined BEF: not on Medal Card. 1901 Census: son of John Pickett, bricklayer's labourer, and Amy Pickett, Gipsy Encampment, Lower Chatham, Kent.

18th August 1917
Pte. James Ewings 38032 DoW
born: Cruwys Morchard   enlisted: Exeter   residence: Rewe, Devon
Buried: Brandhoek New Military Cemetery No.3. Grave II.G.1. Age 19. Joined BEF: not on Medal Card. 1901 Census: son of John Ewings, carter on farm, and Mary Jane Ewings, Eastland, Cruwys Morchard, Devon. 1911 Census: schoolboy, son of John Ewings, road contractor, and Mary Jane Ewings, Sunday School, Cruwys Morchard, nr. Tiverton, Devon. CWGC: family address: Heazille Cottage, Rewe, Exeter.

27th August 1917
Pte. Albert George Campbell 203380 DoW (home)
born: Plymouth   enlisted: Plymouth
Buried: Ford Park Cemetery (Formerly Plymouth Old Cemetery) (Pennycomequick). Grave: General F.14.24. Age 19. Joined BEF: not on Medal Card, but gives name as Allen G. Campbell. 1901 Census: son of Elizabeth Campbell, 23 Tollox Place, Laira, Plymouth. 1911 Census: schoolboy, son of Elizabeth Campbell, widow, 23 Tollox Place, Laira, Plymouth, Devon.

Martin Body

SEPTEMBER 1917

1st September 1917
Pte. Edwin Henry Goddard 204886 DoW (home)
born: Weymouth   enlisted: Weymouth
Buried: Portsmouth (Eastney or Highland Road) Cemetery. Grave H.6.14. Age 18. Joined BEF: not on Medal Card. Formerly 20329, Dorsetshire Regiment. 1901 Census: son of Tom Goddard, Navy slaughterman, and Annie Goddard, 14 Wellington Place, Weymouth, Dorset.

2nd September 1917
Pte. Robert Mower 3/7050 KIA
born: Ipswich   enlisted: Exeter
Buried: Lancashire Cottage Cemetery, nr. Ploegsteert. Grave II.E.8. Joined BEF: 17/12/14 with the 8th Devons. CWGC: husband of Mrs. M. Mower, 2 Langford Cottages, Wonford, Exeter.

3rd September 1917
Pte. William George Bracher 30792 KIA
born: Henstridge   enlisted: Dorchester   residence: Gillingham, Dorset
Buried: Lancashire Cottage Cemetery, nr. Ploegsteert. Grave II.E.10. Age 29. Joined BEF: not on Medal card. Formerly 27584, Dorsetshire Regiment. 1891 Census: son of John Bracher, agent for the Singer Sewing Machine Company, and Sarah Bracher, 1 Court Ash Terrace, Yeovil, Somerset. CWGC: husband of Alice Mary Bracher, Tomlin's Lane, Gillingham, Dorset.
Sgt. Richard James Stephens 290118 KIA
born: no record   enlisted: Exeter
Buried: Lancashire Cottage Cemetery, nr. Ploegsteert. Grave II.E.9. Age 34. Joined BEF: not on Medal Card. 1911 Census: accountant, husband of Ellen Stephens, 43 Churchill Road, St. Thomas, Exeter, Devon. CWGC: husband of Ellen Stephens, 51 Churchill Road, St. Thomas, Exeter.

4th September 1917
A/Cpl. Henry Richard Collins DCM MM 8595 KIA
born: St.Ives, Cornwall   enlisted: Exeter   residence: Barnstaple
Buried: Lancashire Cottage Cemetery, nr. Ploegsteert. Grave II.E.12. Age 25. Joined BEF: 06/11/14 with original cadre. CWGC: son of Mary Jane Skerry (formerly Collins), 11 South Street, Barnstaple, Devon, and the late Henry Richard Collins.
A/Cpl. Collins' DCM citation reads as follows: *"For conspicuous gallantry and devotion to duty while in charge of a party carrying ammunition to the front line. His guide lost the way, and led the party into the enemy's lines, and they were immediately fired on by hostile machine guns. He immediately got his men under cover, and engaged the enemy himself with a Lewis gun, enabling the party to withdraw safely with all the stores. He then withdrew with the gun, and succeeded in handing over the stores to the unit, who were urgently in need of them. Throughout the operations he displayed exceptional courage, resource, and devotion to duty."*
Pte. Henry Shattock 46294 KIA
born: Bristol   enlisted: London   residence: Hoxton, Middx.
Buried: Lancashire Cottage Cemetery, nr. Ploegsteert. Grave II.E.11. Age 21. Joined BEF: 02/01/15 as 2300 of the Royal Fusiliers. 1911 Census: an errand boy, son of Henry Shattock, glazier, and Florence Shattock, 3 Smart's Buildings, Hoxton Street, Hoxton, London. CWGC: son of Mr. H. S. Shattock, 39 Ivy Street, Hoxton, London.

Pte. Charles James Page 3597 DoW
born: Gloucester   enlisted: Gloucester
Buried: Ljissenthoek Military Cemetery. Grave XVIII.F.19. Age 24. No Medal Card. 1901 Census: son of Charles James Page, baker, and Julia Anne Page, 22 Alvin Street, Gloucester. 1911 Census: baker, son of Charles James Page snr., baker and confectioner, and Julia Anne Page, 22 Alvin Street, Gloucester.

5th September 1917
Pte. Frank William John Betts 30904 KIA
born: Kennington, London   enlisted: Southwark   residence: Kennington
No known grave. Ploegsteert Memorial, Panel 3. Age 19. Joined BEF: not on Medal Card. Formerly 8/2450, Devonshire Regiment (Territorials). Son of Oliver Betts, foreman joiner, and Lucy Jane Betts, 5 Harmsworth Street, Newington, London.
Pte. Frederick Amos Brooking 290278 KIA
born: Diptford, Devon   enlisted: Totnes   residence: Diptford, Devon
No known grave. Ploegsteert Memorial, Panel 3. Age 22. Joined BEF: not on Medal Card. 1901 Census: son of James Brooking, worker on roads, and Harriett Brooking, Diptford, South Brent, Devon. 1911 Census: farm labourer, son of James Brooking, farm labourer, and Harriet Brooking, Diptford, South Brent, Devon.
Pte. Arthur Flower 23681 KIA
born: Bath   enlisted: Taunton   residence: Bath
No known grave. Ploegsteert Memorial, Panel 3. Age 30. Joined BEF: not on Medal Card. 1901 Census: son of Sampson Flower, mason, and Julia Flower, 1 Flowers Cottages, Bath, Somerset. 1911 CWGC: son of Mrs. Julia Flower, 3 Alma Cottages, Widcombe, Bath.
Pte. Frank Arthur Bridge 30895 DoW
born: Poplar, Middx.   enlisted: Poplar
Buried: Trois Arbres Cemetery, Steenwerck. Grave I.Y.16. Age 18. Joined BEF: not on Medal Card. Formerly 9/21308, 33 Training Reserve Battalion. 1901 Census: son of William Bridge, dock labourer, and Elizabeth Bridge, Junkin Street, Poplar, London. CWGC: family address: 239 Manchester Road, Cubitt Town, Poplar, London.

6th September 1917
Pte. James Dowding 30932 KIA
born: Christchurch   enlisted: Christchurch
Buried: Lancashire Cottage Cemetery, nr. Ploegsteert. Grave II.E.13. Age 19. Joined BEF: not on Medal Card. Formerly 8/4345, 206 Infantry Battalion. 1901 Census: son of Walter Dowding, garden labourer (domestic), and Jane Dowding, Nea Gardens, Highcliffe, Christchurch, Hants. 1911 Census: schoolboy, son of Walter James Dowding, gardener/domestic, and Jane Dowding, New Cottage, Christchurch, Hants.

9th September 1917
Pte. William Thomas Frawley 16890 DoW
born: Plymouth   enlisted: Plymouth
Buried: Wimereux Communal Cemetery. Grave VI.A.22. Age 25. Joined BEF: not on Medal Card. 1901 Census: son of Eliza Frawley, widow, clothes mangler/wash, 11 Woolster Street, Plymouth, Devon. 1911 Census: adopted son of William John Hooper, Naval Pensioner, and Annie Hooper, 6 Marine Place, Plymouth, Devon. CWGC: nephew of Mr. and Mrs. Hooper, 6 Marine Place, Coxside, Plymouth.

Pte. Benjamin James Paul 30824 DoW
born: St.Buryan, Cornwall   enlisted: Penzance
Buried: Wimereux Communal Cemetery. Grave VI.A.14A. Age 19. Joined BEF: not on Medal Card. Formerly 34881, Duke Of Cornwall's Light Infantry. 1911 Census: schoolboy, son of Annie Paul, married, 22 Alma Place, Penzance, Cornwall.

15th September 1917
Pte. Benjamin James Ridgway 31003 KIA
born: Old Cleeve, Somerset   enlisted: Minehead   residence: Washford
Buried: Motor Car Corner Cemetery, Comines-Warneton, Hainaut. Grave A.30. (In this sector, Motor Car Corner was the nearest point to the front line that military vehicles were allowed to travel). Age 19. Joined BEF: not on Medal Card. 1901 Census: son of James Ridgway, postman and gardener, and Ellen Ridgway, Washford, Old Cleeve, Somerset. 1911 Census: schoolboy, son of James Ridgway, jobbing gardener/auxiliary GPO postman, and Ellen Ridgway, Washford, Somerset.

16th September 1917
Pte. Thomas Jesse Sollars 25197 KIA
born: Painswick, Gloucs.   enlisted: Stroud
No known grave. Ploegsteert Memorial, Panel 3. Age 37.
Joined BEF: not on Medal Card. Annotation to Medal Card: *Death regarded.* 1901 Census: stone mason, son of Charles Sollars, stone mason, and Rose Sollars, Shepscombe Village, Painswick, Gloucestershire. 1911 Census: stone mason, husband of Emma Elizabeth Sollars, father of one, of Far Westrip, nr. Stroud, Gloucestershire. CWGC: son of Mrs. Charles Sollars, of Shepscombe, Stroud, husband of Emma Elizabeth Sollars, Far Westrip, Stroud, Glos.

26th September 1917
Pte. William Fishwick 30849 KIA
born: no record   enlisted: Chorley
Buried: Lancashire Cottage Cemetery, nr. Ploegsteert. Grave II.F.2. Age 20. Joined BEF: not on Medal Card. Formerly 21673, Royal Lancashire, Regiment. 1911 Census: 'dodger bleach works', son of Samuel Fishwick, general labourer, and Jane Fishwick, cotton weaver, 9 Jackson Street, Chorley, Lancashire. CWGC: son of Mr. S. Fishwick, 104 Bolton Street, Chorley, Lancs.
Pte. Harry Opie Thomas 290451 KIA
born: Lanteglos, Cornwall   enlisted: Fowey
Buried: Lancashire Cottage Cemetery, nr. Ploegsteert. Grave II.F.3. Joined BEF: not on Medal Card. CWGC: son of Mr. C. M. Thomas, 2 Victoria Terrace, Fowey, Cornwall.

30th September 1917
2/Lt. Victor Thomas James Rainey KIA
born: Apuldram, Sussex
Buried: Lancashire Cottage Cemetery, nr. Ploegsteert. Grave II.F.1. Age 19. Joined BEF: 20/06/17. 'B' Company. 1901 Census: son of William Rainey, R.I., artist (painter),and Harriet Matilda Rainey, Apuldram, West Sussex. 1911 Census: schoolboy, son of William Rainey, artist, and Harriet Matilda Rainey, Ecclesbourne, Grove Park, Chiswick, Middlesex. CWGC: family address: "Avonmore," Granville Road, Eastbourne.

The 2nd Devons War Diary

OCTOBER 1917

2nd October 1917
L/Cpl. Frank Coles 33199 KIA
born: Cullompton   enlisted: Cullompton
Buried: Pont-D'Achelles Military Cemetery, Nieppe. Grave II.E.5. Joined BEF: not on Medal Card. Formerly 864, Devonshire Regiment.
A/Sgt. George Arthur Moult 30510 KIA
born: Compstall, Cheshire   enlisted: Camborne   residence: Scorrier, Cornwall
Buried: Pont-D'Achelles Military Cemetery, Nieppe. Grave II.E.4. Age 25. Joined BEF: not on Medal Card. 1911 Census: clerk, son of Thomas Emanuel Moult, coachman/domestic, and Lucy Moult, 20 Avenue Road, West Bowling, Bradford, Yorkshire. CWGC: son of Thomas Emanuel Moult and Lucy Moult, 20 Avenue Road, West Bowling, Bradford, Yorkshire.
Pte. William Henry Andrews 17639 KIA
born: Croyde, Devon   enlisted: Exeter   residence: Georgeham
Buried: Pont-D'Achelles Military Cemetery, Nieppe. Grave II.E.7. Age 20. Joined BEF: not on Medal Card. 1901 Census: son of William Andrews, general labourer, and Martha Andrews, Croyde, Georgeham, Devon. CWGC: family address, Putsborough, Georgeham, Braunton, Devon.
Pte. Harold Aldrick Oates 30992 KIA
born: Birmingham   enlisted: Birmingham
Buried: Pont-D'Achelles Military Cemetery, Nieppe. Grave II.E.6. Age 19. Joined BEF: not on Medal Card. Formerly 8/2011, Devonshire Regiment. CWGC records him as the son of Frederick Oates and Mary Ann Oates, of "Springview," Mount Lane, Monkspath, Shirley, Birmingham.
Pte. Herbert Lawrence Prout 15483 DoW
born: Devonport   enlisted: Plymouth
Buried: Trois Arbres Cemetery, Steenwerck. Grave II.A.13. Age 23. Joined BEF: 18/05/15. 1911 Census: 'assisting in bake house', stepson of Christopher Clement Foster, general labourer, son of Ellen Foster, 25 Gibbon Street, Plymouth, Devon. CWGC: son of Ellen Foster (formerly Prout), 14 Gascoyne Place, Plymouth, and the late Abraham Prout.

22nd October 1917
Pte. Alexander Middleton 18001 DoW (Germany)
born: Banff N.B.   enlisted: Walthamstow
Buried: Hamburg Cemetery, Germany. Grave V.A.15. Joined BEF: not on Medal Card.

27th October 1917
Pte. John Henry Codrington 29258 KIA
born: Shirehampton   enlisted: Bristol
Buried: Lancashire Cottage Cemetery, nr. Ploegsteert. Grave III.A.1. Age 29. Joined BEF: not on Medal Card. 1901 Census: son of John N. Codrington, farmer and butcher, and Louisa Codrington, High Street, Shirehampton, Gloucestershire. 1911 Census: ship's clerk, son of J. Robert Codrington, butcher, and Louisa Codrington, 13 High Street, Shirehampton, Bristol, Gloucestershire. CWGC: son of Mrs. L. Codrington, Avonmere Cottage, Shirehampton, Bristol, Gloucestershire.

Pte. Reginald Alfred Freegard 30939 KIA
born: Sutton Benger, Wilts.   enlisted: Devizes
Buried: Lancashire Cottage Cemetery, nr. Ploegsteert. Grave III.V.3. Age 19. Joined BEF: not on Medal Card. Formerly 8/831, 206 Infantry Battalion. Named Freeguard on Medal Card. 1901 Census: son of William Freeguard, cattleman on farm, and Sophia Freeguard, Foxham, Chippenham, Wiltshire. 1911 Census: schoolboy, son of William Freegard, general farm labourer, and Sophia Freegard, Foxham, Chippenham, Wiltshire.

Pte. George Henry Ryder 16963 KIA
born: Totnes   enlisted: Plymouth
Buried: Lancashire Cottage Cemetery, nr. Ploegsteert. Grave III.A.2. Age 19. Joined BEF: not on Medal Card. 1901 Census: son of James Ryder, horseman on farm, and Phyllis Ryder, Higher Dunstone Farm, Yealmpton, Devon. CWGC: son of Phyllis Ryder, Mill Cottages, Lee Mill Bridge, Ivybridge, Devon, and the late James Ryder.

29th October 1917
A/Cpl. Christopher James Kerr 15639 KIA
born: Rochdale   enlisted: Rochdale   residence: Littleborough, Lancs.
No known grave. Tyne Cot Memorial, Panel 38 to 40. Age 26. Joined BEF: 07/07/15 with 1/Devons . 1901 Census: son of Hall Kerr, general engineer, and Hannah Kerr, 3 Pinfold Place, Rochdale, Lancashire. 1911 Census: weaver, cotton cloth, son of Hall Kerr, oiler and presser of machinery, and Hannah Kerr, 13 Caldebrook Terrace, Littleborough, Lancashire. CWGC: family address: 64 Summit, Littleborough, Manchester, Lancashire.

30th October 1917
Pte. Ben Broomfield 45527 KIA
born: Lymington   enlisted: Brockenhurst
Buried: Lancashire Cottage Cemetery, nr. Ploegsteert. Grave III.F.4. Age 31. Joined BEF: not on Medal Card. 1891 Census: son of George Broomfield, trainer, and Charlotte Broomfield, 13 Upper Woodside, Lymington, Hants.

Pte. Josiah Jefferies 48800 KIA
born: Bristol   enlisted: Bristol
No known grave. Ploegsteert Memorial, Panel 3. Age 20. Joined BEF: not on Medal Card but spells name 'Jeffries'. 1911 Census: schoolboy, son of Tom Jefferies, engineers fitter, and Jane Jefferies, 145 Robertson Road, Eastville, Bristol, Gloucestershire. CWGC: son of Tom and Jane Jefferies, 4 Bridge Street, Eastville, Bristol.

The 2nd Devons War Diary

NOVEMBER 1917

6th November 1917
L/Cpl. George Knott 30856 DoW
born: Rotherhithe, Kent   enlisted: Chatham, Kent   residence: Luton, Bedfordshire
Buried: Chatham Cemetery, Kent. Grave PP.208. Age 38. Joined BEF: 05/11/14 as 9975 with 1st Worcester Regiment. 1891 Census: son of William Knott, general labourer, and Margaret Knott, 77 Castle Road, Chatham, Kent. 1901 Census: blacksmith's hammerer, dockyard, 22 Sturla Road, Chatham. 1911 Census: 2/Worcester Regiment, Jhansi, India.

9th November 1917
Pte. Austen Stripp 290498 KIA
born: no record   enlisted: Exeter   residence: East Looe, Cornwall
No known grave. Ploegsteert Memorial, Panel 3. Age 26.
Joined BEF: not on Medal Card. 1901 Census: son of William Slade Stripp, grocer shopkeeper, widower, Fore Street, Bodmin, Cornwall. 1911 Census: draper's assistant, lodging with 6 other draper's assistants at the home of Clara Pyrome, housekeeper, 32 Fore Street, City of London. CWGC: husband of Florence Mavin (formerly Stripp), Belmont, East Looe, Cornwall.
An obituary from an unidentified local newspaper reads: *"STRIPP, AUSTEN, Private, No. 290498, 2nd Battn. (11th Foot) The Devonshire Regt., s. of William Slade Stripp, of East Looe, co. Cornwall, Stationer, by his wife, Sarah, dau. Of Thomas Channing; b. Bodmin, 19 Aug. 1891; educ. Harleigh House School there; was a Chemist's Assistant; enlisted 14 July, 1915; served with the Expeditionary Force in France and Flanders from July 1917; was reported missing after the fighting at Ploegsteert 9 Nov. following, and is now assumed to have been killed in action on that date. He m. at St. Martin's-by-Looe, co. Cornwall, 11 Nov 1915, Florence (Penharvon, Looe, co. Cornwall, eldest dau. Of Edwin Skentelbery: s.p."*

10th November 1917
Pte. James Harris 203270 DoW
born: Tiverton   enlisted: Barnstaple   residence: West Down, Devon
Buried: Pont-D'Achelles Military Cemetery, Nieppe. Grave II.F.11. Joined BEF: not on Medal Card. Formerly 30162, Devonshire Regiment. CWGC: son of Mr. E. Harris, Porch Dairy, North Molton, Devon.

11th November 1917
Pte. Chase George Read 16155 KIA
born: East Ham, Essex   enlisted: Southwark   residence: Walworth, Surrey
Buried: Lancashire Cottage Cemetery, nr. Ploegsteert. Grave III.B.1. Age 26.
Joined BEF: 07/07/15. Formerly with 1/Devons. 1901 Census: names him George Read, son of Ellen Read, widow, housekeeper/domestic, 8 Wellington Road, East Ham, Essex. CWGC: son of Ellen Cheesman (formerly Read), of Walworth, London, husband of Daisy R. Read, 86 Lovelinch Street, Old Kent Road, London.
Pte. Benjamin Edmund Burgess 30806 DoW
born: Kensington   enlisted: Swanage
Buried: Trois Arbres Cemetery, Steenwerck. Grave II.B.9. Age 33. Joined BEF: not on Medal Card. Formerly 17892, Dorsetshire Regiment. 1911 Census: house painter, husband of Alice Burgess, father of 4 children, Court Hill, Swanage, Dorset.

20th November 1917
Captain Cecil Otway Reed Jacob Attached from 2/5th Devons KIA
Born: St. Helens, Lancashire
Buried: Orival Wood cemetery, Flesquieres. Grave II.A.21. Joined BEF: not on Medal Card. Commissioned 26/01/15. Medal Card annotation: *Major Jacob applies for 1914 Star Clasp and emblems 9/10/22*. Formerly Pte. 1648 of 28/London Regiment. 1911 Census: bank clerk, boarding at the house of Arthur Bruton, 7 Cricklade Avenue, Streatham Hill, London.

22nd November 1917
Pte. Ernest Lawrence 3/20272 Executed by firing squad
Buried: Ypres Reservoir Cemetery. Grave I.I.45. At a Field General Court Martial, Pte. Lawrence was sentenced to death on three counts of desertion. His gravestone bears the inscription: *"In memory of my dear son, gone but not forgotten"*. Age 21. No Medal Card. Son of John Lawrence, 101 Clifton Road, South Norwood, London. He was the only 2nd Devon to be executed in WW1.

24th November 1917
Pte. Leslie Baker 19208 KIA
Born: Fulham, Middx.   Enlisted: Plymouth   residence: Woolwich
No known grave. Tyne Cot Memorial panel 38 to 40. Joined BEF: not on Medal Card.
Sgt. Harry Langdon 9330 KIA
Born: Plymouth   enlisted: Plymouth
No known grave. Tyne Cot Memorial panel 38 to 40. Age 26. Joined BEF: 6th Nov 1914, with original cadre. 1911 Census: Army Reservist, lodger, 7 Albany Street, Devonport, Devon.

25th November 1917
Major Harry Archer DSO KIA
No known grave. Tyne Cot Memorial, Panel 38 to 40. Age 38. Joined BEF: 13/05/15. Mentioned in despatches. CWGC: second son of the late Henry James Archer, Rock House, Halberton, and of Mrs. Archer, Alfoxton, near Bridgewater, Somerset; husband of Mary Archer (nee Birmingham), Salem House, Uffculme, Devon. All-round sportsman; captain of Devon County hockey team.
2/Lt. John Howard Cole Willy KIA
No known grave. Cambrai Memorial Louverval, Panel 4. Age 34. No Medal Card . 1901 Census: son of Arthur White Willy, Registrar of Births and Deaths, and Elizabeth E. Willy, Dudmoor House, Kingsbury Episcopy, Somerset; husband of Stephanie M. Willy. 1911 Census: grazier, son of Arthur White Willy, Relieving Officer, and Elizabeth Emily Willy, Kingsbury Episcopi, Martock, Somerset.
Pte. Coleman Benjamin 30903 KIA
born: Birmingham   enlisted: Birmingham
No known grave. Tyne Cot Memorial, Panel 38 to 40. Age 19. Joined BEF: not on Medal Card. Formerly 8/1326, Devonshire Regiment (Territorials). 1901 Census: son of Lewis Benjamin, tailor/presser, and Esther Benjamin, tailoress, 8 Florence Street, Birmingham. 1911 Census: schoolboy, son of Lewis Benjamin, presser tailoring, and Ester Benjamin, 8 Florence Street, Birmingham, Warwickshire. CWGC: family address: 95 Wheeler Street, Lozells, Birmingham, Warwickshire.

Pte. Walter Samuel Clark 291753 KIA
born: Melksham, Wiltshire   enlisted: Trowbridge   residence: Melksham
No known grave. Tyne Cot Memorial, Panel 38 to 40. Age 23. Joined BEF: not on Medal Card. Formerly 3431, Devonshire Regiment. 1901 Census: son of Samuel Clark, general labourer, and Annie Clark, Melksham, Wiltshire. 1911 Census: farm labourer, son of Annie Elizabeth Clark, widow, Littleworth, Whitley, Melksham, Wiltshire. CWGC: son of the late Samuel Clark, I West View, Whitley, Melksham, husband of Mabel Clark, 18 Scotland Road, Melksham, Wilts.

Pte. Ernest Flay 18569 KIA
born: Silverton, Devon   enlisted: Exeter   residence: Bradninch
No known grave. Tyne Cot Memorial, Panel 38 to 40. Age 27. Joined BEF: 06/10/15, 9/Devons. 1901 Census: son of Mary Ann Flay, rag sorter in paper mill, Matthews Road, Bradninch, Devon. 1911 Census: machine mindre's assistant, stepson of John Webb, builder's labourer, son of Mary Ann Webb, Hornbeam Terrace, Bradninch, Devon. CWGC: husband of Lucy Cora Lily Flay, Church Lane, Bradninch, Devon.

Pte. Walter Bernard Channings Hughes 33187 KIA
born: Cullompton, Devon   enlisted: Cullompton
No known grave. Tyne Cot Memorial, Panel 38 to 40. Age 21. Joined BEF: not on Medal Card. Formerly 795 of the Devonshire Regiment. 1901 Census: recorded as boarder, age 5, New Street, Cullompton, Devon.

Pte. Thomas Charles Lineham 59318 KIA
born: Northampton   enlisted: Northampton
No known grave. Tyne Cot Memorial, Panel 38 to 40. Joined BEF: not on Medal Card. Charles T. Lineham on Medal Card. CWGC: Thomas Charles Lineham.

Pte. Harry Elford Mortimore 290424 KIA
born: Modbury   enlisted: Liskeard   residence: Modbury
Buried: Tyne Cot Cemetery. Grave LVII.C.43. Age 23. Joined BEF: not on Medal Card. 1901 Census: son of Alfred J. Mortimore, builder and contractor, and Jessie A. Mortimore, New Road, Modbury, Devon.

Pte. George Smart 291108 KIA
born: Sherston   enlisted: Devizes   residence: Tetbury
No known grave. Tyne Cot Memorial, Panel 38 to 40. Age 28. Joined BEF: not on Medal Card. 1901 Census: son of Henry Smart, cowman on farm, and Reubena Smart, Malmesbury Road, Long Newton, Wiltshire.

28th November 1917
Sgt. George Edward Albert Ellis 5991 KIA
born: Exeter   enlisted: Exeter
No known grave. Tyne Cot Memorial, Panel 38 to 40. Age 34. 'C' Company. Joined BEF: 27/05/15. 1891 Census: son of George Ellis, packer GWR, and Hannah Ellis, brushmaker, 24 Smythen Street, St. John, Exeter. CWGC: family address: 187 Parkhouse Road, St. Thomas, Exeter, Devon, mother's name Hannah Nankivel Ellis.

Pte. Edward James Browning 44222 DoW
born: no record   enlisted: Plymouth
Buried: St. Sever Cemetery Extension, Rouen. Grave P.III.T.8B. Age 19. Joined BEF: not on Medal Card. CWGC: son of Mr. and Mrs. Charles Browning, Rear Go, Cecil Street, Plymouth.

29th November 1917
Pte. Francis Addicott 290274 KIA
born: Plymouth   enlisted: Plymouth
No known grave. Tyne Cot Memorial, Panel 38 to 40. Age 21. No Medal Card. 1901 Census: son of John Addicott, builder's labourer, and Louie Kate Addicott, 4 Gilwell Street, Plymouth, Devon. CWGC: son of Louisa Kate Addicott, 51 Well Street, Plymouth, and the late John Addicott.
Pte. Arthur George Bolt 203297 KIA
born: Colaton Raleigh   enlisted: Exeter   residence: Colaton Raleigh
No known grave. Tyne Cot Memorial, Panel 38 to 40. Age 19. Joined BEF: not on Medal Card. 1901 Census: son of William E. Bolt, farmer, and Emily Bolt, farmer's wife, Stowford, Colaton Raleigh, Devon. 1911 Census: schoolboy, son of William Ellis Bolt, farmer, and Emily Bolt, Stowford Farm, Colaton Raleigh, Devon.
A/Cpl. Arthur Harms 204885 KIA
born: Christchurch   enlisted: Winchester   residence: Aldershot
No known grave. Tyne Cot Memorial, Panel 38 to 40. Age 38. Joined BEF: not on Medal Card. Formerly 203178, Nottinghamshire and Derbyshire Regiment. 1891 Census: nephew of Susanna E. Harms, widow, 2 Hillside, Caversham, Oxfordshire. CWGC: son of Elizabeth Harms, 117 Caversham Road, Reading, Berks, and the late Alfred Harms.
Pte. Louis William Pardon 290285 DoW
born: Roborough,Devon   enlisted: Exeter   residence: Broadclyst
Buried: Nine Elms British Cemetery, Poperinghe. Grave IX.C.13. No Medal Card. 1911 Census: carpenter, husband of Mary Pardon, father of three, New Buildings, Roborough, Torrington, Devon.

30th November 1917
Sgt. James Shaddick 13302 KIA
born: Barnstaple   enlisted: Barnstaple
No known grave. Tyne Cot Memorial, Panel 38 to 40. Age 36. No Medal Card. 1911 Census: general labourer, son of John Shaddick, general labourer/oddworks, and Mary Ann Shaddick, 7 Green Lane, Barnstaple, Devon. CWGC: son of John Shaddick and Mary Ann Shaddick, 7 North Place, Barnstaple; husband of Carrie Shaddick, 10 Cumberland Street, Devonport.
L/Cpl. Albert Henry Dibble 3/8163 KIA
Born: Bristol   enlisted: Bristol
No known grave. Tyne Cot Memorial, Panel 38 to 40. Age 19. Joined BEF: 27/12/14 with 1/Devons. 1901 Census: son of Frederick Dibble, tailor, and Susanna F. Dibble, 7 Manor Street, St. Paul, Bristol. 1911 Census: son of Frederick Dibble, shop assistant, and Susanna Dibble, 71 Chessel Street, Bedminster, Bristol. CWGC: son of Frederick Dibble, 71 Chessel Street, Bedminster, Bristol.
L/Cpl. Herbert Tuckwell 9653 KIA
born: London   enlisted: London
No known grave. Tyne Cot Memorial, Panel 38 to 40. Age 20. Joined BEF: not on Medal Card. 1901 Census: Herbert Tuckwell, school porter, and Annie Tuckwell, 18 Farringdon Road Buildings, Clerkenwell, London. 1911 Census: errand boy, son of Herbert Tuckwell, school porter, and Annie Tuckwell, 72 Victoria Dwellings, Clerkenwell Road, Clerkenwell, London.
Pte. Lionel George Ernest Humphrey 291079 KIA
born: London   enlisted: Woolwich   residence: Belvedere
Buried: Tyne Cot Cemetery. Grave XLIX.B.8. Age 20. Joined BEF: not on Medal Card. Formerly

2738, Devonshire Regiment. 1911 Census: schoolboy, son of Lionel Humphrey, nurseryman, and Kate Humphrey, Audley Villa, Harold Road, Belvedere, Kent. CWGC: son of Lionel Harry Humphrey and Kate Ada Humphrey, 23 Harold Road, Belvedere, Kent.

Pte. Charles Thomas James 29679 KIA
born: Tormoham, Devon   enlisted: Torquay
No known grave. Tyne Cot Memorial, Panel 38 to 40. Age 36. Joined BEF: not on Medal Card. CWGC: son of Mary James, 11 Madeira Cottages, Torquay, Devon, and the late Joseph James.

Pte. Samuel Cook Johnson 16799 KIA
born: Stonehouse   enlisted: Plymouth
No known grave. Tyne Cot Memorial, Panel 38 to 40. Age 24. No Medal Card. 1911 Census: railway messenger, son of Mary Anna Johnson, widow, charwoman, 40 High Street, East Stonehouse, Devon. CWGC: son of the late Samuel Cook Johnson and Mary A. Johnson, 62 Emma Place, Stonehouse, Plymouth.

Pte. Alfred Sydney Jones 17085 KIA
born: Wolborough   enlisted: Newton Abbot
No known grave. Tyne Cot Memorial, Panel 38 to 40. Age 29. Joined BEF: not on Medal Card. 1901 Census: errand boy at the Co-Op stores, son of Samuel Jones, jobbing gardener, and Jessie Jones, 7 Albany Road, Wolborough, Devon. 1911 Census: porter, son of Samuel Jones, general labourer and dealer, and Jessie Jones, 50 The Avenue, Newton Abbott, Devon. CWGC: husband of Emma Jones, Pound Street, Moreton Hampstead, Devon.

Pte. Arthur Smith 54521 KIA
born: Birmingham   enlisted: Birmingham
No known grave. Tyne Cot Memorial, Panel 38 to 40. Joined BEF: 23/03/15. Formerly 1427, Royal Warwickshire Regiment.

Pte. William Alexander Knox 30970 DoW
born: Bethnal Green   enlisted: Stratford
Buried: Nine Elms British Cemetery, Poperinghe. Grave IX.B.16. Age 18. Joined BEF: not on Medal Card. Formerly 8/2476, Devonshire Regiment, also 206 Infantry Battalion. 1901 Census: son of John Knox, bricklayer's labourer, and Elizabeth Knox, 7 Rutland Road, East Ham, Essex. 1911 Census: son of John Knox, widower, labourer, 23 Pond Road, West Ham, Essex.

DECEMBER 1917

3rd December 1917
Lt.Col. Alexander Tillett, DSO MC Commanding Officer, 2/Devons DoW
Buried: Nine Elms British Cemetery, Poperinghe. Grave XIII.A.3. Age 25. Joined BEF: 22/08/14, 1/Devons. In August 1914, Tillett was a junior subaltern in the 1/Devons. After recovering from wounds he was posted to the 2/Devons early in 1915. With 2/Devons, he performed duty of Adjutant for nearly eighteen months and later became second-in-command. Although only twenty-five years old, he proved equal to the task when given command of the Battalion, and posthumous award of DSO was well deserved. Lt. Col. Tillett, the CO, was the only 2/Devons fatality in December 1917.

JANUARY 1918

5th January 1918
Pte. Herbert Douglas Ellis 291853 KIA
born: Exmouth   enlisted: Exeter
No known grave. Tyne Cot Memorial, Panel 38 to 40. Age 19. No Medal Card. 1911 Census: schoolboy, son of Ernest Edward Ellis, architect and surveyor, and Edith Ellis, 44 Polsloe Road, Heavitree, Devon.

Pte. Bertram Cater Fry 30936 KIA
born: Peckham   enlisted: Camberwell   residence: Catford
No known grave. Tyne Cot Memorial, Panel 38 to 40. Age 19. Joined BEF: not on Medal Card. Formerly 9/21320, 206th Infantry Battalion. 1901 Census: son of William Fry, railway signalman, and Jane Fry, 17 Fenwick Road, Camberwell, London. 1911 Census: schoolboy, son of William Fry, railway timekeeper, South East and Chatham Railway, and Jane Fry, 22 Glenton Road, Lee, London.

7th January 1918
L/Cpl. William Johnson 30839 KIA
born: Burnley   enlisted: Wigan   residence: Levenshulme
No known grave. Tyne Cot Memorial, Panel 38 to 40. Joined BEF: 18/03/15. Formerly 1/6658, 1/East Lancashire Regiment.

14th January 1918
Pte. Charles Walter Leonard 204873 KIA
born: London   enlisted: London
No known grave. Tyne Cot Memorial, Panel 38 to 40. Age 19. Joined BEF: not on Medal Card. Formerly 654430, 21/London Regiment. 1901 Census: born Paddington, 1895, son of Georgina Leonard, widow, charwoman, 11 Burlington Mews East, Paddington, Middlesex. 1911 Census: schoolboy, son of Georgina Leonard, widow, 186 Guinness Buildings, Chelsea, Middlesex. CWGC: son of Georgina Leonard, 10 Clifton Crescent, Peckham, London, and the late Edward Leonard.

The 2nd Devons War Diary

FEBRUARY 1918

12th February 1918
Pte. Thomas Adams 64419 Died
born: Stoke Newington   enlisted: Whitehall   residence: Stoke Newington
Buried: Longuenesse (St. Omer) Souvenir Cemetery. Grave IV.F.54. Age 35. No Medal Card. 1891 Census: son of Benjamin Adams, cabinet maker, and Charlotte Adams, 92 Cranbrook Street, Bethnal Green, London. CWGC: son of Charlotte Adams, husband of Lily Ellen Adams, 91 Bouverie Road, Church Street, Stoke Newington, London.

15th February 1918
Pte. Bert Devereux 30927 KIA
born: Tewkesbury   enlisted: Tewkesbury
No known grave. Tyne Cot Memorial, Panel 38 to 40. Age 18. Joined BEF: not on medal card. Formerly 8/2144, 206/Infantry Battalion. 1901 Census: son of Thomas Devereux, labourer in milled corn stores, and Emily Devereux, 2 Clay's Court, East Street, Tewkesbury, Glos. 1911 Census: schoolboy and clothier's errand boy, son of Thomas Devereux, labourer, and Emily Devereux, 10 Clay's Buildings, Tewkesbury, Gloucestershire. CWGC: family address: 10 Clay's Buildings, East Street, Tewkesbury, Gloucestershire.
Pte. Herbert Sidney Haines 21594 KIA
born: Lymington   enlisted: Yeovil   residence: West Coler, Som.
No known grave. Tyne Cot Memorial, Panel 38 to 40. Age 29. Joined BEF: not on Medal Card. 1911 Census: domestic gardener, boarding at The Hall Cottage, West Coker, Yeovil Somerset. CWGC: son of William Haines and Kate Haines, I Bridge Road, Lymington, Hants., husband of Alice Nellie Haines, 50, Gosport Street, Lymington, Hants.

21st February 1918
Lt. George Deas Ferard KIA
No known grave. Tyne Cot Memorial, Panel 38 to 40. Age 21. Joined BEF: 1916. Formerly 6/King's Royal Rifle Corps. Medal Card annotation: *H. Ferard makes application for medals due to the late Lt. G. D. Ferard. 24/5/20.* 1911 Census: scholar, boarding at Winchester College, Southgate Corner, Winchester, Hants. CWGC: son of Henry Cecil Ferard, C.S.I., C.I.E., and Ida Margaret Ferard, 22 Bardwell Road, Oxford.

23rd February 1918
Pte. William John Hobbs 291839 KIA
born: Newport, IoW   enlisted: Newport, IoW
No known grave. Tyne Cot Memorial, Panel 38 to 40. Age 21. Joined BEF: not on Medal Card. 1901 Census: son of John Hobbs, agricultural labourer, and Eliza Hobbs, 13 John Street, Newport, Isle of Wight. 1911 Census: fitter, son of John Hobbs, gravel digger, and Eliza Hobbs, 10 Green Street, Newport, Isle of Wight. CWGC: family address: 7 Green Street, Barton, Newport, Isle of Wight.
Pte. Frederick Charles Lewis 69048 KIA
born: Plymouth   enlisted: Plymouth
No known grave. Tyne Cot Memorial, Panel 38 to 40. No Medal Card.
Pte. Ernest Frank Simpkins 31826 KIA
born: Keevil, Wilts.   enlisted: Andover
No known grave. Tyne Cot Memorial, Panel 38 to 40. Age 19. No Medal Card. 1901 Census:

son of George Simpkins, carter on farm, and Rhoda Simpkins, Asley No.3, Winsley, Turley and Ashley, Westbury, Wiltshire. 1911 Census: schoolboy, son of George Simpkins, carter on farm, and Rhoda Simpkins, Andover, Hants. CWGC: family address: 44 London Road, Andover, Hants.

24th February 1918
Pte. Percy Clarke 33686 DoW
born: Bedminster   enlisted: Bristol
Buried: Nine Elms British Cemetery, Poperinghe. Grave XIII.D.6. Age 19. Joined BEF: not on Medal Card. Formerly 8/9589, Devonshire Regiment. 1911 Census: schoolboy, son of Elizabeth Clarke, married, 52 Park Street, Knowle, Bristol, Gloucestershire.

The 2nd Devons War Diary

MARCH 1918

3rd March 1918
L/Cpl. Arthur Bailey 30853 KIA
born: Brandon, Suffolk   enlisted: Worcester   residence: Lakenheath, Suffolk
No known grave. Tyne Cot Memorial, Panel 38 to 40. Date joined BEF: 21/06/15. Formerly 13942, Worcestershire Regiment.
Pte. Charlie Selley 21176 KIA
born: Stoke Damarel   enlisted: Devonport
No known grave. Tyne Cot Memorial, Panel 38 to 40. Age 26. 'C' Company. Joined BEF: not on Medal Card. 1901 Census: son of Charles John Bolt Selley, shipwright, and Eliza Jane Selley, 15 Clowance Street, Devonport. 1911 Census: waiter, son of Charles Selley, shipwright, and Eliza Selley, 15 Clowance Street, Devonport, Devon. CWGC: family address as Census.

23rd March 1918
Pte. Charles Low 28896 KIA
born: King's Nympton   enlisted: Exeter
No known grave. Pozieres Memorial, Panel 24 and 25. Age 34. No Medal Card. 1901 Census: son of Sarah Low, sailor's wife, South Road to Whompford, King's Nympton, Umberleigh, Devon. 1911 Census: coal merchant, husband of Bessie Catherine Low, 5 Stuart Road, Heavitree, Exeter, Devon. CWGC: family address as 1901 and 1911 Census.
Pte. Herbert Wheeler 31034 KIA
born: Frampton Cotterell   enlisted: Bristol
Buried: Bouchoir New British Cemetery. Grave I.B.48. Age 19. Joined BEF: not on Medal Card. 1911 Census: 'scholar', son of Alice Wheeler, tailoress, Harris Barton, Frampton Cotterell, Glos.

25th March 1918
Sgt. Albert John Isaacs 5274 KIA
born: Exeter   enlisted: Exeter
No known grave. Pozieres Memorial, Panel 24 and 25. Age 37. Date joined BEF: 06/11/14 with original cadre. CWGC records him as being in 'D' Company.   1881 Census: 1 week old son of Albert Henry Isaacs, stonemason, and Sarah Annie Isaac, Court behind 21 James Street, Exeter, Devon. CWGC: family address: 28 Holloway Street, Exeter.
Pte. John Charles Boden 30896 KIA
born: Poplar, Middx.   enlisted: Poplar
No known grave. Pozieres Memorial, Panel 24 and 25. Age 20. Joined BEF: not on Medal Card. Formerly 9/21067, Devonshire Regiment. 1911 Census: schoolboy, son of Robert Boden, steam crane driver, and Sarah Ann Boden, 21 Suffolk Street, Poplar, London. CWGC: son of Robert Francis Boden and Sarah Boden, 21 Suffolk Street, Poplar, London.
Pte. Leonard George Camp 30544 KIA
born: Exeter   enlisted: Exeter
No known grave. Pozieres Memorial, Panel 24 and 25. Age 21. Joined BEF: not on Medal Card. Formerly 1536, Devonshire Regiment. 1911 Census: son of George Camp, head gardener domestic, and Flora Annie Camp, Culver, Devon. CWGC: family address as 1911.
Pte. Charles Henry Field 30938 KIA
born: no record   enlisted: Devizes   residence: Lacock, Wilts.
Buried: Roye New British Cemetery. Grave IV.D.1. Age 21. Joined BEF: not on Medal Card. Formerly 8/855, 206/Infantry Battalion. 1911 Census: farm labourer, son of Charles Field,

general farm labourer, and Mary Field, Grove Lane, Yatton Keynell, Castle Combe, Wiltshire.

Pte. Sidney Thomas Hill 25109 KIA
born: St.Austell   enlisted: Bodmin   residence: Truro
No known grave. Pozieres Memorial, Panel 24 and 25. Age 31.
Joined BEF: not on Medal Card. 1901 Census: butcher's boy, son of John Hill, shepherd, and Phillippa Hill, Menheniot, Liskeard, Cornwall. 1911 Census: gardener domestic, son of John Hill, farm labourer, and Phillippa Hill, Tregrill, Menheniot, Liskeard, Cornwall.

Pte. Harold Hoare 30958 KIA
born: St.Agnes   enlisted: Bodmin   residence: St.Agnes
No known grave. Pozieres Memorial, Panel 24 and 25. Age 19. Joined BEF: not recorded on Medal Card. Formerly 8/4819, 206th Infantry Battalion. 1901 Census: son of John Hoare, timberman in tin mine, and Kate Hoare, St. Agnes, Cornwall. 1911 Census: schoolboy, son of John Hoare, foreman in tin mine, and Katie Hoare, Wheal Friendly, St. Agnes, Cornwall. CWGC: son of Kate Hoare, Rose Mundy, St. Agnes, Cornwall, and the late John Hoare.

Pte. George Howle 69046 KIA
born: no record   enlisted: Worcester   residence: Birmingham
No known grave. Pozieres Memorial, Panel 24 and 25. Age 40. Joined BEF: not on Medal Card. CWGC: son of William Howle and Elizabeth Howle, husband of Elizabeth Howle, 108 Benton Road, Sparkhill, Birmingham.

Pte. Thomas Howard Morris 291421 KIA
born: Birmingham   enlisted: Birmingham
No known grave. Pozieres Memorial, Panel 24 and 25. Age 32. Joined BEF: not on Medal Card. 1911 Census: insurance agent, husband of Elizabeth Howle, 108 Benton Road, Sparkhill, Birmingham, Warwickshire, CWGC: husband of Nellie Morris, 31 Wood Street, Ladywood, Birmingham, Warwickshire.

Pte. Wilfred Richards 30665 KIA
born: no record   enlisted: Cullompton   residence: Silverton
No known grave. Pozieres Memorial, Panel 24 and 25. Age 19. No Medal Card. 1901 Census: son of Frank Richards, journeyman carpenter, and Mary Richards, Fore Street, Silverton, Exeter, Devon. 1911 Census: names him Wilfred Ernest Richards, schoolboy, son of Frank Richards, carpenter (building trade), and Mary Eliza Richards, Fore Street, Silverton, Exeter, Devon.

Pte. Reginald Edwin Horace Rowe 69054 KIA
born: Perranwell, Cornwall   enlisted: Bodmin   residence: Perranwell
No known grave. Pozieres Memorial, Panel 24 and 25. Age 23. Joined BEF: not on Medal Card. 1901 Census: son of William Rowe, coal porter, and Eliza Rowe, Tarandean Hill, Perranworthal, Cornwall. 1911 Census: gardener domestic, son of William Rowe, general labourer, and Eliza Ann Rowe, Terrandean, Perranwell Station, Falmouth, Cornwall. CWGC: son of William Rowe, Bribbaree, New South Wales, Australia, husband of Rhoda Jane Rowe, Perranwell, Cornwall.

Pte. David Daniel Williams 12753 KIA
born: Pontardulais   enlisted: Swansea   residence: Pontardulais
No known grave. Pozieres Memorial, Panel 24 and 25. Age 26. Joined BEF: 02/05/15. Formerly 1/Devons. Medal Card annotation: *Death regarded 25/3/18*. CWGC: brother of Mrs. Catherine Ann Hopkins, 16 Dantwyn Road, Pontardulais, Glam.

Pte. John Arthur Stevens 43330 DoW
born: Penryn, Cornwall   enlisted: Plymouth
Buried: Rosieres British Cemetery. Grave 42. Joined BEF: not on Medal Card.

26th March 1918
2/Lt. Sydney George Carthew KIA
No known grave. Pozieres Memorial, Panel 24 and 25. Age 32. Joined BEF: 06/11/14 with original cadre. Formerly 7296 Sgt. Sydney George Carthew, 2/Devons. 1911 Census: 2/Devons, St. George's Barracks, Malta. CWGC: son of Henry Carthew and Elizabeth Carthew, Cross Cottage, Cheriton Bishop, Devon.
Capt. George Fleetwood Thuillier MC KIA
Born: Rawalpindi, India.
Buried: Assevillers New British Cemetery. Grave VI.E.9. Age 21. Joined BEF: 12/07/16. 1901 Census: born Punjab, India, son of Henry F. Thuillier, Army Captain Royal Engineers, and Helen Thuillier, 3 Clarendon Villas, Dovercourt, Harwich, Essex. 1911 Census: boarder at Priory House Cottage (Dover School), Dover, Kent, with elder brother Henry Thuillier. CWGC: son of Maj. Gen. H. F. Thuillier, C.B., C.M.G., and Mrs. Helen Thuillier.
Pte. Albert Victor Hinves 290998 KIA
born: Southampton   enlisted: Winchester   residence: Southampton
No known grave. Pozieres Memorial, Panel 24 and 25. Age 30. Joined BEF: not on Medal Card. 1911 Census: law clerk, son of Mary Ann Hinves, widow, 11a Lisbon Road, Southampton, Hampshire.
Pte. Richard James Needs 24681 KIA
born: Exeter   enlisted: Exeter
No known grave. Pozieres Memorial, Panel 24 and 25. Age 38. Joined BEF: not on Medal Card. 1891 Census: son of Samuel Needs, labourer, and Mary Ann Needs, 4 Union Place, St. Thomas, Exeter, Devon. 1911 Census: general labourer, husband of Emily Mary Needs, 4 Union Street, Cowick Street, St. Thomas, Exeter. CWGC: husband of Emily Needs, 30 Goldsmith Street, Heavitree, Exeter.
Pte. Henry Herniman Phillpotts 28476 KIA
born: Slapton   enlisted: Newton Abbot   residence: Totnes
No known grave. Pozieres Memorial, Panel 24 and 25. Age 20. Joined BEF: not on Medal Card. CWGC: son of James Phillpotts and Annie Phillpotts, 5 New Walk, Totnes, Devon.
Pte. Horace Edward Woodgate 16609 KIA
born: Exeter   enlisted: Exeter
No known grave. Pozieres Memorial, Panel 24 and 25. Age 24. Joined BEF: not on Medal Card. 1901 Census: son of Harry Woodgate, grocer, and Elizabeth Woodgate, 8 Fortescue Road, St. Thomas, Exeter, Devon. 1911 Census: errand boy, son of Harry Woodgate, widower, grocer, 8 Fortesque Road, Exeter, Devon. CWGC: son of the late Harry Woodgate and Elizabeth Woodgate.
Pte. Reginald Darke Cockwill 15147 DoW
born: Plymouth   enlisted: Totnes
Buried: Rosieres British Cemetery. Age 28. Born: 15/07/1888. Educated at Charles National School, Plymouth, Devon. Enlisted: 01/01/15. Joined BEF: 18/05/15. Medal Card: DoW 26/03/18. Died at No.47 Casualty Clearing Station, from wounds received 25/03/18. 1901 Census: son of John Darke Cockwill, maltster's accountant, and Sarah Cockwill, 8 Edgar Terrace, Plymouth. 1911 Census: grocer's assistant, husband of Evelyn Cockwill, West Street, Ashburton, Devon. Obituary gives the family address as Brooklands, Bridgetown, Totnes, Devon.

27th March 1918

A/Cpl. John Francis Brown 49040 KIA
born: Cockerton, Durham   enlisted: Bletchley   residence: Buckingham
Buried: Heath Cemetery, Harbonnieres. Grave I.A.9. Age 24. Born 11/08/1892. Joined BEF: not on Medal Card. 1901 Census: son of Robert Brown, coal miner/hewer, and Mary Brown, Back Row, Coxhoe, Durham. CWGC: family address: 5 Grosvenor Terrace, Cockerton, Darlington. Mary Brown died 1913.

Sgt. Edgar Davey 206021 KIA
born: Torrington   enlisted: Barnstaple   residence: Torrington
No known grave. Pozieres Memorial, Panel 24 and 25. Age 33. Joined BEF: not on Medal Card. 1901 Census: ordinary agricultural labourer, son of John Davey, general labourer, and Ann Davey, Village, Petrockstow, Torrington, Devon. 1911 Census: inn keeper, husband of Ellen Davey, The Buckingham Arms, Taddiport Street, Torrington, Devon.

Cpl. Albert James 15631 KIA
born: Lapford   enlisted: Lapford
No known grave. Pozieres Memorial, Panel 24 and 25. Joined BEF: not on Medal Card.

A/Cpl. Harry Snell 290009 KIA
born: Plymouth   enlisted: Plymouth
No known grave. Pozieres Memorial, Panel 24 and 25. Age 31. Joined BEF: not on Medal Card. 1901 Census: nephew of Jane Rogers, widow, lodging house keeper, 23 Leigham Street, Plymouth, Devon. 1911 Census: 'effect worker of pictures, animated', nephew of Jane Rogers, widow, apartment house keeper, 3 Hoe Park, Terra, Plymouth, Devon.

Pte. Percy Thomas Ackland 16911 KIA
born: Plymouth   enlisted: Plymouth
No known grave. Pozieres Memorial, Panel 24 and 25. Age 27. No Medal Card. 1911 Census: brewer's clerk, son of William James Ackland, bookbinder, and Edith Ackland, 29 Sea View Terrace, Plymouth, Devon. CWGC: son of the late James Ackland and Edith Ackland, also as the husband of O. M. Jordan (formerly Ackland), 26 Widey View, Compton, Plymouth, Devon.

Pte. Harry Darke Chapple 44152 KIA
born: Membury, Devon   enlisted: Newton Abbot   residence: Exbourne
No known grave. Pozieres Memorial, Panel 24 and 25. Age 21. Joined BEF: not on Medal Card. 1901 Census: son of Robert W. Chapple, widower, butcher, Battens, Membery, Devon. 1911 Census: schoolboy, son of Robert William Chapple, butcher shopkeeper, stepson of Susan Maud Chapple, assistant in shop, Lansdowne Place, Dawlish, Devon.

Pte. Bert Jones 30962 KIA
born: Birmingham   enlisted: Birmingham
No known grave. Pozieres Memorial, Panel 24 and 25. Joined BEF: not on Medal Card. Formerly 8/1669, 206th Infantry Battalion.

Pte. Walter Leslie Law 15400 KIA
born: Todmorden, Lancs.   enlisted: Halifax   residence: Todmorden
No known grave. Pozieres Memorial, Panel 24 and 25. Age 22. 'D' Company. Joined BEF: 18/05/15. 1901 Census: son of Sam Law, cotton seamer, and Sarah Alice Law, 12 Pear Place, Todmorden, Lancs. 1911 Census: cotton weaver, son of Mary Ann Law, widow, 64 Parkinson Street, Burnley, Lancs.CWGC: family address: 878, Burnley Road, Cornholme, Todmorden, Lancs.

Pte. Thomas Saxon 15538 KIA
born: Heywood, Lancs.   enlisted: Rochdale
No known grave. Pozieres Memorial, Panel 24 and 25. Age 21. No Medal Card. 1901 Census:

son of Thomas Saxon, house painter, and Eliza Ann Saxon, 5 Hartland Street, Heywood, Lancs. 1911 Census: apprentice house painter, son of Thomas Saxon, house painter, and Eliza Ann Saxon, 8 Matthew Moss, Rochdale, Lancs. CWGC: family address:12 Matthew Moss, Marland, Rochdale, Lancs.

Pte. Clifford Smart 31014 KIA
born: Kingswood, Somerset   enlisted: Bristol   residence: Kingswood
No known grave. Pozieres Memorial, Panel 24 and 25. Age 19. Joined BEF: not on Medal Card. Formerly 8/9307, 206th Infantry Battalion. Medal Card annotation: *Death regarded 27/3/18*. 1901 Census: son of James Smart, 'clicker' boot trade, and Elizabeth Smart, 10 Seymour Place, Kingswood, Somerset. 1911 Census: schoolboy, son of James Smart, 'clicker', and Elizabeth Smart, 100 Soundwell Road, Kingswood, Somerset.

Pte. Francis William Stoyel 205166 KIA
born: Tiverton   enlisted: Exeter   residence: Tiverton
No known grave. Pozieres Memorial, Panel 24 and 25. Age 20. Joined BEF: not on Medal Card. 1901 Census: son of William Henry Stoyel, cabinet maker, and Mary Ann Stoyel, 3 Bridge Street, Tiverton Devon. 1911 Census: schoolboy, son of William Henry Stoyel, news-agent tobacconist and furniture dealer, and Mary Ann Stoyel, 1 West Exe South, Tiverton, Devon. CWGC: family address: 17/19 Bridge Street, Tiverton, Devon.

Pte. Albert Edward Underhill 68920 KIA
born: Worcester   enlisted: Worcester   residence: Evesham
No known grave. Pozieres Memorial, Panel 24 and 25. Age 19. Joined BEF: not on Medal Card. 1901 Census: son of Thomas Underhill, bracket maker, and Emma Underhill, Evesham, Worcs. 1911 Census: schoolboy, son of Thomas Underhill, basket maker, and Emma Underhill, 7 Common Road, Evesham, Worcs.

Pte. Reginald James Frank Ward 33870 KIA
born: Midgham, Berks.   enlisted: Caversham   residence: Henley
No known grave. Pozieres Memorial, Panel 24 and 25. Age 20. Joined BEF: not on Medal Card. 1901 Census: son of Jabes Ward, cowman on farm, and Mary Ann Ward, near school, Padworth, Berkshire.

28th March 1918
2/Lt. Eugene D. Davis KIA
No known grave. Pozieres Memorial, Panel 24 and 25. Joined BEF: 31/07/15. Formerly s/h7655 Pte. Eugene D. Davis, 10/Royal Fusiliers. Commissioned in Devons 30/10/17.

Pte. George William Friday 3/6883 KIA
born: Southwark   enlisted: Stratford   residence: London N.E.
No known grave. Pozieres Memorial, Panel 24 and 25. Age 21. Joined BEF: 27/04/15 with 1/Devons . 1901 Census: son of George Friday, tailor, 170 New Kent Road, Newington, Southwark, London. 1911 Census: schoolboy, son of Gustav Friday, tailor maker, and Lena Friday, 170 New Kent Road, Walworth, Southwark, London.

Pte. Thomas Garner 17654 KIA
born: Birmingham   enlisted: Birmingham
No known grave. Pozieres Memorial, Panel 24 and 25. Age 28. Joined BEF: not on Medal Card. CWGC: son of Mary Ann Garner, 3 Theresa Road, Sparkbrook, Birmingham, and the late Charles James Garner; husband of Florence Garner, 1 Boughton Place, Theresa Road, Sparkbrook, Birmingham.

Pte. Frederick John Brealy 16035 DoW
born: Crediton   enlisted: Exeter
No known grave. Pozieres Memorial, Panel 24 and 25. Age 23. Joined BEF: not on Medal Card. 1901 Census: son of Honor Brealy, domestic servant. 28 year old Honor, 6 year old Frederick, sister Florence and younger brother Henry, both age 4, are described as 'paupers' at Crediton Union Workhouse, Crediton, Devon. 1911 Census: servant 'cow boy', on the farm of George Thomas Philp, Chilton Farm, Stockley Pomeroy, Devon.

29th March 1918
Pte. Charles Philip Rowe 68053 DoW
born: Bristol   enlisted: Bristol
Buried: Suzanne Military Cemetery No.3. Grave I.D.2. Age 19. Joined BEF: not on Medal Card. 1901 Census: son of James Alfred Rowe, 2nd mate on Trinity launch, and Ethel Palmer Rowe, 18 Clifton Place, Stapleton Road, Bristol, Glos. 1911 Census: schoolboy, son of J.A. Rowe, sanitary inspector, and E. Rowe, 18 The Paddock, Easton Road, Bristol, Glos. CWGC: family address: 18 Clifton Place, Stapleton Road, Bristol, Glos.

30th March 1918
Pte. Percy Cross 20577 KIA
born: Rochdale   enlisted: Rochdale
No known grave. Pozieres Memorial, Panel 24 and 25. Age 21. Joined BEF: not on Medal Card. Son of John William Cross, stationary engine driver, and Sarah Ann Cross, of 424 Whitworth Road, Rochdale, Lancs. 1911 Census: 'cotton weft carrier', son of John William Cross, stationary engineman, and Sarah Ann Cross, 424 Whitworth Road, Rochdale, Lancs. CWGC: family: 5 Rudman Street, Shawclough, Rochdale, Lancs. Sarah Cross shown as died.
Pte. William James Hales 66961 KIA
born: Cullompton   enlisted: Cardiff   residence: Rhondda
No known grave. Pozieres Memorial, Panel 24 and 25. Age 30. Joined BEF: not on Medal Card. 1901 Census: son of George Hales, widower, coal yard labourer, London Inn Court, Cullompton, Devon. 1911 Census: traction engine steerer, boarding at 1a James Terrace, Exeter, Devon. CWGC: family address: Church Lane, Cullompton. Husband of Louisa J. Hales, Reed's Place, Cullompton, Devon.
Pte. Arthur Richard Hannaford 10434 KIA
born: Totnes   enlisted: Exeter   residence: Totnes
No known grave. Pozieres Memorial, Panel 24 and 25. Age 36. Joined BEF: 25/07/15, 8/Devons. 1901 Census: stepson of John Penwill, carter on farm, and Ellen Penwill, Church Lane, Totnes, Devon. 1911 Census: omnibus driver, husband of Beatrice Hannaford, 2 Windsor Cottages, Bridgetown, Totnes, Devon. CWGC: family address: Church Close, Totnes, Devon.
Pte. Frank Henry Gregory 290215 DoW
born: no record   enlisted: Exeter   residence: Exeter
Buried: St. Sever Cemetery Extension, Rouen. Grave P.VII.C.11A. Age 25. 'A' Company. Joined BEF: not on Medal Card. 1901 Census: son of Harry Gregory, railway labourer, and Mary Ann Gregory, Townhill, Broadclyst, Devon. 1911 Census: errand boy, son of Mary Ann Gregory, married, 3 Red Lion Court, Sidwell Street, Exeter, Devon. CWGC: family address: 3 Red Lion Cottages, St. Sidwell's Street, Exeter, Devon.
Cpl. Arthur George Wright 18918 Died
born: London   enlisted: London
Buried: St. Sever Cemetery Extension, Rouen. Grave P.IX.E.5B. Age 39. Joined BEF: 01/10/15.

1911 Census: general labourer, husband of Olive Nellie, Wright, 'out of work', 34 Wedmore Street, Holloway, London. CWGC: husband of Winifred Olive Wright, 54 Inderwick Road, Hornsey, London.

31st March 1918
Pte. Thomas William Diss 15689 KIA
born: Bromley-by-Bow   enlisted: Stratford   residence: Bromley-by-Bow
No known grave. Pozieres Memorial, Panel 24 and 25. Age 24. Joined BEF: not on Medal Card. 1911 Census: labourer, son of Ellen Diss, widow, 11 Hinks Court, Bromley E., Poplar, London.
Pte. Joseph Dixon 16314 KIA
born: Leeds, Yorks.   enlisted: Rochdale   residence: no record
No known grave: Soissons Memorial. Joined BEF: 02/09/15, 8/Devons.
Pte. Alfred Gagneur 9188 KIA
born: Jersey C.I.   enlisted: Jersey C.I.
No known grave. Pozieres Memorial, Panel 24 and 25. Age 25. Joined BEF: 06/11/14 with original cadre. CWGC: son of Mrs. Augustine Marie Julienne Rollond Gagneur, 6 Salisbury Cottage, St. Saviours Road, Jersey.
Pte. William Humber 31814 KIA
born: Southampton   enlisted: Southampton
No known grave. Pozieres Memorial, Panel 24 and 25. Age 19. No Medal Card. 1911 Census: schoolboy, son of John Humber, jobbing builder, and Elizabeth Humber, Bromley, Lemon Road, Shirley, Southampton, Hampshire.
Pte. Frank Marsden 15263 KIA
born: Rochdale   enlisted: Rochdale
No known grave. Pozieres Memorial, Panel 24 and 25. Age 21. Joined BEF: 18/05/15. 1901 Census: son of Henry Marsden, stone mason, and Margaret Marsden, 2 Chapels Court, Rochdale, Lancs. 1911 Census: son of Margaret Marsden, married, 4 Chappells Court, Joshua Street, Rochdale, Lancs. CWGC: father the late Henry Marsden.
Pte. Henry Squire 30551 KIA
born: Exeter   enlisted: Exeter
No known grave. Pozieres Memorial, Panel 24 and 25. Age 23. Joined BEF: not on Medal Card, but gives rank as Corporal. 1901 Census: son of William Davey Squire, palemaker, and Henrietta Squire, 39 Jubilee Street, Exeter, Devon. 1911 Census: tailor's apprentice, son of William Davey Squire, paper maker, widower, 27 Weisfield Road, Exeter, Devon. CWGC: father the late William Squire.
A/Cpl. Henry Thomas 3/8300 KIA
born: Cardiff   enlisted: Swansea   residence: Saltley, Warwicks.
No known grave. Pozieres Memorial, panel 24 and 25. Joined BEF: 04/01/1915. Medal Card annotation: *'death regarded 31/3/18'*.
L/Cpl. Frank Cecil Keeling 266881 DoW
born: Bath   enlisted: Bath
Buried: St. Sever Cemetery Extension, Rouen. Grave P.IX.I.4A. Age 18. Date joined BEF: not on Medal Card. Formerly 3685, Devonshire Regiment. 1901 Census: son of George Keeling, fireman at factory, and Emma Keeling, 2 High Street, Twerton, Bath, Somerset.

Martin Body

APRIL 1918

1st April 1918
Pte. James Dillon 3/6726 KIA
born: St.Helens, Lancs.   enlisted: Exeter   residence: St.Helens
Buried: Moreuil Communal Cemetery Allied Extension. Grave R.22. Age 24. No Medal Card. 1901 Census: son of James Dillon, labourer chemical works, and Maria Dillon, 5 Canal Bank East, St. Helens, Lancs. 1911 Census: coal miner roadman (below), son of James Dillon, labourer above ground, and Maria Dillon, 4 Brown Street, St. Helens, Lancs. CWGC: mother the late Maria Dillon, family address: 104 Berry's Lane, Parr, St. Helens, Lancs.
Pte. Charles Frederick Ekers 31784 KIA
born: Paignton   enlisted: Newton Abbot   residence: Paignton
No known grave. Pozieres Memorial, Panel 24 and 25. Age 19. Joined BEF: not on Medal Card. 1901 Census: son of Hedley H. E. Ekers, house painter, and Mary E. Ekers, 24 Roundham Cottages, Paignton, Devon. CWGC: family address: 8 Roundham Cottages, Paignton, Devon.
Cpl. Frederick Robert Redwood MM 9336 DoW
born: Torquay   enlisted: Torquay
Buried: Namps-Au-Val British Cemetery. Grave I.F.14. Age 27. Joined BEF: 06/11/14 with original cadre. 1901 Census: son of Robert Redwood, general labourer, and Sarah Redwood, 32 Glamorgan Street, Torquay, Devon. 1911 Census: haulier, son of Robert Redwood, mason's labourer, and Sarah A. Redwood, 18 Broadmead Road, Newton Abbot, Devon. CWGC: husband of Beatrice Wyatt (formerly Redwood), 9 Daison Cottages, Lymington Road, Torquay, Devon.
Pte. John Nicholas Andrew 205186 Died
born: Wendron, Cornwall   enlisted: Redruth   residence: Camborne
Buried: St. Sever Cemetery Extension, Rouen. Grave P.IX.G.5A. Age 24. Joined BEF: not on Medal Card.   1901 Census: son of John Nicholas Andrew, tin miner – metal cleaner, and Eliza Jane Andrew, Bolenowe Moor, Camborne, Cornwall. 1911 Census: general labourer, son of John Nicholas Andrew, tin miner, and Eliza Jane Andrew, Bolenowe, Troon, Camborne, Cornwall.

2nd April 1918
Lt. Alfred Lewis Noon DoW
Buried: Namps-Au-Val British Cemetery. Grave I.H.27. Age 20.
Joined BEF: not on Medal Card. 1901 Census: born at Butterleigh, Devon, son of the Rev. Alfred K. Noon and Alice E. Noon, the Vicarage, Butterleigh, Tiverton, Devon. 1911 Census: schoolboy, son of Alfred Knight Noon, clergyman established church, and Alice Elizabeth Noon, the Rectory, Butterleigh, Cullompton, Devon. Educated at Blundell's School.
Pte. Harry Barter 31795 KIA
born: Southampton   enlisted: Southampton
No known grave. Pozieres Memorial, Panel 24 and 25. No Medal Card. 1901 Census: apprentice engineer, stepson of Robert Wilkinson, labourer/navvy, and Rhoda Wilkinson, shop assistant, 22 Page Street, St. Mary's, Southampton, Hants.
Pte. Cecil John Toms Hannaford 203241 KIA
born: Bigbury   enlisted: Newton Abbot   residence: Kingsbridge
No known grave. Pozieres Memorial, Panel 24 and 25. Age 35. Joined BEF: not on Medal Card.   1901 Census: horseman on farm, son of James Ryder Hannaford, cattleman on farm, and Jane S. Hannaford, Rectory Cottage, Bigbury, Kingsbridge, Devon. 1911 Census: farm

labourer, son of James Ryder Hannaford, farm labourer, and Jane Stidson Hannaford, Bigbury, Kingsbridge, Devon.
Pte. George William Crowfoot 26310 DoW
born: Chelmsford   enlisted: Newton Abbot
Buried: Bois Guillaume Communal Cemetery Extension. Grave C.14A. Age 36. 'A' Company. Joined BEF: not on Medal Card. 1891 Census: son of Jane Crowfoot, widow, baker, 9 Legg Street, Chelmsford, Essex. 1901 Census: assistant in a furniture shop, living with his mother, 11 Legg Street, Chelmsford, Essex. 1911 Census: shop assistant, husband of Beatrice Mary Crowfoot, 20 Coronation Road, Newton Abbot, Devon. CWGC: son of the late Mr. and Mrs. Crowfoot, of Chelmsford, Essex. According to a report in the Newton Abbot Western Guardian of 11th November 1918, Pte. Crowfoot, of 'A' Company, died of wounds at Rouen Hospital (No.8 General Hospital) and, prior to enlistment, was employed by Wm. Badcock & Son, Courtney Street, Newton Abbot, Devon. An article in the Mid Devon Advertiser states that he was married and his widow lived in Coronation Road, Newton Abbot. Pte. Crowfoot's name is on the War Memorial at All Saints Church, Highweek, Newton Abbot, Devon.

7th April 1918
Pte. William Claud Berry 292084 KIA
born: Birmingham   enlisted: Birmingham
No known grave. Pozieres Memorial, Panel 24 and 25. Age 19. Joined BEF: not on Medal Card. 1911 Census: schoolboy, son of John James Berry, steel metal worker, and Minnie Berry, 49 Morley Road, Ward End, Aston, Birmingham, Warwickshire. CWGC: son of John Berry, 18 Southern Road, Ward End, Birmingham, Warwickshire.
Pte. George Henry Brock 18398 KIA
born: Ilsington, Devon   enlisted: Newton Abbot   residence: Kingsteignton
No known grave. Pozieres Memorial, Panel 24 and 25. Age 24. Joined BEF: 15/02/15. Medal Card annotation: *'Pres. Dead 7/4/18'*. 1901 Census: son of George Brock, horseman on farm, and Alice Brock, Lanes Tenement, Ilsington, Devon. 1911 Census: farm servant, cattle man on farm, at the farm of Peter Mann, Ware Barton, Kingsteignton, Newton Abbot, Devon.
Pte. Ernest Parsons 45774 KIA
born: Ladock, Cornwall   enlisted: Truro   residence: Wadebridge
No known grave. Pozieres Memorial, Panel 24 and 25. Age 22. Joined BEF: not on Medal Card. 1901 Census: son of William Parsons, cattleman on farm, and Elizabeth A. Parsons, Nansough, Ladock, Cornwall. 1911 Census: horseman on farm, boarding at the home of Henry Watkins, GWR platelayer, Halezy, Grampound Road, Ladock, Cornwall.

9th April 1918
2/Lt. Howard Grimley Floyd Attached from 1/5th Devons KIA
Born: Gravelly Hill, Warwickshire   residence: Bournemouth
Buried: Ramleh War Cemetery. Grave T.13. Age 20. Joined BEF: not on Medal Card. 1901 Census: son of Herbert E. Floyd, wine and spirit merchant, and Elsie R. Floyd, 87 Birchfield Road, Handsworth, Staffordshire. 1911 Census: schoolboy, son of Elsie Rose Floyd, married, matron of nursing home, Montsend Nursing Home, 22-24 Loone Park Road, Bournemouth, Dorset. CWGC: son of Elsie Hope Willson (formerly Floyd), "Spa Croft," 95 Alexandra Road, Parkstone, Dorset, and the late Herbert Edwin Floyd. 9th April 1918 is the date recorded for 2/Lt. Floyd's death in SDGW, CWGC and on the Medal Card, but in 'The Devonshire Regiment 1914-1918, vol.1', he is listed as being KIA in the vicinity of Villers-Bretonneux, between 21st and 27th April 1918. The discrepancy in the dates remains unexplained, but he is more likely

to have been killed during the latter period, rather than on 9th April, when the Battalion was out of the line.

11th April 1918
Pte. Henry Thomas Croxford 291158 DoW
born: Islington, Middx.   enlisted: Holloway
Buried: St. Sever Cemetery Extension, Rouen. Grave P.IX.5.A. Age 25. Joined BEF: not on Medal Card. Formerly 2817, Devonshire Regiment. 1901 Census: son of Henry Croxford, general labourer, and Elizabeth Croxford, Islington, Middlesex. 1911 Census: van guard, son of Henry Croxford, general labourer, and Elizabeth Croxford, 7 and 8 Beaconsfield Buildings, Randells Road, Islington, London. CWGC: family address: 19 Beaconsfield Buildings, York Road, King's Cross, London.

13th April 1918
Pte. Ernest John Ashmore 30273 DoW
born: no record   enlisted: Barnstaple   residence: Morchard Bishop
Buried: St. Sever Cemetery Extension, Rouen. Grave P.VII.K.9A. Age 23. Joined BEF: not on Medal Card. Formerly 2900, Royal North Devon Yeomanry. 1901 Census: son of John Ashmore, general labourer, and Mary Ashmore, Barn Cottage, Morchard Bishop, South Molton, Devon. 1911 Census: farm labourer, son of John Ashmore, farm labourer, and Mary Ashmore, Chapmans, Morchard Bishop, Devon.
L/Cpl. Albert Tidwell 9395 Died
born: Honiton   enlisted: Honiton
Buried:Tourgeville Military Cemetery.Grave I.D.2. Age 24. Joined BEF: 06/11/14 with original cadre. 1901 Census: son of Edwin Tidwell, stockman on farm, and Elizabeth Tidwell, Buckerell, Honiton, Devon. CWGC: brother of William Tidwell, of Buckerell, Honiton, Devon. However, there is no Albert Tidwell recorded in the 1901 Census who had a brother named William, and the William Tidwell who is recorded there had no brother named Albert.

19th April 1918
Pte. Frederick Weed 203551 DoW
born: Islington, Middx.   enlisted: Exeter   residence: Honiton
Buried: St. Sever Cemetery Extension, Rouen. Grave P.XI.L.2A. Age 21. Joined BEF: not on Medal Card. 1901 Census: son of Frederick Weed, fur skinner, and Harriet Weed, 17 Bookham Street, Shoreditch, London. 1911 Census: junior clerk, boarding at the house of Edward Prior, 38 tyler Street, East Greenwich, London. CWGC: brother of Edward John Weed, 47 Welbourne Road, High Cross, Tottenham, London.

21st April 1918
Pte. James Godley 205026 KIA
born: Portsmouth   enlisted: Portsmouth
Buried: St. Pierre Cemetery, Amiens. Grave XII.D.4. Age 30. Joined BEF: not on Medal Card. Formerly 203165, Dorsetshire Regiment. 1901 Census: son of Teresa Kelly, flower hawker, 5 Nobb's Lane, Portsmouth, Hampshire.
Pte. William James Blight 71158 Died (home)
born: Oreston, Devon   enlisted: Newton Abbot   residence: Torquay
Buried: Torquay Cemetery and Extension. Grave F.2.259. Age 19. Joined BEF: not on Medal Card. 1901 Census: son of John F. Blight, groom/gardener/domestic, and Harriet Blight,

Woodlands Lodge, Tormoham, Torquay, Devon. 1911 Census: schoolboy, son of John Farrs Blight, domestic gardener, and Harriet Louisa, Blight, Gardeners Cottage, Woodlands, Chelston, Devon. CWGC: family address, 38 Walnut Road, Chelston, Torquay.

22nd April 1918
Pte. Ernest Leonard Gould 70442 KIA
born: Hampstead, Middx.   enlisted: Bristol
Buried: Blangy-Tronville Communal Cemetery. Grave 41. Age 19. Joined BEF: not on Medal Card. 1901 Census: son of William L. Gould, carpenter, and Susan A. Gould, Chestnut Grove, Staines, Middlesex. 1911 Census: schoolboy, son of Susan Ann Gould, widow, monthly nurse, 67 New Richmond Terrace, Avonmouth, Bristol, Glos. CWGC: Mrs. S. A. Gould's address: 67 Richmond Villas, Avonmouth, Bristol, Glos.
Pte. William Treemare Moore 203004 KIA
born: Torpoint, Cornwall   enlisted: Plymouth   residence: Torpoint
Buried: Adelaide Cemetery, Villers Bretonneux. Grave II.M.1. Age 19. Joined BEF: 05/09/15. 'B' Company. Formerly 5796, 4/Devons. 1901 Census: son of Alexander J. Moore, shipwright, and Helena Moore, 2 Coldstream Terrace, Torpoint, Cornwall. 1911 Census: son of Alexander I. Moore, shipwright, and Helena Augusta Moore, 2 Coldstream Terrace, Torpoint, Cornwall. CWGC: names him William Tremeer Moore.

24th April 1918
2/Lt. Richard Cornelius Arthur Cardew KIA
Buried: Adelaide Cemetery, Villers-Bretonneux. Grave II.I.14. Age 19. Joined BEF: 14/12/17 as 2/Lt. Commissioned 26/09/17. Formerly 235087 Gunner Cardew, Royal Field Artillery. 1911 Census: schoolboy, son of Arthur Cardew, Assistant Secretary to Board of Education (Civil Service), and Alexandra Rhoda Cardew, 4 North View, Wimbledon Common, Wimbledon, London. CWGC: son of Arthur Cardew and Alexandra Rhoda Cardew, 4 North View, Wimbledon, London.
Capt. Henry Harris Jago MC KIA
No known grave. Pozieres Memorial, Panel 24 and 25. Age 23. Joined BEF: not on Medal Card. Formerly Pte. H.H. Jago, PS5115, Royal Fusiliers. 1901 Census: son of William H. Jago, solicitor, and Jeannie Jago, 10 Leigham Terrace, Plymouth, Devon. Brother of 2/Lt. Edward Arthur Jago, KIA 1st July 1916, also while serving with the 2/Devons. In Emmanuel Church, Compton Giffard, Plymouth, in 1919, a Chapel is dedicated to their memory.
2/Lt. Fred Lethbridge DCM KIA
Born: South Molton, Devon
Buried: Adelaide Cemetery, Villers-Bretonneux. Grave II.P.16. Age 30. Joined BEF: 06/11/14 with original cadre. Formerly 8021 L/Sgt. Lethbridge, 2/Devons . Date of commission not recorded on Medal Card. 1901 Census: son of John Lethbridge, farm bailiff, and Elizabeth Lethbridge, Pigwell, Lydford, Tavistock, Devon. 1911 Census: Lance Corporal Lethbridge, 2/Devons, St. George's Barracks, Malta. Earlier in the war Sgt. Lethbridge was awarded the DCM, the citation reading: *"For conspicuous gallantry and devotion to duty. He cut a gap in the enemy wire under heavy machine gun and rifle fire. Later, although wounded, he refused to leave his post until wounded a second time."*
A/Cpl. James Betts 6887 KIA
born: Canning Town   enlisted: Stratford
No known grave. Pozieres Memorial, Panel 24 and 25. Joined BEF: 06/11/14 with original cadre.

L/Cpl. Donald Leo Carden 30912 KIA
born: Cologne, Germany   enlisted: Dorchester   residence: Lyme Regis
No known grave. Pozieres Memorial, Panel 24 and 25. Joined BEF: not on Medal Card. Formerly 8/10155, 206th Infantry Battalion.

Cpl. Ernest Comer 8376 KIA
born: Landcross, Devon   enlisted: Exeter
No known grave. Pozieres Memorial, Panel 24 and 25. Age 29. Joined BEF: 06/11/14 with original cadre. 1891 Census: son of Henry Comer, tiler, and Emma Comer, 5a Handy Cross Cottages, Clovelly Road, Bideford, Devon. 1911 Census: 2/Devons, St. Georges Barracks, Malta. CWGC: son of the late Harry Comer and Emma Comer, husband of Lilian H. Comer, Castle Hill, Hemyock, Cullompton, Devon. A photograph of Cpl. Comer's medal trio, which are part of the author's collection, is included in this book.

Cpl. Patrick Costello MM 9917 KIA
born: Coundon, Durham   enlisted: Spennymore, Durham
No known grave. Pozieres Memorial, Panel 24 and 25. Age 30. Joined BEF: 03/12/14. 1901 Census: son of Richard Costello, labourer in iron works, and Mary A. Costello, 20 James Street, Stockton on Tees, Durham. 1911 Census: 'shop sinker', husband of Norah Costello, 17 Hut, Easington Colliery, Castle Eden, Durham.

Cpl. Arthur Edwin Dorothy 29045 KIA
born: Exeter   enlisted: Exeter
No known grave. Pozieres Memorial, Panel 24 and 25. Age 19. Joined BEF: not on Medal Card. Best match in 1901 Census is Arthur T. Dorothy, son of Walter F. Dorothy, gas engine labourer, and Sarah Dorothy, 8 St. Leonard's Avenue, Exeter, Devon.

Sgt. George Henry Down 37438 KIA
born: Marwood, Devon   enlisted: Exeter   residence: Chulmleigh
Buried: Adelaide Cemetery, Villers-Bretonneux. Grave II.P.20. Age 38. No Medal Card. 1911 Census: horseman on farm, husband of Beatrice Nellie Down, Dean, Landkey, Goodleigh, Devon. CWGC: son of John and Elizabeth Down, husband of Beatrice Nellie Down, New Street, Chulmleigh, Devon.

L/Cpl. Francis George Jago 69049 KIA
born: Plymouth   enlisted: Plymouth
No known grave. Pozieres Memorial, Panel 24 and 25. Age 30. Joined BEF: not on Medal Card. 1901 Census: son of Samuel E. Jago, engine fitter, and Emma Jago, 14 Cornwall Street, Devonport, Devon. 1911 Census: labourer, son of Samuel Jago, engine fitter, and Emma Jago, 7 Albany Street, Devonport, Devon.

Cpl. William John Pike 15596 KIA
born: Yeoford, Devon   enlisted: Exeter   residence: Morchard Bishop
No known grave. Pozieres Memorial, Panel 24 and 25. Age 23. Joined BEF: 10/06/15. 1911 Census: servant, horseman on farm of James Coram Troake, Pedley Barton, East Worlington, Morchard Bishop, Devon. CWGC: son of Samuel Pike and Alice Pike, Pedley Cottage, East Worlington, Crediton, Devon.

Cpl. James Radmore 9099 KIA
born: Newton Abbot   enlisted: Bulford, Hants.   residence: Torquay
No known grave. Pozieres Memorial, Panel 24 and 25. Age 26. Joined BEF: 06/11/14 with original cadre. 1911 Census: 1/Devons, Mooltan and Lucknow Barracks, Uttar Pradesh, India.

Sgt. Joseph Spiller Seldon MM 26061 KIA
born: Broadclyst, Devon   enlisted: London S.E.
Buried: Adelaide Cemetery, Villers-Bretonneux. Grave II.L.22. Age 46. Joined BEF: 22/08/14

with original cadre of 1/Devons as 7059 Pte. Seldon. 1881 Census: son of George Seldon, farmer, and Mary Seldon, Hunnacott, Landkey, Devon. CWGC: family address: Welcombe Farm House, Swimbridge, Devon.

Pte. Abraham Adelson 30894 KIA
born: Hackney   enlisted: Stratford   residence: Hackney
No known grave. Pozieres Memorial, Panel 24 and 25. Age 20. No Medal Card. 1901 Census: son of Morris Adelson, boot maker, and Mina L. Adelson, 15 Ash Grove, Hackney, London. 1911 Census: schoolboy, son of Morris Adelson, 'boot laster', and Minnie Adelson, 4 Carmel Buildings, Bethnal Green, London. CWGC: son of Minnie Adelson, 31 Ellingfort Road, Mare Street, Hackney, London, and the late Morris Adelson.

Pte. Alfred George Allen 71141 KIA
born: Bincombe, Dorset   enlisted: Weymouth   residence: Upway, Dorset
No known grave. Pozieres Memorial, Panel 24 and 25. Age 18. No Medal Card. 1901 Census: son of Harry Allen, groom/gardener, and Fanny Allen, Lower Farm Cottages, Bincombe, Weymouth, Dorset. 1911 Census: schoolboy, son of Harry Allen, gardener and cowman on farm, and Fanny Allen, Bincombe, Dorset. CWGC: family address: "Brooklyn", Steepleton, Dorchester, Dorset.

Pte. Arthur Bailey 53770 KIA
born: St.Michaels, Cheshire   enlisted: Macclesfield
No known grave. Pozieres Memorial, Panel 24 and 25. Age 34. Joined BEF: not on Medal Card. Son of Frank Bailey, fustian cutter, and Emily Bailey, of 53 Mill Lane, Sutton, Macclesfield, Cheshire. 1911 Census: silk weaver, husband of Annie Bailey, card lacer, 141 High Street, Macclesfield, Cheshire. CWGC: parents address: II Lee Street, Macclesfield, husband of Annie Bailey, 141 High Street, Macclesfield, Cheshire.

Pte. Clifford Barker 3/7016 KIA
born: Sheffield   enlisted: Exeter   residence: Sheffield
No known grave. Pozieres Memorial, Panel 24 and 25. Age 21. Joined BEF: 17/12/14. 1901 Census: son of George W. Barker, silver and gold roller, and Amy Barker, 199 Penistone Road, Nether Hallam, Sheffield, Yorkshire. 1911 Census: schoolboy, son of George William Barker, German silver roller, widower, 32 Barrack Lane, Sheffield, Yorkshire.

Pte. Charles Henry Bealey 71151 KIA
born: Taunton   enlisted: Exeter
No known grave. Pozieres Memorial, Panel 24 and 25. Age 35. Joined BEF: not on Medal Card. 1901 Census: son of Charles Bealey, solicitor's managing clerk, and Martha Bealey, Langstone Villa, Weston-Super-Mare, Somerset.

Pte. George Beck 51451 KIA
born: Plymouth   enlisted: Plymouth
Buried: Adelaide Cemetery, Villers-Bretonneux. Grave II.K.1. Age 19. Joined BEF: not on Medal Card. 1901 Census: son of Francis Beck, general labourer, and Bessie Beck, 18 Vauxhall Street, Plymouth. 1911 Census: son of Francis Beck, fisherman, and Bessie Beck, 1 Looe Cottages, Plymouth, Devon. CWGC: family address: 6 High Street, Plymouth, Devon.

Pte. Saxby Brimcombe 68083 KIA
born: Newton Abbot   enlisted: Newton Abbot
Buried: Adelaide Cemetery, Villers-Brettoneux. Grave 11.F.15. Age 19. Joined BEF: not on Medal Card. CWGC: son of Lewis H. Brimcombe and Annie Brimcombe, 13 Abbotsbury Road, Newton Abbot. Name recorded on the War Memorial at All Saints Church, Highweek, Newton Abbot, Devon.

Pte. Charles Edward Brown 71164 KIA
born: Sparshott, Hants.   enlisted: Whitchurch
No known grave. Pozieres Memorial, Panel 24 and 25. Joined BEF: not on Medal Card.

Pte. Charles George Brown 68585 KIA
born: Southampton   enlisted: Southampton
No known grave. Pozieres Memorial, Panel 24 and 25. Joined BEF: not on Medal Card.

Pte. Fernley Buckingham 16706 KIA
born: Plymouth   enlisted: Plymouth
No known grave. Pozieres Memorial, Panel 24 and 25. Joined BEF: not on Medal Card.

Pte. George Sidney Bullock 71166 KIA
born: King's Norton   enlisted: Pershore   residence: Evesham
Buried: Adelaide Cemetery, Villers-Brettoneux. Grave III.M.14. Age 19. Joined BEF: not on Medal Card. 1901 Census: son of William S. Bullock, steam roller and engine repairer, and Laura E. Bullock, Salford Priory, Salford, Stratford on Avon, Warwickshire. 1911 Census: schoolboy, son of William Bullock, engineers fitter, and Laura Bullock, Church Lench, Evesham, Worcs.

Pte. Sidney John Butland 11807 KIA
born: Plymouth   enlisted: Devonport
Buried: Adelaide Cemetery, Villers-Brettoneux. Grave II.P.9. Age 19. Joined BEF: 22/09/15. 1901 Census: son of John Butland, railway guard, and Ellen Butland, 42 Hanwell Street, Plymouth, Devon. 1911 Census: schoolboy, son of John Butland, GWR guard, and Ellen Butland, 29 Ilbert Street, Plymouth, Devon.

Pte. George Candelent 36604 KIA
born: no record   enlisted: Birmingham
No known grave. Pozieres Memorial, Panel 24 and 25. Age 33. Joined BEF: not on Medal Card. Pte. Candelent first served as 36604 with the Devons, then as 306367 with Royal Engineers, then 92314 with Labour Corps, and back to the Devons as 36604. 1891 Census: son of William Candelent, goldsmith, and Esther Candelent, 90 Loyalls Street, Aston, Warwickshire. CWGC: son of the late William Candelent and Esther Candelent, husband of Emily Elizabeth Candelent, 5 Bredon Terrace, Brookfield Road, Birmingham, Warwickshire.

Pte. Richard Carne 31792 KIA
born: Paul, Cornwall   enlisted: Penzance   residence: Paull, Cornwall
No known grave. Pozieres Memorial, Panel 24 and 25. Age 20. Joined BEF: not on Medal Card. 1901 Census: Richard F. Carne, son of Richard Carne, farmer, and Jane Carne, Halwyn and Pensilva, Paul, Cornwall.

Pte. Herbert Ernest Carter 31819 KIA
born: Bedminster   enlisted: Bristol
No known grave. Pozieres Memorial, Panel 24 and 25. Age 19. Joined BEF: not on Medal Card. Formerly 8/2199, 51/Grad battalion Devon. 1901 Census: son of William B. Carter, railway policeman, and Harriett Carter, 42 London Street, Kingswood, Gloucestershire.

Pte. William George Christopher 70417 KIA
born: Witchampton, Dorset   enlisted: Wimborne
Buried: Adelaide Cemetery, Villers-Brettoneux. Grave II.M.12. Age 19. Joined BEF: not on Medal Card. 1901 Census: son of Francis Christopher, carter on farm, and Ellen Christopher, of Deans Leaze, Witchampton, Dorset.

Pte. Walter Cilvert 204437 KIA
born: Andover   enlisted: Andover
No known grave. Pozieres Memorial, Panel 24 and 25. Age 19. Joined BEF: not on Medal

Card. 1901 Census: son of John Cilvert, ironmoulder, and Elizabeth Cilvert, 1 Millway Road, Andover Hants. 1911 Census: schoolboy, son of John Cilvert, iron moulder, and Elizabeth Cilvert, Charlton, Andover, Hampshire. CWGC: family address: 109 Vigo Road, Andover, Hants.

Pte. Albert Collis Colbran 315038 KIA
born: Eastbourne   enlisted: Newton Abbot
Buried: Adelaide Cemetery, Villers-Brettoneux. Grave II.M.8. Age 33, born March 1886. 'B' Company. Joined BEF: not on Medal Card. Formerly 5145, Devonshire Regiment. 1891 Census: son of Horace Colbran, green grocer, and Mary Ann Colbran, 12 Myotte Road, Willingdon, Eastbourne, Sussex. 1911 Census: gardener domestic, husband of Ellen Martha Colbran, Woodpark Cottage, Lustleigh, Newton Abbot, Devon. CWGC: son of Horace Colbran and Mary A. Colbran, Eastbourne, husband of Martha E. Colbran, Beach Cottage, Riverside, Shaldon, Teignmouth, Devon.

Pte. Albert Ernest Cotton 44354 KIA
born: Totton, Hants.   enlisted: Southampton
Buried: Adelaide Cemetery, Villers-Brettoneux. Grave II.I.16. Age 35. Joined BEF: not on Medal Card. 1901 Census: joiner, son of Louisa Cotton, widow, 22 Shirley Park Road, Shirley, Southampton, Hampshire. 1911 Census: joiner/carpenter, son of Louisa Cotton, widow, 20 Shirley Park Road, Southampton, Hampshire. CWGC: husband of M. G. Cotton, "Laurel Bank," Norham Avenue, Shirley, Southampton, Hampshire.

Pte. Cyril Henry Cox 71177 KIA
born: Cheltenham   enlisted: Swindon
No known grave. Pozieres Memorial, Panel 24 and 25. Age 18. Joined BEF: not on Medal Card. 1901 Census: grandson of William Cox, railway signalman, and Fanny Cox, 5 Newent Place, Cheltenham, Gloucestershire. 1911 Census: schoolboy, grandson of William Cox, signalman, and Fanny Cox, 5 Newent Place, Marsh Lane, Cheltenham, Glos.

Pte. Sydney Prince Denham 291410 KIA
born: Manchester   enlisted: Birmingham
No known grave. Pozieres Memorial, Panel 24 and 25. Age 37. Joined BEF: not on Medal Card. Formerly 3078, Devonshire Regiment. 1891 Census: of Emily Denham, living on own means, Spen Lane, Thorpe, Derbyshire. 1901 Census: road asphalter, boarding at 5 Florence Terrace, Birkbeck Road, Ilford, Essex. CWGC: son of Thomas Denham and Emily Denham, Grindon, Staffs, husband of Kate Denham, 3164 Anderton Street, Ladywood, Birmingham.

Pte. Edward Dennis 315052 KIA
born: Combe Martin   enlisted: Exeter
No known grave. Pozieres Memorial, Panel 24 and 25. Age 36. Joined BEF: not on Medal Card. 1891 Census: son of George Dennis, agricultural labourer, and Eliza Dennis, Main Street, Combe Martin, Devon. 1901 Census: servant, carter on farm, Hoyles, Combe Martin, Devon. 1911 Census: market garden labourer, husband of Louisa Dennis, Moorcoms Place, Combe Martin, Devon.

Pte. Albert William Derrick 290766 KIA
born: Swindford, Devon   enlisted: Bristol   residence: Swindford
Buried: Adelaide Cemetery, Villers-Brettoneux. Grave II.O.24. Age 20. Joined BEF: not on Medal Card. 1911 Census: 'caddie', son of Albert W. Derrick, 'paper machine man', and Mary Derrick, Swinford, Bitton, Bristol, Glos.

Pte. Arthur Victor Dibden 30926 KIA
born: Romsey, Hants.   enlisted: Winchester   residence: Romsey
No known grave. Pozieres Memorial, Panel 24 and 25. Age 19. Joined BEF: not on Medal Card. Formerly 8/1123, 206/Infantry Battalion. 1901 Census: son of Harry Victor Dibden,

general labourer, and Ella Jennet Dibden, West Wellow, Southampton. 1911 Census: schoolboy, son of Harry Victor Dibden, horseman on farm, and Ella Jennet Dibden, Near Shoe Inn, Plaitford, Romsey, Hampshire. CWGC: family address: Wellow Wood, Romsey, Hampshire.

Pte. Harry Downey 13185 KIA
born: Surbiton, Surrey   enlisted: Abercynon, Glam.
Buried: Adelaide Cemetery, Villers-Brettoneux. Grave I.E.8. Age 35. 'B' Company. No Medal Card. 1901 Census: son of Elizabeth Downey, widow, plain cook, 18 Smeaton Road, Wandsworth, London. 1911 Census: 'assistant repairer', boarding at the house of David Davies, 27 Upper Terrace, Pontypridd, Glam. CWGC: son of late Henry Downey and Elizabeth Downey, 10 Lancaster Cottages, Richmond Hill, Surrey.

Pte. Leslie Gordon Drew 203214 KIA
born: Plymouth   enlisted: Plymouth
No known grave. Pozieres Memorial, Panel 24 and 25. Age 32. Joined BEF: not on Medal Card. 1901 Census: son of Charles Drew, coal dealer, and Mabel Drew, 127 Exeter Street, Plymouth, Devon. 1911 Census: baker, boarding at the house of William Edward Eke, stationary engineman, 16 Coburg Lane, Plymouth, Devon.

Pte. Frederick Percy Dunn 68791 KIA
born: High Bickington   enlisted: Exeter   residence: High Bickington
Buried: Adelaide Cemetery, Villers-Brettoneux. Grave II.M.16. Age 19. No Medal Card. 1911 Census: schoolboy, son of Walter Dunn, blacksmith and ironmonger dealer, and Mary Ann Dunn, High Bickington, Umberleigh, Devon. CWGC: son of Walter Dunn and Mary Ann Dunn, High Bickington, Umberleigh, Devon.

Pte. Leslie Victor Dunning 70429 KIA
born: Gillingham, Dorset   enlisted: Dorchester   residence: Gillingham, Dorset
No known grave. Pozieres Memorial, Panel 24 and 25. Age 19. Joined BEF: not on Medal Card. 1901 Census: son of Joseph Ward Dunning, brickyard labourer, and Mary Dunning, Cottage, Wavening Lane, Gillingham, Dorset. 1911 Census: schoolboy, son of Joseph Ward Dunning, clay miner, and Mary Dunning, Waverland Lane, Gillingham, Dorset. CWGC: family address: New Road, Gillingham, Dorset.

Pte. Gilbert Hugh Field 70438 KIA
born: Chatham, Kent   enlisted: Worcester   residence: Redditch
Buried: Adelaide Cemetery, Villers-Brettoneux. Grave II.M.6. Age 19. Joined BEF: not on Medal Card. 1901 Census: son of CSM George Harry Field, Royal Engineers, and Mary Ann Field, St. Mary's Barracks, Gillingham, Kent. 1911 Census: schoolboy, son of George Harry Field, licensed victualler/Army pensioner, and Mary Ann Field, Royal Hotel, Market Place, Redditch, Worcs. CWGC: family address: 20 Mason Road, Redditch, Worcs.

Pte. Frederick Fisher 69081 KIA
born: Tiverton   enlisted: Tiverton
Buried: Adelaide Cemetery, Villers-Brettoneux. Grave II.M.15. Age 19. No Medal Card. 1901 Census: son of Jesse Fisher, general labourer, and Harriet Fisher, 19 Little Silver, Tiverton, Devon.

Pte. Arthur Richard Fleman 203477 KIA
born: Mutley, Devon   enlisted: Plymouth
No known grave. Pozieres Memorial, Panel 24 and 25. Age 20. Joined BEF: not on Medal Card. 1901 Census: son of Richard Fleman, carpenter, and Emma Fleman, 40 Belgrave Road, Plymouth, Devon.

Pte. George Anthony Fooks 71191 KIA
born: Bruton, Somerset   enlisted: Weston-Super-Mare
Buried: Adelaide Cemetery, Villers-Brettoneux. Grave II.E.11. Age 18. Joined BEF: not on Medal Card. 1901 Census: son of Frederick Fooks, farmer, and Amelia F. Fooks, Greenscombe, Milton Clevedon, Somerset. 1911 Census: schoolboy at "Britford", Berrow Road, Burnham-on-Sea, Somerset. The living arrangements are unclear because there is no mother or father recorded, but there are three other Fooks offspring, the eldest being Irene Agnes Fooks, aged 18. Also recorded are three middle-aged/elderly people living on 'private means', and a nurse, Celia Amanda Newman. CWGC: son of Amelia F. Fooks, "Britford," Berrow Road, Burnham-on-Sea, Somerset, and the late Frederick Fooks.

Pte. Arthur Charles Ford 290732 KIA
born: Bristol   enlisted: Yeovil
No known grave. Pozieres Memorial, Panel 24 and 25. Age 20. Joined BEF: not on Medal Card. Formerly 2383, Devonshire Regiment. 1901 Census: son of Charles Ford, slaughterman, and Ellen Ford, 6 Morley Road, Bristol. 1911 Census: 'assisting father in the butcher's business', son of Charles Ford, master butcher (born USA), and Ellen Ford, 2 St. Martin's Terrace, West Coker, Yeovil, Somerset. CWGC: family address: Yeovil, Somerset.

Pte. Reginald Gaylard 71195 KIA
born: Odcombe, Somerset   enlisted: Taunton   residence: Odcombe
No known grave. Pozieres Memorial, Panel 24 and 25. Age 18. Joined BEF: not on Medal Card. 1901 Census: son of Henry Gaylard, agricultural labourer, and Emily Gaylard, 16 Church Road, Odcombe, Somerset.

Pte. Herbert Geen 70444 KIA
born: Marwood, Devon   enlisted: Barnstaple   residence: Marwood
No known grave. Pozieres Memorial, Panel 24 and 25. Age 19. Joined BEF: not on Medal Card. 1901 Census: son of John Geen, general labourer, and Eliza A. Geen, Marwood, Devon. 1911 Census: scholar, son of Eliza Geen, widow, plain sewer, Prixford, Marwood, Devon.

Pte. Frederick William Gill 44130 KIA
born: no record   enlisted: Romsey, Hants.   residence: Honiton
Buried: Adelaide Cemetery, Villers-Brettoneux. Grave II.E.10. Joined BEF: not on Medal Card. Annotation to Medal Card: *Mother makes application for medals of dead son 19/8/23.*

Pte. Charles Herbert Goldie 70450 KIA
born: Woodstock, Oxon.   enlisted: Oxford
No known grave. Pozieres Memorial, Panel 24 and 25. Age 18. Joined BEF: not on Medal Card. 1901 Census: son of June L. Goldie, head of family, Oxford Street, Woodstock, Oxon. 1911 Census: schoolboy, son of James Lipsham Goldie, Regimental Sergeant Major, Queen''s Own Oxfordshire Hussars, and Julia Lucy Goldie, St. Thomas House, Paradise Street, Oxford.

Pte. Harry Lifely Golding 43098 KIA
born: Kidderminster, Worcs.   enlisted: Kidderminster
No known grave. Pozieres Memorial, Panel 24 and 25. Age 20. Joined BEF: not on Medal Card. 1901 Census: son of Charley Golding, painter, and Florence Golding, 106 Wood Street, Kidderminster, Worcestershire. 1911 Census: grandson of Lifely Golding, carpenter, and Ann Golding, 12 Crescent Road, Kidderminster, Worcs.

Pte. William Gilbert Greenall 70449 KIA
born: Coombe-in-Teignhead   enlisted: Newton Abbot
No known grave. Pozieres Memorial, Panel 24 and 25. Age 19. Joined BEF: not on Medal Card. 1901 Census: son of Alice Greenall, wife of artificer R.N., 2 Holly Well, Haccombe with Combe, Coombe-in-Teignhead, Newton Abbot, Devon. 1911 Census: schoolboy, son of Alice

Greenall, married, 37 Beaumont Road, Newton Abbot, Devon.
Pte. Percy Charles Griffin 70451 KIA
born: Swindon   enlisted: Devizes   residence: Swindon
Buried: Adelaide Cemetery, Villers-Brettoneux. Grave II.O.25. Age 19. 'A' Company. Joined BEF: not on Medal Card. 1901 Census: son of Charles Griffin, railway guard, and Eliza Griffin, 12 Queen's Road, Swindon, Wilts. 1911 Census: schoolboy, son of Charles Griffin, goods guard, and Eliza Griffin, 12 Alexandra Road, Swindon, Wiltshire. CWGC: family address: 12 Alexandra Road, Swindon, Wiltshire.
Pte. James Albert Hall 69848 KIA
born: Shoreditch   enlisted: Kingsway   residence: Hoxton
No known grave. Pozieres Memorial, Panel 24 and 25. Age 17. No Medal Card. 1901 Census: son of Sydney H. Hall, grocer shopkeeper, and Harriet A. C. R. Hall, 61 Bethune Road, Stoke Newington, London.
Pte. Arthur George Hammond 70458 KIA
born: Cardiff   enlisted: Bristol
No known grave. Pozieres Memorial, Panel 24 and 25. Joined BEF: not on Medal Card.
Pte. Ernest Hancock 204858 KIA
born: Plumstead   enlisted: Woolwich   residence: Plumstead
No known grave. Pozieres Memorial, Panel 24 and 25. Age 23. Joined BEF: not on Medal Card. Formerly 653688, 21/London Regiment. 1901 Census: son of William Hancock, machinist in factory, and Amelia Hancock, 24 Orissa Road, Plumstead, London. 1911 Census: telegraph messenger, son of William Hancock, gun maker machinist, and Amelia Hancock, 24 Orissa Road, Plumstead, London.
Pte. Albert James Hawker 30953 KIA
born: Birmingham   enlisted: Birmingham
No known grave. Pozieres Memorial, Panel 24 and 25. Age 20. Joined BEF: not on Medal Card. Formerly 8/1940, 206/Infantry Battalion. 1911 Census: schoolboy, son of John Hawker, district road foreman, and Cordela Hawker, 57 Thomas Street, Aston, Birmingham, Warwickshire.
Pte. Frederick John Jewell 16976 KIA
born: Plymouth   enlisted: Plymouth   residence: Bugle, Cornwall
No known grave. Pozieres Memorial, Panel 24 and 25. Age 28. Joined BEF: not on Medal Card. 1901 Census: son of Tom Jewell, carpenter, and Susan Ann Jewell, 26 Oakfield Terrace, Plymouth, Devon. 1911 Census: 'waggoner coal stores', husband of Constance Ruby Jewell, living with in-laws, James Stacey, mill man in powder factory, and Hannah Stacey, Trevelmond, Liskeard, Cornwall. CWGC: family address: Station Road, Bugle, Cornwall.
Pte. Charles Henry Job 39774 KIA
born: Gunnislake, Cornwall   enlisted: Plymouth   residence: Gunnislake
No known grave. Pozieres Memorial, Panel 24 and 25. Age 23. Joined BEF: not on Medal Card. Formerly 34858 of the D.C.L.I. 1901 Census: son of Isaac Job, granite quarry labourer, and Martha Job, Calstock Road, Calstock, Cornwall. 1911 Census: son of Isaac Job, general labourer, and Martha Job, Calstock Road, Gunnislake, Tavistock, Cornwall.
Pte. Frederick Thomas Keirl 13145 KIA
born: Cardiff   enlisted: Barry, Glam.
No known grave. Pozieres Memorial, Panel 24 and 25. Age 25. Joined BEF: 27/07/15. On Medal Card as L/Cpl., 9/Devons. 1911 Census: apprentice carpenter, son of James Keirl, mason, and Bartha Keirl, tailoress, 162 Barry Road, Barry, Glam.

Pte. Frederick Maidment 3/7073 KIA
born: Axminster   enlisted: Exeter   residence: Axminster
Buried: Adelaide Cemetery, Villers-Brettoneux. Grave II.F.21. Age 42. Joined BEF: 17/12/14. 1881 Census: son of James Maidment, railway labourer, and Sarah Jane Maidment, Silver Street, Axminster, Devon. CWGC: son of James Maidment, Musbury Road, Axminster, Devon, and the late Sarah Jane Maidment.

Pte. George Middleton 67916 KIA
born: Aston, Warwickshire   enlisted: Birmingham
No known grave. Pozieres Memorial, Panel 24 and 25. Age 19. Joined BEF: not on Medal Card. 1901 Census: son of Rosina Middleton, head of household, 192 Heneage Street, Aston, Birmingham. 1911 Census: schoolboy, son of Henry Middleton, blacksmith's striker tube trade, and Rosina Middleton, 28 Court, 192 Henaege Street, Aston, Birmingham. CWGC: son of Henry Middleton and Rosina Middleton, address as 1901 and 1911.

Pte. Charles Webbell Nicholls 203123 KIA
born: Plymouth   enlisted: Plymouth
No known grave. Pozieres Memorial, Panel 24 and 25. Joined BEF: not on Medal Card.

Pte. James Parker 30783 KIA
born: Teigngrace, Devon   enlisted: Newton Abbot
No known grave. Pozieres Memorial, Panel 24 and 25. Joined BEF: not on Medal Card. Formerly 35016 of the D.C.L.I. 1901 Census: son of Humphrey Parker, farm labourer, and Mary Parker, of Yonder House, Teigngrace, Newton Abbot, Devon.

Pte. Thomas Parry 10241 KIA
born: Poplar, London   enlisted: Exeter   residence: Chesterfield
Buried: Adelaide Cemetery, Villers-Brettoneux. Grave II.B.3. Age 23. Joined BEF: 19/01/15. 1901 Census: son of Sarah Ann Parry, widow, 54 St. Mary's Gate, Chesterfield, Derbyshire. CWGC: brother of Miss Sarah Parry, 1963 Park Avenue, Montreal, Quebec, Canada.

Pte. John Payton 16089 KIA
born: Walthamstow   enlisted: Walthamstow
No known grave. Pozieres Memorial, Panel 24 and 25. Age 20. Joined BEF: not on Medal Card. 1901 Census: son of John Payton and Margaret Payton, 13 Southwold Road, Hackney, London. CWGC: son of the late Mrs. John Payton, 11 Newman Road, Walthamstow, London.

Pte. Arthur John Richards 203627 KIA
born: Shobrooke, Devon   enlisted: Plymouth   residence: Ivybridge
No known grave. Pozieres Memorial, Panel 24 and 25. Age 19. Joined BEF: not on Medal Card. 1901 Census: son of John Richards, wood man, and Ellen Richards, New Parks, Monkhampton, Okehampton, Devon. 1911 Census: nephew of Robert Richards, dairy farmer, and Sarah Richards, 20 Summerland Street, Barnstaple, Devon. CWGC: family address: Monks Mills, Monkhampton, Winkleigh, Devon.

Pte. William Henry Rose 205033 KIA
born: Aldershot   enlisted: Poole   residence: Aldershot
Buried: Adelaide Cemetery, Villers-Brettoneux. Grave II.E.14. Age 20. Joined BEF: not on Medal Card. Formerly 203319, Dorsetshire Regiment. CWGC: son of James Rose and Emily Rose, Hill Cottage, Alderholt, Salisbury, Wilts.

Pte. Frederick John Rowe 10734 KIA
born: Ilfracombe   enlisted: Taunton   residence: Ilfracombe
No known grave. Pozieres Memorial, Panel 24 and 25. Age 31. Joined BEF: 25/07/15. 1911 Census: servant, hotel barman, Britannia Hotel, Ilfracombe, Devon.

Pte. Sydney Crymes Rundle MM 30443 KIA
born: no record   enlisted: Launceston
Buried: Adelaide Cemetery, Villers-Brettoneux. Grave II.I.8. Age 30. Joined BEF: not on Medal Card. 1901 Census: son of John K. Rundle, farmer and butcher, and Hannah Rundle, Colbay Farm, St. Stephen's by Launceston, Cornwall. 1911 Census: butcher, son of Hannah Rundle, butcher and farmer, Ridgegrove, St. Stephens, Launceston, Cornwall.
Pte. Everett Henry Shepherd 16699 KIA
born: Newton Ferrers   enlisted: Plymouth
Buried: Adelaide Cemetery, Villers-Brettoneux. Grave II.P.18. Age 24. No Medal Card. 1901 Census: son of Samuel Shepherd, wood ranger, and Eliza Shepherd, Newton Ferrers, Plymouth, Devon. 1911 Census: general labourer, son of Samuel Shepherd, general labourer, and Eliza Ann Shepherd, Newton Ferrers, Plymouth, Devon.
Pte. Ernest William Sizer 25650 KIA
born: Tunstead, Norfolk   enlisted: Exeter   residence: Starcross
Buried: Adelaide Cemetery, Villers-Brettoneux. Grave II.M.10. Age 32. No Medal Card. 1901 Census: gardener/domestic, son of George Sizer, gardener/domestic, and Mary Sizer, Beach Road, Scratby, Norfolk. 1911 Census: gardener domestic, husband of Jessie Sizer, living with in-laws William Ley, farm labourer, and Sarah Ley, Ratisloe, Poltimore, Exeter, Devon.
Pte. Albert Edward Smithson 43236 KIA
born: Plymouth   enlisted: Plymouth
Buried: Adelaide Cemetery, Villers-Brettoneux. Grave I.F.1. Age 25. Joined BEF: not on Medal Card. 1901 Census: son of Samuel Smithson, Sergeant in the Royal Engineers Militia, and Mary A. Smithson, 15 Cotehele Avenue, Plymouth, Devon. 1911 Census: barman, son of Samuel Smithson, painter/labourer, and Mary Ann Smithson, 80 Embankment Road, Plymouth, Devon.
Pte. Gilbert Stuttard 20844 KIA
born: Oldham   enlisted: Rochdale
Buried: Adelaide Cemetery, Villers-Brettoneux. Grave II.L.24. Age 26. Joined BEF: not on Medal Card. 1901 Census: son of Mark Stuttard, mechanic at woollen mill, and Hannah Stuttard, 270 Spotland Buildings, Rochdale, Lancs. 1911 Census: cotton operative, minder, son of Mark Stuttard, millwright/pattern maker, and Hannah Matilda Stuttard, 270 Spotland Bridge, Rochdale, Lancs.
Pte. John Richard Taswell 68799 KIA
born: Isle Abbots, Somerset   enlisted: Castle Cary   residence: Kingsdon
No known grave. Pozieres Memorial, Panel 24 and 25. Age 19. Joined BEF: not on Medal Card. 1901 Census: son of Fredrick James Taswell, ordinary labourer on farm, and Ellen Taswell, Round Oak, Isle Abbots, Bridgwater, Somerset. 1911 Census: schoolboy, son of Frederick James Taswell, farm labourer, and Ellen Taswell, Highbrooks, Long Sutton, Langport, Somerset. CWGC: family address: Langport Road, Somerton, Somerset.
Pte. Harold Taylor 203620 KIA
born: Plymouth   enlisted: Plymouth
Buried: Adelaide Cemetery, Villers-Brettoneux. Grave I.E.1. Age 25. Joined BEF: not on Medal Card. 1901 Census: son of Ernest James Taylor, house painter, and Ellen Taylor, 38 Belgrave Road, Plymouth. 1911 Census: barman, son of Ernest James Taylor, house painter, widower, 10 Ivydale Road, Plymouth, Devon. CWGC: husband of Hilda Biddle (formerly Taylor), 46 Chudleigh Road, Laira, Plymouth, Devon.
Pte. Arthur Joseph Upward 205035 KIA
born: Shaftesbury   enlisted: Southampton   residence: Romsey
No known grave. Pozieres Memorial, Panel 24 and 25. Age 21. Joined BEF: not on Medal

Card. Formerly 202882, Dorsetshire Regiment. 1901 Census: son of Joseph W. Upward, stockman on farm, and Julia J. Upward, Whitenap, Romsey, Hants. 1911 Census: schoolboy, son of Joseph William Upward, cowman on farm, widower, Whitenap Lane, Romsey, Hants. CWGC: son of William Joseph Upward, Whitenap Park, Romsey, Hants.

Pte. Clifford Edward Wallis 42625 KIA
born: no record   enlisted: Exeter
No known grave. Pozieres Memorial, Panel 24 and 25. Age 22. Joined BEF: not on Medal Card. 1901 Census: son of Clifford B. Wallis, national schoolmaster, and Eleanor A. Wallis, assistant mistress, The School House, Bishopsteignton, Newton Abbot, Devon. 1911 Census: scholar, son of Clifford Blinman Wallis, head teacher, and Eleanor Anne Wallis, assistant teacher, The School House, Bishopsteignton, Devon.

Pte. William Walsh 13997 KIA
born: Waterford, Ireland   enlisted: Wattstown, Glam.
Buried: Adelaide Cemetery, Villers-Brettoneux. Grave II.P.1. Age 30. 'B' Company. Joined BEF: not on Medal Card, records number as 13007. 1901 Census: son of William Walsh, widower, groom, 19 Lansdown Crescent, Bath, Somerset. 1911 Census: 'collier hewer underground', one of three brothers lodging at the home of George Jones, grocer's haulier, and Sarah Ann Jones, 42 Ruth Street, Bargoed, Merthyr Tidfil, Glam. CWGC: husband of Jessie Walsh, 48 Pleasant View, Wattstown, Ynishir (Rhondda), Glam.

Pte. Ralph Vinning Walters 67936 KIA
born: Buckfastleigh   enlisted: Newton Abbot   residence: Buckfastleigh
No known grave. Pozieres Memorial, Panel 24 and 25. Age 19.
Joined BEF: not on Medal Card. 1901 Census: son of James Walters, general labourer, and Elizabeth Walters, of Tanyard, Sherwells Court, Buckfastleigh, Devon. 1911 Census: schoolboy, son of JamesWalters, carter, and Elizabeth Walters, Sherwill's Court, Silver Street, Buckfastleigh, Devon. CWGC:family address: Sun House, Buckfastleigh, Devon.

Pte. Reginald Stewart Wheeler 31827 KIA
born: Gloucester   enlisted: Gloucester
Buried: Adelaide Cemetery, Villers-Brettoneux. Grave II.F.8. Age 19. Joined BEF: not on Medal Card. 1901 Census: son of Hansell Wheeler, widow, sweet stuff shop keeper, Lower Westgate Lane, Gloucester. 1911 Census: schoolboy, boarding at the house of Harry Walden, moulder, and Ann Walden, 20 Lower Westgate Street, Gloucester, Glos.

Pte. Luther James Willcocks 28025 KIA
born: Plymouth   enlisted: Plymouth
Buried: Adelaide Cemetery, Villers-Brettoneux. Grave II.F.19. Age 26. 'D' Company. Joined BEF: 05/11/14 with 25 Field Ambulance, R.A.M.C. 1135. 1901 Census: son of Alice Willcocks, widow, laundress, 35 Lees Street, Plymouth, Devon. 1911 Census: shop assistant, son of Alice Willcocks, widow, 30 Looe Street, Plymouth, Devon. CWGC: son of Alice Willcocks and the late Luther Willcocks, 64, Belgrave Road, Mutley, Plymouth.

Pte. Harold Edward Mansfield Williams 51575 KIA
born: Birmingham   enlisted: Birmingham
Buried: Adelaide Cemetery, Villers-Brettoneux. Grave I.E.7.   Age 21. No Medal Card. 1901 Census: son of Bernard J. Williams, police constable, and Sarah Williams, 35 Shottery Road, Old Stratford, Warwickshire. CWGC: family address: 380B, Victoria Road, Aston, Birmingham.

Pte. Frederick James Wood 316093 KIA
born: Sidmouth   enlisted: Exeter
Buried: Adelaide Cemetery, Villers-Brettoneux. Grave II.B.2.   Age 19. No Medal Card. 1901 Census: son of Frederick Wood, tailor journeyman, and Mary Elizabeth Wood, Honiton, Devon.

1911 Census: son of Frederick Wood, journeyman tailor, and Mary Elizabeth Wood, Chapel Lane, New Street, Honiton, Devon. CWGC: family address: Chapel Street, Honiton, Devon.

Pte. Walter Woodbury 8236 KIA
born: Tiverton enlisted: Exeter
No known grave. Pozieres Memorial, Panel 24 and 25. Age 33. No Medal Card. 1901 Census: son of James Woodberry, butcher, and Harriet Woodberry, 44 Gold Street, Tiverton, Devon. CWGC: family address: 56 Bampton Street, Tiverton, Devon, and that he served II years in the 2/Devons.

Pte. Leonard Stanley Wright 62347 KIA
born: Exeter enlisted: Exeter
No known grave. Pozieres Memorial, Panel 24 and 25. Age 21. Joined BEF: not on Medal Card. Formerly 844 and 33194, Devonshire Regiment. 1901 Census: son of Walter Charles Wright, printer/compositor, and Eliza Wright, 33 Oxford Street, St. Thomas, Exeter, Devon. 1911 Census: plumber's apprentice, son of Walter Charles Wright, compositor, and Eliza Wright, 19 Beaufort Road, St. Thomas, Exeter, Devon. CWGC: family address: 36 Oxford Street, St. Thomas, Exeter, Devon.

Pte. Harry Avery 71143 DoW
born: North Tawton, Devon enlisted: Okehampton residence: North Tawton
Buried: Adelaide Cemetery, Villers-Brettoneux. Grave I.F.8. Age 18.
Joined BEF: not on Medal Card. 1901 Census: son of William Avery, gardener (not domestic), and Mary Avery, Globe Cottages, North Tawton, Devon. 1911 Census: schoolboy, son of William Avery, labourer contractors, and Mary Avery, address as above.

Pte. Arthur Brooker 30907 DoW
born: Lambeth enlisted: Lambeth
Buried: St. Sever Cemetery Extension, Rouen. Grave P.IX.N.7A. Age 30. Joined BEF: not on Medal Card. Formerly 9/20858, 206th Infantry Battalion.

Pte. Edward Broughton 68114 DoW
born: Derby enlisted: Newark, Notts.
Buried: St. Pierre Cemetery, Amiens. Grave XII.B.2. Joined BEF: not on Medal Card. CWGC: son of Mr. J. Broughton, 21 Tenter Buildings, Newark, Notts.

25th April 1918

Pte. William Manning 30555 KIA
born: Exeter enlisted: Exeter
No known grave. Pozieres Memorial, Panel 24 and 25. Age 22. Joined BEF: not on Medal Card. 1901 Census: son of William Manning, laundry assistant, and Ellen Manning, laundress, 1 Colleton Grove, Exeter, Devon. 1911 Census: tailor, son of William Manning, laundry man, and Ellen Manning, laundress, address as above.

A/Cpl. Bert Pannell 11278 KIA
born: Exmouth enlisted: Exeter residence: Exmouth
Buried: Crouy British Cemetery, Crouy-Sur-Somme. Grave I.A.18. Age 23. Joined BEF: 19/01/15, 1/Devons. 1901 Census: Albert Pannell, son of Frank Pannell, baker journeyman, and Sarah Pannell, London Road, Colyton, Devon. 1911 Census: porter, son of Henry Pannell, labourer, and Annie Pannell, 4 Halls Buildings, Exmouth, Devon.

Pte. Albert Edward Hawkes 18664 KIA
born: Vauxhall enlisted: London S.W.
Buried: Mont Huon Military Cemetery, Le Treport. Grave V.G.5A. Age 20. Joined BEF: 15/12/15 with 8th Devons. 1901 Census: son of Harry James Hawkes, sorter post office, and

Elizabeth M. Hawkes, 22 Wickersley Road, Battersea, London. 1911 Census: schoolboy, son of Harry James Hawkes, civil servant porter, and Elizabeth Maria Hawkes, 124 Strathville Road, Southfields, Wandsworth, London. CWGC: son of Mrs. E. M. Hawkes, 28 Maskell Road, Lower Tooting, London.

26th April 1918
Pte. Leonard Warren 316007 KIA
born: Camborne   enlisted: Redruth   residence: Camborne
No known grave. Pozieres Memorial, Panel 24 and 25. Age 20.
Joined BEF: not on Medal Card. 1901 Census: son of John Warren, tin miner, and Eunice Warren, the family boarding at Parken Bowen, Camborne, Cornwall. 1911 Census: schoolboy, son of Emmie Warren, char woman, widow, 58 College Street, Camborne, Cornwall.
Pte. Herbert Frank Crofts 70425 DoW
born: Castle Bromwich   enlisted: Warwick   residence: Castle Bromwich
Buried: Longpre-Les-Corps Saints British Cemetery. Grave A.16. Age 19. Joined BEF: not on Medal Card. 1911 Census: schoolboy, son of Mary Ann Crofts, widow, Castle Bromwich, Birmingham, Warwickshire. CWGC: youngest son of the late Joseph Crofts and Mary Ann Crofts, Castle Bromwich, Birmingham, Warwickshire.
Pte. Ernest Arthur Murch 290322 DoW
born: Bradninch, Devon   enlisted: Exeter   residence: Hele, Devon
Buried: Crouy British Cemetery, Crouy-Sur-Somme. Grave I.B.25. Age 24. Joined BEF: not on Medal Card. 1901 Census: son of John Murch, carpenter, and Emma Jane Murch, 16 Ellerhaye Cottages, Silverton, Devon. 1911 Census: 'cutter boy, paper mill', son of John Murch, carpenter at paper mill, and Emma Jane Murch, 1 Ellerhays Cottages, Hele, Cullompton, Devon. CWGC: family address: 1 Ellerhayes Cottages, Hele, Cullompton, Devon.

27th April 1918
Pte. William Burt 292147 DoW
born: Bedminster   enlisted: Bristol
Buried: St. Pierre Cemetery, Amiens. Grave XIII.B.3. Age 26. Joined BEF: not on Medal Card. 1901 Census: son of William Burt, wood carver, and Elizabeth M. Burt, 6 Pearson Street, Balsall Heath, Birmingham. 1911 Census: 'smith striker', son of William Burt, widower, 6 Sargent Street, Bedminster, Bristol, Glos. CWGC: husband of Alice Burt (likely to be from a second marriage), 14 Temple Street, Bedminster, Bristol, Glos.
Pte. Fred Farrar 15262 DoW
born: Heywood, Lancs.   enlisted: Rochdale   residence: Heywood
Buried: Longpre-Les-Corps Saints British Cemetery. Grave A.9. Age 44. Joined BEF: 18/05/15. 1891 Census: apprentice iron moulder, son of George Farrar, iron moulder, and Margaret Farrar, 33 Nelson Street, Heywood, Lancs. 1901 Census: iron founder/moulder, husband of Alice Charlotte Farrar, cotton cardloom hand, 40 Hannah Street, Middleton, Lancs. 1911 Census: iron founder, husband of Charlotte A. Farrar, 20 Clarke Street, Heywood, Bury, Lancs.

28th April 1918
L/Cpl. George Medland 28394 DoW
born: Lew Down, Devon   enlisted: Exeter   residence: Lew Down
Buried: Crouy British Cemetery, Crouy-Sur-Somme. Grave II.A.16. Age 39. Joined BEF: not on Medal Card. 1891 Census: son of George Medland, farm labourer, and Mary Medland, Holster Yard, Marystow, Devon. 1911 Census: farm labourer, husband of Ellen Medland, Holster Yard,

Lewdown, Tavistock, Devon.

29th April 1918
Pte. Harry Cecil Gaskill 204358 DoW
born: Birmingham   enlisted: Birmingham
Buried: Crouy British Cemetery, Crouy-Sur-Somme. Grave I.D.23. Age 19. Joined BEF: not on Medal Card. 1901 Census: son of Harry Gaskill, law clerk, and Harriet Ann Gaskill, 5 Castleford Grove, Yardley, Worcs. 1911 Census: schoolboy, son of Harry Gaskill, law writer, and Harriett Ann Gaskill, 107 Fallows Road, Aston, Birmingham, Warwickshire. CWGC: family address: Sparkhill, Birmingham.

30th April 1918
Pte. Walter Fitzgerald Campkin 41365 DoW
born: Alderney C.I.   enlisted: Aldershot
Buried: Longpre Military Cemetery. Grave 39.B.6. No Medal Card. One of 56 men who died in the 12th and 55th Casualty Clearing Stations.
Pte. Gerald Edgar Gidley 67891 DoW
born: Wolborough   enlisted: Newton Abbot
Buried: St. Sever Cemetery Extension, Rouen. Grave P.XI.J.12B. Age 19. Lewis gunner. Birthday: 16/12/1898. Educated: Newton Abbot Secondary School. Enlisted: 19/04/17. Joined BEF: 01/04/18. 1901 Census: son of John Gidley, grocer/storeman, and Eliza Jane Gidley, 25 Bowden Hill, Wolborough, Newton Abbot, Devon. 1911 Census: schoolboy, son of John Gidley, grocer's van driver, and Eliza Gidley, 1 Bearne's Lane, Newton Abbot, Devon. CWGC: son of Eliza Jane Gidley (nee Turpin), Grove House, Newton Abbot, Devon, and the late John Gidley, of the Royal Marine Artillery. An article in the Newton Abbot Western Guardian of 9th May 1918, relates that G.E.Gidley died of gunshot wounds to the chest, leg and arm. The Easter 1918 edition of the Abbotonian Magazine states that he was a pupil at Newton Abbot Secondary School in 1912-1913. He was also a Sunday School teacher, was in charge of the 2nd Highweek Boy Scout Troop and was instrumental in forming the Wolf Cub Scouts. Before enlisting, he was employed by Messrs. J. Gibbons, of Newton Abbot. The Devonshire Roll of Honour in Exeter Cathedral incorrectly records his name as George Edgar Gidley.
Pte. Thomas Holmes 30951 KIA
born: Stepney   enlisted: London   Buried: St. Sever Cemetery Extension, Rouen. Grave P.XI.M.IIB. This cemetery is far from the battlefield, which suggests that he probably DoW. Joined BEF: not on Medal Card. Formerly 8/2426, 206th Infantry Battalion.
Pte. Arthur William John Lewis 31823 DoW
born: Bristol   enlisted: Bristol
Etretat Churchyard Extension. Grave II.D.4. Age 19. No Medal Card. 1901 Census: son of John Lewis, stone sawyer, and Bessie M. Lewis, 12 Elm Road, Bristol. 1911 Census: son of John Lewis, general labourer, and Bessie Magdalene Lewis, 71 Thornleigh Road, Horfield, Bristol, Glos. CWGC: family address: 71 Thornleigh Road, Horfield, Bristol, Glos.
Pte. William Toms 45535 DoW
born: Highcliff, Hants.   enlisted: Winchester   residence: New Milton
Buried: St. Sever Cemetery Extension, Rouen. Grave P.XI.J.10B. Age 19. Joined BEF: not on Medal Card. 1901 Census: son of Emanuel Toms (age 63 in 1901) farm labourer, and Ellen Toms (age 28 in 1901), Chewton Common, Highcliff, Hants. 1911 Census: schoolboy, son of Emanuel Toms, unemployed invalid, and Ellen Toms, Walkford Glen Cottage, Highcliffe, Christchurch, Hants.

The 2nd Devons War Diary

MAY 1918

1st May 1918
Pte. James Job Dance 292080 DoW
born: Birmingham   enlisted: Birmingham
Buried: Crouy British Cemetery, Crouy-Sur-Somme. Grave I.D.15. Age 19. Joined BEF: not on Medal Card. Formerly 3759, Devonshire Regiment. 1901 Census: son of Joshua Henry Dance, furniture remover, and Mary Ann Dance, 55 Ruston Street, Ladywood, Birmingham. 1911 Census: schoolboy, son of Joshua Henry Dance, carter, and Mary Ann Dance, 63 Sherborne Street, Ladywood, Birmingham, Warwickshire. CWGC: address: Sherbourne Street, Ladywood, Birmingham, Warwickshire.

3rd May 1918
Pte. Albert James Johnson 18585 DoW
born: Antony, Cornwall   enlisted: Plymouth
Buried: Mont Huon Military Cemetery, Le Treport. Grave VI.H.9A. Age 35. Joined BEF: 15/12/15, 8/Devons. 1891 Census: son of John Johnson, farm labourer and pensioner, and Emma Johnson, Quarry Street, Antony, Torpoint, Cornwall. CWGC: husband of A. M. Johnson, 15 Albany Street, Devonport.

5th May 1918
Pte. Walter Francis Gazey 70447 DoW
born: Dymock, Glos.   enlisted: Gloucester   residence: Dymock
Buried: Mont Huon Military Cemetery, Le Treport. Grave VI.G.7B. Age 19. Joined BEF: not on Medal Card. 1911 Census: schoolboy, son of Bartholomew F. Gazey, farm labourer, and Rebecca Gazey, Cut Hill, Redmarley, Newent, Glos. CWGC: son of Mr. and Mrs. Gazey, Angus Villa, Old Road, Maisemore, Glos.

11th May 1918
Pte. Sidney Claud Friend 44242 DoW
born: Whitchurch, Devon   enlisted: Plymouth   residence: Whitchurch
Buried: St. Sever Cemetery Extension, Rouen. Grave P.XI.G.9A. Age 20. Joined BEF: not on Medal Card. 1901 Census: records him as the son of William James Friend, general labourer on land roads, and Rhoda Friend, of Village, Whitchurch, Devon. 1911 Census: schoolboy, son of William James Friend, general labourer highway, and Rhoda Friend, 2 Paisey Cottages, Whitchurch, Tavistock, Devon. CWGC: family address: 2 Paisy Cottage, Whitchurch, Tavistock, Devon.

13th May 1918
Pte. Albert Congrave 74134 KIA
born: Birmingham   enlisted: Birmingham
Buried: La Ville-Aux-Bois British Cemetery. Grave I.A.12. Age 18. Joined BEF: not on Medal Card. 1911 Census: schoolboy, son of James Arthur Congrave, railway engine driver, and Gertrude Congrave, 73 Ellesmere Road, Saltley, Birmingham, Warwickshire. CWGC: son of Arthur Congrave and Gertrude Congrave, address as 1911 Census.

14th May 1918
Pte. John Joseph Letts 315159 KIA
born: Aston   enlisted: Birmingham
Buried: Hermonville Military Cemetery. Grave III.G.5. Age 19. Joined BEF: not on Medal Card. 1901 Census: son of Thomas H. Letts, tinplate worker, and Annie A. Letts, 31 Lower trinity Street, Aston, Birmingham. 1911 Census: 'spoon worker, sorter', son of Thomas Henry Letts, lamp maker, and Annie Amelia Letts, 15 Hack Street, Aston, Birmingham, Warwickshire.

16th May 1918
L/Cpl. William James Webb 33907 DoW
born: South Molton   enlisted: Barnstaple   residence: South Molton
Buried: Vailly British Cemetery. Grave III.A.35. Age 30. No Medal Card. 1901 Census: son of William James Webb, solicitors clerk, and Mary Ann Webb, 33 Cooks Cross, South Molton, Devon. 1911 Census: law clerk, son of Mary Ann Webb, widow, 40 Cooks Cross, South Molton, Devon. CWGC: family address: 7 Broad Street, South Molton, Devon.

26th May 1918
Cpl. Arthur Shortridge 15392 KIA
born: Bideford   enlisted: Exeter   residence: Bow, Devon
No known grave. Soissons Memorial. Age 23. Joined BEF: not on Medal Card. 1901 Census: son of William H. Shortridge, general labourer, and Harriet Shortridge, Clifton Street, Bideford, Devon. 1911 Census: pottery labourer, son of Harriet Shortridge, widow, 16 Torrington Lane, Bideford, Devon.
L/Cpl. Walter George Tucker 24881 KIA
born: Harberton   enlisted: Exeter   residence: Starcross
No known grave. Soissons Memorial. Age 20. Joined BEF: not on Medal Card. 1901 Census: son of William George Tucker, railway signalman, and Charlotte Tucker, 2 Branscoff Cottages, Wolborough with Newton Abbot, Devon. 1911 Census: schoolboy, son of William Tucker, station master, and Charlotte Tucker, Orpheus, Victoria Road, Dartmouth, Devon. CWGC: family address: 1 Mayfield Terrace, Wiveliscombe, Somerset.
Pte. Horace Gilbert Badman 70407 KIA
born: Street, Somerset   enlisted: Weston-Super-Mare   residence: Street
No known grave. Soissons Memorial. Age 19. Joined BEF: not on Medal Card. 1901 Census: son of Kate Badman, 48 West End, Street, Somerset. 1911 Census: son of Harry Badman, stoker, and Kate Badman, 75 West End, Street, Somerset.
Pte. Leslie Honychurch Blake 205129 KIA
born: Torrington   enlisted: Torrington
No known grave. Soissons Memorial. Age 20. Joined BEF: not on Medal Card. Formerly 225304, Royal North Devon Yeomanry. 1901 Census: son of Thomas G. Blake, chamois leather worker, and Charlotte Blake, Milliner, 201 New Street, Torrington, Devon. 1911 Census: 'errand boy in stationer's shop', son of Thomas Gent Blake, 'leather grounder', and Charlotte Blake, 201 New Street, Torrington, Devon. CWGC: son of the late Thomas Gent Blake.
Pte. Dennis Petrie Devereux 70431 KIA
born: Birmingham   enlisted: Birmingham
No known grave. Soissons Memorial. Age 19. Joined BEF: not on Medal Card. 1901 Census: son of Ernest Devereux, foreman cycle trade, and Elizabeth Devereux, 70 Nelson Road, Aston Manor, Warwickshire. 1911 Census: schoolboy, son of Ernest Devereux, general engineer tool maker, and Elizabeth Devereux, address as above. CWGC: family address: 195 Clifton Road,

Aston, Birmingham, Warwickshire.
Pte. Mark Farrow 5881 KIA
born: Swaffham Prior, Cambs.   enlisted: London   residence: Swaffham Prior
Buried: La Ville-Aux-Bois British Cemetery. Grave I.K.16. Age 37. Joined BEF: not on Medal Card. 1891 Census: son of William Farrow, agricultural labourer, and Ann Farrow, 31 High Street, Swaffham Prior, Cambridgeshire.
Pte. Joseph Henry Hall 37141 KIA
born: Cardiff   enlisted: Exeter   residence: Hemyock, Devon
No known grave. Soissons Memorial. Age 34. Joined BEF: not on Medal Card. 1901 Census: saddle and shoemaker, son of William Hall, saddle and shoemaker, and Ann Hall, Cornhill, Hemyock, Devon. 1911 Census: boot maker, husband of Amy Georgina Hall, Cornhill, Hemyock, Devon.
Pte. Leonard Gregory Keen 74069 KIA
born: High Wycombe   enlisted: Aylesbury   residence: High Wycombe
No known grave. Soissons Memorial. Age 18. 'C' Company. Joined BEF: not on Medal Card. 1901 Census: son of William Keen, chair manufacturer, and Lavinia Keen, Westville House, Wycombe, Bucks. 1911 Census: schoolboy, son of William Keen, chair manufacturer, and Lavinia Keen, High Chester, West Wycombe, Bucks. CWGC: family address: 180 West Wycombe Road, High Wycombe, Bucks. Mother the late Lavinia Emily Keen.
Pte. Denis Rupert Walker 291760 KIA
born: Chearsley, Bucks.   enlisted: Aylesbury
No known grave. Soissons Memorial. Age 29. Joined BEF: not on Medal Card. 1901 Census: nephew of Sarah Badrick, lacemaker, Chearsley, Aylesbury, Bucks. 1911 Census: shepherd on farm, son of Alfred Walker, carman on farm, and Ada Walker, New Cottages, Chearsley, Aylesbury, Bucks. CWGC: son of Alfred William Walker, and Ada Sophia Walker, address as above.
Pte. Frederick Mitchell 74076 KIA
born: Cattisfield, Herts.   Enlisted: Frome, Somerset.   Residence: Bath
No known grave. Soissons Memorial. Age 18. Joined BEF: not on Medal Card. Census records not found.

27th May 1918
Lt.Col. Rupert Henry Anderson-Morshead DSO KIA
No known grave. Soissons Memorial. Age 32. 2/Devons Commanding Officer. Joined BEF: 06/11/14 with original cadre. During the war he left to command 1/Devons but returned to the 2nd. Awarded posthumous DSO. 3 times mentioned in despatches. Croix de Guerre with Palm (France). Medal card annotation: *Mrs. L Anderson-Morshead makes application for 1914 Star in respect of the services of her husband the late Lt. Col. R. H. Anderson-Morshead. 12/5/19. Address: Wayside, Lingfield, Surrey.* 1911 Census: Lieutenant Anderson-Morshead 2/Devons, St. George's Barracks, Malta, but is noted as 'absent'. CWGC: son of John Yonge Anderson-Morshead and Helen Beatrice Anderson-Morshead, Lusways, Sidmouth, Devon, and husband of Lucy Helen Anderson-Morshead, of Green Hedges, Lingfield, Surrey. On the 90th anniversary of the battle in which he died, a service of remembrance was held in his memory at Salcombe Regis Church.
Pte. Sidney Allingham 290744 DoW
born: Wool, Dorset   enlisted: Wareham
SDGW: DoW 05/02/1915, but CWGC shows date as 27/05/1918 – Army number 290744 suggests that later date is correct. Joined BEF: not on Medal Card. 1911 Census: schoolboy,

born 1900, son of Alfred Allingham, general farm labourer, and Elizabeth Allingham, New Road, Wareham, Dorset. CWGC: son of Alfred Allingham, flour mill carter, and Elizabeth Allingham, 3 Bindon Cottages, Wool, Dorset.

2/Lt. Stanley James Cussell Attached from Army Service Corps. KIA
No known grave. Soissons Memorial. Age possibly 25. No Medal Card. There is a Stanley John Cussell in the 1911 Census, born 1893 at Leytonstone, Essex, electrical clerk, son of John Stratton Cussell, hatter's salesman, and Alice Cussell, 193 Cann Hall Road, Leytonstone, Essex.

2/Lt. Frederick Charles Leat KIA
Buried: Jonchery-Sur-Vesle British Cemetery. Grave I.F.33. Age 21. Joined BEF: 16/11/15. Formerly SPTS/4033, Private then Sergeant, Royal Fusiliers. Commissioned 30/10/17 as 2/Lt. in the Devons. 1901 Census: son of Charles Leat, policeman, and Petronella Leat, 1 Harbour Avenue, Plymouth, Devon. 1911 Census: schoolboy, son of Charles John Leat, policeman, and Petronella Potter Leat, the Police Station, Exeter Street, Plymouth, Devon. CWGC: family address: 95 Oakfield Terrace, Plymouth.

2/Lt. Cyril Elmore Pells KIA
No known grave. Soissons Memorial. Age 27. Joined BEF: 14/04/18, after commission. Formerly Private 765308, 28/London Regiment. Son of Arthur Pells, architect, and Caroline A. Pells, Alexandra Road, Beccles, Suffolk. 1911 Census: apprentice in the optical scientific instrument trade, boarding at Bury Street, Ruislip, Middlesex. CWGC: family address: "Briarwood," Grange Estate, Beccles, Suffolk. Husband of Mary Anita Pells (nee Reeve), San Luis Obispo, California, U.S.A.

Lt. Louis Nicholas Lindsay Tindal MC KIA
No known grave. Soissons Memorial. Possible age 25. Joined BEF: 17/08/16. 1891 and 1901 Census records: possibly the son of James Tindal, tailors cutter, and Isabella Tindal, 4 Fairfield Road, Newcastle-Upon-Tyne.

L/Cpl. Frederick Charles Baker 30908 KIA
born: Alverstoke, Hants. enlisted: Winchester residence: Alverstoke
No known grave. Soissons Memorial. Age 21. No Medal Card. 1911 Census: schoolboy, son of Alfred Baker, general labourer, and Martha Elizabeth Baker, 83 Village Road, Alverstoke, Hants. CWGC: son of Alfred Baker and Martha Elizabeth Baker, 6 The Avenue, Alverstoke, Gosport, Hants.

L/Sgt. Walter Hampton Bridgman 205160 KIA
born: Broadwood, Cornwall enlisted: Barnstaple residence: Launceston
No known grave. Soissons Memorial. Age 19. Joined BEF: not on Medal Card, but recorded as Corporal. 1911 Census: 'farmer's son', son of Richard Bridgman, farmer, and Rebecca Bridgman, Downicary, Lower Hill, Broadwood, Devon. CWGC: son of Richard and Rebecca Bridgman.

L/Cpl. Ronald John Lear MM 22138 KIA
born: Plymouth enlisted: Plymouth
No known grave. Soissons Memorial. Age 22. Joined BEF: not on Medal Card. 1901 Census: son of John Lear, blacksmith, and Sarah Lear, 1 Brunswick Place, Devonport, Devon. 1911 Census: son of John Lear, blacksmith, and Sarah Lear, 2 St. Barnabus Villas, Devonport, Devon. CWGC: family address: 5 Moor View, Laira, Plymouth, Devon.

Sgt. William James Ridd 9696 KIA
born: Barnstaple enlisted: Barnstaple
No known grave. Soissons Memorial. Joined BEF: 14/08/14 with original cadre of 1/Devons.

Pte. William Blake 40853 KIA
born: Withleigh, Devon   enlisted: Tiverton
Joined BEF: not on Medal Card. No other records identified.

Pte. Edward George Cakebread 70424 KIA
born: Tyseley, Worcs.   enlisted: Warwick
No known grave. Soissons Memorial. Age 19. Joined BEF: not on Medal Card. 1901 Census: son of George Cakebread, platelayer (railway), and Bertha Cakebread, 6 Tudor Terrace, Aston, Birmingham, Warwickshire. 1911 Census: schoolboy, son of George Cakebread, jobbing gardener, and Bertha Cakebread, Ulverley Terrace, Olton, Solihull, Birmingham, Warwickshire. CWGC: family address: 7 Ulverley Terrace, Warwick Road, Olton, Acock's Green, Birmingham, Warwickshire.

Pte. Cecil Robert Cull 74003 KIA
born: Portsmouth   enlisted: Portsmouth
No known grave. Soissons Memorial. Age 19. Joined BEF: not on Medal Card. Formerly 21543, Wiltshire Regiment. 1901 Census: son of John Cull, prison clerk, and Louisa Cull, 135 St. Mary's Road, Portsmouth, Hants. 1911 Census: schoolboy, son of John Cull, prison clerk, and Louisa Jane Cull, 23 St. Mary's Road, Portsmouth, Hants. CWGC: family address as 1911 Census.

Pte. Britton John Edwards 66836 KIA
born: Axminster   enlisted: Newton Abbot   residence: Teignmouth
No known grave. Soissons Memorial. Age 35. Joined BEF: not on Medal Card. 1891 Census: grandson of John Dymond, farmer, Rose Farm, Stockland, Devon. 1901 Census: bank clerk, boarding at 15 Camden Road, Bridgwater, Somerset.

Pte. Robert Coley Gee 70440 KIA
born: Warley, Worcs.   enlisted: Stourbridge   residence: Langley, Warwicks.
No known grave. Soissons Memorial. Age 19. Joined BEF: not on Medal Card. 1901 Census: son of Charles H. Gee, steam engine fitter, and Ada W. Gee, 30 Hancox Street, Warley, Worcs. 1911 Census: brush maker, son of Mary Ann Gee, widow, cook, 287 Vicarage Road, King's Heath, Worcs.

Pte. Bertram Frank Hawkins 52298 KIA
born: Fareham, Hants.   enlisted: Gosport   residence: Wickham, Hants.
Buried: Sissonne British Cemetery. Grave H.5. Age 19. Joined BEF: not on Medal Card. Son of John Sadler Hawkins, general labourer, and Selina Hawkins, 55 North Wallington, Fareham, Hants. 1911 Census: son of John Sadler Hawkins, casual worker, general labourer, and Selina Hawkins, dressmaker, Bridge Street, Wickham, Hampshire. CWGC: family address: 29 Mill Road, Fareham, Hants.

Pte. Henry Pembroke Innes 290949 KIA
born: Holloway, Middx.   enlisted: Winchester   residence: Portsmouth
No known grave. Soissons Memorial. Age 39. Joined BEF: not on Medal Card. 1891 Census: son of James Innes, hotel keeper (pub) and Grace A, Innes, 41 High Street, Portsmouth, Hants. 1901 Census: artist/sculptor, visiting 318 Holloway Road, Islington, London. 1911 Census: artist, son of James Innes, hotel proprietor, and Grace A. Innes, of The Dolphin, High Street, Portsmouth, Hants.
An obituary in an unidentified local newspaper reads: *"INNES, HENRY PEMBROKE, Private, No. 290949, 2nd Battn. (11th Foot) The Devonshire Regt., s. of James Innes, of Hurstbourne, Jubilee Road, Waterlooville, by his wife, Grace Amelia (-); b. Holloway, London, N., 30 July 1879; educ. Mile End House School, Portsmouth; was a Black and White artist; volunteered for active service, and enlisted in the Devonshire Regt. 16 Sept. 1916; served with the Expeditionary Force*

in France and Flanders from 25 July, 1917, and was killed in action at the Chemin des Dames 27 May 1918. Buried where he fell. On 27 May, 1918, the 2nd Devons were apparently on the Aisne, in front of Pontavert and Roucy, and this day they suffered their heaviest losses, being cut off and surrounded, 552 officers and men being killed. Mr. Innes, who was a student at Hatherley's, had a picture exhibited in the Royal Academy at the age of 17. He m. at St. James's, Littlehampton, 16 Oct. 1909, Winifred (41, High Street, Portsmouth), only dau. Of John Kear, and had two sons; Malcolm Richard Henry, b. 28 Oct 1910, and Norman David, b. 30 Dec. 1914."

The figure in the obituary of 552 officers and men killed is incorrect, the number of men of the 2nd Devons actually killed over this period being 95. There were, however, 552 casualties (dead, wounded and prisoners), in less than a fortnight, which undeniably represents a calamity of the highest order.

Pte. Alfred Leonard Jones 74064 KIA
born: Tewkesbury   enlisted: Birmingham
No known grave. Soissons Memorial. Age 18. Joined BEF: not on Medal Card. CWGC: son of George Jones and Ellen Jones, Church End, Bushley, Tewkesbury, Glos.

Pte. Albert Ernest William Murton 18617 KIA
born: Stonehouse   enlisted: Plymouth
No known grave. Soissons Memorial. Age 22. Joined BEF: not on Medal Card. 1901 Census: son of Albert E. Murton, skilled labourer dockyards, and Ada Murton, tailoress, 10 Waterloo Street, East Stonehouse, Devon. 1911 Census: office boy, son of Albert E. Murton, fitter's assistant, and Ada B. Murton, 10 East Street, East Stonehouse, Devon. CWGC: family address: 10 East Street, Stonehouse, Plymouth.

Pte. Alfred Pearce 43323 KIA
born: Chelsea   enlisted: Plymouth
Buried: Marfaux British Cemetery. Grave V.I.3. Attached to Army Service Corps. Joined BEF: not on Medal Card.

Pte. Frank Ernest Penn 74128 KIA
born: Birmingham   enlisted: Birmingham
No known grave. Soissons Memorial. Age 18. Joined BEF: not on Medal Card. 1901 Census: son of William J. Penn, bricklayer's labourer, and Amelia Penn, No.6 Court, Gooch Street, Birmingham, Warwickshire. 1911 Census: schoolboy, son of John William Penn, bricklayer's labourer, and Amelia Penn, 197 Gooch Street, Birmingham, Warwickshire. CWGC: family address: 1b, 113 Great Colmore Street, Birmingham, Warwickshire.

Pte. Frank Edward Preece 30994 KIA
born: Birmingham   enlisted: Cheltenham
Buried: Jonchery-Sur-Vesle British Cemetery. Grave I.F.34. Age 19. Joined BEF: not on Medal Card. Formerly 8/1547, 206/Infantry Battalion. 1901 Census: son of Edward C. Preece, carpenter, and Amphaliss Preece, 45 Fallows Road, Aston, Birmingham, Warwickshire. 1911 Census: schoolboy, son of Amphaliss Preece, widow, dressmaker general sewing, 5 Hermitage Street, Cheltenham, Glos.

Pte. Stanley Wilks 31829 KIA
born: High Wycombe   enlisted: High Wycombe
No known grave. Soissons Memorial. Age 19. Joined BEF: not on Medal Card. 1911 Census: schoolboy, son of John Wilks, bricklayer builder, and Minnie Wilks, 13 Lower Gordon Road, High Wycombe, Bucks. CWGC: son of John Wilks and Minnie Wilks, address as given in 1911 Census.

Pte. Frederick Thomas Westaway 30374 Died
born: Holsworthy   enlisted: Barnstaple   residence: Holsworthy
No known grave. Soissons Memorial. Age 22. Joined BEF: not on Medal Card. 1901 Census: son of Elijah Westaway, engraver on stone/temporary hotel proprietor, and Salome Ann Westaway, Temperance Hotel, Higher Village, Bradworthy, Holsworthy, Devon. 1911 Census: schoolboy, son of Elijah Westaway, monumental mason, and Salome Ann Westaway, High Park View, Bradworthy, Holsworthy, Devon.

28th May 1918
Pte. William Bertram Bennett 30905 DoW
born: Handsworth   enlisted: Worcester
Buried: Sissonne British Cemetery. Grave L.13. Age 19. Joined BEF: not on Medal Card. Formerly 8/1591, Devonshire Regiment (T.R.). 1911 Census: schoolboy, son of George Bennett, coachman, and Ann Maria Bennett, laundress, Rose Tree Villa, Pickersleigh Road, Malvern, Worcs.
Pte. Henry William Cosnett 70421 DoW
born: Pershore, Worcs.   enlisted: Pershore
Buried: Marfaux British Cemetery. Grave V.D.2. 19. Joined BEF: not on Medal Card. 1911 Census: schoolboy, son of Herbert Strickland Cosnett, baker journeyman, married, 15 Mary Street, Walsall, Staffs.

29th May 1918
A/Cpl. Bertie Doidge 21657 KIA
born: Tavistock   enlisted: Tavistock
No known grave. Soissons Memorial. Age 31. Age 30. Joined BEF: not on Medal Card. 1891 Census: son of Thomas Doidge, agricultural labourer, and Harriet Doidge, dressmaker, Dixon's Lane, Tavistock. 1901 Census: nephew of John Doidge, farmer, and Harriet Doidge, West Rowden, Marford, Tavistock, Devon. 1911 Census: grocer's assistant, son of Thomas Doidge, labourer, and Harriet Doidge, 25 West Bridge Cottages, Tavistock, Devon. CWGC: brother of Mrs. G. Matthews, of 2, "B" Block, Married Quarters, 1/Dorsets, St. Andrews, Malta.
A/Cpl. Arthur Ernest Hawthorne 12401 DoW
born: Bromsgrove, Worcs.   enlisted: Birmingham   residence: Langley Green
Buried: Sissonne British Cemetery. Grave C.4. Age 26. Joined BEF: 27/07/15 with 9/Devons. 1911 Census: house painter, son of Alfred Hawthorne, 'hammerman', and Ann Hawthorne, 15 Henry Street, Langley Green, Oldbury, Staffs.
30th May 1918
Pte. William Arthur Alfred Mills 30986 KIA
born: Lambeth   enlisted: Lambeth
Buried: Chambrecy British Cemetery. Grave V.E.7. Age 19. Joined BEF: not on Medal Card. Formerly 9/20893, 206/Infantry Battalion. 1901 Census: son of William Hugh Mills, railway porter, and Laura Ellen Mills, 28 Hartington Road, Lambeth, London. CWGC: family address: 8 Tradescant Road, South Lambeth, London.

31st May 1918 The men listed as KIA on 31st May 1918 includes men who died on 27th May.
Sgt. Joseph William Stanley Collins 240142 KIA
born: Plymouth   enlisted: Plymouth
Buried: Sissonne British Cemetery. Grave J.7. Age 31. Joined BEF: not on Medal Card. 1901 Census: grocery shop assistant, son of Joseph Anthony Collins, foreman of bakery, and

Henrietta Collins, 13 Dunstan Terrace, Plymouth, Devon. 1911 Census: grocery assistant, husband of Lily Collins, 3 Quarry Park Road, Peverell, Plymouth, Devon. CWGC: husband of Lily Priscilla Collins, 3 Ford Park Cottages, Mutley, Plymouth, Devon.
A/Cpl. Thomas Cox 291761 KIA
born: March, Cambs.   enlisted: Birmingham
Buried: Jonchery-Sur-Vesle British Cemetery. Grave I.E.35. Joined BEF: not on Medal Card.
Cpl. Ernest James Cornish 20435 KIA
born: Luton, Devon   enlisted: Exeter
Buried: Jonchery-Sur-Vesle British Cemetery. Grave I.G.36. Age 21. Joined BEF: not on Medal Card. 1901 Census: son of Stephen G. Cornish, blacksmith, and Catherine A. Cornish, 25 Queen Street, Leighton Buzzard, Bedfordshire. 1911 Census: errand boy, son of Stephen Ernest Cornish, iron moulder, and Catherine Annie Cornish, 36 Baker Street, Leighton Buzzard, Bedfordshire.
A/Cpl. Henry Westwood Frost 30934 KIA
born: Solihull   enlisted: Birmingham
No known grave. Soissons Memorial. Age 19. Joined BEF: not on Medal Card. Formerly 8/1734, 206/Infantry Battalion. 1911 Census: schoolboy, son of Amy Frost, married, 42 Church Road, South Yardley, Solihull, Warwickshire. CWGC: records death on 27/05/1918, SDGW on 31/05/1917. Son of Mrs. A. W. Frost, 42, Church Rd., South Yardley, Birmingham, and the late Mr. D. W. Frost.
L/Sgt. Frederick Goldsmith 27662 KIA
born: Brighton   enlisted: Brighton
No known grave. Soissons Memorial. Age 34. Joined BEF: not on Medal Card. 1901 Census: smith/stoker railway works, son of George Goldsmith, iron founder, and Mary A. Goldsmith, 56 Carlton Hill, Brighton, Sussex. 1911 Census: draper's traveller, son of George Goldsmith, former iron moulder, and Mary Ann Goldsmith, laundress, 56 Carlton Hill, Brighton, Sussex.
A/Cpl. Albert Jeffery 8558 KIA
born: Cullompton   enlisted: Cullompton
No known grave. Soissons Memorial. Age 29. Joined BEF: 07/11/14 with original cadre. 1911 Census: 2/Devons, St. George's Barracks, Malta. CWGC: son of Henry Jeffery and Elizabeth Jeffery, Pound Square, Cullompton, Devon.
L/Cpl. Albert Edward Lilley 206022 KIA
born: Bideford   enlisted: Barnstaple   residence: St.Columb
No known grave. Soissons Memorial. Age 28. Joined BEF: not on Medal Card. CWGC: son of John Lilley and Edith Lilley, Searle Terrace, Northam, Devon; husband of Florence E. Coles (formerly Lilly), Middle Lodge, St. Columb, Cornwall.
Cpl. Percy Charles Parker MM 3/6759   KIA
born: Hennock, Devon   enlisted: Exeter   residence: Hennock
No known grave. Soissons Memorial. Age 21. Joined BEF: 29/06/15. CWGC: son of Charles Parker, Hennock, Bovey Tracey, Devon.
Sgt. Charles Edmund Smith 20390 KIA
born: no record   enlisted: in the field   residence: East Budleigh
No known grave. Soissons Memorial. Age 22. Joined BEF: 19/01/15. CWGC: brother of Mr. F. W. Smith, Cromley Cottage, East Chudleigh, Devon.
L/Cpl. Alec Edward Wilder 31033 KIA
born: London   enlisted: Lewisham
No known grave. Soissons Memorial. Age 21. Joined BEF: not on Medal Card. 1911 Census: schoolboy, son of Benjamin E. Wilder, foreman carpenter, and Kate Wilder, 3 Boyne Road,

Lewisham, London. CWGC: son of Ben E. Wilder and Kate Wilder, 6 Church Terrace, Lewisham, London.

Pte. Richard Henry Andrew 45606 KIA
born: Halberton   enlisted: Teigntown   residence: Churchtown
No known grave. Soissons Memorial. Age 26. Joined BEF: not on Medal Card. CWGC: son of the late William Andrew and Thurza Andrew; husband of Lilian Andrew, Amble Street, Kew, Wadebridge, Cornwall.

Pte. Charles William Cyril Barker 70741 KIA
born: Eastleigh, Hants.   enlisted: Bournemouth
No known grave. Soissons Memorial. Age 19. Joined BEF: not on Medal Card. 1911 Census: schoolboy/milk boy, son of Lilian Caroline Barker, widow, 'daily help washing and cleaning', 2 Cranmer Road, Winton, Bournmouth, Dorset. CWGC: son of Lilian Caroline Barker, 2 Cranmer Road, Winton, Bournemouth, Dorset, and the late Charles Barker.

Pte. Frederick John Bullock 70396 KIA
born: Hartley Wintney, Hants.   enlisted: Hartley Wintney   residence: Mattingly, Hants.
No known grave. Soissons Memorial. Age 19. Joined BEF: not on Medal Card. CWGC: son of Henry Bullock and Emily Bullock, Stoker's Farm, Mattingley, Basingstoke.

Pte. Percy Butler 70402 KIA
born: Weston-on-the-Green, Oxon.   enlisted: Oxford   residence: Weston-on-the Green
No known grave. Soissons Memorial. Age 19. Joined BEF: not on Medal Card. 1901 Census: son of Joseph Butler, shepherd on farm, and Florence M. Butler, 5 Church Road, Weston-On-The-Green, Oxon. 1911 Census: son of Joseph Butler, shepherd, and Florence Mary Butler, Clipping Farm, Islip, Oxon.

Pte. John William Chapman 74007 KIA
born: Spaldwick, Hunts.   enlisted: Huntingdon
No known grave. Soissons Memorial. Age 19. No Medal Card. 1901 Census: son of Frank Chapman, carpenter, and Mary Chapman, Stow Road, Spaldwick, Hunts. 1911 Census: schoolboy, son of Frank Chapman, carpenter, and Mary Elizabeth Chapman, Stow Road, Spaldwick, Hunts.

Pte. Ernest William Church 31820 KIA
born: Wells, Somerset   enlisted: Weston-Super-Mare   residence: Wells
No known grave. Soissons Memorial. Age 20. Joined BEF: not on Medal Card. Formerly 8/1744, 51/Grad. Battalion. Son of William Church, cowman on farm, and Amy Caroline Church, Asylum Farm, Frome Road, Wells, Somerset. 1911 Census: schoolboy, son of William Church, cowman on farm, and Amy Caroline Church, Farm Yard, Frome Road, Wells, Somerset.

Pte. Samuel Stone Clist 21194 KIA
born: Hemyock, Devon   enlisted: Tiverton   residence: no record
No known grave. Soissons Memorial. Age 35. Joined BEF: not recorded on Medal Card. 1891 Census: son of William Clist, gardener, and Margaret Clist, Village, Hemyock, Collumpton, Devon. 1901 Census: servant/cattleman on farm, Culmbridge, Hemyock, Devon. CWGC: family address: Culmstock Road, Hemyock, Devon.

Pte. George Valentine Vincent Cooke 30296 KIA
born: no record   enlisted: Barnstaple
No known grave. Soissons Memorial. Age 26. Joined BEF: not on Medal Card. 1901 Census: son of William Cooke, retired butler, and Ann Cooke, Shirwell Cross, Shirwell, Devon. 1911 Census: grocer's assistant, son of William Cooke, retired butler, and Ann Cooke, 16 Pulchress Street, Barnstaple, Devon. CWGC: son of the late Mr. and Mrs. William Cooke, Barnstaple, Devon, and husband of LouisaElizabeth Cooke, The Farm, Instow, Devon.

Pte. William Henry Daniel 16797 KIA
born: Parkham, Devon   enlisted: Bideford
No known grave. Soissons Memorial. Age 24. Joined BEF: 15/12/15. 1911 Census: servant, farm waggoner, son of John Daniel, farmer, and Joanna Daniel, 8 Gilscott, Alwington, Fairy Cross, Bideford, Devon. CWGC: father's address: Hall, Fairy Cross, Alwington, Bideford, Devon.

Pte. Arthur Jesse Edney 69004 KIA
born: Bristol   enlisted: Bristol
No known grave. Soissons Memorial. Age 20. Joined BEF: not on Medal Card. 1901 Census: son of George H. Edney, cabinet maker, and Caroline Edney, 44 Holwell Road, Bristol. 1911 Census: schoolboy, son of George H. Edney, cabinet maker, and Caroline Edney, 10 New George Street, Bristol, Glos. CWGC: family address: 74 St. George's Road, College Green, St. Augustine's, Bristol.

Pte. Robert Herbert Henry Edwards 68811 KIA
born: Urchfont, Wiltshire   enlisted: Devizes
No known grave. Soissons Memorial. Age 19. Joined BEF: not on Medal Card. 1901 Census: grandson of Thomas Edwards, widower, blacksmith, son of Robert Edwards, blacksmith and Jane Edwards, The Street, Urchfont, Wilts. 1911 Census: schoolboy, son of Robert Edwards, blacksmith, and Jane Edwards, The Street, Urchfont, Devizes, Wilts. CWGC: family address: The Smithy, Urchfont, Devizes, Wilts.

Pte. Herbert Thomas James Fortune 290779 KIA
born: Calne, Wilts   enlisted: Devizes   residence: Chippenham
No known grave. Soissons Memorial. Age 20. Joined BEF: not on Medal Card. Formerly 2431, Devonshire Regiment. 1901 Census: son of Thomas Fortune, milk factory hand, and Mary Jane Fortune, Lowden, Chippenham, Wilts. 1911 Census: market gardener, son of Thomas Fortune, market gardener, and Mary J. Fortune, Frogwell, Chippenham, Wilts. CWGC: family address: "Fair View," Sheldon Road, Chippenham, Wilts.

Pte. Frank Eugene Gamblen 30942 KIA
born: Catford   enlisted: Camberwell   residence: Lewisham
No known grave. Soissons Memorial. Age 19. Joined BEF: not on Medal Card. Son of Thomas Frederick Gamblen, bricklayer, and Edith E. Gamblen, of 14 Roxley Street, Lewisham, London. CWGC: family address: 50 Taunton Road, Lee, London.

Pte. Ernest Howard Guest 68373 KIA
born: Ashwood Bank, Worcs.   enlisted: Worcester   residence: Redditch
No known grave. Soissons Memorial. Age 19. Joined BEF: not on Medal Card. 1901 Census: recorded as Howard Guest, son of Joseph Guest, needles bender, and Agnes Sarah Guest, Retreat Street, Feckenham, Worcester. CWGC: family address: Council Buildings, Astwood Lane, Astwood Bank, Redditch, Worcs.

Pte. Charles Herbert Haines 291419 KIA
born: Fiddington, Somerset   enlisted: Southampton
No known grave. Soissons Memorial. Age 25. Joined BEF: not on Medal Card. 1901 Census: son of Thomas Haines, coachman/domestic, and Elizabeth Haines, Main Street, Fiddington, Bridgwater, Somerset. 1911 Census: ironmonger's assistant, son of Thomas Haines, gardener domestic, and Elizabeth Haines, Bishops Lydeard, Taunton, Somerset. CWGC: family address: Bishop's Lydeard, Taunton, Somerset.

Pte. Frederick Samuel Hardy 71207 KIA
born: Morton, Dorset   enlisted: Dorchester
No known grave. Soissons Memorial. Age 19. Joined BEF: not on Medal Card. 'A' Company. 1911 Census: schoolboy, son of Amelia Louise Hardy, married, charwoman, 12 Friary Lane,

Dorchester, Dorset. CWGC: son of Mrs. L. Hardy, 11 York Terrace, East Fordington Hill, Dorchester, Dorset.

Pte. Frederick Charles Harris 290393 KIA
born: Helston, Cornwall   enlisted: Helston
No known grave. Soissons Memorial. Age 20. Joined BEF: not on Medal Card. 1901 Census: son of Thomas John Harris, tanner's carter, and Ann C. P. Harris, St. Johns, Sithney, Helston, Cornwall. CWGC: son of Thomas John Harris and Charlotte Ann Harris, Silver Hill, Helston, Cornwall.

Pte. Sydney Hugh Hellings 71209 KIA
born: Barnstable   enlisted: Trowbridge   residence: Melksham
No known grave. Soissons Memorial. Age 19. Joined BEF: not on Medal Card. 1901 Census: son of Henry Hellings, Army pensioner, and Mary H. Hellings, 6 Hardaway Head, Barnstaple, Devon. 1911 Census: schoolboy, son of Henry Hellings, Army pensioner, and Mary Helen Hellings, Kings Street, Melksham, Wilts.

Pte. William Thomas Heysett 29702 KIA
born: Lewtrenchard, Devon   enlisted: Exeter   residence: Lewtrenchard
No known grave. Soissons Memorial. Age 21. Joined BEF: not on Medal Card. 1901 Census: son of William Heysett, ordinary agricultural labourer, and Rhoda Heysett, Holdstrong, Lewtrenchard, Devon. 1911 Census: son of William Heysett, widower, general farm labourer, Holdstrong, Lew Trenchard, Lew Down, Devon. CWGC: son of the late William Heysett and of Mary Emma Heysett (stepmother), Eastcott, Coryton, Lewdown, Devon.

Pte. Frederick George Holbrook 74053 KIA
born: Harptree, Somerset   enlisted: Bristol
No known grave. Soissons Memorial. Age 18. Joined BEF: not on Medal Card. Son of Edward Austin Holbrook, quarryman/labourer, and Elizabeth E. Holbrook, of Venns Lane, Clutton, Somerset. CWGC: family address: Cambrooke House, Temple Cloud, Bristol.

Pte. Ewart Gladstone Hopes 30952 KIA
born: Bristol   enlisted: Bristol
No known grave. Soissons Memorial. Age 19. Joined BEF: not on Medal Card. Formerly 8/2358, 206 Infantry Battalion. 1901 Census: son of Charles Hopes, grocer, and Blanche Eliza Hopes, 1 Milton Park, Bristol. 1911 Census: scholar, son of Charles Hopes, commission agent, and Blanche Eliza Hopes, 11 Roseberry Terrace, Bristol, Glos. CWGC: family address: 1 Church Road, Horfield, Bristol, Glos.

Pte. Frederick Jackson 74006 KIA
born: Birmingham   enlisted: Birmingham
No known grave. Soissons Memorial. Joined BEF: not on Medal Card.

Pte. John Edwin Henry Jeans 30963 KIA
born: Camberwell   enlisted: Portsmouth
No known grave. Soissons Memorial. Age 19. Joined BEF: not on Medal Card. Formerly 8/9604, 206/Infantry Battalion. 1911 Census: schoolboy, son of William John Jeans, removal and railway carriers manager, and Charlotte Mary Jeans, 6 St. Bartholomew's Terrace, Rochester, Kent. CWGC: son of William John Jeans, 72 High Street, Blue Town, Sheerness, Kent.

Pte. William Charles Jenvey 290816 KIA
born: Lymington, Hants.   enlisted: Winchester   residence: Lymington
Buried: Sissonne British Cemetery. Grave I.1. Age 20. Joined BEF: not on Medal Card. 1911 Census: schoolboy/newspaper boy, son of Charlotte Jenvey, married, 'charring and washing', Middle Road, Lepington, Hants. CWGC: son of John Jenvey and Charlotte Eliza Jenvey,

Inkerman Cottage, Middle Road, Lymington, Hants.
Pte. Wilfred Keep 30973 KIA
born: Lane End, Bucks.   enlisted: High Wycombe   residence: Lane End
No known grave. Soissons Memorial. Age 19. Joined BEF: not on Medal Card. Formerly 8/1345, 206/Infantry Battalion. 1901 Census: son of Nicholas James Keep, bricklayer, and Fanny Keep, Daisy Cottages, Marlow, Bucks. 1911 Census: schoolboy, son of Nicholas James Keep, bricklayer, and Fanny Keep, Ditchfield, Lane End, High Wycombe, Bucks. CWGC: family address: "Ditchfields," Lane End, High Wycombe, Bucks.

Pte. Thomas William Knight 74067 KIA
born: Twyford, Hants.   enlisted: Winchester   residence: Twyford, Hants.
No known grave. Soissons Memorial. Age 18. Joined BEF: not on Medal Card, but names him Wm. T. Knight, as does SDGW. 1901 Census: son of the late W. Thomas Knight, butcher, and Rosa Knight, laundress, High Street, Twyford, Hants. 1911 Census: schoolboy, son of Rosa Knight, charwoman, High Street, Twyford, Winchester, Hants. CWGC: family address: Park Lane, Twyford, Hants.

Pte. George Edward Loader 31786 KIA
born: Portsmouth   enlisted: Portsmouth
No known grave. Soissons Memorial. Age 18. Joined BEF: not on Medal Card. 1911 Census: schoolboy, son of Edward Thomas Loader, Naval pensioner/general labourer Portsmouth Dockyard, and Alice Rosina Loader, 3 Malins Road, Portsmouth Hants. CWGC: son of Mr. and Mrs. Edward T. Loader, 3 Malins Road, Landport, Portsmouth, Hants.

Pte. Leonard Middleton 74078 KIA
born: Birmingham   enlisted: Birmingham
No known grave. Soissons Memorial. Age 18. Joined BEF: not on Medal Card. 1901 Census: son of Joseph Middleton, gun stocker, and Susan Middleton, 71 Bracebridge Street, Aston, Birmingham. CWGC: son of Susan Middleton, 109 Mansfield Road, Aston, Birmingham, and the late Joseph Middleton.

Pte. Charles Herbert Miller 30987 KIA
born: Hackney, Middx.   enlisted: Hackney
No known grave. Soissons Memorial. Age 19. Joined BEF: not on Medal Card. Formerly 9-21468, 206/Infantry Battalion. 'D' Company. 1911 Census: son of Charles Miller, baker, and Eliza Miller, 16a Priory Place, Hackney, London. CWGC: son of Charles Robert Miller and Eliza Miller, 6 Percy Villas, Retreat Place, Hackney, London.

Pte. Walter Mitchell 16907 KIA
born: Axminster   enlisted: Exeter   residence: Axminster
No known grave. Soissons Memorial. Age 29. Joined BEF: not on Medal Card. 1911 Census: carpenter, son of William Mitchell, carpenter, and Jane Mitchell, South View, Exminster, Devon. CWGC: son of William Mitchell and Jane Mitchell, of Exminster, Devon.

Pte. William Ernest John Ockford 204887 KIA
born: Torquay   enlisted: Poole
No known grave. Soissons Memorial. Age 38. Joined BEF: not on Medal Card. Formerly 203294, Dorsetshire Regiment. 1891 Census: son of William G.H. Ockford, printer, newsagent, tobacconist and stationer, and Clara A. Ockford, 3 Market Street, Tormoham, Torquay, Devon. 1911 Census: manager book retailer, 111 High Street, Poole, Dorset. CWGC: husband of Amy Ockford, Poole, Dorset.

Pte. Herbert Henry Owen 74082 KIA
born: Reading, Berks.   enlisted: Reading
Buried: Hermonville Military Cemetery. Grave III.E.1. Age 18. Joined BEF: not on Medal Card.

Son of Walter N. Owen, biscuit factory labourer, and Lydia M. Owen, of 28 School Terrace, St. Giles, Reading, Berks. 1911 Census: schoolboy, son of Walter Owen, 'corder warehouse', and Lydia Maria Owen, 28 School Terrace, Reading, Berks. CWGC: family address: 156 Cumberland Road, Reading, Berks.

Pte. Robert Priddle 8138 KIA
born: Taunton   enlisted: Exeter   residence: Loxbeare, Devon
No known grave. Soissons Memorial. Age 29. Joined BEF: 06/11/14 with original cadre. 1911 Census: 2/Devons, St. George's Barracks, Malta.

Pte. Frank Ralph 16969 KIA
born: Plymouth   enlisted: Devonport   residence: Plymouth
Buried: Jonchery-Sur-Vesle British Cemetery. Grave I.E.34. Joined BEF: not on Medal Card.

Pte. Ernest Gordon Redman 291210 KIA
born: Southampton   enlisted: Southampton
No known grave. Soissons Memorial. Age 31. Joined BEF: not on Medal Card. Formerly 2869 of the Devonshire Regiment. 1901 Census: son of Thomas Redman, painter/paperhanger, and Florence Redman, 11 Little Lyon Street, Southampton, Hants. 1911 Census: house painter, husband of Ellen Annie Catherine Redman, 85 Northumberland Road, Southampton.

Pte. James Simpson 70063 KIA
born: no record   enlisted: Falkirk
No known grave. Soissons Memorial. No Medal Card.

Pte. Beluchistan Thomas Smith 74000 KIA
born: Devizes, Wilts.   enlisted: Dover   residence: Aldershot
No known grave. Soissons Memorial. Age 18. Joined BEF: not on Medal Card. 1901 Census: son of Evelyn L. M. Smith, widow, 4 Whillock's Court, Devizes, Wiltshire. CWGC: son of Evelyn Mary Langley (formerly Smith), "Baluchistan," Mytchett Road, Frimley Green, Surrey, and the late James Smith (Sergeant 1/Wiltshires).

Pte. Frank Clarence Sweet 33160 KIA
born: Cullompton   enlisted: Cullompton
No known grave. Soissons Memorial. Age 20. Joined BEF: not on Medal Card. 1901 Census: son of Frank Sweet, carpenter, and Sarah Jane Sweet, 6 Tiverton Road, Cullompton, Devon. 1911 Census: schoolboy, son of Frank Sweet, builder, and Sarah Sweet, Elm House, Higher Bull Ring, Cullompton, Devon.

Pte. William David Thorne 74109 KIA
born: Handley, Dorset   enlisted: Wimborne   residence: St.Giles, Dorset
No known grave. Soissons Memorial. Age 18. Joined BEF: not on Medal Card. Formerly 8/11243, Devonshire Regiment. CWGC: son of Mrs. Alice Maria Thorne, of St. Giles, Salisbury.

Pte. William Chamberlain Turvey 74110 KIA
born: Nuneaton, Warwickshire   enlisted: Nuneaton
No known grave. Soissons Memorial. Age 18. Joined BEF: not on Medal Card. 1901 Census: son of William Turvey, felt hatter, and Sarah Turvey, 55 Bothill Street, Nuneaton, Warwickshire. 1911 Census: schoolboy, son of William Turvey, felt hat finisher, and Sarah Turvey, Broad Street, Nuneaton, Warwickshire. CWGC: family address: 28 Broad Street, Nuneaton, Warwickshire.

Pte. Christopher Harry Williams 74115 KIA
born: Worcester   enlisted: Birmingham
No known grave. Soissons Memorial. Age 18. Joined BEF: not on Medal Card. 'C' Company. CWGC: son of Capt. Henry Williams and Charity Williams, 71, Green Lane, Handsworth, Birmingham, Warwickshire.

Pte. Arthur Leslie Wilson 74027 KIA
born: Chigwell, Essex   enlisted: Bath
No known grave. Soissons Memorial. Age 34. Joined BEF: not on Medal Card. CWGC: son of Henry Wilson and Margaret Wilson, Edgware Road, London, husband of Amy Elizabeth Wilson, 13 Weymouth Square, Snow Hill, Bath.

Pte. Thomas Henry Wright 69064 DoW
born: Cheriton, Hants   enlisted: Gosport, Hants.   residence: Titchfield
Buried: Jonchery-Sur-Vesle British Cemetery. Grave I.F.38. No Medal Card.

Pte. Thomas Charles Welsh 290403 Died
born: no record   enlisted: Liskeard, Cornwall   residence: Menheniot, Cornwall
No known grave. Soissons Memorial. Joined BEF: not on Medal Card.

The 2nd Devons War Diary

JUNE 1918

1st June 1918
Pte. Charles Henry Cheshire 71170 DoW
born: Birmingham   enlisted: Birmingham
Buried: Sissonne British Cemetery. Grave L.5. Age 18. Joined BEF: not on Medal Card. 1901 Census: son of William Cheshire, gas stoker, and Alice Cheshire, 44 Baker Street, Aston, Birmingham, Warwickshire. 1911 Census: schoolboy, son of William Cheshire, gas stoker, widower, 6 Carlton Road, Aston, Birmingham, Warwickshire.
Pte. Alfred Charles Hook 30950 DoW
born: Walworth   enlisted: Camberwell
Buried: Sissonne British Cemetery. Grave L.4. Age 19. Joined BEF: not on Medal Card. Formerly 9/20802, 206/Infantry Battalion. 1911 Census: son of E.A. John Hook, engineer fitter, and Minnie Hook, 73 Villa Street, Walworth, Southwark, London. CWGC: son of Mr. E. A. J. and Mrs. H. M. Hook, 35 Faversham Road, Catford, London. SDGW states that Pte. Hook died of wounds in Germany, but he more likely died as a prisoner while still in France, hence his burial in Sissonne British cemetery. The village of Sissonne was in German hands during almost the whole of the 1914-1918 War. Sissonne British Cemetery was designated after the Armistice, and was a concentration of graves from the German Cemetery, other burial grounds, and the battlefield.
Cpl. John Cadamy 8599 Died
born: Devonport   enlisted: Plymouth
Buried: La Ville-Aux-Bois British Cemetery. Grave 11.J.9. Age 29. Joined BEF: 06/11/14 with original cadre. 1901 Census: son of Edward Cadamy, mason's labourer, and Matilda Cadamy, 6 Marine Fields, Plymouth, Devon. 1911 Census: 2/Devons, St. George's Barracks, Malta. SDGW records that Cpl. Cadamy died in Germany, but CWGC says his grave lies in La Ville-Aux-Bois British Cemetery, in the area where the 2/Devons were in action at the time. La Ville-Aux-Bois British Cemetery was designated after the Armistice and was a concentration of isolated graves from a wide area. Like Pte. Hook, he may have been wounded and captured.

5th June 1918
Pte. Charles Leonard Richards 74098 DoW
born: Kingsbridge   enlisted: Exeter
Buried: Marfaux British Cemetery. Grave VII.D.2. Age 18. Joined BEF: not on Medal Card. CWGC: son of Mrs. E. A. Creber, 16 Duke Street, Kingsbridge, Devon.

6th June 1918
Pte. Robert Manifold 69193 KIA
born: no record   enlisted: Bristol   residence: Macclesfield
CWGC: no record. Joined BEF: not on Medal Card.
Pte. Alfred Thomas Cross 70422 DoW
born: Morton, Oxon.   enlisted: Oxford   Residence: Morton
Buried: Vailly British cemetery. Grave I.AA.17. Joined BEF: not on Medal Card. Formerly 8/18259, 206th Infantry Battalion.
Pte. Wallace Rowe 69059 DoW
born: Roche, Cornwall   enlisted: Bodmin   residence: Roche
Buried: Montcornet Military Cemetery. Grave E.7. Age 19. Joined BEF: not on Medal Card. 1901 Census: son of Hart Rowe, china clay labourer, and Hillie A. Rowe, Pease Hill, Roche,

Cornwall. 1911 Census: schoolboy, son of Hart Rowe, cattle dealer, and Hettie Rowe, Reeshill, Roche, Cornwall. CWGC: son of Hart Rowe and Hettie A. Rowe "Hendra", Roche, Cornwall.

8th June 1918
Pte. Archibald Robert Vincent 315303 DoW
born: Hemyock   enlisted: Exeter   residence: Hemyock
Buried: Rethel French National Cemetery. Grave 1764. Age 21. Joined BEF: not on Medal Card. 1901 Census: son of William Vincent, farmer, and Sarah Jane Vincent, Alexandrahayes, Hemyock, Devon. Recorded as died in Germany. 1911 Census: schoolboy, son of Sarah Jane Vincent, farmer, widow, Alexandrahayes, Hemyock, Devon.
Pte. Arthur Ernest White 74132 Died
born: Bristol   enlisted: Bristol   residence: Keynsham
Buried: Terlincthun British Cemetery, Wimille. Grave XVI.B.16. Age 18. Joined BEF: not on Medal Card. CWGC: son of Thomas Rood White and Sarah Ann White, Chew Bridge, Keynsham, Bristol, Glos.

27th June1918
Pte. William (Billy) Nelson Alexander 291457 Died
born: Bray, Berks.   enlisted: Reading   residence: Maidenhead
Buried: Etaples Military Cemetery. Grave LXVI.F.27. Age 21. No Medal Card. 1901 Census: son of Frederick Alexander, blacksmith, and Alice Alexander, Red Lion Yard, Maidenhead, Berkshire. 1911 Census: schoolboy, son of Alice Alexander, married/laundress, 30 Risborough Road, Maidenhead, Berkshire. CWGC: son of the late Mr. and Mrs. F. Alexander.

28th June1918
Sgt. John Parkyn 9198 DoW
born: Guernsey C.I.   enlisted: Guernsey
Buried: Crediton (Holy Cross) Churchyard. Grave: North-east of church. Age 49 or 25. Joined BEF: 06/11/14 with original cadre. 1901 Census shows two possible identities: father and his son, both named John. John Parkyn (father) is shown as a 32 year old reservist, married to Ellen Parkyn. John Parkyn (son) born in 1893 in St. Peter Port, Guernsey. Family address for both men is York Hill, Alderney, Channel Islands.
Pte. Bertie Harold Davis 71182 DoW
born: Meonstoke, Hants.   enlisted: Kensington   residence: Meonstoke
Buried: Sissonne British Cemetery. Grave H.18. Age 18. Joined BEF: not on Medal Card. 1901 Census: son of Charles G. Davis, general labourer, and Sarah Davis, Bucks Head Hill, Meon Stoke, Hampshire. 1911 Census: schoolboy, son of Charles George Davis, general labourer, and Sarah Davis, Meonstoke, Hants.
Pte. James Greenlees 32233 Died
born: Glasgow   enlisted: Hamilton N.B   residence: Rutherglen N.B.
Buried: St. Sever Cemetery Extension, Rouen. Grave Q.II.C.13. Age 19. Joined BEF: not on Medal Card. Formerly M/281173, Army Service Corps, 33799, Ox and Bucks Light Infantry. CWGC: son of William Greenlees and Janet Greenlees, Westfield, Rutherglen, Glasgow.

29th June1918
Pte. Henry John Bishop 64352 Died
born: Barwell Somerset   enlisted: Fulham, Middx.   residence: Chelsea
No known grave. Soissons Memorial. Joined BEF: 27/07/15.

Pte. William Clark 45248 Died
born: Birmingham   enlisted: Birmingham
Buried: Birmingham (Witton) Cemetery. Grave: Screen Wall. 188. 41325. Age 26. Joined BEF: not on Medal Card. 1911 Census: 'temperer' son of Emma Clark, widow, 24 Court, 5 House, Heneage, Birmingham, Warwickshire. CWGC: son of George Clark and Emma Clark, husband of Maud Annie Clark, Back, 95 Grosvenor Road, Aston, Birmingham, Warwickshire.

JULY 1918

2nd July1918
A/Cpl. Reginald Thomas Cox 9974 DoW (Germany)
born: Exeter   enlisted: Exeter
Buried: Cologne Southern Cemetery. Grave XIV.F.14. Age 20. Joined BEF: not on Medal Card. 1901 Census: son of Robert Cox, gardener (not domestic), and Ellen Cox, 5 Birts Lane, Heavitree, Exeter, Devon. CWGC: son of Mrs. Ellen Godbeer, 7 Stafford Road, St. Thomas, Exeter.

4th July1918
Pte. George Davis 74036 DoW
born: Bath   enlisted: Taunton   residence: Bath
Buried: Niederzwehren Cemetery. Grave VII.J.4. Joined BEF: not on Medal Card.

14th July1918
Pte. Albert Edward Punt 204840 KIA
born: Thornton Heath   enlisted: London
Buried: Peronne Communal Cemetery Extension. Grave V.E.10. Age 21. Joined BEF: not on Medal Card. Formerly 653632, 21/London Regiment. 1911 Census: baker's boy, son of Walter Punt, coachman/domestic, and Elsie Punt, 60 Stanley Grove, Croydon, Surrey. CWGC: son of Mr. and Mrs. Walter Punt, 71 Windmill Road, West Croydon, Surrey.

15th July1918
Pte. Oliver Charles Webber 292187 DoW
born: no record   enlisted: Bristol
Buried: La Chapelette British and Indian Cemetery, Peronne. Age 19. Grave VI.B.1. Joined BEF: not on Medal Card. 1911 Census: schoolboy, son of Martha Webber, widow, 37 Wellington Street, Cathay, Bristol, Gloucestershire.

23rd July1918
A/Cpl. Herbert Walter Francis 74041 DoW
born: Bournemouth   enlisted: Dorchester   residence: Parkestone
Buried: Ligny-St.Flochel British Cemetery, Averdoingt. Grave I.F.16. Age 18. No Medal Card. CWGC: son of Walter Henry Francis and Rhoda Francis, "Wardour," Alexandra Road, Parkstone, Dorset.

The 2nd Devons War Diary

AUGUST 1918

3rd August1918
Pte. Fred Caryl Hooper 16873 DoW (Germany)
born: Offwell, Devon   enlisted: Axminster   residence: Offwell
Buried: Niederzwehren Cemetery. Grave III.C.12. Age 30. Joined BEF: not on Medal Card. 1901 Census: son of Alfred Hooper, walling mason, and Elizabeth Hooper, Honiton Hill, Widworthy, Honiton, Devon. Recorded as DoW in Germany. 1911 Census: packer on railway line, son of Alfred Hooper, mason journeyman, and Elizabeth Hooper, Honiton Hill, Offwell, Honiton, Devon.

4th August1918
Pte. Edward B. Young 71308 KIA
born: Radstock   enlisted: Taunton   residence: Radstock
Buried: Thelus Military Cemetery. Grave V.C.2. Age 19. Joined BEF: not on Medal Card. 1901 Census: son of Alfred Acquila Young, coal labourer, and Annie S. Young, 41 Whitelands, Radstock, Somerset. 1911 Census: schoolboy, son of Acquila Young, coal miner hewer, and Sophia Young, 41 Lower Whitelands, Radstock, Somerset.CWGC: family address: 7 Morley Terrace, Radstock, Bath, Somerset.

8th August1918
A/Cpl. Frederick William Henry Hannaford 290440 Died
born: Torquay   enlisted: Exeter   residence: Torquay
Buried: Montcornet Military Cemetery. Grave G.2. Age 21. Joined BEF: not on Medal Card. 1901 Census: son of William John Hannaford, turncock, borough waterworks, and Rhoda Louise Hannaford, 14 Marchwood Terrace, Torquay, Devon. 1911 Census: 'errand boy – paper', son of William John Hannaford, market gardener, and Rhoda Louise Hannaford, Upton House Cottage, Torquay, Devon. CWGC: family address: 8 Windsor Road, Torquay, Devon.

12th August1918
Pte. Thomas Alfred Anthony Bush 9808 Died
born: Salisbury   enlisted: Exeter
Buried: Roisel Communal Cemetery Extension. Grave IV.N.6. Age 23. Joined BEF: 22/08/14 with original cadre of 1/Devons . 1911 Census: servant 'retailing milk', at the farm of Thomas James Pile, dairyman, 3 Teign Street, Teignmouth, Devon.

24th August 1918
Pte. Stanley Vernon Clacy 30915 DoW
born: Strawhall, Berks.   enlisted: Winchester   residence: Stockbridge
Buried: Aubigny Communal Cemetery Extension. Grave IV.D.34. Age 18. Joined BEF: not on Medal Card. 1901 Census: son of Frederick J. Clacy, head game keeper, and Edith R. Clacy, Stubbings Cottages, Bisham, Berkshire. 1911 Census: son of Frederick Joseph Clacy, game keeper, widower, Leckford, Stockbridge, Hants.

Martin Body

SEPTEMBER 1918

10th September 1918
Pte. William Mander 74077 DoW (Germany)
born: Dudley, Worcs.   enlisted: Worcester   residence: Dudley
Buried: Cologne Southern Cemetery. Grave XVIII.A.6. Age 18.
Joined BEF: not on Medal Card. 1911 Census: news boy – part time, son of Zachariah Mander, brass polisher, and Tamar Mander, 19 Vauxhall Street, Dudley, Worcs.

11th September 1918
Cpl. Alfred Blackman 32144 Died
born: Burnham, Bucks.   enlisted: Maidenhead
Buried: La Targette British Cemetery, Neuville-St.Vaast. Grave III.C.4. Age 21. Joined BEF: not on Medal Card. Formerly 12256, Hampshire Regiment. 1901 Census: son of Emma Blackman, sameday woman (wash), Alma Row, Burnham, Bucks. 1911 Census: schoolboy, son of Emma Blackman, widow, laundress, Alma Row, Burnham, Bucks.
Pte. Henry Hughes 32093 Died
born: Admington, Glos.   enlisted: Birmingham
Buried: La Targette British Cemetery, Neuville-St.Vaast. Grave III.C.5. Age 28. Joined BEF: 18/12/15, Hampshire Regiment. Medal Card: *accidentally killed 11/9/18*. 1901 Census: son of Esther Hughes, widow, Cottage, Admington, Gloucestershire.

12th September 1918
Pte. George Sharland 10761 KIA
born: Withycombe Raleigh   enlisted: Exeter   residence: Withycombe
Buried: Montcornet Military Cemetery. Grave D.1. Age 37. No Medal Card. 1901 Census: farm labourer, son of Samuel Sharland, farm labourer, and Elizabeth Sharland, Lyndhurst Road, Withycombe Raleigh, Exmouth, Devon. 1911 Census: son of Samuel Sharland, farm labourer/haulier, and Elizabeth Sharland, 63 The Village, Withycombe, Exmouth, Devon. CWGC: family address: Broadham House, Withycombe Raleigh, Exmouth, Devon.

15th September 1918
Pte. Albert Cecil Yauldren 32224 KIA
born: Winchester   enlisted: Southampton   residence: Winchester
Buried: La Targette British Cemetery, Neuville-St.Vaast. Grave III.C.II. Joined BEF: not on Medal Card. CWGC: son of William Henry Yauldren and Edith Maude Yauldren, 70 Lower Brooks Street, Winchester, Hants.

27th September 1918
Lt. Charles Wilfred Eales KIA
No known grave. Vin-En-Artois Memorial, Panel 4. Age 25. Joined BEF: 05/15, 176 Company, 2nd Division, Royal Engineers. Medal Card annotation: *Mrs. Grace A. Eales makes application for 1914-15 Star, British Medal and Victory Medal due to her late son. 01/07/20.* CWGC: son of Grace A. Eales, of Lewannick Vicarage, Launceston, Cornwall, and the late Rev. Henry William Eales.
Sgt. Herbert William Hill 14072 KIA
born: Totnes   enlisted: Totnes
No known grave. Vin-En-Artois Memorial, Panel 4. Age 24. Joined BEF: not on Medal Card.

1901 Census: son of William Walter Hill, gardener (domestic), and Jane Hill, 19 South Street, Totnes, Devon. 1911 Census: under gardener (domestic), son of William Walter Hill, gardener (domestic), and Jane Hill, Shinners Bridge, Dartington, Totnes, Devon. CWGC: family address: 1 Station Road, Totnes, Devon.

Pte. John Turner Adams 15175 KIA
born: Oldham   enlisted: Rochdale
Buried: Bois-Carre British Cemetery, Thelus. Grave III.F.15. Age 33. No Medal Card. 1891 Census: son of William Henry Adams, ironfounder, and Sarah Adams, 7 Barclyde Street, Castleton, Rochdale, Lancs. 1901 Census: working in cotton mill, son of Sarah Adams, 11 Freehold Street, Rochdale, Lancs. 1911 Census: 'cotton mule piecer', husband of Sarah Ann Adams, 'cotton drawing frame tenter', 233 Kensington Street, Rochdale, Lancashire. CWGC: husband of Sarah Ann Adams, 231 Kensington Street, Rochdale.

Pte. Sidney Allingham 290744 KIA
born: Bindon, Dorset   enlisted: Wareham
Buried: Bois-Carre British Cemetery, Thelus. Grave III.F.13. Age 18. SDGW records Pte. Allingham as DoW 05/02/1915, but CWGC lists date as 27/09/1918. Army number is a late series which suggests that the later date is probably correct. Joined BEF: not on Medal Card. 1901 Census: son of Alfred Allingham, flour mill carter, and Elizabeth Allingham, 3 Bindon Cottages, Wool, Dorset. 1911 Census: schoolboy, son of Alfred Allingham, general farm labourer, and Elizabeth Allingham, New Road, Wareham, Dorset.

Pte. William James Bowsher 70397 KIA
born: Beckhampton   enlisted: Marlborough
Buried: La Targette British Cemetery, Neuville-St.Vaast. Grave IV.C.8. Age 18. Joined BEF: not on Medal Card. 1901 Census: son of Samuel J. Bowsher, labourer (stone digging) and Emily Bowsher, 73 Frog Lane, West Overton, Wiltshire. 1911 Census: schoolboy, son of Samuel Bowsher, labourer, and Emily Bowsher, Lockeridge, Marlborough, Wiltshire.

Pte. Henry Brougham 32138 KIA
born: Birmingham   enlisted: Birmingham
No known grave. Vin-En-Artois Memorial, Panel 4. Age 19. Joined BEF: not on Medal Card. Formerly 38901, Royal Warwicks. 1901 Census: son of Henry Brougham, carter, and Elizabeth Brougham, 173 Byron Road, Aston, Birmingham. 1911 Census: schoolboy, son of Henry Brougham, 'currier', and Elizabeth Brougham, 2 Newbridge Villas, Coventry Road, South Yardley, Solihull, Warwickshire. CWGC: family address: 57 Preston Road, South Yardley, Birmingham.

Pte. Cyril Alfred Brunham 32235 KIA
born: Codman End   enlisted: High Wycombe   residence: Lane End
Buried: La Targette British Cemetery, Neuville-St.Vaast. Grave III.D.1. Age 19. Joined BEF: not on Medal Card. Formerly 19524, Ox and Bucks Light Infantry. 'A' Company. CWGC: son of Mr. and Mrs. Stephen Brunham, Lane End, Ditchfield, Bucks.

Pte. Harold Travers Dore 78710 KIA
born: Reading   enlisted: Reading
Buried: La Targette British Cemetery, Neuville-St.Vaast. Grave IV.C.9. Age 22. Joined BEF: not on Medal Card. 1901 Census: son of George D. Dore, coachman, and Emily M. Dore, 29 Waterloo Road, St. Giles, Reading, Berkshire. 1911 Census: milk boy, son of George Dore, coachman, and Emily Dore, address as above.

Pte. George William French 207153 KIA
born: no record   enlisted: Horsham
Buried: La Targette British Cemetery, Neuville-St.Vaast. Grave III.D.3. Joined BEF: not on

Medal Card. Formerly 74163, Royal Sussex Regiment.
Pte. Jonathan Edward Futter 74164 KIA
born: Cantley, Norfolk   enlisted: Wroxham, Norfolk   residence: South Burlingham
Buried: La Targette British Cemetery, Neuville-St.Vaast. Grave III.D.2. Age 20. Joined BEF: not on Medal Card. 1901 Census: son of Miles Futter, stockman on farm, and Elizabeth Futter, Near Bases Farm, Burleigham St. Edmund, Norfolk. 1911 Census: schoolboy, son of Miles Futter, farm labourer, and Elizabeth Futter, South Burlingham, Lingwood, Norwich, Norfolk. CWGC: family address: Beighton, Norwich.
Pte. Stanley Griffin 76009 KIA
born: Pontynewydd, Mon.   enlisted: Newport, Mon.   residence: Pontynewydd
Buried: La Targette British Cemetery, Neuville-St.Vaast. Grave III.D.4. Age 29. Joined BEF: not on Medal Card. Formerly 028037: Army Ordnance Corps. 1901 census: son of Thomas Griffin, shopkeeper, and Rhoda Griffin, Richmond Road, Upper Llanfrechva, Pontynewydd, Monmouthshire. 1911 Census: tinworker/sorter, son of Rhoda Griffin, widow, Glen View, Pontynewydd, Mon. CWGC: husband of Mrs. A. M. Griffin, 23 Mill Street, Newport, Mon.
Pte. Thomas Theobald Jackaman 204843 KIA
born: Camberwell   enlisted: Camberwell   residence: Peckham Rye
Buried: La Targette British Cemetery, Neuville-St.Vaast. Grave IV.C.5. Age 31. Joined BEF: not on Medal Card. Formerly 654513: 21/London Regiment. 1901 Census: son of George A. Jackaman, widower, general labourer, 45 Banstead Street, Camberwell, London. 1911 Census: general labourer, husband of Mary Ann Jackaman, 24 Eastney Street, Greenwich, London.
Pte. William Jarvis 18893 KIA
born: South Huish, Devon   enlisted: Kingsbridge   residence: Salcombe
Buried: La Targette British Cemetery, Neuville-St.Vaast. Grave IV.C.6. Age 35. Joined BEF: not on Medal Card. 1901 Census: gardener (domestic), son of John Jarvis, farmer, and Sarah A. Jarvis, Lower Batson, Salcombe, Devon. 1911 Census: jobbing gardener, husband of Emily Kathleen Jarvis, 23 Island Street, Salcombe, Devon. CWGC: husband of Emily Kathleen Jarvis, 2 Island Street, Salcombe, Devon.
Pte. Albert George Piner 205473 KIA
born: Thornton Heath   enlisted: Exeter   residence: Thornton Heath
Buried: Bois-Carre British Cemetery, Thelus. Grave III.F.16. Age 18. Joined BEF: not on Medal Card. 1901 Census: son of William Piner, brick maker, and Gertrude Piner, 19 Tankerton Terrace, Croydon, London. 1911 Census: schoolboy, son of William Piner, brickfield labourer, and Gertrude Maria Piner, 55 Spa Road, Thornton Heath, Croydon, Surrey.
Pte. Arthur Richard Carter Rickard 57010 KIA
born: Saltash, Cornwall   enlisted: Liskeard   residence: Saltash
Buried: La Targette British Cemetery, Neuville-St.Vaast. Grave IV.C.7. Age 19. Joined BEF: not on Medal Card. 1911 Census: schoolboy, son of William Rickard, leading man of joiners at H.M. Dockyard, Devonport, and Annie Rickard, Albert Villas, Burraton, St. Stephens, Saltash, Cornwall.
Pte. Wilfred Roberts 74194 KIA
born: Heathfield, Sussex   enlisted: Eastbourne
Buried: La Targette British Cemetery, Neuville-St.Vaast. Grave III.D.12. Age 20. Joined BEF: not on Medal Card. Formerly 1451: Royal Sussex. 1911 Census: schoolboy, son of Frank Roberts, 'farmer's son working on farms', and Mary Elizabeth Roberts, Bodle Street, nr. Hailsham, Sussex. CWGC: son of Mrs. M. E. Roberts, of The Stores, Bodle Street, Hailsham, Sussex.

Pte. Frederick Townsend 32214 KIA
born: Avon   enlisted: Stroud   residence: Avening
Buried: Bois-Carre British Cemetery, Thelus. Grave III.F.14. Joined BEF: not on Medal Card. Also on Medal Card as 66580, Devonshire Regiment.

A/L/Cpl. George Woodley 8423 Died
born: Exeter   enlisted: Exeter   residence: Salcombe
Buried: Sucrerie Cemetery, Ablain-St.Nazaire. Grave V.F.12. Age 28. 'C' company. Joined BEF: 06/11/14 with original cadre. 1901 Census: son of Richard Woodley, ordinary agricultural labourer, and Mary Ann Woodley, Knowle Cross, Whimple, Devonshire. 1911 Census: 2/Devons, St. George's Barracks, Malta.

Martin Body

OCTOBER 1918

4th October 1918
Pte. Jack Elliott 70434 Died
born: Bournemouth   enlisted: Bournemouth
Buried: Landrecies Communal Cemetery. Grave 2. (Grave amongst civilians). Joined BEF: not on Medal Card.

7th October 1918
Pte. Harry Penny 203402 KIA
born: Plymouth   enlisted: Plymouth
Buried: St.Nicholas British Cemetery. Grave II.E.15. Age 30. Joined BEF: not on Medal Card. 1911 Census: 'boots', son of Herbert S. Perry, lithographer, and Henrietta Penny, 40 Cotehele Avenue, Plymouth, Devon.
Pte. David Henry Waterman 32087 KIA
born: Breamore, Hants.   enlisted: Brockenhurst   residence: Breamore
Buried: St.Nicholas British Cemetery. Grave II.E.14. Age 26. Joined BEF: 20/09/15 as 15413, Hampshire Regiment. 1901 Census: son of Charles Waterman, shepherd on a farm, and Mary E. Waterman, "Warditch," Whitsbury, Salisbury, Hants. 1911 Census: shepherd on farm, son of Charles Waterman, shepherd on farm, and Mary Waterman, Whitsbury, nr. Breamore, Salisbury, Hants.
L/Cpl. Charles George Leaman 33232 DoW (Germany)
born: Crediton   enlisted: Crediton   residence: Copplestone
Buried: Niederzwehren Cemetery. Grave III.B.1. Age 28. Joined BEF: not on Medal Card. Formerly 968, Devonshire Regiment. 1911 Census: 2/Devons, St. George's Barracks, Malta.

8th October 1918
2/Lt. Gordon Eyre Baxter KIA
Born: Steeple Ashton, Wilts.
Buried: St.Nicholas British Cemetery. Grave II.F.5. Age 28. Joined BEF: 22/04/15 as No 929, King Edward's Horse, commissioned 26/06/17. 1901 Census: son of Stanley Eyre Baxter, dairy farmer, Great House Farm, Leigh-on-Mendip, Somerset. CWGC: son of Stanley Eyre Baxter and Emma Louisa Baxter, Waranga, Omapere, Hokianga, New Zealand.
Sgt.James Henry Moses Prescott 8433 KIA
born: Dartmouth   enlisted: Torquay   residence: Dartmouth
Buried: St.Nicholas British Cemetery. Grave II.F.6. Age 29. Joined BEF: not on Medal Card. 1901 Census: son of Sarah J. Prescott, widow, dressmaker, 6 Coast Guard Cottages, Erith, Kent. CWGC: son of Sarah J. Prescott, of Dartmouth, Devon, and the late William Prescott, husband of Fanny R. Prescott, 19 Newcombe Street, Heavitree, Exeter.
Pte. John Harold Moore 70295 KIA
born: Stourbridge   enlisted: Stourbridge
Buried: St.Nicholas British Cemetery. Grave II.F.7. Joined BEF: not on Medal Card.
Pte. Ernest Wood 33147 Died (home)
born: Bradninch, Devon   enlisted: Bradninch
Buried: Bradninch Burial Ground. Grave 150. Age 24. Joined BEF: not on Medal Card. 1901 Census: son of William Wood, gardener/labourer (not domestic), and Mary Wood, Cullompton Hill, Bradninch, Devon. 1911 Census: labourer in paper mill, son of William Wood, farm labourer, and Mary Wood, Cullompton Hill, Bradninch, nr. Cullompton, Devon.

The 2nd Devons War Diary

10th October 1918
Pte. Ernest Jones 76008 KIA
born: Hurst, Lancs.   enlisted: Ashton-Under-Lyme   residence: Hurst, Lancs.
Buried: Ste.Catherine British Cemetery. Grave J.14. Joined BEF: not on Medal Card. Formerly 019692, Army Ordnance Corps.

11th October 1918
Pte. Louis Reggy Tungate 32254 KIA
born: Tivetshall, Norfolk   enlisted: Swaythling, Hants.   residence: Norwich
Orchard Dump Cemetery, Arleux-En-Gohelle. Grave VI.H.49. Age 20. Joined BEF: not on Medal Card. 1901 Census: son of Mrs. Anna Maria Tungate, housekeeper, grandson of William Tungate, ordinary agricultural labourer, Seames Green, Pulham, St. Mary Magdalen, Norfolk. 1911 Census: farm labourer, eldest son of William Tungate, 'Council labourer on roads', and Anna Maria Tungate, Semere Green, Pulham Market, Norfolk. CWGC: Anna Maria Tungate's address: Rectory Road, Tivetshall St. Mary, Norwich, Norfolk.
Pte. Cecil Wilcox 32218 KIA
born: Leamington   enlisted: Leamington
Buried: Ste.Catherine British Cemetery. Grave J.17. No Medal Card.
Pte. Albert Edward John Winstone 63236 KIA
born: Leckhampton   enlisted: Gloucester
Buried: Ste. Catherine British Cemetery. Grave J.13. Age 23. Joined BEF: 18/07/15, 10/Worcesters. Medal Card annotations: *Mrs. E. Winstone makes application in respect of the services of her late husband Pte. A.E.J.Winstone for 1914-15 Star. 24/3/19. Major F.E.Rickersby recommends medals to be forwarded to Mrs. Winstone (undated).* 1911 Census: farm labourer, son of Albert E. Winstone, farm labourer, and Ellen A. Winstone, Little Whitcombe, Badgworth, Glos.

13th October 1918
Cpl. Walter Scott Robertson 32245 DoW
born: Dublin   enlisted: Southampton
Buried: Etaples Military Cemetery. Grave LXVI.J.19. Age 32. Joined BEF: 27/08/14 as 6909 of original cadre of 1/Hampshires. 1901 Census: draper's porter, boarding at 174 High Street, Southampton, Hants. CWGC: son of the late Robert Robertson and May Robertson.

15th October1918
L/Cpl. Ernest G. Jones 30965 DoW
born: Birmingham   enlisted: Birmingham   residence: King's Norton
Buried: Duisans British Cemetery, Etrun. Grave VII.B.87. Age 20. Joined BEF: not on Medal Card. CWGC: son of William Jones and Mary Ann Jones, 1676 Pershore Road, Cotteridge, King's Norton, Birmingham, Warwickshire.

16th October1918
A/Cpl. William R. Weekes 290208 Died
born: Torquay   enlisted: Torquay
Buried: Etaples Military Cemetery. Grave LXVI.J.11. Age 21. Joined BEF: not on Medal Card. 1901 Census: son of Albert John Weekes, general labourer, and Mary Elizabeth Weekes, laundress, 2 Albert Street, Torquay, Devon. CWGC: family address: 6 Princess Street, Babbacombe, Torquay, Devon.

20th October 1918
Pte. Frederick William Frise 74043 Died
born: Horrabridge   enlisted: Plymouth   residence: Horrabridge
Buried: St.Avold Military Cemetery. Grave 18. Age 19. Joined BEF: not on Medal Card. 1901 Census: son of Frederick Frise, stone mason, and Jessie Elizabeth Frise, Dostabrook Cottages, Horrabridge, Devon. 1911 Census: schoolboy, son of Frederick W. Frise, farm labourer, and Jessie Frise, Dostabrook, Horrabridge, Devon.
Pte. William Daniel Shears 290282 Died
born: no record   enlisted: Exeter
CWGC: no grave or memorial reference. Age 33. No Medal Card. 1911 Census: stonemason's labourer, husband of Clara Louisa Shears, 4 Weslyan Courts, Sidwell Street, Exeter, Devon.

21st October 1918
Pte. Ernest Leonard Edwards 70824 Died
born: Branksome, Dorset   enlisted: Bournemouth
No known grave. Malbork Memorial. Age 19. Joined BEF: not on Medal Card. 1901 Census: recorded as Leonard E. Edwards, son of James George Edwards, bootmaker, and Mary Edwards, 3 Cromer Road, Branksome, Dorset. 1911 Census: schoolboy, son of James George Edwards, boot repairer, and Mary Edwards, 15 Wynyard Road, Winton, Bournemouth, Hants. CWGC: family address: "Heather Bank," 15 Wynyard Road, Winton, Bournemouth, Hants.

24th October 1918
Pte. Frederick George Smith 230165 Died
born: Torpoint   enlisted: Plymouth
Buried: Harlebeke New British Cemetery. Grave XIX.B.2. Joined BEF: not on Medal Card.

25th October 1918
Lt. Leslie Vinnicombe Died Attached to the Railway Transportation Establishment (R.T.E.). Buried: Staglieno Cemetery, Genoa. Grave I.C.33. Age 30. Not with 2/Devons when died. Joined BEF: 06/04/15 as L/Cpl 6978, 12th Lancers. Later A/Cpl 41921, Machine Gun Corps. Commissioned as Lieutenant 12/11/16, in the Devonshire Regiment (no record of commission on Medal Card). 1891 Census: son of Thomas Hedger Vinnicombe, hotel proprietor, and Lizzie Frances Vinnicombe, 48 High Street, Sittingbourne, Kent. 1901 Census: boarder-pupil at Cleveland House School, Melcombe Regis, Dorset. 1911 Census: railway clerk, boarding at 10 Grosvenor Road, Richmond, Surrey. CWGC: family address: The Leas Hotel, Folkestone, Kent.

27th October 1918
Pte. Patrick Diamond 32153 KIA
born: no record   enlisted: Bath   residence: no fixed abode
Buried: Valenciennes (St.Roch) Communal Cemetery. Grave II.D.11. Joined BEF: not on Medal Card. Formerly 17334, Hampshires.
Pte. Samuel Hackett 32033 KIA
born: Rowley Regis, Staffs.   enlisted: Brierley Hill
Buried: Valenciennes (St.Roch) Communal Cemetery. Grave II.F.16. Age 19. Joined BEF: not on Medal Card. Formerly 43225, Hampshires. 1901 Census: son of Shadrack Hackett, labourer at stone quarry, and Mary Anne Hackett, 33 Hawes Lane, Rowley Regis, Staffordshire. 1911 Census: schoolboy, son of Mary Anne Hackett, widow, Village, Rowley Regis, Birmingham, Warwickshire.

Pte. Jim Morris 61823 KIA
born: Monmouth   enlisted: Tredegar   residence: Blackwood, Mon.
Buried: Valenciennes (St.Roch) Communal Cemetery. Grave II.F.15. Joined BEF: not on Medal Card.

Pte. Francis John Trute 30367 KIA
born: no record   enlisted: Barnstaple   residence: Swimbridge
Buried: St.Amand-Les_A-Eaux Communal Cemetery. Grave: in South-East part. Age 31. Joined BEF: not on Medal Card. 1901 Census: son of William Trute, horseman at tannery, and Ann Trute, Swimbridge Village, Devon. 1911 Census: railway platelayer, husband of Edith Maud Trute, Swimbridge, Devon. CWGC: husband of Edith Maud Trute, Vellator, Devon.

Pte. Sidney Herbert Waller 24825 Died
born: Bristol   enlisted: Exeter
Buried: Worms (Hochheim Hill) Cemetery. Grave: Screen Wall. Age 41. Joined BEF: not on Medal Card. 1891 Census: provision clerk, son of Jabez Edgar Waller, ironmonger's assistant, and Elizabeth Waller, 5 Wilms Road, Wandsworth, London. CWGC: husband of Lily Waller, 5 Coleridge Road, St. Thomas, Exeter, Devon.

28th October 1918
Pte. George Frederick Clift 74149 DoW
born: Hackney, Middx.   enlisted: Hackney
Buried: Mont Huon Military Cemetery, Le Treport. Grave VIII.O.4B. Age 30. Joined BEF: not on Medal Card. Formerly 11402, Royal Sussex. 1891 Census: son of James Clift, tailor, and Charlotte Clift, 142 Hertford Road, Hackney, London. 1901 Census: son of Charlotte Clift, widow, 142 Hertford Road, Hackney, Kingsland, Middlesex. 1911 Census: postman, son of Charlotte Clift, widow, 142 Hertford Road, Hackney, Kingsland, Middlesex. CWGC: son of James Clift and Charlotte Clift, 142 Hertford Road, Kingsland, London.

29th October 1918
Pte. Victor Hedley Andrews 69515 DoW
born: Thornford, Dorset   enlisted: Sherborne
Buried: Douai British Cemetery, Cuinchy. Grave A.6. Age 19. 'D' Company. Joined BEF: not on Medal Card. CWGC: son of Henry Andrews and Eliza Ruth Andrews, 405 Thornford Road, Thornford, Sherborne, Dorset.

Pte. Reuben George Shergold 69068 DoW
born: Salisbury   enlisted: Salisbury
Buried: Douai British Cemetery, Cuinchy. Grave A.2. Age 20. Joined BEF: not on Medal Card. 1911 Census: schoolboy, son of Henry Shergold, shepherd on farm, and Edith Emma Shergold, South Mill, Avebury, Salisbury, Wilts. CWGC: son of Henry Shergold and Edith Emma Shergold, Albert Place, South Newton, Salisbury, Wilts.

Pte. Henry George Preece 74085 Died (home)
born: Bayford. Herts.   enlisted: Hertford
Buried: Milverton (St.Michael) Churchyard. Grave: In North-West part. Age 19. Joined BEF: not on Medal Card. 1901 Census: son of Edwin Henry Preece, coachman domestic, and Elizabeth Joyce Preece, The Green, Bayford, Herts. 1911 Census: schoolboy, son of Edwin Henry Preece, coachman domestic, and Elizabeth Joyce Preece, Bayford Green, Hertford, Herts. CWGC: son of Edwin Henry Preece, The George Hotel, Milverton, Devon.

31st October 1918
2/Lt. John Sayes KIA
Buried: Valenciennes (St.Roch) Communal Cemetery. Grave II.F.17. Age 27. No Medal Card.
1901 Census: son of Elijah Sayes, coal hewer, and Emily Sayes, Ellwood, West Dean, Coleford, Glos. 1911 Census: student at Culham Training College, Sutton Courtenay, Abingdon, Berks.
L/Cpl. George Pearson 3/6834 KIA
born: Hackney   enlisted: Stratford   residence: Edmonton
Buried: Valenciennes (St.Roch) Communal Cemetery. Grave II.F.9. Joined BEF: 03/12/14.
Cpl. Robert Whitlock MM 32186 KIA
born: Woodstock, Oxon.   enlisted: Yeovil
Buried: Valenciennes (St.Roch) Communal Cemetery. Grave II.F.8. Age 30. Joined BEF: 24/07/15, 14892, Somerset Light Infantry. 1901 Census: carpenter's assistant, son of John Whitlock, glove maker, and Rhoda Whitlock, Browns Lane, Woodstock, Oxon. 1911 Census: glove leather dresser, husband of Mary Whitlock, Tintinhull, Martock, Somerset.
Pte. Albert Victor Bates 68855 KIA
born: Wednesbury   enlisted: Stratford-on-Avon   residence: Redditch
Buried: Odomez Communal Cemetery. Grave: South of Calvary. Age 20. No Medal Card.
1911 Census: scholar 'tool making and cycle works', son of Henry Newman Bates, tool maker, and Laura Bates, 45 Marsden Road, Redditch, Warwickshire. CWGC: son of Henry Bates and Laura Newman Bates, 45 Marsden Road, Redditch, Warwickshire.
Pte. Charles Henry Thomas Brooks 291773 KIA
born: Plymouth   enlisted: Plymouth
Buried: Valenciennes (St.Roch) Communal Cemetery. Grave II.F.10. Age 19. Joined BEF: not on Medal Card. 1901 Census: son of Robert H. Brooks, cab driver, groom, and Selina Brooks, 35 Millbay Road, Plymouth.
Pte. Frederick Edward Carter 32189 KIA
born: Portsmouth   enlisted: Southampton   residence: Portsmouth
Buried: Valenciennes (St.Roch) Communal Cemetery. Grave II.D.25. Joined BEF: not on Medal Card. Formerly 8/11685, 51/Grad. Battalion.
Pte. Arthur Charles Dixon 12830 KIA
born: Hampton, Middx.   enlisted: Kingston-on-Thames
No known grave. Vin-En-Artois Memorial, Panel 4. Age 19. Joined BEF: 22/09/15 with 10/Devons. 1901 Census: son of Thomas Alfred Dixon, crane driver, water works, and Helen Dixon, Avenue Road, Hampton, Middlesex. CWGC: family address: 19 Belgrade Road, Hampton, Middx.
Pte. Thomas Dixon 69164 KIA
born: Grimsby   enlisted: Hull
No known grave. Vin-En-Artois Memorial, Panel 4. Joined BEF: not on Medal Card.
Pte. Harry Glanville 74046 KIA
born: Clyst Hydon, Devon   enlisted: Exeter   residence: Clyst Hydon
Buried: Valenciennes (St.Roch) Communal Cemetery. Grave II.F.11. Age 18. Joined BEF: not on Medal Card. 1901 Census: son of Elizabeth Glanville, Symons, Clysthydon, Devon. 1911 Census: son of Harry Glanville, steam wagon driver, and Elizabeth Glanville, Palmers, Clysthydon, nr. Whimple, Devon.
Pte. John Lentle 25615 KIA
born: Luppit, Devon   enlisted: Honiton
Buried: Valenciennes (St.Roch) Communal Cemetery. Grave II.F.13. Age 33. Joined BEF: not on Medal Card. 1891 Census: son of William Lentle, agricultural labourer, and Emma Lentle, 2

Birds Overday, Luppitt, Devon. 1901 Census: servant, agricultural labourer, Gulley Lane, Luppitt, Devon. 1911 Census: farm labourer, married, Penn Cottage, Luppitt, Honiton, Devon.

Pte. Arthur Edward Watson 32048 KIA
born: Buckland, Berks.   enlisted: Abingdon   residence: Buckland
Buried: Valenciennes (St.Roch) Communal Cemetery. Grave II.F.7. Age 18. Joined BEF: not on Medal Card. Formerly 43360, Hampshires. 1901 Census: son of Edward Watson, agricultural labourer, and Lucy Francis Watson, Buckland, Berks. 1911 Census: schoolboy, son of Edward Watson, farm labourer, and Lucy Francis Watson, Buckland, Faringdon, Berks.

Pte. Montague Augustus White 315580 KIA
born: no record   enlisted: Maidenhead
Buried: Odomez Communal Cemetery. Grave: South of Calvary. Age 33. Joined BEF: not on Medal Card. 1901 Census: assistant in general shop, son of Alice M. White, supported by husband, 4 Pennystone Road, maidenhead, Berks. 1911 Census: fishmonger roundsman, son of Alice Marie White, housekeeper, 3 Glenholme Villas, Rutland Place, Maidenhead, Berks. CWGC: son of Benjamin White and Alice Maria White, husband of Edith White, 30 Spencers Road, Maidenhead, Berks.

Pte. James Frank Bye 32021 DoW
born: Ruscombe, Berks.   enlisted: Ruscombe
Buried: Valenciennes (St.Roch) Communal Cemetery. Grave II.D.14. Age 23. Joined BEF: 18/12/15 as 12355, Hampshires. 1901 Census: son of James F. Bye, coachman domestic, and Mary A. Bye, Castle End, Ruscombe, Twyford, Berks. 1911 Census: farm labourer, son of James Frank Bye, groom/domestic, and Mary Ann Bye, Castle End Cottages, Ruscombe, Twyford, Berks.

NOVEMBER 1918

2nd November 1918
Pte. John Charles Rew 32067 DoW
born: London N.   enlisted: Marylebone   residence: Wood Green
Buried: Douai British Cemetery, Cuinchy. Grave A.9. Age 23. Joined BEF: not on Medal Card. Formerly 11370, Hampshires. 1901 Census: son of John H. Rew, horse keeper groom, and Mary A. E. Rew, 58 Euston Street, St. Pancras, London. 1911 Census: brewer's employee, son of Johnny K. Rew, horse keeper, and Mary Ann Emma Rew, 99 Drummond Street, St. Pancras, London.

3rd November 1918
Pte. Richard Harmon Gallop 32052 DoW
born: Stony Stratford   enlisted: Bletchley   residence: Stony Stratford
Buried: Brebieres British Cemetery. Grave B.1. Age 19. Joined BEF: not on Medal Card. Formerly 8/5147, 51/Grad Battalion, 28436, Hampshires. 1901 Census: son of William H. Gallop, iron moulder, and Harriet C. Gallop, Park Road, Claverton, Bucks. 1911 Census: son of Harriet Clara Gallop, married, 7 Swan Terrace, Stony Stratford, Northants.
Pte. Bertie Harold Westwood 31024 Died
born: no record   enlisted: Warwick   residence: Birmingham
Buried: Birmingham (Brandwood End) Cemetery. Grave: Screen Wall.C.1."C." 455. Joined BEF: not on Medal Card. Formerly 8/1735, 206th Infantry Battalion.

4th November 1918
Pte. Archibald Ball 32019 DoW
born: Skirmit, Bucks.   enlisted: Abingdon   residence: Boars Hill, Oxon.
Buried: Etaples Military Cemetery. Grave XLIX.B.13. Joined BEF: 18/12/15 as 12500, Hampshires.

5th November 1918
Pte. James Henry Fowler 316052 DoW
born: Bideford, Devon   enlisted: Exeter   residence: Northam
Buried: Brebieres British Cemetery. Grave C.1. Age 19. Joined BEF: not on Medal Card. 1901 Census: son of Mary Ann Fowler, husband Captain (away), 1 Highfield Place, Bideford, Devon. 1911 Census: schoolboy, son of Mary Ann Fowler, married, 24 Meddon Street, Bideford, Devon.
Pte. Stanley Frank Kemish 74068 DoW (Germany)
born: Romsey, Hants.   enlisted: Southampton   residence: Romsey
Buried: Cologne Southern Cemetery. Grave XVIII.A.31. Joined BEF: not on Medal Card.

6th November 1918
L/Cpl. Charles Robert Rowe 23786 DoW
born: Bristol   enlisted: Plymouth
Buried: Sarralbe Military Cemetery. Grave: Morhange German Cemetery. Mem. 11. Age 31. Joined BEF: not on Medal Card. 1901 Census: son of Robert J. Rowe, cabinet maker journeyman, and Elizabeth Jane Rowe, 20 Whimple Street, Plymouth, Devon. CWGC: husband of Sarah Elizabeth Morris (formerly Rowe), Woodend, Marston, Beds.

Pte. Ernest William Creek 8456 Died
born: Combe Martin, Devon   enlisted: Combe Martin
Buried: Douai British Cemetery, Cuinchy. Grave A.25. Age 30. Joined BEF: 05/11/14 with original cadre. 1891 Census: son of William Creek, butcher and farmer, and Ellen Creek, Wards, Combe Martin, Devon. 1911 Census: 2/Devons, St. George's Barracks, Malta. CWGC: husband of Mabel Annie Creek, of Devonia House, Combe Martin, Devon. Ernest Creek served throughout the Great War with 2/Devons, only to die, possibly from Influenza, five days before Armistice Day.

12th November 1918
Pte. James Sheard 63211 DoW (home)
born: Beeston, Yorks.   enlisted: Dewsbury, Yorks.   residence: Charwell, Yorks.
Buried: Leeds (Beeston) Cemetery. Grave: New part. 1608. Age 27. No Medal Card. 1901 Census: son of Edward Sheard, blacksmith's stoker, and Mary Sheard, 18 Bank Terrace, Morley, Yorkshire. 1911 Census: woollen picker, son of Mary Sheard, widow, 64 Gilderson New Road, Morley, Dewsbury, Yorkshire. CWGC: husband of Elizabeth Alice Sheard, 3 Cross Flatts Crescent, Beeston, Leeds.

13th November 1918
Sgt. Roderick Lewis Davies 33943 DoW
born: Gartheli, Cardiff   enlisted: Bridgend, Glam.
Buried: Etaples Military Cemetery. Grave L.C.17. Age 27. Joined BEF: not on Medal Card. Formerly 5583, Welsh Regiment, 54098, also of the Welsh Regiment. 1901 Census: son of Stephen Lewis Davies, farmer, and Ann Davies, Pantyrhwchfawr, Llangyli, Cardiganshire.

26th November 1918
Pte. Henry Snell 69218 Died
born: Crediton   enlisted: Exeter   residence: Crediton
Buried: Douai British Cemetery, Cuinchy. Grave C.18. Age 30. Joined BEF: not on Medal Card. 1911 Census: 'carter/road, son of William Snell, 'carter on the road', and Emma Snell, 5 Baptist Chapel Court, Crediton, Devon. Husband of Sarah Ann Snell, Baptist Chapel Court, Crediton, Devon. CWGC: family address: 67 High Street, Crediton, Devon.

Martin Body

DECEMBER 1918 to JANUARY 1920

3rd March 1919
Cpl. Edmund George Josephson MM 32154 DoW (home)
born: Aldershot   enlisted: Aldershot
Buried: Plymouth (Efford) Cemetery. Grave: Church C.7565. Age 22. No Medal Card. 1911 Census: apprentice compositor, son of Edmund Josephson, Army pensioner, barrack warden, and Maud Josephson, at Wellington Lines, Aldershot, Hants. CWGC: son of Edmund Josephson and Maude Josephson, "Oakdene," Pinewood Road, Ash, Surrey. Born at Stanhope-Lines, Aldershot.

In the SDGW database there are records of three men of the 2/Devons who died after the War Diary's last entry:

27th June 1919
L/Sgt. Peter John Herbert 17669 KIA (Russia)
Born: Stepney, Middx.   enlisted: Woolwich, Kent   residence: Stepney, Middx.
No known grave. Archangel Memorial. Age 20. Joined BEF: not on medal card. 1901 Census: son of Peter Herbert, watchmaker, and Ellen Herbert, 18 Cayley Street, Limehouse, London. 1911 Census: son of Peter John Herbert, packing case maker/carman, and Ellen Herbert, 122 Carr Street, Stepney, London. CWGC: son of Peter John and Ellen Herbert, 33 Arnold Road, Bow, London.

15th September 1919
L/Cpl. Henry Hardy Moody 8637 DoW (Russia)
Born: Aldershot, Hants.   enlisted: London
Buried: Archangel Allied Cemetery. Grave D.10. Joined BEF: 22/08/14 with the original cadre of the 1/Devons.

4th January 1920
Pte. Arthur H. Norcott 45538 DoW (England)
Born: Stonehouse, Glos.   enlisted: Ringwood, Hants.
Buried: Stonehouse (St.Cyr) Churchyard. Grave: In North-East corner. Age 41. Joined BEF: not on medal card. 1901 Census: gardener/domestic, at Moulton, Newmarket, Suffolk. 1911 Census: gardener/domestic, husband of Theresa Norcott, father of three, Burley Street, Ringwood, Hants. CWGC: son of Mr. and Mrs. Charles Norcott, husband of Theresa Norcott, Burley Street, Burley, Brockenhurst, Hants. Had been a prisoner of war in Germany.

The 2nd Devons War Diary

Martin Body

The 2nd Devons War Diary

PART 3

AN ALPHABETICAL LIST OF THE LOST MEN

Surname	Fore Names	Rank	Number	Date Died
Acomb	Horace	2/Lt.		21/08/1916
Ackland	Percy Thomas	Pte.	16911	27/03/1918
Adams	John Turner	Pte.	15175	27/09/1918
Adams	Thomas	Pte.	64419	12/02/1918
Addicott	Francis	Pte.	290274	29/11/1917
Adelson	Abraham	Pte.	30894	24/04/1918
Adey	Albert	Pte.	45524	24/02/1917
Alexander	William (Billy) Nelson	Pte.	291457	27/06/1918
Algate	Robert John	Sgt.	8282	16/08/1917
Allen	Alfred George	Pte.	71141	24/04/1918
Allen	Percy Fricker	Pte.	8557	18/01/1915
Allingham	Sidney	Pte.	290744	05/02/1915
Alsop	Walter George	Pte.	9044	05/02/1915
Anderson-Morshead	Rupert Henry	Lt/Col.		27/05/1918
Andrew	John Nicholas	Pte.	205186	01/04/1918
Andrew	Richard Henry	Pte.	45606	31/05/1918
Andrew	Charles	L/Cpl.	14193	31/07/1917
Andrews	Francis William George	Pte.	17814	01/07/1916
Andrews	Frank	Pte.	12718	01/07/1916
Andrews	James Alfrey	Capt.		01/07/1916
Andrews	Victor Hedley	Pte.	69515	29/10/1918
Andrews	William Henry	Pte.	17639	02/10/1917
Annenberg	Albert	Pte.	3\6916	08/11/1916
Anning	Montague William	Pte.	18950	23/03/1917

Appleton	Charles	Pte.	9195	24/11/1914
Arberry	Arthur John	L/Cpl.	11429	18/07/1916
Archer	Harry	A/Maj.		25/11/1917
Armstrong	Bertram John	Pte.	15487	18/05/1916
Ascott	George John	Pte.	17560	31/12/1916
Ash	Thomas Laurence	Pte.	16955	07/07/1916
Ashmore	Ernest John	Pte.	30273	13/04/1918
Ashton	Arthur Samuel Charles	Pte.	17166	03/08/1917
Auton	Josiah Henry	Pte.	16928	31/12/1916
Avery	George Henry	Pte.	11301	01/07/1916
Avery	Harry	Pte.	71143	24/04/1918
Avery	William James	L/Cpl.	18768	06/10/1916
Badcock	Alfred Hugh	Pte.	12787	13/03/1915
Badman	Horace Gilbert	Pte.	70407	26/05/1918
Baglow	George	Pte.	9534	10/02/1915
Bagwell	Wilfred	Sgt.	7537	21/12/1914
Bagwell	William Henry	Pte.	11244	15/03/1915
Bailey	Arthur	L/Cpl.	30853	03/03/1918
Bailey	Arthur	Pte.	53770	24/04/1918
Bailey	John	Pte.	8602	27/12/1914
Bailey	Samuel James	Pte.	8325	01/07/1916
Baker	Albert John	Pte.	25081	16/04/1917
Baker	Frederick Charles	L/Cpl.	30908	27/05/1918
Baker	George James	Pte.	9141	20/08/1916
Baker	James	Pte.	3\5778	18/12/1914
Baker	James	Pte.	26245	14/04/1917
Baker	Leslie	Pte.	19208	24/11/1917
Baldwin	George Henry	Pte.	9929	01/07/1916
Ball	Archibald	Pte.	32019	04/11/1918
Ball	Bertie John James	Pte.	33563	08/11/1916
Banks	James	Sgt.	8590	01/07/1916
Barker	Charles William Cyril	Pte.	70741	31/05/1918
Barker	Clifford	Pte.	3\7016	24/04/1918
Barnes	Thomas Robert	Pte.	9839	01/07/1916
Barrett	William James	Cpl.	7989	01/07/1916

Barter	Harry	Pte.	31795	02/04/1918
Bartlett	Cornelius Joseph	Pte.	26866	31/07/1917
Bates	Albert Victor	Pte.	68855	31/10/1918
Bates	Herbert James	Pte.	16172	01/07/1916
Bates	Reginald Plumptre	Lt.		10/03/1915
Bates	William John Farrow	Pte.	26524	31/07/1917
Batten	Frederick	Pte.	203255	16/08/1917
Batters	Norman John	Sgt.	7642	31/07/1917
Baxter	Gordon Eyre	2/Lt.		08/10/1918
Bayliss	Frederick George	Sgt.	8143	06/10/1916
Bealey	Charles Henry	Pte.	71151	24/04/1918
Beazley	Ernest	Pte.	3\7100	27/10/1916
Beck	George	Pte.	51451	24/04/1918
Beddow	Cecil Victor	2/Lt.		01/07/1916
Beer	Frederick John	Pte.	20349	06/07/1916
Beer	Henry	Pte.	3\7318	18/12/1914
Beer	William Henry	Pte.	9399	10/03/1915
Behenna	Herbert Stanley	Pte.	27615	31/07/1917
Belsham	Henry Charles Jacob	Pte.	3\6975	07/06/1915
Benjamin	Coleman	Pte.	30903	25/11/1917
Bennett	Arthur John	Pte.	11408	09/05/1915
Bennett	William Bertram	Pte.	30905	28/05/1918
Berry	Albert George	Pte.	11839	15/03/1915
Berry	William Claud	Pte.	292084	07/04/1918
Betts	Frank William John	Pte.	30904	05/09/1917
Betts	James	A/Cpl.	3\6887	24/04/1918
Beynon	Lancelot	Pte.	12632	11/03/1915
Bickford	Edward	Pte.	15376	01/07/1916
Bicknell	Thomas	Pte.	6732	17/05/1915
Bidder	Walter Robert	Pte.	3\6464	18/12/1914
Biggs	Walter James	Pte.	9798	18/12/1914
Billing	Reginald Herbert	Pte.	30848	29/07/1917
Bingle	Alfred John	Pte.	33554	28/07/1917
Birkett	Joseph	L/Cpl.	27607	14/04/1917
Bishop	Fred	Pte.	8837	01/01/1915

Bishop	Henry John	Pte.	64352	29/06/1918
Blackman	Alfred	Cpl.	32144	11/09/1918
Blake	Charles John	Pte.	30810	28/07/1917
Blake	Leslie Honychurch	Pte.	205129	26/05/1918
Blake	Sidney Alfred	Sgt.	7129	30/01/1915
Blake	William Henry	Pte.	9351	18/12/1914
Blake	William	Pte.	40853	27/05/1918
Blight	Sidney	Pte.	14295	16/08/1917
Blight	William James	Pte.	71158	21/04/1918
Blunt	Frank Hilton	Pte.	8346	21/10/1916
Boam	Edgar	Cpl.	14569	01/07/1916
Boden	John Charles	Pte.	30896	25/03/1918
Bolt	Arthur George	Pte.	203297	29/11/1917
Bolt	John	Pte.	203383	31/07/1917
Bolton	William	Pte.	9862	01/07/1916
Bond	Frank	Cpl.	8415	10/03/1915
Boon	Frederick William	Pte.	9308	07/02/1915
Bourhill	James Frederick	Cpl.	33173	31/07/1917
Bovin	Frank	Pte.	9209	17/12/1914
Bowden	Charles John	Pte.	9075	09/05/1915
Bowden	David John	Pte.	3\7321	09/05/1915
Bowden	Ernest John	L/Cpl.	8687	01/07/1916
Bowden	James	Pte.	3\7266	01/02/1915
Bowden	Sydney	Pte.	11273	10/03/1915
Bowden	William	Pte.	28992	05/02/1917
Bowles	Albert	Pte.	9148	01/07/1916
Bowsher	William James	Pte.	70397	27/09/1918
Boyland	William John	Pte.	3\6824	17/03/1915
Bracher	William George	Pte.	30792	03/09/1917
Bradford	Ernest	Pte.	8320	30/11/1914
Brant	Ernest Edward	Pte.	29704	31/07/1917
Braund	Frederick James	L/Cpl.	9158	17/05/1915
Braund	William Ernest	Pte.	9277	18/12/1914
Bray	James	Pte.	8883	07/02/1915
Brealy	Frederick John	Pte.	16035	28/03/1918

Brice	Cyril Vivian	Pte.	3\7604	10/03/1915
Brice	George	Pte.	8151	29/07/1917
Bridge	Frank Arthur	Pte.	30895	05/09/1917
Bridgman	John	L/Cpl.	16299	18/01/1917
Bridgman	Walter Hampton	L/Sgt.	205160	27/05/1918
Brimcombe	Saxby	Pte.	68083	24/04/1918
Bristow	Harold John	Pte.	9864	09/06/1915
Bristowe	Robert Owen	Lt.		10/03/1915
Brittain	Montague Thomas	Pte.	15119	01/07/1916
Broadway	Robert	Pte.	26122	14/04/1917
Brock	George Henry	Pte.	18398	07/04/1918
Broderick	Alfred William	Pte.	18328	17/07/1916
Brogan	George Henry	Pte.	19184	31/07/1917
Brooker	Arthur	Pte.	30907	24/04/1918
Brooking	Frederick Amos	Pte.	290278	05/09/1917
Brooks	Charles Henry Thomas	Pte.	291773	31/10/1918
Brooks	Thomas	Pte.	5839	31/07/1917
Brooks	William	Pte.	8077	12/03/1915
Broomfield	Ben	Pte.	45527	30/10/1917
Brougham	Henry	Pte.	32138	27/09/1918
Broughton	Edward	Pte.	68114	24/04/1918
Brown	Alfred John	Pte.	13139	12/03/1915
Brown	Charles Edward	Pte.	71164	24/04/1918
Brown	Charles George	Pte.	68585	24/04/1918
Brown	John	Pte.	44263	25/06/1917
Brown	John Francis	A/Cpl.	49040	27/03/1918
Brown	Thomas	Pte.	8286	28/11/1914
Browning	Edward James	Pte.	44222	28/11/1917
Brunham	Cyril Alfred	Pte.	32235	27/09/1918
Bryant	Herbert Felix	Pte.	17039	14/03/1917
Buckingham	Charles	Cpl.	7393	23/01/1916
Buckingham	Fernley	Pte.	16706	24/04/1918
Bulford	Stanley	Pte.	9832	13/02/1915
Bulley	John Henry	Sgt.	8372	10/05/1915
Bullock	Frederick John	Pte.	70396	31/05/1918

Bullock	George Sidney	Pte.	71166	24/04/1918
Burge	John	Pte.	9404	09/05/1915
Burgess	Benjamin Edmund	Pte.	30806	11/11/1917
Burgess	Fred	Pte.	3\7063	11/08/1917
Burgoyne	John Henry	Sgt.	7978	01/07/1916
Burley	William	Pte.	3\5234	25/06/1917
Burnham	George	Pte.	8497	10/03/1915
Burrell	John Henry	Pte.	19005	01/07/1916
Burston	Walter	Pte.	8741	16/12/1914
Burt	James Henry	Pte.	203644	31/07/1917
Burt	William	Pte.	292147	27/04/1918
Buscombe	Thomas Percival	Pte.	30823	31/07/1917
Bush	Thomas Alfred Anthony	Pte.	9808	13/08/1918
Butland	Sidney John	Pte.	11807	24/04/1918
Butler	Henry	Pte.	14135	01/07/1916
Butler	John	Pte.	30882	24/07/1917
Butler	Percy	Pte.	70402	31/05/1918
Butler	Thomas	Pte.	70412	31/05/1918
Butler	Walter Charles	Pte.	26466	16/08/1917
Butt	John	Pte.	4328	27/11/1914
Buttle	Francis William	Pte.	8756	18/12/1914
Bye	James Frank	Pte.	32021	31/10/1918
Cadamy	John	Cpl.	8599	01/06/1918
Cahill	Vincent	Pte.	3\7535	13/03/1915
Cakebread	Edward George	Pte.	70424	27/05/1918
Callaghan	Sidney	Sgt.	9378	14/04/1917
Camp	Leonard George	Pte.	30544	25/03/1918
Campbell	Albert George	Pte.	203380	27/08/1917
Campbell	Joseph	Pte.	8889	11/02/1915
Campkin	Walter Fitzgerald	Pte.	41365	30/04/1918
Candelent	George	Pte.	36604	24/04/1918
Cann	Charles Frederick	L/Cpl.	8626	02/06/1915
Cann	Frederick	Pte.	8974	01/07/1916
Cann	William	L/Cpl.	7772	01/07/1916
Carden	Donald Leo	L/Cpl.	30912	24/04/1918

Carder	Leslie George	Pte.	20160	01/07/1916
Cardew	Richard Cornelius Arthur	2/Lt.		24/04/1918
Carey	Charles James	Pte.	43324	31/07/1917
Carey	Leonard Arthur	2/Lt.		01/07/1916
Carmody	John	Pte.	18073	25/07/1917
Carne	Richard	Pte.	31792	24/04/1918
Carney	Thomas	Pte.	15017	01/07/1916
Carpenter	Arthur	Pte.	19063	06/10/1916
Carpenter	Arthur Charles	L/Cpl.	9147	01/07/1916
Carpenter	Edward James	Pte.	6950	09/05/1915
Carpenter	Fred	Pte.	11320	09/11/1916
Carpenter	Henry	Pte.	15478	01/07/1916
Carr	Walter Frederick James	Dmr.	9150	01/07/1916
Carreau	John	Pte.	9475	09/05/1915
Carroll	Thomas	Pte.	9173	21/06/1915
Carter	Charles	Pte.	9674	01/07/1916
Carter	Frederick Edward	Pte.	32189	31/10/1918
Carter	Herbert Ernest	Pte.	31819	24/04/1918
Carter	Walter Henry	L/Cpl.	9991	01/07/1916
Carthew	Sydney George	2/Lt.		26/03/1918
Carver	George Sholto Douglas	2/Lt.		01/07/1916
Caseley	Henry Francis	L/Cpl.	14184	10/05/1915
Challis	William George	Pte.	11136	01/07/1916
Chapman	George	Pte.	12719	06/11/1916
Chapman	John William	Pte.	74007	31/05/1918
Chapple	Harry Darke	Pte.	44152	27/03/1918
Chard	William	Pte.	20035	23/03/1917
Chase	Archibald Charles John	Pte.	8274	20/12/1914
Cheshire	Charles Henry	Pte.	71170	01/06/1918
Chick	William John	Pte.	30846	31/07/1917
Chipperfield	Bertie George	Pte.	12241	29/07/1916
Chivall	Simon	Pte.	9561	10/03/1915
Choak	John James	Pte.	9383	11/03/1915
Christopher	William George	Pte.	70417	24/04/1918
Chudley	Alfred	Pte.	3\7248	18/12/1914

Church	Ernest William	Pte.	31820	31/05/1918
Cilvert	Walter	Pte.	204437	24/04/1918
Clacy	Stanley Vernon	Pte.	30915	24/08/1918
Clark	Albert Edward	Pte.	3\7080	25/02/1915
Clark	Thomas	Pte.	14211	01/07/1916
Clark	Walter Samuel	Pte.	291753	25/11/1917
Clark	William	Pte.	45248	29/06/1918
Clarke	Frederick Edwin James	Pte.	12737	31/07/1917
Clarke	Harry Ernest	Pte.	3\6937	21/05/1915
Clarke	Percy	Pte.	33686	24/02/1918
Clarke	Stanley Vingoe	2/Lt.		06/07/1917
Clatworthy	William Henry	Pte.	17530	31/12/1916
Clegg	Jonas	Pte.	15113	01/07/1916
Clift	Dudley Charles	Pte.	3\7122	16/07/1916
Clift	George Fredrick	Pte.	74149	28/10/1918
Clist	Samuel Stone	Pte.	21194	31/05/1918
Cockwill	Reginald Darke	Pte.	15147	26/03/1918
Codrington	George Henry	Pte.	29258	27/10/1917
Cody	Kingsley	Pte.	19149	01/07/1916
Colbran	Albert Collis	Pte.	315038	24/04/1918
Coldwells	Francis Baker	2/Lt.		01/07/1916
Cole	Frederick George	Pte.	9132	31/10/1916
Cole	George	Pte.	26146	29/10/1916
Coles	Frank	L/Cpl.	33199	02/10/1917
Collings	Francis	Pte.	16940	01/07/1916
Collins	Frederick George	L/Cpl.	9538	14/07/1916
Collins	Henry Richard	A/Cpl.	8595	04/09/1917
Collins	John	Pte.	6410	18/12/1914
Collins	Joseph William Stanley	Sgt.	240142	31/05/1918
Comer	Ernest	Cpl.	8376	24/04/1918
Congrave	Albert	Pte.	74134	13/05/1918
Connolly	Edward Charles	Pte.	9097	25/11/1914
Conway	Albert	Pte.	16347	01/08/1917
Cook	Ernest	Pte.	14602	01/07/1916
Cooke	George Valentine Vincent	Pte.	30296	31/05/1918

Coome	Henry	Pte.	9104	12/12/1914
Copp	Sidney Archibald	Pte.	20042	01/07/1916
Copsey	Ernest Victor	Dmr.	7756	12/05/1915
Corby	Joseph	Cpl.	26735	31/07/1917
Cornish	Ernest James	Cpl.	20435	31/05/1918
Cornish	John	L/Cpl.	8384	01/07/1916
Cornish	William	Sgt.	8588	13/09/1916
Cose	Albert	Pte.	25859	16/08/1917
Cosnett	Henry William	Pte.	70421	28/05/1918
Costello	Patrick	Cpl.	9917	24/04/1918
Cotton	Albert Ernest	Pte.	44351	24/04/1918
Couling	William Charles	Cpl.	6737	16/08/1917
Court	Ernest John	Sgt.	5897	18/12/1914
Cox	Arthur George Gilbert	L/Cpl.	11648	16/09/1916
Cox	Charles Edward	L/Cpl.	8767	01/07/1916
Cox	Cyril Henry	Pte.	71177	24/04/1918
Cox	Ernest Charles Stephen	Pte.	14744	01/07/1916
Cox	Reginald Thomas	A/Cpl.	9974	02/07/1918
Cox	Thomas	A/Cpl.	291761	31/05/1918
Crate	Henry John	Pte.	3\6302	11/11/1916
Creek	Ernest William	Pte.	8456	06/11/1918
Crimp	Alfred Samuel	A/Cpl.	20523	01/08/1917
Crofts	Herbert Frank	Pte.	70425	26/04/1918
Crook	Clarence Henry	Pte.	3\6616	17/03/1915
Cross	Alfred Thomas	Pte.	70422	06/06/1918
Cross	Percy	Pte.	20577	30/03/1918
Crossley	Albert Edward	Pte.	16216	16/09/1916
Crout	George	Pte.	9783	19/12/1914
Crowfoot	George William	Pte.	26310	02/04/1918
Croxford	Henry Thomas	Pte.	291158	11/04/1918
Cull	Cecil Robert	Pte.	74003	27/05/1918
Curd	John Jonas	Pte.	11168	01/07/1916
Curran	William Michael	A/Cpl.	8498	10/03/1915
Curtis	Archelaus	Pte.	8541	18/12/1914
Curtis	James	Pte.	8572	20/02/1915

Cussell	Stanley James	2/Lt.		27/05/1918
Dance	James Job	Pte.	292080	01/05/1918
Daniel	William Henry	Pte.	15797	31/05/1918
Daniel	William John	Pte.	3\8117	01/07/1916
Daniels	Albert Emmanuel	Pte.	33169	20/06/1917
Darch	William Henry	Pte.	9763	22/08/1916
Darke	Robert Horwood	Pte.	14216	05/02/1915
Dart	Edgar	Pte.	16768	01/07/1916
Davey	Edgar	Sgt.	206021	27/03/1918
Davey	Ernest John	Cpl.	14130	01/07/1916
Davey	Ernest William	Pte.	8781	09/05/1915
Davey	William	Pte.	7070	18/11/1916
Davies	Brinley	Pte.	11919	01/07/1916
Davies	George	Pte.	12064	01/07/1916
Davies	Roderick Lewis	Sgt.	33943	14/11/1918
Davies	Thomas Henry	Pte.	16944	01/07/1916
Davis	Albertus Hamilton	Pte.	204875	31/07/1917
Davis	Bertie Harold	Pte.	71182	28/06/1918
Davis	Eugene D.	2/Lt.		23/03/1918
Davis	George	Pte.	74036	04/07/1918
Davis	Maurice Harry	Pte.	203373	16/08/1917
Davis	Sidney James	Pte.	9327	18/12/1914
Dawe	Ernest James	Sgt.	8728	23/11/1915
Day	Percy William	Pte.	43802	31/07/1917
Dear	Frank	Cpl.	7560	11/05/1916
Denham	Sydney Prince	Pte.	290410	24/04/1918
Denham	Wilfred Henry	Sgt.	8315	10/03/1915
Dennis	Edward	Pte.	315052	24/04/1918
Densham	William Charles	Pte.	3\6654	30/10/1915
Derrick	Albert William	Pte.	290766	24/04/1918
Derry	Charles	Pte.	267370	27/07/1917
Deveney	Albert John	Pte.	10910	01/07/1916
Devereux	Bert	Pte.	30927	15/02/1918
Devereux	Dennis Petrie	Pte.	70431	26/05/1918
Diamond	Patrick	Pte.	32153	27/10/1918

Dibble	Albert Henry	L/Cpl.	3\8163	30/11/1917
Dibble	William	Pte.	7729	01/07/1916
Dibden	Arthur Victor	Pte.	30926	24/04/1918
Diccox	Albert	Pte.	22313	14/04/1917
Dicker	Arthur	Pte.	3\6993	09/05/1915
Dillon	James	Pte.	3\6726	01/04/1918
Dimond	Thomas	Pte.	19041	05/09/1916
Diss	Thomas William	Pte.	15689	31/03/1918
Dixon	Arthur Charles	Pte.	12830	31/10/1918
Dixon	John	Sgt.	4348	10/03/1915
Dixon	Joseph	Pte.	16314	31/05/1915
Dixon	Thomas	Pte.	69164	31/10/1918
Dodd	Frederick William	Pte.	15365	01/07/1916
Dodds	William	L/Cpl.	9800	31/10/1916
Doidge	Bertie	A/Cpl.	21657	29/05/1918
Donoghue	Denis	L/Sgt.	49039	31/07/1917
Dore	Harold Travers	Pte.	78710	27/09/1918
Dorey	Leonard Willie	Pte.	8645	01/07/1916
Dorothy	Arthur Edwin	Cpl.	290453	24/04/1918
Dorrington	Frederick Herbert	L/Cpl.	16112	21/06/1917
Dowden	Clifford	Pte.	8900	09/05/1915
Dowding	James	Pte.	30932	06/09/1917
Dowell	Fred	Cpl.	8463	18/12/1914
Down	George Henry	Sgt.	37438	24/04/1918
Down	Thomas Henry	Pte.	30553	02/04/1917
Downey	Harry	Pte.	13185	24/04/1918
Doxey	Walter	Pte.	15160	01/07/1916
Drake	Wilfred Wallace	2/Lt.		16/08/1917
Drew	Fred	Pte.	3\8083	10/03/1915
Drew	Frederick	Pte.	8269	01/07/1916
Drew	Leslie Gordon	Pte.	203214	24/04/1918
Drewe	Ernest Edwin	Sgt.	3\7772	07/08/1917
Dun	David	Pte.	267960	31/07/1917
Dunham	Arthur	Pte.	16968	01/07/1916
Dunn	Frederick Percy	Pte.	68791	24/04/1918

Dunning	Leslie Victor	Pte.	70429	24/04/1918
Dunsford	Christopher George	L/Cpl.	9499	31/01/1915
Dymond	Bert Fred	Pte.	3\7124	09/05/1915
Eales	Charles Wilfred	Lt.		27/09/1918
Ebdon	Samuel Mark	A/Cpl.	8747	01/07/1916
Edney	Arthur Jesse	Pte.	69004	31/05/1918
Edwards	Alfred George	Pte.	19037	18/07/1916
Edwards	Alfred George	Pte.	9574	11/02/1915
Edwards	Britton John	Pte.	66836	27/05/1918
Edwards	Ernest Leonard	Pte.	70824	21/10/1918
Edwards	Robert Herbert Henry	Pte.	68811	31/05/1918
Edwards	Thomas Augustine	Pte.	11317	05/07/1915
Edwards	William Alfred	Pte.	8898	30/11/1914
Edwards	William Henry	Pte.	3\6867	25/01/1915
Edwards	William Henry	Pte.	13224	10/05/1915
Edworthy	Ernest	Pte.	16941	01/07/1916
Ekers	Frederick	Pte.	31784	01/04/1918
Eller	Herbert	Pte.	13180	14/04/1917
Elliott	Charles	Pte.	10338	01/07/1916
Elliott	Jack	Pte.	70434	04/10/1918
Ellis	George Edward Albert	Sgt.	5991	28/11/1917
Ellis	Herbert Douglas	Pte.	291853	05/01/1918
Ellis	William	Pte.	11224	10/05/1915
Elson	William Henry	Pte.	8406	18/12/1914
Elston	John	Pte.	15101	01/07/1916
Elsworthy	George	Sgt.	8917	09/05/1915
Emmett	Samuel John	Pte.	26082	31/07/1917
Endacott	Arthur	Pte.	11339	18/06/1915
England	Fred	Pte.	16684	18/07/1916
English	James Coverdale	Cpl.	3\8168	31/07/1917
Eva	Ernest Daniel	A/Cpl.	8850	12/03/1915
Evans	Alfred Edwin	Pte.	30771	16/08/1917
Evans	Evan Stanley	Pte.	8176	07/02/1915
Evans	Frank Charles	Pte.	6916	18/12/1914
Evans	John	Pte.	12710	09/05/1915

Evans	John	Pte.	8768	01/07/1916
Evans	Owen	Pte.	13204	13/03/1915
Evans	William	Pte.	8177	12/03/1915
Ewings	James	Pte.	38032	20/08/1917
Farley	Frederick William	Pte.	18942	01/07/1916
Farley	George	Pte.	8871	01/07/1916
Farley	Sidney Herman	Pte.	9579	11/03/1915
Farmer	Charles Abraham	L/Cpl.	15593	31/07/1917
Farrar	Fred	Pte.	15262	27/04/1918
Farrow	Mark	Pte.	5881	26/05/1918
Featherstone	Reginald Benjamin	Capt.		18/12/1914
Ferard	George Deas	Lt.		21/02/1918
Field	Charles Henry	Pte.	30938	25/03/1918
Field	Gilbert Hugh	Pte.	70438	24/04/1918
Fielden	Joshua	Pte.	15591	04/07/1916
Fisher	Frederick	Pte.	69081	24/04/1918
Fisher	Harry	Pte.	13363	10/03/1915
Fishlock	John Henry	Pte.	25578	14/08/1917
Fishwick	William	Pte.	30849	26/09/1917
Fitzgerald	John	Pte.	9869	01/07/1916
Fitzgerald	Walter Campkin	Pte.	41365	30/04/1918
Flay	Ernest	Pte.	18569	25/11/1917
Fleman	Arthur Richard	Pte.	203477	24/04/1918
Flower	Arthur	Pte.	23681	05/09/1917
Flowers	Arthur	Pte.	12711	01/07/1916
Floyd	Howard Grimley	2/Lt.		09/04/1918
Fogg	Horace George	Sgt.	9961	01/07/1916
Fooks	George Anthony	Pte.	71191	24/04/1918
Ford	Arthur Charles	Pte.	290732	24/04/1918
Ford	Samuel John	Sgt.	8811	13/01/1915
Fortune	Herbert Thomas James	Pte.	290779	31/05/1918
Foster	Edward Thomas	Pte.	11777	01/04/1915
Foster	Stanley John	Pte.	8038	20/03/1915
Foster	Thomas	L/Cpl.	8465	01/07/1916
Fowler	James Henry	Pte.	316052	05/11/1918

Surname	Forename(s)	Rank	Number	Date
Foxwell	James	Cpl.	14783	29/10/1916
Francis	Herbert Walter	A/Cpl.	74041	23/07/1918
Franklin	William John	Pte.	27079	31/07/1917
Frawley	William Thomas	Pte.	16890	09/09/1917
Freegard	Reginald Alfred	Pte.	30939	27/10/1917
French	George William	Pte.	207153	27/09/1918
French	Richard Ernest William	Pte.	30831	31/07/1917
Freshney	Samuel	Pte.	3\6913	23/05/1915
Friday	George William	Pte.	3\6883	28/03/1918
Friend	Sidney Claud	Pte.	44242	11/05/1918
Friend	Walter	Pte.	6863	09/05/1915
Frise	Frederick William	Pte.	74043	20/10/1918
Froom	John	Pte.	3\7846	13/01/1915
Frost	Henry Westwood	A/Cpl.	30934	31/05/1918
Fry	Bertram Cater	Pte.	30936	05/01/1918
Fryer	Edward	Pte.	3\8119	09/05/1915
Fuller	William	L/Cpl.	8128	31/05/1915
Furneaux	John	Pte.	9120	26/11/1914
Futter	Johnathan Edward	Pte.	74164	27/09/1918
Gagneur	Alfred	Pte.	9188	31/03/1918
Gallop	Richard Harmon	Pte.	32052	03/11/1918
Gamblen	Frank Eugene	Pte.	30942	31/05/1918
Garland	Reginald Gilbert	Pte.	23172	30/01/1917
Garner	Thomas	Pte.	27654	28/03/1918
Gaskill	Harry Cecil	Pte.	204358	29/04/1918
Gaylard	Charles	Pte.	11826	31/07/1917
Gaylard	Reginald	Pte.	71195	24/04/1918
Gazey	Walter Francis	Pte.	70447	09/05/1918
Geake	William Charles Hamilton	Pte.	26133	22/06/1917
Gee	Robert Coley	Pte.	70440	27/05/1918
Geen	Herbert	Pte.	70444	24/04/1918
Gibson	Nathaniel	Pte.	8694	12/03/1915
Gidley	Frederick	Pte.	26291	25/07/1917
Gidley	Gerald Edgar	Pte.	67891	30/04/1918
Gidley	Richard	Pte.	15432	01/07/1916

Gifford	Ralph James	Pte.	3\6297	01/07/1916
Gigg	Sidney Francis Harry	Pte.	8705	10/03/1915
Gilbert	Frank	Pte.	3\6934	23/01/1915
Gilbert	George Henry	Pte.	18859	19/06/1916
Gilbert	William Peter Northey	Pte.	3\7135	01/07/1916
Giles	Reginald William	Pte.	3\6194	24/12/1914
Gill	Albert	Pte.	21647	14/04/1917
Gill	Frederick William	Pte.	44130	24/04/1918
Gill	Richard Ernest	Pte.	26096	07/03/1917
Gill	Walter	Cpl.	20067	18/06/1917
Gillard	Bertram George	Pte.	9637	12/03/1915
Gillard	George Dilwyn	Pte.	3/8185	09/05/1915
Gillard	Sidney	Pte.	9185	11/12/1915
Gilliland	John Lurburam	Sgt.	9261	01/07/1916
Gilpin	John Richard	L/Cpl.	26684	04/08/1917
Glanfield	Giles	Pte.	8555	12/03/1915
Glanville	Harry	Pte.	74046	31/10/1918
Gloyne	Albert	Pte.	30859	24/07/1917
Goddard	Edwin Henry	Pte.	204886	01/09/1917
Godfrey	Herbert William	Pte.	11508	16/03/1915
Godley	James	Pte.	205026	21/04/1918
Goldie	Charles Herbert	Pte.	70450	24/04/1918
Golding	Harry Lifely	Pte.	43098	24/04/1918
Golding	William Albert	Sgt.	8502	01/07/1916
Goldsmith	Frederick	L/Sgt.	27662	31/05/1918
Gollop	Albert James	Pte.	3\6803	11/05/1915
Gollop	William John	Sgt.	8621	31/07/1917
Gooding	Frederick	Pte.	8515	18/12/1914
Gooding	Henry	Pte.	8776	19/03/1915
Gooding	James	Pte.	9622	18/12/1914
Goodman	Harold Harry	A/Capt.		16/08/1917
Goodwin	Albert Stanley	Pte.	30807	27/07/1917
Gough	Francis William	Pte.	23163	06/05/1917
Gould	Eric Melville	2/Lt.		01/07/1916
Gould	Ernest Leonard	Pte.	70442	22/04/1918

Govus	Fred Charles Victor	Pte.	7146	01/07/1916
Gower	William Ernest Percy	Pte.	30821	31/07/1917
Grabham	Albert	Pte.	33204	25/02/1917
Gratton	Alfred Frank	A/Cpl.	3\6619	05/10/1916
Gratton	William Lewis	Pte.	3\7817	13/03/1915
Gray	Harry	Pte.	30809	16/08/1917
Grayer	Wilfred	Pte.	8189	19/01/1915
Green	Alfred Lewis	Pte.	8408	01/07/1916
Green	Harry	Pte.	10118	11/03/1915
Green	John	Pte.	3/8191	05/02/1915
Green	John	Pte.	3\6875	01/07/1916
Green	John Henry	Pte.	29683	23/03/1917
Greenall	William Gilbert	Pte.	70449	24/04/1918
Greenaway	William	Pte.	15602	23/09/1916
Greenbank	Arthur	Pte.	15612	01/07/1916
Greenlees	James	Pte.	32233	28/06/1918
Gregory	Francis Henry	Pte.	290215	30/03/1918
Gregory	Richard	Pte.	8316	25/12/1914
Gribble	Percy Henry	Pte.	8534	12/03/1915
Griffin	Percy Charles	Pte.	70451	24/04/1918
Griffin	Stanley	Pte.	76009	27/09/1918
Griffiths	David Daniel	Pte.	3\8194	01/07/1916
Grigg	William George	Pte.	11123	01/07/1916
Gudge	Albert George	Pte.	9083	28/03/1915
Guest	Ernest Howard	Pte.	68373	31/05/1918
Hackett	Samuel	Pte.	32033	27/10/1918
Haines	Charles Herbert	Pte.	291419	31/05/1918
Haines	Herbert Sidney	Pte.	21594	15/02/1918
Hales	William James	Pte.	66961	30/03/1918
Hall	Frank Burnett	Pte.	30845	16/08/1917
Hall	Henry John	Pte.	15022	01/07/1916
Hall	James	Pte.	9231	12/02/1915
Hall	James Albert	Pte.	68948	24/04/1918
Hall	Joseph Henry	Pte.	37141	26/05/1918
Hall	Robert	Pte.	8528	27/03/1917

Hall	William Kelly	Pte.	9970	30/06/1915
Hames	Harold Arthur	Pte.	14299	09/05/1915
Hamlyn	Edgar James	Pte.	6871	15/05/1917
Hamlyn	Frederick George	Pte.	8916	26/01/1915
Hamlyn	Henry Thomas	Pte.	14149	01/07/1916
Hammond	Arthur George	Pte.	70458	24/04/1918
Hancock	Ernest	Pte.	204858	24/04/1918
Hancock	John Courtney	Pte.	15142	01/07/1916
Hannaford	Arthur Richard	Pte.	10434	30/03/1918
Hannaford	Augustine	Pte.	3\7532	01/07/1916
Hannaford	Cecil John Toms	Pte.	203241	02/04/1918
Hannaford	Frederick William Henry	A/Cpl.	290440	08/08/1918
Hannaford	John Parker	L/Cpl.	15493	16/09/1916
Hannah	Charles William Cooper	2/Lt.		28/09/1916
Harding	Arthur	Pte.	3\8199	01/07/1916
Harding	Harry James	Pte.	3\6830	18/12/1914
Harding	Reggie	Pte.	3\8200	18/03/1915
Hardy	Frederick Samuel	Pte.	71207	31/05/1918
Hare	Fearnley	Pte.	9121	12/03/1915
Harms	Arthur	A/Cpl.	204885	29/11/1917
Harrild	William	L/Cpl.	8787	14/03/1915
Harris	Charles Thomas	Pte.	33182	01/08/1917
Harris	Frederick Charles	Pte.	290393	31/05/1918
Harris	Frederick William	A/Cpl.	8520	17/08/1917
Harris	Herbert	Cpl.	8525	09/05/1915
Harris	James	Pte.	203270	10/11/1917
Harris	John Henry	A/Cpl.	9219	10/08/1917
Harris	William James	Pte.	15957	01/07/1916
Harvey	George	Pte.	17881	31/07/1917
Harvey	Hedley John	Pte.	8276	09/02/1915
Harvey	Stanley	L/Cpl.	9191	25/08/1916
Harvey	Walter	Pte.	9250	18/12/1914
Haskings	Samuel	L/Cpl.	85071	12/03/1915
Hatton	Ernest John	Sgt.	3\5673	01/07/1916
Hawker	Albert James	Pte.	30953	24/04/1918

Hawkes	Albert Edward	Pte.	18664	25/04/1918
Hawkes	Samuel John	Pte.	25943	29/10/1916
Hawkins	Bertram Frank	Pte.	52298	27/05/1918
Hawkins	Ernest	Pte.	15592	02/07/1916
Hawkins	Edward Frederick	Pte.	9009	10/03/1915
Hawthorne	Arthur Ernest	A/Cpl.	12401	29/05/1918
Haydon	John	Pte.	7606	14/04/1917
Hayman	Edmund Alfred	Cpl.	11060	09/02/1917
Hayter	Charles	Pte.	9406	12/01/1915
Hayward	Frederick	Pte.	27671	08/03/1917
Haywood	George	Pte.	14782	09/05/1915
Heaman	Robert George	Pte.	15510	28/08/1915
Hearn	William	Pte.	8860	18/12/1914
Heath	Ernest	Pte.	16665	13/08/1916
Heath	William	L/Cpl.	15285	06/10/1916
Hebdon	Albert William	Sgt.	15097	16/08/1917
Hedges	Albert Frederick	Pte.	45533	14/04/1917
Hegson	John	Pte.	15128	06/10/1916
Hellings	Sydney Hugh	Pte.	71209	31/05/1918
Helsdon	Alfred	Pte.	21010	01/07/1916
Hemborough	Henry William	Cpl.	9047	01/07/1916
Henderson	Frank	Pte.	10998	24/07/1917
Hendrie	George	L/Sgt.	20072	31/07/1917
Herbert	Peter John	Sgt.	17669	27/06/1919
Herring	Norman Hamilton	Sgt.	9325	01/07/1916
Hewitt	Ralph	L/Cpl.	9212	18/12/1914
Heysett	William	Pte.	29702	31/05/1918
Heyworth	Ernest	Pte.	15613	01/07/1916
Hicks	Edwin Charles	L/Cpl.	8554	06/10/1916
Highland	William James	Pte.	8927	18/12/1914
Hill	Archie	Pte.	16195	01/07/1916
Hill	Herbert William	Sgt.	14072	27/09/1918
Hill	John	Pte.	7853	02/06/1915
Hill	Sidney Thomas	Pte.	25109	25/03/1918
Hill	William Henry	Pte.	3\7068	26/03/1915

Hinves	Albert Victor	Pte.	290998	26/03/1918
Hoare	Harold	Pte.	30958	25/03/1918
Hoare	Joseph George	Pte.	11348	09/05/1915
Hobbs	Richard Henry	Pte.	21649	07/09/1916
Hobbs	Thomas Henry	Pte.	20792	29/07/1916
Hobbs	William Henry	Pte.	3\7137	01/07/1916
Hobbs	William John	Pte.	291839	23/02/1918
Hodge	Thomas John	Pte.	8467	30/12/1916
Hodge	William John	Pte.	3\6561	11/08/1916
Hodges	Wilfred George	Pte.	9241	09/05/1915
Hodson	Alfred	Pte.	9130	13/01/1915
Hodson	Charles Henry	Pte.	11293	12/03/1915
Hogg	James	Sgt.	7062	14/01/1915
Holbrook	Frederick George	Pte.	74053	31/05/1918
Hole	John	L/Sgt.	6940	19/11/1914
Holmes	Albert Edward	Cpl.	12608	27/03/1917
Holmes	Thomas	Pte.	30951	30/04/1918
Holmes	William Edward	Pte.	3\5827	18/12/1914
Hook	Alfred Charles	Pte.	30950	01/06/1918
Hooper	Fred Caryl	Pte.	16873	03/08/1918
Hooper	Stephen	Pte.	9447	18/12/1914
Hopes	Ewart Gladstone	Pte.	30952	31/05/1918
Horrell	Arthur	Pte.	9714	06/02/1915
Horsam	William Frederick	Pte.	3\7325	18/12/1914
Horsham	Norman	L/Cpl.	33197	22/04/1917
Horton	Arthur	Pte.	8367	12/03/1915
Horwood	William George	Pte.	3\6843	01/07/1916
Hosegood	Gilbert	2/Lt.		10/09/1916
Howard	James	L/Cpl.	8914	22/04/1916
Howard	Lionel	Pte.	11310	17/05/1915
Howells	David	L/Cpl.	9549	09/05/1915
Howle	George	Pte.	69046	25/03/1918
Hubbard	Charles Frederick	Pte.	52849	31/07/1917
Hughes	Henry	Pte.	32093	11/09/1918
Hughes	Tom	Pte.	12874	13/03/1915

Hughes	Walter Bernard Channings	Pte.	33187	25/11/1917
Hughes	William Richard	Pte.	14219	28/03/1915
Humber	William	Pte.	31814	31/03/1918
Humphrey	Lionel George Ernest	Pte.	291079	30/11/1917
Humphreys	Frank	Pte.	11170	27/10/1916
Hunt	William Arthur	Pte.	7517	09/05/1915
Hunt	William Henry	Pte.	20041	01/07/1916
Hurrell	Percy	Pte.	44096	31/07/1917
Hutcheson	Alfred William	Pte.	15587	01/07/1916
Hutchinson	Bernard	Sgt.	7228	01/07/1916
Huxter	Charles	Pte.	17900	13/01/1917
Ings	William	Pte.	30798	01/08/1917
Innes	Henry Pembroke	Pte.	290949	27/05/1918
Innus	Henry William	Pte.	17160	23/03/1917
Irwin	Alfred John	Sgt.	8032	19/04/1917
Isaacs	Albert	Pte.	8698	07/02/1915
Isaacs	Albert John	Sgt.	5274	25/03/1918
Jackaman	Thomas Theobald	Pte.	204843	27/09/1918
Jackson	Frederick	Pte.	74066	31/05/1918
Jackson	Richard Wallace	Pte.	16579	14/04/1917
Jackson	Thomas	Pte.	15282	18/06/1915
Jacob	Cecil Otway Reed	Capt.		20/11/1917
Jago	Edward Arthur	2/Lt.		01/07/1916
Jago	Francis George	L/Cpl.	69049	24/04/1918
Jago	Henry Harris	A/Capt.		24/04/1918
James	Albert	Cpl.	15631	27/03/1918
James	Charles Thomas	Pte.	29679	30/11/1917
James	William Edward	Pte.	14220	25/01/1915
James	William Samuel	Pte.	12913	12/03/1915
Jarrett	Frederick	Pte.	8667	10/11/1916
Jarvis	William	Pte.	18893	27/09/1918
Jeans	John Edwin Henry	Pte.	30963	31/05/1918
Jefferies	Josiah	Pte.	48800	30/10/1917
Jeffery	Albert	A/Cpl.	8558	31/05/1918
Jenkins	Stanley Thomas	Pte.	12922	09/05/1915

Jenvey	William Charles	Pte.	290816	31/05/1918
Jewell	Frederick John	Pte.	16976	24/04/1918
Job	Charles Henry	Pte.	39774	24/04/1918
Johnson	Albert James	Pte.	18585	03/05/1918
Johnson	James	Pte.	14980	22/04/1917
Johnson	Samuel Cook	Pte.	16799	30/11/1916
Johnson	William	Pte.	3\6130	18/12/1914
Johnson	William	L/Cpl.	30839	07/01/1918
Johnston	Frank Robert	Pte.	10024	12/05/1915
Jones	Alfred Leonard	Pte.	74064	27/05/1918
Jones	Alfred Sydney	Pte.	17085	30/11/1917
Jones	Bert	Pte.	30962	27/03/1918
Jones	David John	Pte.	13056	01/07/1916
Jones	Ernest	Pte.	76008	10/10/1918
Jones	Ernest G	L/Cpl.	30965	15/10/1918
Jones	Frederick Charles	Pte.	47597	31/07/1917
Jones	Frederick Thomas	Pte.	15391	01/07/1916
Jones	Idris	Pte.	12752	09/05/1915
Jones	Robert David	L/Cpl.	12920	01/07/1916
Jones	William	Pte.	14258	01/07/1916
Jones	William Henry	Pte.	14154	01/07/1916
Jones	John William	Pte.	12754	11/03/1915
Jordan	John Robert	L/Cpl.	20382	31/07/1917
Josephson	Edmund George	Cpl.	32154	03/03/1919
Joslin	Robert Luke	Pte.	7492	30/10/1916
Joy	Thomas Cyril Bruce	T/Capt.		11/12/1915
Kearns	John	Sgt.	7443	05/05/1916
Keates	Wilfred	Pte.	30795	31/07/1917
Keeling	Francis Cecil	L/Cpl.	266881	31/03/1918
Keen	Leonard Gregory	Pte.	74069	26/05/1918
Keen	Lewis Albert	Pte.	9131	01/07/1916
Keens	Alfred George	Pte.	13149	01/07/1916
Keep	Wilfred	Pte.	30973	31/05/1918
Keirl	Frederick Thomas	Pte.	13145	24/04/1918
Kellehar	Edward Patrick	Pte.	6464	21/08/1916

Kelley	John William	Pte.	17659	30/04/1916
Kemish	Frank Stanley	Pte.	74068	05/11/1918
Kemp	William	Pte.	30789	31/07/1917
Kerr	Christopher James	A/Cpl.	15639	29/10/1917
Kershaw	John	Pte.	15266	21/08/1916
Kerswill	Thomas George	Pte.	25781	06/10/1916
Kettlewell	George Frederick	Pte.	11148	11/08/1917
King	William Richard Edwards	Pte.	9275	24/01/1915
Kingdom	Albert	Pte.	7024	10/03/1915
Kingdom	Gordon	L/Cpl.	8207	01/07/1916
Kitchener	Frank David	Pte.	17615	16/07/1916
Knapman	Frederick John	Pte.	9837	03/09/1916
Knapman	George Frederick	Pte.	3\6520	18/12/1914
Knapman	John James	Pte.	19021	14/08/1917
Knapman	William John	Pte.	8972	30/10/1916
Knight	Albert Edward	Pte.	3\6617	18/12/1914
Knight	Thomas William	Pte.	74067	31/05/1918
Knott	George	L/Cpl.	30856	06/11/1917
Knox	William Alexander	Pte.	30970	30/11/1917
Ladd	Albert Edward	Pte.	9947	09/05/1915
Lafone	Claude Alexander	Capt.		12/03/1915
Lake	Thomas	Pte.	8543	24/01/1915
Lambell	William Henry	Pte.	9350	01/07/1916
Lamble	William Hubert	Pte.	21288	14/04/1917
Lang	Percy Thomas	Pte.	9528	18/12/1914
Langdon	Albert John	Pte.	3\5789	26/05/1916
Langdon	Harry	Sgt.	9330	24/11/1917
Langwasser	Leo Jacob	Pte.	3\6829	01/07/1916
Larcombe	Donald Colway	Pte.	15988	14/04/1917
Larcombe	Francis George	A/Cpl.	26094	30/03/1917
Lavers	Douglas William	Pte.	3\7285	31/10/1916
Law	Walter Leslie	Pte.	15400	27/03/1918
Lawrence	Charles William	Pte.	204880	31/07/1917
Lawrence	Ernest	Pte.	3/20279	22/11/1917
Lawry	Charles	Pte.	6400	09/11/1916

Leaman	Charles	Pte.	8820	25/01/1915
Leaman	Charles George	L/Cpl.	33232	07/10/1918
Lear	Ronald John	L/Cpl.	22138	27/05/1918
Leat	Frederick Charles	2/Lt.		27/05/1918
Lee	John	Pte.	8302	02/07/1916
Lee	William	L/Cpl.	3\8231	05/06/1916
Legge	Ronald George	Capt.		18/12/1914
Lenihan	James	Pte.	5116	11/03/1915
Lentle	John	Pte.	25615	31/10/1918
Leonard	Charles Walter	Pte.	204873	14/01/1918
Leslie	William Thomas	Pte.	204888	27/07/1917
Lethbridge	Fred	2/Lt.		24/04/1918
Letts	John Joseph	Pte.	315159	15/05/1918
Lewis	Arthur William John	Pte.	31823	30/04/1918
Lewis	Frederick Charles	Pte.	69048	23/02/1918
Lewis	William James	Pte.	3/8 3 27	05/07/1916
Leworthy	Frederick James	Pte.	9446	01/12/1914
Leworthy	William James	Pte.	9462	07/09/1916
Ley	Maurice Carew	2/Lt.		01/07/1916
Lilley	Albert Edward	L/Cpl.	206022	31/05/1918
Lineham	Thomas Charles	Pte.	59318	25/11/1917
Linton	John Phillips	Pte.	16937	14/08/1916
Little	Frederick John	Pte.	9766	18/12/1914
Litton	Arthur Henry	Pte.	11340	27/05/1917
Lloyd	Francis Burrows	2/Lt.		03/10/1916
Lloyd	Frederick David	Pte.	18108	29/07/1917
Loader	George Edward	Pte.	31786	31/05/1918
Lodge	Thomas Henry	L/Cpl.	8529	12/08/1917
Lomas	Albert Henry	Pte.	9891	13/03/1915
Loveridge	Herbert	Pte.	20601	01/07/1916
Low	Charles	Pte.	28896	23/03/1918
Luxton	George	Sgt.	6779	01/07/1916
Luxton	Thomas Arthur	Pte.	8551	18/12/1914
Maidment	Frederick	Pte.	3\7053	24/04/1918
Mander	William	Pte.	74077	10/09/1918

Manifold	Robert	Pte.	69193	06/06/1918
Mann	Christopher	L/Cpl.	9318	15/10/1916
Manning	Alfred C. H.	Pte.	15274	10/08/1917
Manning	John Henry	Pte.	7187	08/03/1917
Manning	William	Pte.	30555	25/04/1918
Marchant	George	Pte.	9182	05/06/1916
Marchant	Harold Edgar	T/2/Lt.		05/06/1916
Margetts	William Henry (Oxford)	L/Cpl.	9335	11/03/1915
Marks	Joseph	Pte.	5290	18/12/1914
Marsden	Frank	Pte.	15263	31/03/1918
Martin	Charles	Pte.	11419	14/11/1915
Martin	Herbert	Pte.	9162	01/07/1916
Martyn	William Henry	Pte.	203574	31/07/1917
Marwood	Fred	Pte.	11560	21/06/1917
Masey	Charles Keefe	Pte.	11526	12/03/1915
Matthews	David	Pte.	12963	01/07/1916
May	Alfred	Pte.	7471	16/02/1915
May	Robert	Pte.	3\6737	08/07/1916
May	Thomas	Pte.	15520	13/07/1916
May	Thomas Henry	Sgt.	9734	01/07/1916
Mayle	Harry	Pte.	8930	18/02/1916
McCarthy	Bernard F.	Pte.	8514	26/02/1915
McGowan	John Spence	2/Lt.		01/07/1916
McMorran	Roy Alexander	Cpl.	20514	31/07/1917
Medland	George	L/Cpl.	28394	28/04/1918
Meers	Fred	Pte.	6564	09/05/1915
Middleton	Alexander	Pte.	18001	22/10/1917
Middleton	George	Pte.	67916	24/04/1918
Middleton	John	Pte.	26333	31/07/1917
Middleton	Leonard	Pte.	74078	31/05/1918
Miller	Charles Herbert	Pte.	30987	31/05/1918
Miller	Edwin	Pte.	11617	10/03/1915
Miller	Frederick Charles	Pte.	15698	31/07/1917
Millman	Ernest Charles	Pte.	3\6526	16/03/1917
Mills	Ernest	Pte.	1263	18/02/1915

Mills	William Arthur Alfred	Pte.	30986	30/05/1918
Milton	Richard	Pte.	3\7533	07/02/1915
Mitchell	Alfred	Pte.	11323	01/07/1916
Mitchell	Charles	L/Cpl.	9356	02/10/1915
Mitchell	Francis	Pte.	3\5311	01/07/1916
Mitchell	Frederick	Pte.	74076	26/05/1918
Mitchell	Frederick Arthur	Pte.	3\8063	07/07/1915
Mitchell	Robert	Pte.	9444	18/12/1914
Mitchell	Walter	Pte.	16907	31/05/1918
Monday	William Thomas	Pte.	3\6888	31/07/1917
Monk	George	Pte.	9257	18/12/1914
Moody	Frederick George	Pte.	11151	01/07/1916
Moody	Henry Hardy	L/Cpl.	8637	15/09/1919
Moore	Bertie	Pte.	6962	06/05/1917
Moore	John Harold	Pte.	70295	08/10/1918
Moore	William James	Pte.	3\6569	18/12/1914
Moore	William Treemare	Pte.	203004	22/04/1918
Morrell	George	Pte.	5886	18/12/1914
Morris	Jim	Pte.	61823	27/10/1918
Morris	Thomas	Pte.	3\6515	18/12/1914
Morris	Thomas Howard	Pte.	291421	25/03/1918
Mortimore	Harry Elford	Pte.	290424	25/11/1917
Moulson	Samuel	Pte.	8450	25/01/1915
Moult	George Arthur	A/Sgt.	30510	02/10/1917
Mower	Robert	Pte.	3\7050	02/09/1917
Mulcahy	Daniel Patrick	Pte.	204889	27/07/1917
Munro	John Joseph	Pte.	3\7629	11/03/1915
Murch	Ernest Arthur	Pte.	290322	26/04/1918
Murphy	John Philip	Pte.	9851	29/10/1916
Murray	Bryson Roy	Cpl.	9184	01/07/1916
Murton	Albert Ernest William	Pte.	18617	27/05/1918
Narracott	Frederick John	Pte.	15576	31/10/1916
Needs	Richard James	Pte.	24681	26/03/1918
Neve	Harry	Pte.	25536	02/08/1917
Newcombe	William	Cpl.	8912	31/07/1917

Newcombe	William Henry	Pte.	11501	27/08/1915
Newton	Thomas Michael	Pte.	3\6577	09/05/1915
Nicholls	Charles Webbell	Pte.	203123	24/04/1918
Nicholls	George	Pte.	8428	10/03/1915
Nicholls	Harry	Pte.	11221	09/05/1915
Nickols	John	Pte.	9401	18/12/1914
Nile	Sydney Charles	Pte.	3\6216	18/07/1916
Noon	Alfred Lewis	Lt.		02/04/1918
Norcott	Arthur	Pte.	45538	04/01/1920
Norman	Fred	Pte.	45537	27/06/1917
Norman	Harry Charles	Pte.	32096	27/10/1916
Norman	Sydney George	Pte.	9640	18/12/1914
Northcott	Frank Leonard	Pte.	16805	01/07/1916
Northcott	William Alfred	Pte.	9639	25/05/1915
Nott	Frederick	Pte.	16191	13/08/1917
Oates	Harold Aldrick	Pte.	30992	02/10/1917
Ockford	William Ernest John	Pte.	204887	31/05/1918
Offord	James Bertram	Pte.	20508	08/06/1916
Ogden	Frank Taylor	Pte.	15504	01/07/1916
Older	Edgar Lytton	Pte.	15528	01/07/1916
Oliver	John Abner	Pte.	26019	16/08/1917
Oliver	Thomas	Pte.	12867	10/03/1915
Orchard	Harry	Pte.	11111	01/07/1916
Osborn	Charles	Cpl.	8121	18/12/1914
Osborn	Frank Ernest	L/Cpl.	8355	01/07/1916
Owen	David John	Pte.	7606	18/07/1916
Owen	Herbert Henry	Pte.	74082	31/05/1918
Paddon	Horace Leonard	L/Cpl.	7315	10/03/1915
Page	Charles James	Pte.	33597	04/09/1917
Page	William	Pte.	11326	01/07/1916
Palmer	David	Pte.	3\8265	01/07/1916
Palmer	Horace Cecil	Pte.	33192	22/09/1916
Palmer	Walter Henry	Pte.	45962	31/07/1917
Pannell	Bert	A/Cpl.	11278	25/04/1918
Pannell	Edward Thomas	Pte.	8793	24/06/1916

Pardon	Louis William	Pte.	290285	29/11/1917
Parker	James	Pte.	30783	24/04/1918
Parker	John	Pte.	9180	11/03/1915
Parker	John Herbert	Pte.	11916	24/02/1915
Parker	Percy Charles	Cpl.	3\6759	31/05/1918
Parker	William	Pte.	26141	21/10/1916
Parkyn	John	Sgt.	9198	28/06/1918
Parnell	William Henry	Pte.	20788	06/10/1916
Parr	James	Pte.	8881	14/03/1915
Parry	Thomas	Pte.	10241	24/04/1918
Parsons	Ernest	Pte.	45774	07/04/1918
Parsons	Frederick James	Pte.	33209	30/09/1916
Parsons	Harold James	Pte.	16914	22/08/1916
Parsons	Harry	Pte.	11347	09/05/1915
Passmore	Daniel	Pte.	9585	18/12/1914
Paul	Benjamin James	Pte.	30824	09/09/1917
Payne	Christopher	Pte.	11269	01/07/1916
Payton	John	Pte.	16089	24/04/1918
Pearce	Alfred	Pte.	43323	27/05/1918
Pearce	Frederick Charles	Pte.	3\6757	12/03/1915
Pearce	James	Pte.	3\7062	11/03/1915
Pears	Alfred Richard	Cpl.	16512	06/05/1917
Pearse	Samuel	Pte.	9007	05/08/1915
Pearson	George	L/Cpl.	3\6894	31/10/1918
Peckins	William Henry	Pte.	1504	01/07/1916
Peers	Alexander	Pte.	8527	01/07/1916
Pells	Cyril Elmore	T/2/Lt.		27/05/1918
Pendrigh	Alexander Conrad Cuthbertson	2/Lt.		31/07/1917
Penn	Frank Ernest	Pte.	7412	27/05/1918
Penny	Harry	Pte.	203402	07/10/1918
Penwarn	Joseph Henry	Sgt.	8480	25/10/1916
Perkin	Frederick	L/Cpl.	9068	05/08/1917
Perry	John	Pte.	30786	31/07/1917
Perry	William Everard Hill	T/2/Lt.		14/04/1917

Perryman	Herbert	Pte.	7467	09/05/1915
Perryman	John W.	Pte.	8968	11/03/1915
Peters	Frederick Thomas	Pte.	203283	21/06/1917
Petherick	Arthur	Pte.	15451	01/07/1916
Phillips	Archibald Harry	Pte.	9294	05/06/1916
Phillips	Henry	Pte.	3\6480	29/12/1914
Phillips	Robert	Pte.	16889	04/07/1916
Philpotts	Henry Herniman	Pte.	28476	26/03/1918
Pickett	John Thomas	Pte.	51556	17/08/1917
Pike	Walter Thomas	Pte.	9066	28/02/1915
Pike	William John	Cpl.	15596	24/04/1918
Pine	Albert	L/Cpl.	8411	09/05/1915
Piner	Albert George	Pte.	205473	27/09/1918
Pinson	William Joyce Neville	Pte.	14451	30/03/1917
Pitt	Frederick John	Pte.	45122	16/08/1917
Pommeret	Francis Ange	Pte.	16858	07/01/1917
Poole	James Tope	Pte.	3\6878	24/10/1916
Poolman	Ernest George	Pte.	18572	17/07/1916
Pope	William Charles	Pte.	3\6422	15/05/1915
Potter	Leonard George	Pte.	8711	21/11/1914
Preece	Charles Henry	Pte.	20170	01/07/1916
Preece	Frank Edward	Pte.	30994	27/05/1918
Preece	Henry George	Pte.	74085	29/10/1918
Preedy	Alban	Capt.		01/07/1916
Prescott	John Henry Moses	Sgt.	8433	08/10/1918
Price	David Thomas	Pte.	3\8271	27/09/1915
Priddis	William James	Pte.	25869	14/04/1917
Priddle	Cecil	Pte.	8570	19/07/1915
Priddle	Robert	Pte.	8138	31/05/1918
Prigg	Harry Robert	Pte.	21718	20/04/1917
Prior	Rowland	A/Cpl.	8440	10/11/1916
Prout	George Henry	L/Cpl.	8921	01/07/1916
Prout	Herbert Lawrence	Pte.	15483	02/10/1917
Prowse	Charles	L/Cpl.	15075	01/07/1916
Prynn	Cyril Ernest	Pte.	44099	31/07/1917

Pugsley	William George	Pte.	19103	01/07/1916
Punt	Albert Edward	Pte.	204840	14/07/1918
Purchase	Reginald Hawkin	Pte.	8610	14/03/1915
Purvey	Frederick Leonard	Pte.	9804	01/07/1916
Quick	Alfred	Pte.	8601	27/11/1914
Radford	Walter	Pte.	30865	16/08/1917
Radmore	James	Cpl.	9099	24/04/1918
Radmore	Richard Henry	Pte.	16945	31/05/1918
Rainey	Victor Thomas James	2/Lt.		30/09/1917
Ralph	Frank	Pte.	16969	31/05/1918
Randall	James	Pte.	6692	11/03/1915
Randle	George Taylor	Sgt.	7742	07/05/1915
Read	Chase George	Pte.	16155	11/11/1917
Read	George William Stanley	Pte.	1015	15/08/1916
Reading	Charles Edward	Pte.	43173	30/06/1917
Redman	Ernest Gordon	Pte.	291210	31/05/1918
Redwood	Frederick Robert	Cpl.	9336	01/04/1918
Reed	Frederick Youlden	Pte.	11516	30/10/1916
Reed	George	Pte.	8493	13/03/1915
Reed	William	Cpl.	8280	01/07/1916
Reekes	Charles Henry	Pte.	15514	07/10/1915
Rees	Albert David	Pte.	7381	06/01/1915
Reeves	Edward Alec	Pte.	9563	07/06/1915
Reeves	Henry Rueben	Pte.	205046	25/11/1916
Reeves	Kenneth William	Pte.	17793	01/07/1916
Rennie	John Archibald	2/Lt.		25/07/1916
Rew	John	Pte.	32067	02/11/1918
Reynolds	John	Sgt.	8273	18/12/1914
Reynolds	William	Pte.	7274	18/12/1914
Rice	John	Pte.	3\6484	01/03/1915
Rice	Mark	Pte.	3\6730	01/07/1916
Richards	Arthur John	Pte.	203627	24/04/1918
Richards	Charles Leonard	Pte.	74098	05/06/1918
Richards	Reginald George	Pte.	3\6783	01/07/1916
Richards	Thomas Henry	Pte.	11395	29/10/1916

Richards	Wilfred	Pte.	30665	25/03/1918
Rickard	Arthur Richard Carter	Pte.	57010	27/09/1918
Ridd	William James	Sgt.	9696	27/05/1918
Rider	Alfred	Pte.	6757	13/09/1916
Ridges	Harry	Pte.	8795	03/01/1915
Ridgeway	Ernest	Pte.	18701	01/07/1916
Ridgway	Benjamin James	Pte.	31003	15/09/1917
Riggs	Herbert George	Pte.	8126	27/11/1914
Roach	William John	Pte.	9349	16/05/1915
Roberts	Frederick James	Pte.	9582	09/05/1915
Roberts	Jack	Pte.	11889	30/05/1915
Roberts	John Francis	L/Cpl.	8885	09/09/1916
Roberts	Philip	Pte.	3\8283	01/07/1916
Roberts	Reginald Louis	L/Sgt.	9987	04/05/1917
Roberts	Robert Henry	Pte.	33576	06/10/1916
Roberts	Samuel	L/Cpl.	3\6924	09/05/1915
Roberts	Wilfred	Pte.	74194	27/09/1918
Robertson	Walter Scott	Cpl.	32245	13/10/1918
Rodd	Charles Bouchier	2/Lt.		30/10/1916
Rogers	Alfred Morris	2/Lt.		18/07/1916
Rogers	Ernest Alfred	Pte.	18652	01/07/1916
Rogers	William John	Pte.	933	18/12/1914
Rolston	William	Pte.	3\7145	01/01/1915
Rookes	William John	Pte.	33161	30/10/1916
Rose	William Henry	Pte.	205033	24/04/1918
Rowe	Charles Philip	Pte.	68053	29/03/1918
Rowe	Charles Robert	L/Cpl.	23786	06/11/1918
Rowe	Frederick John	Pte.	10734	24/04/1918
Rowe	James	Pte.	3\7131	09/01/1915
Rowe	John	Pte.	8468	01/07/1916
Rowe	Percy Harold	Pte.	25313	22/09/1916
Rowe	Reginald Edwin Horace	Pte.	69054	25/03/1918
Rowe	Sidney Albert	Pte.	33215	14/04/1917
Rowe	Thomas	Cpl.	7000	01/07/1916
Rowe	Wallace	Pte.	69059	06/06/1918

Rowe	Walter	Pte.	8863	18/12/1914
Rowland	Walter	Pte.	12757	23/03/1917
Rundle	Sydney Crymes	Pte.	30443	24/04/1918
Russell	George Robert	Pte.	3\6979	13/03/1915
Ryder	George Henry	Pte.	16963	27/10/1917
Saddler	Frank	Pte.	203419	01/08/1917
Salter	Harold Lionel	Pte.	8569	01/02/1915
Salter	Samuel	Pte.	3\6990	01/02/1915
Samuels	Sydney Joseph	Pte.	44148	30/03/1917
Sampson	Ernest Edwin	Pte.	9641	04/01/1915
Sampson	John	Pte.	20944	10/08/1917
Sanders	Charles Enos	Pte.	16788	15/09/1916
Sanders	George	Sgt.	8598	10/03/1915
Sanders	Joseph	Pte.	30784	14/08/1917
Sanders	Reginald	Pte.	3\6797	14/04/1917
Sando	Joseph Charles	L/Cpl.	204874	01/08/1917
Saunders	Charles	Pte.	11219	01/07/1916
Saunders	James	Pte.	10015	01/07/1916
Saxon	Thomas	Pte.	15538	27/03/1918
Sayes	John	T/2/Lt.		31/10/1918
Schofield	Charles Edward	Pte.	19070	14/04/1917
Searson	William	Pte.	13371	01/07/1916
Seldon	Joseph Spiller	Sgt.	26061	24/04/1918
Seldon	Stanley Jerome	Pte.	9030	18/12/1914
Sellek	Edgar James	Pte.	11349	09/05/1915
Selley	Charlie	Pte.	21176	03/03/1918
Selley	Richard	Pte.	10016	11/03/1915
Sercombe	Henry	Pte.	8903	18/12/1914
Shaddick	James	Sgt.	13302	30/11/1917
Sharland	George	Pte.	10761	12/09/1918
Sharratt	George	Pte.	23885	31/07/1917
Shattock	Henry	Pte.	46294	04/09/1917
Shaxon	William	Sgt.	8029	01/07/1916
Shaxton	Percy	Pte.	11359	26/08/1915
Sheard	James	Pte.	69211	12/11/1918

Shears	William Daniel	Pte.	290282	20/10/1918
Sheldon	William Henry	Pte.	10983	06/10/1916
Shelley	Arthur George	Pte.	204882	16/08/1917
Shepherd	Everett Henry	Pte.	16699	24/04/1918
Shepherd	John	Pte.	3\7113	22/03/1916
Sheppard	Sydney Daniel	Pte.	3\6773	08/03/1917
Shergold	Reuben George	Pte.	69068	29/10/1918
Shortridge	Arthur	Cpl.	15392	26/05/1918
Shute	Charles	Pte.	8800	11/03/1915
Simmonds	Robert	Pte.	11321	30/10/1916
Simpkins	Ernest Frank	Pte.	31826	23/02/1918
Simpkins	George Edward	Pte.	9688	13/04/1915
Simpson	James	Pte.	70063	31/05/1918
Simpson	William John	A/Cpl.	8713	11/03/1915
Sinclair	William	Pte.	8841	20/11/1914
Sizer	Ernest William	Pte.	25650	24/04/1918
Skelley	Stanley	Pte.	16956	01/07/1916
Skinner	Frederick James	Pte.	9361	01/07/1916
Skinner	George	Pte.	7895	09/05/1915
Skinner	John William	Pte.	8790	18/12/1914
Skinner	Mark	Pte.	19229	21/08/1916
Smale	Charles Donald	Pte.	7457	03/08/1916
Smale	John	Pte.	30813	16/08/1917
Smart	Clifford	Pte.	31014	27/03/1918
Smart	George	Pte.	291108	25/11/1917
Smith	Albert	Pte.	12650	13/03/1915
Smith	Arthur	Pte.	54521	30/11/1917
Smith	Arthur Herbert	A/Capt.		06/10/1916
Smith	Beluchistan Thomas	Pte.	74000	31/05/1918
Smith	Charles Edmund	Sgt.	20390	31/05/1918
Smith	Charles Hamlet	Pte.	204848	24/07/1917
Smith	Ernest	Pte.	11196	12/03/1915
Smith	Frederick George	Pte.	290165	24/10/1918
Smith	Harry	Pte.	17562	01/07/1916
Smith	Henry	Pte.	7605	10/03/1915

Surname	Forename(s)	Rank	Number	Date
Smith	James	Pte.	8735	11/03/1915
Smith	Lewis James	Pte.	7106	18/12/1914
Smith	Mia	Pte.	47713	31/07/1917
Smith	William	Pte.	33125	08/11/1916
Smith	William Henry	Pte.	25707	21/11/1916
Smithson	Albert Edward	Pte.	43236	24/04/1918
Snell	Frank	L/Cpl.	9160	06/10/1916
Snell	Harry	A/Cpl.	290009	27/03/1918
Snell	Harry	Pte.	69218	26/11/1918
Sohier	Henry Lyman	Sgt.	9848	14/04/1917
Sollars	Thomas Jesse	Pte.	25197	16/09/1917
Soper	George	Pte.	3\5165	14/05/1916
Southcott	George	Pte.	26767	21/06/1917
Sparrow	Walter Frank	Cpl.	8293	13/03/1915
Spencer	Charles James	Capt.		18/12/1914
Spicer	Albert Edward	Pte.	9077	17/03/1915
Spiller	Charles	Pte.	11232	18/07/1916
Spiller	Herbert James	Pte.	15052	27/10/1916
Spoerry	Julius Englebert	Cpl.	8057	07/07/1915
Sprague	Charles Frederick	L/Cpl.	8760	09/05/1915
Squire	Henry	Pte.	30551	31/03/1918
Squires	Albert Ernest	Pte.	26282	05/02/1917
Squire	Frederick Josiah	Pte.	11263	10/05/1915
Stacey	Edwin	Pte.	30841	28/07/1917
Stacey	Samuel	Pte.	15162	31/01/1916
Stamp	Harry	Pte.	15590	01/07/1916
Steer	Jack	Pte.	8802	23/07/1917
Stentiford	Frank	Pte.	15494	10/08/1917
Stephens	Richard James	Sgt.	290118	03/09/1917
Stephens	William	Pte.	18507	22/07/1916
Stevens	Frank Mitchelmore	Pte.	3\5264	20/11/1914
Stevens	James Garfield	Pte.	30775	27/07/1917
Stevens	John Arthur	Pte.	43330	25/03/1918
Stone	Harry Thomas	Sgt.	10195	01/07/1916
Stoneman	Harry	Pte.	9591	16/03/1915

Stoyel	Francis William	Pte.	205166	27/03/1918
Stoyles	Walter	Pte.	8319	13/03/1915
Strawbridge	William Henry	Cpl.	9550	01/07/1916
Stringer	Alfred	Pte.	17100	06/10/1916
Stripp	Austen	Pte.	290498	09/11/1917
Stuttard	Gilbert	Pte.	20844	24/04/1918
Sunderland	Alfred Joseph Elton	Lt/Col.		31/07/1917
Sussex	Frederick William	Cpl.	8540	22/04/1916
Sutton	Ernest Charles	Pte.	30797	28/07/1917
Sweet	Frank Clarence	Pte.	33169	31/05/1918
Tancock	Harry	Sgt.	8804	12/11/1916
Tanner	Joseph	Pte.	6402	01/07/1916
Tapscott	Alfred Samuel	Pte.	30541	31/07/1917
Tarr	Arthur	Pte.	8925	13/05/1915
Tarr	John	Pte.	15096	04/05/1915
Taswell	John Richard	Pte.	68799	24/04/1918
Tattersall	Frank Hamlet	Pte.	18739	01/07/1916
Taylor	Arthur Martin	T/2/Lt.		01/08/1917
Taylor	Charles	Pte.	3\6854	01/07/1916
Taylor	Harold	Pte.	203620	24/04/1918
Taylor	Levi	Pte.	3\7783	13/03/1915
Taylor	William	Pte.	11393	06/10/1916
Teague	John	Pte.	10220	06/07/1916
Tennant	Charles Alan Ramsay (Bunny)	2/Lt.		09/05/1915
Thomas	George James	Pte.	14174	01/07/1916
Thomas	Henry	A/Cpl.	3/8300	31/03/1918
Thomas	Harry Opie	Pte.	290451	26/09/1917
Thomas	Henry James	Pte.	8425	09/05/1915
Thompson	George Edward	Pte.	15240	01/07/1916
Thorne	Ernest Frederick	Pte.	25876	16/08/1917
Thorne	William David	Pte.	74109	31/05/1918
Thresher	John	Pte.	8688	13/07/1916
Thuillier	George Fleetwood	A/Capt.		26/03/1918
Tidwell	Albert	L/Cpl.	9395	13/04/1918

Tillett	Alexander	Lt/Col.		03/12/1917
Tindal	Louis Nicholas Lindsay	Lt.		27/05/1918
Tomkins	Horace	Pte.	47702	06/08/1917
Toms	Charles	Pte.	30811	01/08/1917
Toms	William	Pte.	45535	30/04/1918
Townsend	Frederick	Pte.	32214	27/09/1918
Trace	Henry	Pte.	9003	10/03/1915
Treays	James	Pte.	44126	01/08/1917
Triggs	Charles Victor	Pte.	20582	01/07/1916
Trout	Sidney	Pte.	10125	09/05/1915
Truman	William Thomas Mudge	A/L/Cpl.	21023	23/03/1917
Trute	Francis John	Pte.	30367	27/10/1918
Tucker	Walter George	A/Cpl.	24881	26/05/1918
Tuckerman	James Madick Moses	Sgt.	8459	12/03/1915
Tuckwell	Herbert	L/Cpl.	9653	30/11/1917
Tungate	Louis Reggy	Pte.	32254	11/10/1918
Turner	Arthur	Pte.	8999	25/03/1915
Turner	John William	Pte.	11222	11/03/1915
Turner	Mark	CSM	7293	30/06/1916
Turvey	William Chamberlain	Pte.	74110	31/05/1918
Twigg	John	Pte.	14175	09/05/1915
Twitchett	Ernest Edward	L/Cpl.	8623	06/01/1915
Underhill	Albert Edward	Pte.	68920	27/03/1918
Upward	Arthur Joseph	Pte.	205035	24/04/1918
Vanstone	Brinley	Pte.	3\8310	10/03/1915
Vass	Ernest George	Pte.	11491	01/07/1916
Vaughan	William	Pte.	12735	22/08/1915
Venn	Robert	Cpl.	33171	08/03/1917
Vernon	James Albert	Sgt.	8317	31/07/1917
Vesey Fitzgerald	William Herbert Lesley	2/Lt.		14/08/1916
Vile	James	Pte.	9056	01/07/1916
Vincent	Archibald Robert	Pte.	315303	08/06/1918
Vincent	Frederick Joseph	Pte.	15606	01/07/1916
Viney	John Edward	Pte.	18965	06/10/1916
Vinnicombe	Leslie	Lt.		25/10/1918

Wade	Richard Lloyd	Pte.	3\8311	01/07/1916
Wakeham	Charles James	Pte.	20787	01/07/1916
Waldron	Albert	Pte.	203594	21/06/1917
Walker	Charles	Pte.	11283	10/05/1915
Walker	Denis Rupert	Pte.	291760	26/05/1918
Walker	Frederick Cecil Banes	2/Lt.		09/05/1915
Walker	John Thomas	Pte.	15404	08/09/1916
Walker	Samuel	Pte.	10127	09/05/1915
Walker	William James	Pte.	13547	01/07/1916
Waller	Sidney Herbert	Pte.	24825	27/10/1918
Wallington	Robert James	Pte.	12194	17/05/1917
Wallis	Clifford Edward	Pte.	42025	24/04/1918
Wallser	Henry	Pte.	8854	13/03/1915
Walsh	William	Pte.	13007	24/04/1918
Walsh	William Joseph	L/Cpl.	8402	06/10/1916
Walters	Bert	Pte.	11089	23/02/1915
Walters	Ralph Vinning	Pte.	67936	24/04/1918
Walton	Arthur	Pte.	15272	01/07/1916
Ward	James	Pte.	11169	09/05/1915
Ward	Reginald James Frank	Pte.	33870	27/03/1918
Warfield	Edward Albert	Pte.	205161	16/08/1917
Warne	Richard Henry	Pte.	8739	02/10/1915
Warne	William Benjamin	Pte.	7430	30/03/1917
Warren	Arthur Courtenay	Pte.	3\6496	25/01/1915
Warren	James	Pte.	16884	18/04/1917
Warren	Leonard	Pte.	316007	26/04/1918
Warren	Richard	Pte.	8720	12/03/1915
Warren	William David	Pte.	9681	13/03/1915
Waterman	David Henry	Pte.	32087	07/10/1918
Watkins	David John	Pte.	12864	10/03/1915
Watkins	Eustace Arundel De St. Barbe Sladen	Capt.		31/01/1915
Watkins	Francis	Pte.	13072	11/07/1916
Watson	Arthur Edward	Pte.	32048	31/10/1918
Watts	Arthur Francis	Pte.	3\6202	01/07/1916

The 2nd Devons War Diary

Watts	Harold Vaughan Iremonger	2/Lt.		11/08/1917
Watts	Jack Edward	Cpl.	8313	09/05/1915
Way	Bernard Walter	Pte.	11946	31/12/1916
Webb	John	Pte.	19236	21/08/1916
Webb	William James	L/Cpl.	33907	17/05/1918
Webber	Alfred George	Pte.	3\8315	01/07/1916
Webber	Frederick Thomas Hitchcock	Pte.	33189	10/05/1917
Webber	George	Sgt.	7410	17/06/1916
Webber	Oliver Charles	Pte.	292187	15/07/1918
Webber	Archibald Walter	Pte.	205164	16/08/1917
Webber	William Charles	Pte.	9347	19/10/1916
Webster	George	L/Sgt.	3\7039	09/05/1915
Wedge	Joseph	L/Cpl.	14607	10/03/1915
Weed	Frederick	Pte.	203551	19/04/1918
Weeks	Charles Henry	Pte.	3\6362	14/04/1917
Weeks	George Edwin	Pte.	8641	14/03/1915
Weeks	John	Pte.	11205	12/03/1915
Weeks	Thomas	Pte.	17542	01/07/1916
Weeks	William Henry	Pte.	18151	19/06/1917
Weeks	William R.	A/Cpl.	290208	16/10/1918
Welsh	Thomas Charles	Pte.	290403	31/05/1918
West	Albert	Pte.	3\8316	29/10/1916
Westaway	Frederick Thomas	Pte.	30374	27/05/1918
Westaway	John	Pte.	9440	18/12/1914
Westcott	Charles George	Pte.	8655	18/12/1914
Westcott	George	Pte.	11509	15/07/1915
Westlake	William	Pte.	12595	01/07/1916
Weston	Ernest John	Pte.	8891	18/12/1914
Westwood	Bertie Harold	Pte.	31024	03/11/1918
Wheaton	George	Pte.	8770	18/12/1914
Wheeler	Herbert	Pte.	31034	23/03/1918
Wheeler	Reginald Stewart	Pte.	31827	24/04/1918
White	Alfred	Pte.	30791	31/07/1917
White	Arthur Ernest	Pte.	74132	08/06/1918

White	Arthur Tom	Pte.	33238	20/03/1917
White	Charles Henry	L/Cpl.	15086	01/07/1916
White	Frederick George	Pte.	8545	18/12/1914
White	Frederick Maurice	Pte.	3\6874	26/08/1915
White	George	Pte.	6819	21/11/1914
White	John	Pte.	35585	24/07/1917
White	John	Pte.	8146	01/07/1916
White	Montagu Augustus	Pte.	315580	31/10/1918
White	Sidney George	Sgt.	8485	09/06/1917
Whitlock	Robert	Cpl.	32186	31/10/1918
Whitty	Sidney	Pte.	9649	09/05/1915
Wicks	Thomas	Pte.	9821	01/07/1916
Widdecombe	Thomas Charles	Pte.	9870	14/12/1914
Widger	William	Pte.	9502	24/12/1914
Wilcocks	Henry	Pte.	26117	06/05/1917
Willcocks	Luther James	Pte.	20825	24/04/1918
Wilcox	Cecil	Pte.	32218	11/10/1918
Wild	Harold	Pte.	15389	14/03/1917
Wilder	Alec Edward	L/Cpl.	31033	31/05/1918
Wilkey	Frederick James	Pte.	9518	18/12/1914
Wilks	Stanley	Pte.	31829	27/05/1918
Willcocks	John Gordon	Pte.	3\6199	18/02/1915
Willcocks	Luther James	Pte.	28025	24/04/1918
Willey	Frederick Charles	Pte.	3\5013	31/07/1917
Williams	Charles Lewis	Cpl.	42693	10/04/1917
Williams	Christopher Harry	Pte.	74115	31/05/1918
Williams	David Daniel	Pte.	12753	25/03/1918
Williams	Harold Edward Mansfield	Pte.	51575	24/04/1918
Williams	Ralph Washington	Pte.	16949	01/08/1917
Williams	Robert Richard	Pte.	3\6855	15/04/1915
Williams	Samuel	Pte.	3\6821	04/08/1917
Williams	Walter	Pte.	8949	08/01/1917
Williams	William	Pte.	12875	23/02/1915
Willie	Harold	Pte.	11536	27/07/1916
Willis	Walter	Pte.	12888	12/03/1915

Willshire	Thomas Louis	Pte.	10985	12/12/1916
Willy	John Howard Cole	T/2/Lt.		25/11/1917
Wilson	Arthur Leslie	Pte.	74027	31/05/1918
Wilson	George Frederick	Pte.	8714	03/07/1916
Wilson	Walter John	A/Cpl.	3\6977	10/03/1915
Wilson	William Currey	Pte.	16879	01/07/1916
Windsor	Mark Gilham	2/Lt.		10/03/1915
Winn	Arthur	Pte.	290394	16/08/1917
Winstone	Albert Edward John	Pte.	69236	11/10/1918
Wood	Ernest	Pte.	33147	08/10/1918
Wood	Frederick James	Pte.	316093	24/04/1918
Woodberry	Walter	Pte.	8236	24/04/1918
Woodgate	Horace Edward	Pte.	16609	26/03/1918
Woodley	George	A/L/Cpl.	8423	27/09/1918
Woolacott	Herbert	Pte.	9084	01/07/1916
Woolacott	William	Sgt.	4884	18/12/1914
Wooldridge	Alfred	Pte.	10146	18/12/1914
Woolf	Edward Samuel	Pte.	3\7082	16/01/1915
Woolfries	Edwin	Pte.	30843	31/07/1917
Woolway	Thomas	Pte.	15220	01/07/1916
Worth	Arthur	Pte.	8788	18/12/1914
Wright	Arthur George	Cpl.	18918	30/03/1918
Wright	George Clinton	2/Lt.		10/03/1915
Wright	Leonard Stanley	Pte.	62347	24/04/1918
Wright	Thomas Henry	Pte.	69064	31/05/1918
Wright	William James	Pte.	27954	31/07/1917
Yates	Charles Hulbert	Pte.	11187	01/07/1916
Yeo	John	Pte.	3\7088	11/03/1915
Yeo	Robert	Pte.	9453	22/08/1916
Yauldren	Albert Cecil	Pte.	32224	15/09/1918
Young	Arthur	Pte.	8833	23/02/1915
Young	Edward B.	Pte.	71308	04/08/1918

Martin Body

THE END

The 2nd Devons War Diary

GLOSSARY

1st Devons - 1st battalion, The Devonshire Regiment
2nd Devons - 2nd battalion, The Devonshire Regiment
3rd Devons - 3rd battalion, The Devonshire Regiment
2/Lt. - 2nd Lieutenant
A.D.C. - Aide de Camp
A.E.F. - American Expeditionary Force
A.I.F. - Australian Imperial Force
A.D.M.S. - Assistant Director of Medical Services
A.S.C. - Army Service Corps
B.E.F. - British Expeditionary Force
Bde. - Brigade
Bn. - Battalion
Brig. - Brigadier
Cap. - Captain
C-I-C - Commander In Chief
C.I.G.S. - Chief (of the) Imperial General Staff CMG
C.M.G. - Companion of the Order of St. Michael and St. George
C.O. - Commanding Officer
Coy. - Company
Cpl. - Corporal
C.Q.M.S. - Company Quartermaster Sergeant
C.R.E. - Corps of Royal Engineers
C.S.M. - Company Sergeant Major
C.W.G.C. - Commonwealth War Graves Commission
D.C.L.I. - Duke of Cornwall's Light Infantry
D.C.M. - Distinguished Conduct Medal
D.L.I. - Durham Light Infantry
D.S.C. - Distinguished Service Cross
D.S.O. - Distinguished Service Order
F/F - France/Flanders
F.G.C.M. - Field General Court Martial
Flammenwerfer - German Flame Thrower
Gen. - General
G.H.Q. - General Headquarters
G.O.C. - General Officer Commanding
H.E. - High Explosive
H.Q. - Headquarters
I.W.M. - Imperial War Museum
I.O. - Intelligence Officer
K.C.B. - Knight Commander of the Order of the Bath
K.O.Y.L.I. - King's Own Yorkshire Light Infantry
L/Cpl. - Lance Corporal
L.G. - Lewis Gun
L.G.O. - Lewis Gun Officer
L/Sgt. - Lance Sergeant
Lt. - Lieutenant
Lt. Col. - Lieutenant Colonel
L.T.M. - Light Trench Mortar
Maj. - Major
M.C. - Military Cross
M.G. - Machine Gun

M.G.C. - Machine Gun Corps
Minenwerfer (Minnie) - German Trench Mortar
M.M. - Military Medal
M.O. - Medical Officer
N.C.O. - Non Commissioned Officer
O.C. - Officer Commanding
O.R. - Other rank
P.A.S.L.I. - Prince Albert's Somerset Light Infantry
Pte. - Private
R.A.M.C. - Royal Army Medical Corps
R.E. - Royal Engineers
R.F.A. - Royal Field Artillery
R.F.C. - Royal Flying Corps
R.G.A. - Royal Garrison Artillery
R.G. - Rifle Grenade
R.Q.M.S. - Regimental Quartermaster Sergeant
R.S.M. - Regimental Sergeant Major
S.D.G.W. - Soldiers Died (in the) Great War (database)
Sgt. - Sergeant
S.M.L.E. - Short Magazine Lee Enfield rifle
T.M. - Trench Mortar
T.M.B. - Trench Mortar Battery
U.S.A.M.C. - United States Army Medical Corps
V.C. - Victoria Cross
Whizz-bang - German 77mm high velocity field gun shell
W.O. - War Office or Warrant Officer
Y.M.C.A. - Young Men's Christian Association

The 2nd Devons War Diary

Bibliography

Arthur, Max. 2003, *Forgotten Voices of the Great War*, Second Edition, Ebury Press, London.

Atkinson, C.T., 2001, *The Devonshire Regiment 1914-1918*, Volumes 1 and 2, Second Edition, The Naval &Military Press Ltd., Uckfield, East Sussex.

Bell, Ernest W. 1977, *Soldiers Killed on the First Day of the Somme*, First Edition, Ernest W. Bell, Bolton, Lancashire.

Blake, R., 1952, *The Private Papers of Douglas Haig, 1914-1919*, First Edition, Eyre & Spottiswoode, London

Boraston, J.H., Lt.Col., and Bax, C.E.O., Capt, 1926, *The Eighth Division In War. 1914 – 1918*, First Edition, The Medici Society, London

Colwill, R.A., 1927, *Through Hell to Victory*, 2nd Edition, Reginald A. Colwill., Torquay.

Hammerton, J.A., 1914-1918, *The War Illustrated – A Pictorial Record of the Conflict of the Nations*, The Amalgamated Press Ltd., London.

Levine, J., 2008, *Forgotten Voices on the Somme*, First Edition, Ebury Press, London

MacDonald, Lyn, 1998, *To the Last Man: Spring 1918*, First Edition, Viking, London

Messenger, Charles, 2006, *Call to Arms, The British Army 1914-18*, 2nd Edition, Cassell, London.

Middlebrook, Martin, 1983, *The First Day on the Somme*, Third Edition, Allen Lane, London.

Rogerson, Sidney, 2007, *The Last of the Ebb*, Second Edition, Greenhill Books, London

Putkowski, Julian, and Sykes, Julian, 1999, *Shot at Dawn*, Eighth Edition, Leo Cooper, Barnsley, South Yorkshire.

Saunders, Tim, 2004, *West Country Regiments on the Somme*, First Edition, Pen & Sword Books, Barnsley, South Yorkshire.

Sheldon, Jack, 2005, *The German Army on the Somme*, First Edition, Pen & Sword Books, Barnsley, South Yorkshire.

Warner, Phillip, 1975, *Stories of Famous Regiments*, First Edition, Arthur Barker, London.

Westlake, Ray, 1994, *British Battalions on the Somme*, First Edition, Leo Cooper, Barnsley, South Yorkshire.

Official History of the Great War 1914 – 1918. Military Operations France & Belgium, 2010, CD-ROM, Imperial War Museum/Naval & Military Press Ltd., Uckfield, East Sussex.

Soldiers Died in the Great War 1914-19, CD-ROM, Naval & Military Press Ltd., Uckfield, East Sussex.

National Archives Document WO/95/1712, *The 2nd battalion, Devonshire Regiment, War Diary, 1914-1919*, Kew, London.

www.ingramcontent.com/pod-product-compliance
Lightning Source LLC
Chambersburg PA
CBHW020631230426
43665CB00008B/130